Indian Administration

Retrospect and Prospect

P.D. SHARMA
B.M. SHARMA

RAWAT PUBLICATIONS
Jaipur • New Delhi • Bangalore • Mumbai • Hyderabad • Guwahati

ISBN 81-316-0064-5 (Hardback)
ISBN 81-316-0065-3 (Paperback)

Published by
Prem Rawat for **Rawat Publications**
Satyam Apts., Sector 3, Jawahar Nagar, Jaipur 302 004 (India)
Phone: 0141 265 1748 / 7006 Fax: 0141 265 1748
E-mail: info@rawatbooks.com
Website: www.rawatbooks.com

New Delhi Office
4858/24, Ansari Road, Daryaganj, New Delhi 110 002
Phone: 011-23263290

Also at Bangalore, Mumbai, Hyderabad and Guwahati

Typeset by Rawat Computers, Jaipur
Printed at Nice Printing Press, New Delhi

Indian Administration: Retrospect and Prospect

Contents

3 UNION-STATE RELATIONS IN FEDERAL POLITY 88

4 THE SECRETARIATAL ORGANISATIONS OF UNION GOVERNMENT 109

5 ADMINISTRATIVE ORGANISATION AND WORKING OF UNION MINISTRIES 147

6 EXECUTIVE AGENCIES AND COMMISSIONS 213

7 ADMINISTRATION IN STATES: ISSUES AND PERSPECTIVES 270

8 DISTRICT ADMINISTRATION AND DECENTRALISED GOVERNANCE: FROM DYARCHY TO SELF-GOVERNMENT 296

9 CIVIL SERVICES IN INDIA 337

10 POLICE ADMINISTRATION AND CRIMINAL JUSTICE SYSTEM IN INDIA 382

11 ACCOUNTABILITY AND DEMOCRATIC ADMINISTRATION IN THE NEW MILLENNIUM 422

Preface

Indian administration, as it obtains today, is a cherished legacy of the British Raj. In retrospect, the origins of administrative institutions and agencies in India may be traced back to the all knowing classical texts of ancient Hindu literature, from which Kautilya culled his *Arthashastra*. The universality of these Kautilayan principles makes them relevant for the students and scholars of "India, that is, Bharat", even after centuries of upheavals of history. The Mughal rule strived to plant an imperial administration on the non-Islamic people of the sub-continent, the traces of which are still alive in the district administration of the Patwari and the Thanedar. It goes to the credit of the British, who built a brand new apparatus of public administration in India to unify the colony and to subjugate its people to a system called the 'Rule of Law'.

The Government of India Acts of 1909, 1919 and 1935 provided the political framework, within which the administration of India got shaped and institutions like Secretariat, Public Service Commission, Comptroller and Auditor General, Collectorate and Municipal Corporation were born and adjusted to the socio-political realities of the colony. This retrospective introspection offers a backdrop on which the Constituent Assembly of partitioned India painted a political landscape known as the Republican Constitution of free India.

After centuries of servitude 'we the people' resolved to live in dignity and gave to our people liberty, equality and justice under a democratic regime, which shall ensure a socialist and secular way of life. This constitutional philosophy elaborately explains the basic premise on which the Indian administration has to be built, tested and reformed for the succeeding generations of this ancient land of ours.

The union government, though federal in form, operates to keep the national unity of India in tact in letter as well as in spirit. The pressures of democracy have already forced the Indian polity to decentralise itself at the level of the district and below, but the vision of a modern nation-state lingers in the emergency provisions of the Constitution, union-state relations and institutionalisation of planning and centralised development through Planning Commission and National Development Council. The parliamentary democracy necessitates a Cabinet Secretariat, a Central Secretariat and an office of the Prime Minister. The Finance Commission, the Election Commission and the Planning Commission have their inevitable repercussions on the administrations of the union and state governments.

The Indian Constitution also prescribes the governmental structure of the states and the rural and urban local bodies at village, block and district levels in the national frame itself. These structures need Governors, Chief Ministers, Chief Secretaries, district level officials and elected public representatives. The variety and novelty of some of these political and administrative structures need an objective study by the academics. How should an Indian district be governed in future is a vexed question and the younger generations of students of public administration must devote their thought and energy to chart out the institutional arrangement for resurgent India. Development administration and welfare administration are the key areas of future study in the era of liberalisation, privatisation and globalisation and as the struggle for social justice and gender parity advances, India of tomorrow will be engaged in her second war of independence against her own elites, who are practising the politics of urban vs. rural, men vs. women, poor vs. rich and the educated vs. uneducated in open as well as clandestine manner. It is a historical battle and public administration cannot afford to be indifferent and still less a non-participatory spectator, without inviting peril.

The Indian Civil Service, which managed the affairs of a huge colony for more than two centuries, today confronts crises of legitimacy and viability. The policies of reservation and the role of bureaucracy in development had metamorphically transformed it to induct a new elan of transparency and accountability. The students and scholars of Indian administration should understand this reality and explore newer models of civil service effectivity with unprecedented efforts in the areas of training, research and reform.

Preparing a textbook on Indian Public Administration seems like snapping a running object. New reforms, experiments and research findings need to be incorporated to the existing corpus of administrative knowledge. Moreover, the students engaged in the pursuit of studies for university degrees and other competitive examinations for entry in civil service and other public service careers have different kinds of needs and demands, which a comprehensive textbook alone can fulfil.

We are glad that the present volume strives to cater to the needs of students and scholars of Indian Public Administration by systematising and abstracting the relevant information from primary and secondary sources. Some of the administrative concepts and institutions in India are of very recent origin. They too are new and the readers should update these materials with the help of studies published in the learned journals of public administration.

We are conscious of the omissions and limitations of the first edition. The subsequent editions and revisions will incorporate the suggestions offered by the student community.

Our text resources are based on varied materials, studies, books, learned journals and government reports in the field. We express our gratitude to all those writers, researchers and officials from whose writings we have been benefited. Our special thanks are due to our publishers, Rawat Publications, Jaipur, who took extra pains in updating the computer copy of the manuscript and doing an excellent job of production.

Jaipur
14th January, 2009

P.D. Sharma
B.M. Sharma

1

Administrative History of India

Administrative history can be viewed as that aspect of history which has its bearing and linkages with the political and governing institutions of a given country. Public administration in ancient and mediaeval India consisted of structures, procedures and behaviours which the ruling dynasties or emperors had and employed for running their respective systems of government. The historian and researchers like Sir Jadunath Sarkar, Dr Beni Prasad and Dr Iswari Prasad have devoted a great part of their research effort in isolating and identifying the structures and the nature of their administrative working. Still, the fact remains whether this administration was an offshoot of monarchical politics or can it be evaluated as an administrative system observing uniform and universal laws or practices of governance.

Notwithstanding the endless debates and controversies about historicity of history, one has to admit that contemporary literature has to be and is a potential source of history. The historians who narrate the administrative accounts of rulers in history tend to club them with their political successes and failures of individual rulers. Then there is a tendency to see ancient India as a romantic lore and describe administrative institutions in a nationalistic perspective. *Hindu Polity* by K.P. Jayaswal is an example in point, where in all ancient institutions have been eulogised to project the glory that was India.

Much more difficult is the problem of extricating literary superfluity and falsehoods from the brazen truths of history. Those who describe administration on the basis of literary accounts of epics or even *Arthshastra* and *Sukraneeti* have to be on their guard because 'should' may not be the 'is' or the vice versa. Kautilya while conceptualising the principles of state craft or diplomacy is prescribing as well as describing the day-to-day working of a Mauryan state. One can read Arthshastra as an informal constitution of the Mauryan empire or as the *Memoirs of an Insider* like that of late Narsimha Rao. Whatever Acharya Vishnu Gupta mentions or suggests does not necessarily constitute the basics of Indian administration. Machiavelli wrote the History of Florence and the Prince but it shall be erroneous to assert that public administration of Italy can be gleaned from the writings of a Nicholo Machiavelli. Similarly the administrations of an Allauddin Khilji or Akbar or an Aurangzeb do not represent any continuity. The successful rulers had rotten public administration systems and the vice versa. In fact, the modern nation-state and its political ideologies have devised the bureaucratic structures of its public administration on a clean slate. Hence, to look for the ancestry of administrative organisations and to discover their underlying principles is a ritual of digging out legacies, which stand metamorphosed by modern developments of Indian history.

The advent of the British and their interface with Indian realities caused a sea change. The English rulers systematically destroyed the ancient and medieval relics of administrative inheritance. They literally built most of the things from the scratch and there is scarcely any aspect of Indian civil and military apparatus which can be called genuinely un-British or non-British. The district administration which still has some faint impact of the Mughal administration is an anomaly, which Panchayati Raj threatens to devour. The students of Indian administration should read the administrative history of India with a great amount of caution realising that when its three epochs have very little continuity, there is an epoch making change which the English rule initiated in India.

I
Ancient Period

This phase of administrative history of India is usually traced from Vedic times and spans up to the advent or establishment of Mughal rule in the peninsula. The Vedic literature, Buddhist treatises, Jain literature, Puranas, Dharam Shastra, Manusmriti, Sukraneeti, epics like *Ramayana*, *Mahabharata* and *Arthshastra* of Kautilya can be skimmed to get a glimpse of organisation and functions of administration during this period. The excavations indicate that government in Mohenjo-Daro and Harappa was systematic. In the Indus valley civilisation, there were planned roads and drainage which show that there existed a municipal government which looked after the needs and made systematic arrangements for the governance of cities. Moreover, one type of houses, a common system of weights and measures and a common script point out that there existed an imperial civilisation in the valley. In the *Rigvedic* period, administrative units were called as *kul*, *gram*, *vish* and *rastra*. Gram or the village consisted of several households. The smallest unit was the family. The head of the village was known as *Gramini*. A group of villages constituted a Vish under a Vishpati. Numerous Vishas consisted a *Jan* under an administrative officer called *gopa* who represented the king. The state was a developed form of these villages. The form of government in the Rigvedic era was monarchical and the kingship was hereditary. But the kings were benevolent. The officers like *Senani* and *Gramini* assisted him. He had ministers also, the chief of whom was the *purohit*. Two democratic bodies known as the *Sabha* and the *Samiti* controlled the king. The sabha worked as the council of elders while the samiti was a public body.

न सा सभा यत्र न सन्नि वृद्धाः ने ते वृद्धा ये न वदन्ति धर्मम्

The post-Vedic period witnessed the rise of powerful kingdoms. There was a natural increase in the number of officers in administration. Departments like finance, inspection and defence existed even in earlier times. The sabha and samiti used to put limit on the despotism of the king. The local government was active under a special minister, whose task was to control rural administration and settle disputes. The head of the judicial administration was the king himself and several other officers advised him at different levels.

The form of government in the epic age of *Ramayana and Mahabharata* was monarchical and public administration was sufficiently developed. The head of the administration was the king and the ministers and councillors advised him in matters of government. The main purpose of the state was to fulfil its Dharma, to encourage morality, to increase prosperity and happiness of the people and to safeguard their interests. The state has been called 'Saptanghi' in Mahabharata by Ved Vyas. The principal form of government was monarchy and king set an example of high ideals and performance of one's duties. From the point of view of administration, there used to be a council of ministers and officers picked upon the basis of merit. The Buddhist literature refers to the existence of *Mahajanpadas*. During this period, numerous republics along with four big kingdoms of Magadha, Avanti, Vats and Kaushal flourished. In the republics, the real power belonged to Sabhas which included the common people as well as the elite. The king was the head of the republic and was elected for a fixed term and was accountable for his actions to the council or Sabha.

The state in ancient India, though a monarchy widely differed in its nature, scope and operations. The research does not establish a particular pattern of administration. Even epic periods are incomparable. Similarly the Mauryan administration of Kautilya had little in common with the administrative system maintained by the Guptas, like Harsh Vardhan. Military, police and judicial functions, being central, the public officials whether political or administrative were loyal workers to the king, who symbolised the state. We have little evidence whether these officials worked as instructed, but they were supposed to be efficient, accountable and benevolent. Broadly speaking the common features of public administration during this ancient period (i.e., from Vedas to Mughals) can be summed up as under:

(1) The imperial government of kings and emperors had administrative advisers or advisory institutions like sabha, samiti and councils.
(2) The administrative officers had a hierarchy and were supervised at each level and ultimately by the king.
(3) Administrators were expected to act as trustees and public welfare was exhorted as a legal and moral duty.
(4) Rule of law was visualised as dharma.
(5) The personnel administration and merit bureaucracy were there in the given frame of monarchy.

Arthshastra of Kautilya

A graduate of Taxshila University, Acharya Vishnu Gupta was the teacher, adviser and guide of emperor Chandra Gupta. Born in 325 BC, he was known as Kautilya or Chanakya who was a saint in politics. The Chinese traveller Fahiyan in his Fn Kuo Ki writes, "that country is bound to be affluent whose Prime Minister leads a simple life of the commoner". Out of several books written by Kautilya, Arthshastra is regarded as the classic wherein the encyclopaedic wisdom of the Acharya has unfolded itself into 15 *adhikarans* (अधिकरण), 180 *prakarans* (प्रकरण), 150 *chapters* (अध्याय) and 60,000 *shlokas* (श्लोक).

It is a monumental work that encompasses various disciplines of present day social science. The Acharya believed that livelihood is Artha. The land inhabited by people is also called Artha. Hence this work which explains the means of attaining and retaining the land and the livelihood has been titled as Arthshastra.

"मनुष्याणां वृत्तिरथः, मनुष्यती भूमिरिव्यर्थः
तस्या पृथिवा लाभापालनोपत्यः शास्त्रमशर्थ शास्त्रिमिति"

A cursory glance at the contents and the chapters enable us to see the wide range and penetrating insights into politics and public administration which Kautilya has handled in this encyclopaedic volume of Social Science.

Adhikaran I: Tendencies in State Craft – It explains the nature and functions of *amatya* council, *purohit*, *mantri*, *doot* and *raj bhawan*. It identifies enemy activities and roles of the king and the crown prince vis-à-vis morality.

Adhikaran II: This part depicts the duties and function of administrative heads of departments, important among them are *samaharta, sannidhata* and heads of treasuries, army, parade activities, agriculture and a wide variety of spies indulging in and controlling espionage.

Adhikaran III: It describes the principles and procedures to be followed in judicial administration. Suits pertaining to marriage loans, property, contracts, gambling and purchase-sales deeds have been outlined in great details.

Adhikaran IV: Punishment is the theme of this adhikaran and the Acharya explains the ways and means to protect the empire against conspiracies, espionage systems assassinations and crimes like rape and treason.

Adhikaran V: The duties of public servants have been outlined in this part. Revenue collection, patronage to public servants and punishment to the delinquents have been enumerated with perception and insight.

Adhikaran VI: This part talks about controlling the enemy kingdoms and establishment of peace.

Adhikaran VII: It is the lengthiest part of Arthshastra, commencing from six elements and then examining the various kinds of treaties managing conflicts and discords with in and outside the state.

Adhikaran VIII: It is a fascinating account of political ailments and their eradication in each category of diseased brains.

Adhikaran IX: Here in Kautilya exhibits his deep understanding of military strategies, necessary to be planned before an invasion. His analysis of army organisation, placement of forces, treason and anticipation of disaster needs a special mention.

Adhikaran X: It describes varieties of field fights and ambushes by the soldiers. Even cantonment management and organising *chakravyahus* can be read with great interest.

Adhikaran XI: Enumerates the techniques of divide and rule.

Adhikaran XII: Defence measures for the state against enemy tactics have been explored in this specific adhikaran.

Adhikaran XIII: Forts and their special protection is the subject matter of this part.

Adhikaran XIV: Use of poison in warfare was a special kind of combat technique in Kautilya's times.

Adhikaran XV: Here the Acharya talks about the basic principles of economy which have a decisive bearing on politics and management of the public exchequer.

Apparently this wide-ranging study enunciating the principles of defence administration, military strategy, diplomatic manipulations, punishment systems and land revenue cannot be clubbed under one rubric or academic discipline. The interdisciplinary nature apart, the administrative contents of adhikaran one, two, fifth and sixth make it a book of public administration. The divine origin of state, the benevolent nature of monarchy, the principles of organisations of justice and finance along with sharp insights in merit-based bureaucracy bring Kautilya in line with Weber and Taylor. Though he is often compared with Machiavelli's State Craft and Study of Power, a sober study makes him a real contemporary of Plato and Aristotle in the context of Mauryan empire and its conflicts.

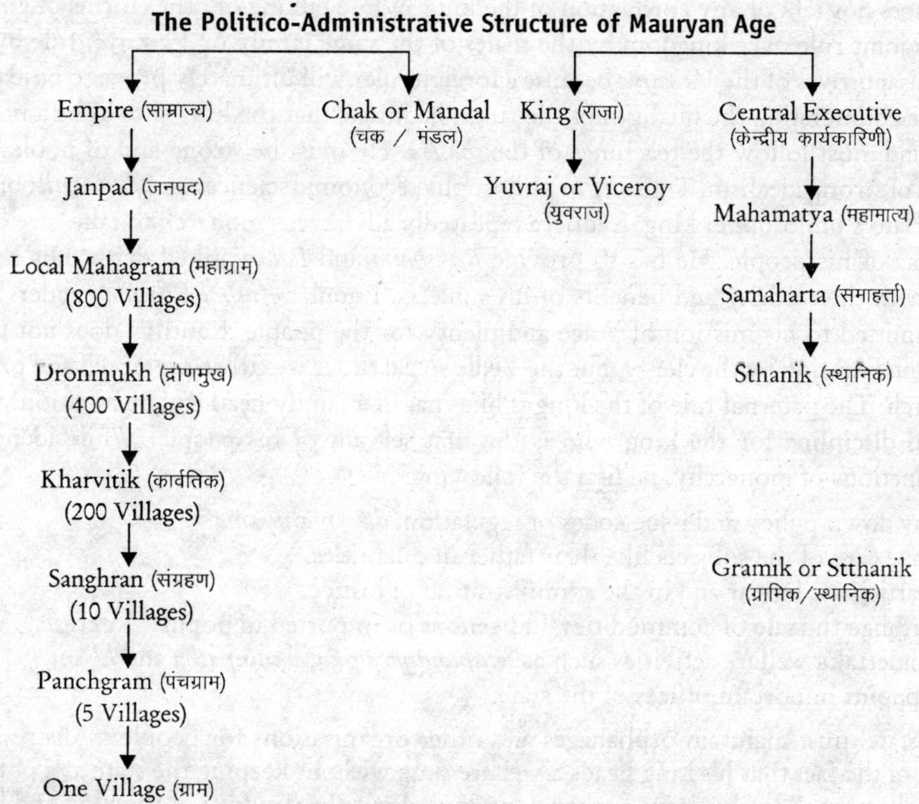

The Political System in Arthshastra

The historical structure of the empire handling unprecedented problems of survival compelled Kautilya to develop his philosophy, vision and theories of state, government and administration. Although, Kautilya did not propound any specific theory about origin, nature and functions of state, yet compared with Western thinkers of his time and later his ideas come close to propound the following:

(1) Divine origin of monarchical state.
(2) Benevolent monarchy with restraints.
(3) The amatya and the mantri parishad as advisors.
(4) The welfare state based on Dharma, Artha and Kama.
(5) The saptang doctrine of seven prakritis.

The Monarchical Government

Unlike the mediaeval writer's of the West, the king of Kautilya does not enjoy any derived or delegated powers from any ecclesiastical organisation. In fact, Arthshastra does not talk of divine origin or social contract. Even scriptures have not been quoted to make the king powerful. But Manu being the son of Vivasvat, the rulers were regarded as descendent of Sun God. The element of divinity is bestowed upon the king by implication so that people may treat kings with respect. The king is like Indra and Yama in his rewards and punishments. Monarchy is an accepted norm and Kautilya does not talk of any coronation of the king. While talking of other forms of government, (*Dvatrajya* joint rule over kingdom by the males of the same family or *Vairajya*, rule by a foreign ruler) he disapproves of the *Vairajya* because a foreign ruler will ultimately prove to be exploitative.

While enumerating the qualities of the ruler, he insists that the king should be a native of the territory and must follow the teachings of the *shastra.* He must be strong and of noble birth with high sense of strong idealism. Training in philosophy, economic sciences and *dandaniti* bring him at par with Plato's philosopher king. Kautilya repeatedly advises his monarch to take care of the yoga and kshema of his people. He has to provide *Rakshana* and *Palana* liked deity. His happiness is identical with the security and benefits of his subjects. Popular *Kushal Kshema* renders him a real king, committed to his mission of peace and plenty for the people. Kautilya does not talk of any advise or intervention by the clergy, but the Vedic social order was to be preserved and protected by the monarch. The paternal rule of the king is like that of a family head and he mentions varnas and ashrams as discipline for the king who is the first servant of his people. While identifying the specific functions of monarchy, he lists the following:

(1) To lay down policy and issue codes of regulation, *dharmaniyama.*
(2) To take care of the subjects like their father in calamities.
(3) To participate in war and in the administration of justice.
(4) To arrange the sale of commodities, indigenous or imported in popular interests.
(5) To undertake welfare activities such as *setubandha*, *vraja*, *vanikpatha* and *khani.*
(6) To appoint important offices of the state.

The state must maintain orphanages and other organisations for people in distress, which is indicative of the fact that his king heads a welfare state without keeping the state as a police state of revenue collectors. Kautilya is more than conscious about the dandniti of the king and has advised caution to avoid the anger (kop) of his people. Punishment is necessary to prevent anarchy, but the subjects should not be pushed to disaffection (Apacarita). The threat of a popular revolt serves as a check on the wanton use of coercive power. It also shows that popular contentment is the basis of an enduring state.

The king of Kautilya personified his state. He has to be a dharmik person and dharma here is a term equivalent to the modern notion of secular kingship. He follows the shastras but never interprets them in his personal interest. Kautilya expects him to be disciplined, decisive, fearless and above all humble. Expansion of the kingdom is his 'Raj Dharma' (असन्तुष्टा द्विजा नष्टा सन्तुष्टाःच महीभृता) and he has to be a conqueror par excellence. Kautilya goes to the extent of punishing the incapable rulers and asks people to organise for their removal. The kings who violate established codes of moral conduct may even be killed.

The Work Schedule of the Ruler

The king according to Arthshastra has to have a very busy and productive life. His twenty-four hours have been divided into eight parts of three hours each. The day and night schedules are prescribed as under:

With such a busy routine, the king can have a time management of his heavy responsibilities. It demonstrates Kautilya's vast and precious experience as an amatya. His prince is a conqueror so he should find time to discuss matters with his senapati and supervise the espionage system along with inspection of arms. But his duties towards his people must take precedence and he should devote considerable time of his day in personnel, treasury and municipal management. But these trying functions can be performed with ease and wisdom when adequate rest, amusement, sleep and religious study and worship are made available to him along with the advise of his competent ministers. In brief, Arthshastra can be gainfully read by all the rulers in all parts of the world. The text raises perennial questions and offers universal answers about the state, government and its political managers.

Day	
First Part	Familiarisation with the defence matters and budgetary position
Second Part	Inspection of the janpad and municipal work
Third Part	Personal matters like bath, meals, etc.
Fourth Part	Treasury and selection matters
Fifth Part	Consultation with ministers and secret matters
Sixth Part	Personal amusement and leisure
Seventh Part	Inspection of arms
Eighth Part	Discussions with Senapati and planning
Night	
First Part	Meeting with important persons
Second Part	Meals and studies
Third Part	Entertainment and amusement
Fourth and Fifth Parts	Sleep
Sixth Part	Contemplation of shastras or other duties
Seventh Part	Meeting with secret agents and dealing with spies
Eighth Part	Prayers and worship

The Council of Ministers

The council of ministers was headed by the Prime Minister. The Mahamantri or Mahamatya was the most influential minister. The ministers were responsible only to the king who was free to appoint the ministers. Kautilya gives elaborate details about the selection procedure and qualities of ministers. Some of the qualities of ministers listed by him are: (1) 'kuleen' or of a good family or of a high caste, (2) clever, ambitious and adventurous, (3) patient, popular and well versed in shastras including Arthshastra, and (4) efficient, loyal and faithful. The king used to consult his ministers individually and collectively. The 'mantri parishad' was a constitutional institution and was consulted in making high appointments. The offices of deputy and assistant ministers could be created when needed. Individual ministers and the council could have a joint session and the majority decisions prevailed. The king was bound to accept majority decisions, and ministers were free to resign in protest. The system of written records was highly developed and the orders were usually given in writing. Kautilya even provides for a training programme for the crown prince and member of the royal family. Character building finds a special place and the training aimed at physical and mental development of the officials.

The Amatya (अमात्य) comes at top in his hierarchy. He occupied a special position uncomparable with any office in recent times. As a public official, he comes close to the present Cabinet Secretary. Amatya looked after administration and its details. Kautilya separates the two offices of the minister and amatya. The selection to this high position was made by the king who was to be guided by the wise words of scholars like Bharadwaj, Vishalaksha, Parashar, and others. Kautilya believes that only those persons should be appointed as amatya who are capable, reliable, loyal, scholarly and well connected. In his opinion, amatya should be selected from among persons who were efficient, highly intelligent and could take decisions. He ensures high emoluments, good residence and other facilities.

The Tirthas

All the amatyas, mantris and heads of departments have been categorised into 18 tirthas. These are:

(1) Purohit (पुरोहित): Head Priest
(2) Senapati (सेनापति): Commander-in-Chief controlling (i) Elephants, (ii) Horses, (iii) Chariots, (iv) Soldiers, (v) Head of Navy, (vi) Officers of PWD and Medical Department.
(3) Yuvraj (युवराज): Crown Prince
(4) Dauvarik (दौवारिक): Chief of Palace Administration
(5) Antarvarisika (अन्तर्वशिक): Chief of Royal Guard
(6) Prasasta (प्रशास्ता): Magistrate
(7) Samaharta (समाहर्ता): Controller General of Income and Expenditure. His charge included control over a variety of officials of state such as (i) Devtadhayaksha, (ii) Akshyapataradhayaksha, (iii) Panyaadhayaksha, (iv) Knpayadhayaksha, (v) Pautradhayaksha, (vi) Manaadhayaksha, (vii) Sulkadhayaksha, (viii) Sutraadhayaksha, (ix) Sitaadhayaksha, (x) Suraadhayaksha, (xi) Sunaadhayaksha, (xii) Ganikaadhayaksha, (xiii) Ganadhayaksha, (xiv) Mudraadhayaksha, and (xv) Vivitaadhayaksha.
(8) Sannidhata (सन्निधाता) had control over: (i) Koshadhyaksha (कोषाध्यक्ष), (ii) Koshtkaradhyaksha (कोष्ठाकाराध्यक्ष), (iii) Ayudhgaradhyaksha (आयुधागाराध्यक्ष), (iv) Bandhanagaradhyaksha (बन्धनागाराध्यक्ष), and (v) Suwarnadhyaksha (सुवर्णाध्यक्ष).
(9) Pradesta (प्रदेष्टा): Commissioner
(10) Nayak (नायक): Town Guard
(11) Paur (पौर): Mayor of the Town
(12) Vyavaharik (व्यावहारिक)
(13) Karmantika (कार्मान्तिक) controlled: (i) Akaradhyaksha (आकाराध्यक्ष), (ii) Lohadhyaksha (लोहाध्यक्ष), (iii) Lakshanadhyaksha (लक्षणाध्यक्ष), (iv) Roopdarashak (रूपदर्शक), (v) Lavanadhyaksha (लवणाध्यक्ष).
(14) Mantri Parishad (मन्त्रि–परिषदाध्यक्ष): Chief Council of Ministers
(15) Dandpal (दण्डपाल): Officer of Army Department
(16) Durgpal (दुर्गपाल): Guardian of Forts
(17) Antpal (अन्तपाल): Officer Incharge of Boundaries
(18) Atavik (आटविक): Officer of Incharge of Forests

Thus, Kautilya believes in divine benevolence but not in divine origin of monarchy. It makes the king accountable to God through precepts of dharma. The council and the office of amatya stood as a positive check to restrain the abuse of powers although it did not imply any parliamentary form of government or the cabinet system of modern times. The functions made the king *Praja Vatsal* and the adviser in the council though loyal were not the yes men to carry out his orders.

The Saptang Doctrine of State

The Sukraneeti propounded the organic theory of state comparing the king amatya, and treasury with the head, eye and mouth of a human being. Kautilya carries the parallelism further by calling forts as hands and territory as feet of the body politics. His seven prakritis are: (i) The King (राजा), (ii) The Amatya (अमात्य), (iii) Territory (जनपद), (iv) Durg (दुर्ग), (v) Kosh (कोष), (vi) Dand (दण्ड), and (vii) Mitra (मित्र).

These seven organs are essential and interlinked. Kautilya outlines their functions and explains their varieties and problems of management. While examining the notion of janpad he enunciates the principle of decentralisation and suggests a low level hierarchy of local self-government as under:

- Local janpad for 800 villages
- Dronmukh for 400 villages
- Kharvtik for 200 villages
- Sangrahan for 10 villages

There were cooperatives to run rural governments and sthaniks looked after the purs in urban centres. Kautilya classifies army into six varieties and durg and dand enumerate the military canons and administration of justice. The saptang doctrine implies that all the seven organs of the state should be in good health and proper coordination. The king and his amatya should protect the territory through strategic weapons stored in the forts. The state treasury should not be depleted in wasteful exploits. A proper use of punishment techniques should ensure domestic peace but external peace can reign when neighbouring and border states are ruled by trusted friends and dependable allies. The saptang doctrine reminds the ruler about his basic duties, i.e., security of the state and safety of his people. They include all the four elements of Aristotelian state viz., population, territory, government and sovereignty. In fact, preservation and exercise of sovereignty require durg, kosh, dand and mitras in neighbourhood.

The Mandal Theory and Foreign Affairs

Kautilya like Machiavelli discusses the survival problems of state in the midst of a hostile milieu that generates conflicts. He calls the neighbouring state a 'Sahaj Shatru' and an enemy of an enemy state as – natural ally. He classifies states into a quadrivium to plan and conduct foreign policy. These types are: (1) *Vijgishu*, a state whose ruler is always engaged in expansion. This forms the centre. (2) *Ati* states surrounding the *Vijgishu* and are usually inimical to the centre. (3) *Madhyam* which is capable of helping as well as fighting against the ruler. (4) *Udasin* state which observes neutrality in its relations with other states. Kautilya has classified neighbouring kings into twelve categories on the basis of their behaviour and geopolitical situations and conditions.

Like Machiavelli's Florence Kautilya and his king confronted turbulent situations and espionage systems of foreign powers posing a threat to the survival of state. This similarity produced a striking identity of views on foreign affairs in the writings of these two stalwarts of East and West. The doctrines of International law, which are chaotic even today, suggest the universality of human nature and both Kautilya and Machiavelli warn their pupils about chicanery and frauds of the neighbouring rulers. But unlike Machiavelli, Kautilya gives elaborate details about how to handle diplomats and the diplomatic immunities which they should enjoy. The Mandal theory is comparable with the Realist Theory of International Politics as propounded by Hans J. Morgantheau. Kautilya envisages a welfare polity but he is extra conscious about the survival needs of the state surrounded by natural enemies of all sorts. A successful king according to Kautilya should strengthen and increase the prosperity of his country but should miss no opportunity to weaken his enemy. But these military and diplomatic exploits should not disturb the normal functions of the state. Kautilya elaborately describes the methods of conquering enemies and advises the ruler not to merge the enemy territory to avoid future complications. He directs that ambassadors should be treated with high respect and allowed immunities and privileges due to their exalted status. The embassy precincts should be accepted as a part of the country to which the embassy belonged. Privileges like the right of passage and freedom to express their mission should be respected without any offence for the words spoken by them. Hanuman and Angad, enjoyed these immunities as envoys of Ram. But if they refuse to return even without permission of having intimated the unfavourable message to the enemy, they should be punished. The right to ask for termination of mission and the permission to leave the country should be respected by the king.

The Mandal theory of international relations is relevant even today. According to it there are twelve kinds of states which base their foreign policy on six elements in the system. These twelve states are:

(1) Vijigusu (विजीगीषु): Central state desirous to expand
(2) Aari (अरि): The state opposite and first enemy
(3) Mitra (मित्र): The enemy of enemy state but friendly to the central state
(4) Arimitra (अरिमित्र): Enemy of Vijigusu
(5) Mitra Mitra (मित्र मित्र): Friend of friendly state
(6) Arimitra Mitra (अरिमित्र मित्र): Enemy of friend, hence enemy of dwijigusu (दिजीगीषु)
(7) Parthigrah (पार्थिग्राह): Enemy behind vijigusu state
(8) Aakrand (आक्रंद): State behind panigrahan state but friendly to dwijigusu
(9) Panigrahan Sar (पाणिग्रहण सार): Friend of panigrahan hence enemy of vijigusu (विजीगीषु)
(10) Akrand Sar (आक्रंद सार): Friend of Akrand hence friend of dwijigusu (दिजीगीषु)
(11) Madhayam (मध्यम): More powerful than dwijigusu and its enemy
(12) Udasin (उदासीन): Apathetic, but can help

Kautilya has presented these situations and locations almost like a geometric theorem. To handle this complex web of relationships, he advances his Shadyug which takes the following factors into account (1) *sandhi* (संधि), (2) *vigrah* (विग्रह), (3) *yan* (यान), (4) *aasan* (आसन), and (5) *sasram dwadhibhav* (संश्रम द्वैधीभाव). He gives a long list of espionage organisation and diplomats who had to indulge in *sam* (साम), *dam* (दाम), *dand* (दण्ड), *bhed* (भेद), *maya* (माया), etc. to protect the interests of their respective states. His warnings and counsels to the diplomats are of universal import and can be literally accepted by modern ambassadors in the age of terrorism.

Administration and Administrators in Arthshastra

The salient features of the administrative state of Kautilya can be summed up as under:

(1) The hierarchical organisation of departments under political command following the principles of unity of command, control and coordination.
(2) Specialised cadres of personnel, duly classified under 30 adhyakshas, further classified into four categories, namely:
    (a) Incharge of state goods
    (b) Incharge of state establishments
    (c) Incharge of mining and industry
    (d) Incharge of trade and communication

(3) Recruitments, promotion, salary and training system for civil services of the state based on merit. The programme and personnel policies are indicative of Human Resource Development approach of modern times.
(4) Planned management of budget under fifteen account heads with special emphasis on control.
(5) A decentralised pattern of land management at janpad level and below with officers like sthanika, gopa, gram swamin, gramika and samaharti, etc.
(6) Yoga and kshema were stressed as the ultimate objective of the state and its public officials, entrusted with specific and responsibilities of public welfare. It was not a tax gathering police station to terrify people.

Although bureaucracy will be a wrong concept to be employed to public officials of a Mauryan state, still a detailed account of a variety of officials, their eligibility qualifications, functions and relationships are systematically mentioned in Arthshastra. The *mukt* (मुक्त), *upyukt* (उपयुक्त), and *tatpurush* (तत्पुरुष) were the three categories of officials in every department. The eligibility qualification for the public officials have been enumerated as *satva* (सत्त्व), *pragya* (प्रज्ञा), and Vakshakti (वाक्‌शक्ति). Kautilya goes further and even suggests various tests to discover and measure these qualities. These test were *dharmopdha* (धर्मोपधा), *arbhodadha* (अर्भोदधा), *ayopdha* (अयोपधा) and *karmapadha* (कार्मापधा). In each case loyalty of the official to the King and his integrity not to succumb to worldly allurements was insisted upon. Even intelligibilities like *mulahar* (मुलाहर) (i.e., squandering of patrimony), *tadicchki* (तदच्चिकी) (over spending) and kandarp (कदर्प) (unwanted miserliness) have been identified to avoid unworthy recruitment. The amatya (अमात्य) and matrin (मत्रिन्) had 18 tirthas (departments) which outlines the range of bureaucratic functions of Kautilya's state. In addition to the Yuvraj (युवराज) often functioning as senapati (सेनापति), the following public officials constituted the top and lower echelons of administrative hierarchy.

(1) The Purohit (पुरोहित): He was the prime functionary among the 18 tirthas. A scholarly and a person of blue blood, he was a father figure in the administration. He was overall incharge of the entire government and its administrative departments. The early Hindu books talk high of this office, who was supposed to keep the state government in a state of equilibrium. It was a key office and combined the two modern positions of a chief minister and the chief secretary.
(2) Senapati (सेनापति): He was a member of the council of ministers and a trusted soldier who used to manage a chaturangni armed force as chief. He looked after the following departments:
    (i) Elephant Force (हस्त्याध्यक्ष) with gajshalas
    (ii) Horse Cavalry (अश्वाध्यक्ष) and horse register
    (iii) Chariot Force (रथाध्यक्ष) with ammunitions
    (iv) Infantry (पत्याध्यक्ष) with variety of contingents
    (v) Naval Officer (नौकाध्यक्ष) to guard waterways, rivers and coasts
(3) Yuvraj (युवराज): He was the hair apparent to the throne. His human qualities and administrative abilities have been listed in great details.
(4) Dauvarik (दौवारिक): He was incharge of royal household.
(5) Antarvasik (अन्तर्वशिक): He was the chief of army and bodyguard of the king. He looked after security problems of royal family and servants. There were not a part of state bureaucracy being too close to the king, they have also been referred as *antermatyaja* (अन्तरमत्याज).

(6) Prashasta (प्रशास्ता): He was a sort of an engineer incharge for the upkeep of road, bridges and transport of soldiers.

(7) Samaharta (समाहर्ता): He was the chief of general administration and managed the treasury. His other functions have been narrated as controlling of:
   (i) Durgs,
   (ii) Rasta,
   (iii) Khani, and
   (iv) Setu

   (a) Van (वन), (b) Vraj (व्रज), and (c) Vanikpath (वणिक्पथ) were also under his jurisdiction.

   The tax revenue from the sale of vegetables (one sixth of produce), fines from delinquent traders, estate duty, taxes and other dues were recorded. Expenditure incurred upon deities, ecclesiastical affairs, royal household, diplomats, defence forces and protection of animals were checked and controlled by him. His juniors included:
   (i) Devtaadhyaksha (देवताध्यक्ष): He looked after the temples and their income.
   (ii) Akshpatalaadhyaksha (अक्षपटलाध्यक्ष): He was the head of accounts department.
   (iii) Panyaadhyaksha (पण्याध्यक्ष): He arranged supply of commodities at reasonable price to people.
   (iv) Kupyaadhyaksha (कुण्याध्यक्ष): His functions were to manage the supply of woods and forest produce.
   (v) Peeatvaadhyaksha (पौतवाध्यक्ष): His office checked the weight and measures and examined the sample of adulterated goods in the market.
   (vi) Manaadhyaksha (मानाध्यक्ष): He was to enforce the rules pertaining to weather, time and calendar.
   (vii) Shulkadhyaksha (शुल्काध्यक्ष): Officer incharge of excise.
   (viii) Sutradhyaksha (सूत्राध्यक्ष): Officer for textiles and leather goods.
   (ix) Sitadhyaksha (सीताध्यक्ष): Head of agriculture and land produce.
   (x) Suradhyaksha (सुराध्यक्ष): Prohibition officer arranging and forbidding sale of liquor.
   (xi) Sunadhyaksha (सूनाध्यक्ष): Officer controlling slaughter houses.
   (xii) Ganikadhyaksha (गणिकाध्यक्ष): Officer controlling prostitutes and comfort girls.
   (xiii) Gaoadhyaksha (गोअध्यक्ष): Officer incharge of animal slaughter.
   (xiv) Mudraadhyaksha (मुद्राध्यक्ष): Immigration officer.
   (xv) Vivitadhyaksha (विवीताध्यक्ष): Officer for pastures and grasslands.

(8) Treasury Officer (सान्निधाता): He used to arrange for the construction of prison houses, food depots, forest property stores, ordinance depots and marketing centres, etc., to collect revenue and control public expenditure. He worked with the following officers in his department.
   (i) Koshadhyaksha (कोषाध्यक्ष): He accepted precious metals for the treasury and kept details about their purity and price, etc.
   (ii) Kostagaradhyaksha (कोष्ठागाराध्यक्ष): He managed the supply of ghee, oil corn and excess grains in each category.
   (iii) Ayudagaradhyaksha (आयुधागाराध्यक्ष): He was an ordinance officer, who used to control arms stored in basement. He supervised defence and production of ornaments.
   (iv) Bandhanagaradhyaksha (बन्धनागाराध्यक्ष): He was the jail superintendent looking after male and female prisons and was responsible for their maintenance.

(v) Suvarnadhyaksha (सुवर्णाध्यक्ष): Head of gold and silver mints. Artisans used to manufacture ornaments under his care and supervision.

(vi) Pradesta (प्रदेष्टा): He was a judicial officer for the protection of weaker sections. Petty crimes were reported to him and he acted like a magistrate.

(vii) Nayak (नायक): He conducted military operation during the war. The army columns were organised and horse and elephants were arranged as per strategy of the enemy.

(viii) Paur (पौर) also called as Nagarik: He worked with gops and sthaniks.

(ix) Vyavaharik (व्यावहारिक): He was the head of the religious court. He adjudicated in matters pertaining to marriages, contracts, sale of property, loans, gambling, etc.

(x) Karmantik (कार्मान्तिक): An official looking after mines, forests and factories. The following junior officials helped him:

  (1) Aakaradhyaksha (आकराध्यक्ष): He used to test metals, minerals.
  (2) Lakshanadhyaksha (लक्षणाध्यक्ष): Officers responsible for coinage and management of mints.
  (3) Roopdarshak (रूपदर्शक): Examiner of coins and counterfeit currency in the empire.
  (4) Lohaedhyaksha (लौहाध्यक्ष): Specialist for fasting of steel, copper, glass, etc.
  (5) Lavanaadhyaksha (लवणाध्यक्ष): Officer incharge for sale and storage of salt.

(xi) Head of Mantri Parishad (मन्त्रि–परिषदाध्यक्ष): He was a sort of secretary to the council of ministers. He kept record of the minutes of the meetings.

(xii) Dandpal (दण्डपाल): He was a police-cum-military officer through whom the king used his powers of punishment and coercion.

(xiii) Durgpal (दुर्गपाल): He looked after the forts which needed construction repairs and protection.

(xiv) Antpal (अन्तपाल): He was an officer guarding borders of the empire. He controlled entry points and immigration through vehicles, etc.

(xv) Aatvik (आटविक): A forest officer, looking after nomic tribes and preservation of forest woods, etc.

All these officers enjoyed wide ranging powers but it will be wrong to assert that they were extra powerful. The punishments for dereliction of duties were harsh and public welfare was the major consideration in evaluating the services of these officials. The way Kautilya describes the designation, nature and functions of these officials is indicative of the administrative operations of his Mauryan state. He was the architect of this administrative apparatus and his theoretical knowledge and field experience of administration offer deep and penetrating insights into public administration. Officers like Vyavaharik, Ganikadhyaksha, Suradhyaksha and Sunadhyaksha prove that administrators were widely engaged in social service activities and control of animal slaughter houses and public morals. The Sannidhata had dozens of officials for basic public functions. Specialisation apart, the entire public bureaucracy had wide ranging functions including weather forecasts, forests and customs. This Mauryan bureaucracy of Arthshastra needs research and the modern public personnel systems can gainfully be revamped from this historical experience.

Public administration in ancient India as we understand it today was conditioned by ethical considerations of a monarchic state, confronting internal conflicts and political chicanery around. Kautilya and all others who were engaged in enunciating the principles or describing the administrative institutions are partly normative and partly empirical in their approach. The administrative insights are based on the realities of the situation and the idealistic cures to rectify the ailments. No wonder a Kautilya looks Machiavellian and comes close to Max Weber or Winslow Taylor. In fact, the similes are far fetched and unfair. Rationality being the universal basis of administrative activity creates an ideal type of Weberian bureaucracy in Arthshastra also but the anarchic situations of the empire ask Kautilya to exhort upon his pupil to distinguish between private and public morality. The time and space make a big difference, but the root problems of state craft and diplomacy are constant and enduring. This period of Indian history, notwithstanding its glories and shame, soon eclipsed with the advent of invaders or bandits from Persia. The invasions of Sindh witnessed the rise of Sultans and later on the Mughal emperors of Indian history who systematically destroyed the ancient system to establish a military state in India.

II
The Muslim Period (1206–1757)
(The Emergence of Islamic Military State in India)

This period stands divided into two parts: (a) The Delhi Sultanate period, and (b) The Mughal empire. There is conspicuous continuity in the two periods and put together the period is called as 'Muslim Period' or mediaeval period of Indian history.

It is difficult to work out the date when Hindu period ended, but the invasions of Mohammad Bin Kasim and conquest of Sindh in 8th century was an epoch making event. The Sultanate of Delhi began with Shahbuddin Ghori in 1192 and his provincial Governor Qutubuddin Aibek ascended the throne in 1206. The Sultanate period lasted till 1526 when its last Sultan Ibrahim Lodi lost the Sultanate to Babur in the first battle of Panipat in 1526. The following dynasties of Afgan rulers ruled Delhi from 1206 to 1526.

Slave Dynasty	1206 to 1290
Khilji Dynasty	1290 to 1320
Tughlak Dynasty	1320 to 1414
Saiyyad Dynasty	1414 to 1451
Lodi Dynasty	1451 to 1526

Several outstanding names like Iltutmush Balban, Razziya Sultan, Allauddin Khilji, Mohamad Bin Tughlak stand out as empire builders and great administrators. Babur, a Chagtai Turk of Timur. and Chingiz parentage founded the New Mughal dynasty, but his sudden demise in 1530 put his son Humayun in great difficulties. He tumbled through life and faced bitter wars and exile at the hands of Sher Shah, till his final victory in 1555. He died after few months and his minor son Jalaluddin Mohammad Akbar had to win the second battle of Panipat to ascend the throne of Delhi. He founded the Mughal rule in India. The first four *Padshahs* or emperors were good rulers and the dynasty flourished under Akbar, Jahangir, Shah Jahan and Aurangzeb. But the empire disintegrated after Aurangzeb's death and a number of new power centres arose on its ruins. The later Mughals were helpless onlookers and the British East India Company captured the reigns of power after the battle of Plassey in 1757. The last Mughal king, Bahadur Shah Zafar, was dethroned and exiled in 1858.

The Sultanate Administration

It was basically military and its rulers were despots. The Sultans established a systematic administration wherein the Sultan was supreme. He had all the political, legal and military powers and was responsible for judicial administration. The Sultans had advisors but they were non-entities. The military rule of the Sultans divided India into regions under principal generals. The king had ministers but their opinions did not matter much. The chief of these ministers was *wazir* who was the head of administration. The wazir had his secretariat and a chain of civil officers. The head of the military department and two civil *dewans* looked after religious matters, holy institutions and correspondence. The Sultanate was divided into *prants* and administrated by civil departments. The *prants* were divided into *shikos* headed by *shikdars*. The shikos were divided into *sarkars*, sarkars into *parganas* and parganas into villages. The urban administration was run by a centralised bureaucracy, but the villages had some sort of self-rule. The chart below explains the administrative organisation of the Sultanate.

This history of India from 1526 to 1555 is the story of Mughal-Afgan conflicts for supremacy. Akbar's decisive victory marks the beginning of Mughal empire in India. His expansionist policy coupled with liberal secular approach enabled him to consolidate the empire. The process continued for some time but when Aurangzeb reversed this policy the disintegration started which his unworthy successors could not arrest and reverse. The European traders who had arrived in India with their merchandise soon jumped into the fray and the battle of Plassy won by Lord Clive gave a decisive turn to political events of Indian history.

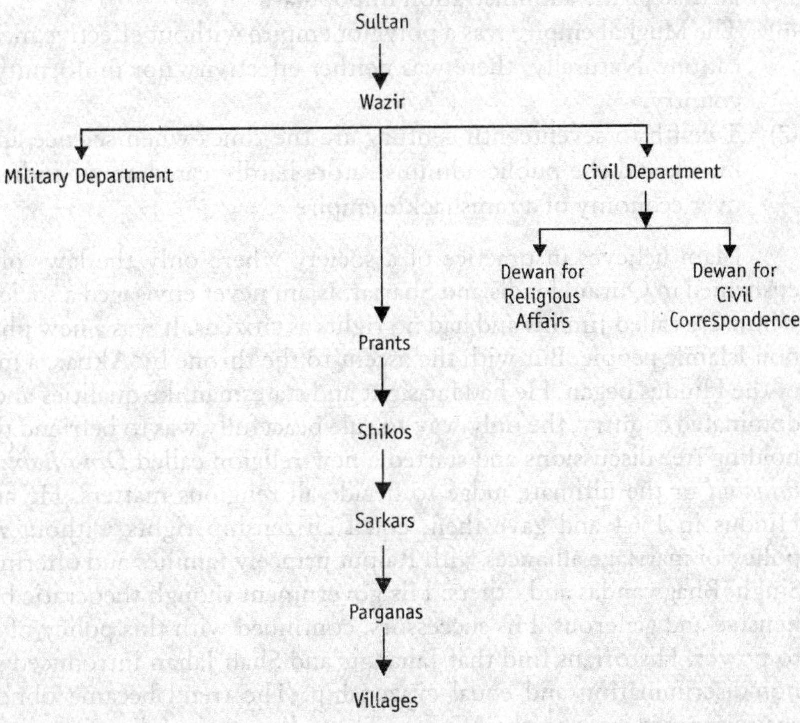

The Islamic State and Its Administration

A few exception apart the Mughal state was an Islamic military state purposely designed and perpetrated on the non-Islamic people of India. The administration which the alien rulers brought from Central Asia could neither wipe out the native system nor could it be superimposed on a vast country of India's size and diversities. Naturally, all sorts of graftings were attempted and as the Mughal government settled down, its revenue and police functions became prominent. Allauddin Khilji and Sher Shah initiated the process of welfarism which Akbar took over with special efforts in the fields of military, revenue, police and judicial administrations. The following features of Mughal state and mediaeval administration deserve consideration:

(1) In Indo-sarcemic character of institutions and practices were in perso Arabic graftings and were attempted on the traditional settings of Hindu period.
(2) The military nature of civil rule based on Mausabdari and Rayaatwari system designed in the absence of a standing national militia.
(3) The Islamic nature of monarchy which can broadly be called as centralised despotism of a Padshah.
(4) Police functions and revenue collection being the two major functions of the state. The entire administrative exercise was concentrated to these two segments of administration without any notion of development.
(5) The fusion of religion and politics bedevilled the administrative system and tax practices like *Jazia* kept the administration unpopular.
(6) The Mughal empire was a polyglot empire without effective means of transport and communications. Naturally, there was neither effectivity nor uniformity of rules in governance of the country.
(7) Twelfth to seventeenth century are the times when science and technology had not made a knock and the public administrators hardly cared about industrial developments or control over economy of a ramshackle empire.

Islam believes in practice of a society where only the laws of God operate. These laws are enshrined in Quran, Hadis and Shariat. Islam never envisaged a society dominated by non-Muslims who were called Jimmis and had no rights as citizens. It was a new phenomenon of Islamic rule over non-Islamic people. But with the ascent to the throne by Akbar, a marked change in the treatment of the Hindus began. He had far-sight and statesmanlike qualities and soon realised that in a Hindu dominated country, the only way to rule peacefully was to befriend them. He started the practice of holding free discussions and started a new religion called *Din-i-Ilahi*. He declared himself to be the *mujahid* or the ultimate judge to decide all religious matters. He abolished the 'jazia' tax on the Hindus in 1564 and gave them equal citizenship rights without religious discriminations. The policy of marriage alliances with Rajput princely families and offering high posts to chiefs like Man Singh, Bhagwandas and others. His government though theocratic became more tolerant, comprehensive and generous. His successors, continued with this policy of tolerance till Aurangzeb came to power. Historians find that Jahangir and Shah Jahan introduced some changes in this policy of non-discrimination and equal citizenship. The trend became obnoxious when Aurangzeb once again imposed jazia on the Hindus. The policy evoked dissatisfaction and led to rebellions and the downfall of the empire could not be averted.

The Padshah or the Emperor

In 1526, Babur proclaimed himself as the Padshah, which denotes stability and over lordship of ruler, the Shah. It literally means a sovereign owing allegiance to none. Padshahship implied political and religious headship and supreme commandership of the armed forces. As a head of judiciary, he became the fountain of justice and an ultimate lawgiver to the people. Although Islam does not recognise divine representativeness of kind but the Mughal rulers cherished the doctrine of divine rights. They lived in luxury and enjoyed privileges. Sizda, Khutba Jharoka were practised and all sorts of discriminations and persecutions were allowed to legitimise the imperial power of the Padshah. During Mughal dispensation, the emperor enjoyed real sovereignty which was indivisible and inalienable. Within his realm, the Padshah stood supreme as the symbol of unity and peace performing major functions of government. As head of state, the emperor headed the civil and military administrations, and made appointment and dismissal of all high officials. The *farmans* bore his signatures and seal. The expenditure and sources of revenue were decided by him without being formally accountable to the people. But, most of the Mughal emperors did not abuse their powers. Paternalistic benevolence covered their despotism. The emperors toured the country extensively and the idea of a fixed capital did not meet their favour. Akbar, used to do his all administrative work in an open *darbar* called the *Diwan-i-Aam*. As per code of Islam, the emperor should have been chosen by the people. But the Muslim rulers did not practise even the law of primogeniture in India. Their children raised banners of revolt and fought bloody wars for the throne which became one of the reasons of disintegration of the mighty empire.

The Indo-Arabic Nobility

The Mughal government was a combination of native and perso Arabic system. The Mughal nobility was a heterogeneous group of influential people around the throne. It consisted of members of ruling elites from among Turks, Tartars, Persians, Hindus and native Muslims. It was purely official and did not operate on the basis of heredity. Some of them occupied significant positions in the army and bureaucracy. Inter marriages among these nobles caused cliques and palace infights for power and birth of successors. Still the non-hereditary and heterogeneous character of this Indo-Arabic nobility presented the rise of a counter elite to rise in rebellion. The healthy and pernicious influence of these notables and nobles shaped the composition and working of council of ministers and the administrative officials at each level of hierarchy.

The Council of Ministers

Under Muslim rule there is no provision in the law to have colleagues. The Muslim ministers were merely assistants to the Padshah who was free to consult them at will and was not bound by their advice. The high officers in Mughal administration were responsible to the king but the Muslim law was silent about their number and mode of appointment including qualifications necessary for holding such posts. Practically, all Mughal rulers in India had some important officers to assist them but they bear no resemblance to the council of ministers. The wazir and the diwan were always there but the rest of the officials were determined exclusively by the emperor. They were mere delegates of the royal polity. They advised the sovereign but this advice was not binding. They provided no checks on the royal will and, in no sense can be called his colleagues. One may call them 'secretaries rather than ministers'. They influenced his policy either by gentle persuasion or veiled warning. Babur and Humayun appointed wazirs but Akbar's patron Bairam Khan styled himself as *Vakil-i-Sultanat* and became all-powerful. He may be compared with a modern Prime Minister. Akbar was the first emperor to separate the two offices of vakil and wazir. The office of the vakil continued till the time of Shah Jahan, but was of little consequence. The Sultanate legacy of four wazirs or ministers got revived. These ministers were: (1) Diwan responsible for revenue and finance; (2) *Mir Bakshi* in charge of the army and administration; (3) *Chief Sadar* or *Sadra-ul-Sadar* in charge of judiciary and religion; and (4) *Mir Saman* in charge of royal store houses and *karkhanas*. In fact, these four offices of ministers were the pillars of the Mughal empire.

The Mughal Government at Centre

A host of authentic information about the organisation of the central government of Mughal rulers can be gleaned from varied original sources like *Dastur-ul-Amar*, *Padshahnama Tuzuk Jahangiri*,

Tabkati Akbari and the like. In addition to the Padshah and his wazir, there were advisers close to the royal household. Historian J.N. Sarkar maintains that "the Mughals did not have any formal cabinet" and the ways of working were unwritten and largely informal. Still there was a semblance of a portfolio system and the following heads constituted the council of the Padshah.

(1) Diwan (दीवान): Exchequer and revenue
(2) Khan-i-saman (खानशामा): Imperial household high steward
(3) Bakshi (बक्षी): Military pay and accounts office
(4) Qazi (काजी): Canon law, both civil and criminal
(5) Sadar (सदर): Religious endowments and charity
(6) Muhatsib (मुहात्सिब): Censorship of public morals
(7) Mir Aatish (मीर आतिश): The Artillery
(8) Daroga Dak Chowki (दरोगा डाक चौकी): Intelligence and posts

These officials political as well as administrative looked after their respective charges. It was something comparable to a departmental system but mostly concentrating on personnel problems in the absence of effective control mechanism. Some historians will like to call them secretaries rather than ministers in a theocratic and despotic monarchy.

Provincial Administration of the Suba

Akbar decreed a ten-year *Ain-i-Dahsala*, i.e., a new revenue system which reorganised the imperial territory into twelve *subas*. The *suba* had an administrative system which was a sort of miniature replica of the central government of the emperor. The *Subedar*, also known as *Shipah Salar* headed the province and was responsible for revenue, law and order, and judicial administrations. The functional hierarchy operated as under:

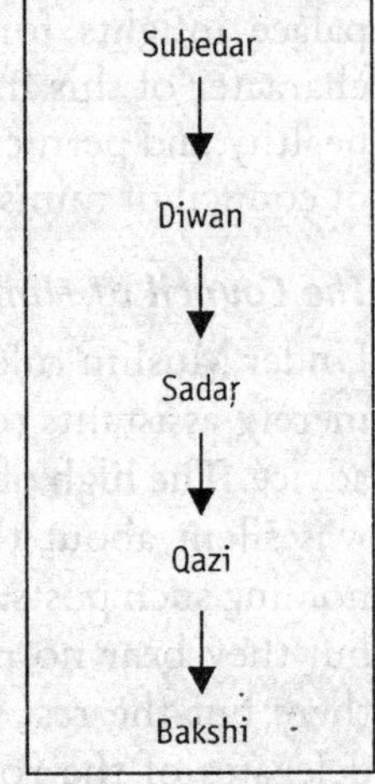

These provincial functionaries did not receive executive orders from their counterparts at centre nor did they function under the subedar in a strict hierarchy. Their functions were broad and the officials below at sarkar or paragana levels looked for their guidance.

Administration at Sarkar, Paragana and Village Levels

Administration at this level and below was elaborate and real. The emperors created geographical units with the expansion of empire but its military and urban bias continued. The following chart presents the units and the official's incharge of these units.

The provinces subdivided into sarkars were comparable to modern districts and these, in turn, were subdivided into parganas. The head of the province was called subedar who was appointed by the emperor himself. The high officials were selected for their military prowess and administrative qualities. In addition to high salaries and allowances; they held high *mansabs*. They were transferred to different provinces after every three to five years. The subedar had three kinds of duties, namely: civil, military and judicial. As head of civil administration, his main duty was to maintain law and order. He also headed the provincial army and was responsible for the upkeep of armed forces. He was also the supreme judge in the province and held the final court of appeal from the lower courts. In revenue and financial matters the diwan was final word and he was appointed by the king himself. The subedar was the head of the military and civil administrations and all officers from fauzdar downwards were under him. The diwan controlled revenue officials in the province and the subedar was dependent on diwan in financial matters. But conversely the diwan had to depend on the subedar in military and law and order matters.

The Mughal province divided into sarkars was comparable with the present day districts. There was dual administration and the executive and revenue wings constituted the district administration. The head of the executive wing was the *fauzdar* who was the highest officer in the sarkar. He was a prototype of the present day collector and district magistrate. He held a mansab and worked under the control of the provincial subedar. Similarly, the *amal guzar* was the revenue official in charge of financial and revenue matters. He was the highest revenue officer in the district and worked under the control of the provincial diwan with a number of subordinates assisting him in his duties. Each sarkar in turn was subdivided into parganas and each pargana was a cluster of villages. The pargana was an administrative and revenue unit, something akin to the present *tehsil* or *taluq*. In addition to these units, there were acquired administrative areas under the direct control of the central government like the ports, frontier posts, forts, *chaklas* and *thanas* or police stations.

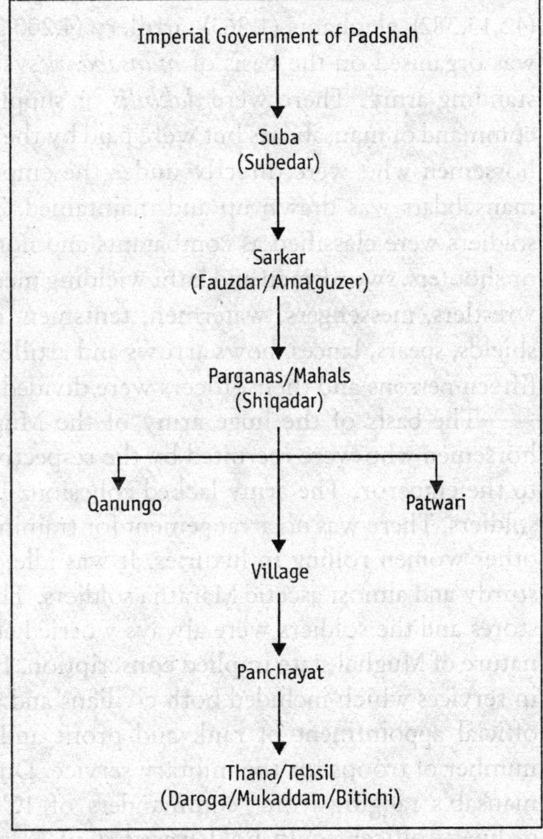

There was really no arrangement for local government. The villages were largely left untouched by the Mughal administration and stray gram panchayats looked after village matters. There was nothing like the present municipal administration.

Historians like Sir J.N. Sarkar, hold the view that the Mughals were essentially urban people and preferred to lead a city life. The villages were neglected and even despised, the village life was dreaded by Mughal official as punishment. The state did not undertake welfare activities. It was apathetic to people unless there was some violent crime or defiance of royal authority in the villages. Sarkar maintains that "every village was left free to continue the noiseless tenor of its life along the old grooves, untroubled by the government if it did not trouble the government". The provincial government interacted with the villages through the faujdars, the lower level officials of the revenue department, the contact of *zamindars* with subedars, and the inspections of the subedars. The contact was quite limited and could never become intimate.

Mansabdari System and the Army

Unlike the armed forces of Mauryas and Guptas the Mughal built their own army organisation with the help of native Hindu rulers and princely chieftains. Akbar made special efforts in this field. According to *Ain-i-Akbari*, the total number of the Mughal army was – cavalry (3,86,618), infantry

(42,13,382), elephants (1,863), artillery (4,200 guns), and navy (4,500 ships of all types). The cavalry was organised on the basis of *mansabdari* system. The Mughals did not have any need for a large standing army. There were *dakhilis* or supplementary troopers also who were placed under the command of mansabdars but were paid by the state. Then, there were the *Ahadis* or a special class of horsemen who were directly under the emperor. Periodical musters or a descriptive roll of the mansabdars was drawn up and maintained. The system of branding horses was strict. The foot soldiers were classified as combatants and non-combatants. The former included archers, gunmen or shooters, swordsmen and lathi wielding men. The non-combatants consisted of attendants, *sayies*, wrestlers, messengers, watermen, tentsmen, etc. The armoury of foot soldiers included swords, shields, spears, lances, bows arrows and artillery. The infantrymen were organised into platoons of fifteen persons and their officers were divided into four categories.

The basis of the huge army of the Mughals was the mansabdari system. The soldiers and horsemen who were recruited by the respective mansabdars were more loyal to their masters than to the emperor. The army lacked cohesion. The mansabdars rarely maintained their full quota of soldiers. There was no arrangement for training these soldiers. The army had all sorts of *begums* and other women rolling in luxuries. It was idle, lethargic and spiritless and could not cope with the sturdy and almost ascetic Maratha soldiers. There was no adequate arrangement for provisions and stores and the soldiers were always worried about these matters than actual warfare. The military nature of Mughal state implied conscription. Hence, it led to the creation of the mansabdari system in services which included both civilians and army officers. Every public officer held a mansab or official appointment of rank and profit and every mansabdar was expected to supply a given number of troops for the military service. During Akbar's reign, there were thirty-three grades of mansab's ranging from 'commanders of 10' to 'commanders of 10,000'. The highest rank an ordinary officer could hold was that of a commanders of 5,000. The senior upper grades were reserved for members of the royal family. These mansabdars were directly recruited, promoted, suspended or even removed by the emperor himself. Each grade carried a definite rate of pay, out of which the holder was expected to maintain a quota of horses, elephants, loading animals and carts. The rank was not hereditary and any officer could be entrusted at any moment with an entirely new duty. The system had numerous pitfalls because the mansabdars rarely fulfilled the condition of maintaining their required quota. The public officials were paid in cash and or in jagirs. *Ain-i-Akbari* holds the testimony that the Mughal officers enjoyed 'inordinately high salaries'. After making deductions for the maintenance and other incidental expenses, a Mansabdar of 5,000 used to get a net salary of 18,000 a month. The general character of the public services remained unchanged during the reign of Aurangzeb but it became worse in later years.

Administration of Police and Judiciary

The central government of the Mughals did not have any office comparable to a present day Home Minister. The emperor was responsible for peace and order in the four corners of the empire. There were *faujdars* in the provinces. The *kotwal* under the control of faujdar appointed headmen for *mohallas* to look after the reports about law and order situations. The law and order situation in the villages were reported only when there were violent crimes. The policing of the rural areas was by and large a local affair. The *chaukidars* were maintained by the villagers themselves out of the village land or through a share of the crops. They were neither paid nor supervised by the police officers of state. The Mughal government did not undertake any responsibility for rural peace and security. Rather, it made the villagers responsible for the safety of their own property and that of travellers in the neighbouring roads. A reference of all-powerful kotwals or darogas is found in almost all sources. The *Ain-i-Akbari* delineates the duties of a kotwal as under:

(1) To detect thieves and criminals,
(2) To oversee prices and check weights and measures,
(3) To keep vigil and do night patrolling,
(4) To keep register of houses and movements of citizens and foreigners,
(5) To employ spies,
(6) To gather information about income of people,
(7) To prepare inventory of persons with property and without heirs,
(8) To prevent slaughter of horses, camels and buffalos, and
(9) To prevent the burning of women.

The list presents an awareness of police responsibilities and the rudiments of a thana police which survives even today. However, the arrest, custody, prosecution and trial systems of Mughal times is uncomparable with the modern English court system which follows the rule of law and assistance by the learned members of the bar.

The Mughal emperors regarded it as their sacred duty to dispense impartial justice and to organise a judicial system accessible to their subjects. The liberals among them did not strictly enforce the Islamic law which was not acceptable to a large majority of Hindu population. The organisation of a just and impartial judicial system was viewed as a sacred duty. Humayun, introduced a *tabal adal* or a system of judicial trumpets which his grandson Jahangir continued by providing the golden chain. The chain was 28 metres long and had sixty bells which could be pulled by the aggrieved at anytime. Shah Jahan was more orthodox but he too was famous for his impartial justice. Aurangzeb though a *sunni* wanted to establish the rule of the *shariat* throughout his empire, yet he too was honest and impartial in the dispensation of justice. The department of law was headed by the *Qazi* who tried criminal suits according to Islamic law and acted as a Chief Justice in suits involving religious affairs. The *ulema* was the spokesperson of Islamic law of which the Qazi was the guardian. The civil cases also fell under his jurisdiction of the Qazi and his court.

The Administration of Land Revenue

The Sultan of Delhi laid the foundations of land revenue system for rural India. The system underwent radical changes at the hands of Akbar whose revenue minister, Todarmal has been credited for the land administration of our times. The administration of land revenue was organised in three parts, namely, (a) land mapping and land registration; (b) land revenue assessment on the basis of land classification as *polaz*, *parti*, *banjar*; and (c) land revenue realisation which was done by an army of civil servants under various exceptions and concessions. The wazir or the diwan were in charge of the system at the centre. The emperors took interest in supervision and Akbar appointed Diwan-i-tan and Diwani-i-Khalsa to assist his wazir. The two junior functionaries called as *mushriff* and *mustaufi* helped them in controlling the accounts of revenues to the treasury. There was a public record office and the diwan signed revenue documents including major collection and payments. The provincial diwans reported to the imperial diwan about local collections. Amount of one crore of dam (i.e., 2.5 lakh rupees) was the national limit of revenue and hence the revenue official at the district level was called *Krori*. In the collection of revenue, the karori was assisted by the *amin* in assessing the revenue which was collected by the fotedar. Todarmal introduced this system in Gujarat. The *Ilahi Gaj* was Tanals and *Zarib* joined by iron rings assured a constant measure. *Chachar*, *polaz*, *parti* and banjar lands were given different assessments. The share of the state was fixed at one-third of the produce. The system was based on rayalwadi, under which this cultivator was the assessee. The malguzar collected the revenue. The Mughal state was essentially a revenue gathering state without its due returns to the farmer. Hence, historian Sarkar finds terrible antagonism between the revenue administrator and *riyaya* of the kingdom. There were leakages in the land revenue administration and the offices of patwari and tehsildars were seeped in corruption. The petty revenue officials were poorly paid and collected illicit money through *nazaranas* or gifts from the exploited peasantry.

Personnel Administration of the Mughals

The Mughal mansabdari personnel system was a mixture of Hindu feudalism and Persian borrowings. It combined the military and civil administration in a meaningful manner. Historian Irwin calls it a system of positional hierarchy which classified the levels and quantum of salaries of official. These rankings were from 10 to 10,000 which Akbar raised to 12,000. These mansabdars have three categories determined on the basis of number of horses or elephants each mansabdar had to maintain. According to Blochman, the civil assignments were given on the basis of merit and training was provided to induct efficiency. Promotion system followed a mixed criteria with loyalty as the major characteristic. Layner finds bravery, tact and commitment as additional qualification for promotion. But there were no institutions and inviolable rules for recruitment and promotion of officials in Mughal bureaucracy. The officials were paid in cash as *tanakha* and even pensions were granted to widows and the children of the deceased public servants. The principle of decentralisation was practised in administration, partly because of the lack of tight control. It made the junior officials petty tyrants and their discretion was enormous in the want of written codes and personal supervision of the high officials. But the system of punishment was very rough and cruel. It created an ethos of fear resulting in discipline of civil service. The Mughal bureaucracy was noticeably different from the officials of Hindu era. The administrative operations had the semblance of a system.

The Mughal phase of administrative history adds a colourful chapter and brings administrative organisation and personnel to be a point from where the Britishers could take off. The Islamic nature of state was superimposed but the non-Islamic elements of the country made it somewhat secular. The military pattern and nature of administration were emphasised in civil affairs also, but the mixture of the two could evolve a unique and comprehensive system of administration in various fields of governmental activity. Historians judge this administrative phenomenon as an advance on the previous phase but find it loose, corrupt, discriminatory and even tyrannical. The vast empire though unitary, practised decentralised administration which gradually gave birth to Indian federalism. Being the public administration of a monarchy it could not accept the principles of rule of law or popular accountability but it did give uniformity of institutions and their bureaucratic working on an all-India level. As the situation differed from emperor to emperor, the discontinuities entered into the system. The later Mughals could not handle the administrative apparatus which Akbar bequeathed and Aurangzeb dismantled. Yet the dilapidated structure had strength and resilience to get revived by the British.

III
British Period (1758–1947)
(The Foundations and Legacies)

The East India Company received a charter of monopoly trading right from the British crown to carry out mercantile activities in eastern waters in 1600 A.D. As a trading corporation, its charter has to be reviewed and its employees selectively indulged in native politics without any effective control of the Court of Directors of the Company and the Board of Control appointed by the British Parliament. The deteriorating situation threatened the security of the mercantile establishments and the local officials conspired to the extent that a cleave could manage to defeat Nawab Sirajuddulla in the battle of Plessey in 1757. This enabled the Company to control civil administration of Bengal, Bihar and Orissa and the journey of colonialism began leading to Company's termination after the Indian revolt of 1857. These hundred years of free booting and misrule attracted the attention of British Parliament, which had to pass the Regulating Act in 1774 and recurring Charter Acts in 1813, 1833 and 1853 to manage the situation from London.

The Company management as per directions from the British Parliament laid the foundations of British administration in India. Consciously as well inadvertently they had to send civilians to India when voyages were risky and even disastrous. The Regulating Act created the office of the Governor-General of India and British luminaries like Warren Hastings, Lord Cornwallis, Lord Wellesley and Lord Dalhousie initiated varieties of administrative innovations to change the Mughal character of government at top as well as at bottom. The foundations of British Raj laid down during the century from 1757 to 1857 can be highlighted as under:

(1) Political management from London;
(2) Caderisation of civil services and training of public servants; and
(3) Secretarial and infrastructural developments.

Administration from London

The administration of East India Company under Regulating Act 1774 and Pitts India Act 1784 was conducted by two controlling authorities, namely, (a) Board of Control, and (b) Court of Directors. The former was a superior body and was appointed by the British Parliament. It was vaguely accountable to Parliament in the sense that it kept the British Parliament informed and got the Successive Charter Acts passed and renewed. The Court of Directors was nominated by the proprietors of the Company and it used to control the commercial policies and day-to-day activities of the Company as a private corporation. Notwithstanding anomalies and contradictions the Company administrators picked up very able civilians who could constitute a mini Iron Frame, which later developed into a mega Steel Frame when the crown took it over in post-1857 era.

The Civil Service Cadres

To attract brilliant and able English young men to join the Company service and to come to unknown alien land, i.e., India was a horrifying adventure. This forced the Company to constitute two distinct kinds of civil services for the governance of the colony.

(i) The Covenanted Civil Service

It was to encadre Englishmen or European only and they had to "enter into a covenant to serve the Company faithfully and give security for doing so in various categories of services like judicial, political, revenue and mercantile". They were supposed to be loyal, trustworthy and honest and enjoyed special privileges. Its hangovers can be seen among gazetted categories of civil servants even today.

(ii) The Uncovenanted Civil Service

This service was recruited from army natives, Parsis and Portuguese, etc. It was not a cadre and was a conglomeration of odd jobs on ad hoc basis. These services were not required to sign any covenant, therefore, they were called uncovenant.

The uncovenanted civil servants were like non-gazetted public servants more especially in menial categories or semi skilled class of company workers. The three Presidencies of Bombay, Calcutta and Madras locally recruited functionaries and their service conditions, salaries, training systems, etc., differed from place to place and from position to position. Lord Cornwallis believed that every Indian is corrupt and Lord Clive forced their Company servants to sign service bonds declaring not to indulge in private trades and corrupt practices. The situation was forced intolerable by the select committee of the British Parliament in the seventies which paved the way for the passing of the Regulating Act 1774.

Viceroy Wellesley added a new chapter to the history of civil service in India when he sent a note to Company directors on July 10, 1800. The Viceroy argued that the public servants who come at a very tender age from Britain have to shoulder very heavy responsibilities in a very unfriendly milieu of the colony. On approval, he decided to establish Fort William College at Calcutta, so that these young officers could be trained on the pattern of Oxford and Cambridge colleges. Lord Wellesley wanted language training centres in three Presidency towns also but the Court of Directors of the Company were not favourably inclined. Despite his honest intentions to improve the system the viceroy had to retrace his steps in 1802. The grandiose plans of provincial and National Training Programme of company servant had to be given up, although a number of Indian civil service luminaries like Munro, Malcolm, Elphinstone and Philip Woodruff were the products of this Wellesley endeavours. On the closure of the Fort William College, the Court of Directors decided in 1806 to open another East India College at Hartford Castle in London. Later in 1809, it was shifted to Haileybury and became a premier civil service training institute of Europe. The Company directors took personal interests in its two year training programmes and in the selection of trainers and the trainees. Woodruff in his celebrated memories, the men who ruled India speaks very high about the quality of this training and its impact on young probationers. Its teaching standard and syllabi were comparable with that of British universities, but the Charter Act of 1853 and Macaulay report of 1854 recommended for its closer, which became effective since January 31, 1858. The Macaulay Committee on Indian civil services tried to develop the Granville proposal of competitive examination for entry into civil services in great details and made the following recommendations in 1854:

(a) The patronage system in Indian civil services should be replaced by a system of competitive merit examinations.

(b) The lower and upper age limits for these competitors should be 18 and 23 years respectively. It will enable successful British graduates to earn their eligibility.

(c) The syllabi for the competitive examinations should be of generalist nature so that the left over of the examinations may continue their studies in universities and nobody can succeed to become an administrator in India without the basic knowledge of European science and literature.

(d) These recruits were to continue their higher studies for the rest of their lives with special reference to Indian problems and native languages.

(e) The probation period of one to two years had to be rigorous and was to be used to weed out the misfits.

The committee found Haileybury experiment inadequate and recommended for the abolition of the college. The merit oriented career civil servants, who were to be distributed to various presidencies of the crown with generalist training was the corner stone which even today stands as a hub of all civil service reforms in free India. The purpose of this innovation was to create a generalist meritocracy which could liberalise, modernise and colonise the vast empire of the British.

The Infrastructural Developments (1757 to 1857)

One of the significant characteristic feature of company administration from 1757 to 1857 was the concentration of authority at the centre. This centralisation was intended to ensure a close control over the presidencies of Bombay and Madras. The Regulating Act of 1773 restricted the power of the presidencies from making laws or treaties without the sanction of the Governor-General in council. The Pitt's India Act of 1784 placed Indian affairs under the direct control of the British government by establishing a Board of Control representing the British cabinet. The board was "authorised and empowered from time to time to superintend, direct and control all acts, operations and concerns which in any way relate to civil or military government revenues of British territorial possessions". The Court of Directors of the East India Company were required to pay due obedience (and be) governed and bound by such orders as they shall, from time to time, receive from the said court.

The Regulating Act of 1773 created a council of four members and ordained that all decisions of the council were to be taken by a majority of votes of those present. The 1786 amendment authorised the Governor-General "to override his council and act on his own responsibility in respect of measures whereby the interest of the Company or the safety or tranquillity of the British possessions in India or in any part thereof are or may in the judgement of the Governor-General be essentially affected". The Governor-General in council conducted government affairs till 1859 when Lord Canning introduced portfolio system. In 1756, a secret committee of four members was constituted to safeguard secrecy of transactions.

In 1763, the business of the Company was organised into public department and the secret department. The former was to continue to officiate over all affairs relating to shipping, revenue, fortifications, accounts and appointments. Later in 1765, Lord Clive was appointed as President and Governor with command over the Company's military forces. In 1776, a military board (in reality a military department) was formed for the purpose of recording all orders affecting the army posted in other departments, all general orders of whatever nature and all 'memorials of officer respecting rank'. In 1786 the Court of Directors ordered that the government of the country be carried on by the Governor-General in council through the medium of four boards, namely, (1) the Board of Council, (2) a Military Board, (3) a Board of Revenue, and (4) a Board of Trade. A Hospital Board was also created in 1786 and its designation was changed to Medical Board ten years later. In 1793, a separate judicial department was created to deal with matters hitherto dealt with by the revenue department. Thus, by the end of the 18th century, the 'Supreme Government' stood under four sections, each in charge of a secretary: public (including commercial); secret – political and foreign; revenue and judicial; and military. A chief secretary was in general control of all the departments.

The name of the Board of Revenue at Calcutta was changed to Sadar Board of Revenue in 1829 and another such board was created at Allahabad in 1833. The overgrown presidency of Bengal was divided into two distinct presidencies, namely, (1) the Presidency of Fort William in Bengal, and (2) the Presidency of Agra. The Governor-General of Bengal became the Governor-General of India, besides being also the Governor of Bengal.

The origin of Indian central secretariat can be traced to the office of the factory writers. A secretary to the council of the Governor-General in Madras and Bengal Presidencies had five or six junior servants for his secretarial assistance. This structure, created by Hastings, was further strengthened by his successor, Lord Cornwallis. The Cornwallis reforms in public service introduced a highly liberal system of remuneration, in lieu of the petty salaries which kept them poor and dishonest. The Charter Act of 1833 made the Governor-General of Bengal the Governor-General of India and his government became the Government of India. Thus, the legislative powers formerly enjoyed by the governments of Madras and Bombay were taken away by this all India government. The right of patronage of the Court of Directors was terminated yet workload in the offices of the English judges and magistrates continued to increase and facilitate the entry of Indians in large numbers. Lord Cornwallis devised several corrective measures to prevent the abuse of power by officials. The Cornwallis Code applicable to administrations of revenue, police, criminal and civil justice and allied functions made serious efforts to:

(1) define the boundaries of authority of officials;
(2) create a regular system of appeals to redress public grievances; and
(3) prevent miscarriage of justice in the system.

It can be called an attempt to introduce rule of law which laid the foundations of civil service as it exists in present day India. Both Hastings and Cornwallis started a process of establishing administrative boards in different departments of the government in Calcutta and Madras. By 1785, government of the Presidency of Madras created four boards, namely:

(1) Board of Trade,
(2) Board of Revenue,
(3) Military Board, and
(4) Medical Board.

In 1785, the Court of Directors of the Company in their London meeting decided that the administration of the Company will be carried out by the Governor-General in Council at Calcutta through the instrumentality of four boards, namely, the Board of Revenue. These boards continued till the last days of the Company's rule in 1857. The Governor-General-in-Council separated the secretariat of the Government of India from that of Bengal Secretariat by an order of April 29th 1843. A separate secretary for the financial department was already there and other departments were separated in May 1843. The political, foreign and secret branches were clubbed and put under another secretary and the new department was called the foreign department of the Government of India. The charge of the remaining branches (revenue, general, marine, judicial, legislative and ecclesiastical) was given to a third secretary and the department was called the home department of the Government of India.

Thus, the growth of Indian administration during the pre-mutiny or Company era is significant and fore shadows the coming events of the period from 1858 to 1947. East India Company, though a private corporation took charge of government in a piecemeal manner. There was little conscious design and the Indian empire fell on the Company servants who handled the situations as and when they arose. The traders and missionaries developed colonial interests and the administration was chiselled in a state of absent-mindedness under compulsions of varied motives. Naturally, this phase had to take into account the desires of political and commercial masters at London, who did not have effective means of communication to control their servants in India and for whom the empire was a distant daydreaming. The Governors and Governor-General created two levels of governance which was to be grafted to the Mughal administrative structures of a suba and a pargana. Civil service caderisation and some sort of secretariat system was the need and every statute from Regulating Act to Charter Acts of 1813, 1833 and 1853 is tinkering with the system to give it a sememblance of meritocracy and secretariat bureaucracy with a portfolio system of working. The infrastructure is being built through the establishment of committee and commissions, working in the areas of judiciary, education, police, railways, home and ecclesial affairs. The rudiments of a home government a civil service cadre and a secretariat working are the foundational achievements of English rulers of this period. In spite of their pious and not so very pious intentions, the Sipoy revolt of 1857 could not be averted and the events moved that fast that the government of the crown had to intervene decisively by terminating the East India Company and its misrule in 1858. The phase called India under the crown from 1857 to 1947 is an era of 90 years, wherein the constitutional and administrative saplings planted and grafted by the British reasonably matured. When Englishmen decided to quit the colony these administrative institutions and practices had become so strong and inextricably mixed up with the totality of the system, that they survive even today as extremely precious legacies of the Raj.

1857 and After

The revolt of 1857 shook the foundations of the Company and shocked the English rulers to sense of seriousness. Lord Palmerston introduced a Bill in the House of Commons, maintaining that the principles of parliamentary responsibility and ministerial accountability were being flagrantly violated by the Company rulers in India. Prime Minister Disraeli on March 26, 1858 made a vain bid to transfer Indian government to the British crown. Later on Mr Stanley presented a 14-point proposal, which was passed as an act for the better government of India by British Parliament on August 2nd, 1858. It established a Home Government of the Secretary of State for India as a responsible cabinet minister of the Crown and Lord Canning in his Allahabad Durbar on November 1st, 1858 officially proclaimed that the Company regime stands terminated and India will usher into a new order under the crown.

During the 90-year period of crown's rule, India became a colony of British government and the English Parliament operated as sovereign master managing the colonial affairs of India through a responsible minister of the English cabinet.

An India Council was created to aid and assist this secretary, who was a responsible minister for Indian affairs in British cabinet. This home government located in London remained in existence up to August 15th, 1947 and the successive acts dissolved its powers and functions to the Governor-Generals and Governors in instalments. During this span of 90 years of Crown's rule in India, the English Parliament enacted the following statutes which inducted constitutional, political and administrative changes in the governance of the colony:

(1) India Council Act 1861
(2) India Council Act 1892
(3) India Council Act 1909
(4) India Council Act 1919
(5) India Council Act 1935

All these Acts installmentally reorganise and reform the constitutional system which has been called a council system of government in India. As the system made a headway, the Morley Minto reforms of 1909 and Montague Chelmsford reforms of 1919 created a quasi-limited parliamentary system at the centre as well as in the provinces. In 1926, the Simon Commission recommended a federal frame of government for British and princely India encompassing the subcontinent. As the princely rulers were not enthusiastic about the proposed federation and national politics was sharply divided on key issues, India continued to be governed by the Act of 1919 till the English rulers resolved to quit of after having partitioned it in 1947.

The constitutional landmarks were pressurised by the upsurge of national movement after the birth of Indian National Congress in 1885. As the political progress was slow the administration had to tighten its grip on the working of government in London, Delhi and provincial capitals. All the five statutes very meticulously created a nuclear political system of councils which were partly to be nominated and partly to be elected indirectly as well as indirectly at both the levels of the centre and the province. Before 1919, the purpose was to create institutions and let the Indians learn under a parental command. After the Queen's proclamation of 1918, this policy highlighted the gradual development of self-governing institutions and to place India on the road to self-government. As a consequence, the control of home government and secretary of state was increasingly relaxed by every Act that followed of and to balance this, the power of the Governor-General were enhanced to safeguard against the risk of provincial diarchy in 1919. In 1935 when the dose of provincial autonomy became inevitable the response of the British government was all-powerful Governor-General and the Governor armed with extraordinary powers of special responsibilities, discretion, individual judgement and emergency. This balancing exercise apart, the colonial government made a tall claim of associating Indians in all walks of public life. Consequently, the characteristic features of each statute witnessed:

(1) The expansion of legislative councils at centre and in the provinces.
(2) The enlargement of elective element with a restraining system of communal elections (1909) indirect elections and limited suffrage to keep the system attuned to colonial interests.
(3) Slow and gradual liberalisation of policy in each Act to enable Indians to learn parliamentary principles and practices of debate and popular accountability.
(4) Progressive Indianisation of Indian government, more specially at lower levels and in the civil services positions of the country.

Where the Acts of 1861, 1892 and 1909 are known for their councils which were legislative and executive in nature, the Acts of 1919 and 1935 are remembered for their dyarchical and autonomy reforms in provincial governments. Keith, Conpland and several other commentators call them realistic, but the nationalist historians like G.N. Singh find them a hoax, a mischievous attempt to declare Indians incompetent and rule the colony through Governor-Generals, Governors and collectors. All these political acrobatics were essentially aimed to pacify nationalists and to rob the wine from their sails. The failures of council system and dyarchical reforms gave a free hand to the bureaucracy, which not only consolidated its powers and functions but became a government, i.e., politics and administration both at the exclusion of people and their representatives.

The evolution of administration during 90 years of Crown's rule can be examined under the following heads:

(1) The advisory system in home government
(2) The reorganisation of departments in the secretariat
(3) The strengthening of civil service
(4) The fiscal management
(5) The devolution, local government and the districts

The Home Government of the SSI

The Government of India Act, 1858 created the office of secretary of state for India. The powers which were formerly exercised by the Court of Directors and the Board of Control were transferred. The Act authorised the secretary of state to superintend, direct and control all acts, operations and concerns relating to the government or revenues of India. He was assisted by a council of 15 members called Council of India or India Council. The council, under the direction of the secretary of state, conducted the business transacted in United Kingdom.

The 1919 Act relaxed this control over the provincial Governors, especially in the areas of transferred departments under diarchy. Moreover, the British government agreed to pay his salary from British revenues. The Act of 1935 made no reference to home governments, powers of superintendent, direction and control, but it made little difference in practice. However, the provincial part of Indian government was made free from the control of home government. The Indian Council was also replaced by three advisers. They were senior bureaucrats, and were apparently too powerful to share authority with the Governor-Generals and Governors.

Evolution of Secretariat System in India

The central secretariat remained located in Calcutta till 1843. It had a secretary-general, three assistants and some clerical staff for routine work. The secretariat was organised in three departments, viz., (1) Public, (2) Secret, and (3) Commercial.

The resolution of 1843 can be seen as a great landmark in the evolution of secretariat system. The resolution created four distinct departments and assigned their functions as under:

(1) Military Department: All matter pertaining to the military.
(2) Foreign Department: Foreign and diplomatic relations.
(3) Home Department; Justice, education and law.
(4) Finance Department: Treasury, finance and ways and means.

As the British rule deepened its roots and the empire expanded the number of departments increased and their functions and organisation were streamlined. The following dates are significant in this evolution from 1843 to 1919.

1855 A new department of public works was created by taking some of the functions of home department.

1869 A new department known as legislative department was separated from the home department of Central government.

1871 The home department was further split and a new department was born by assimilating three allied functions. It was called department of revenue, agriculture and commerce.

1879 (a) The department of revenue, agriculture and commerce was abolished due to consideration of economy. Commerce was incorporated in finance and revenue and agriculture returned to parent home department. (b) Home department was renamed as department of home, revenue and agriculture.

1880 The new home department was bifurcated into: (a) Department of home, and (b) Department of revenue and agriculture, which included land revenue, surveys, horticulture, minerals, famine, meteorology and emigration.

1905 (a) Railway branch of public works department was abolished. (b) A new Railway Board was created with control over expanded railway system. (c) Another new department of commerce and industry was created and the old commerce functions were handed over to it. Some railway references were later added as a part of commerce and industry.

1906 (a) The Railway Board was designated as new railway department. (b) The military department was reorganised on Lord Curzon's resignation. Two new departments were created. They were: (i) Department of army, and (ii) Department of military supplies. (iii) the C-in-C controlled the army but the military supplies were placed under a member of Governor-General's council. But it proved a makeshift arrangement for a reamalgamation.

1910 The home department gave away some of its functions to the newly born department of education on December 9th, 1910.

The Montford Reforms of 1919 made radical changes inevitable in the organisation of the secretariats of the Central government and that of the provinces for dyarchical reforms. After the World War, the problems were of pressing nature and the declaration of 1918 implied that the welfare administration of the government will expand. So the departments of health, industries, labour and education got priority in the secretarial reorganisation.

1921 (1) Medical administration transferred from home to education department.
(2) A reorganised department of industries had some activities of commerce department.

1923 (1) Public works department was merged with the department of industries and labour.
(2) Central Board of Education and Bureau of Education was abolished.
(3) Department of revenue and agriculture merged into department of education and health which was redesignated as department of education, health and lands.

The period from 1919 to 1946 is the Gandhian era of national politics. The constitutional landmarks like dyarchy, provincial autonomy, Simon Report, the Government of India Act 1935 brought consequent administrative changes in the organisation and working of the government departments. These structural changes can be enumerated as under:

1937 (1) The foreign and political department was split into: (a) the external affairs department, and (b) the political department. (2) The Board of Education was revived. (3) The department of industries and labour got bifurcated into: (a) department of labour, and (b) department of communications. (4) Subjects rurality to industry copyright and ecclesiastical affairs were handed over the department of commerce and education and defence respectively.

1941 Three new departments were created to met the pressure of war. They were: (a) Department of information and broadcasting (b) Department of civil defence, and (c) Department of Indians overseas.

1942 (1) A new department of food was given the responsibility of procurement and distribution of food stuffs. (2) The department of communications was split into: (a) Department of posts and air, and (b) Department of war transport. (3) The new department of transport took care of ports, road utilisation, railway priorities, petrol rationing and water transport.

1943 Civil supplies department was added to industries department

1944 (1) Central road fund and Motor Vehicle Laws transferred to war transport department. (2) The department of Indian overseas was renamed as Department of Commonwealth Relations. It was merged with foreign affairs department in 1947 and come to be known as department of external affairs and commonwealth relations. (3) A new department of planning and development was created to plan post-war reconstruction. But it had to be abolished two year later because of administrative exigencies.

1945 The department of education, health and lands was re-carved into: (a) Department of education, (b) Department of health, and (c) Department of agriculture.

1946 (1) The supply department was merged with the department of industries. (2) The 1942 bifurcation was done away with and the amalgamated department of communication and transport was born. (3) the labour department got bifurcated into: (a) Department of labour, and (b) Department of works, mines and power.

1947 Advent of independence elevated the status of departments into ministries and on August 29, 1947, the central secretariat of Union government was formally reorganised into 12 ministries.

The Portfolio System

Till 1858, the transactions of the Company government were carried out by the council as a Board and the successive Governor-Generals felt the heavy burden of official work. Wellesley had little respect for law and conventions of bureaucracy. He ignored his council in taking decisions. Lord Dalhousie took some remedial measures, which lightened the workload of the Governor-General. However, the unorthodox methods of Wellesley and the orthodox procedural reforms of Dalhousie could not improve the situation and the tumultuous events from 1850 to 1858 aggravated the need for more drastic reforms.

In 1859 Lord Canning introduced the portfolio system as a reform. The innovation was that a member of council would be appointed in charge of one or more departments of the government by the Governor-General and he would issue orders on behalf of the Governor-General-in-Council. Section 8 of the Act of 1861 accorded statutory recognition to this practice. It authorised the Governor-General to make rules and orders for convenient transaction of the executive business of the Government of India. Reference to the Governor-General was necessary in matters where provincial governments were overruled. It can be called a crude beginning of the cabinet system under the Governor-General. This introduction of the portfolio system yielded results. The wheels of the government turned with greater speed and efficiency. The members of the council came to be recognised as heads of their respective departments and they acquired a greater degree of initiative and responsibility over the functioning of their departments.

This continuous reorganisation of administrative departments and clubbing them into portfolios on the pattern of British White Hall administration was a Parliament innovation. The White Hall System of Secretariat working was the model and it was Indianised as per local needs and constitutional requirements at each level. Certainly, it marked a positive departure from the Mughal system of administration and laid the foundation of present day central secretariat. The Civil Service Reforms corresponded with this secretarial change and together. They changed the nature and scope of public administration.

As the secretariat system evolved the British rulers adjusted the needs and competences of their civil servants to their hierarchical positions of bureaucracy. Then secretariat procedures and practices had to be regularised and established. This work was accomplished by the following committees:

(1) Secretariat Procedure Committee – 1919
(2) Llewellyn Smith Committee – 1920
(3) Wheeler Committee – 1935
(4) Maxwell Committee – 1937
(5) Tottenham Committee – 1945

The first committee recommended for the constitution of Staff Selection Board to supervise the recruitment process through qualifying examinations and interview. The Imperial secretariat service entry was governed by these procedures till the Federal Public Service Commission took it over. The secretariat procedure committee recommended a pyramidal organisation for every department, with a secretary at the top, and two deputy secretaries below. It recommended the abolition of the post of under-secretaries except in the finance department. The purpose of these changes was to expedite official business. The Llewellyn Smith Committee re-examined the tenure system operating from Lord Curzon's time since 1905. It observed that the tenure of the office of secretaries and deputy secretaries should remain fixed at four years so that stability may be ensured in the working of the secretariat. The Wheeler Committee studied the problem of delays in the working of the secretariat and recommended the practice of double noting to speed up the work. The major recommendation of Maxwell Committee was that the secretary of the department should be responsible to the minister and he was the competent officer to guide the minister. It categorised staff into assistants and clerks and specified their functions. The Tottenham Committee reported on the organisation of departments, the question of staffing and the reorganisation of the entire secretariat system. It recommended that distinct duties be assigned to different grades of secretarial officers and agreed nomenclatures for each grade. It 're-cherished' the old Imperial secretariat service into central secretariat service. The subsequent secretariat system that emerged relies on procedures that specify levels of responsibility, patterns of noting, filing, record keeping, etc. The bureaucratic legacies continue even after half a century of freedom and administrative innovations.

The Bureaucratic Steel Frame

The servants of East India Company who were responsible to the court of directors become servants of the Crown in 1858 and the secretary of the state for India was designated as their guardian. This change of guards implied a sea change in the contents, quality and civil service procedures of bureaucracy which got rid of commercial control of the business elite of England. The Indian employees were asked to owe allegiance to a foreign power and were repeatedly asked to rule their own people in the interest of Queen Victoria. As Blunt points out these Anglo-Indian rulers developed an isolation from the people and did incredible things to please the masters.

With the birth of Indian National Congress in 1885 and the pressure of moderate loyalists in Congress the demand for Indianisation of Indian administration and especially of civil services became highly pressing. The removal of Sir S.N. Benerjee from Indian Civil Service and the decision to reduce the entry age from 21 years to 19 years by Lord Lytton raised organised protests. In 1870, the Viceroy Lytton constituted a committee consisting of B.W. Calwin (chairman) and C. Benard, J. Westland and D. Barkar as members. It recommended the Constitution of a statutory civil service for the natives. Nominations for entry in the service were invited by provincial governments and they were appointed in the province concerned with the approval of Secretary of State for India. The service could not attract the right kind of civil servants and was abolished after nine years of experimentation.

Atchison Commission 1887

The Government of India appointed this commission under the chairmanship of the then Deputy Governor of Punjab Mr Atchison and six Indian members. They were: (i) R.C. Mittar, (ii) Raja W.P. Singh, (iii) Sir Syad Ahmad, (iv) Kazi Shahbuddin, (v) S.R. Mudaliar, and (vi) K.L. Nalkar. The term of commission was to do justice to persons of Indian origin in recruitment to senior posts in Indian civil service as obtained in the year 1886. The commission took depositions from relevant people and organisation and inter alias recommended:

(1) A provincial civil service should be constituted to conduct administration of provinces. The commission earmarked 108 posts for this service from the ICS and unconverted services of the Company. The number of posts in convented service was to cut down and a proportionate increase of posts in provincial civil services may be made by amalgamating the unconvented positions. This could meet the demand of Indianisation and merit availability for lower services.

(2) The Imperial and provincial civil services were to be recruited on the basis of examinations, promotion and nomination. As far as possible every province should have a provincial civil service but certain departments may continue to be manned by Indian civil service.

(3) The third level of subordinate services may be created in provinces and their salaries, service conditions and promotions may be adjusted with provincial services in consultation with the Government of India.

This three-fold classification of civil services as: (i) Imperial, (ii) Provincial, and (iii) Subordinate goes an landmark in the history of bureaucracy in India. The old classification of covenanted and uncovenanted services was abolished. The new arrangement could suit to the administrative needs of the expanding colony and still more to the aspirations of educated people on a rational basis of merit selection and local talent. The subordinate service as a new category was welcome relief to the native population who even today look to the government as its guardian and job giver in non-gazetted cadres. The commission broadly reorganised the existing covenanted, statutory and uncovenanted services into imperial, provincial and subordinate public services with adjustment of seats and salaries.

Islington Commission 1917

The Atchison Commission recommendations could not be implemented satisfactorily. To diffuse the rising discontent, the British government appointed another commission under the chairmanship of Lord Islington the Governor of Newsland in 1912. The commission took five years to present its report about:

(1) Selection procedures, training and probation.
(2) Salary, leave, pension and service conditions.
(3) Complaints of non-Europeans about entry into Imperial and provincial Services.
(4) Necessary changes in recruitment procedures.

With these terms of reference, Lord Islington examined the situation in the following public services which had come into existence from 1861 to 1910. On the basis of its study, the commission recommended a three-fold categorisation of public services:

(1) Public services, which have British component such as ICS and imperial police.
(2) Public services comprising Indian and British components, such as finance, medical services.
(3) Public services which need not be recruited in Britain, such as technical services.

All these services may be divided into two classes or two groups of services, performing menial work or semi-skilled work. The commission felt that engineering services of railways, post and telegraph, etc., may be merged in Imperial and provincial services. The commission earmarked 25 out of 189 for Indian incumbents in Indian civil service. It equalised salaries and service conditions which were discriminatory for the natives in the past.

Lee Farnham Commission 1923

The World War I and the Montford reforms of 1919 changed the political scenario which demanded a revision of service conditions in civil service. Lee recommended a liberal bonanza in terms of pay hike and other allowances at time when countries were passing through adverse circumstances. It was condemned as 'Lee Loot' because Lee Commission added an overall burden of 1.25 crore rupees on Indians for the luxuries of public servants. There were 3975 public servants in 9 public services of the country which the Islington Commission recognised. Lee recommended that recruitment in five services namely education service, agriculture service, veterinary service, forest service (in some provinces) and engineering service should be stopped and only the provincial government should fill the vacant posts. The Indian Medical Service was allowed to continue because the European members of Indian services were strongly fighting for its continuation.

Name of Service	*Year of Creation*
Indian Forest Service	1862
Indian Engineering Service	1892
Indian Veterinary Service	1892
Indian Medical Service	1897
Imperial Police	1905
Indian Education Service	1906
Indian Agriculture Service	1907

As per provisions of the Act of 1935, a Public Service Commission was to be established in India. The Lee Commission desired that it should be a body comprising of five non-political members so that Indian civil services may be insulated from the all-pervading influence. The Commission recommended that two of the members of this body should be judicial officials. The recommendation was implemented in 1936 when Federal Public Service Commission was born with Lee Farnham as chairman and eight other members. The four Indians appointed in the Commission were (1) Bhupendra Nath Baru, (2) M. Habibullah, (3) Har Kishan Kaul, and (4) N.M. Samarth.

The Merit System

The Macaulay Report 1854 for the first time inducted the element of merit in the civil service of the colony. From 1858 to 1919, the Indian civil service members were recruited by open competition in London. The British government and the Secretary of State for India were extremely conscious of the administrative demands which civil service made upon people in an alien land. It was more than a Weberian bureaucracy and the merit needs had to be matched with character and personality traits of the age and educational equipment of the incumbents.

On the eve of Montford reforms there were five methods of recruitment of senior civil servants in India. They were:

(1) Open competition examination in London.
(2) Separate competitive examination in India.
(3) Promotion from the Provincial Civil Service.
(4) Nomination of Indians on the basis of provincial and communal representation.
(5) Appointments of 25 per cent members of ICS from the bar to fill the posts of sessions judges.

The senior civil service posts were classified as superior and inferior on the basis of responsibilities and emoluments. The senior posts were not even one hundred. Lord Montague recommended the highest pay scale for the secretary in the department. Seniority promotions and better service conditions were ensured on the basis of annual returns whereby subordinate officials were graded by superior officials. Before Montford reforms, the departments recruited their junior officials. The Secretariat Procedure Committee (1920) made the upper division clerks of the secretariat a part of imperial secretarial service, which was recruited by the Central Staff Selection Board. Gradually, the junior officials who were natives found themselves in unsatisfactory conditions with regard to leave, allowances and other privileges to which the British civil servants were entitled. This lead to corruption, truancy and exploitation of natives by natives. The situation in the provincial services was much worse and the subordinate service could not attract the right kind. The Atchism Commission recommended the transfer formula but the gap between ICS and PCS could not be bridged and survives as an anomaly even today. The provincialisation of post vis-à-vis all India service always presented the dilemma of merit gap, which has been a reflection of regional imbalances in education.

Decentralisation and Fiscal Management

The Accountant General of Fort William in Bengal controlled the finances of the Government of India. The accounts officers of the presidencies of Madras, Bengal, Bombay and Agra submitted their financial accounts to him. Control was exercised by the Finance Secretary of the Finance Department of the British government. Attempts were made to separate the Indian accounts from the local accounts of Bengal. The Secretary to the Government of India in the finance department was nominated as the *ex officio* Accountant General of India with powers to supervise and examine Indian accounts. Secondly, a general department of accounts was created in place to separate accounts for each presidency. Before 1857 revenue was obtained from two sources: (1) land revenue, and (2) taxes on trade and personal property. Similarly, the expenditure was kept under two heads, (i) security or defence and (ii) social and development services which included education and public health.

The Financial Resolution of 1860 introduced budget system in the council. Like UK, the financial estimates for each year were to be arranged, considered and sanctioned by the Government of India before the year commenced. It presented the anticipated income and proposed expenditure of the colony. A central revenue department was created in Calcutta to integrate and coordinate the operations of all the revenue yielding authorities. The Imperial Audit Department was also set up to examine whether the departments were adhering to the norms and provisions of the budget. The Resolution (1860) provided for the creation of a Budget and Audit Committee which, inter alia recommended that the posts of the Accountant General and Auditor General were merged into the Accountant and Auditor General. An Audit Board, consisting of an Auditor General and the chief of the military finance department was set-up to act in all organisational and policy matters which affected the budget estimates, audit and accounts.

Paper currency was introduced in India in 1860. The Bank of Bengal became the agent for the printing, issuing and circulation of the notes. The district treasury was placed under the collector of the district in the year 1882. The systematic mechanism of control evolved in 1919 when the C and AG was made responsible to the Central Legislature. He was given the power to inspect 'any government office of account' and a Central Public Accounts Committee was created in 1922 with elected and official members, and the Finance member as its *ex officio* chairman. It considered the Auditor General's reports on the reappropriation amounts. Thus, through these two bodies, the Indian Legislature was to exercise control over the administration of public finance. A Standing Finance Committee with the finance member as its chairman was another practical step for this control. It had some of the functions of a Public Estimates Committee. In addition, Public Accounts Committees were created in each Governor's province. Under the Act of the Central Legislature, the Government of India established the Reserve Bank which began its function with effect from 1 April 1935. The Board of Revenue became a controlling authority for revenue purposes and had a number of civil servants, to serve as a link between the government and the collectors. In 1829, divisional commissioners were appointed to supervise the collectors, in four to five districts, in the exercise of their powers. They were made responsible to the Board of Revenue.

Local Government and Ripon Resolution

Introduction of local government was never the priority of the British Raj in India. The Mughal system of empire suited them but their training in local institutions back home reminded them of the Whiteman's burden. Moreover as a sea faring class they took keen interest in the port towns of India and Calcutta, Bombay and Madras are the discernable contributions of the English rule in every respect. Madras Corporation, born as early as 1688 was a tangible step. It was followed by municipal charters of 1726 setting up corporations at Calcutta and Bombay. These corporations were to have elected councils, mayors, Justice of Peace and Sheriffs to manage the port towns with primary and secondary municipal functions. The early Viceroys thought of town municipalities but little progress could be made unless Lord Ripon declared it as a matter of policy. Earlier Viceroy Lord Mayo has taken some steps, but the district authorities were not supportive to the encouragement of rural panchayats. The 1864 resolution admitted that the people of the country were capable of administering these local affairs and every view of duty and policy should induce the government to leave as much as possible of the business of the country to be done by people. In 1870, Lord Mayo decided about financial devolution of powers and earmarked funds for the management of education, sanitation and public works to local institutions. Consequently the provincial governments enacted municipal legislation and elective principle was extended. The decentralisation policy implied attempts to develop local bodies with powers of levying local rates and cesses, etc.

Lord Ripon who is called the father of local self-government in India took genuine interest and his policy resolution of 1882 stands as a landmark in the annals of local government in India. It denotes a shift of policy. The resolution said, it is not primarily with a view to improvement in administration that this measure is put forward and supported, it is desirable as an instrument of political and popular education. The resolution advocated that:

(1) Self-government institutions with special emphasis on the necessity for meeting the requirements of the rural areas;
(2) The reduction of the official element in the local bodies to not more than third of the total strength;
(3) The exercise of control from within and not from without; and
(4) A larger measure of financial decentralisation and adoption of election as a means of constituting local bodies wherever possible.

The result of the resolution was a series of acts regarding municipal bodies and a variety of legislative enactments as regards rural areas. The Decentralisation Commission in his report of 1909 examined the problem of local government in great detail. The commission emphasised the need of village panchayats and recommended the adoption of special measures for their revival and growth. It made special recommendations for lessening of government control over local bodies and augmenting the sources of their income. Unfortunately, the Government of India and the provincial governments could not carry out the policy of Ripon in real spirit. The Montague-Chelmsford Report on Indian Constitutional Reforms examined the system of local government in the country in 1918 and concluded that, the educative principle had been subordinated to the desire for immediate results. It was reiterated that local bodies would henceforth be vested with greater autonomy and outside control would be minimal. Executive action was initiated to implement these principles in 1920. Thus, notwithstanding the acceptance of LSG in principle only cosmetic reforms were introduced by converting the pargana administration of Mughals into a collectorate.

The Prefecturate of the District Magistrate

The British administration of provincial Governors resolved to have the office of collector as early as 1872. The purpose was to keep the Mughal land revenue system continuing and fill the coffers of the British treasury. This colonial interest was vital and the Drain Theory of Dadabhai Nauroji brings home the point why panchayati institutions were neither conceived nor designed during the entire period of British history. In the absence of any district model back home in England, the English rulers thought of a French Prefecturate and superimposed it on the Mughal system as a collectorate. The collector as an Indian Prefect could control the local institutions and other officers of land administration hierarchy from *Patwari* to sub divisional officers. The police administration was so devised that the magisterial power of the district bureaucracy could function as total government and the villagers felt the presence of White Masters at every echelon of government.

The Indian Police Act was enacted in the year 1861 to create a Provincial Police System to deal with the problems of disorder and crime at the level of the district and below. The police hierarchy from the thana level to the level of the district and above was streamlined to put under a unified command of the Superintendent of Police in the district and an IGP at the provincial headquarters. The armed and civil wings of police were created to handle routine and emergent problems of law and order. The executive arm philosophy of police was openly proclaimed by asking the District Magistrate (DM), i.e., the collector to undertake surveillance functions over police duties of the SP. The Police Act was followed by the preparation of penal books, popularly known as Indian Penal Code (IPC), Criminal Procedure Code (Cr.PC) and Indian Evidence Act.

The beginnings being crude, the police administration under the charge of Mughal thanedars, darogas and kotwals could not come up to people's expectations but the rule of system was planted to get legitimised over a period of time. The White Supremacy was asserted through the powers of DM and the constabulary was left to operate as per local situations. The post-mutiny situation and later the nationalist convulsions of history in different periods shaped the callous and corrupt behaviours of police force which have become a anachronism after independence. The 1902–03 Police Commission confirmed the supremacy of magistracy for imperial reasons and the tilt can be seen in all the clauses envisaged in criminal procedures and police-DM relations even today.

Police as an instrument of law enforcement and order maintenance was designed by the British with distrust and without any notion of human rights. Naturally, this legacy of British Raj serves a negative purpose of order maintenance under civil bureaucracy. As J.C. Curry in his book *Indian Police* points out that "The drumvirati (of SP and Collector) in the administration of law and order is a check and balance mechanism" and even a Dharam Veer National Police Commission has not dared to revise it.

Administration of Land Revenue

The district administration was an anathema for the British Raj since its very inception. Firstly, English rulers knew nothing about the intricacies of rural administration of the vast colony. Secondly, they were not very enthusiastic to change the Mughal system of Akbar which was paying rich dividends in the form of land revenue. Thirdly, the absence of local institutions discouraged them to go down below the level of collector. Then, there was mass illiteracy and any attempt to disturb the statues quo would help the national movement to weaken their moorings. So the colonial interests of collecting land revenue prevailed and the district collector with the powers of a district magistrate could play a mini-Governor of the district. The arrangement suited to the natives who could exploit the situation like their predecessors.

The land revenue administration was kept under the care of the collector who controlled this hierarchy through his sub divisional officers and tehsildars. The *nizamat* was kept in tact and magisterial powers were given to the lower functionaries against whom appeals pertaining land disputes could lie with the collector. Land mapping, registration, revenue assessment and revenue collection was done by the district functionaries who had practically no developmental functions of planning or welfare measures before 1947. The disaster management was emerging duty of this rural bureaucracy which was too loyal and too much exploitative of the peasantry.

The strong and weak collectors were theoretical controversies and as the Nationalist movement passed through its radical and extremists phase the collector as DM became all-powerful. Later, the Gandhian phase of mass movement added to the ever-expanding powers of the collector who reduced the police apparatus to play the mere executive arm of the government. Thus, land, revenue, and law and order at the level of the district and below shaped the district administration as a powerful tool in the hands of Englishmen to keep rural India outside the purview of local institutions. The Mughal military state destroyed local bodies and the English rulers could take recourse behind the alibis that local reforms in countryside cannot be possible without an infrastructure of popular government. Consequently, the district bureaucracy thrived and educated urban Indians kept the rural people under their feudal tutelage without their participation in the administrative process. This legacy survives even in the 21st century and the constitutional bodies of Panchayati Raj are struggling with dyarchy to get their democratic rights from the district bureaucrats of state administration.

The Legacies

A comparative look at the three periods of Indian administrative history reveals that there is a tremendous amount of continuity and change in the evolution of Indian administration in terms of structures, procedures and behaviours. Each period of history bequeathed a legacy to the succeeding period which revised and consolidated the heritage as per needs of the changed times. The Hindu period was imperial and republican and hence public administrators were assigned specific roles by Acharya Vishnu Gupta in his *Arthshastra*. The Mughal rulers strived to impose a Islamic state on non-Islamic people and therefore certain administrative institutions were obliterated and newer institutions like wazir, Qazi and daroga were installed. The success was partial and the mixed legacies created ambivalent situations of mixed administration at district pargana and central levels. When East India Company took over diwani rights of Bengal the Mughal legacies were anglicised and adjusted with the colonial needs of the mother country. The native governments did not have any uniform pattern of administration. The British rulers received their administrative legacies from the Mughal empire and they have left their own legacies to administrators of free India. Even after half a century of freedom it appears, as if the present day secretariats, field offices, meritocracy, financial management and district collectorates are nothing but British handimaids of history. The roots may be Hindu or Mughal, but the structural forms and their operational behaviours are the legacies of the British Raj. The lag between these British institutions and societal behaviours in India can explain the nature and gravity of administrative problems like inefficiency, corruption, rule boundedness, public grievance and poor public accountability. To be more precise the administrative legacies of the British Raj are:

(1) Parliamentary form of democratic government in a centralised quasi-federal structure of a plural society.
(2) A secretariat system of ministries with administrative departments at the Union and state levels.
(3) A merit-oriented and merit-based open bureaucracy as a support structure to democratic politics.
(4) A rule bonded system of financial management through budget as a tool of control of public expenditure.

Indian administration has a history of systemic training in all the four areas and these legacies constitute the core of Indian administrative organisation. Independence has added several new dimensions to the Indian polity and society and it is in a state of constant convulsions and transformations to shape a new kind of administration as per demands of this change. Some of these new dimensions of change are: (1) development; social, economic and political (2) social justice without discriminations of caste-colour, caste, sex and creed (3) a welfare polity with equal participation of women and weaker people as free citizens (4) growth of science and technology and their application to the life of the community, and (5) Fundamental Rights and Duties asking the people to assert and make public administration amenable to popular demands and aspirations. These developments in Indian society which is still traditional, rural plural and poor pose problems to elected governments and the law abiding public servants are blamed for this ambivalence. The answer lies in revamping the administrative system and renovating the fossilised values of a mediaeval society.

The administrative history of India besides being chequered and long has witnessed the vicissitudes and ravages of time. Its continuity is somewhat unbroken but the changes too have been metamorphic and revolutionary. Each phase leaves a legacy which serves as the foundation for the other phase of history. The Hindu, Mughal and British eras do not represent mere change of rulers or dynasties, but every time there is an attempt to renew and build anew. Administration more than politics has been the experimenting ground for the rulers and if Mughals inducted Persian thought and Institutions, the English rulers as traders and Crown's representatives converted India into a Bureaucratic preserve of the white and black elites loyally wedded to the British masters frame of civil service and the generalist nature of all India services. The district bureaucracy and even the federal administrative relations are the cherished legacies which are directly confronting the elective institutions of representation at every level. The revolution of rising expectations of restive people specially in the countryside are pressurising the administrative functionaries to accommodate the demands of human rights, popular welfare and public accountability.

2

Constitution and Administration

A Constitution represents a higher law of the land. The civil, criminal and other varieties of administrative laws are enacted with in the parameters of this higher law which can be amended by the sovereign Parliament of the nation. In India, the independent judiciary is the guardian of the Constitution and its sanctity along with fundamental rights of citizens is judicially guaranteed under one of the fundamental rights, i.e., Right to Constitutional Remedies. The Constitution, which was hammered out, by the veteran nationalists and freedom fighters of the country meeting in Constituent Assembly prescribes an institutional framework, which keeps the day-to-day administration of the country in operation as per intentions of the legislature, directions of the executive and overseeing of the judiciary. The administrative machinery and the administrative personnel which work in accordance with administrative laws, rules, regulations, directions, ordinances and codes and manuals, etc., are the creatures of subordinate law which has to be congruent with parliamentary statues and other dictates of the constitutional bodies. Constitutions generally do not prescribe administrative institutions and their working, but being a part of the executive wing of the government, the administration has to be accountable directly as well as indirectly to higher organs of government or even to the people of a democratic polity. The founding fathers of Indian Constitution who freely borrowed from other Constitutions of the world did very little to reconcile the administrative legacies of British Raj to the constitutional system of government they wanted to establish. Naturally, when political institutions have been constitutionalised in a democratic frame the administrative institutions and behaviours are taking their time to get acculturated to political change, which is faster than administrative change in free India. The district administration and politics about which the Indian Constitution was meaningfully silent in 1950 has now been amended to induct Panchayati Raj Polity in 1993 to usher into a new era of administration in the countryside.

The relationship between Constitution and administrative system can be studied under three specific heads of the phenomenon.

(1) Constitutional philosophy or value premise, which all institutions of polity, society and government should respect, imbibe and practise in their respective operations.
(2) The constitutional framework within which the political institutions of central, state and district governments work to achieve the constitutional goals which the people keep prescribing for themselves through their elected representatives.

(3) The administrative working of the civil services and varied administrative organisations which have to operate under the regime of rule of law and implement the policies of the governments according to the letter and spirit of the Constitution.

All this implies that politics and administration are the creatures of the Constitution and hence subordinate to it. The people elect the members of legislatures. The legislative bodies select and permit executive or cabinets to run the government, which in turn should take the services of the administrators to implement the law an their policies for the good governance of the people. The legislature, executive and judiciary all the three are the best judge in their respective spheres. But, if it is a matter of interpretation of the Constitution then an independent and neutralist non-political judiciary has to protect and defend the Constitution from perversion and disfigurement. Consequently, public administration which is a subordinate branch political executive has to work under its control and supervision, but the other wings of government and the people who are the beneficiaries and victims of administrative operations have a right to seek public accountability of administration in the interest of fundamental rights (now human rights) of citizens and welfare of the society as a whole. The Indian Constitution besides being detailed and bulky elaborately lays down the roles of all the organs of government. It enumerates Fundamental Rights and Duties and enjoins upon the future governments to take care of the Directive Principles enunciated in the Constitution while formulating and executing the state policies. The administration of extra constitutional bodies and the infrastructure that has proliferated must permeate with the spirit of the Constitution, which Parliament must feel, executive should obey and the judiciary must defend and preserve.

The philosophy of the Indian Constitution can be understood from the evolutionary landmarks of constitutional history of India since 1858. The Act enunciated the principle of absolute imperial control of home government without any native participation. The provisions of the Act established a rigidly centralised unitary system of government without any separation of functions. The Governor-General was supposed to run the administration under the superintendence, direction and control of the secretary of state for India with the help of a bureaucratic apparatus. The Indian Council Act 1861 expanded the size of the Executive Council with additional non-official member to transact legislative business of the colony. The subsequent instalment of 1892 retained the non-official element but created a majority of official members in the legislative council at the centre. It was the Morley Minto reform of 1909 when the Council System was given the semblance of a legislative body of 67 members. The electoral system though extremely limited and absolutely communal was introduced. The deliberative functions of the council were increased. Still, Lord Morley firmly declined that the reform had any intention to introduce a parliamentary form of government in India. Ten years later, when Montague Chelmsford surveyed the scene, the constitutional framework was totally overhauled in the light of the Queen's proclamation of 1917. The 1919 Act, introduced dyarchical reforms in provincial government, bisecting the subjects into reserved and transferred. The former part was to be controlled by the Governor with the half of his ICS advisers while the latter transferred half was to be administered by responsible Indian minister under a variety of restraints and constraints. The reforms relaxed central control over provincial governments without any conscious division of federal nature. The central legislature was made bicameral and more representative. Even the so-called liberalisation, expansion and Indianisation did not restrain the powers of the Governor-General and the Governors, who reduced the entire scheme to a force. The Gandhian era witnessed all sorts of proposals including the report of the Simon Commission, Round Table discussions, Communal Award and Poona Pact, etc. The Government of India Act 1935 envisaged a federal system with provincial autonomy and diarchy in provincial and central governments respectively. The 1935 Federation though unborn, laid the foundation of the present constitutional arrangement in the distribution of subjects in three lists, emergency powers of Governors and Governor-General and reservation of seats in legislatures of the parliamentary system.

The Republican Constitution of India was prepared and passed by the Constitutional Assembly, which was constituted under the Cabinet Minister Plan of 1945. But then its demand can be traced back to Mahatma Gandhi's protest movements of 1922 and Round Table discussions of 1930–31. Earlier, the Nehru Report attempted to draw a Constitution of India under the Chairmanship of Pandit Motilal Nehru in consultation with Ali brothers. The failure of provincial autonomy in 1939 forced the Indian National Congress to formulate the demand in clearer terms and Cripps' Proposal of 1942 gave respectability to this legitimate demand of Indian. While the World War II was on and the Japanese were knocking at the doors of India the coalition Government of His Majesty decided to despatch veteran statesman Sir Stafford Cripps to India to negotiate constitutional reforms with leaders of Indian National Congress and Muslim League. Sir Cripps unfolded his mission by presenting his proposals in the following form:

(a) that the Constitution of India was to be framed by an elected Constituent Assembly of the Indian people;
(b) that the Constitution should give India dominion status, equal partnership of the British Commonwealth of Nations;
(c) that there should be one Indian Union comprising all the provinces and Indian states; but
(d) that any province (or Indian state) which was not prepared to accept the Constitution would be free to retain its constitutional position existing at that time and with such non-accepting provinces the British government could enter into separate constitutional arrangements.

But the two parties failed to come to an agreement to accept the proposals. The Muslim League argued that India should be divided into two autonomous states on communal lines, and that some of the provinces, earmarked by Mr Jinnah, should form an independent Muslim state, to be known as Pakistan; instead of one Constituent Assembly, there should be two Constituent Assemblies, i.e., a separate Constituent Assembly for building Pakistan. When *Qaidi-Azam* Jinnah refused to accept a maimed and motheaten Pakistan, Mahatma Gandhi called Cripps – a Devils advocate presenting a post-dated cheque on a crashing bank. He advised him to take next plane home. The efforts were renewed in 1945 when the government of Earl Atlee sent a Cabinet Mission under the leadership of Lord Pathirc Sarwence, the last Secretary of State of India. He along with Sir Stafford and A.V. Alexander presented the Cabinet Mission Plan in concrete details in two parts. First, the Constitution of the Constituent Assembly on the basis of indirect election from provincial assemblies and nomination of some members by the rulers of princely states.

There were serious differences in the perceptions of Congress and League leaders about the details, which could not be sorted out in earlier Simla Conference, convened by Viceroy Lord Wavell. The second part of the proposal pertained to the guidelines of the future Constitution of India. The Muslim League was sharply opposed to it, while Congress had its own reservations about grouping of provinces.

The broad features of the scheme were:

(1) There would be a Union of India, comprising both British India and the states, and having jurisdiction over the subjects of foreign affairs, defence and communications. All residuary powers would belong to the provinces and the states.

(2) The Union would have an executive and a legislature consisting of representatives of the provinces and states. But any question raising a major communal issue in the legislature would require for its decision a majority of the representatives of the two major communities present and voting as well as a majority of all the members present and voting.

(3) The provinces would be free to form groups with executives and legislatures, and each group would be competent to determine the provincial subjects, which would be taken up by the group organisation.

The scheme was recommendatory, and it was contemplated by the Mission that it would be adopted by agreement between the two major parties. An explosive situation arose after the election for forming the Constituent Assembly was held. The Muslim League joined the election and its candidates were returned. But a difference of opinion had in the meantime arisen between the Congress and the League regarding the interpretation of the 'grouping clauses' of the proposals of the Cabinet Mission. The British government intervened at this stage and explained to the leaders but League members did not attend the Constituent Assembly meeting. The League urged for the dissolution of the Constituent Assembly on the ground that it was not fully representative of all sections of the people of India. The British government in a statement on 20th February, 1947, declared that British rule in India would in any case end by June, 1948, after which the British would certainly transfer authority to Indian hands; and if by that time a fully representative Constituent Assembly failed to work out a Constitution in accordance with the proposals made by the cabinet delegation which inter alia stated:

His Majesty's government will have to consider to whom the powers of the Central government in British India should be handed over, on the due date, whether as a whole to some form of Central government for British India, or in some areas to the existing provincial government, or in such other way as seems most reasonable and in the best interests of the Indian people.

Still the League did not consider it necessary to join this assembly, and went on pressing for another Constituent Assembly for 'Muslim'. The British government responded by sending Lord Mountbatten to India as the Governor-General, in place of Lord Wavell, to expedite transfer of power, for which they had fixed a time limit. Lord Mountbatten brought the Congress and the League into a definite agreement that the two 'problem' provinces of the Punjab and Bengal would be partitioned so as to form absolute Hindu and Muslim majority blocks within these provinces. The League would then get its Pakistan – which the Cabinet Mission had denied by excluding Assam, East Punjab and West Bengal, while the Congress which was taken a the representative of the people of India other than the Muslims would get the rest of India where the Muslims were in minority. The actual decisions as to whether the two provinces of the Punjab and Bengal were to be partitioned was, however, left to the vote of the members of the Legislative Assemblies of these two provinces, meeting in two parts, according to a plan known as the 'Mountbatten Plan'. It was given a formal shape by a statement made by the British government.

I
Making of the Constitution

"The Provincial Legislative Assemblies of Bengal and the Punjab (excluding European members) will, therefore, each be asked to meet in two parts, one representing the Muslim majority districts and the other the rest of the province ... . The members of the two parts of each legislative assembly sitting separately will be empowered to vote whether or not the province should be partitioned. If a simple majority of *either part* decides in favour of partition, division will take place and arrangements will be made accordingly. If partition were decided upon, each part of the legislative assembly would decide, on behalf of the areas it represented, whether it would join the existing or a new and separate Constituent Assembly."

It was also proposed that there would be a referendum in the North Western Frontier province and in the Muslim majority district of Sylhet as to whether they would join India or Pakistan. The representatives of the Muslim majority areas of the two provinces (i.e., West Punjab and East Bengal) voted for partition and for joining a new Constituent Assembly. The referendum in the North Western Frontier and Sylhet was in favour of Pakistan. On the 26th July, 1947, the Governor General announced the setting up of a separate Constituent Assembly for Pakistan.

The British Parliament lost no time to draft the Indian Independence Bill upon the basis of the above plan, and the bill was passed and placed on the Statute Book, as the Indian Independence Act, 1947. It was introduced in Parliament on July 4, received the Royal assent on July 18, 1947, and came into force from the date. The Act provided that as from the 15th August, 1947 'India' as defined in the Government of India Act, 1935, will have two independent dominions, to be known as *India* and *Pakistan*. The Constituent Assembly of each dominion was to have unlimited power to frame and adopt any Constitution and to repeal any Act of the British Parliament, including the Indian Independence Act. Under the Act, the Dominion of India was to get the residuary territory of India excluding the provinces of Sind, Baluchistan, West Punjab, East Bengal, and the North Western Frontier province and the district of Sylhet in Assam which had voted in favour of Pakistan at a referendum, before the Act came into force.

The Constituent Assembly, which had been elected for undivided India held its first sitting on the 9th December, 1946, reassembled on the 14th August, 1947, as the sovereign Constituent Assembly for the dominion of India. It had been elected by indirect election by the members of the Provincial Legislative Assemblies (lower house only), according to the scheme of the Cabinet Mission Plan, which envisaged that:

(1) Each province and each Indian state or group of states were allotted the total number of seats proportional to their respective populations roughly in the ratio of one to a million. As a result, the provinces were to elect 292 members while the Indian states were allotted a minimum of 93 seats.
(2) The seats in each province were distributed among three main communities, Muslim, Sikh and general, in proportion to their respective populations.
(3) Members of each community in the Provincial Legislative Assembly elected their own representatives by the method of proportional representation with single transferable vote.
(4) The method of selection in the case of representatives of Indian states was to be determined by consultation.

Under the plan of June 3, 1947, a separate Constituent Assembly was set up for Pakistan, The representatives of Bengal, Punjab, Sind, North Western Frontier province, Baluchistan and the Sylhet district of Assam ceased to be members of the Constituent Assembly of India, and fresh elections were held in the new provinces of West Bengal and East Punjab. When the Constituent Assembly reassembled on the 31st October, 1947, the membership of the House was reduced to 299, out of which 284 were actually present on the 26th November, 1949, and appended their signatures to the Constitution as finally passed. The outline of the proposed Constitution emerged in the deliberations of various committees of the assembly such as the Union Constitution Committee, the Union Powers Committee, Committee on Fundamental Rights, and, the Assembly Drafting Committee constituted on the 29th August, 1947. The Drafting Committee, under the chairmanship of Dr Ambedkar, embodied the decision of the assembly with alternative and additional proposals in the form of a 'Draft Constitution of India' which was published in February, 1948. The Constituent Assembly considered the provision of the draft, clause by clause and the second reading was completed on 17th October, 1949. The Constituent Assembly again sat on the 14th November, 1949, for third reading and the Constitution was declared as passed and adopted when President Dr Rajendra Prasad signed the approved draft on 26th November, 1949.

The Preamble

The Constituent Assembly through indirectly elected composed of ardent patriots, veteran freedom fighters, legal luminaries of bar and above all tested well-wishers of the masses. While the various committees of Constituent Assembly under the chairmanship of Nehru, Patel, Ambedkar, K.M. Munshi and others were busy in preparing a workable draft, the Constituent Assembly which was presided by Dr Rajendra Prasad debated an objective resolution which was to guide its deliberations till end. The three schools in the Constituent Assembly were apparently riving with each other for conserves. The first and foremost was the Gandhian school whose adherents and proponents were numerous and in the absence of the Mahatma in the assembly (He was assassinated on January 30, 1948) they could not make any dent and the resultant document is called Ungandhians by the critics. The second school which stood for the advocacy of British pattern and European institution called it an opportunity to lay the foundations of a modern India. The third school strived to work out a mixed model and take the Indian constitutional history to its logical culminations. Dr Ambedkar and Pandit Nehru along with K.M. Munshi, P.D. Tondon, Nasiruldin Ahmed, B.N. Rau and dozen's of others prevailed upon the members and on January 22, 1947, the Constituent Assembly adopted the following objective resolution after a brief but meaningful debate on the floor of the house.

- "This Constituent Assembly declares its firm and solemn resolve to proclaim India as an Independent Sovereign Republic and to draw up for her future governance a Constitution.
- Wherein the territories that now comprise British India, the territories that now form the Indian states, and such other parts of India as are outside British India and the states as well as such other territories as are willing to be constituted into the Independent Sovereign India, shall be a union of them all; and
- Wherein the said territories, whether with their present boundaries or with such others as may be determined by the Constituent Assembly and thereafter according to the law of the Constitution, shall possess and retain the status of autonomous units, together with residuary powers,

and exercise all powers and functions of government and administration, save and except such powers and functions as are vested in or assigned to the union, or as are inherent or implied in the union or resulting therefrom; and

- Wherein all power and authority of the Sovereign Independent India, its constituent parts and organs of governments are derived from the people; and
- Wherein shall be guaranteed and secured to all the people of India justice,, social, economic and political; equality of status, of opportunity, and before the law; freedom of thought, expression, belief, faith, worship, vocation, association and action, subject to law and public morality; and
- Wherein adequate safeguards shall be provided for minorities, backward and tribal areas, and depressed and other backward classes; and
- Wherein shall be maintained the integrity of the territory of the republic and its sovereign rights on land, sea, and air according to justice and the law of civilised nations; and
- The ancient land attaints rightful and honoured place in the world and make its full and willing contribution to the promotion of world peace and the welfare of mankind."

Pandit Nehru called it a pledge, a resolve and an understanding for a dedication because of our tryst with destiny. The founding fathers did not debate this philosophy but only reiterated in again and again to build an Indian of their dreams. It was their 'political will' which they wanted to pan on the posterity with an exertion that their children will not fail them. In fact the language of this objective resolution repeat the phraseology of that pledge which Congress leadership took on the bank of river Ravi in its Lahore session. Ever since its inception the moderates, the radicals and Gandhites in Indian National Congress were strongly against the British to establish an independent nation-state wedded to the ideals of liberalism, secularism and welfare. Although, partition of the country was a great set back to this philosophy, yet they stead fastly stuck to their guns. Allen Glad Hill eulogistically maintains that 'it was heroic on the part of the Indian people' to stick to the liberal philosophy of a secular State. In its long and cherished history of freedom struggle the veteran nationalist leaders had seen very many deviation, conflicts and revisions of their nationalist ideology. Partition of the nation-state and assassinations of its torch bearer like Mahatma Gandhi were the price that the nation has already paid. Naturally, these was a near unanimity or a strong consensus about the constitutional philosophy which the preamble of the Constitution eloquently states. In fact it is the telegraphic summary of the entire Constitution, every letter of which has been given meaning and substance by institutionalisation in the legal framework. The 42nd Amendment of 1976 only adds to it and widens the ambits of this constitutional philosophy. The preamble states:

> WE, THE PEOPLE OF INDIA, having solemnly resolved to constitute India into a SOVEREIGN SOCIALIST SECULAR DEMOCRATIC REPUBLIC and to secure to all its citizens: JUSTICE, social, economic and political; LIBERTY of thought, expression, belief, faith and worship; EQUALITY of status and of opportunity; and to promote among them all; FRATERNITY assuring the dignity of the individual and the unity and integrity of the Nation.
>
> IN OUR CONSTITUENT ASSEMBLY this twenty-sixth day of November, 1949, do HEREBY ADOPT, ENACT AND GIVE TO OURSELVES THIS CONSTITUTION.

Though, unjustifiably, the Supreme Court of India has viewed it as a lamp post directing the ship of the state from harbour 'we the people of India' have resolved it and this solemn resolution has resulted in this organisational framework, which the people of India have enacted, adopted and given to themselves through the medium of Constituent Assembly. It is very much oη the tune of the charter of United Nations and the Constitution of United States. We the People, denote several philosophical nuances:

(1) People have framed this Constitution through their representatives.
(2) People are sovereign and all govern mental powers inhere in people.
(3) People alone have the final authority and nobody can subjugate them or trample their wishes and aspiration.
(4) People, alone can change, amend or revise this Constitution, and even the 'basic structure' has to be protected and presumed for the people, if not by the representatives of the people.

These People of India are sovereign and they will operate their republic government in a democratic manner without distinctions or discriminations of caste, colour, sex and creed. The democratic nature of the sovereign republic will keep the government accountable to the people who shall exercise this sovereign majesty though adult suffrage, practice of rule of law and availability of fundamental rights. The political institutions will ensure liberty, equality and justice to all without privileged groups and feudal behaviours of the governmental functionaries.

The nation-state has to be preserved at all costs and with this 'the dignity of the individual' has to be respected and enhanced ... . The 42nd Amendment by adding socialism and secularism to the philosophy wants to assert that socio-political milieu and economic conditions must be such that rights may became meaningful and attainable. The integrity of the nation is more important than the unity of the nation, just because if the latter is not adequate the former should not be jeopardised. The elaboration and still more the interpretation of the preamble makes the philosophy dynamic and terms like democracy, socialism, secularism and social justice are acquiring new meanings and contents by the operational dynamics of Constitution institutions. For centuries, Indian state and society not only suffered the indignities of the alien rule but developed perverted and stagnant behaviours of caste, class and committees. Feudalism and colonialism drained out its vitality and injustices of sorts have become the order of the day. The preamble awakens and warns the future rulers of the country against this scourge of inhuman practices, parochial attitudes and feudal legacies of the part. The value premises so meaningfully embodied in the preamble may not have teeth but their reiteration explain the intention, which is obviously reflected in every provision of the document. These values which administrators have to imbibe need elaboration for a clearer understanding of our constitutional polity so meticulously built by the founding fathers to modernise the mediaeval society in this ancient land.

Democratic Republicanism

Addressing a seminar on 'Parliamentary Democracy' in 1956, Pandit Jawaharlal Nehru, the chief architect of the Constitution defined the democratic order as under:

> Democracy has been spoken of chiefly in the past, as political democracy, roughly represented by every person having a vote. But a vote by itself does not represent very much to a person who is down and out, to a person, let us say, who is starving or hungry. Political democracy, by itself, is not enough except that it may be used to obtain a gradually increasing measure of economic democracy, equality and the spread of good things of life to others and removal of gross inequalities.

This extension of political concept of democracy to social and economic aspects of people and the cultural ethos of Indian society was an innovation. Poor and oppressed people cannot operate a republic. It is good to hear an elected head so that military chiefs or political dictators or superiors may not subvert democratic institutions and their accountability to people, but mere elected republic should not be confused with democratic polity. Dr B.R. Ambedkar, the Chairman of the Drafting Committee of the Constitution had to intervene effectively in the Constituent Assembly. In his concluding speech, he eloquently mentioned:

> Political democracy cannot last unless there lies at the base of it social democracy. What does social democracy mean? It means a way of life, which recognises liberty, equality and fraternity, which are not to be treated as separate items in a trinity. They form a union of trinity in the sense that to divorce one from the other is to defeat the very purpose of democracy. *Liberty cannot be divorced from equality, equality cannot be divorced from liberty. Nor can liberty and equality be divorced from fraternity.*

The parliamentary democracy in the unwritten Constitution of England without any Supreme Court to review and interpret has a special structure and meaning to the Island nation. Unlike India, it did not have a superimposition of political institutions and rule of law as we had in our colonial history, yet our elite was enamoured by British institutions. The 1919 and 1935 Acts were a workable compromise of parliamentarism with Indian conditions of political feudalism, regional disintegration and communal conflicts. The framers of Indian Constitution institutionalised democratic values of French Revolution, namely, liberty, equality and fraternity in the following characteristics of the constitution:

(1) Adult suffrage without any distinction of caste, colour, sex and creed, but due safeguard to the poor weak and vulnerable minorities through reservation in elections.
(2) Sovereignty of Parliament with powers of judicial review to an independent judiciary, impeachable by the legislature.
(3) Rule of law along with accountability of all political institutions to sovereign people, whose fundamental rights have to be jealously protected by all the organs of government by a system of check and balance of powers.
(4) Justice and fraternity as watch words of polity envisaged in the Directive Principles of State Policy along with right against exploitation and socio-cultural rights.

Fundamental Rights

Thus, when political institutions have been made representative and responsible, constitutional efforts have been made to empower people, especially the members of weaker sections to live in dignity with rights of liberty, equality and religious freedom. Initially, Constitution enshrined seven fundamental rights of citizens as a part of democratic polity. But, the Right to Property later by Amendment 44th converted into a legal right, because of the progressive laws of property compensations. These rights are:

(1) Right to Equality
(2) Right to Freedom
(3) Right against Exploitation
(4) Right to Freedom of Religion
(5) Cultural and Educational Rights
(6) Right to Constitutional Remedies

Right to equality envisages that discriminations cannot be allowed in a democratic polity and social offences like untouchability are heinous crimes to be punished by law. Abolishing all distinctions on the basis of colour, caste, sex, creed or place of birth the specific right to equality heroically liberates our people from a social bondage of centuries. The founding fathers have gone to the limit of mentioning details like access to shops, public restaurants, hotels and places of public entertainment which cannot be denied to weaker sections or untouchables under any excuse of religious purity. Though quite comprehension in its meaning and scope this right permits the state to make special provisions for women, children or socially and educationally backward classes for their initial advancement. Notwithstanding agitations against reservation policy embodied in the Constitution, it is justified on the ground of equality of opportunity to all deprived citizens in matters relating to employment under the State Articles 14, 15, 16, 17 and 18 talk about:

1. Socio-cultural equality and abolition of discriminations
2. Equality before law and public employment
3. Ban on untouchability
4. Equality of opportunities and status with positive discrimination through reservations
5. Abolition of titles

All this fulfils a national commitment of social justice which the founding fathers made during the freedom struggle under the Father of the Nation.

The right to equality without *Right to Liberty* loses its meaning. The founding fathers have guaranteed a set of freedom (Article 19) which include:

(1) Freedom of speech, thought, belief, faith, worship and expression;
(2) Assemble peaceably and without arms;
(3) Form associations or unions;
(4) Move freely throughout the territory of India;
(5) Reside and settle in any part of the territory of India; and
(6) Practice any profession or carry on any occupation, trade or business.

These liberties are subject to reasonable restrictions on the individual in the interest of the sovereignty and integrity of the nation, public order and morality and in the interest of the general public or the minorities. The Constitution offers protection against arbitrary arrest and excessive punishment. No person shall be convicted of any offence except for violation of a law in force. He shall not be detained in custody without being informed and shall be produced before the nearest magistrate within a period of twenty-four hours of such arrest (Article 22). The Constitution forbids *exploitation* or "traffic in human beings, begging and other similar forms of forced labour are prohibited and any contravention of this provision is an offence punishable in accordance with law" (Article 23). But the state can impose compulsory service for public purposes without discriminations of religion, race, caste, or class. Hazards is Employment, and exploitation of children stand prohibited (Article 24). Articles 25 to 28 of the Constitution provide the citizens with *Right to Religious Freedom*. All persons are entitled to freedom of conscience and the right to preach profess, practice and propagate any 'religion' without an effort to convert people. No person can be compelled to pay taxes, the proceeds of which are specifically appropriated in payment of expenses for the promotion or maintenance of any particular religion or religious denomination. *The Socio Cultural Right* conserves the citizens, right to cultural identity and no citizen can be denied admission into any educational institution maintained by the state. Article 31 deals with the *Right to Property*, but it has been dropped as a constitutional right claiming judicially guaranteed compensation by the 44th Amendment of the Constitution in 1977. The Constitution provides a machinery for the enforcement of these rights. The Supreme Court has been given the power to issue injunctions, or orders or writs under Article 32. This *Right to Constitutional Remedies* operates in the following manner:

(1) Habeas Corpus: This writ is a command of the court to a person who is detaining another person, to bring the body of the person in his custody at a stipulated time and place for a specified purpose.
(2) Mandamus: It is an order that commands a person or a body to do that what constitutes his or its duty as legal performance.
(3) Prohibition: This writ is issued to prevent a junior court not to exceed its jurisdiction or act contrary to the norms of natural justice.
(4) Certiorari: This writ is used to order the shifting of a suit from a lower court to a higher court to prevent an excess or abuse of jurisdiction before the commencement of the trial.
(5) Quo Warranto: It grants an injunction to restrain a person from acting in an office to which he is not entitled. The court may declare the office vacant.

Article 38 of the Constitution states: "The state shall strive to promote the welfare of the people by securing and protecting as effectively as it may, a social order in which justice, social, economic and political shall inform all the institutions of the national life." The 'liberty' of thought, expression, belief, faith and worship has been viewed in the perspective of the fundamental right to profess, practice and propagate any religion and ensurement of the freedom of conscience. [Article 19(1)]. The Preamble mentions essential individual rights and these are guaranteed against the entire subject, to the implementation of the Directive Principles, and the 'Fundamental Duties', introduced (Article 51A) by the 42nd Amendment. These duties talk about respect for ideals and institutions of freedom struggle and the Constitution. Promotion of communal harmony, dignity of women and preservation of composite culture and environment have been stressed upon. The Constitution exhorts upon the lay citizens to abjure violence, develop scientific temper and strive towards excellence.

The critics maintain that the scheme of rights is too vague and full of contradictions. It gives by one hand and takes back by the other. The constraints of, 'morality' decency and public order, can be stretched to any extent. Then emergency provision can run rough shed over the entire scheme. The right to property has already been deleted and anti-reservation agitations may permit all high caste citizens to make their inroads in the sections called SC, ST and OBC. The claims of poor, women and minorities totally revolutionise what the founding fathers had as a part of their intentions.

The Constitution of India is a living and vibrant document. It talks about the basics to which every successive generation has a right to add and delete. The constitutional philosophy of liberty, equality and justice stands vindicated. Now when the Fundamental Duties and the Directive Principles of State Policy are getting integrated with Human Rights, the Constitution of India makes provisions for the dignity of the individuals and unity of the nation which ultimately creates a democratic society wherein there will be a capacity and a passion for the enjoyment of liberty.

Socialist Welfarism

Socialism in the west has been propounded in the context of industrial revolution and lassie faire capitalism of the nineteenth century. Karl Marx added a revolutionary dimension to it by presenting a class analysis for civil war. In India, the industrial revolution has begun after independence and capitalism too was also having imperialist overtones. So, Pandit Nehru, Jai Prakash Narain, Acharya Narendra Dev and Ashok Mehta in their respective expositions talk of social welfarism, which has been the hallmark of socialist thought even in Europe. Mahatma Gandhi's Sarvodaya socialism was a dream of social equality and social justice without powerful intervention of the state. Pandit Nehru's efforts of planned development have been called 'a socialism of production' rather than that of distribution. A poor developing and agricultural economy must be industrialised to banish poverty and eradicate backwardness of the masses. A number of Directive Principles of State Policy such as equal pay for equal work, equitable distribution of national wealth, protection of old age maternity and children from abuse are pronounced socialist principles which the Indian Constitution proclaims. The realisation of objectives would certainly mean an expansion of the functions of the state. The goal envisaged by the Constitution, therefore, is that of a 'welfare state' and the establishment of a 'socialist state' which the Avadi session of Congress (1955) explained as a 'socialistic pattern of society' in the following words.

"In order to realise the object of Congress, and to *further the objectives stated in the Preamble and Directive Principles of State Policy* of the Constitution of India, planning should take place with a view to the establishment of a *socialistic pattern of society*, where the principal means of production are under social ownership or control, production is progressively speeded up and there is equitable distribution of the national wealth". The trend has been from a 'socialistic pattern' towards a 'socialistic state', which is not only bringing industries and private enterprises under State ownership but also carrying on trade and business as a state function. This goal of *socialism* has been ensured by inserting the word 'socialist' in the preamble, by the Constitution (42nd Amendment) Act, 1976. However, 'socialism' envisaged by the Indian Constitution is not the Western scheme of state socialism, which involves 'nationalisation' of *all* means of production, and the abolition of private property. Prime Minister Indira Gandhi clarified it:

"We have always said that we have our *own brand* of socialism. We will nationalise the sectors where we feel the necessity. Just nationalisation is not our type of socialism."

The Indian Constitution, therefore, does not seek to abolish private property, it only accepts it as a legal but not a fundamental right of the citizens. It helps the state to preserve its welfare policies for the poor. The word 'socialist' has been read with Article 39(b) by the Supreme Court and High Courts to uphold the constitutionality of laws of nationalisation of private property in accordance with procedure established by law. Articles 14 and 16 of the Constitution have enabled the Supreme Court and the High Courts to deduce a fundamental right to equal pay for equal work; and strike down statues which fail to achieve socialist goal in the name of due process interpretation of law. Because of this, centrality of Nehru brand of socialism, a number of radical economic reforms have taken place in India since 1991 through policies of economic liberalisation, privatisation and disinvestment of the public sector which Prime Minister Narsimha Rao initiated in varied ways. The role and responsibility of the government in accelerating equitable economic development have not been reduced as a result of these attempts to restructure the economy but the impact is apparent on the nature of the mixed economy of Nehru era.

The Directives and Duties

The socialist ethos of Indian Constitution can be appreciated by going through the Directive Principles of State Policy and Fundamental Duties of citizens. The state has been directed to strive to promote the welfare of the people by securing and protecting a social order in which justice, shall inform all institutions of national life. The state shall strive to minimise the inequalities income and eliminate inequalities in status, facilities and opportunities amongst individuals and groups of people residing in different areas or engaged in different vocations. The citizens, will have the right to an adequate means of livelihood. The ownership and control of the material resources of the community will be so distributed that they will sub serve the common good. The operation of the economic system will not result in the concentration of wealth and means of production to the common detriment. Equal pay for equal work for both men and women will be assured. The health and strength of workers, and children of tender age will not be abused. Citizens will not be forced by economic necessity to enter vocations unsuited to their age, gender or strength. Children will be given opportunities and facilities to develop in a healthy manner and in conditions of freedom and dignity and childhood and youth will be protected against exploitation and against moral and material abandonment. The state shall ensure that the operation of the legal system promotes justice on the basis of equal opportunity and shall, provide free legal aid by suitable legislation so that opportunities for securing justice are not denied to a citizen by reason of economic or other disabilities. The state shall take steps to organise village panchayats and endow them with such powers and authority as may be necessary to enable them to function as units of self-government. The state shall make effective provision for securing the right to work, to education and to public assistance in cases of unemployment, old age, sickness and disablement. The Constitution directs that the state shall make provision for securing just and humane conditions of work and for maternity relief. It shall endeavour to secure, to all workers, a living wage, and conditions of work ensuring a decent standard of life and full enjoyment of leisure and socio-cultural opportunities. The state shall take steps to secure the participation of workers in the management of undertakings, shall endeavour to secure a uniform civil code for citizens of different religious persuasions throughout the country. The Directives urge upon the state to promote the educational and economic interests of the weaker sections of the people and protect them from social injustice and other forms of exploitation. The state shall initiate measures to raise the level of nutrition and the standard of living of its people to improve public health as its primary duty. It shall endeavour to bring about prohibition of the consumption of intoxicating drinks and of drugs which are injurious to public health (Article 47). The Constitution enjoins upon the state to endeavour to organise agricultural and animal husbandry on modern and scientific lines and take steps for improving the breeds and prohibiting the slaughter of cow and calves and other milch and draught cattle. It shall endeavour to protect and improve the environment and to safeguard forests and wildlife of the country. It shall be the obligation of the state to protect historic monument and places or objects of artistic interest, declared of national importance by the Parliament from spoilation and disfigurement. The Constitution asks the state to take steps to separate the judiciary from the executive in the public services of the state. Article 51 states,that the state shall make special efforts to promote international peace and security; maintain just and honourable relations between nations; foster respect for international law and treaty-obligations and encourage settlement of international disputes by arbitration.

The Constitution further adds a list of duties for the citizens vide Article 51(A) which has been inserted by the 42nd Amendment Act of 1976. It prescribes that it shall be the duty of every citizen of India:

(a) to abide by the Constitution and respect its ideals and institutions, the National Flag and the National Anthem;
(b) to cherish and follow the noble ideals which inspired our national struggle for freedom;
(c) to uphold and protect the sovereignty, unity and integrity of India;
(d) to defend the country and render national service when called upon to do so;
(e) to promote harmony and the spirit of common brotherhood amongst all the people of India transcending religious, linguistic and regional or sectional diversities, to renounce practices derogatory to the dignity of women;
(f) to value and preserve the rich heritage of our composite culture;
(g) to protect and improve the natural environment including forests, lakes, rivers and wildlife and to have compassion for living creatures;
(h) to develop the scientific temper, humanism and the spirit of inquiry and reform;
(i) to safeguard public property and to abjure violence;
(j) to strive towards excellence in all spheres of individual and collective activity, so that the nation constantly rises to higher levels of endeavour and achievement.

These duties are addressed to the citizens but are without any legal sanctions against their violation. The mixed economy of Nehru period could not be sustained in Indira Gandhi's period when she found the rightist forces apathetic and even inimical to welfare measures of state. The emergency situation in 1975 has been a matter of debate but the Amendment 42nd which added ten Fundamental Duties of citizens by Article 51(A) drastically changed the Avadi spirit of the socialistic pattern of society. The successive regime especially that of Narsimha Rao desperately struggled with the collapse of the closed economy working against the development of the weak and poor. He valiantly took the cudgels and made socialism compatible with socialist welfarism by enlarging the national cake. Today, when the country has embarked on the path of liberalisation, privatisation and globalisation, our economy can be called socialistic. Public enterprise failed us, so private ownership can yield more production. The issues of distribution being unimportant in a mass society seeped in poverty and scarcity, the western socialist clichés do not help. Hence, the term 'socialist republic' is synonymous with welfarism and social justice. The Directive Principles enjoin upon the state to create a socialistic pattern of society without capitalistic exploitation and concentration of wealth. The value premise of popular welfare, absence of inhuman conditions of work and exploitative relations in industry have constitutional socialism compatible with globalised liberal economy of 21st century.

The scheme of Directive Principles of State Policy read with the Charter of Fundamental Duties balance the socio-economic rights with socio-political duties. Both the schemes are not justiceable but their inclusion implies their implementation. The citizen may not go to law court but the authorities of the state have to account for their failures before the electorate at the time of elections. Moreover the Supreme Court under justices like P.N. Bhagwati, J.C. Verma, Kuldeep Singh and their compares has emphatically taken a position that directives need primacy and the socio-economic rights are a part of the total scheme. Judicial activism has given a new content to the scheme and measures like equal pay for equal work, social security of vulnerable sections, prohibition, right to primary education, separation of judiciary even Uniform Civil Code have been high on the agenda of executive implementation. Fundamental Duties have become a part of school textbooks and Human Rights jurisprudence is emerging with a vehemence.

Secular Pluralism

One of the dimensions of democracy can be called secularism because it essentially implies the extension of democratic principles of liberalism and individualism in the realism of religion. The protestant reformers were asking for freedom of conscience and secularism stood for a protest against the theological hegemony of the Pope. The democratisation of ecclesiastical institution was called secular reaction in Europe.

India had no organised Hindu or Muslim spiritual institutions, comparable with the Christian church. On the other hand, it had an indigenous component of secularisation from the mediaeval times. The *Sufi* and *Bhakti* movements in medieval India gave a tremendous impetus to bringing the people of various communities closer. Khwaja Moinuddin Chisti, Baba Farid, Kabir, Guru Nanak, Dadu, Tukaram, Mira Bai and many others contributed to the development of a composite culture, which was not possible through any political or administrative system. Guru Nanak saw no distinction between man and man. The spirit of tolerance and coexistence became a landmark of secular attitude and outlook. Ashoka's famous twelfth rock edict on 'Religious Toleration' echoes it. It triumphed in the reign of Akbar, who, being a liberal Muslim ruler, was alive to the dangers of religious bigotry and tried to promote national solidarity by his catholic eclecticism and secular policies. His *Din-i-Illahi* (divine faith) and *Sulh-i-Kul* (peace with all) were imbued with the spirit of secularism. This spirit was strengthened and enriched through our long freedom movement. The Constitution drafted by Pandit Moti Lal Nehru in 1928 had a specific provision regarding secularism.

Dr Rajendra Prasad paying a tribute to Indian eclecticism did not allow the European concept to enter into the Constitution because religion (dharma) in the Indian context can never be 'one final Book way' of knowing the truth. Religion in India has different meanings to different people as individuals, as citizens and as co-religionists. Seth Govind Das, a veteran freedom fighter and litterateur firmly maintained that secularism can neither be a religion, nor indifference to religion, nor mere tolerance and coexistence of religions. Those who viewed it as anti communalisms were dismissed on the ground that religious groups are not communities (*sampradayas*). There can be respectable sampradayas like Vallabhacharya, Radha Vallabh, etc. Broadly speaking, it is used not as opposed to religion but as divorced from all religion or religious having nothing to do with the conduct of state affairs. In India the word has been used not in anti-religious sense, but meaning treatment to all religious on an equal footing and ruling out any discrimination of any Indian on the ground of his religion. Use of the term 'secularism' in this sense can be characterised as 'Indianism', which has no place in *Oxford English Dictionary*. The usage of equal respect to all has identified the word secular with tolerance among the different religions in India. Infact "Secularism does not mean irreligion or atheism or even stress on material comforts. It proclaims that it lays stress on the universality of spiritual values which may be attained by a variety of ways." In India, secularism means equal status to all religions. D.E. Smith in his book *India as a Secular State* defines, "the Secular State as a state which guarantees individual and corporate freedom of religion, deals with the individual as a citizen irrespective of his religion, is not constitutionally connected to a particular religion nor does it seek either to promote or interfere with religion." The founding fathers wished to evolve Indian polity on these lines.

Secularism Conceptualised

This conceptual problem apart the 42nd Amendment added secular character to Indian Republic. It is specially relevant because our neighbouring countries like Afghanistan, Bhutan, Bangladesh, Nepal, Pakistan and Sri Lanka have opted for the theocratic model of their states. The bewildering diversities of religion, caste, creed, language and ethnic groups make it imperative upon the Indian state to develop a secular ethos of pluralism and multi-religious society over the sub-continent. It is a fact that more Muslims reside in India than in Pakistan. States like Punjab, Kerala, Nagaland and Kashmir do not have Hindu majority and when Hindus are a majority in India they happen to be a global minority in the era of globalisation. Naturally, Indian polity has to be evolved on secular lines which according to the philosophy of the Constitution means:

(1) State will have no religion of its own and all citizens of its own and all citizens will be given similar treatment without any distinction of religion, caste or creed.
(2) Right to religious freedom is a fundamental right of every citizen and he or she can preach, profess and practice any religion without indulging into religious conversions.
(3) Religion will be treated as a personal domain and state will encourage all religions to organise their festivals, fairs and morality to peace, dignity and morality.
(4) With religious freedom it is a fundamental duty of every citizen to develop scientific temper and fight against religious fundamentalism, obscurantism, superstitious and discriminations.

Indian Constitution embodies a concept of positive and dynamic secularism. The state does not interfere but is not apathetic to religious affairs. For instance, Constitution abolishes untouchability under Article 17. It permits the state to make reservation for the backward classes in public services (Articles 16 and 235). It guarantees reservation of seats in Parliament to Scheduled Castes, Scheduled Tribes and Anglo-Indians. It permits advisory councils and special commissions for the welfare of victims of religious misbehaviour. The entire Sixth Schedule is devoted to the people of this variety. Moreover, the Indian state would not support any religion out of public funds, nor would it penalise the profession and practice of any religion or the right to manage religious institutions as provided in Articles 25 and 26. There has been controversies and interpretations of the term 'secular'. The dispute appears to be whether the state should respect all religions equally or should disassociate itself totally from religion. While the plan of equal respect for all religions seems to be acceptable to all communities, the premise of separation of the state from religion, rooted in the European notion of a secular state, has not led to any consensus on its meaning or implications. The attempt to bring about a constitutional amendment of separation between religion and politics was not acceptable to the major non-Congress political parties in 1993. Every group must recognise common Indianness and be prepared to subordinate its petty interests to the common national good. All political parties should build a secular society through a decentralised, democratic, political and administrative set-up. There has to be a federal union of autonomous states. Both these conditions have been accepted and provided for in the Constitution. A secular society or polity cannot be legislated but can certainly be evolved by making conditions conducive. Hinduism, Islam and Christianity have been metamorphosed by scientific and technological revolutions of our times. The state should patiently wait and allow scientific temper to grow to secularise religions of a plural society.

Indissolvability of the Union

The founding fathers were immensely obsessed with the unity and integrity of Indian nation-state, which was being delivered under the shadows of partition. The history may not repeat itself, so the lesson of history as Dr B.R. Ambedkar perceived it, was to have a strong centralised state to arrest disintegration of dismemberment. For this, the term 'federation' was avoided and an indissolvable union was proclaimed. The fear of disruption was so intense that union-state relations were specially designed on the pattern of 1935 Act and even three kinds of emergencies were justified to keep the nation-state together. Even the 42nd Amendment stresses to protect the integrity of the country, which is more than mere unity of the units. The legislative, administrative and financial relations between union and states have been so devised that centre has an upper hand and quasi-federation can be interrupted as 'federal in form but unitary in spirit'. This overcentralisation of the structure has created an infrastructure of the Constitution which according to G.N. Singh reduces the state to municipalities. After the 73rd and 74th Amendments, the states feel further weakened and the technological advances are facilitating centre sway over every nook and crony of government activity. The Indian Constitution gives a new meaning or version to the theory of federalism. Cooperative federalism, incremental federalism, centralised federalism and now panchayati federalism, explain the varied experiment, which in each case asks the administration of the state to adjust with the prevailing waves of democracy and federalism. A federation is characterised by several features. The Indian Constitution enshrines a federally governed state by providing two levels of government – the Central government and the state government (and now the local government also). The powers and functions of the Central government, the state and the local government have been defined in a written Constitution; all governments are autonomous within their respective areas of operations. Disputes regarding the powers and functions of the Central government and the state government are decided by an independent judiciary.

Three-Tier Federalism

The Indian Constitution fulfils all these conditions. It visualises two and now of three levels of government after 73rd Amendment each being autonomous in its own sphere of functioning. There is the constitutional distribution of functions between the two levels of government. The Central government has jurisdiction over 97 subjects; strictly speaking, there are 96 subjects, the ninety-seventh being "any other matter not enumerated in List II or List III including any tax not mentioned in either of those Lists". This is really the residuary power. The State List includes 66 subjects, which are within the exclusive legislative jurisdiction of the state legislature. Also, there is a Concurrent List consisting of 47 subjects over which both the governments have concurrent jurisdiction subject, of course, to the superiority of the Central government. The disputes between the Central government and the states are to be decided by the Supreme Court. Nevertheless, the Constitution has created an extraordinarily powerful Central government, Article 249 authorises Parliament to enact legislation on any subject in the State List, provided the Rajya Sabha by a two-thirds majority empowers it to do so. Under Article 312, Parliament is empowered to create new all India services common to the Centre and the state, provided the Rajya Sabha passes resolution to this effect by a two-thirds majority. This Article was pressed into service in 1963, when the Central government, acting on the recommendation of the Rajya Sabha, decided to set up three new All India Services – the Indian Forest Service, the Indian Medical and Health Service, and the Indian Service of Engineers. However, only the Indian Forest Service alone could be created. The state government is placed under an obligation to exercise its executive power so as to ensure compliance with the laws made by the Parliament. Article 257 gives the mandate that the executive power of every state shall be exercised so as not to impede or prejudice the exercise of the executive power of the Union, and the executive power of the Union shall extend to the giving of such directions to a state as may appear to the Government of India to be necessary for that purpose. Similarly Articles 200 and 201 empower the Governor who is a presidential appointee to reserve a bill passed by the state legislative assembly for the consideration of the President who has the power to veto it without giving any reasons. The powers of the Central government become far-reaching unrestricted in times of emergency. The Union can virtually function as a unitary state (a) when the security of the country is threatened, (b) when there is failure of the Constitution in a state, or (c) when there is threat to the financial stability of any state.

An unusual feature of Indian federalism is that there is nothing permanent about the very identity of the states. Article 3 of the Constitution provides that the Parliament may by law (a) form a new state, (b) increase the area of any state, (c) diminish the area of any state, (d) alter the boundaries of any state, or (e) alter the name of any state. And, as Article 4 confirms, such a law is not to be construed as an amendment of the Constitution. It is also to be stressed that the Central government has made ample use of this provision contained in Article 3.

Dignity of the Individual

The debates of the Constituent Assembly for almost three years centred around the theme of the common man who stood exploited depowerised and humiliated for centuries in Indian history. The concern was genuine and sensitive to the care. Naturally it became the hall mark of the Constitution of the nation-state. The dignity of this individual not only assured but also made an ongoing concern of all the parliamentary institutions based on adult suffrage. The judiciary was specifically asked to protect his fundamental rights under judicial review and the state was given directive to take measures for his emergence and powerisation in new Indian society. Lack of fraternalism among citizens has caused this callousness and exploitation of man by man. This fraternity cannot, be installed unless the dignity of each of its members is maintained. The preamble, therefore, says that the state in India, will assure the dignity of the individual. The Constitution seeks to achieve this object by guaranteeing equal fundamental rights to each individual, so that he can enforce his minimal rights. Seeing that these justifiable rights may not be enough to uphold the dignity of an individual if he is not free from wants and misery, a number of directives have been included in Part IV of the Constitution exhorting upon the state to shape its social and economic policies whereby, "all citizens, men and women equally, have the right to an adequate means of livelihood" [Article 39(a)], "just and humane conditions of work" (Article 42), and "a decent standard of life and full enjoyment of leisure and social and cultural opportunities" (Article 43). To remove poverty and to bring about a socio-economic revolution, the list of Directives has been widened by the 42nd Amendment Act, of 1976, and it has been provided that such welfare measures for the benefit of the masses may not be defeated by capitalists and vested interests by insisting on their fundamental rights. Measure for the implementation of any of the directives are no longer immune from attack in the courts on the ground that such measure contravenes any person's fundamental rights under Article 14 or 19. The philosophy has been further highlighted by emphasising that each individual shall not only have the fundamental rights in Part III of the Constitution to ensure his liberty of expression, faith and worship, equality of opportunity and the like, but also a corresponding fundamental duty, such as to uphold the sovereignty, unity and integrity of the nation, to maintain secularism and the common brotherhood amongst all the people of India.

Thus, the Constitutional philosophy epitomises the essence of the freedom struggle. The English rulers were driven out not because they were collecting wealth and draining out the energy of the colony but to build a new nation of their dreams. This dream envisioned self-government, self-respect for citizen and mutual love and cooperation among people pursuing diverse faiths, varied languages and numerous styles of living. Neither ancient Indian nor mediaeval or British India could be the imitable models of future. Those who wrought for freedom had the opportunity to lay the foundations of contemporary Indian society to play its role in the comity of nations. The Constitution and its value premises have started shaping the Indian people and public administration of the country is being revamped to adjust and respond to the needs of a democratic Socialist Secular Society, wedded to the sublime ideals of liberalism and nationalism.

II
The Institutional Framework

A Constitution has been defined as something that fixes the structure of the government. This structure has not only to be outlined but the roles, relations and functions of its various organs have to be interrelated in relation to objectives and principles underlying the system. The Constituent Assembly conclusively prescribed a Parliamentary Federal System, which is unique in many ways. The two-tier Government of India with its third-tier structure of local government as amended has an elaborate structure of its three organs namely the legislature, the executive and the judiciary. This institutions framework of the Central government can be depicted as under:

The Office of the President

The executive power of the Union government lies in the President who exercises it either directly or through officers subordinate to him. He is the supreme commander of the defence forces of the union. Executive actions are formally taken in his name. This power, is to be exercised in accordance with the Constitution, which lays down positive qualifications and negative disqualifications for the high post. The positive requirements are that he should be a citizen of India; should have completed the age of 35 years; and should be qualified for election as a member of House of People (Lok Sabha). Negatively, he should not hold any office of profit; and should not be a member of either house of Parliament or of a house of the legislature of any state. The President is indirectly elected by an electoral college consisting of the elected members of both houses of Parliament and the elected members of the legislative assemblies of the states. The members of state assemblies have been included in the electoral college to prevent the President from being elected merely by the vote of the party in power at the centre. The Constitution lays down a mandatory time limit and the election cannot be postponed beyond the expiration of the President's tenure. Thus, the election would have to be completed even though there may be some vacancies in Parliament or in some the state assemblies, or even if the assembly of any state stands dissolved. The procedure ensures uniformity and 'weightage' is determined by the weight of population of each state. Thickly populated states like Uttar Pradesh, have a larger number of votes than the less populous state like Goa. The principle of federal parity between the states taken together and the union has been achieved by the Mudalier formula of weightage of votes. The election is held in accordance with the system of proportional representation by means of the single transferable vote. It ensure the

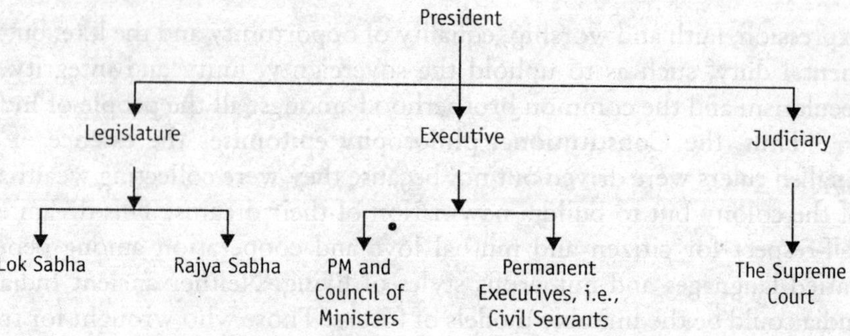

minorities a better voice in the selection of the head of the state. If a candidate gets an absolute majority of the votes cast, he would be deemed to have been elected without any recount. But, if no candidate has secured an absolute majority of the votes cast, the subsequent preferences, would have to be taken into account. The voting at the election is by secret ballot and every vote for or against may become a 'conscience vote'.

To secure uniformity in the scale of representation among the states themselves as well as parity between states as whole and the Union, the total population of each state is divided by the total number of elected members in the state assembly (MLAs). The quotient or the figure obtained is further subdivided by 1,000. The multiples of one thousand give the number of votes to be cast by each elected member of the state. If the remainder exceeds 500, then the number of votes is increased by one. So mathematically speaking the formula given in the Constitution is:

$$\text{Weightage of votes of a MLA} = \frac{\text{Population of state}}{\text{number of elected members of the state assembly}} \div 1000$$

The method determining the number of votes to be cast by each elected Member of Parliament (MP) is to divide the total number of state votes by the strength of the Parliament. The formula is:

Weightes of votes each Member of Parliament has

$$= \frac{\text{Total votes assigned to be elected members of the legislative assemblies of all states}}{\text{Total number of the elected members of both the houses of parliament}}$$

The principle of proportional representation, single transferable vote and secret ballot permissible under the 11th Amendment Act, provide that the elections of the President and the Vice-President cannot be challenged on the ground that the electoral college was incomplete. In case of the inability of the President, the Vice-President takes over the presidency. If he too is not available, the Chief Justice of the Supreme Court acts as the President. If that too is not possible, the Parliament will decide as to who should be given this responsibility. The American Constitution provides a list of 11 successors to the American presidency. However, in India, the conventions are yet to be evolved. The President can be impeached under Articles 56(1)(b) and 61, but the rigid provisions make the removal difficult. Unlike a no-confidence resolution it implies disgrace or imputation of moral turpitude which is not a disapproval of the government policy. The motion may be introduced in either of the two chambers. The initiating house frames the charges which are signed by one-fourth members of that house and a 14 days notice is sent to the President. Then, it will have to be passed by a two-third majority in that House. The second house investigates these charges. The President can personally appear before it to defend himself/herself or send his representative. If the charges are proved and the motion is passed by a two-third majority in the second house also, the President is considered removed from that time and day.

This kind of presidency was purposely designed to keep the President in the nominal role of a crown and additionally to present him as a national head of a federal form of government. An ornamental head by a system of election was a contradiction in terms yet Ramaswamy Mudaliar found out a via media whereby the President can be an indirectly elected head of a government and nation, which might continue to have a variety of regional cultures and political parties in a plural society. The formula equalises the weight of votes between centre and states and can make the President a glorified dignitary without much intervention in the day-to-day affairs of the government by the Prime Minister. Like the British Crown, he can gracefully enjoy the right to be consulted, right to encourage and right to warn but unlike the American President he will not rule the nation of which he happens to be the first citizen and a gracious representative.

Although, Dr Ambedkar fondly hoped that the Indian President will be the nominal figurehead of the government, but he had to write down the powers and functions of the President, which the British sovereign happens to enjoy through conventions. The written feature of the Constitution and the federal nature of the Indian Union make a big difference in the power of the Indian President. The convention and amendments keep on filling up the blanks, which the founding fathers perhaps deliberately kept to evolve the presidency in terms of Indian political genius. These powers of the President like that of any head of the state arm the President with wide ranging functions along with meaningful discretion. Still, the constrains and limitations on the working of the President are numerous. They are partly written, but a great deal of the same is emerging with the working of parliamentary federalism of India absent in UK and USA. A look at the vast array of powers of the Indian President enshrined in the Constitution explain the design of this office which the founding fathers cherished in their vision.

Powers of the President

Article 53 vests powers in the President who carries out the business of government or affairs of state excepting functions, which are vested by the Constitution in any other authority. This ambit of the executive power has been expanded by the Supreme Court:

> The executive function comprises both the determination of the policy as well as carrying in into execution, the maintenance of order, the promotion of social and economic welfare, the direction of foreign policy, in fact, the carrying on or supervision of the general administration of the State.

But, there are several *constitutional limitations* under which he has to exercise his executive powers. He must exercise these powers according to the Constitution which requires that ministers (other than the Prime Minister) can be appointed by the President only on the advise of the Prime Minister. If the President violates any of the mandatory provisions of the Constitution, he can be removed by the process of impeachment. The executive powers are exercised by the President in accordance with the advise of his council of ministers. Prior to 1976, he was not bound to act in accordance with the advice tendered by the council of ministers. The 42nd Amendment Act, 1976 has amended Article 74(1) as under:

> There shall be a Council of Ministers with the Prime Minister at the head to aid and advise the President who shall, in the exercise of his functions, act in accordance with such advice.

The word 'shall' makes it obligatory for the President to act in accordance with ministerial advice. But the 44th Amendment Act added a Proviso to Article 74(1) which says:

> Provided that the President may require the Council of Ministers to reconsider such advice, either generally or otherwise and the President shall act in accordance with the advice tendered after such reconsideration.

The net result after the 44th Amendment, therefore, is that except in certain marginal cases referred to by the Supreme Court, the President shall have no power to act in his discretion. If the council of ministers adheres to their previous advice, the President shall have no option but to act in accordance with such advice. The power to return for reconsideration can be exercised only once, on the same matter. The various powers that are included within the comprehensive expression 'executive power' can be classified as under:

Powers Pertaining to Administration

Not being a real head of the executive like the American President, the Indian President does *not* have any administrative function to discharge nor does he has the power of control and supervision over the departments of the government. The various departments of government of the Union are carried on under the control of the respective ministers and the President remains the *formal* head of the administration. All executive action of the Union is taken in the *name* of the President. Though, he is not the 'real' head of the administration, all officers of the Union are his 'subordinates' and he has a right to be informed about the affairs of the government. The administrative power also includes the power to *appoint* and *remove* the high dignitaries of the state. In making appointments, the President is required to consult persons other than his ministers as well. Thus, in appointing the judges of the Supreme Court, the President shall consult the Chief Justice of India and such other judges of the Supreme Court and of the High Courts, as he may deem necessary. The President also has the power to remove (i) his ministers, individually; (ii) the Attorney-General of India; (iii) the Governor of a state; (iv) the chairman or a member of the Public Service Commission of the Union or of a state on the report of the Supreme Court; (v) a judge of the Supreme Court or of a High Court or the Election Commissioner, on an address of Parliament. The Indian Constitution makes the 'Union Public Services and the Union Public Service Commission' – a legislative subject for the Union Parliament, and by making it obligatory on the part of the President to consult the Public Service Commission in matters relating to appointment, except in certain specified cases.

Powers as Commander of Armed Forces

The military powers of the Indian President are much less than those of the American President and the English Crown. The supreme command of the defence forces is vested in the President, but the Constitution expressly lays down that the exercise of this power shall be regulated by law. The President's powers as Commander-in-Chief cannot be construed, as a power independent of legislative control. The Constitution enjoins that certain acts cannot be done without the authority of law. The President must approach the Parliament. Article 114(3) demands that money for raising, training and maintenance of the defence forces has to be passed by the Parliament.

Powers in International Affairs

The diplomatic powers and functions comprise "matters which bring the Union into relation with foreign country". The legislative power about these matters and the power to make treaties and implementing them belongs to Parliament. But, the final power in these matters vests in

Parliament. The task of negotiating treaties and agreements, subject to ratification by Parliament the President who acts on the advice of his ministers. He has the power of appointing Indian diplomats to other countries and of receiving foreign diplomats as recognised by Parliament.

Powers over Legislation

The legislative powers of the Indian President are varied and comprehensive. Like the English Crown, our President has the power to summon or prorogue the houses of Parliament and to dissolve the lower house. He can summon a joint sitting of both houses of Parliament in case of deadlock between them (Articles 85 and 108). He addresses both houses of Parliament assembled together, at the first session after each general election to the House of the People and at the commencement of the first session of each year, and "informs Parliament of the causes of its summons". Apart from the right to address, the President has the right to send messages to either house of Parliament about pending Bills, or to other matters which the House must consider. The President has the power to send messages not only on legislative matters but 'otherwise' also.

The President has been given the power to nominate twelve members to the Council of States, persons who possess special knowledge or practical experience of literature, science, art and social service. He is also empowered to nominate not more than two members to the House of the People from the Anglo-Indian community, if it is not adequately represented in the house.

Powers in Matters of Finance

It is the duty of the President to cause to be laid before Parliament: (a) the Annual Financial Statement (Budget) and the supplementary statement, if any; (b) the report of the Auditor-General relating to the accounts of the Government of India; (c) the recommendations made by the Finance Commission, together with an action taken report; (d) the report of the Union Public Service Commission, explaining the reasons for non-acceptance of the advice; (e) the report of the special officers for Scheduled Castes and Tribes; Backward Classes and linguistic minorities.

The Constitution requires the previous sanction of the President for introducing legislation on certain matters. The courts are debarred from invalidating any legislation on the ground that the previous sanction was not obtained, and the President has assented to the legislation (Article 255). These matters are:

- Formation of new states or the alteration of boundaries of existing states (Article 3).
- Providing for matters specified in Article 31A(1).
- A Money Bill [Article 117(1)].
- A Bill which would involve expenditure from the Consolidated Fund of India even though it is not a Money Bill.
- A Bill affecting taxation in which states are interested, or affecting the principles laid down for distributing moneys to the states and State Bills imposing restrictions upon the freedom of trade. Every Bill needs the assent of the President. He has three options – he may assent; or withhold his assent; or (in the case of Bills other than Money Bills) return the Bill for reconsideration of the Houses, with or without a message. A Money Bill cannot be returned for reconsideration. In case of return, if the Bill is passed again by both houses of Parliament, it would be obligatory upon him to declare his assent to it. From the standpoint of effect on legislation, executive vetos have been classified as absolute, qualified, suspensive and pocket vetos. The Indian President enjoys a combination of all the three. If, instead of refusing his assent

outright, he remits the Bill or any part of it for reconsideration, a re-passage of the Bill by an ordinary majority would compel the President to give his assent. The effect of a return by the President is thus merely 'suspensive' and this power is not there in the case of Money Bills.

Powers over State Legislation

The Constitution does not prescribe any time limit within which the President should assent or refuse or to return the Bill. Article 111 says 'as soon as possible' after the Bill is presented to him. This absence of a time limit, permits the Indian President to exercise something like a 'pocket veto' or a desk veto for an indefinite time. The President may disallow or return a Bill of the State Legislature for reconsideration reserved by the Governor. Reservation of a State Bill for the assent of the President is a discretionary power of the Governor who may assent or withhold his assent or reserve the Bill for the consideration of the President. If a Money Bill is so reserved, the President may either declare his assent or withhold his assent. But in the case of the Bill, other than a Money Bill, the President may, direct the Governor to return the Bill to the legislature for reconsideration. In this latter case, the legislature must reconsider the Bill within six months but it shall not be obligatory upon the President to give his assent. He may keep a Bill of the state legislature pending for an indefinite period of time, without expressing his mind. There is no provision in the Constitution for a direct disallowance of state legislation by the President, but the bills reserved by the State Governor for assent of the President can be disallowed. There is no way to override the President's veto on state legislation. So, the Union's control over state legislation is absolute, and the President is entitled to refuse his assent without assigning reasons.

The Power to Proclaim Ordinances

The President enjoys the power to legislate by ordinances whenever the parliamentary enactment on the subject is needed. The ambit of this ordinance-making power is co-extensive with the legislative powers of Parliament, with its constitutional limitations. Thus, an ordinance cannot contravene the fundamental rights like an Act of Parliament. Article 13(3)(a) lays down that 'law' includes an 'ordinance' which has to be laid before Parliament when it reassembles. It automatically ceases to have effect at the expiration of six weeks. The ordinance-making power is available to the President only when *either* of the two houses of Parliament has been prorogued or is otherwise not in session. Even when the legislature is not in session, the President promulgates an ordinance only when he is satisfied that there are circumstances which render it necessary for him to take 'immediate action'. The promulgation of an ordinance is not dependent upon the existence of an armed rebellion or external aggression.

The Power to Pardon

The 'pardoning power' comprises a group of allied powers each of which has a distinct legal consequences, viz., pardon, reprieve, respite, remission, suspension, commutation. A pardon rescinds both the sentence and the conviction and absolves the offender from all punishment and disqualification. Commutation merely substitutes one form of punishment for another of a lighter character. The sentences of death; rigorous and simple imprisonments; fine, amount of sentence can be reduced without changing its character. Respite means awarding a lesser sentence instead of the penalty prescribed, in view of some special fact, like pregnancy of a woman offender. Reprieve means a stay of execution of a sentence, pending a proceeding for pardon or commutation. The

President has the pardoning power in respect of all cases of punishment by a Court Martial, (the Governor does not have such powers) offences against laws made under the Union and Concurrent Lists. The only authority of pardoning a sentence of death is the President.

The Residuary Powers

The President has been vested with powers which may be called residuary in nature. He has the constitutional authority to make *rules* and regulations relating to matters, such as, (1) authentication of his orders; (2) custody of and withdrawal of money from the public accounts of India; (3) the number and service conditions of members of the Union Public Service Commission; (4) the procedure of joint sittings of the houses of Parliament; (5) the manner of enforcing the orders of the Supreme Court; (6) emoluments payable to a Governor appointed for two or more states; (7) the discharge of the functions of a Governor in contingency and (8) specifying of Scheduled Castes and Scheduled Tribes.

He is empowered to give instructions to a Governor to promulgate an ordinance if a Bill containing the same provisions requires the previous sanction of the President. He can refer any question of public importance for the opinion of the Supreme Court. He has the power to appoint commissions for the purpose of reporting on specific matters, such as, commissions to report on the Administration of Scheduled Areas and Welfare of Scheduled Tribes and Backward Classes; the Finance Commission; Commission on Official Language; and Inter-State Council. The President enjoys several special powers relating to 'Union Territories', or territories which are directly administered by the Union. The administration of such territories is responsible to him alone. He has the final legislative power (to make regulations) relating to the Andaman and Nicobar Islands; the Lakshadweep; Dadra and Nagar Haveli; and may even repeal or amend any law applicable to such territories. He enjoys special powers in respect of the administration of Scheduled Area and Tribal Area in Assam. A Tribes Council may be established by the direction of the President in any state having Scheduled Areas and also in states having Scheduled Tribes therein *but* not Scheduled Areas.

The President enjoys protection from criminal proceedings against him in courts of law. This privilege is covered under Article 361 of the Constitution which does not restrict the instrumentality of Article 61. He cannot be arrested and produced before any court. No criminal proceedings can be instituted nor can a writ be filed against his or her actions. However, a civil suit can be filed against him, for an action that he or she has performed in his or her personal capacity before or after joining service.

Powers During Emergencies

Articles from 352 to 360 of the Indian Constitution talk about three kinds of emergencies in which the President of India may play a special kind of role because these situations leave a wide lee way for the President to take decisions in his discretion. National emergency, break down of the Constitution in a state and financial emergencies are abnormal situations which have been stipulated to tide over the crises till the situation returns to normal. In fact, it is a hangover from the Government of India Act 1935 under which the Governors and Governor-Generals used to take care of the political situation in imperial interest. The national leaders who were highly critical of these provisions found them indispensable to keep the country together and avoid mishaps in the working of democracy. The Constituent Assembly members were sceptical about the intensity and scope of emergencies. Yet, there was a general agreement that the fragile Union needed a protective ring around it and, hence, the presence of these provisions was considered appropriate. Viewed from the constitutional angle alone, these powers can turn the President into an unabashed autocrat, but the practice of this power will be within restraints of the system.

(i) National Emergency

The Article 352 states that if the President is satisfied that a grave emergency exists due to which the security of India or any part thereof is threatened, whether by war or internal disturbance, he may proclaim an emergency. Its duration, in the first instance will be two months. Within two months, it has to be ratified by the Parliament. If the Lok Sabha stands dissolved, the consent of the Rajya Sabha has to be sought within two months. If the Rajya Sabha does not pass it, the emergency becomes void. If it gets passed, then too, it should be approved by the newly constituted Lok Sabha within one month. After it has been passed by both the houses, it will continue as long as the President desires. However, the period cannot exceed more than six months at a time.

In India, emergency under this article has been declared three times. During this kind of emergency, the term "if the President is satisfied" could mean that he does not have to consult the cabinet. It is not necessary that an external aggression must be actual, potential threat or anticipation of danger is adequate. The life of the Lok Sabha can be extended by one year's at a time by the President with the possibility of indefinite renewal. During this time, the Parliament is empowered to frame laws on the subjects of the State List. The President can issue directives to governments. He will have the right to alter or amend the distribution pattern of financial resources between the Centre and the states. Even the fundamental rights can be suspended selectively or in the entire country. In 1975, when Prime Minister Indira Gandhi got National Emergency declared by President Fakhruddin Ali Ahmad, the President played no role and followed the parliamentary procedure. But the national emergency did not disturb the state governments and fundamental rights were selectively suspended in some states only. Amendment 42nd was the product of this situation and three judges of the Supreme Court were superceded. But then Amendment 44th restored the status quo anti and elections were held to repair the damaged system.

(ii) President's Rule in States

The second kind of emergency under Article 356 is popularly known as President's rule in a state which can be declared by the President on the Governor's report that the government of the state cannot be run in accordance to the provisions of the Constitution. The proclamation has to be approved by both the houses in the same manner as the first kind of emergency, but by a simple majority. The proclamation, in the first instance, is applicable for two months and, after ratification by the Parliament for a period for six months, unless revoked earlier. It can be extended again and again for six months each time but should not exceed more than three years. The consent of the Governor is imperative because the President must have trust in his own nominee. The Governor's report cannot be open to public inspection. It may bring a suspension of fundamental rights and the President can dissolve the state legislature or put the same in a state of suspended animation. The state cabinet may be dissolved and the laws and budget of the state will be passed by the Union Parliament. The Parliament can authorise the President to sanction expenditure from the Consolidated Fund of the state but the President will not interfere with the jurisdiction of the state High Court.

(iii) Financial Emergency

Article 360 states that if the President is satisfied that a situation has arisen whereby the financial stability or credit of India or any part of it is threatened, he may proclaim a financial emergency. This state should also be approved by the Union Parliament. This is also applicable for two months in the first instance, but the Parliament, by simple majority can extend the period. During this time, the President can issue directions to the state governments to observe such canons of financial propriety as may be specified in the directions. He may order reduction of salaries and allowances of all or any class of persons serving in connection with the affairs of a state. A provision can be made requiring all money bills to be reserved for the consideration of the President after they are passed by the legislative assembly of the state. The financial emergency has never been declared although we have been very close to it. This situation gives sweeping powers to the President in the Union executive to discipline the state government from taking overdrafts from the Reserve Bank of India or other banks.

The amendments 38th, 42nd, 44th and the 59th have revised the situation. The 38th Amendment Bill which was passed in 1975, made it clear that the President could issue different proclamations of emergency on different grounds, whether or not there was a proclamations already in existence and in operation. It also made the satisfaction of the President in the matter final and conclusive and not challengeable on any ground. By the 42nd Amendment, the period of six months in relation to Article 356 was raised to one year. The words 'armed rebellion' have been substituted in place of 'internal disturbance' vide the 44th Amendment. It could be the actual breakdown of the state machinery or an attempt by the ruling party to overthrow opposition governments. Therefore, the insertion of the words 'armed rebellion' is more meaningful. The President can issue a proclamation only if the unanimous decision of the cabinet in this regard has been communicated to him in writing. Moreover, the Presidential order cannot suspend the fundamental rights of an arrested person to move a court and ensure that an individual is not deprived of his immunity from ex-post facto penal law. The mere satisfaction of the President is sufficient in this case. All fundamental rights, can be suspended and the press can be forced to fall in line. No judicial authority could call Presidential 'satisfaction' in question. In the term, 'satisfaction of the President' in reality, becomes the will of the PM then the human rights get jeopardised.

Notwithstanding the utility of emergency provisions, all governments in India will have to strike a balance between the threatened chaos and repression of human rights in a democratic polity. The founding fathers were apprehensive and Mr Kamath staged a symbolic walkout calling the day of enactment as a day of shame and sorrow. Several members condemned the emergency provisions as 'a chapter of reaction and retrogression'. The President was seen as democratic despot in a totalitarian democracy. The misgivings have proved right as well as imaginary. Instances of presidents like V.V. Giri, Fakruddin Ali Ahmad, Gyani Zail Singh and even K.R. Narayanan are being quoted to push the arguments on either side. Mistrust in the strength of democratic institutions is natural but the role given to the Parliament is relevant and effective. The ratification of emergency by the Union Parliament must make the vigilant Parliament assert and prevent the abuse of emergency provisions by a cynical incumbent of the high office.

Similarly, it will be pessimistic to see malafide intentions of the Union government in declaring the Presidents' rule in a state. Union government has a key role in maintaining internal security and restoring political stability in all the states. Article 356 has been a much maligned provision of our federal arrangement.

It is true that its political abuse against other party governments, mostly coalitional, has caused much hue and cry. But the Supreme Court has intervened quite constructively in Bomai Case and Buta Case and the procedures about Governor's Report, Cabinet decisioning and Presidential assent have become reasonably streamlined after the 44th Amendment. Formerly the Presidents were forced to act as a mere rubber stamp and the Governors were seen as 'Villains of Peace'. As democracy matures the President, the Prime Minister and the Governors are realising it to their predicament that the provision has little discretion for any individual incumbent. The Union Council of Ministers and its Prime Minister should accept the responsibility and nobody can be made a scape-goat for the errors of commission or omission. The check and balance system of decisioning has emerged as a healthy check upon the suspect intentions of the President. It is a welcome development which represents the will of the founding fathers.

As a political head of the parliamentary government the Indian President should be a phantom king without crown. In Dr Ambedkar's view he should represent the nation but should not rule over the nation. He conceded that unlike the British monarch he will not be a golden zero or a mere rubber stamp. He enjoys the suspensory veto of returning the bills to the Council of Ministers or ask for a reconsideration of its advice. The Prime Minister has a constitutional obligation to keep him informed about administrative decisions and legislative proposals. He may call for these proposals at his own initiative. Even individual minister's decisions may be referred by him to the Council of Ministers. All this implies that ministerial advice does not mean an instant acceptance. He is within his Presidential prerogative to make specific objectives or suggestion asking the minister in council to reconsider the entire matter. The non-acceptance of presidential advice by the Council of Minister is not easy and he can create situations in which the Prime Minister will have to persuade his colleagues to tender due regard and weightage to Presidential dissent. Of course he does not have the last word and will accept the democratic verdict of the House which the Prime Minister represents.

Notwithstanding the federal nuances of the Union government, the President in India has to work with the Prime Minister. The Constituent Assembly declared him a Formal Head in unambiguous terms. Critics have their own reservation and think that impeachment is too weak an instrument to keep him within limits. Petty differences apart even the Presidents like Zail Singh and K.R. Narayanan never allowed the dignity of the high office to be compromised. The amendments 42nd and 44th have little to do with the Presidential ambitions. In fact the office of the Prime Minister was made extra powerful under 42nd Amendment. The 44th Amendment constitutionalised the Prime Ministerial position by making the President a democratic check on populist dictatorship. In its ultimate the Indian President accepts the position that like the British Crown. He has a right to be consulted, right to encourage and even right to warn. No sensible President of a plural democracy must demand or need anything more. Matters like dissolving the Lok Saha and selection of the incumbent for the office of Prime Minister in case of hung parliaments may cause temporary aberrations but no indirectly elected President will be in a position to run the country without a popular mandate which the party and its majority leader represents. Suggestions like that of National government for sometime, as advanced by former President Venktaraman might be worth a trial during emergency, but a huge democracy of India's size and diversities may replace party politics by alliance politics and make the Prime Minister more powerful. So long India opts to stay in a parliamentary frame any confrontation between the President and the Prime Minister will sooner than later go in favour of the latter.

The Council of Ministers and the Prime Minister on its behalf is expected to aid and advice the President. The legal quibblings must be resolved in the light of British conventions. Advises are merely recommendatory and aid implies running of the government under the seal and signatures of the head of the state. The advise is tendered and aid is rendered by the cabinet which represents the popular aspirations through elected representatives. The President must respect this advise. If the Prime Minister disrespects the popular verdict his government can be voted out by a vote of non confidence. But no President can be impeached just because he violated the advice of the Council of Ministers. The British Crown is a working hypothesis and so is the Indian President. If the Prime Minister or cabinet are not there, the President must create the alternate government of a new Prime Minister. If he wants to get the Lok Sabha dissolved prematurely, the President may not accept the advice and experiment with alternative government in national interest.

Unlike the British system, the Indian Constitution binds the President to consult various dignitaries other than the Prime Minister in different areas of government. Chief Justice of India, Chief Election Commissioner are consulted under Article 217(3) and Article 103(2) respectively. The Constitution specifically provides that these consultations or advises will not be inquired into by the law courts. Naturally the aid and advise are a part of parliamentary procedure. The Cabinet is not an advisory body but a decision-making political executive. The Governors in the state have some discretion because they can withhold assents for President's consideration. But the President has no such discretion. If he delays or denies he would be violating Article 74 of the Constitution which inter alia states "The President SHALL act in accordance with the advice (given by the PM and his Council of Ministers). The President may reprive the Council of Ministers to reconsider such advice - and shall act in accordance - after such reconsideration. Whether any and if so what advice, was tendered shall not be enquired into any court." This closes all controversies and puts all doubts to rest. In fact the Presidency will never become what the President chooses to make it.

The President and the Prime Minister

The Constitution provides a Council of Ministers with the Prime Minister at the head to aid and advise the President. The amendments made during and after emergency of 1975 have substantial changes in the content of Article 74th. The 44th Amendment Act, attempted to follow a middle path. The amended provision runs as under "the President may require the Council of Ministers to reconsider such advice, either generally or otherwise, and the President shall act in accordance with the advice tendered after such reconsideration. The question whether any, and if so what, advice was tendered by ministers to the President shall not be inquired into in any court".

The controversy regarding the role of the President originated from different interpretations of Articles 53, 74 and 75. The President has to exercise his power in accordance with the Constitution. The Council of Ministers with the Prime Minister will aid and advise the President. But Article 75 states: "The ministers shall hold office during the pleasure of President, and the Council of Ministers shall be collectively responsible to the Parliament".

The terms 'aid and advise' may mean that the ministers have to act as advisers to the President and it is for the President to make decisions. But the interpretation runs counter to the spirit of the parliamentary government. The President can dismiss his council of ministers. But the council of ministers is responsible to the House of the People. If the President dismisses a council of ministers which enjoys confidence of the House of the People, the whole constitutional framework would topple down. Thus, a correct interpretation of the seemingly conflicting provisions leads to the conclusion that the President is a constitutional head of the state. Still it cannot be denied that there was ambiguity in the text of provisions.

Still the President is not a cypher or a mere rubber stamp. The proviso to Article 74(1) empowers the President to ask the council of ministers to reconsider the advice tendered to him. Besides, Article 78 confers significant powers on the President. It is the duty of the Prime Minister to communicate to the President all decisions of the council of ministers relating to the administration of the affairs of the union and proposals for legislation. The Prime Minister should furnish such information relating to the administration of the affairs of the Union and proposals for legislation as the President may call for. He should submit for the consideration of the council of ministers any matter on which a decisions has taken by a minister but which has not been considered by the council. Thus, although the President has to act on the advice of the ministers, acting on ministerial advice does not mean immediate acceptance of the ministers first thought. The President can state his objections to any proposed course of action and ask his Minister-in-Council, if necessary, to reconsider the matter. It is only in the last resort that he must accept their final advice.

The Constitution defines, in general terms, the relationship between the head of the state and the actual head of the government, i.e., the Prime Minister. The discussion in the Constituent Assembly, as well as the working of the Constitution since 1950 leave no doubt on the point that the President is a mere formal head of the Indian Union. There are some scholars, however, who have argued at length to prove that the President is a 'constitutional autocrat'. In the words of K.V. Rao, "our Constitution creates a very powerful executive, perhaps the most powerful in the world; our Constitution concentrates that power in the President who is king for five years, and on whom the only check against abuse is the impotent impeachment". So far nothing concrete has happened to prove that the President is anything but a mere formal head. The 42nd Amendment of the Constitution in 1976 (which came into operation on January 3, 1977) made the position more explicit. The 44th Amendment added, "The President may require the council of ministers to reconsider such advice, either generally or otherwise, and the President shall act in accordance with the advice tendered after such reconsideration". Matters like the right of the President to be informed, his right to act only on the advice of his council, the right to dismiss a government at his discretion, the right to decide if new elections are to be held in place of the dissolved Lok Sabha, the right to reconsider a legislation if assented by the President, the open confrontation will finally go in favour of the Prime Minister.

The jurists maintain that there is virtually no point in an aid being binding. Aid is just assistance, and cannot be regarded as an admonition. At the same time, it is not so superfluous as to be merely an adulation. An advice is not an order and, therefore, is not mandatory in any sense. Yet Article 74 makes it clear that the PM and his ministers alone are responsible to advise the President on all matters. Since the Constitution does not assign any other specific role to the PM and his ministers, rendering aid and tendering advice becomes critical. The advice is not superfluous and cannot be ignored. Besides, "advice, as a term, has to fulfil a purpose. It must be of an assistance rather than an obstruction". The aid and advice may not be binding because the President cannot be impeached for violating this advice. When a PM suggests dissolution of the house, the President can refuse to accept the advice, because an alternative government may not be formed or the fresh elections could be detrimental to national interests.

The Constitution provides that the President must consult certain other authorities in certain further cases. He has to consult the Chief Justice of India in the matter of determination of the age of a High Court Judge under Article 217(3). In the matter of a disqualification of a Member of Parliament, he must consult the Election Commission under Article 103(2). The Forty-fourth Amendment Act says: "The President shall obtain the opinion of the Election Commission and shall act according to such opinion". The 44th Amendment ensures that the President abides by the aid and advice of the council of ministers, although, it does not mean immediate acceptance of the ministry's first thought and compliance with such advice. He can state his objections and ask the ministry to reconsider such advice. However, if the ministry sticks by its decision, the President has to sign it in the second instance. Several articles of the Constitution also point to the reality that the advice is binding. Article 78(a) demands that the PM communicate all decisions of the council of ministers to the President. The Governors explicitly have the right to act in their discretion. The President has no such areas of discretionary authority. Besides if the President does not heed the advice, he can be impeached for violation of Article 74 of the Constitution. Similarly, the President is not answerable to any court for the exercise and performance of the powers and duties of his office. It follows that he may commit no wrong. Article 74 provides that what advice was tendered cannot be enquired into by courts. So, no legal relief can be obtained against the President if he refuses to abide by the advice. The courts are barred by the Constitution from compelling production of the advice.

Still, there are a number of open ended questions to which the Constitution provides no answer. The President is always performing duties on someone else's advice, so he cannot be impeached for something he has not done individually. He need not obey any unconstitutional advice. He owes no personal responsibility to the nation, for these politico judicial riddles. Naturally 'The Presidency' to quote Dr Rajendra Prasad, "will be what the President will choose to make it".

Vice-President

The Constitution provides for a Vice-President of India who must possess the following qualifications:

(1) He must be a citizen of India.
(2) He must have completed the age of thirty-five years.
(3) He must possess qualifications prescribed for the election of a member of the Rajya Sabha.
(4) He must not hold any office of profit under the Government of India or of any state or under any local or other authority subject to the control of the said government.
(5) He shall not be a member of either House of Parliament or a House of the legislature of any state, and if a member of either House of Parliament or a House of the Legislature of a state be elected Vice-President, he shall be deemed to have vacated his seat in that House on the date on which he enters upon his office as Vice-President.

The Vice-President is elected by an electoral college consisting of the members of both Houses of Parliament in accordance with the system of proportional representation by means of the single transferable vote and secret ballot. The electoral college constituted for the election of Vice-President consists of all the members of the two houses of Parliament. Every member of electoral college has only one vote. The Vice-President shall hold office for a term of five years from the date on which he enters upon his office. He may, by writing under his hand addressed to the President, resign his office. He can also be removed from his office by a resolution of the Council of States passed by a majority of the then members of the council and agreed to by the House of the people, but no resolution for this purpose shall be moved unless at least 14 days notice has been given of the intention to the resolution. He stays in the office even after the expiration of his term until his successor enters upon office. The Vice-President of India occupies the second highest office in the country and enjoys a rank next to the President. But no special constitutional functions have been entrusted to him. He is the *ex officio* Chairman of the Rajya Sabha and acts as the spokesman of the council to the President. In the event of the occurrence of any vacancy in the office of the President by reason of his death, resignation or removal or otherwise, the Vice-President takes over as President until the date on which a new President enters upon his office. When the President is unable to discharge his function owing to absence, illness or any other cause, the Vice-President discharges his functions until the date on which the President resumes his duties. The authority, powers and role of the President are taken over by the Vice-President under Article 65(1) but Article 71(2) reads: that "If the election of a person as President and Vice-President is declared void by the Supreme Court, the acts done by him in the exercise and performance of the powers and duties of the office of President or Vice-President, as the case may be, on or before the date of decision of the Supreme Court, shall not be invalidated by reason of that declaration". This implies that even if the election of the Vice-President acting as the President has been invalidated, the acts done by him in the capacity of the President will not be declared void. While acting as the President, he will have all the immunities of the President and will draw the same emoluments, allowances and privileges as the President. However, while he acts as the President, he will not draw the salary of the Chairman of the Council of States and will not perform the duties of the office of the Chairman of the Rajya Sabha.

Prime Minister and His Council of Ministers

The British constitutional system was called Parliamentary Government by Marriot. Later, Sir Ivor Jenninga called it cabinet form of government. Now writers like Morris Jones state that it is a prime ministerial kind of government. This shift in the nature of government from Hanover to Windsor dynasties represents the growth of democracy culminating in the omnipotence of the Prime Minister. Conventionally, this development is a result of the bi-party system and the absence of a Supreme Court as an interpreter of an unwritten Constitution.

The Indian situation can never be a carbon copy of the West Minister Model. The earlier Act of 1919 and 1935 did not create any Parliament nor could a Governor-General combined the offices of the President and the Prime Minister. The Governor-General's Executive Council notwithstanding its advisory functions could ever be conceived as a cabinet accountable to legislature. So the founding fathers have to think of a President in place of the crown and a council of ministers in place of the Governor-General's Executive Council. But when they devised the office of the Prime Minister, the cabinet principles of British government dominated their thought process and the earlier experiments of diarchy and provincial autonomy got their culmination in the institution of council of ministers and the Prime Minister.

The British parliamentary, broadly speaking, has developed the following principles, which the Indian Constitution seeks to enshrine irrespective of our multiparty and federal situations. These principles are:

(1) The elected Parliament is the sovereign body and it express its sovereignty through a small committee called the cabinet.
(2) The cabinet will be formed by the leader of the majority party in the house whom the head of the state will invite to constitute his council of minister or cabinet.
(3) All the members of cabinet should belong to majority party in the Parliament and must have homogeneity of views. The coalitions must sit opposite with its shadow cabinet.
(4) The council of ministers and the Prime Minister have to be responsible to the Parliament and they should resign if a vote of no confidence is passed against their policies and actions by the Lower House of the Parliament.
(5) The responsibility of the cabinet has to be collective and they will sink and swim together like a team playing the game.
(6) The Prime Minister will act as a leader, a primus inter pares who will be cultural to the formation working and dissolution of his team in and outside the House.
(7) The cabinet observes the principle of secrecy. Before a minister enters upon his office, the President administers to him the oath of office and of secrecy according to the form prescribed in the Third Schedule of the Constitution. Secrecy implies safeguarding the decisions and deliberations of the cabinet from public gaze. If the deliberations were open, the quality of the cabinet decisions would suffer and the opposition may get a chance to embarrass the government. The head is informed about the decisions of the council of ministers, but he too cannot let out official secrets to anyone outside the official hierarchy. The Indian Constitution by and large accepts these basic principles but the electoral situation, multiparty realities and federal tensions make a world of difference. The decline of Congress Party and emergence of regional parties in a cooperative federation have drastically revised these principles, but the Constitution is continuously striving to work a synthesis so that the "Prime Ministerial form of government" in India may remain a cabinet and parliamentary government close to the West Minister Model.

The Indian Constitution meticulously avoids the term cabinet, which in practice means the group of senior member council of ministers occupying key portfolios. They are always invited to discuss policy matters and constitute the steering wheel inside the council of minister which is a larger body comprising deputy minister; ministers of state and parliamentary secretaries. The Prime Minister determines the size, the portfolios, the cabinet status and even the office of the Deputy Prime Minister and ministers without portfolio. The size has now been fixed at 15 per cent of the size of the Parliament.

The Council of Ministers

The Council of Ministers is a three-tier organisation comprising three levels of ministers: (1) cabinet ministers, (2) ministers of state with independent charge of portfolios, and (3) ministers of state and deputy ministers. At the head of the council stands the Prime Minister. There have also been deputy prime ministers, since Pandit Nehru's time. But the convention has not taken roots. The interim government formed in 1946 at the Centre was the first government to function as a cabinet in India. On 15th August 1947, Nehru as Prime Minister formed a new government consisting of a prime minister, a deputy prime minister and twelve other ministers. N. Gopalaswami Ayyangar was included into the cabinet without portfolio to examine the governmental structure. He recommended three categories of ministers and their functions and powers as provided for in the Rules of

Business. He preferred the terms 'deputy minister' to 'parliamentary secretary' and the term 'minister of state'. Later the Ayyangar report sought to bring out the distinction between the three categories of ministers. Ayyangar recommended that the ministers of state and deputy ministers should be members of the council of ministers but not of the cabinet. He defined the role of the deputy ministers as corresponding to that of the parliamentary secretaries. Their duties included answering questions in Parliament on behalf of their ministers: assisting in piloting bills; explaining to the public the policies and programmes of the government; maintaining liaison with members of Parliament, political parties and the press, and studying of investigating problems assigned to them by their ministers. Unlike the deputy ministers, the ministers of state were entrusted with specific administrative responsibility. This can be done in placing independent charge of a ministry like a cabinet minister. He may be placed in charge of a department within the portfolio of the cabinet minister. The minister of state may assist the cabinet minister, who in addition may entrust the former with certain specific items of work under the latter's overall responsibility. The Administrative Reforms Commission did not agree with the suggestion to abolish the institution of the deputy minister because it provides "a training ground to build party cadres for higher ministerial appointments"; and it also "has an edge over the post of parliamentary secretary providing opportunities for acquiring experience in executive work". A deputy minister relieves the senior minister of a part of his burden by being given the charge of an important programme or overseeing the implementation of some policies and programmes, or a wing or a department with powers of minor policy decisions, and of parliamentary work. The three-tier system in the ministerial setup, comprising: (1) cabinet ministers, (2) ministers of state, and (3) deputy ministers continues alongwith parliamentary secretaries. The number of different categories of ministers constituting the council of ministers has been changing from time to time but the three-tier system has come to stay.

The cabinet is a small body comprising senior members of the council who are influential. The Prime Minister in council decides all the policy matters of national governance. The memberships restricted so that decisions may be taken promptly and collectively. These ministers hold important portfolios and take unanimous decisions. Their "responsibilities transcend departmental boundaries into the entire field of governance". It has entrenched itself deeply in the political system and the Prime Minister chooses the so-called "inner cabinet" to act as his close confidants or advisors. This small body is the power centre and assists the Prime Minister in crucial decision-making. The ministers of state may be given independent charge of individual ministry and may be performing similar functions and exercising similar powers as those of cabinet ministers. The rest may not be given independent charges and they have to work under the cabinet ministers. The latter are not invited to cabinet meetings. The deputy ministers are junior ministers in the council's hierarchy. They are ministers within the definition of the Constitution. The 'Salaries and Allowances of Ministers Act, 1952' technically makes a minister a member of the Council of Minister which includes a Deputy Minister also.

The contest for Prime Ministership has provided three different method of selecting the leader as Prime Minister.

(1) By consensus,
(2) By secret ballot, and
(3) By compromise.

He recommends to the President the names of members whom he deems fit to work in his team. The Prime Minister has a free hand to choose the team and distribute the portfolios as he deems proper. There are several kinds of constraints and competing claims of regional, communal, party leadership and gender representation in forming the team. But then it is the sole prerogative of the Prime Minister to apportion due weightage to various claims and prepare a list of colleagues who represent the country and the ruling party and who enjoys his confidence. The conventions are respected. Important ministries are reserved for senior colleagues. They may be bifurcated to accommodate and train junior claimants in the party. The Administrative Reforms Commission (ARC) recommended that "the office of the Deputy Prime Minister should be duly recognised in the Transaction of Business Rules". But the government preferred to leave it to the discretion of the Prime Minister. The Constitutional arrangement under Article 75 provides that ministers will be appointed by the President on the advice of the Prime Minister. They will hold office during the pleasure of the President. An oath of office and secrecy is administrated to every minister individually and if he is not a member of either house of Parliament, he should get elected to any house with in a period six months.

India is a huge country and the regional interests even with in a political party bring competing pressure on the Prime Minister. Then the reservation policy has its formal and informal impacts on the composition and working of the Council of Ministers. The alliance system before and after elections has evolved the practice of defining a Common Minimum Programme whereby the alliance members bring pressures on Prime Ministers' leadership through their respective party chiefs. The coalitional experiment which seems to be a workable reality in Indian federal milieu has told heavily on the position of the Prime Minister. Unlike his British counterpart his hands in choosing the team and assigning portfolios are not free. His strength has started varying with the position of parties in his coalitional alliance. The Prime Minister is absolutely free to reshuffle his pack. He need not consult any colleague or even his party leaders. But the Indian developments in a federal polity do not follow the British pattern. Mrs Sonia Gandhi's refusal to accept prime ministership created a situation unknown to British politics. The extra constitutional centre of power outside the cabinet and in addition to the Prime Minister is a typical Indian experiment which goes a long way to revise the working of Parliamentary democracy in India.

As regards the size of the Council of Ministers ARC suggested a range between 40 to 45 ministers, 16 cabinet ministers, 15 to 18 ministers of state and the remaining being deputy ministers. The exigencies of political situations have not permitted the Prime Minister to observe these limits. Yet a ceiling exists that the total membership should not exceed 10 per cent of the strength of both the houses. The number of cabinet ministers and deputy ministers may be more in coalitional teams but the Prime Minister enjoys the freedom to form his council of ministers and the cabinet.

Functions and Role of the Cabinet

Being a central executive body of the government the cabinet performs wide ranging functions which make its role critical and decisive. The entire administration and even the Parliament rotates around it and seeks its leadership in resolving conflicts and managing the affairs of government. These functions can be enumerated as under:

(1) Formulation, execution, evaluation and revision of public policy in various spheres which the party in power seeks to progress and practice.

(2) Coordination among various ministries and other organs of the government which might indulge in conflicts, wastefulness, duplication of functions and empire building.
(3) Preparation and monitoring of the legislative agenda which translated the policies of the government in action through statutory enactments.
(4) Executive control over administration through appointments, rule making powers and handling of crises and disasters – natural as well as political.
(5) Financial management through fiscal control and operation of funds like Consolidated Fund and Contingency Funds of India.
(6) Review the work of planning and Planning Commission.

These functions are all pervading and interdependent. The members individually as well as collectively and through the Prime Minister perform these functions within the parameters of the Constitution. The council of ministers exercises the executive authority of the Union Government. It is the cabinet which steers the ship of the state. Under our Constitution, the cabinet can issue directives to state government under certain circumstances and under the state of emergency it can virtually control the working of the state governments.

Policy Making Functions

The cabinet is a policy-formulating body. All kinds of policies, national, internal, external and international are thrashed out in the cabinet, which then presents them to the Parliament for approval. Once the policy has been determined by the cabinet, it is for the ministry/department concerned to carry it out. A cabinet minister is in-charge of a specific ministry or department and it is his duty to administer the subjects included in his portfolio. In addition, he also shares a collective responsibility with other members of the cabinet for the overall policy for anything of high importance that is done in every branch of public business besides his own.

Laws Making Functions

The Parliament is the repository of legislative authority and can enact repeal and amend legislation but in practice, it is the cabinet which takes initiative in legislative matters and directs Parliament. It is the cabinet which prepares the legislative measures, introduces them and pilots them through the two houses of Parliament.

Financial Functions

The annual budget is prepared by the cabinet which determines what taxes are to be imposed and how the public revenues are to be spent. The Parliament, even the Lok Sabha is free to debate upon and discuss all items of the budget but it can hardly make any substantive change in it unless the government agrees to such a change. An adverse vote in Parliament on any money bill is deemed to be an expression of censure of the cabinet which may result in its resignation.

Administrative Functions

All major appointments reserved for action by the President under the Constitution, e.g., Attorney-General, members of the Union Public Service Commission, Chief Election Commissioner, Judges of the Supreme Court and High Courts, Governors of states, etc., are made by him on the recommendation of the Prime Minister and in consultation with the minister of the department concerned. The Secretary is responsible for carrying out the policies laid down by the cabinet and approved by the Parliament. He can instruct the departmental functionaries and supervise their working. A minister is expected to face questions in the Parliament. He may or may not abide by the advice of his civil servants but he should see to it that the civil servant's freedom to advise is not curtailed.

Coordination Functions

The conduct of foreign relations, reception and dispatch of diplomatic agents and recognition or non-recognition of new states are done after the approval of the cabinet. Treaties are also negotiated and signed after the approval of the cabinet is obtained and the Parliament is duly informed about these. The cabinet also controls the foreign tours of the President and other ministers. Decisions in matters which are of complicated and controversial nature, the ministers consult the Prime Minister before taking any action. Matters, particularly those affecting other departments/ministries, the matter may be referred to the cabinet for collective decisioning. Such cases are referred to as 'coordination cases' or cabinet questions which can be decided only by the cabinet. In addition, there are matters about which Rule 4 of the Transaction of Business Rules lays down that "when the subject of a case concerns more than one department, no order shall be issued until all such departments have concurred of failing such concurrence, a decision thereon has been taken by or under the authority of the cabinet". The cabinet decides, at the beginning of each session, what bills will be put forth in that session. The inaugural speech of the President is also prepared by the cabinet. The President summons, prorogues and dissolves the House on the advice of the cabinet headed by the PM. All ordinances issued by the President are also prepared by the cabinet. It is a subsidiary power of legislation which takes the form of administrative orders.

All important Money Bills are framed in the cabinet and are initiated and seen through in the legislature by it. The cabinet is responsible for the entire expenditure of the state and for raising revenues to meet it. Similarly, the 'Emergency Provisions' authorise the President to issue a proclamation whereby the authority is really exercised by the cabinet during the period specified. The real centre of authority and power has been shifting from the full cabinet, which itself is a committee of the council of ministers, to a still smaller body. Such smaller bodies usually consist of the Prime Minister and three or four influential colleagues who share his confidence and are habitually consulted by him. Thus, it is difficult to identify at any given time the actual number and kind of persons whom the Prime Minister may choose to consult. But the fact remains that nobody formal or informal can supplant the cabinet, which continues to act as a political 'court of appeal'.

The Planning Commission works in close collaboration with the cabinet. The Prime Minister is the chairman of this Commission, which controls the entire economic planning for the country. He also heads the National Development Council, which acts as a coordinating forum for the Centre and the states. The cabinet not only executes the policies but also provides leadership to the legislature during legislation. It is this hyphen that joins and the buckle that fastens the administrative and the legislative wings of the government. It formulates policies, makes decisions and drafts bills on all significant matters which in their judgement require legislative attention. The Cabinet advises the President and the advice of the cabinet is binding on him. It is the sole decision-making body on policy matters and these decisions are conveyed to the President who endorses them. Although the work of administration is divided into several departments, they are not autonomous in their working. All key appointments and decisions about wars, peace, treaties and mobilisation of troops are brought before Cabinet for processing. The three kinds of emergencies, their grounds, duration and termination are suggested by the home ministry but the cabinet should advice the Prime Minister to send their mandate to the President. The Amendment 44th and Bomai case judgment about Presidential Rule by the Supreme Court of India have clarified the position in favour of the council of ministers.

The Transaction of Business Rules do not require that matters which are not strictly within their purview be brought before the cabinet. In matters of vital importance, the Prime Minister has consulted a small group of his colleagues generally in the Political Affairs Committee of the cabinet or its predecessor bodies, and sometimes only individual members privately, before taking a decision. The rules permit the Prime Minister, to anticipate a decision of the cabinet where such approval is required. In such an eventually, the case is reported to the cabinet and any member can ask for a discussion and reconsideration of the decision. Therefore, while it may be true that not all the members of the cabinet know of some of the major decisions referred to, it will not be quiet correct to say that there has been any constitutional or legal violation of the Business Rules.

In administration, conflicts and differences are usual occurrences. More than one department might be engaged in similar activities leading to duplication and overlapping. It is among the Prime Minister's major functions to see that numerous activities undertaken by various departments lead to the realisation of desired objectives. Inter-ministry policy and working are subject to cabinet discipline, and the onerous task of coordinating the work of the different ministries and to enforce discipline is the job of the Prime Minister.

The Office of the Prime Minister

The appointment of the Prime Minister is made by the President but he has to invite the leader of the majority party in the Lok Sabha to become the Prime Minister and under normal circumstances the appointment is just a constitutional formality. He can be placed at par with the powerful President of US and in some respects he is even superior to him, with a parliamentary majority behind him. He is the fountain of authority, final arbiter of policy and the ultimate repository of real power in a parliamentary government. The Indian Constitution states that the Prime Minister shall be appointed by the President and the other ministers shall be appointed by the President on the advice of the Prime Minister. The convention requires that the President should appoint the leader of a party or a group of parties who commands majority support in the House of the People. His continuance in office depends on 'the pleasure of the President'. All ministers are collectively responsible to the House of the People. The chief function of the Prime Minister is to render aid and tender advice to the President. The Constitutional position is that "There shall be a Council of Ministers with the Prime Minister at the head, to aid and advise the President who shall in the exercise of his functions act in accordance with such advice". Amendment 44th provides that "the President may require the Council of Ministers to reconsider such advice, either generally or otherwise, and the President shall act in accordance with the advice tendered after such consideration". The Ministers hold office during the pleasure of the President. The Prime Minister has to convey to the President all decisions of the council relating to the administration of affairs of the Union and proposals for legislation. These duties of the Prime Minister "enables the President to exercise his rights to be consulted, to encourage and to warn". He is bound by the advice except in exceptional circumstances. One such example can be that the President decides to summon a meeting of each house of Parliament and more than six months have not elapsed between two consecutive sessions. The Prime Minister should keep the President informed. The President can sanction legal prosecution of the Prime Minister, if the latter is found guilty by a court of law as was the case with late Prime Minister Narsimha Rao.

The Indian Prime Minister though lately heading coalition governments has emerged more powerful than the luminaries adoring the office in sixties and seventies. The Constitution empowers him with multi splendoured powers and as the government launches its newer programmes of economic development and social welfare the patronage and functions of the Prime Minister multiply many fold. Moreover the stabilisation of the democratic system enables the Prime Minister to consolidate his power and coalitional uncertainties have paradoxically made him a leader of commanding heights. The problems of insurgency and emergence of weaker people make citizens look to him for the implementation of new policies of globalisation and liberalisation. It is a worldwide phenomenon and the Prime Minister and his team must faithfully implement the mandate of the people against all odds. The constitutional position apart, the political ethos of the country and the mass media present the incumbent in an unprecedented image of a savour and the challenge has to be met by the national leader, who can scarcely ignore the pressures of the situation.

Some of the reasons responsible for this all pervading and decisive role of the Prime Minister are:

(1) He is the chief executive of the government, and there is very little in the Constitution except judicial restraints to deter him, if he enjoys a majority in the Parliament.
(2) He is the leader of the House or the majority party in the house. Naturally Parliament echoes His Masters Voice. Even in a hung Parliament he has privileges and discretions to bring the frivolous opposition around.
(3) He is the chief financial manager of the Budget and commands the federal economy in the context of it global nuances.
(4) He often controls his political party with an iron hand because the party uses his image during elections. Moreover party leaders look to him for the advancement appointments and assign.
(5) All important appointments and assignments lie with the office of Prime Minister. He controls military and international affairs by his policies and even emergency by his policies and even emergency provisions can be used by him to safeguard his power position.
(6) As Chairman of Planning Commission and National Development Council he plays an extra-constitutional federal role in the development of the nation, which makes him a national hero with lots of patronage.

The concept of primus inter pares does not seem to be appropriate in the context of Indian Prime Minister. He is more of a keystone of the cabinet arch. He represents the entire government, perhaps much more meaningfully and in a *de facto* manner than the entire council of state. The President appoints ministers on his advise. He decides the size and has a forehand in the allocation of portfolios. He is central to the formation, reshuffle and even to the dissolution of the council or any member thereof. He decides about the time and agenda of cabinet meetings and individual proposals from ministers are concerned only when accepted by him. He is familiar with the working of ministries and has to ensure their effective functioning through coordination and persuasion. He fosters teamwork and arbitrates difference of views and personality. To make his team, work he fits people to posts and positions to people. Collective responsibility implies acceptance of cabinet decisions by all individually as well as collectively before the Parliament. The

Prime Minister articulates this political uniformity. He ensures that proceedings of the Parliament are conducted with dignity. He approves the legislative agenda of the house and guides the bids at each stage. The twelve members that the President appoints to the Rajya Sabha are appointed on the advice of the PM. He can also act as a mediator if the Rajya Sabha and the Lok Sabha have differences of opinion. The Prime Minister has to maintain a hold over all the party organisations at the central, regional and local levels. He should have the support of not the parliamentary party alone but also of its organisational wings. The PM ensures that the party members carry out the policies and programmes of the government faithfully. He can use his office status and authority to keep the rank and file in discipline. Unchallenged leadership in the various committees of the party and its various boards helps in keeping the PM a boss rather than a mere colleague. The budget and the important Money Bills are prepared under the close supervision and scrutiny of the PM. He is the chairman of the Planning Commission which formulates Five-Year Plans and other important economic programmes of the nation. The Prime Minister is the chief representative of the nation in international affairs. He participates in international conferences, pays official visits to foreign countries, maintains relations with the UN and other international organisations, negotiates with heads of states, signs MOUs and agreements, advises the President to declare war and conclude peace, and advises the President to grant or withhold recognition to nations. He has to maintain a very close collaboration with key ministries. The emergency powers of the Indian President are, in fact, the powers of the PM.

The Cabinet Committees

A democratic system functions by participation and interaction. The Parliament and cabinet are august bodies, which work in accordance to formal rules and procedures. Moreover administrators who are at edge of the government are non-political functionaries. But they have relevant data and useful in sights that can enrich the policies and enable the government to operationalise its agenda. The Constitution prescribes ministerial responsibility for administrative actions. Naturally the administrators should be heard and controlled to explain their actions or lapses to the representatives of the people. A cabinet decision and a parliamentary enactment including the budget has to pass through several committee screenings to reach to adequacy or acceptability. The cabinet committees wield real power of decision on less important general policy matters. Other matters, which must be dealt with in the cabinet, are also whittled in committees. Only the delicate and complex points, or those on which ministers differ, remain for discussion by the cabinet. What has saved the cabinet, as the central decision-making body, is the elaborate network of cabinet committees, which have acted as a clearing house. This device enables ministers to bargain and compromise with each other and this reduces pressure of work upon the cabinet. Consequently, the cabinet is left free to devote itself to more important matters. The committee system safeguards the principle of collective responsibility, which is an essential feature of the cabinet system. Thus, ministers of state and deputy ministers who are not members of the cabinet are members of one or more committees. This is a way in which they can and are brought into a closer association with the work of the cabinet. Thus, all ministers continue to be partly responsible for the government's action. Cabinet committees increase the effectiveness of political control over public services. The public servants are called upon by the committees to justify their proposals and comment on problems under review. This procedure establishes a close interface between a politicians and public servants and ensures that those who formulate policy are reasonably well informed. It also eliminates the possibility of any one department carrying a disproportionate weight of opinion. The committees also act as a collective check on individual ministers and on the Prime Minister too. In view of the growth in the volume and complexity of the government business, a proper division of labour and effective delegation within cabinet requires committees to perform functions devolved on them by the cabinet. They focus supra-ministry attention on particular sectors of administration. Effective coordination is their major contribution. The ad hoc cabinet committees settle specific problems submitted to them and are automatically dissolved as soon as the task is fulfilled. The standing committees have wider competence and their duration is indeterminate. They may be terminated by the fresh decision of the cabinet or the Prime Minister. The committees are set up either by the cabinet on the proposal of the Prime Minister or directly by the Prime Minister himself. Unlike UK, these committees in India are presided by Prime Minister and their membership is confined only to members of the cabinet. The number of such committees has also been changing from time to time.

In 1948, there were only two standing committees, i.e., (1) Defence Committee, and (2) the Economic Committee. The Defence Committee was set up in 1947 and consisted of five or six members. The Economic Committee was created soon after and consisted of six members. In due course some more committees were created, namely, the Priorities Committee, the Rehabilitation Committee and the Resources Committee. The N. Gopalaswamy Ayyangar report on the reorganisation of the machinery of the Central government stressed upon the need of division of labour and effective delegation which should be rationalised and established on a permanent basis. He suggested that a distinction should be drawn between three types of committees: (1) ad hoc, (2) standing, and (3) subcommittee. Standing committees are regarded as part of the permanent machinery of government for which appropriate secretariat organisation may be provided on a permanent basis; procedures may be laid down in the Rules of Business and maintained by appropriate machinery prescribed therefore; and the committees may be enabled to develop specialised knowledge and experience of the nature of these problems and the policies and principles adopted in solving them. Leftover matters should be dealt with by the ad hoc committees, which could be created on a temporary basis to deal with such matters. In addition, Ayyangar suggested the need for setting up subcommittees, one in each of the four bureaus under which ministries would be grouped under his plan. Ayyangar wanted four permanent standing committees, (1) Defence Committee, (2) Economic Committee, (3) Administrative Organisation Committee, and (4) the Parliamentary and Legal Affairs Committee, but the Prime Minister should be the chairman of only two committees, namely, defence and economic. He should preside over the meeting of these standing committees, should be entrusted with the authority to take binding decisions on matters within their jurisdiction. Four Standing Committees namely (1) defence; economic; (2) parliamentary; (3) legal affairs and (4) administrative organisation were constituted in 1950. A fifth standing committee was soon added to the list in the form of the Appointments Committee. The Prime Minister was given authority to determine the composition of these committees. The cabinet secretariat serviced the defence and economic committees, the department of parliamentary affairs and the law ministry provided secretarial assistance to the parliamentary and legal affairs committee. The home ministry was earmarked as host ministry for secretarial servicing of appointment and administrative organisation committees.

These five existing standing committees were abolished in the year 1950 and three ad hoc committees dealing with transient matters were formed. Ten new standing committees were created on economic affairs, heavy industry, defence, foreign affairs, rehabilitations, scientific matters, parliamentary and legal affairs, information and broadcasting and appointments. Ashok Chanda, the then Controller and Auditor General of India, in his note to the cabinet on the working of the cabinet committees found wide variation in the strength of various standing cabinet committees. The chairmanship of the Prime Minister of all cabinet committee is difficult for the cabinet to play a revisionary role. Moreover, the committees did not always include as members only ministers concerned with their subject matter. In his note Chanda asked: "to introduce decentralised coordination by grouping ministries with interrelated functions together and placing these groups under the central supervision of senior ministers without portfolio". No attention was paid to these recommendations. But an emergency committee had to be constituted in the wake of the Chinese invasion in 1961. It consisted of the Prime Minister as the chairman, finance, home and defence ministers as its members. In course of time, its influence waned and the Study Team on the Machinery of Government of India, in its report (1967) recommended its replacement by the committee of defence and foreign affairs. The study team observed:

> But such committees can provide an effective alternative only if they are operated in a manner substantially different to what is today the case. Some of the committees have hitherto not been meeting regularly, while some others have almost fallen into disuse. The composition of the committees also leaves much to be desired.

Most of the cabinet committees are loaded with cabinet ministers. Some ministers of state do not figure at all in any cabinet committee, even though they are in independent charge of ministries; No deputy minister is included anywhere. The subjects covered by the cabinet committees in existence range from the most important to the most trivial. The committees are empowered to take decisions only if matters have been referred to them by order of minister concerned or by the cabinet; thus neither the Prime Minister nor the chairman of a committee can refer a matter for decision in committee.

To remove these basic deficiencies in the working of the cabinet committees, the study team recommended that:

- Committees should cover between them all important areas of governmental activity.
- The Prime Minister should not be the chairman of any committee unless it should be a very important committee like that of defence, foreign affairs and economic affairs.
- The membership of each committee should not exceed eight.
- As far as possible, all ministers in-charge of subjects covered by a committee should be represented on it.
- These committees should meet regularly so that sustained attention is given to complex problems and their progress in implementation of important policies and programmes is kept under review.
- These committees should be serviced by well-manned cells in the cabinet secretariat.
- The number of cabinet committees should be brought down from the existing thirteen to eleven.
- *Ad hoc* committees may be retained but their scope should be restricted to investigating particular issues and reporting back to the cabinet or the concerned committee as the case may be.
- The distinction between standing committees and ad hoc committees should be made clear in the Rules of Business.

The Administrative Reforms Commission in its report in 1969 revised these recommendations of the study team. The Commission wanted that:

- There should be eleven standing committees, one each for defence; foreign affairs; economic affairs; parliamentary affairs and public relations; food and rural development; transport, tourism and communications; social services (including social welfare and family planning); commerce; industry and science; internal affairs (including centre-state relations); administration; and appointments. The membership of each committee should not normally exceed six and should include all ministers-in-charge of subjects covered by the committee.
- Every standing committee should be supported by a committee of secretaries which will consider in advance all matters to be taken up by the cabinet committee. The ad hoc committees should be retained but should be confined to mere investigation and not decision-making.

The Union Government did not accept these recommendations but these were kept in view during the 1974 reconstitution of these committees. The year 1977 witnessed a great increase in the number of committees because of increase of work. The membership of the cabinet committees varies from three to eight. Their chairmanship is shared between the Prime Minister and the home minister of all the committees as it does of the senior most ministers in terms of their political stature or the importance of the portfolios held by them. Sometimes these committees function as a 'super cabinet' in providing higher direction to the government. The ARC (1966–70) found that some of the cabinet committees have not met regularly. Several important subjects were not covered by the cabinet committees. Further, they can take up a matter only if it is referred to them by the minister concerned or by the cabinet. It is also essential that each cabinet committee meets regularly so that sustained attention is given to complex important policies and progress is kept under constant review. This is primarily because there is less institutionalisation and more personalisation in the functioning of the government. Three or four such committees have existed under all governments in power at the Centre; the Political Affairs Committee, the Economic Affairs Committee, Committee on Parliamentary Affairs and the Appointment Committee. The following cabinet committees have been functioning since 1994:

(1) Cabinet Committee on Political Affairs
(2) Cabinet Committee on Natural Affairs
(3) Cabinet Committee on Parliamentary Affairs
(4) Cabinet Committee on Appointments
(5) Cabinet Committee on Accommodation
(6) Cabinet Committee on Foreign Investment
(7) Cabinet Committee on Drug Abuse Control
(8) Cabinet Committee on Price
(9) Cabinet Committee on Minority Welfare
(10) Cabinet Committee on Economic Affairs
(11) Cabinet Committee on Trade and Investment
(12) Cabinet Committee on Expenditure
(13) Cabinet Committee on Infrastructure

There is also in existence a powerful group known as the crisis management team comprising of some senior ministers as well as outsiders enjoying the personal trust of the Prime Minister. A subject needing cabinet decision may either come directly to the appropriate committee or may be referred to it by the cabinet for detail scrutiny before the latter takes a decision. Some of the cabinet committees have come to exercise real authority and the cabinet endorses the decision already taken there. Since, it is difficult for the cabinet to meet very frequently and go in depth into each specific issue of policy and decision, it takes recourse to the committee system. The cabinet committees are useful instruments of taking policy initiatives and effecting coordination in defined fields. They act as arms to the cabinet and as forums for conflict resolution and inter-ministry coordination. The Rules of Business provide for the setting up of standing committees of the cabinet to help expedite the decisional process and to ensure coordination in governmental business. Flexibility is their essential virtue and their number changes from ministry to ministry and from situation to situation. The ARC desired that each of the cabinet committees should be supported by a member of the committee of secretaries. The Government of India did not like to evolve any fixed pattern in the structure of cabinet committees. It opined that a committee of secretaries should serve more than one cabinet committee.

The Parliament and Parliamentary Committees

The administration being a part of the executive constantly interacts with the ministers and formally takes order from the President. The Lok Sabha is directly elected by the people of India on the basis of adult suffrage. The Rajya Sabha is indirectly elected by members of state legislatures on the basis of proportional representation for the seats allotted to states in the Constitution. Both these houses perform various functions such as:

(1) law making,
(2) formulation of policy,
(3) control of the council of ministers and Prime Minister,
(4) passing of the budget,
(5) amending the Constitution, and
(6) ventilation and removal of public grievances.

The Lower House has the monopoly of initiating Money Bills and passing the vote of no confidence in the cabinet or in the Prime Minister. The Rajya Sabha in India has equal powers of amending the Constitution and has special powers of shifting state subjects to Union List and creating new all India services. Naturally the administrative system of the country has to interact with the working of the sovereign Parliament directly and also because of the system of ministerial responsibility.

The functions of the Parliament are varied and considerable in volume but the time at its disposal is limited. It cannot make very detailed scrutiny of all legislative and other matters that come up before it. A good deal of its business has to be transacted in committees. Both the houses of Parliament have a similar committees structure with some exceptions. Their appointment, terms office, functions and procedure of conducting business are also more or less similar and are regulated under rules made by the two houses. Broadly speaking, parliamentary committees are of two kinds. (1) Standing Committees, and (2) *ad hoc* Committees. The former are elected or appointed every year or periodically and their work goes on a continuous basis. The latter are appointed on an ad hoc basis as and when the need arises and they cease to exist as soon as they complete the work assigned to them. The financial committees are (1) Committees on Estimates, (2) Public Accounts, and (3) Public Undertakings. They constitute a distinct group and keep an unremitting vigil over government expenditure and performance. While members of the Rajya Sabha are associated with committees on Public Accounts and Public Undertakings, the Committee on Estimates is composed of members from the Lok Sabha only. Besides, these financial committees, the Rules Committee of the Lok Sabha has set up 17 department-related standing committees. They were set up on 8th April, 1993. Other standing committee in each house are: (1) Committees on Inquire; (2) Committee of Privileges; (3) Business Advisory Committee; (4) Rules Committee; (5) Committee on the Welfare of Scheduled Castes and Scheduled Tribes; (6) House Committee; (7) Joint Committee on Salaries and Allowances; (8) Joint Committee on offices of Profit; (9) The Library Committee; and (10) Ethics Committee.

Ad hoc Committees may be broadly classified under two heads: (1) Committees which are constituted from time to time by two houses to inquire into and report on specific subjects, like conduct of certain members, Draft Five-Year Plans, Bofors Contracts, Stock Market Scam, etc., (2) Select or Joint Committees on Bills which are appointed to consider and report on a particular bill. These committees are distinguishable from other ad hoc committees in as much as they are concerned with bills and the procedure to be followed by them as laid in the Rules of Procedure and directions by the Speaker/Chairman. According to the Rules of Procedure and Conduct of Business in the Lok Sabha, there are twelve committees of Parliament.

(1) *The Business Advisory Committee*: It regulates the timetable of the work of the house. The Speaker is its Chairman and has 15 members.
(2) *The Committee on Private Members' Bills and Resolutions*: It is a committee of fifteen whose function is to examine all private members' Bills from different points of view and recommend them to be placed before the house.
(3) *Select Committees on Bills*: Select committee for any Bill is constituted when a motion on the Bill referred to a Select Committee. Its members are appointed by the house. The committee may hear expert evidence and representatives of special interests before them.
(4) *The Committee on Petitions*: The committee is nominated by the Speaker and has strength of fifteen members.
(5) *The Estimates Committee*: To enable the Parliament to discharge its financial functions efficiently through a detailed examination of the budget estimates. Its function include:
    (i) to report what economies, improvements, efficiency or administrative reform, underlying the estimates, may get effected;
    (ii) to suggest alternative policies to bring about efficiency and economy in administration;
    (iii) to examine whether the money is within the limits of the policy implied in the estimates; and
    (iv) to suggest the form in which the estimates should be presented to Parliament.
(6) *The Public Accounts Committee*: It is called the twin-sister of the Estimates Committee. It is concerned with the manner and results of spending public funds. It is its duty to scrutinise the appropriation accounts and the report of the Comptroller and Auditor-General of India. Unlike the Estimates Committee, it has at its disposal the expert advice of the Comptroller and Auditor-General based upon a detailed examination of the government's accounts.
(7) *The Committee of Privileges*: It consists of fifteen members nominated by the Speaker. It is concerned with the examination of questions of privileges and the determination of any breach of privileges in the cases which are referred to it.

(8) *The Committee on Subordinate Legislation*: It scrutinises and reports to the house whether the powers to make regulations, rules, sub-rules, bye-laws, etc., conferred by the Constitution or delegated by Parliament are being properly exercised within the limits of such delegation.

(9) *The Committee on Government Assurances*: This committee scrutinises the various assurances, promises, undertakings, etc., given by ministers, from time to time, on the floor of the House and to report on the extent to which such assurances have been implemented.

(10) *The Committee on Absence of Members from the Sittings of the House*: It considers all applications from members for leave of absence from the sittings of the House and examine every case where a member has been absent for a period of sixty days or more, without permission, and report whether the absence should be condoned or the seat be declared vacant for a new appointment.

(11) *The Rules Committee*: This committee considers matters of procedure and conduct of business in the house and recommends amendments or additions to these rules that may be deemed necessary.

(12) *The Committee on Public Undertakings*: It examines: (1) the reports and the accounts of the public undertakings, (2) the reports, if any of the Comptroller and Auditor-General on the public undertakings, and (3) in the context of the autonomy and efficiency of the public undertakings whether their affairs are being managed in accordance with sound business principles and prudent commercial practices.

The parliamentary committees are larger in size and are recommendatory. They are not mandatory but the chairmanships of Prime Minister makes a big difference in their acceptance and effectivity. The parliamentary committees are primarily to train the younger members of the Parliament in parliamentary procedure. They offer opportunities to the members of the Parliament to understand the dynamics of democracy. The interface is mutually advantageous. Some departmental select committees or ad hoc committees keep administration on their toes and the parliamentarians learn how to shape the administrative realities.

The three parliamentary committees, namely, Public Accounts, Estimates and Public Undertaking are the repositories of legislative wisdom and senior members from all political parties especially from the opposition work for financial rectitude and check on wasteful expenditure. The parliamentary committee control is genuine close and extra ordinarily detailed. The administrators do the homework and heads roll when the Public Accounts Committee puts the government in the dock. The Congressional Committees, in USA are called the government. In Indian parliamentary democracy these committees are not very powerful, but their observations and recommendations cannot be taken in a light manner. In fact, some of the committees look like mini-parliament. Even the cabinet committees go by their recommendations. Although parliamentary and cabinet committees are not a part of the Constitution but the constitutional functionaries like Prime Minister and his cabinet members have to go by conventions which these committees establish and uphold. The presence of senior administrators, their confidential depositions, the flexibility of approach in scrutinising problems and data, add value to the labours of these committees. They work silently beyond the gaze of media and their sober and legal work enable the cabinet and Parliament to take difficult decisions.

The Judiciary

The Constitution provides a single integrated judiciary for the country under the supervision of the Supreme Court. The High Courts at state level are independent and separate from the executive and legislature at all levels. Unlike UK, it protects and preserves a written federal Constitution which enshrines a parliamentary democracy at the Centre and at the states in its unique frame. The American doctrine of Judicial Review with the 'due process of law' has been duly revised by underlining the notion of procedure established by law. The senior judges are appointed by the President on the recommendation of the Chief Justice but they are initially picked up by the executive. Unlike USA, there is no legislative whetting of the names but once appointed they are free to operate without any interference from the executive and the legislature.

The judiciary has been assigned three specific roles in the constitution: (1) to hear appeals and dispose of litigation, (2) to defend and preserve the Constitution under the system of judicial review, and (3) to protect the fundamental rights of citizens. Along with several quasi-Judicial organisations the courts in India have extended their jurisdiction under the doctrine called judicial activism. This third chamber judiciary development has interpreted the Constitution in a positive manner and the judicial judgements are bordering on constitutional amendments. Tensions notwithstanding, the Indian judiciary is trying to preserve and defend the basic structure of the Constitution and simultaneously respecting the sovereignty of the Parliament. The administration has to respect the jurisdiction of the courts and it is developing a new democratic ethos through court interventions.

More recently, the practice of public interest litigation has pushed the courts into the arena of human rights jurisprudence which is evolving quite fast with the constitution of Human Rights Commissions at the Centre and in the states. The judiciary as a guardian of citizen rights is taking cognition suo motto and senior administrators are being summoned to explain their administrative lapses and misconduct of their juniors. This kind of positive judicial activism is pressurising the executive to stay alert. This in turn has forced the government to prepare a new legislative agenda for democratic functioning of a transparent and sensitive public administration. The retired judges and chairpersons of Women's Commission, Minorities Commission, SC and ST Commission and Child Commission are engaged in overseeing activities which are called 'Policing the police and sensitising the bureaucracy'. It has enhanced accountability of public administrators and judicial, control guidance and directive supervision of administration has emerged as a phenomenon, which renders judiciary an integral part of public administration system in India.

Thus, the Constitution prescribes the parameters and rules of the game for administration which is essentially a part of the executive. The President in Parliament, the President as Head of the State and the President as the fountain of justice operates as a parliamentary democracy in the centralised federal political system of India. The President, the cabinet and the Prime Minister run the day-to-day government with the help of permanent civil servants. The Parliament controls the political masters, their political policies and the administrative operations of the various ministries and executive agencies. The judiciary as a guardian of the Constitution plays the honest referee and the civil servants have to abide by the dictum of rule of law which ensures fundamental and human rights to all the citizens without any distinction of colour, caste, sex or creed. This linkage of public administration with the political executive, the sovereign Parliament, the guardian judiciary and the vigilant People of India making it a central activity and a vital agency in the good governance of a dynamic democracy. The right to information granted to lay citizens of India further strengthens the accountability of administrators through the instrumentality of an independent judiciary. As democracy advances and the decentralised institutions of panchayati governance take roots, the processes of democratising bureaucracy will be hastened in due course.

3

Union-State Relations in Federal Polity

"India that is Bharat is an indissoluble union of states". Naturally, all debates about 'Federalism', 'Quasi federation' or 'Centralised federal polity' are interpretational and skirt around the US model which is classical in constitutional theory. The term 'Foedris' which requires 'Union' not unity has its extremist ends in cultural federalism in a unitary state and confederationalism of contractual units. USSR and Switzerland have been the best examples which are called cultural federations with in the ambit of a strong centralised state and a weak decentralised government with cantonal autonomy of direct democracy respectively. In between there are varieties of models like Canada, Germany, Australia, South Africa and USA from where the founding fathers of Indian Constitution freely borrowed and fitted the characteristic borrowings in the 1935, federal frame prepared by the British to resolve Indian problems of 'Unity in Diversity'. In its essence, this model of Indian federalism is unique and is unfolding its resilience in operation with every parliamentary and state vidhan sabha elections in India.

The federal and unfederal features of Indian quasi-federalism vis-à-vis American federalism of Jacksonian era are:

Federal features	*Unfederal features*
Division of subjects	Division by three lists
Double governments	Three-tier federalism
Parity representation of units and strong second chamber	Unequal representation in the weakest second chamber of the world
Rigid amendment procedure	Rigid in basic structure, otherwise flexible
Judicial guardianship with due process of law	Judicial supremacy with procedure established by law
Weak centre and strong autonomous units	Strong centre with weak states
A contractual contrivance	Suspendable during emergencies

These interventions in classical theory of federalism were warranted by several historical, cultural and political factors of building a nation-state under the tragic shadows of partition. Moreover, the princely India which Sardar Patel has integrated in three years time justified a centralised federal structure to foster national integration in a continental country of diversities cherishing the vision of a 'Bharat Mata'. In fact, when all federations represent a process of coming together of the federating states the Indian federation is a process of breaking up the unitary Indian states into federating units. The Maurya, Gupta and Mughal empires welded the people of diverse faiths, origins and languages of the subcontinent on whom the colonial rule of the British superimposed an administrative unity of the ruling elites. The complex situation has become simply incomparable to fit into any ideal type framework. Hence the term 'indissolvable union' was chosen and a separate part was devoted to the centre-state relations during normalcy and emergency. Parts XI, XII, XIII, and XVII provide elaborate details on the basis of these relations which are interpreted as unitary as well as federal. The part (XI) is divided into two chapters, Chapter I, entitled Legislative Relations deals with the distribution of legislative powers. Chapter II, entitled Administrative Relations is divided into three parts (1) general, (2) disputes relating to waters and (3) coordination between states. The Part XII, entitled Finance Property, Contracts and Suits has four chapters. Chapter I deals with the distribution of revenues between the Union and the states and miscellaneous financial provisions including expenditure, custody, grants, and provides for the constitution of a Finance Commission (Article 280). Chapter II deals with borrowing by the Government of India and the states. Chapter III deals with property, contracts, rights, liabilities and suits. Chapter IV is concerned with the Right to Property. Then there is Part XVIII which deal with Emergency Provisions.

Unlike USA, where every state has its own Constitution, the Indian Constitution prescribes a uniform structure of governments for the states as an integral part of the Indian Constitution. The division of subjects follows the scheme of 1935 Government of India Act, which enumerates the subjects in its VII Schedule. The Union List consists of 97 subjects which include subjects like defence, armed forces, arms and ammunition, atomic energy, foreign affairs, diplomatic representation, United Nations, treaties, war and peace, citizenship, extradition, railways, shipping and navigation, airways, posts and telegraphs, telephones, wireless and broadcasting, currency, coinage and legal tender, foreign loans, the Reserve Bank of India, foreign trade, inter-state trade and commerce, banking, bills of exchange, insurance, stock exchange, patents, control of industries, regulation and development of mines, minerals and oil-resources.

The State List has 61 subjects which envisage the possibility of different kinds of treatment to different items in the different states. Some of these items are public order, police, administration of the justice, prisons and reformatories, local government, public health and sanitation, intoxicating liquors, burials and burial grounds, libraries and museums controlled by the state, inter-state communications, agriculture, animal husbandry, water-supplies and irrigation, land rights, fisheries, trade and commerce within the state, gas and gas-works, markets and fairs, money-lending, theatres, betting and gambling. The state legislature has the exclusive power of legislation with regard to everyone of the items included in the State List.

The subjects in the Concurrent List are 47 in number. These areas require uniformity of legislation throughout the Union. The list includes subjects such as: power, lunatic asylums, civil procedures and criminal laws, economic and social planning, marriage and divorce, education, vital statistics including registration of births and deaths, newspapers, legal, medical and other professions, trust and trustees. Both the Union Parliament and state legislature possess simultaneous rights to frame laws on concurrent items. But in case, a Union law on a concurrent topic conflicts with a State Act on the same subject, the former has precedence. The residuary powers of legislation are vested in the Union. This power as in the Canadian Constitution includes the power of making laws, imposing any taxes not mentioned in either of the State or Concurrent Lists. The American Supreme Court developed it as a convention, now called 'Doctrine of Implied Powers'.

Legislative Relations

This distribution of legislative powers is based on two considerations:

(1) The territory over which the federation and the units shall, respectively, have their jurisdiction.
(2) The subjects to which their respective jurisdiction shall extend.

The state legislature suffers from a limitation to which Parliament is not subject, namely, that the territory of the Union being divided amongst the states, the jurisdiction of each state must be confined to its own territory. It is not possible for a state legislature to enlarge its territorial jurisdiction under any circumstances. The Union Parliament has, on the other hand, the power to legislate for 'the whole or any part of the territory of India' which includes not only the states but also the union territories or any other area. It also possesses the power of 'extra-territorial legislation' (Article 245[2]), which no state legislature possesses. But this territorial jurisdiction of Union Parliament is subject to three limitations:

(1) As regards some union territories, such as the Andaman and Lakshadweep groups of Islands, regulations may be made by the President to have the same force as Acts of Parliament and such regulations may repeal or amend a law made by Parliament in relation to such territory.
(2) The application of Acts of Parliament to any Scheduled Area may be barred or modified by notifications made by the Governor.
(3) The Governor of Assam may, by public notification, direct that an Act of Parliament shall not apply to an autonomous district or an autonomous region in the State of Assam or shall apply to such district or region or part thereof subject to such exceptions or modifications as he may specify.

Still the Union Parliament has overriding powers. In the event of inconsistency between laws made by Parliament and the state legislatures on any matter in that Union List the former shall prevail. Parliament is further empowered to legislate for two or more states by consent and addition of such legislation by any other state. The residuary power of legislation are with the Union Parliament which has been given exclusive power to make any law on any matter not enumerated in the Concurrent or State List.

Not only this, the Constitution permits the Union government to encroach upon the State List subject in more than one condition. It talks of circumstances under which the Centre can expand the scope of its legislative jurisdiction and circumscribe the powers of the states. These situations are:

(1) If the Council of States declares by a resolution of two-third of its members present and voting, that it is necessary in the national interest that Parliament shall have power to legislate over such matters. Each such resolution may give a lease of one year to the law in question. A law made by Parliament would not cease to have effect on the expiration of a period of six months. The resolution of the Council of States may be renewed for a period of one year at a time.
(2) If a proclamation of 'Emergency' made by the President is in operation, Parliament shall have similar power to legislate with respect to state subjects. The Union law shall cease to be operative after a period of six months.
(3) If the legislatures of two or more states resolve that it shall be lawful for Parliament to make laws with respect to any matters included in the State List relating to those states, the

Parliament can grant extension of jurisdiction of Union Parliament by consent of the state legislatures.

(4) If the President makes a proclamation about the failure of constitutional machinery in the states.

(5) If compliance of international obligation or treaty relations demand Union legislation, upon the subject which falls in the State List.

All this makes the Union legislature powerful and all pervading. The interpretation of the three lists has further strengthened the Union government by a convention of 'Doctrine of Implied Powers', developed by the Supreme Court. The states have also reconciled to this subordinate position and it is not questioned even politically in the era of coalitional governments.

Administrative Relations

Thus, the legislative relations are effectively tilted in favour of the Centre which has an exclusive jurisdiction over vital subjects of Union List. Subjects of Concurrent List virtually belong to the Centre. The residuary subjects are again with the Union government and the subjects of State List can be nibbled away by the Union under varying conditions or pretexts. This overcentralisation in legislative realm has lead to Centre's predominance in administrative and other fields. In general, the latter follows the scheme of distribution of the legislative powers. Consequently, the executive power of the state becomes co-extensive with its legislative powers. It means that the executive power of state shall extend only to its own territory and with respect to those subjects over which it has legislative competence. Conversely, the Union shall have exclusive executive power over the matters with respect to which Parliament has exclusive power to make laws and the exercise of its powers conferred by any treaty or agreement. On the other hand, a state shall have exclusive executive power over matters included in State List. As regards matters included in the Concurrent Legislative List the executive function shall ordinarily remain with the states, but the Union may, take up the administration of Union laws relating to concurrent subjects while the executive power relating to subject will remain with the states. The Constitution vests executive functions upon the Union to implement any treaty or international agreement belongs exclusively to the Union, whether the subject appertains to the union-state or Concurrent List. The Union government has the power to give directions to the state governments to ensure due compliance of Union laws or existing laws which apply in that state.

The administrative relations between Union and state operate in a manner that Centre's supremacy is more than visible. During emergencies the Indian federal arrangement can be suspended and squeezed into a unitary operation. But even during normal times the Centre can descend upon the state through its powers of delegation, direction and grants in India. The provisions of all India services, Inter-state councils and later State Commerce Commission establish Centre's hegemony and writers like G.N. Singh maintain that states have been reduced to the status of municipalities. The comment may be uncharitable but Articles like 256, 246, 257 and 263 are potent weapons by which the administrative activities by states can be made to fall in line to the wishes of the Centre. Article 256 of the Constitution specifies the respective obligations of the Union and the state governments and lays down, "The executive power of every state shall be so exercised as to ensure compliance with the laws made by the Parliament and any existing laws which apply in that state and the executive power of the Union shall extend to the giving of such direction to the state as may appear to the Government of India to be necessary for that purpose." This Article provides that the executive authority of the state has to be so exercised that the laws made by Parliament and the existing laws of the states are properly enforced. If the state government fails to enforce such laws, the Union government can issue direction to the state government to do so.

Article 257 makes the situation explicit when it says: "The executive power of every state shall be so exercised as not to impede or prejudice the exercise of the executive power of the Union, and the executive power of the Union shall extend to the giving of such directions to a state as may appear to the Government of India to be necessary for that purpose." Thus, the Union government can give directions to the state governments even in areas of State List such as construction of highways, waterways, means of communications declared to be of national or military importance. The Union government can also give directions regarding the measures to be taken for the protection of railways within the boundaries of the state. In case of dispute about the quantum of the payment, it is decided by the arbitrator appointed by the Chief Justice of India.

The Centre can ensure compliance of these directions and even President's rule may be imposed upon the state for non-compliance of the Presidential directions. Article 258 provides that Parliament may delegate powers to the state governments and their officers in so far as the statute is applicable in the respective states. Conversely, a state government with the consent of the Government of India confer administrative functions upon the later, relating to state subjects.

Then, there are three all India services common to the Union and the states and their tenure system not only makes the state administrative services junior but all top positions in state administration are manned by these all India public servants. The Union government can create more all India services if the Rajya Sabha passes a resolution by two-third majority in national interests. The conditions of services of persons appointed to all India services are prescribed by the Union government but their salaries, allowances and pensions are paid from the exchequers of the state governments. Here the Centre has a distinct edge over the state.

Article 275 maintains that the Parliament has the power to make grants as it may deem necessary to give financial assistance to states which is in need of such assistance. By means of the grants, the Union would be in a position to correct inter-state disparities in financial resources which are not conducive to an all-round development of the country and also to exercise control and coordination over the welfare schemes of the states on a national scale. Besides this, general power to make grants to the states for financial assistance, the Constitution provides for specific grants for schemes of development, for welfare of Scheduled Tribes and for raising the level of administration of Scheduled Areas.

Article 263 empowers the President of India to establish inter-state council in national public interest. The council may have the duty of inquiring into and advising upon disputes which might arise between states. The President has established a Central Council of Health, a Central Council of Local Self-Government, and a Transport Development Council for the purpose of coordinating the policy of the states relating to these matters. In fact, the primary object of an inter-state council being coordination and federal cohesion. The Sarkaria Commission has recommended the constitution of a permanent inter-state council which should be charged with the duties of Article 263. Such a council, consisting of six Union cabinet ministers and the chief ministers of all the states has been created in April, 1990.

Setting up of Inter-State Commerce Commission (Article 301–05) on the lines of US Independent Regulatory Commission for nationwide conduct of trade and commerce adds an administrative dimension to union-state relations. Then the Union government can and have created innumerable extra constitutional agencies such as Planning Commission, National Development Council, National Integration Council, National Security Council which go a long way in giving an upper hand to the Union government to direct the affairs of the states. Then the mutual delegation of functions (Article 73) and immunity from mutual taxation (Article 285 and 289) ultimately work in the expansion of administrative jurisdiction of Union government in matters of the states.

Financial Relations

Thus, the constitutional arrangement follows the philosophy of centralisation. The legislative and administrative relations are neither at the level of parity nor short any kind of transitional state of federal devolution. India as a national state is the overriding consideration which was supported by centralising or centripetal tendencies in the working of the super powers federations towards the end of the Second World War. The states in India were not only weak but also poor and unevenly developed. So the founding fathers of Indian Constitution spent a lot of effort in designing the financial relations between Union and states which are reasonably rigid in a flexible mould. The Constitution devotes two parts – one on the allocation of resources and the second on the distribution of grants in aid between Union and the state.

The Constitution has provided a reasonably long list of Union and state resources of revenue and has then classified them how these resources will be mopped up or realised for transfer to the treasuries of the Union and state governments. This arrangement has deliberately been left open to be revised and readjusted to the fluctuations of national and state economies by a Finance Commission. Although, an expert and independent body, the Finance Commission is an agency of Centre and the state have to appear before it for the augmentation of their revenue resources. The centre has a built-in advantage and the grants-in-aid arrangements that states will have to present their case before the commission determines the quantum and character of these grants. Obviously the sources of the Union government are more elastic while the state governments, not with standing their political colours have to satisfy themselves with traditional services which are too meagre to meet the developmental burdens.

Resources of the Union government include corporation tax, currency, coinage and legal tender, foreign exchange, duties of customs including export duties, duties of excise on tobacco and certain goods manufactured or produced in India, estate duty in respect of property other than agricultural land, fees in respect of any of the matters in the Union List, but not including any fees taken in any court, foreign loans, lotteries organised by the Government of India or the government of a state, post-office savings bank, post and telegraph, telephones, wireless, broadcasting and other like forms of communication, property of the Union, public debt of the Union, railways, rates of stamp duty in respect of bills of exchange, cheques, promissory notes, etc., Reserve Bank of India. Taxes on income other than agricultural income, taxes on the capital value of assets, exclusive of agricultural land, of individuals and companies, taxes on the sale or purchase of newspapers and on advertisements published therein, terminal taxes on goods or passengers, carried by railways, sea or air, and taxes other than stamp duties on transaction in stock exchanges and future markets.

In contrast to this, huge resources that the state sources of finance enumerated in the Constitution are capitation taxes, duties in respect of succession to agricultural land, duties of excise on certain goods produced or manufactured in the states such as alcoholic liquid, opium, etc., estate duty in respect of agricultural land, fees in respect of any of the matters in the State List, but not including fees taken in any court, land revenue, rate of stamp duty in respect of documents other than those specified in the Union List, taxes on agricultural income, taxes on land and buildings, taxes on mineral rights, subject to limitations imposed by Parliament relating to mineral development, taxes on the consumption or sale of electricity, taxes on sale and purchase of goods, taxes on advertisements other than those published in newspapers, taxes on vehicles, taxes on animals and boats, tax on goods and passengers carried by roadways and waterways, taxes on trades professions, taxes on luxuries, tolls and taxes on employment, entertainment and gambling.

The Indian Constitution follows the 1935 arrangement in classifying the levying, collection and appropriation of these resources which are exclusively assigned or are shared between the Union and the states. This five-fold distribution is as follows:

(1) Taxes exclusively assigned to the Union: In this category, certain items of revenue have been exclusively assigned to the Union. These include customs and export duties, income tax, excise duties on tobacco, jute, etc., corporation tax on capital value of assets of individuals and companies; estate duty and succession duty in respect of property other than agricultural land; and income from the earning departments like the Railway and Postal departments.

(2) Taxes exclusively assigned to the states under Article 269: This category contains items of revenue which fall under the exclusive jurisdiction of the state. These are: land revenue; stamp duty (except on documents included in the Union List); succession duty and estate duty; taxes on goods and passengers carried by road or inland waters; consumption or sale of electricity; tolls; taxes on employment; duties on alcoholic liquors for human consumption, opium, India hemp and other narcotic drugs; taxes on the entry of goods into local area; taxes on luxuries, entertainments, amusements, betting and gambling, etc.

(3) Taxes leviable by Union but collected and appropriated by states under Article 268: The revenue from the following items is collected and appropriated by the states. Stamp duties on bills of exchange, cheques, promissory notes, bills of lading, letters of credit, policies of insurance, transfer of shares, etc. Excise duties on medicinal, toilet preparations containing alcohol or opium of Indian hemp or other narcotic drugs. Though all the above items are included in the Union List and the Union government can levy taxes on them, yet all these duties are collected by the states and form part of the revenue of the state who collects them.

(4) Taxes levied and collected by Union but assigned to states under Article 269: The taxes on the following items are levied and collected by the Union but wholly assigned to the states within which they are levied.

- Duties in respect of succession to property other than agricultural land;
- Estate duty in respect of property other than agricultural land;
- Terminal taxes on goods or passengers carried by rail, sea, or air;
- Taxes on railway freights and fares;
- Taxes other than stamp duties on transactions in stock exchanges and future markets; and
- Taxes on the sale or purchase of newspapers and on advertisements published therein.

(5) Taxes levied and collected by Union and shared with states: The taxes from the following items are levied and collected by the Union government but shared with the states in certain proportion with a view to securing an equitable distribution of the financial resources:

- Taxes on income other than agricultural income;
- Excise duties, other than those on medicinal and toilet preparations.

The Constitution provides that the Parliament may by law give grants-in-aid to the needy states out of the revenue of the Central government. The amount of such grants is determined by the Parliament in accordance with the needs aim to help such states which need Centre's special support for special kinds of needs and calamities. Knowing well the inelasticity of state's resources and the pressure of development on state exchequers the provision of grants in aid by the Centre seems justified.

This need necessitated the provision of a Finance Commission which the President of India appoints every fifth year:

(1) To assess and fix the allocation of revenue to the Central and state governments. and
(2) To determine the principles and proportions on which the grants in aid can compensate the revenues of the states.

This ongoing arrangement and distribution of resources by an expert economic body with the approval of the Parliament presents a democratic solution of the question. If it does not work well, then Article 360 of the Constitution empowers the President to make a declaration of emergency stating that a situation has arisen whereby the financial stability or credit of India is threatened. The consequences of this declaration are:

(1) During the period, the executive authority of the Union shall extend to the giving of directions to any state to observe such canons of propriety as may be specified in the directions.
(2) These directions may include: A provision requiring all Money Bills or other Financial Bills to be reserved for the consideration of the President. A provision to issue directions for the reduction of salaries and allowances of all or any class of persons serving in connection with the affairs of the Union and states including the judges of the Supreme Court and the High Court.

The duration of such proclamation will be a period of two months; unless before the expiry of that period, it is approved by resolutions of both houses of Parliament. If the House of the People is dissolved within the aforesaid period of two months, the proclamation shall cease to operate on the expiry of 30 days from the date on which the House of the People first sits after its reconstitution, unless before the expiry of that period of 30 days it has been approved by both houses of Parliament. It may be revoked by the President at any time, by making another proclamation.

Towards Centralisation

This prescribed union-state relationship of the Constitution has passed through very many vicissitudes and strains since 1950. The dependence syndrome of state on the Union government has caused flutter if not open protests. Several committees and commissions were appointed even during Nehru era when the governments in most of the states belonged to the ruling Congress party. The Planning Commission and its role as an extra constitutional body generated a debate but the issue could be resolved within the framework of the Constitution. In six years of working of the

Constitution, the India polity witnessed three constitutional amendments Third, Sixth and Seventh which have a direct bearing on union-state relations.

The Third Amendment Act modified item 33 of the Concurrent List and increased the power of the Union government over the production, distribution, and prices of many commodities including the foodgrains in 1954.

The Sixth Amendment Act 1956 added a new item 9-A to the Union List and thereby reduced the powers of the state legislature with regard to imposition of sales tax by states.

The Seventh Amendment Act added Section 350-A to the Constitution whereby special powers were given to the Centre to give primary education to the linguistic minority groups in their own language. Under this amendment, the Central government was authorised to appoint a special officer to look after the special interests of the linguistic groups. It also transferred 'industries' from the State List to the Union List.

Even during Nehru period, the Supreme Court of India following the American convention of doctrine of implied powers interpreted the Constitution on the assumption that whatever is not clearly given or assigned to the states may be taken as implied with the centre. The Supreme Court, held in a number of cases that the Central government was competent to levy taxes on all those goods and things which were manufactured by the state government. An autonomous corporation created and controlled by the state government is liable to the payment of income tax as imposed by the Central government. It is the jurisdiction of the state government to decide as to which medium of instructions should be used in the affiliated colleges, but at the same time, this power of the state will become invalid if it lowers the standard of an institution of higher learning as higher education is in the domain of the Central government. Thus, the Supreme Court has taken a stand which has led to the increase of the Central government's powers at the cost of state activity. The Indian Constitution lays down the rules of comity, which the units have to observe in their horizontal and vertical relationships. These rules and agencies relate to matters such as recognition of the public acts, records and proceedings of each other, extra-judicial settlement of disputes, coordination between states and freedom of inter-state trade and commerce. It has contributed to the growth of centralisation in Indian polity.

The Pinpricks and Protest

In the post-Nehru era, the non-Congress coalitions at Centre and states disturbed this union-state equilibrium with a political jolt. The states mounted their campaigns for increased autonomy. The Administrative Reforms Commission constituted in 1967 asked the Setalvad Study Team to make a comprehensive analysis of union-state relations for their recommendations. It was the beginning of identification of the problem. Following the ARC report 1969, the Tamil Nadu government constituted a commission to examine intergovernmental relations under the chairmanship of Justice P.V. Rajamannar in 1969. The provision of President's rule under Article 356 was the real hub of controversy when eleven instances of President's rule were witnessed in four years time from 1967 to 1971. The M.C. Setalvad study team of ARC recommended the following:

(1) An inter-state council with five representatives one each from five zonal councils may be set up.

(2) The office of the Governor be filled by a person having ability, objectivity and independence and the incumbent must regard himself a creation of the Constitution.

(3) An inter-state council be composed of the Prime Minister and other central ministers holding key portfolio and chief ministers and others may be invited or co-opted.
(4) Guidelines for the Governor to regulate the exercise of discretionary powers may be detailed.
(5) The relationship between the Finance Commission and the Planning Commission should be rationalised.

The Tamil Nadu Rajmannar report of 1971 is another comprehensive document of 282 pages wherein Justice Rajmannar reopened some of these perennial issues and suggested:

(1) An inter-state council, consisting of chief ministers with Prime Minister as chairman be set up to resolve inter-state disputes.
(2) The Governor of a state should be appointed in consultation with the state government and should be ineligible for second term.
(3) The jurisdiction of Article 356 pertaining to President's rule be restricted to avoid its abuse by the Centre.
(4) Some subjects from Union List be transferred to the State List and a redefinition of items in Union List be attempted.
(5) The residuary powers of legislation and taxation should be vested in the state legislature.

This crystallisation of issues in union-state relation in the year 1977 promoted the West Bengal Marxist government to articulate the need for redefinition and a document was prepared as a charter of demands against the Union government. It picked up specific articles of the Constitution and suggested varieties of amendment to extend the sphere of state autonomy. Some of the major recommendations of West Bengal document on Centre-state relations are appended below:

(1) The state legislature should have exclusive power to legislate on matters not enumerated in Union or Concurrent List. For this Article 248 be suitably amended.
(2) The preamble should describe India a 'Federation of state' and the term Union should be deleted.
(3) Rajya Sabha should be directly elected with equal representation of states and its powers should be equal with that of Lok Sabha.
(4) Article 302 which restricts states trade and commerce should be deleted.
(5) Article 368 should be so amended as to ensure that no amendment of the Constitution was possible without the concurrence of two-thirds of the members present and voting in each house of Parliament.
(6) Languages mentioned in the Eighth Schedule should be allowed in the work of the Central government and the state governments at all levels. English should continue to be used for all the official purposes of the Union along with Hindi as long as the people of the non-Hindi regions so desire.
(7) Article 249 is an encroachment upon state autonomy and should be deleted.
(8) All India services (IAS and IPS) should be abolished and there should be only Union and state services and Centre should have no jurisdiction over the personnel of state services.
(9) Article 3 of the Constitution should be suitably amended so as to ensure that the name and area of a state cannot be changed by Parliament to prevent specific conflict between two or more states in respect to territory.

(10) The special status of Kashmir within the Indian Union, as laid down in Article 370 of the Constitution should be retained.
(11) Articles pertaining to President's Rule, Financial Emergency and Reservation of Bills for President's assent should be done away with.
(12) The Seventh Schedule and its lists should be reformulated and states should have exclusive control over police, law and order, CRPF, certain categories of industries, etc.
(13) A separate article should be included in the Constitution to constitutionalise the existence and operations of Planning Commission and National Development Council. The Centre supervise these organisations to play its role as a coordination agency.
(14) States must be accorded more powers for improving tax on their own and to determine the units of public borrowings.

The Sarkaria Effort

This West Bengal Document was a well thought out and precisely drafted memorandum and it aimed to arrest the increasing tendency of centralisation. It went much beyond Article 356 and its implications but covered several maiden areas like all India services, Seventh and Eighth Schedules and problems of union policy through CRPF. The roles of Governor, Planning Commission, Finance Commissions, NDC were viewed from the state's angle. The memorandum goes to the extent of suggesting that Union List should contain only five subjects, namely, (1) Foreign Relations, (2) Defence, (3) Currency, (4) Communications, and (5) Economic Coordination. The radical suggestions to delete several articles go a long way to change the basic nature and structure of the Indian Constitution. But the demand for restructuring Centre-state relations continued unabated by non-Congress states like Andhra Pradesh, Karnataka, West Bengal, Kerala, Assam, Tripura, Tamil Nadu and Jammu & Kashmir. This forced Government of India to set up a commission under the chairmanship of Justice R.S. Sarkaria to go into the question and recommend appropriate changes with in the constitutional framework in August 1983. The Commission took four years to complete its deliberations and submitted its report on October 27, 1987. The Commission made a total of 247 recommendations of which 24 were rejected, 10 were not considered wholly relevant and 36 accepted with modifications. One hundred and nineteen recommendations are reported to have won the government's full acceptance.

The centrist tendency and the office of the Governor in union-state relations dominated the Sarkaria findings and recommendations. The Commission felt that:

(1) The chief minister of a state should be chosen by the Governor according to a four-step formula.
(2) Article 356 should be retained but should sparingly be used after due warning to erring state.
(3) State legislature should not be dissolve before the Presidential proclamation.
- Leader of the pre-election alliance.
- Leader of the largest single party.
- Leader proving his or her majority in front of the Governor.
- Leader whom the Governor thinks the House will support or accept.

The other recommendations pertain to more all India services in technical fields and inter-governmental councils to sort out Centre-state disputes. The dynamics democracy and development has significantly changed the framework in which the states now find themselves operating.

It signifies a need for a wide ranging re-examination of Centre-state relations so that they are enabled to have adequate powers as well as resources to meet their growing patterns of needs. This should be possible without weakening the Centre. The problems call for greater bi-level or tri-level sensitivity to the need for sound political processes and conventions in the land. With the constitutionalisation of the Panchayati Raj in 1993, federalism has become a three-tier governmental arrangement, and the needs and aspirations of the community-level government must also be constitutionally monitored. For this, the Constitution has already created an institutional framework of zonal councils and control boards. Then, there are informal consultation devices through conferences.

The Zonal Councils

The States Reorganisation Act, 1956 divided the country into five zones, Northern, Southern, Eastern, Western, and the Central and created a council for each zone.

(1) The Northern Zone covers the states of Haryana, Himachal Pradesh, Jammu & Kashmir, Punjab as also the Union Territory of Delhi;
(2) The Southern Zone comprises the states of Andhra Pradesh, Karnataka, Kerala, Tamil Nadu and Pondicherry;
(3) The Eastern Zone includes Assam, Bihar, Manipur, Nagaland, Orissa, Tripura and West Bengal;
(4) The Western Zone consists of Gujarat and Maharashtra; and
(5) The Central Zone which includes two large states of Madhya Pradesh and Uttar Pradesh.

Each of these zones has a separate zonal council. These councils have been mainly formed to promote inter-state cooperation and coordination.

The different zones have been constituted by taking into account the natural divisions of the country; requirements of economic development and cultural and linguistic affinity of the region. The river systems and means of communication and their requirements of security and law and order are the privacy considerations. A zonal council consists of the union home minister who is the chairman of all the councils and the chief ministers included in the zone. The latter act as vice-chairman of the council by rotation each holding office for a period of one year at a time. Further, there is the provision for associating the 'advisers' with the zonal council to assist in the performance of its duties. These advisers are: one person nominated by the Planning Commission; the Chief Secretary and the development commissioner of each of the states in the zone.

The zonal council has been entrusted with tasks such as matters in the field of economic and social planning, which offsets the risk of its relapsing into a body engrossed wholly with disputes – border, linguistic, etc. Further, the association of the Planning Commission with the zonal council results in the latter acquiring a much-desired economic and social bias. The zonal council is empowered to appoint committees of its members and advisers and associate with these committees such ministers either for the Union or for the states and such officers ... as may be nominated by the council. The Act also provides each zonal council with a secretariat staff consisting of a secretary, a joint secretary and such other officers as the chairman may consider it necessary to appoint. The Chief Secretaries of the states represented in the council act as secretaries of the councils by rotation and hold office for one year at a time. The joint secretary is chosen from among officers not in the service of any of the states represented in the council and is appointed by the chairman. The administrative expenses of the office, including the salaries and allowances of the secretariat staff other than the secretary, are borne by the Central government out of finance provided by Parliament for the purpose.

The zonal council is essentially an advisory body which can only discuss matters of common interest and forward its recommendations to the Centre and the states concerned. It is not an executive body, the Act authorises the holding of joint meetings of zonal councils if deemed necessary. The objective is to promote for closer cooperation among the states and territories. These councils discuss the ways and means of implementing the central policy in matters like food, conservation, savings and water conservation. They have also discussed regional problems affecting the member states including such problems as official state and national languages, border disputes, watershed development, regional hydroelectric power resources, food distribution, and police protection. Provision has also been made for holding of joint meetings of zonal councils whenever two or more regions face common regional problems. The decision of these zonal councils are not binding on the state. They are a charge on central budget and the Centre provides a forum for inter-state discussions without any preconceived notions of policy imposition. The state may discuss problems of mutual interest or horizontal and vertical conflicts of jurisdictional nature that pertains to Union and state governments in the zone.

North Eastern Council (NEC)

The seven sisters of northeast present a unique to polography and historical setting of hill life which marks a noticeable difference from the political cultural life of plains. Having their common borders and cultural proximity to countries like China, Bangladesh, Bhutan and Myanmar these small units of north hill region have perennial problems of insurgency and integration with the main land. The British period of Indian history maintained cautions peace in the region and allowed unabated missionary activities which inducted several unique characteristics of disintegrating nature. A host of tribes and tribals which were kept isolated from the dreams of development now find themselves in the midst of completing loyalties to tribe, religion, region and nation. The process of planned development threatens to detribalise their culture and the anglicised among them wish to assert their regional identity through insurgent movements. In 1950, the region has one state of Assam and two union territories of Manipur and Tripura. Around 1962, the disintegration movements began and in ten years four tribal states were carved out from the former state of Assam.

(1) Nagaland in 1962, covering an area of 16,579 sq km and 12,09,546 people.
(2) Meghalaya in 1972, covering an area of 22,429 sq km and 17,74,778 people.
(3) Arunachal in 1972, covering an area of 83,743 sq km and 8,64,558 people.
(4) Mizoram in 1972, covering an area of 21,081 sq km and 6,89,756 people.

Manipur and Tripura, the former union territories were given the statehood in the year 1972 without any change in their borders. This added two regular states to the region.

(5) Manipur, covering an area of 22,327 sq km and 18,13,749 people.
(6) Tripura, covering an area of 10,49,169 sq km and 27,57,205 people.

Thus, after the reorganisation of the North Hill map into six states the eldest seventh sister, i.e., Assam was reduced to a small unit now comprising 74,438 sq km of area, inhabiting 2,22,94,562 residents in its bounds. The panorama in these seven hill states of the north-east widely differs within the region and of the region with the rest of the country. There are difficulties of transport and communications, power and trained manpower. The region has no much required infrastructure both administrative and economic which has led to a poor investment climate both private and public in the industrial sector, the lack of proper development, conservation and exploitation of its rich resources. Over the years, all these have multiplied to create a severe adverse economic imbalance in the region. Besides all the political units are too small to develop their natural resources and are also underdeveloped and financially weak. Consequently, it was felt that this region may be given special treatment and the adoption of a special set of priorities suited to its special and peculiar needs for accelerated development. A scheme providing the smaller ethnic groups the status of separate states keeps them knit together for economic endeavours and has brought them into a relationship of joint action in matters of common interests.

The North Eastern Council was created under the NEC Act of 1971. There already existed the Eastern Zonal Council for the region. This body was created to assuage the feelings of neglect in the region and to reduce the regional imbalances. The NEC Act was passed by the Parliament in December 1971 and Presidential order was given effect from August 1972. The council consists of the following: (1) The Governors, (2) The chief ministers of the seven states, and (3) the President may also nominate a union minister to be a member of the council if he deems it necessary. The President nominates two of the members of the council to act as chairman and vice-chairman respectively. In addition, all states have a minister to represent it on the council. The council has its secretariat with the secretary assisted by advisers on planning, finance and security and other technical and non-technical staff as determined by the Government of India. The council is a policy making body. The secretariat assists the council's members in the matter of drawing up of plans and their execution. The office of the council is located in Shillong.

A committee of ministers for economic development of the northeastern region has also been reconstituted at Delhi. It comprises the Home Minister as Chairman, the Finance Minister, Minister or Ministers in the Union government from the region and the Deputy Chairman of the Planning Commission as members. Other central ministers are represented in the meetings by minister/minister of state/secretary as special invitees in matters relating to them. The chief ministers of the northeastern states are also special invitees to the meetings. The committee meets twice a year. The duty of the committee is to oversee the progress of major central sector programmes being undertaken by the central ministries and departments in the region. It also provides a high level forum where the chief ministers of the states can interact with the central ministries to coordinate the speedy implementation of major projects which have significance for the region as a whole.

The North Eastern Council is essentially a coordinating body for infrastructural growth of the region. Section 4 of the NE Council Act 1971 prescribes its functions as under:

(1) Recommending to the state or central governments the undertaking of necessary surveys and investigations of projects in any state represented in the council to facilitate consideration of the feasibility of including new projects in the regional plan.
(2) Recommending the allocation of expenditure to the member states regarding projects in the regional plan.
(3) Formulation of unified and coordinated regional plan for matters of common interest and importance in the fields of economic and social planning, inter-state transport and communications and power of flood control projects.
(4) Deciding the location of projects and schemes in the regional plan.
(5) Fixation of priorities of projects and schemes and their phasing.

(6) Reviewing and coordinating the implementation of the projects in the regional plan.
(7) To review, measures taken by the concerned states for the maintenance of security and public order and to recommend to the Centre.
(8) Reviewing the progress of the scheme and recommending to the Government of India the amount of financial assistance to be provided to the agency entrusted with the execution of the projects.

The region is extremely rich in natural resources and the council should attempt to supplement the efforts of the constituent units in developing adequate infrastructure for the speedy economic uplift of the region. The council also plans to provide the mechanism and the forum for joint consultation and concerted action in the sphere of planning and implementation of industrial, agricultural, power, communication projects and flood control projects, gradual substitution of traditional method of cultivation by improved ones, development of trained manpower and exploration and utilisation of vast mineral and forest wealth in the region.

The council advises the Central government and the government of each state concerned to make recommendations with regard to matters: (a) of common interest in the field of economic and social planning; (b) concerning inter-state transport and communications; and (c) relating to power or flood control projects of common interest. It also reviews the implementation of the programmes included in the regional plan and recommends measures for effecting the necessary coordination in the matter of their implementation. Where a particular programme is of benefit to two or more states, the council may recommend the manner in which (a) the programme may be executed, (b) the benefits therefrom may be shared, or (c) the expenditure thereon may be incurred. It also recommends to the Central government the quantum of financial assistance to be given to the state or states entrusted with the execution of any programme included in the regional plan. The council reviews the measures taken by the states represented in the council for the maintenance of security and public order and recommend to the governments of the states about measures necessary in this regard.

The NEC has been approaching the ministries of railways, finances and home to launch projects to build communication lines and infrastructural facilities to end the isolation of the states in the region. Among the schemes detailed by the council there have been 34 road projects, six water transport schemes, two roadway schemes and four telecommunication schemes. Similarly proposals relating to the development of power generation and of agriculture, veterinary and animal husbandry services in the region have also been considered by the council. The council has appointed a number of expert committees for overall economic development of the region.

(1) *The Road Committee* is to review the existing communication facilities and recommend steps for improvement of the existing system and construction of new roads.
(2) *The Electricity Committee* is to examine the legal, technical and administrative implications of a single electricity board for the region.
(3) *The Technical Power Committee* is working out a programme for investigation of the thermal and hydro potentialities in the region, and draw up a schedule for bulk transmission and distribution of power.
(4) *The Barak River Project Committee* is to draw up an integrated soil conservation, a forestation and power generation scheme for the river basin and watershed areas.

The major activities sponsored and financed by the North Eastern Council are assessment of resource potential, industrial surveys, and preparation of data bases for development planning and development of infrastructure, especially construction of roads, bridges and power generation, manpower planning and development, improvement and development of agriculture and promotion of industries have been the major priorities. The region is earthquake-prone and it is deterrent to development. The council is evolving measures for disaster management.

Notwithstanding the limitations and the situational imperatives of the problems, the NEC has made a good beginning. It has supported the expansion of facilities for studies in modern agriculture, animal husbandry, nursing, dental surgery and pharmacy courses. It has also assisted financially to develop mental hospitals, Tezpur Cancer Institute, Guwahati; Pasteur Institute, Shillong; Textile Institute, Guwahati; Fishering Training Institute, Joysagar and Assam Administrative Staff College, Guwahati. It has also set up the Northeastern Handicrafts and Handloom Corporation to promote marketing of handicrafts and handloom products. Now, the council has a new shell of programmes of popularising the use of renewable resources of energy, protection and multiplication of endangered species of plants and orchids and provision of special health and welfare services. Some institutions such as Regional Medical College, Imphal; Tripura Engineering College, Agartala; Regional Police Training College, Barapani (Shillong); Training Institute of Judicial Officers, Guwahati, etc., set up by the council are supplying necessary manpower in the region. The council is thus making effort to build up effective manpower to train local people. It is a forum for the member units to discuss their common problems of supply of essential goods, difficulties of roads and air communication and development of post and telegraph and such other subjects of common interest. Still, it is a fact that long-standing problems of the region are far from being solved. Ethnic tensions and terrorist activities bordering on insurgency persist and need an effective presence of paramilitary forces. But, then the experiment evokes optimism and the NEC will not go the zonal councils way. The Union government has taken initiative and massive packages are being sanctioned to pump funds for development and regional integration. Moreover, the council has its own staff, advisers and experts which are professionally engaged in shaping the future of the north-east which is extra ordinarily rich in resources and man power.

Inter-State Council

There is no specific provision in the Constitution to have a dispute resolving mechanism although Article 263 permits the Centre to create a council to probe into Centre-state relations. The Kerala government and later the ARC favoured its establishment but the Union government ... postponing on the plea that there were several forums for thi... in the creation of a body where it might not have ... favoured it and proposed that the Inter-State Council ...

(1) The Prime Minister
(2) The Finance Minister
(3) The Home Minister
(4) Five representatives, one each from every zonal c...
(5) Such Union Minister or Chief Minister as are con...

The ISC was initially recommended for a period ... which took up the matter in great details. The Commiss... tative bodies in the area of union-state relations. They ... abandonment or merger. The conferences were not prop... tries waste a lot of their time in Delhi. The consultative m... does not have follow up mechanism in sensitive ar...

government cause embarrassment to state authorities and the report cites Berubari as a classical case of Centre's callousness to sensitivities of West Bengal government. The Sarkaria plea forced the Union government to constitute the inter-state council in May 1990. The council comprises the Prime Minister as Chairman, Chief Ministers of all states, Administrators of union territories without legislature and six Union cabinet ministers nominated by the Prime Minister as members. It is a recommendatory body and has been asked to investigate and discuss such subjects, in which some or all the states or the Union have a common interest, as may be brought before it. It can make a recommendation upon any such subject for the better coordination of policy and action with respect to that subject; and also deliberate upon such other matters of general interest to the states as may be referred to it by the chairman. The Inter-State Council Order 1990 provides that the council shall meet at least thrice in a year. Its meetings are held in camera and ten members constitute the quorum. Decisions are taken by consensus and the chairman's opinion on it shall be final. There is also a provision for a secretariat for the council.

As an additional Constitutional body along with Planning Commission, Zonal Councils and Finance Commission, etc., the inter-state council has been a weak or even a defunct body. The other organisations have taken over its role in varied ways.

Control Boards

The dispute between two or more states arise mostly relating to boundaries or water distribution or the problem of electricity grids. The best example of boundary dispute is that of Belgaum between the States of Maharashtra and Karnataka. The new boundaries drawn by the Reorganisation Act of 1956 has in some cases placed pockets of linguistic minorities on the wrong side of the border. The constitution makers were fully aware of the problem of water distribution and included Article 262(1) in the Constitution to enable Parliament to provide for the adjudication of any dispute or complaint with respect to the use, distribution or control of the waters of, or in any inter-state river or river valley. There are many common rivers originating in Nepal and flowing through India towards their destination. Then there are rivers like Kaveri flowing through a number of states, namely, Karnataka and Tamil Nadu. The Narmada river similarly flows through three states namely Madhya Pradesh, Maharashtra and Gujarat. The Parliament first tried to solve this problem by creating a Corporation. The Parliament with the active concurrence of the two affected states of Bihar and West Bengal, legislated to create the Damodar River Valley Corporation in 1950. This forum, however, was not found satisfactory and the Union government decided to experiment with control boards as the best form and there are nearly 14 such boards in the country. The Kosi Control Board and the Nagarjuna Control Board are two such examples. These Boards are not tatutory but are created by a resolution of the Union or a state government and as such have no erent administrative or financial powers. Such powers have to be specially delegated to them by ating authority. These boards are placed in charge of various projects enjoying administrative cial powers. These boards have common functions. They differ considerably in staffing l authority structure. Thus one of the control boards has a State Governor (in his ity), another has a central minister and a third a state minister while some have state chairmen. The functions of these boards are:

rogress of different units of the project and recommend adjustments.

ntracts, the cost of which exceeds the powers of sanction of the chief

(3) To scrutinise, modify and recommend project estimates for approval of the government concerned;
(4) To examine and approve delegation of powers, both technical and financial to those engaged in the execution of the project;
(5) To provide for resettlement of persons displaced as a result of project work;
(6) To approve project design; and
(7) To lay down schedules of rates for various classes for work;

These wide ranging functions have made these boards effective and functional.

Inter-State Water Tribunals

The National Water Policy of 1987 recognises river basin as a unit for the purpose of harnessing the water potential. Major river basins of the country are almost all inter-state and there exist differences about their use and distribution of control of waters of these rivers. The Centre makes efforts to resolve disputes by negotiations amongst states concerned. Adjudication through Tribunals is resorted to if warranted. Sharing of the water disputes of the Krishna, Godavari and Narmada by the concerned basin states has been settled by respective tribunals. The Kaveri and Yamuna disputes stand blocked by terrorist activities. The Kaveri water dispute was referred to the Tribunal in 1990. The Karnataka government went in appeal to the Supreme Court. The court asked the Karnataka government to release water to Tamil Nadu, but the dispute still hangs fire. On the international front, India shares river water with Pakistan, Bangladesh and Nepal. As per international agreement there is:

(1) Indus water treaty with Pakistan signed 18th September 1960.
(2) Indo-Bangladesh Joint Rivers Commission set up in July 1972.
(3) Indo-Nepal Sub-Commission on water resources set up in August 1988.

These arrangements have eased out tension, but the problem keeps on plaguing the countries of the basin when there are floods or the water level recedes during summer.

Regional Electricity Boards

Electricity as a source of energy bedevils union-state relations. The new energy policy has augmented electricity generation and conservation. An autonomous body known as 'Energy Management Centre' was established in 1989. It serves as a nodal agency for energy conservation projects. Full benefits of the system need interconnections of the regional power systems. For these advantages, the Union government has constituted regional electricity boards to advise on the integrated operation of all the power systems within their jurisdictions. They function under the administrative control of the Central Electricity Authority. For this purpose, the country stands organised into five regions as under:

(1) Northern Regional Electricity Board covers Uttar Pradesh, Delhi, Rajasthan, Haryana, Punjab, Himachal Pradesh and Jammu & Kashmir.
(2) Eastern Regional Electricity Board covers West Bengal, Bihar, Orissa and DVC System.
(3) North-Eastern Regional Electricity Board covers Assam, Manipur, Tripura, Meghalaya, Arunachal Pradesh and Nagaland.
(4) Western Regional Electricity Board covers Maharashtra, Gujarat and Madhya Pradesh.
(5) Southern Regional Electricity Board covers Andhra Pradesh, Tamil Nadu, Kerala and Karnataka.

The total installed capacity in 1947 was as low as 1,400 MW and activity was mainly concentrated around urban areas. By 2004, power generation capacity had risen to 1,12,058.42 megawatt. This electric power had three dimensions – generation, distribution and consumption and both Central and state governments have been active on all the three fronts. The subject 'power' appears in the Concurrent List and as such the responsibility of its development lies with both governments. The state governments have generally entrusted the task of development to autonomous corporation companies or state electricity boards. They are responsible for generation and distribution of electricity in their respective states. The Central government, on its part, has formed a central authority with responsibility to develop a national power policy and coordinate activities of various agencies or state electricity boards. The authority advises Department of Power on technical, financial and economic matters. The country has been demarcated into five regions – North, West, South, East and North-east. Regional electricity boards were set up in 1964–65 in each of these regions.

(1) The Northern Region covers Haryana, Himachal Pradesh, Jammu & Kashmir, Punjab, Rajasthan, Uttar Pradesh, Chandigarh and Delhi.
(2) Western Region covers Gujarat, Madhya Pradesh, Maharashtra, Goa, Daman and Diu and Dadra and Nagar Haveli.
(3) Southern Region covers Andhra Pradesh, Karnataka, Kerala, Tamil Nadu and Pondicherry.
(4) Eastern Region covers Bihar, Orissa, West Bengal and Sikkim.
(5) North-Eastern Region covers Arunachal Pradesh, Assam, Manipur, Meghalaya, Mizoram, Nagaland and Tripura.

These boards are merely advisory bodies. They review the progress of power development schemes in the region; plan and ensure integrated operation of all the power systems in the region; prepare a coordinated overhaul and maintenance programme for the generating plants in the region; determine the operation schedules to be followed by all the plants in the region; determine the amount of surplus power available for exchange between the states; and determine tariff structures governing exchange of power within the region. No single state can possibly solve the problem of energy deficiency and hence has arisen the need for the formation of regional power grids. Significant progress has been made in the expansion of transmission and distribution facilities in the country. Fairly well interconnected systems are presently available in all regions of the country except the north-eastern region. Inter-state and inter-regional transmission lines would form part of the national power grid. It will promote integrated operation and transfer of power from one system to another with ultimate objective of ensuring optimum utilisation of resources.

Every successive Five-Year Plan has added to the energy capability of the nation and the national and regional power grids have resolved the power shortage crises in under developed states. Moreover it has helped in rapid and uniform industrial development of the country. The states feel reassured of their energy requirements and are inviting global investments on the basis of this infrastructural facility of the grids.

Institutional Channels for Union-State Consultation

Union-state relations flash in newspaper headlines when there are negative conflicts and irreconcilability of interests. There is an infinite area where the two levels of government cooperate, collaborate and create conditions conducive for mutual help. All this goes on informally and under the guise of conventions and practices. Inspired by British example of conventional working, the federal polity in India has arrived at a state of cooperative federalism wherein the union-state relations keep swinging without tilting the balance towards one way or the other. It is true that there is centralism, but the states have been persuaded to create a third tier of Panchayati Raj where they confront pressures from below as well as above. Not only the Governor, the Planning Commission and the union ministries on state subjects are an anachronism but the NDC, All India conference, state functionaries and informal consultative channels keep the various levels of governments interacting to mitigate misunderstandings and tensions. The experience of more than half a century of union-state relations is a pointer that the ideological barriers of state and union governments have not eroded the faith in National Polity. Democracy has sustained federalism by consultation and the need and urge of development have not transgressed the limit of a federal polity. In developing this political faith, the following conferences or institutional channels of consultation have helped. Some of them are:

(1) The Governor's Conference.
(2) The National Development Council.
(3) The Chief Minister's Conference.
(4) The Chief Secretaries Conference.
(5) The Conference of Inspector-Generals of Police.
(6) The Central Council of Local Self-Government.
(7) The Conference of Municipal Corporations.

The first three function at the political level. The next two are officer's conferences operating on the administrative plane. The last two deal with local government, thus, indicating the extent of the Centre's interest, even at the level of panchayati democracy. Then, there are a variety of conferences at political professional and administrative levels. Their formal and informal agendas cover the entire gamut of union-state relations. The state ministers are periodically invited by their counterparts in Delhi and together they exchange notes which include plan discussions, grants in aid matters, special projects and inter-state policy concerns. Some of these conference which are hosted in Delhi as a matter of routine are:

(1) Conference of Panchayati Raj Ministers.
(2) Conference of Health Ministers.
(3) Conference of Food Ministers.
(4) Conference of State Home Ministers.
(5) Conference of State Finance Ministers.
(6) Conference of State Education Ministers.
(7) Conference of State Ministers of Agriculture.
(8) Conference of State Ministers of Cooperation.
(9) Conference of State Labour Ministers.
(10) Conference of State Ministers of Community Development.
(11) Conference of State Ministers of Social Welfare and Welfare of Backward Classes.
(12) Conference of State Housing Minister.
(13) Conference of State Ministers of Irrigation and Power.
(14) Conference of State Ministers for Town and Country Planning.
(15) Conference of State Information Ministers.
(16) Conference of State Ministers of Cultural Affairs.

In addition to the political functionaries, the practice of annual consultation is very much on the increase among academicians, judicial functionaries, administrative secretaries and technological experts. Various committees or panels of Planning Commission and National Development Council have generated consensus on vexed questions of National Policy. These conferences often do not even have a fixed agenda or periodicity of their meetings. Out of a plethora of such conferences, the following can be seen as policy instruments in areas of concurrent jurisdiction:

(1) Conference of Chief Justices of High Courts.
(2) Conference of Vice-Chancellors.
(3) Conference of Mayors.
(4) Conference of Directors General of Police.
(5) Conference of Chief Engineers.
(6) Conference of Directors of Health.

These conferences do not follow any pattern. The union ministries play the host and relevant functionaries attend their sessions as special invitees or hosts. The decisions are sometimes recorded but mostly they serve as forums for informal exchange or discover the consensus. The conferences explore the common ground and federal tensions get dissolved if not resolved over a cup of coffee in an amicable manner. Thus, the union-state relations in the federal polity of India have constitutional, political and administrative dimensions. Technically not a federation, India is a federalised union committed to national unity. Obviously the Constitution following the 1935 pattern provided for legislative, administrative, financial and emergency relationships. The urge for quick and equitable economic development has cemented the strong bonds among states and between the states and the Centre. The constitutional provisions apart, the Planning Commission and the National Development Council rendered the polity extra centralised. Then the basic trends of unification as represented by national army, single judiciary man media and all India services promoted integration and unification. The zonal councils, inter-state councils, North-eastern Councils, and control boards came into existence to supplement the efforts that go to establish an equilibrium between centralised nation-state and decentralised development in a federal polity. The working of the quasi-federal model witnessed innumerable tensions and the constitutional and extra constitutional reforms were suggested by ARC, Justice Rajmannar and Justice Sarkaria. Despite Marxist West Bengal protest the union-state relations moved on an even keel and the Union government showed resilience and accommodation of state demands in the post-Nehru and post-Indira Gandhi eras. The coalitional experiment of hung parliaments has brought Indian polity face to face with regional federalism and as horizontal democracy matures federalism gets roots as vertical democracy in Indian polity. Public administration has a very critical and even decisive role in building bridges between party governments and national development by different parties at union-state and panchayati levels. The administration has to educate political leaders to develop federal perspective and it has to take people along irrespective of their regional affiliations and differences. India has already entered into an age of mass technology and the processes of national development cannot be reversed to the detriment of the millions. Those who talk of switching over to Presidential form of government on the model of US Federalism are ill advised to reverse a political process which has carved out a unique Panchayati Raj-based nation-state with atomic powers and in the front rank economies of the world.

4

The Secretariatal Organisations of Union Government

The term 'secretariat' literally means the 'place' where secretaries sit and work. The secretary to a minister in a parliamentary system of government provides secretariat assistance based on filtering and funnelling of information which is processed by the machinery of the secretariat. All secretariats are staff agencies which process ideas, information and research conclusions of general, technical and auxiliary nature. The secretarial staff represents the chief executive and collects and collates information to be funnelled in the policy making machine for churning. The secretary's plan, process and filter a variety of advises and decisions which keep the executive and the legislature functioning. The secretarial aid and assistance means all help which the minister desires for running the department and keeping the cabinet and Parliament informed. This continuous and systematic aid and advise offered by civil service at the headquarter to the rulers of state is below the key function of secretarial organisation from which flow the planning and coordinational activities of government. The President, the Parliament and the Supreme Court have their respective secretarial establishments but the secretariats for the assistance of the cabinet and the ministries of Union government are of special significance in operating a democratic administration of a vast country of Indian varieties. White Hall is the traditional seat of government from where the ministers of Her Majesty's government function individually as well as collectively. The cabinet secretariat as an organic growth of White Hall establishment sprang up in 1916 during the war, primarily because of Prime Minister Lloyd George's desire to have a war secretariat, to serve the Committee of Imperial Defence. Headed by the secretary of the cabinet, under the direction of the Prime Minister, this cabinet office in Britain comprises (1) the cabinet secretariat, (2) the Central Policy review staff, (3) the historical section and (4) the central statistical office. It operates as an instrument in the coordination of policy at the highest level. Its functions include circulating the memoranda and other documents required for cabinet or cabinet committee business; preparing agenda for meetings of the cabinet and its committees; recording their discussions and circulating the minutes; keeping in touch with the progress of action on decision; and safeguarding the security of documents. The Central Policy review staff advises ministers collectively on major issues of policy. The historical section is responsible for the preparation of official histories of selected events. The central statistical office coordinates the statistics collected by departments and produces statistics needed for central economic and social policies and management, such as the national accounts, balance of payments, financial statistics and measures of output.

Evolution of Cabinet Secretariat in India

The origin of cabinet secretariat in India can also be traced back to war operations of 1945. A coordination committee of the war resources and reconstruction was constituted by the Viceroy Lord Wavell for secretarial assistance to his Executive Council. Earlier Lord Wellington (1931–36) acted as secretary to the Executive Council in addition to his duties. But Viceroy Wavell's note of October 22, 1945 to Secretary of State Lord Pathic Lawrence asked for his official approval. The note stated: "Sir Eric Coates is setting up a small secretariat, which I hope may develops later into a real council secretariat capable of serving the Executive Council and its committees and also perhaps a committee of Indian defence. Sir Eric Coates is to take over shortly as secretariat of the Executive Council in addition to his present duties, and the secretariat will then become proper cabinet secretariat, as was always intended."

Thus, there emerged an institution which induced government wide thinking and action. It provided a much needed chance of come to grips with the Government of India itself. The Viceroy visualised the secretariat as an agency of coordination and to 'develop it into a real secretariat' of the Executive Council. The Secretary of State for India supported Lord Wavell's idea of 'a small secretariat'. He felt that a political executive – with a fair-sized secretariat of its own will function effectively. This secretariat functioned under Sir Eric Coates and the coordination committee of the War Resources and reconstruction of the Viceroy's Executive Council finally blossomed into the cabinet secretariat. H.M. Patel was appointed as Joint Secretary of the Executive Council Secretariat and when Sir Eric Coates was replaced by A.E. Porter as Council Secretary, the Executive Council's secretariat became the cabinet secretariat. Pandit Nehru personally favoured a powerful Prime Minister's secretariat while Sardar Patel stood for a strong cabinet secretariat to develop parliamentary practices in India. H.M. Patel and V.P. Menon sought Lord Ismay's opinion in the matter and Lord Mountbatten also wrote a personal note leaving the position to Nehru's discretion. He, however, hoped that "he will retain and use a proper cabinet secretariat". Realising the gravity of the problem Nehru accepted the cabinet secretariat as a final administrative arrangement.

The central personnel agency was created in the cabinet secretariat in 1949. The economic committee of the secretariat called economic wing was formed in the cabinet secretariat in June 1950. It intended to develop into a central economic office. Later it was transferred to the finance ministry which had already set up a central economic office. In the same year, the work relating to the joint communication – Electronics Committee, which was a sub-committee of the Chiefs of Staff Committee was transferred from the ministry of defence to the cabinet secretariat and attached to military wing.

Paul H. Appleby report of 1953 created an O&M division to improve administrative efficiency in all branches of government. This division remained a separate wing of the cabinet secretariat till 1964, when a new department called Administrative Reforms was set up in the ministry of home affairs. The Central Statistical Organisation, an attached office of the cabinet secretariat, was given the authority and status of a department of the government in 1961. Accordingly, the department of statistics was created as a part of the cabinet secretariat to advise and issue general directions. In 1961, the department had two attached offices: (i) the Central Statistical Organisation, and (ii) the computer centre. In addition, it had one subordinate office – known as the directorate of National Sample Survey. With the Chinese aggression in October 1962 and the consequent declaration of a state of national emergency, the cabinet decided to set up an emergency committee to see matters which normally fell within the jurisdiction of the Defence Committee and the Foreign Affairs Committee of the cabinet. To provide secretarial assistance to these committees, an emergency wing was created in the cabinet secretariat. In 1965, a new intelligence wing, was added to the cabinet secretariat to provide secretarial assistance to the Joint Intelligence Committee. A unit called the Director-General of Resettlement was also set up in cabinet secretariat for the formulation and implementation of schemes of relief and rehabilitation in the areas affected. It was later abolished and residuary work was transferred to the department of rehabilitation. In 1966, the Bureau of Public Enterprises was shifted from the ministry of finance to the cabinet secretariat but was soon retransferred to the ministry.

The Department of Administrative Reforms in the home ministry was transferred to the cabinet secretariat in 1973. Prior to this the services and establishment wing of the home ministry operated as a kind of central personnel agency in conjunction with the establishment division of the finance ministry. The Deshmukh Study Team felt that "the fashioning of an effective central personnel agency in the field of personnel administration was one of the important reforms required in the Government of India". The Administrative Reforms Commission agreed with this suggestion and recommended that "a new department of personnel should be set up and located in the cabinet secretariat, directly under the Prime Minister. In pursuance of this recommendation the department of personnel was established in the cabinet secretariat in August 1970. After an interval of ten years the organisation and methods agency got shifted from the cabinet secretariat to the home ministry with the elevated status of a department. However, after nearly a decade the Department of Administrative Reforms was once again located in the cabinet secretariat in 1973. By 1975, the cabinet secretariat had two departments under it, namely, (i) the Department of Personnel and Administrative Reforms, and (ii) the Department of Cabinet Affairs. A reorganisation of the Central Government in 1977 added the Department of Personnel and Administrative Reforms which were attached to the home ministry. The department of personnel was finally separated from the home ministry and made a new ministry in 1985.

The Organisation of Cabinet Secretariat

The cabinet secretariat inherited the structure from the secretariat of the Executive Council of the Viceroy. Its duty is to prepare the agenda of the cabinet meetings, to provide information necessary for its deliberations, and to draw up records of the discussions and decisions both of the cabinet and its committees. As a department, it is organised in three wings: (1) the civil wing, (2) the military wing, and (3) the intelligence wing. The civil wing provides:

(a) Secretarial machinery for the cabinet.
(b) Secretarial services for the various standing committees and ad hoc committees of the cabinet as also to a number of committees of secretaries which function under the chairmanship of the Cabinet Secretary.
(c) It also deals with the framing of the rules of business of the Union government.

The military wing is responsible for all secretarial work connected with the meetings of:

(a) Defence Committee,
(b) National Defence Council,
(c) Military Affairs Committee, and
(d) A number of other committees concerned with defence matters.

(e) The intelligence wing concerns itself with matters relating to the Joint Intelligence Committee of the cabinet. In addition to the three wings, there was a Joint Communication Electronics Committee located in the cabinet secretariat in 1977.

Besides, Cabinet Secretary, there are three other secretaries in the cabinet secretariat. They head three wings respectively. (1) Security, (2) Coordination, and (3) Research and Analysis Wing (RAW). The Secretary (Coordination) is responsible for preparing agenda and other important papers for cabinet meetings. He is assisted by Additional Secretary Coordination, Joint Secretary Coordination and a Joint Secretary for Joint Interrogation Committee who is normally an IPS officer responsible for coordinating and holding meetings of all important branches of civil police and armed forces and for presenting the relevant details to the Cabinet Secretary. The Secretary (Security) is also an IPS officer who is responsible for the security of the Prime Minister and his colleagues. His is assisted by Director, Special Protection Group who looks after the physical protection of the Prime Minister and his blood relations. Former prime ministers are also included in this charge. Another officer working under the Secretary (security) is Joint Secretary (security). The Secretary (RAW) is responsible for collation of external intelligence. He also works as Director General (Security) and heads Special Frontier Force and Aviation Research Centre. The Secretary (RAW), Director (SSB), Director (ARC) and Inspector General (SSF) constitute the security wing. The director (SSB) has under him one joint director/divisional organiser and some advisors whose number and portfolios change from time to time.

An important organ of the cabinet secretariat emerged in 1988 in the form of Directorate of Public Grievances, which is an independent appellate body of non-statutory nature. The directorate entertains grievances from the public against the decisions and actions of the Central government institutions like public sector banks, Life Insurance Corporation, railways, post offices, telecommunications, etc.

The number of members and size of staff in the cabinet secretariat in 1990 was as under:

	Officials
Department of Cabinet Affairs	223
Statistical Department	493
Computer Centre	62
National Sample Survey Directorate	1,955

The officers in different wings, centres and departments fall in different categories and cadres. Their titles and designations do not follow any accepted pattern as obtained in the ministries of government. Figure 2 explains the wings and their hierarchy.

The strength and structure of cabinet secretariat is flexible. As it handles several very sensitive and confidential matters like security, military affairs, RAW, etc. Its exact strength or nature of work and the kind of officers in its purview are not known and cannot be made known in national interests.

Functions of Cabinet Secretariat

One of the former cabinet secretaries perceived the functions of his secretariat as: (i) submitting of papers to the cabinet and its committees and prior to submission to ensure that they are in order and contain all the required information, (ii) to record the minutes and to follow up the decisions taken, (iii) to coordinate the functioning of the government and working of committees of secretaries, and (iv) to advise on 'special and urgent problems' which arise from time to time.

The Prime Minister being the in charge of his cabinet and its secretariat the entire gamut of governmental activity comes under the purview of this organisation. The Cabinet Secretary who is

Figure 1: Organisation of Cabinet Secretariat

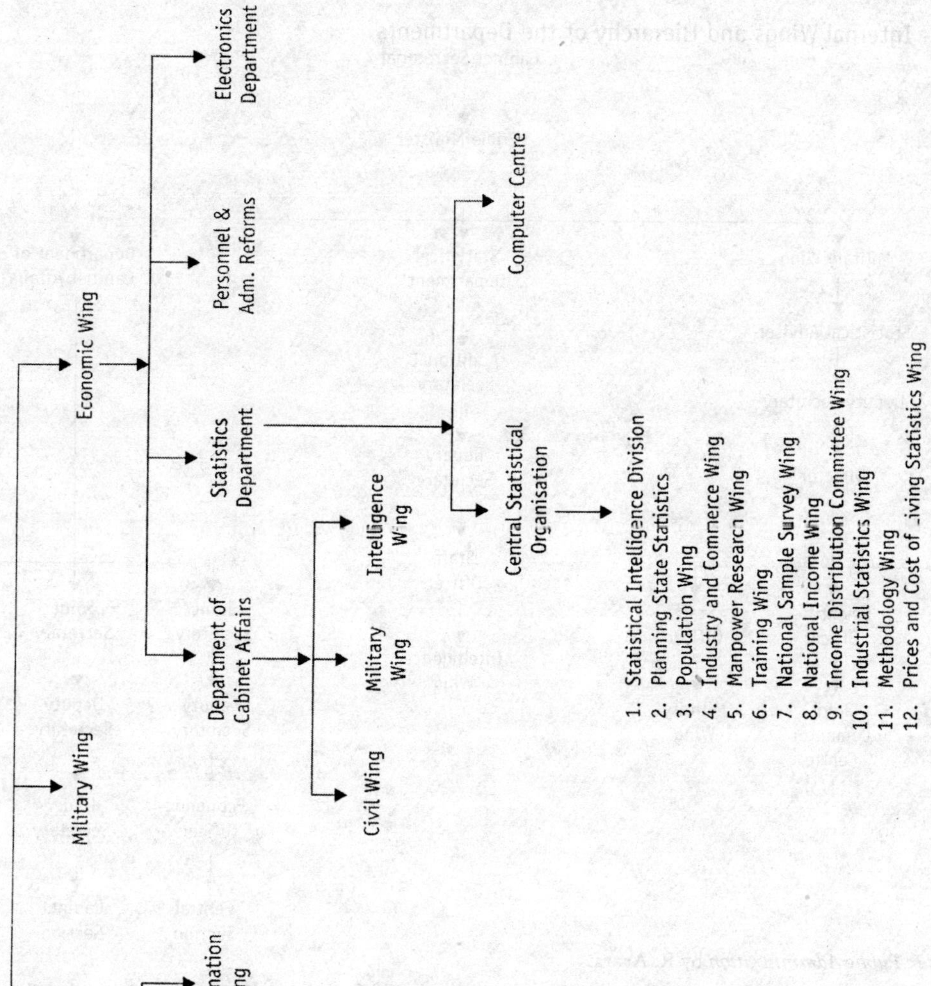

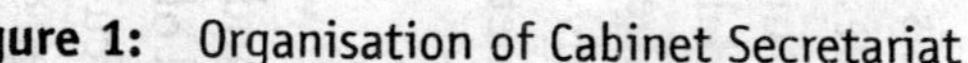

Source: Indian Public Administration by R. Arora.

Figure 2: Internal Wings and Hierarchy of the Departments

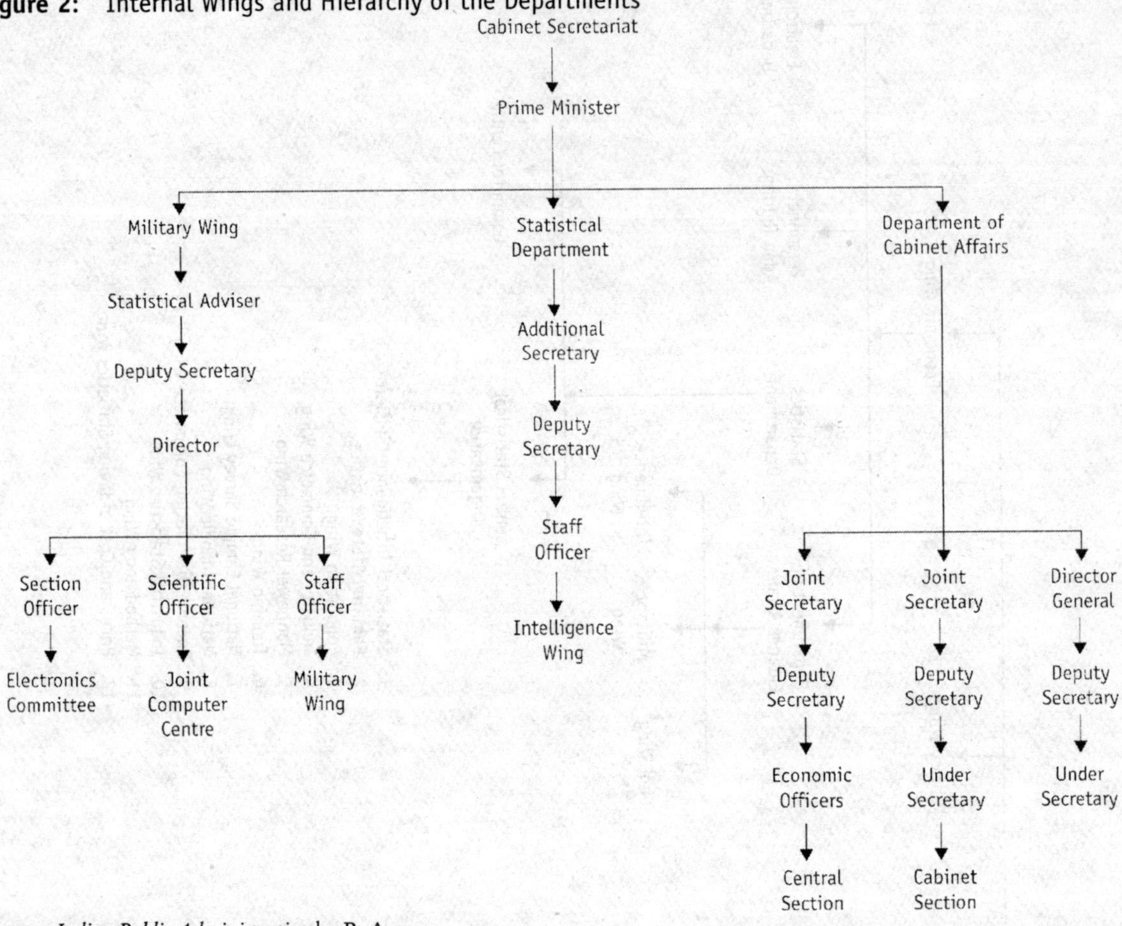

Source: Indian Public Administration by R. Arora.

the administrative head acts as an ex-officio chairman of the Civil Service Board. The Rules of a Business 1961 assign two specific functions to the cabinet secretariat, namely, (1) secretarial assistance to cabinet and its committees, and (2) rules of business. The Transaction of Business Rules (1961) make the cabinet secretariat responsible for facilitating smooth transaction of business in ministries or departments of government. It assists in decision-making, ensuring inter-ministerial coordination and resolution of conflicts through standing and ad hoc committees of secretariat. The President, Vice-President, ministries and chief secretaries of states are kept informed of major activities of the government. The expanding scope of activities and functions entrust the cabinet secretariat with following kinds of roles:

Role in Relations to Cabinet and Its Committees

It includes: (1) preparation of agenda for the meetings of the cabinet, (2) providing information and material necessary for its deliberations, (3) keeping a record of the discussions in the cabinet and of the decisions taken there, circulation of memoranda on issues awaiting cabinet's approval, (4) circulation of the decisions to all the ministries and preparation and submission of monthly summaries on a large number of specified subjects to the cabinet, and (5) it also oversees the implementation of the cabinet decisions by the concerned ministries and other executive agencies. The Fourth Schedule of the Transaction of Business Rules 1961 enumerates the list of papers which the cabinet secretariat circulates to various functionaries of government. These papers are:

(1) Quarterly reports on prices of food articles
(2) Economic review reports
(3) Political reports from states and union territories
(4) Five-Year Plan reviews
(5) Monthly summaries from ministries (fortnightly)
(6) Administrative Reforms reports
(7) Notes from ministries, trade agreements
(8) Reports of UPSC
(9) Reports on agriculture production, public sector undertakings
(10) Papers the PM wishes to share

To accomplish this it can call for information from the various ministries/departments. In accordance with the instructions issued by the cabinet secretariat, each ministry sends it a monthly statement showing the progress in the cases relating to cabinet decisions. In case, a ministry is falling behind schedule, the matter is taken up with it to accelerate the implementation process.

Role as a Department

The cabinet secretariat originates various kinds of proposals which pertain to the appointment of ministers, ministers of state, deputy ministers and parliamentary secretaries and the allotment of portfolios to the ministers. Once the recommendation of the Prime Minister on the appointment of a minister is accepted by the President, matters like the swearing-in ceremony, assumption of office, and so on are handled by this department. Likewise, works relating to resignation, relinquishment of charge, change in portfolios of minister's falls in its charge. Ministries are merged or reorganised and the subjects dealt with by them are re-allotted or readjusted or transferred from one ministry to another. The proposals which arise or are received in this connection are processed in this department. The department does not supersede other ministries nor does it relieve them of their responsibilities. It is the duty of the department to assist in resolving difficulties or delays which may arise in any field of activity between the ministries and departments; and to watch the progress of important administrative measures of the Government of India which affect more than one ministry. The department assists in coordinating the major administrative activities and policies of the Government of India; and watches the implementation of decisions in which the cabinet as a whole or the Prime Minister is interested. The department issues circulars and instructions for the guidance of ministries. It also conveys the directives of the cabinet or the Prime Minister on administrative and allied matters.

The Coordinational Role

A committee of the Executive Council of the Viceroy was intended for dealing with the coordination in respect of both civil and military affairs, primarily relating to economic and industrial matters. The secretary to the council, though without executive authority, performed duties on behalf of the council. He assisted in coordinating the major administrative activities and policies of government to resolve difficulties or delays in the administrative field. The coordination committee of the Council received matters which used to come for its decision or instructions. The Secretary of the coordination committee of the Executive Council and his secretariat served all ministers and was at the disposal of ministries for consultation. The work of coordination previously done by the coordination committee of the Executive Council is now undertaken by the whole cabinet and its committees.

The machinery for coordination consists of the cabinet assisted by a number of standing committees. A number of such committees deal with matters relating to emergency, appointments, economic coordination, parliamentary and legal affairs, external economic relations, family planning, food and agriculture, transport, tourism, defence supplies, location of offices in Delhi, post-devaluation problems and the like. At the official level a number of standing committees of secretaries with the Cabinet Secretary as chairman have been set up. Some of them, viz., the Committee of Economic Secretaries, the Secretaries' Committee on Foreign Affairs and the Scientific Advisory Committee to the cabinet assist and advise the cabinet on matters which fall within the scope of their functions. In cases where there is a difference of opinion among various ministries, the cabinet secretariat assists in resolving such differences and in arriving at agreed or acceptable decisions. The decisions of the cabinet, the committees of the cabinet and of the secretaries committees are communicated to the ministries and department concerned. The Cabinet secretariat keeps an eye on their implementation.

Role as Decision Implementing Body

The cabinet secretariat keeps a watch on the progress in the implementation of the decisions of the cabinet secretariat. A monthly statement showing the progress on the cases relating to each ministry is sent to the cabinet secretariat. These statements are scrutinised and the matters are taken up with the ministries at a higher level with a view to expediting implementation action.

These varied roles of the cabinet secretariat ensures that the cases presented are complete and, the rules for business transactions have been complied with. Where two ministries disagree or the finance ministry differs from the administrative ministry, the different points of view are included in the agenda papers of the cabinet meetings. This is done in matters of policy and a vast field of administrative activity is outside the preview of cabinet decisions. The cabinet ministers are hard pressed for time and, hence, the secretaries meet under the aegis of the cabinet secretariat and sort out their differences.

The department of cabinet affairs is the agency that undertakes this coordination and implementation of cabinet decisions. It is essentially a secretariat to aid and advice the cabinet and through it to the prime minister, president, parliament and various ministries of the central secretariat. Some of these areas on which aid and advice are tendered pertain to:

(1) Proposals to summon or prorogue the Parliament or dissolve the Lok Sabha.
(2) Cases involving legislation including the issuing of ordinances.
(3) Address and messages of the President to the Parliament.
(4) Proposals for sending delegations of persons abroad in any capacity.
(5) Cases involving negotiations with foreign countries on treaties, agreements, etc.
(6) Cases which a minister puts to the cabinet for decision and direction.
(7) Proposals to appoint public committees of enquiry and consideration of reports of such committees of enquiry.

(8) Cases involving financial proposals.
(9) Proposals to vary or reverse decisions.

All this has evolved under rules and the conventions. In 1968, the Administrative Reforms Commission thoroughly examined the work procedures of the cabinet secretariat. The commission recommended that:

(1) The cabinet secretariat should keep the PM informed about activities in the ministries.
(2) Submit memorandums to the PM about all important decisions of ministers.
(3) Receive reports of all committees and present them for discussion.
(4) Assist the PM and cabinet in the formulation of new policies.
(5) Have eight cells to keep the cabinet committees informed.
(6) Have cells working under a joint secretary and report serious matter to cabinet.
(7) Bring the differences between two ministries immediately to the notice of the cabinet.
(8) Keep himself in touch with other secretaries.
(9) Be informed by the secretaries to get proper orders from the PM.
(10) Not be treated as a mere department but should be treated as a key agency for total governance.

Most of these recommendations have been implemented. The secretariat gets the cases processed by the cabinet either by discussion or by circulation for opinion or discussion in committees. The minutes of the meetings are recorded but a lot of business is transacted through informal working of the committees interactions and experience sharing through dialogues.

Cabinet Secretary

The Cabinet Secretary is the senior-most civil servant of the country who heads the cabinet secretariat. He is the principal adviser to the Prime Minister and his office combines an articulate interaction of politics and administration at the top echelons of the Union government. He is not the chief secretary of the Union government but has an enormous amount of semblance with the chief secretary of the state government. The debate about his bureaucratic position and functioning has political overtones. He has emerged as a very powerful executive working as the pivot of the cabinet system. He is the head of civil service and an advisor, who can be called the conscience keeper to all the officials. As an administrative leader of bureaucracy he commands the confidence of the Prime Minister and his cabinet colleagues. As a respectable official, he heads 'the private department of the Prime Minister'. Naturally, there exists a great overlap of functions between the activities of the PM's office and the Cabinet Secretary's secretariat. He works as secretary to the head of the cabinet, i.e., Prime Minister, who alter ego he represents. The PM highly values mature advise of this experienced and venerable civil servant. It is a spring board to several key appointments which speaks volumes about its status and criticality.

Unlike his British counterpart the Cabinet Secretary in India has a shorter tenure. His senior-most position renders him an occupant for few months or years because of the army of juniors. The average tenure in UK has been about ten years. There have been only four cabinet secretaries in Britain, over a span of fifty years since Maurice Hankey was appointed in 1916; the fifth one took over in September 1973. Hankey himself served as Cabinet Secretary for twenty-two years while in India, there have been nine cabinet secretaries in twenty-five years, an average of well under three years.

The evolution of the office of CS has followed the ups and downs of his secretariat which the leadership styles of Indian Prime Ministers has influenced decisively. The history has provided the base but the Secretary of the Executive Council of the Governor-General could not settled down the model. As early as 1935, M.N. Malhotra put up a note about his recruitment position role but the government observed an evasive silence. The main qualifications insisted upon were an intimate knowledge of the systems of cabinet government and a personality which will make for the smooth working of the new procedure. Another time when a debate took place about the position of E.C. Mieville as Cabinet Secretary, a fear was expressed that the Cabinet Secretary would be a kind of super-secretary. The Government repudiated the criticism up till 1950, the Cabinet Secretary was of the joint secretary's rank. The Ayyangar Committee examined his position vis-à-vis his colleagues and recommended "He should be an administrative officer of the highest rank ... and he should be entrusted, as head of the cabinet secretariat, with the positive function of securing coordination as well as timely and effective action by all departments of the Government of India in all matters in which the cabinet as a whole or the Prime Minister is interested ... . While not laying on the Cabinet Secretary any specific functions which would impair the initiative and responsibility of heads of departments, I think it would be desirable to establish the convention that he should be the *ex-officio* president of the committee of secretaries set up to advise the Prime Minister and other ministers on selection for administrative appointments."

The report made a plea for conventions and further recommended that he should be an *ex officio* president or the committee of secretaries set up to advise the Prime Ministers and other ministers on selections for administrative appointments. His status in the service should be such as to entitle him to be regarded as the first member of the public services and one is whose judgement and impartiality the government, as well as the services, could rely implicitly. The Ayyangar recommendation was accepted and since 1950 the Cabinet Secretary has been the senior-most civil servant of the land. The Administrative Reforms Commission (1966–70), fixed his term for three years so that the functionary may provide effective leadership to the civil service. Accordingly, the principal functions assigned to the Cabinet Secretary today are to serve as:

(a) the link between the Prime Minister's office and various administrative ministries.
(b) the principal adviser to the Prime Minister.
(c) the link between the political system and the civil services of the country.
(d) the head of the cabinet secretariat, providing an umbrella organisation for various news agencies which cannot be located in any particular ministry or department.
(e) the head of the civil service – its conscience keeper.
(f) the principal adviser to the cabinet and the cabinet committees.
(g) a monitor and coordinator of activities of various ministries and departments.

The Deshmukh Study Team of the ARC and later the ARC report on the machinery of government eloquently pleaded for the empowerment of this office. The Deshmukh Study Team opined that "none of the tenure provisions ... should stand in the way of a deserving person becoming Cabinet Secretary". The Cabinet Secretary should be selected from amongst outstanding secretaries who have at least two years to go for normal superannuation, without seniority coming into the picture. On selection, he should be appointed for a four-year term. If this takes him beyond the date of his normal superannuation, his service should be deemed as automatically extended. If not, he should compulsorily retire strictly at the close of his four-year term. The ARC report supported the suggestions and in commissions' judgement the Cabinet Secretary should stay in his job for a period of three to four years. In order to bring out the pre-eminent position of the Cabinet

Secretary vis-à-vis other secretaries to government, the Deshmukh Study Team suggested that he be given a higher salary. The Administrative Reforms Commission, however, thought that "it was likely to affect the present cordial feeling among his colleagues that he is one of them" and did not agree to the Team's recommendation.

To facilitate senior management at apex level the chief of the cabinet secretariat should not be handicapped. He should manage his house with competence. His role and relevance vis-à-vis his juniors and senior political functionaries can be effective if his position is improved by taking the following measures.

(1) The Cabinet Secretary should meet other secretaries periodically by rotation.
(2) The position of the Cabinet Secretary should be recognised in the Government of India Transaction of Business Rules.
(3) The Cabinet Secretary should be given a salary which puts him in a pre-eminent position vis-à-vis other secretaries.
(4) Cases involving differences of opinion between two or more ministers should be reported by the secretary concerned to the Cabinet Secretary, who should decide the question after obtaining the orders of the Prime Minister.

The Administrative Reforms Commission recognised that the Cabinet Secretary is the principal staff adviser of the Prime Minister, the cabinet and the cabinet committees. Hence, the advice should be tendered by him at his own level. This implies that the role of the Cabinet Secretary in policy matters should be restricted to cases with which he can deal personally. The Cabinet Secretary provides the eyes and ears for the Prime Minister to keep in touch with the process of official business in the Central government. But he is not a watchdog or an invigilator on behalf of the Prime Minister. The Cabinet Secretary is a staff and he has no line functions in relation to the ministries. His role is to help, not to oversee. He acts on his own authority and responsibility. He may be called upon to serve on occasions as a sort of general multipurpose official. His influence must inevitably grow with the passing of time during which he is seen to work in close proximity to the Prime Minister. But then he is a transient officials, of short duration. The CS deals with cabinet affairs and keeps contact with the ministers. He remains in touch with the secretaries in charge of the different ministries. He keeps his vigilant eye on the smooth working of the system of communication and consultation of the Central government but is not expected to control or supervise it. The Cabinet Secretary, has no administrative authority to interfere but being the senior-most civil servant, he is looked up to offer leadership guidance and consultation to the entire system. His relationship with public servants, makes him a guardian of all the permanent officials. He resolves interdepartmental difficulties. He ensures the high morale of the civil servants and protects the interests of civil servants vis-à-vis political leaders. The personality of the Cabinet Secretary is reflected in his role as a visionary leader and a motivator. The Cabinet Secretary prepares the minutes of the decisions of the cabinet. He maintains secrecy and the differences of opinion among ministers are kept secret. The Cabinet Secretary ensures a proper implementation of the decisions and contacts the ministry concerned to ask what they have done about a certain matter. The PM is in direct charge of the cabinet secretariat and the Cabinet Secretary being responsible to him plays a variety of roles.

The Cabinet Secretary advises the PM on matters such as the classification of subjects, their grouping into suitable portfolios, allocation of particular portfolios amongst the ministers or transferring a subject or a department from one ministry to another. While tendering this advice he may consult other secretaries or the Committee of Secretaries on Administration which he heads to advises the PM. He also acts as the chairman of the Chief Secretaries' committee and provides stability and continuity to government. He advises and assists the President, the caretaker PM and the new PM and his cabinet as per provisions of the Constitution. The law prescribes that the sanction of the Cabinet Secretary needs to be obtained before the prosecution can be launched. Several judicial rulings agree with the personal judgements of the Cabinet Secretary. He may consult the legal experts in the government or some senior ministers or the Prime Minister but no appeal can be made against his decisions.

Prime Minister's Office

The rise of the Prime Minister's secretariat and the cabinet secretariat in India during the past decades is an indicator of the growing centralisation of policy and decisional authority in the position of the Prime Minister. These staff agencies have acted together as overall supervising agencies over the line organisation. They have influence which is disproportionate to their 'formal' role. With the creation of a multitude of governmental and semi-governmental agencies, the role of the chief executive has expanded and a number of experts have been inducted into the cabinet secretariat. Still the core responsibility for providing assistance rests with the committee of secretaries. All these staff agencies suffer from the same handicap as the cabinet itself. They do not have time and expertise to undertake an in-depth scrutiny of policy issues and lack secretarial support consequently the state of policy making bothers the PM.

Prime Minister Indira Gandhi developed her office into PM's secretariat which downgraded and even bypassed the cabinet secretariat during emergency. During the Rajiv Gandhi period, the cabinet secretariat substantially grew in stature and influence. It was working virtually as a 'super-cabinet'. Rajiv Gandhi appointed in the cabinet secretariat eminent persons like G.K. Menon, Pupul Jayakar, Sam Pitroda, R.N. Palit, who lent lustre to the cabinet secretariat and their expertise shaped it into a powerful organisation. P.V. Narsimha Rao's way of working was less controversial and he could strike a reasonable balance between his political and administrative advisers. Atal Bihari Bajpai perhaps inadvertently tilted the scale in favour of the Prime Minister's office when he appointed Brijesh Mishra as his personal secretary in PM office. He dominated the administrative scene to the extent that cabinet secretaries dwindled into oblivion. Later when he became the adviser of National Security Council the glory of PM's office caused an eclipse of the cabinet secretariat. The fall of the Bajpai government reorganised the 'advise apparatus' of Prime Minister Manmohan Singh. After the demise of J.N. Dixit and new incumbents in cabinet secretariat and PM office, the situation stands normalised and conducive to democratic working of a new coalition with Sonia Gandhi as adviser and leader of parliamentary party of Congress in Parliament.

The role and significance of the Cabinet Secretary can be assessed only in the context of the role which the cabinet and Prime Minister play in a parliamentary democracy. As the power has already shifted from the Parliament to cabinet, the cabinet secretariat becomes the nerve centre of government. Now as the trend is towards a prime ministerial form of government, his principal administrative adviser, i.e., the Cabinet Secretary emerges as a facilitator in all-critical decision-making. He is a help as well as check on the prime ministerial style of working. As an adviser, a motivator and an implementer of decisions he is one official who can keep a check on the growing power of the PM's office. As a head of the directorate of public grievances, he handles a variety of problems of public against the decisions and actions of institutions like Public Sector Banks, LIC, Railways, P&T Department, Airlines and Ministry of Surface Transport, etc. In fact, the position and importance of Cabinet Secretary depend upon his style of working and the clout that he has with the Prime Minister. His strength lies in keeping a balance with the PM's office and any imbalance in relationships can jeopardise the democratic process.

The developments of the office of Prime Minister from Robert Walpole to Lady Margaret Thatcher have made a qualitative deference in the nature of parliamentary government in England. The World Wars created situations in which the Parliament passed on its power to the cabinet which could collectively lead the country to victory. The postcolonial Britain needed a strong centralised government of a Prime Minister and the Iron Lady Mrs Thatcher transformed the cabinet system to the prime ministerial form of government. The first among equals become the hyphen that joins and the buckle that fastens the legislative and executive wings of the government. Mackintosh, Crossman, Crick, Hanson and Wiseman opined that not only the British cabinet has become Prime Ministerial, the Prime Minister himself is becoming like the US President. Prime Minister's position is pre eminent and his office is being presidentialised. It was called parliamentary government because of supremacy of the Parliament, and later cabinet government, because the cabinet had assumed, as Ramsay Muir said, dictatorial powers. But today, the Prime Minister is the key man both in the cabinet and in the Parliament. He makes and unmakes the government as its head.

The reasons for this transformation are many and obvious. The PM contests Parliament election in his name and popular mandates are given to his personal leadership. As a party senior, he selects candidates who are elected by popular verdict. Naturally, the Parliament echoes His Master's voice. Even opposition members are afraid of his power to get the house dissolved prematurely. The cabinet is just a committee picked up by him and goes out of existence if he resigns or loses confidence of the House. The President of India like the crown can do very little to change his judgement. In India, he heads the Planning Commission also. This central position of the PM has become extra powerful because of the backing of very many advisers and experts who work for him. He has created 'an Advise Apparatus' to advice the President and this Advise Apparatus functions in very many capacities. Even the institutional frame of these advisers is quite varied and powerful. Some of the staff agencies attached to the Prime Minister are:

(1) National Security Council
(2) Planning Commission of India
(3) Prime Minister's Office Secretariat

National Security Council (NSC)

The National Security Council was established on November 19, 1997. Its need was felt because the PM wanted expert and popular advice in defence policies of the government. After the Pokharan blast, the nuclear security of an atomic power like India with atomic proliferation around especially in Pakistan, the security of the nation could not be left to the political whims of the elected leaders and even to the discretion of military chiefs. Hence, a NSC was conceived of under the chairmanship of the PM to undertake strategic defence review and decide long-term policy options.

Although the composition of this advisory body is still in an embryonic stage and is shrouded in confidentiality, yet its functioning marks a new beginning. This six-member body under the

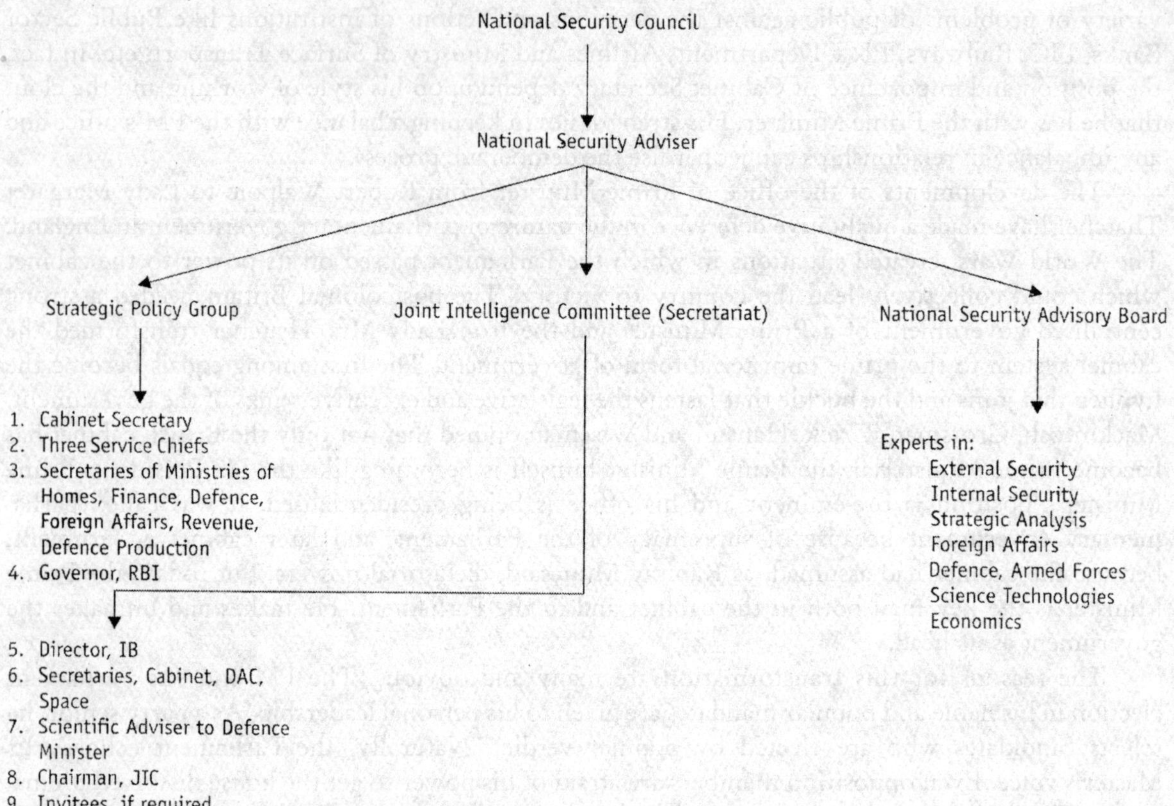

Source: Indian Administration, Avasthi & Avasthi.

chairmanship of Prime Minister Atal Bihari Bajpai was constituted in 1998 on the recommendations of a three-member task force under the chairmanship of K.C. Pant. The other members of task force were Jaswant Singh and Jasjit Singh, Director, IDSA. The three-tier structure works under the principal secretary or National Security Adviser. He is the channel for servicing the NSC. Brijesh Mishra was the first adviser. He was followed by late J.N. Dixit. The members of the council are:

(1) Minister of Home, Defence, Foreign Affairs and Finance
(2) Deputy Chairman of Planning Commission
(3) Other ministers, if and when invited

Principal Secretary to the Prime Minister is the NSC Adviser and is the channel for servicing the NSC.

The joint intelligence committee serves as the secretariat of the National Security Council. The board meets at least once a month or more frequently if need be patterned in the lines of US National Security Council. Its organs provide a long-term prognosis and analysis for the NSC so that it may consider policy options and recommend the same to the Prime Minister. The matter of giving institutional support to the Indian Prime Minister was discussed by the ARC. While everyone agreed with the need for such support, there were differences as to the way in which it should be done. Thus, one school of thought favoured using the machinery already available within ministries and to strengthen it suitably. The other school of thought, on the contrary, recommended strengthening the prime minister's office staff by developing new agencies or 'thinking cells' to give direct assistance to the Prime Minister for providing leadership as administrative head. The Study Team recommended a middle path and proposed the setting up of such institutional support as will not duplicate the work of existing ministries and will be concerned only with overall issues. Such an agency should be located in the cabinet secretariat rather than in the prime minister's office and quality experts alone should be appointed to it. The existing institutional support structure needs streamlining. Whether the NSC be located in PM's office or in cabinet secretariat is a debatable issue ultimately determining the nature of the office of the PM. If located in cabinet secretariat; the NSC will be handicapped by bureaucratic procedures and rules. But the office of the Prime Minister with NSC located in it acquires a commanding position yielding enormous discretion to Prime Minister in matters of defence, especially nuclear inroads. The present NSC is an autonomous body and late J.N. Dixit, a retired Foreign Secretary had no other office. The design is fairly loose and leaves a lot of leeway for the Prime Minister to redesign this advise apparatus of great future potential. Its close relationship with the prime ministers office is a functional necessity but the Cabinet Secretary and his cabinet secretariat should do the check and balance for the PM in consultation with the military, intelligence and security wings of the government.

The Planning Commission

It is an extra-constitutional body created by an executive order in March 1950. As Pandit Nehru had an obsession for planned development, he created this commission to identify and mulch the nations resources for planned development. Realising that its effectivity requires his personal support, he decided to become the Chairman of Planning Commission leaving the administration of planned development to the case of the deputy chairman. The ARC study team was extremely critical of this situation which could erode the sovereignty of Parliament and functioning of parliamentary democracy. To balance the situation, a National Development Council was created with union ministers as members, Planning Commission and chief ministers of state which is often criticised as the federal cabinet of the Prime Minister. During last several decades, this advisory staff apparatus of the Prime Minister works through PMG office and has extended its frontiers in varied directions. It is supervised by the PM in his capacity as chairman and has been kept outside the preview of the cabinet secretariat.

PM's Office/Secretariat

The debate over the term office and secretariat decisively indicates that office is less powerful than secretariat. The former helps while the latter aids and advised. The office represents an open, ruleless situation which the PM can use or manipulate the way he or she needs or wants. The secretariat works as per procedures prescribed. Both can be linked up with other organs of government, but the Prime Minister may take help from personal secretaries, experts and staff members in the office but the institutions way of processing the advise needs a secretariat. Obviously PM's office is the expansion of his personality but the PM secretariat will imply the objective analysis and legal processing of the advise tendered to or tendered by the Prime Minister.

Britain established PM's secretariat in 1939 when Sir Winston Churchill was heading the War Cabinet. In India, it was created as a secretariat in September 1946 when Nehru was heading the interim government. Viceroy Lord Wavell in his note of September 10, 1946 writes: "Although

(Jawaharlal) Nehru is not Prime Minister or Chief Minister, it is inevitable that he should have all sorts of miscellaneous correspondence to deal with as head of the popular part of the Government. I have arranged for him to be given as his principal private secretary one of the cabinet secretariat staff, who will also continue to be joint secretary to the cabinet. His private secretariat will be integrated with the cabinet secretariat, and I think this will be easier for Nehru and also limit the occasions on which he goes off at a tangent." The Prime Minister's Secretariat was not designed to be the residuary legatee of the Government of India. Nehru began with principal private secretary. Later, M.O. Mathai joined as a special assistant. In 1954, it consisted of one principal private secretary and three assistant private secretaries. Nehru largely operated through the cabinet secretariat and the departmental ministers. Shastri needed a strong institutional prop to gain national credence, particularly at a time when India was passing through a period of severe economic strain. He inducted L.K. Jha into the Prime Minister's office and conferred on him a high status to strengthen the body. Jha played a crucial role in the Shastri-era and the importance of the Prime Minister's office increased. In 1969, the Prime Minister's secretariat underwent a sea change when Indira Gandhi concentrated all powers unto herself. The PM office became the real seat of power. She introduced P.N. Haksar who gave the Prime Minister's office a status which aroused fear in the government. In 1974, P.N. Haksar was replaced by P.N. Dhar and he converted the PM Office into a super secretariat. The Janata Government (1977) under Morarji Desai curbed the powers and functions of this all powerful office. Its staff was curtailed and it was renamed as the Prime Minister's office. Indira Gandhi brought P.C. Alexander as her Principal Secretary and the Prime Minister's office became a very powerful institution of policy and decision-making in the government. Rajiv Gandhi strengthened the office further (1984) and included three full-time secretaries, three additional secretaries, five joint secretaries and an army of OSDs and directors. There were, besides, a large number of 'advisers' and the Prime Minister's office became the nerve centre of Union Government.

Under a coalitional arrangement, the Prime Minister functions more as a chairman than as a leader of a single party. There are many in the ministry with different loyalties. Indeed, a pre-determined quota system does bind the coalition and the Prime Minister finds himself operating within the constraints imposed by it. In fact, the organisation of the office of PM has not followed a fixed bureaucratic pattern. As the functions and relevance of functions change so change the number and positions of the personnel. During Nehru period, it was manned by 129 officials which touched 242 in 1975 when Mrs Gandhi declared national emergency. The Fifth Pay Commission fixed its sanctioned strength to 483 in four categories, viz., Group A – 33, Group B – 152, Group C – 161 and Group D – 137.

The strength explains the increase of functions at higher-level move especially in security areas. Figure 3 outlines the organisational analysis of this high profile office of the PM.

Then, there are several junior functionaries who belong to all the four classes of various services. Located at Raisina Hill, New Delhi, the PMO spreads to South and North Blocks of central secretariat building. It includes anti-corruption unit and a public wing that deals with public grievances. The files going to PMO from ministries depends on whether the PM is holding direct charge of the ministry or whether there is a cabinet minister or minister of state (independent charge) in charge of the ministry. In the case of the latter, most matters are dealt with by the cabinet minister/minister of state-in-charge. Only important policy issues, which the minister concerned feels should be submitted to the Prime Minister for orders or information, are received in the PMO.

Figure 3: PMO: Organisational Analysis

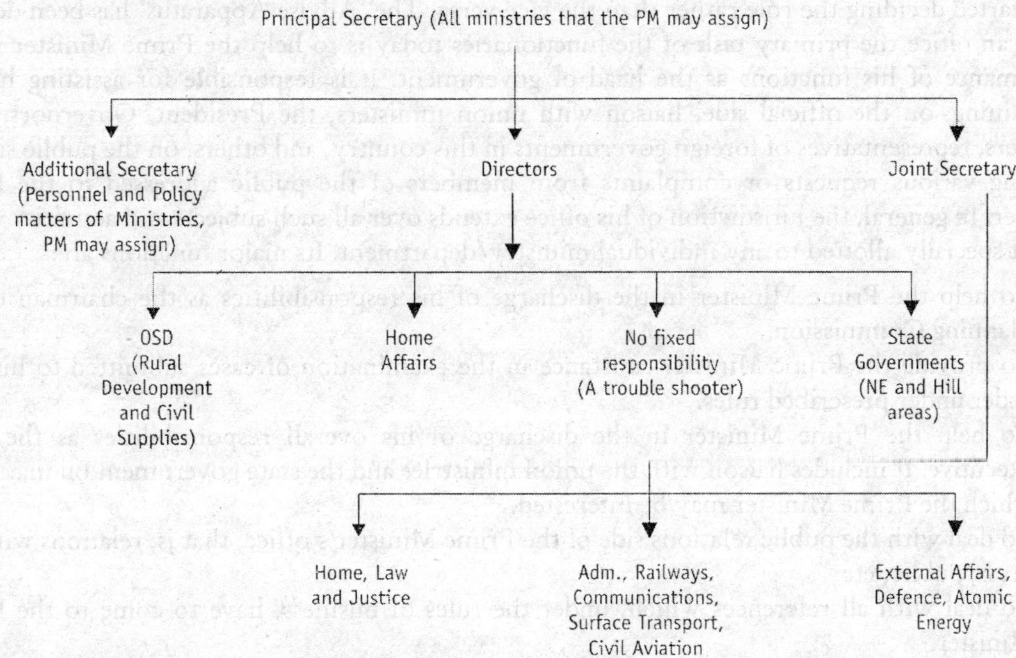

Source: Indian Public Administration, R.K. Arora.

In cases, where the Prime Minister is the minister-in-charge, all matters requiring ministerial approval not delegated to the minister of state/deputy minister, if any, are submitted for orders. The Prime Minister has traditionally been the minister-in-charge of the departments of space, atomic energy, and ministry of personnel, public grievances and pensions. Since the Prime Minister is Chairman of the Planning Commission, relevant files are forwarded to the PMO for his comments and clearance. Some of the matters that require the Prime Minister's personal attention include defence-related matters; decorations, both civilian and defence, important policy issues; proposals for appointment of Indian heads of missions abroad and requests for grant of agreement for foreign head of missions; important decisions relating to the cabinet secretariat; appointments to State and Central Administrative Tribunal committees, commissions, policy matters relating to the administration of the civil services and administrative reforms. Special packages announced by the Prime Minister for states are monitored in the PMO and periodical reports submitted to Prime Minister. All judicial appointments for which Presidential approval is required, Parliament questions relating to the ministries and departments of which Prime Minister is the minister-in-charge are taken care of by Prime Minister himself. The Prime Minister's National Relief Fund (PMNRF) and the National Defence Fund (NDF) are operated directly from the PMO.

The issues that come before PM's office are handled by the Principal Secretary. Bringing a high profile bureaucrat on this post overshadow the position of Cabinet Secretary. Mrs Gandhi made it a powerful organisation by inducting stalwarts at different times. They were not advisers but the extra constitutional centres of power. The post-Gandhi era maintained the continuity in Rajiv days but Narsimha Rao clipped the wings. Brijesh Mishra inadvertently rose to power because of Bajpai's balanced way of working. With Manmohan Singh the office has settled down to its normal functions. Historically, the functions and roles have gone together. Now, it appears that functions have started deciding the role rather than the vice versa. The 'Advise Apparatus' has been defused and as an office the primary task of the functionaries today is to help the Prime Minister in the performance of his functions as the head of government. It is responsible for assisting him in maintaining, on the official side, liaison with union ministers, the President, Governors, chief ministers, representatives of foreign governments in this country, and others, on the public side, in handling various requests or complaints from members of the public addressed to the Prime Minister. In general, the jurisdiction of his office extends over all such subjects and activities which are not specially allotted to any individual ministry/department. Its major functions are:

(1) To help the Prime Minister in the discharge of his responsibilities as the chairman of the Planning Commission.
(2) To provide the Prime Minister assistance in the examination of cases submitted to him for order under prescribed rules.
(3) To help the Prime Minister in the discharge of his overall responsibilities as the chief executive. It includes liaison with the union ministries and the state government on matters in which the Prime Minister may be interested.
(4) To deal with the public relations side of the Prime Minister's office, that is, relations with the press, public, etc.
(5) To deal with all references which, under the rules of business, have to come to the Prime Minister.

However, it does not perform functions which devolve on the Prime Minister in his capacity as the head of the cabinet, except to the extent to which matters are handled in personal correspondence between him and individual ministers or party policies of domestic nature. Still, it remains a nerve centre of power which mirrors the incumbents character and style of functioning. The PM indicates his priorities and the size of the cabinet pushes the PM to lean on a smaller group which the PM picks up each time.

Thus, the prime ministerial form of government arms the popular leader of masses to conform his cabinet and Parliament of the nation. His ever-expanding powers tend to make him extra responsible for which he should be duly informed and systematically assisted by all sorts of expert's advice. This staff help through cabinet secretariat and PM's office alongwith NSC keeps him on the track. His decisions in the realm of policy making or their implementation and revision should be duly whetted by his advisory apparatus which he should keep in good trim. If the advisers or secretaries view with each other for power or submit themselves for ulterior motives the PM will have to bear the responsibility. He should use the advice the way he wants and should induct these advisers after a careful scrutiny. A sound democratic government needs prime ministerial leadership much more than the expertise and loyalty of the counsellors.

Central Secretariat

Below the political and quasi-political structure of the constitutional government, there exists an administrative organisation of the central secretariat through which the ministers and the Prime Minister manage the administrative affairs that pertain to the Union government. This monolith structure at New Delhi and below is too large and too complex to be outlined in a uniform pattern. Moreover, the British rulers evolved it as per needs of administration of the colony. After independence, it has not only expanded in terms of its agencies and functions but has undergone a qualitative change to administer national security and economic development of a plural Indian society modernising itself through democratic processes of popular participation. The ministries, departments, corporations, boards, agencies, offices which collectively constitute the organisation of central secretariat, have different patterns of staffing and work according to varying procedures at the headquarter and in the field. A host of staff agencies attached to ministries and an army of civilians working in subordinate offices keep the central secretarial moving and its changing dynamic determines the quality of governance of the Union government.

The term 'secretariat' literally means the place where secretaries sit or deliberate. The three essential components of the secretarial organisation are the minister, the secretary and the executive head along with a retinue of public servants at various levels of hierarchy. The minister and the secretary are served by the secretariat which is essentially a conglomeration of various ministries/departments of the Central government. Significant enough, the secretariat works as a single unit with collective responsibility as in the case of the council of ministers. Under rules, each secretariat department is required to consult any other department that may be interested or concerned before disposing of a case. Secretaries thus are secretaries to the Union government as a whole and not to any particular minister. A secretariat officer of and above the rank of an under secretary speaks on behalf of the President of India, that is, the entire Central government. Canning, in 1858, granted each secretary the right of direct access to the Governor-General. Even today, the Prime Minister is free to send for any secretary for consultation. The secretariat is the government and is a policy formulating, coordinating and supervisory agency, operating through ex-executive agencies in the field. The demarcation between secretariat and field functions has been rather too thin and the British rule encouraged a policy of free flow between the executive field services and policy making headquarter.

Evolution of Central Secretariat

The effort of English rulers was to develop a Whitehall model of secretariat in India and civil servants in Whitehall were its principal architect. The civil servant in Whitehall had more delegation of power and the junior officials could do much more without referring to their seniors, and the seniors were people trained in the same way as juniors. Unlike Whitehall, the Indian model had two sets of parallel hierarchies, one in the secretariat and the other under the heads of executive departments. No such distinction is found in Britain where a ministry is an integrated agency including within itself both policy formulating and executing agencies. Historian, B.B. Mishra in his celebrated book *Central Administration of the East India Company* describes the design, role and purpose of the central secretariat as under:

> The Central Secretariat of Fort William in Bengal was designed to furnish the requisite information for the formulation of policy and to carry out the orders of the Company's Government. Before the year 1757, the President and the Council at Fort William transacted all their business in one general department with the help of a Secretary and a few assistants. On the arrival of packets from England, the Secretary laid them before the council for orders and the instructions which, when issued, were conveyed for execution to the authorities concerned.

Lord Cornwallis strengthened the secretariat and created the office of the Secretary-General later to be known as the Chief Secretary with all powers and responsibility. Wellesley's reorganisation of the secretariat increased the secretarial work in bulk and responsibility. He raised the status of secretaries to government, by raising their salaries and augmenting responsibilities from execution of routine business, their function extended to advise and planning. Towards the end of the eighteenth century, the supreme government consisted of a Governor-General, three councillors, and a secretariat of four departments, each under a secretary, and a chief secretary in overall control of them. After the Montford Reforms (1919), there were nine secretarial departments and the total strength of the secretariat touched 29 to which 17 more officers of the two boards can be added. This figure of 46 remained unchanged till the Second World War.

The world wars made a real contribution in evolving the secretariat as a policy making body. Its numbers swelled and the functions had to be redesigned in the light of war scarcities and war support policies of the colony. The task of policy making got separated from execution and Lord Curzon introduced the transitory cadre of staff on deputation. This split system made the secretaries, secretaries to government rather than to the minister and the size and centralisation could be kept under check. Curzon redesigned the central secretariat by asking it to concentrate on the following functions:

(1) Policy formulation.
(2) Framing rules and principles of procedure.
(3) Exercise of financial control.
(4) Work pertaining to legislation.
(5) Directing the executive agencies in the performance of their tasks.
(6) Evaluation of the work of the executive agencies.

Around 1940, the specific functions of secretariat were identified as a nodal agency. The field functions were gradually abandoned and the original functions were elaborated as assisting the minister in policy making and frame legislation and rules and regulations. Sectoral planning and programme formulation; with budgeting and operational programmes were accepted as secretariat functions. Supervision and control over executive departments and coordination and interpretation of policies were insisted upon to assist the minister in the discharge of his parliamentary responsibilities.

These advisory and coordinating staff roles crystallised the functions of the secretariat as assisting the minister in making and modifying policy proposals. It must draw rules and do sectoral planning. Budget making was regarded as a secretarial function of the Finance Ministry. Supervision of executive and autonomous field agency gradually come under its purview. Coordination was insisted upon as the key function and it assisted the minister in the discharge of his parliamentary responsibilities. All these advisory and coordinating staff roles ultimately boiled down to the following functions of the secretariat:

(1) Making and modifying policies from time to time.
(2) Supervision and control over the execution of policies and programmes by field agencies, and evaluation of the results.
(3) Coordination and interpretation of policies, assisting other branches of the government and maintaining contacts with state administrations.
(4) Sectoral planning and programme formulation.
(5) Framing legislation, rules and regulations.
(6) Initiating measures to develop greater organisational competence.

(7) Discharging their responsibilities to the Parliament.
(8) (i) Budgeting and control of expenditure.
(ii) According administrative and financial approval to operational plans and programmes and their subsequent modifications.

The secretariat is called a nodal agency, a think-tank because it supplies vital information with regard to policies and activities in the light of precedents. It provides ready reference for a detailed scrutiny of the issues after consulting the ministries of law and finance. The secretariat officials are transferred to the field and the field officers execute the decisions of the government as desired. It functions as the channel of communication between the states or agencies such as the Planning Commission and the Finance Commission. It functions from an apex position, which lends balance, consistency and continuity to the administration. It serves as a nucleus for the total machinery of a ministry and facilitates inter-ministry coordination and accountability to Parliament. It is an institutionalised system, for the proper functioning of the government. The President makes rules for the convenient transaction of business of the Government of India. The Government of India (Allocation of Business Rules), and the Government of India (Transaction of Business Rules) enable the minister or other officials to exercise his power. The rule states that when a particular official of a ministry does any act, he does so, on behalf of the Government as a whole. The transaction of Business Rules defines the authority, responsibility and obligations of each ministry in the matter of disposal of business allotted to it. The secretariat has had to concern itself with details of administration. It has to collect information from various sources and agencies to be made available to Parliament, during question hour. The ministers want to redress popular grievances, which adds to the work of the secretariat. The task of coordinating the functioning of state governments in a federal polity is also done by the central secretariat. The functions and responsibilities of the central secretariat have been on the increase and the authority has also followed. The superior position of the secretariat is recognised by the government which offers higher salaries and special pay to those who join the secretariat.

The Organisational Structure

There is no uniform terminology describing the various segments of administrative structure of the Union government. The central secretariat is a collection of a variety of ministries and departments. But the cabinet secretariat is a ministry comprising more than one department. The term "ministry" came into vague only after independence in 1947. A ministry is the charge allotted to a minister which may include one or more departments, each under the charge of a secretary. Many large ministries like defence, external affairs, finance and home have more than one department included in their charge. A department, is an organisational unit consisting of a secretary with a part of the central secretariat under his administrative control. If a ministry has more than one department, it may have more secretaries, but only one senior will represent the ministry. Formerly, such secretaries were designated as the secretary-general or the principal secretary. So even if all the secretaries draw the same salary, they may not necessarily enjoy equal rank.

There are three levels of secretaryships at the top management in the secretariat. Additional secretaryships and joint secretaryships are filled by members of the Indian Administrative Service. In technical and specialised departments, the personnel are drawn from other services. In departments of Science and Technology, for instance, the secretary is from IAS. The functionaries manning the middle management comprising the levels of director, deputy secretary and under secretary are drawn from the IAS but with some sprinkling of officers belonging to other services. The officers come on tenure and the continually is provided by the office comprising section officers, assistants, upper division clerks. The manning of secretariat positions by different services is governed by administrative practice and is not mandatory. There is no reservation in favour of any particular service. The levels of decision-making in the secretariat are at the levels of the under secretary, the deputy secretary and the secretary. The post of the joint secretary between the secretary and the deputy secretary existed as an exception but the joint secretaryship is a regular feature in all the departments of the Government of India. To remove stagnation at the levels of the deputy secretary and the joint secretary the posts of director and additional secretary have been created. These new functionaries had not been recommended by any pay commission. Deputy secretary was not to report to the director but would refer the file direct to the joint secretary. Under the same logic, a joint secretary would dispose of matters at his own level and more important matters are referred to the secretary/director. The internal hierarchy of the Ministry is as under:

(1) Department – Secretary/Additional/Special Secretary
(2) Wing – Joint/Additional Secretary
(3) Division – Director/Deputy Secretary
(4) Branch – Under Secretary
(5) Section – Section Officer
(6) Office – Assistant, Clerk, Subordinate

The lowest unit is the section under a section officer and it consists of a number of assistants, clerks, 'daftaries', typists and peons. It is also referred to as the office. Two sections constitute the branch which is under the charge of an under secretary, also known as the branch officer. Two branches ordinarily form a division which is normally headed by a deputy secretary. When the volume of work in a ministry exceeds the manageable charge of a secretary, one or more wings are established with a joint secretary in charge of each wing. At the top of the hierarchy comes the department which is headed by the secretary himself or in some cases by an additional/special secretary. In some cases, a department may be as autonomous as a ministry and equivalent to it in rank.

Top Management

The Secretary, Additional Secretary and Special Secretary constitute the top management. The Secretary is the principal adviser to the minister on matters of policy and administration within his ministry/department. His responsibility for the administration as head is complete and undivided. He represents his ministry and keeps himself informed of the working of his department and the files disposed of by his subordinates. He issues instructions and certain cases are submitted to him directly. In a ministry there may be as many secretaries as the number of departments. The senior most secretary, coordinates the work of other secretaries. The secretaries are appointed out of a panel prepared for these posts. The department of personnel and training, cabinet secretariat and the Prime Minister's office do the screening work. For appointment to individual ministries, the secretary's name is approved by the Appointments Committee of the cabinet and finally assented to by the Prime Minister. It is his duty to supply to the minister facts before any policy decision is taken. The secretary may brief the minister about the adverse consequences of policy alternatives. He assists the minister in the formulation of policies, and has the responsibility of keeping a watch over its execution. The secretary represents his ministry in all national and international committees and conferences along with the minister. He also represents his ministry/department before the various committees of the Parliament. His decision are regarded as authentic government decisions in the courts of law. He issues general or specific instructions about cases to be submitted to him directly. Weekly summaries on the cases disposed of at lower levels in his ministers/ department are submitted for his perusal. Mr Gopalaswami Ayyangar suggested, "A secretary should not be immersed in files and burdened with routine. It is essential that he should have time to grasp the overall picture, size up the problems facing government in the field allotted to his charge, and think and plan ahead. All these are his proper functions and must be efficiently performed. Failure to make adequate provision in this respect cannot be compensated by mere increase in the establishment under his control. The Administrative Reforms Commission visualised the secretary's role primarily as one or "coordinator, policy guide, reviewer and evaluator".

The introduction of more than one level of authority in top management has disturbed the hierarchy. The introduction of a new post designated as Special Secretary is a example of this disturbance. In 1951, a special secretary enjoying the pay, status and authority of a secretary, was appointed to the ministry of agriculture. This was a unique post and the principles on which the post was created and its relations with the permanent secretary were kept undefined. A similar post was revived in the ministry of external affairs to take charge of the administration of foreign service. There are several posts of special secretaries for which pay is determined in each case on merit.

The Organisation and Procedure Committee referred to the new levels of joint/additional/ special secretaries. The interposition of such officers between the secretary and his deputy has always been disliked and almost every committee has recommended either the abolition of these posts or a drastic reduction in their number. These posts may have been created originally to relieve the overburdened secretary but there is no specific unit of administration of which this officer is put in charge. Sometimes he is placed in charge of a department and does the work of a secretary; at other times he is put at the head of a wing and performs the tasks of a joint secretary. About the nature and role of these posts, Richard Tottenham suggested that "there should be no distinction of function but only of pay between a joint and an additional secretary. In both cases their correct function is to relieve the secretary of a block of work and to deal direct with the member so far as that work is concerned. They should only be required in those departments ... which are too large for a single secretary, but which cannot be divided into separable divisions. The justification for giving them more pay than a deputy secretary is that they are supposed to exercise a much higher degree of responsibility. When they are correctly employed, they take decisions at the same level as a secretary ... . The nature of their responsibilities differs little from that of a deputy secretary." However, the personnel study team of the Administrative Reforms Commission as well as the commission itself suggested the creation of a definite level of additional secretary. It also envisaged cases in which a wing of the ministry may be headed by an additional secretary himself instead of a joint secretary. Thus, the level of additional secretary has come to stay in the secretariat enabling him to concentrate on the more important policy matters.

Middle Level Management

The Joint Secretary, Deputy Secretary or Director level is called the Middle Level Management. When a secretary has an unmanageable charge of one or more wings, a joint secretary may take charge of each wing. In such cases, the joint secretary is vested with the maximum measure of independent functioning and responsibility in respect of business falling within his wing. Most of the cases which deal with policy matters in a ministry are submitted by the under secretary to the higher officers for consideration. The joint secretary of a department/ministry is a key administrative functionary and his imprint on policy and decision-making in government is immense. A Joint Secretary is generally in-charge of a wing in the ministry. He is vested with the maximum measure of independent functioning and responsibility in respect of the items of work falling under his wing. A small ministry has at least one joint secretary, whereas a large ministry, may have three or more joint secretaries. According to Gorwala the joint secretaries ought to be in reality the secretaries and joint to a more senior secretary for the convenience of administrative work. As in the case of additional secretaries, the emergence of the new level of joint secretaries between the secretary and his deputy secretaries has been criticised by all committees appointed by the government to recommend improvements in the administrative machinery. Mr Gopalaswami Ayyangar observed: "The interposition is *prima facie* an unsatisfactory arrangement. Even at its best, I consider the arrangement to be unsatisfactory. Inherent in this arrangement is a duplication of real responsibility to the minister. It tends to addition to work of the secretary; loss of initiative and consequently uneconomical utilisation of the services of the joint secretary who becomes a glorified deputy secretary, and an avoidable increase in the hierarchical stages of the secretariat personnel, with consequent delay and inefficiency."

The post of a director is not much different in terms of responsibilities from that of a deputy secretary. In hierarchy, the post status below the joint secretary is placed above the deputy secretary. The specific functions assigned to him are mentioned in the standing orders of 1960. Much depends on the division of work effected by the secretaries of the department/ministry.

A deputy secretary in a department acts on behalf of the secretary. He holds charge of a secretariat division and is responsible for the disposal of government business under his charge. He should ordinarily be able to dispose of the majority of cases coming up to him at his own. He acts on behalf of his secretary and discharges the majority of functions of his own volition. In due course, this post got devalued with the interpolation of new cadres like those of joint or additional secretaries. Most of the policy measures are initiated and submitted by a deputy secretary for the approval of the joint secretary or of higher officials. Normally, a division comprises two branches, each under an under secretary. A deputy secretary has to supervise, direct and guide the activities of the branch. Important files go upward in such a way that the deputy secretary may take decisions.

Lower Level Management

The under and assistant secretaries constitute this lower level. An under secretary holds the charge of a branch. He is also referred as the branch officer. He works as a link between the deputy secretary and the section officer under him. He is responsible to the deputy secretary for the smooth running of the branch and exercises control for speedy disposal of work and maintenance of discipline in the sections. One of the great losses in recent years in the working of secretariat departments is the practical disappearance of the drafts of the under secretary. Since British days, a level below the under secretary is called the assistant secretary. These posts were created as a result of the recommendation of the Secretariat Committee of 1919. The Maxwell Report (1937), recommended its abolition. The report said "Ordinarily there should be no grade of assistant secretary but the posts should in due course be automatically replaced by posts of under secretaries."

Officer on Special Duty (OSD)

To accommodate persons or to meet unexpected emergency needs of flexibility in administration, this post is created. While justifying the practice of appointing officers on special duty, the government contended that "OSD are appointed on two different criteria. First, when the government is convinced that the officer will prove economical. Secondly, when the government is convinced that it is an obligation to take action in the interest of the large staff employed. There are certain service conditions of employees which require details relating to facts from first hand information by a field officer. Then there are officers who are put on a combination of both these duties." An OSD is appointed normally from among the existing personnel to attend to particular work. Moreover, if some work is of a purely temporary character, it may be meaningfully concentrated in one hand. This arrangement facilitates coordination, and imparts a sense of importance and urgency to that work.

The designation OSD has a distinctiveness in the hierarchy, which has an attraction. The post of OSD is not necessarily indicative of any status, particularly if the incumbent belongs to the middle management level. Because of its innate flexibility, the post of OSD lends itself to use as a training post. After grooming the OSD is formally inducted into the new position. The designation has a peculiar charm for public servants. It may mean any position at a given time depending upon 'the nature and type of work'. It is this flexibility in the arrangement that suits the top boss. The OSD can be appointed with greater ease and bigger frequency than originally envisaged. The number of OSD, is always more than needed in terms of the nature of work given to them. These officers stay in their special posts 'indefinitely', while the post is inherently of a temporary nature. This suits both the officer concerned and the senior.

The Office System

A high degree of cooperation between the officer and his office is essential so that the officer may rely on his office to supply such materials as he may need to preserve continuity of administration. The functions of the office can be carried out automatically through cases sent to office without specific directions. The other functions can be performed only by direction of the seniors. Functions under the first category include seeing of all papers or notes arranged and paged with correct marginal references. The office verifies facts and points out the laws and rules. Relevant facts and figures available in the department are put up as precedents or papers containing previous decisions and policy. The office puts up drafts for approval and brings to notice matters requiring action or orders. The second category of functions require the officials to examine the case and see that all matters requiring decisions are brought forward and to tabulate and summarise information, where necessary. The officials prepare drafts in accordance with orders for timely execution. The office consists of section officers, assistants, upper division clerks and lower division clerks, typists, stenographers and Class IV workers.

Secretarial Staff

(a) *Section Officers:* Superintendents are in charge of their respective sections. They are called section officers also and are also responsible for handling of important and intricate cases.

Their supervisory duties in the manual are numbered as: distribution of work among his staff; training, helping and advising the staff; coordination of work in the section, ensuring prompt and efficient disposal or work in the section and adoption of proper methods for progressing of cases; timely submission of arrear statements and other periodical returns; proper maintenance of section diary, file register, assistants' diary and other necessary registers; ensuring compliance with instructions regarding treatment and safeguarding of secret papers; seeing that other departments are consulted before the issue of orders; preventing the growth of omnibus files; issuing reminders, acknowledgements, etc.; final disposal of routine cases; maintenance of order and discipline in the section.

(b) *Assistants and Upper Division Clerks:* Assistants work under section officers. Each assistant is allotted a certain number of headings to deal with. His duties as described in the manual are: to examine and put suitable notes and drafts on cases promptly and submit them to his section officer after properly referencing and paging them; to maintain properly the assistant's diary, standing guard files and other registers; and to keep papers and files it tidy condition. Upper Division Clerks perform functions similar to those of assistants except that they are not ordinarily required to deal with cases which are of an important nature. It sustains the entire super-structure which performs a 'memory' function important in the context of the tenure system. It was highlighted in the Wheeler Report (1937).

A typical office normally has a Section Officer (Class I and Class II), four assistants and a number of upper and lower division clerks. The section officer presides over the office. At the lowest rung of the ladder stands the lower division clerk whose task is to perform purely routine duties, such as collection of previous papers, maintenance of files and registers, despatch of mail, etc. The upper division clerk has a similar set of functions to perform but, in addition, he notes on simple cases and assists in their disposal. The section officer ensures that the notes prepared by his subordinates are factually correct. He is the first line supervisor in the secretariat hierarchy and is expected to settle minor cases in his own discretion. The lower division clerk is recruited directly through a competitive examination by the Staff Services Commission since 1976. Direct recruitment to the level of upper division clerk is done in the promotional frame from LDCs. The posts of assistants and section officers are filled partly by direct open recruitment and partly by promotion of upper division clerks and assistants.

The Conventional Growth

The central secretariat has developed a host of conventions which have gradually been formalised and amended as per rules and recommendation of committees appointed from time to time. From Lord Curzon's time till independence the secretariat was rather a closed system which could be run by a personnel system called tenure system. It was found workable and careful and continues till today. The load of work on secretariat caused delays and hence on the recommendation of Deshmukh panel it adopted a desk system which has been operative since 1973. Similarly Central Staffing Scheme which was adopted in 1957 continues in Central Secretariat Service and in Central Administrative Pool and Finance and Commerce Pools of the secretariat. These conventional developments which started as experiments have come to stay:

(A) Desk system
(B) Tenure system

(C) Central staffing scheme
(D) Central Administrative Pool (CAP) and Finance and Commerce Pool (FCP)

(A) *The Desk System:* The Deshmukh Study Team of ARC (1972) recommended the introduction of an innovation known as the desk officer system. It goes as a landmark in the reorganisation of the structure of the secretariat. It is aimed at eliminating dilatoriness procedures in the functioning of the secretariat and equipping it to cope more effectively with the new and increasing demands. This system has since been introduced and adopted by almost all the ministries. Under this system, the work of a ministry or department at the lowest level is organised into different functional desks each manned by an officer of appropriate rank, that is under secretary, section officer or assistant, who handles the case himself with the adequate stenographic/clerical assistance. For each desk, there is a team of two officers which can be constituted in any manner – one under secretary and one section officer; two section officers; and one section officer and one assistant. The level of the desk functionary depends upon the nature and complexity of work. In exceptional cases, the desk can be constituted of more than two officers and even officers of higher grades can be posted to it. Each functionary is assisted by a stenographer and is known as desk officer, assistants and their equivalents are known as desk attaches. There is no change in the designation of the under secretary working on the desk. Functionally, the under secretary will submit cases to the joint secretary, the desk officer to the deputy secretary/director and the desk attache to the under secretary if it is not a desk, otherwise to the deputy secretary/director. Thus, the inherent principle of the system is speed combined with quality. It envisages level jumping and initial examination of cases at more responsible levels. The system eliminates the section officer level where several assistants and stenographers used to delay matters and kept the files pending. The desk officer reports to deputy secretary/director and the desk attaches sends paper to under secretary or directly to the deputy secretary/director. It adds to the speed and improves the quality of decisions.

The Fifth Pay Commission pleaded for the strengthening of the system. Since 1973, several revisions have been made and it works as under:

(1) Index record has been added to the system.
(2) Guard file and card indices maintain detailed record of events.
(3) Every desk officer has clerical facilities added.
(4) Adequate provision of leave reserve has been made.
(5) Policy Advisory Committees are being contemplated to facilitate the work of the desk.

(B) *Tenure System:* There was no Central Secretariat Service for the central officials before 1948. The senior positions were manned by provincial officers borrowed on deputation. Lord Curzon who had a special love for the man working in the districts introduced this practice called tenure system in 1905 with a belief that India may be governed from Simla to Calcutta but has to be administered from the plains. His biographer, Lovat Fraser writes that "the Viceroy had a vision of keeping the district and provincial officers at the top echelons of national hierarchy. These officers move to Delhi for a specified period of 3 to 5 years to any union ministry and then revert back to their respective states and services. The system institutionalises the need for change at higher levels and the Maxwell Committee viewed its range from Governor-General's council members to junior under secretaries. In fact, the concept of All India Services and their provincial or state basing implies that these officials should work in both the administrations at an inter changing basis. The strength of all India services is so fixed with reserve quota so that officers for deputation may be spared by the state and both the administrations may garner the mutual advantages of the tenure system. A number of committees which followed found the system healthy and workable. Mobility apart, it is enriching to generalists and even technical officers to look forward for pastures anew".

The Secretariat Procedure Committee also known as Llewellyan Smith Committee of 1919 pleaded for the extension of the tenure period from three to four years. The government agreed to keep the posts of secretary and deputy secretary in central secretariat as temporary to keep living contact with the provinces. But for the some reason it hesitated to accept committees recommendation, because each year spent by an officer in the secretariat weakens that contact. It may be desirable to enlarge the category of officers who has experience of secretariat work. The field to draw upon is already small and the lengthening of the tenure of office might result in the contraction of this field. So the Government of India decided to maintain the existing arrangements whereby, except in same departments, the tenure of office was kept limited to three years, but extended if need be. The Simon Commission also commended the continuance of this practice of rotation of officers between the secretariat and the field. The commission remarked that efficient secretariat service, depends upon a constant interchange of personnel between the districts and the secretariat, the provinces and the centre ... . Experience is an asset to the provinces or districts and the intimate knowledge of the filed is invaluable in the provincial and the central secretariats.

The Wheeler Committee (1936) and Maxwell Committee (1937) discussed the merits and demerits of the tenure system in details. Wheeler's argument for tenure system were:

(1) the experience will train civil servants to assume responsibilities and cultivate a sound judgement,
(2) the short period of three years neither alienates nor disrupts,
(3) the stint of service in the central secretariat, would benefit the provinces,
(4) it is preferable to rotate such benefits among all officers to prevent jealousies and discontent, and
(5) It is an easy way out to remove unsuitable officers and post them elsewhere.

The Maxwell Committee (1937) reiterated the same arguments of the Wheeler Committee for the continuance of the tenure system. The Committee said that it would increase an officer's touch with reality, widen his horizon and possibly add to his technical equipment. Similarly, officers serving in the field should possess a secretariat experience and an acquaintance with the outlook, the methods and the difficulties of the Central government.

The opponents of the system argue that (1) tenure system does not ensure specialisation. In fact, (2) it strengthens the office at the cost of district experience. The two experiences are contradictory rather than supplementary. In view of this, the Bengal Administration Enquiry Committee, known as Rowland's Committee recommended that the secretariat positions should be occupied by officers with a minimum period (12 years) of field experience. The officers who possess this necessary experience may be asked to opt for the secretariat or the field. Those who opt for the secretariat should spend the rest of their career in the secretariat. The tenure system dates back to the period when the country had unitary government and the Central government was a 'Government of the Provincial Governments'. As the Maxwell Committee opined: "It was this factor more than any other which provided both the need and the justification of a system whereby the officers were lent for short periods by the provinces to the Government of India. The officer coming from a province brought administrative experience and practical knowledge of subjects with which the Central government was concerned and, when his tenure was completed, he was able to return to administration with a deeper insight into those subjects and better understanding of the purposes which his administrative duties were intended to fulfil." The replacement of the unitary government by a federal one under the Republican constitution blurs the line of demarcation between the Centre and the states. But the new arrangement still sticks to the original pattern of staffing because its advantages outweigh the disadvantages. Technically, the Indian government does not possess a permanent civil service of its own, except the Central Secretariat Service. It has always been the policy to fill the middle and higher management positions by deputation of officers from the state government as well as from the various central services. Administrative Reforms Commission Study Team on Personnel Administration (1967) gave its unqualified support for the tenure system and suggested the demolition of all barriers hindering uneven flow of personnel between the secretariat and the field. It made a positive recommendation that the tenure system be rigidly enforced and "officers must go back to the parent departments or state governments as the case may be for a substantial length of time – not less than the period spent outside the department/state before being considered for another assignment".

In fact, the 'tenure system' does not governed all the posts under the Government of India. The exceptions are found in the foreign affairs, Indian audit and accounts, posts and telegraphs, customs and income tax departments. Men once joining these services are ordinarily lost to their states of origin. The large and frequent interchange of personnel between the Centre and the states has increasingly tended to dry up. The Wheeler Committee gave figures to prove that the complaint of the provinces that they did not reap the benefit of reversion of their officers is well founded. Some officers tend to do a protracted spell of secretariat duty. Others obtain high posts. They do not revert to the provincial secretariats. A distinct tendency to promote to successive secretarial posts in the same department is noticeable. Other departments tend to look less and less to the states and increasingly to fill appointments from those already in the secretariat or in other central appointments. The ARC Study Team also endorsed this conclusion and wrote, "We find that the basic idea underlying the tenure system of regular interchange between the secretariat headquarter organisations and field positions tends to be defeated by people remaining indefinitely outside parent departments and changing positions between one organisation and another. Reversion to departments/states is just to complete a formality. We do not consider this a happy state of affairs."

The rigorous discipline of the tenure system postulates appointment of the best, which is not a simple exercise in view of the clash of interests. Posts in the secretariat are limited and aspirants drawn from various all-India and central services are too many. Moreover, the ability of a civil servant is ascertained from his annual performance appraisal and the standardisation has been unworkable because of differing norms of evaluation that prevail in the states and in the services. The tenure system is not rhythmic and the personal relations defeat the reverse flow. On return from the secretariat, the civil servants are not welcome to their state and field agencies and are put to 'sidelines'. The discipline has become weak and those who had early deputation are reaping the fruits. A typical civil servant makes all kinds of efforts to prolong his stay in Delhi and he tries to become eligible for another deputation. This prevents induction of officers with fresh experience and officers otherwise eligible for secretariat postings remain unutilised. Posting in the secretariat are governed by the Central Staffing Scheme and the doors are open to all higher civil services. But in practice, there are officers who have liking for central postings in ministries and agencies that manage economic affairs, with an eye on international organisations like the World Bank or IMF and the like.

Imbalance of salary structures, amenities available at the capital, proximity to the centre, greater opportunities for travels abroad, better educational and career opportunities for children have proved too powerful incentives for officers to stay on in New Delhi. Moreover, state governments are not always willing to part with their best officers. The basic changes in the secretarial landscape have put the 'tenure system' under very heavy strain. There is a qualitative change in the nature of the functions which has led to the creation of several pools like the Commerce and Finance Pool, the Central Administrative Pool and the Central Economic Pool, the Industrial Management Pool and services like the Indian Economic Service and the Indian Statistical Service. The political change has led to the creation of two levels of government, each responsible for policy and administration. The 'tenure system' has its difficulties in a federal polity with autonomous states.

(C) *Central Staffing Scheme*: The Government of India announced a Central Staffing Scheme (1957), according to which the senior positions from deputy secretary and onwards are filled through implementation in the following six categories in the central secretariat:

(1) Officers of the Central Administrative Pool.
(2) Officers borrowed from the state cadres of the all India services and from other Class I services of the states (other than the state civil service) on tenure deputation.
(3) Officers borrowed on tenure deputation from central services, Class I including officers serving in public industrial undertakings.
(4) Officers of the selection grade of the central secretariat service.
(5) State civil service officers whose names are included in the select list for appointment to the IAS.
(6) Other state civil service officers, in consultation with the Union Public Service Commission.

The bulk of the posts are filled by officers of the Indian Administrative Service, Class I central services and the selection grade of the Central Secretariat Service. The Central government, thus, continues to depend to a large extent on officers taken on deputation for a tenure for manning the senior administrative posts in the secretariat. The officers of the Indian Foreign Service hold almost all the secretariat posts in the ministry of external affairs. Similarly, the officers of the Railway Service and of the Central Legal Service, are deputed to the ministries of railways and law and justice respectively. If joint secretary is to be promoted on the higher position then deputation period is adjusted in the way that he may serve as additional secretary for minimum three years. The period for additional secretary is four years. If the joint secretary is promoted as additional secretary then his total tenure becomes minimum five and maximum seven years. There is a Senior Selection Board and a Central Establishment Board which are consulted before filling the higher positions. The SSB is chaïred by Cabinet Secretary and it recommends for posts of joint secretary and above. The CEB is headed by the secretary of personnel department. The Board recommends incumbents for promotion above the positions of under secretary and below that of joint secretary.

(D) *The Central Administrative Pool and Finance and Commerce Pool:* There exists a gap in the manning of the senior secretariat positions. It implies that certain growing areas of administration need specialised attention. This led to the formation of the Finance Commerce Pool of officers of the Indian Civil Service and other superior services like the Indian Audit and Accounts Service and the Customs Service in 1938. These officers were expected to specialise in matters covering finance and commerce. The discontinuation of recruitment to this pool after 1946 and depleting of the strength caused by retirement of British officers, transfers arising out of partition and routine retirements necessitated a re-examination of the entire question of manning superior secretariat posts. A proposal was mooted in 1950 to form the Indian Civil Administrative (Central) cadre to man the superior posts in the secretariat. It was felt that the new cadre would in fact create a new central service and thus nullify the 'tenure system'. Hence, the proposal was modified in favour of the constitution of the Central Administrative Pool. After consultation with the state governments it was decided in 1970 to constitute a Central Administrative Pool as a reserve for manning senior administrative posts of the rank of deputy secretary and above in the Central government. The basic idea was to select and earmark officials for higher positions, in the field of economic administration. The pool was to include officers drawn from the Indian Administrative Service, Class I officers of the central services including the Central Secretariat Service and Class I officers of state services. These officers were either to be permanently seconded to the pool or selected for it. It was also proposed that persons with specialised qualifications would be directly recruited from outside the services from higher age levels. The initial total strength of the pool was fixed at about 120 and the control of the pool was vested in the home ministry advised by the Central Establishment Board. The proposal met a storm of protests from the states and from the Indian Administrative Service Associations which led to its suspension. The officers seconded to it have been freed from the operation of the tenure rule and have continued in the union government till superannuation.

Central Secretarial Service

There are three kinds of services in the central secretariat:

(1) The first one, known as CSS is organised in four grades, namely, (a) Selection grade, (b) Grade I, (c) Section officers grade, and (d) Assistant.

(2) The second is called Central Secretariat Stenographers Service (CSSS). This also has 4 grades. viz., (a) Private secretary's grade, (b) Grade A and B merged, (c) Grade C, and (d) Grade D.

(3) The third one in called as Central Secretariat Clerical Service (CSCS). It has two grades, namely, (a) Upper division grade, and (b) Lower division grade.

Except for the selection grade, Grade I of CSS and private secretary's grade in CSSS, all other grades in the three secretariat services constitute decentralised cadres. It simply means that appointments and promotions in these grades are made cadre-wise which comprises posts in one ministry/department or its attached offices. The selection grade, Grade I and the new private secretary's grade of the CSSS are made on all secretariat basis. The task of monitoring, assessing overall requirements of different cadres, fixing zones of promotions and arranging centralised recruitment through open examinations is done by the Ministry of Personnel. The Central Secretariat Service provides staff for most of the attached and subordinate offices and is common for all ministries. The Estimates Committee recommended decentralisation of the lower two grades of the Central Secretarial Service. The ministry of home affairs has divided the two lower grades of assistants and section officers into ministrywise cadres and the control over these levels now vests in the administrative ministry concerned. The control over Grade I and selection posts now vests in the department of personnel and training. The scheme also provides a liberal deputation reserve which enables the officers of the service to be appointed to outside executive posts under the Central government. The Institute of Secretariat Training and Management provides systematic pre-entry training to new entrants in Grades III and IV of this service.

Expansion of Central Secretariat

The expansion of the secretariat took place largely during the war and the need for reorganisation of the secretariat was felt even before the transfer of power in 1947. The 'Whitehall System' of staffing was considered at some length and the secretarial staffing was introduced as an experiment in the ministry of finance. The Second Pay Commission (1959) recommended the merger of grades II and III into one running class II grade. A new selection grade was to consist of the posts of deputy secretaries and above. Posts in the cadre of deputy secretaries were reserved for the promotion of under secretaries in the Central Secretariat Service. Similarly a provision was made to reserve posts in the select list for director's grade and posts in the select list for the posts of joint secretaries. The grade-wise position of the Central Secretariat Service has: (1) Selection Grade; (2) Grade I; (3) Sections Officer's Grade; and (4) Assistants Grade posts. Officers in various grades are deployed on a regular basis in the attached offices participating in the Central Secretariat Service Scheme. The service provides staff for all posts from the level of assistants upto under secretaries. The new service is a common service for all the ministries. The Estimates Committee (93rd report), recommended decentralisation in the interest of better personnel management and better utilisation for the training received in each ministry. The ministry of home affairs has divided the two lower grades of assistants and section officers into ministry-wise cadres, But for purposes of promotion to Grade I, the field of choice consists of all officers in the section officers' grade in all sub-cadres which the department of personnel controls. The scheme visualises a liberal "deputation reserve" to enable officers to be appointed to outside executive post in attached offices and directorates and in local administrations under Central government. The Secretariat Training School (1948) upgraded as institute now provides systematic pre-entry training to new entrants in Grades III and IV of this service. The selection grade posts are filled by promotion on the basis of merit from the officers of grade I, having five years' services in that grade. For promotion to Grade I, the field for eligibility consists of permanent section officers having at least ten years of service in that grade. Recruitment to the vacancies in the grade of section officers is made in three ways.

(1) One-sixth of the substantive vacancies are filled through the Union Public Service Commission on the results of the Indian Administrative Service examination.
(2) The remaining substantive vacancies, as also the temporary vacancies, are filled by promotion of assistants to the extent of two-thirds of the vacancies, and
(3) through a limited departmental examination conducted by the Union Public Service Commission for the remaining one-third.

For the grade of assistants, the quota of direct recruitment has been fixed at 50 per cent and the remaining 50 per cent vacancies are filled by promotion or meritorious upper division clerks of the Central Secretariat Clerical Service. The study team on personnel administration on the working of the above scheme found that the members of these services are actually manning 70 per cent of positions at under secretary's level and about 50 per cent at deputy secretary's levels.

Subordinate and Attached Offices

The rules of procedure classifies the executive offices as: (1) Subordinate offices, and (2) Attached offices. There is no uniform pattern of these organisations and their relationships differ from organisation to organisation even in one ministry. After independence their number has increased enormously and the pressure of work increasingly makes it confusing to differentiate between the two. Broadly speaking, they follow the line of a staff arrangement but some of the attached offices have developed their subordinate offices as line agencies to staff. The ministry normally works through its subordinate offices and their agencies in the field; while the attached offices advise, aid, research and help in planning and training personnel for the ministry at head quarters. The execution of the policies of the government requires decentralisation of executive action and/or direction by the ministry to its subordinate and attached offices. The head of an executive agency who may be called as the director-general, inspector-general, director, commissioner, controller, chief controller, registrar carries out the policies of the government which is formulated in the secretariat.

The attached offices or executive agencies are responsible for giving executive direction required in the implementation of the policies of the ministry to which they are attached. They advise the ministry on technical aspects of questions. Policies require adequate data, precedents, technical and other relevant information and the attached offices supply the same. The internal organisation of these offices differs from unit to unit. The head is generally a technical officer and his status varies from that of an additional or joint secretary to that of director or deputy secretary. He has several technical as well as non-technical subordinates, the ratio of which differs from one attached office to another. The relationship between the executive agencies and the secretariat, depends upon structural patterns. Some of the patterns are:

(1) *Interated pattern:* It is followed in the models of the Railway Board and the Post and Telegraph Board in their respective Ministries.
(2) *The 'link' officer pattern*: It has a senior officer of the ministry as the head of the executive agency while functioning under the concerned ministry.
(3) *The coordinated pattern*: It has a common office wherein the secretariat office as well as the executive agency may coexist.
(4) *Ex officio secretariat status*: the head of an executive agency may be accorded this status.
(5) *The separation pattern*: Here the secretariat and its executive agencies or attached office are based on policy administration separation.

The system has the in-build advantage of ensuring uniform policies in matters of various executive agencies of a ministry and multi-level scrutiny of proposals, but duplication of work, delays and conflicts and distrust between the secretariat and the attached offices also surface because of the arrangement.

The subordinate office as a field agency executes the policies and decisions of the government. An attached office directs it but it can work directly under the ministry concerned if the volume of work is heavy. The subordinate offices may also assist the ministries in handling technical matters in the field of their specialisation. The criteria to classify organisations as attached or subordinate offices are not neat. In practice, there are organisations which are responsible for actual execution of the policy but are inferior in hierarchy. The attached offices are at par with the secretariat in all matters. The Central Pay Commission (1947) found it derogatory and invidious because the scale of pay of the office staff, whether it serves in a secretariat branch or in the office of the chief executive at the headquarters of government or in a local office, should be determined purely with reference to the nature of the work, the qualifications required and the field or recruitment necessary for getting suitable personnel.

The reorganisation of departments and ministries in the secretariat has a purpose of making the system result-oriented. For effective results, the business of the government should be organised around 'nodal points' of related activities and create appropriate administrative unit for effective implementation of specific tasks. The nodal concept of organisation organises the entire functioning of the government under some ministries with a large number of second rank ministers placed in operational control of specific areas under the overall guidance of senior ministers. During the colonial rule, the Government of India was accommodated in the North and South Blocks. Today, the Central government ministries and departments cover a large number of their own buildings in the capital. The *Allocation of Business Rules* makes the Central government directly responsible for thousands of jobs. Then, there are State governments directly responsible for developmental and regulatory activities. The secretariat has witnessed a rapid expansion during the 20th century as is evident from the data officially published.

The number of posts of:

(1) Secretaries in 1900 was 7. It increased to 12 in 1930, 32 in 1960 and 71 in 1994. Towards the end of the century, it touched 111 and touched 141 in 2001.
(2) The additional secretaries were born in 1994 and their number, which was 58 in 1994 swelled to 105 in 2000 and 141 in 2001.
(3) The joint secretaries were only 12 in 1930, but a steady increase in their numbers can be called phenomenal, i.e., from 81 in 1960 to 281 in 1994 to 449 in 2000 and 511 in 2001.
(4) The posts of 195 directors were created in 1994 which increased to 516 in 2000, touching 628 in 2001.
(5) The number of deputy secretaries rose from 9 to 230 in sixty years. But this number dwindled to 160 by 1994, but again rose to 442 in 2000 and 578 in 2001.
(6) The total number of under secretaries marked an uninterrupted increase from 9 in 1900 to 1363 in 2001.

The trend analysis denotes that there is an all round increase at all levels in every cadre. In one hundred years, the secretaries have multiplied twenty times that is from 7 to 141. The number of joint secretaries has swelled from 1 to 511 and the deputy and under secretaries have mushroomed from 9 to 578 and 1363 respectively. The year 1994 is a dividing line when secretariat witnessed an unprecedented bulge and 58 additional secretaries and 195 directors positions were created to clear the promotional stagnation. The numbers of joint secretaries and under secretaries have swelled to take care of new developmental ministries. More interestingly is the fact that more than 80 per cent of these senior positions have been manned by officers from IAS cadre. 81 out of 111 secretaries, 5 out of 12 special secretaries and 61 out of 105 additional secretaries hailed from the IAS fraternity. The middle level management of joint secretaries, directors and deputy secretaries had a heavy influx from the IAS cadre to fill as many as 268 (out of 449) 166 (out of 516) and 127 (out of 442) positions in the three cadres respectively. At the under secretary level, the number thinned down to 12 out of 552. In fact, 33 per cent staff of this secretariat does housekeeping jobs which besides being insignificant are of infructuous nature. Most of the ministries have more than one secretary to advise to the minister.

Criticism and Suggestions

The organisation and working of the secretariat is generally criticised on the grounds that it is an overgrown institution. It has too many officials working in the offices and the departments to dispose of self-created work. The secretariat officers suffer from a sense of superiority, even arrogance and vanity, which are reflected in their behaviours towards the executive agencies. These personnel between the secretariat and the field, is unsystematically distributed tilting in favour of the former. The Union secretariat presently performs a lot of work, which should be done in the non-secretariat organisations. It has added a number of executive functions and has prevented the secretariat from concentrating on policy making. Consequently, the encroachment has weakened the authority of the executive agencies. The preponderance of generalists dominate the secretariat. In fact, it needs a larger number of technocrats and specialists to handle complex problems of modern administration.

The secretariat procedures cause delay due to lack of adequate delegation of authority to executive agencies; cumbersome procedures of doing work in the secretariat; and the practices of postponing decisions, over consultation and excessive coordination. The methods of work in the secretariat are uniform, i.e., the same for the dealing with specialised and non-specialised matters. The practice of uniform method of work based on the system of 'noting' are unhelpful in dealing with specialised and technical matters.

There is an element of truth in each of the points of criticism. The recommendations made by the Administrative Reforms Commission in its report of the Machinery of the Government of India deserve careful consideration of the Government and the researchers of public administration.

(A)

(i) Non-secretariat organisations engaged primarily in planning, implementation, coordination and review of single development programme or several allied programmes, covering a substantial area of the activities of the ministry and having a direct bearing on policy making should be integrated with the secretariat of the concerned ministry. Such amalgamation is especially significant in the case of activities of scientific and technical character and activities, which call for a high degree of functional specialisation.

(ii) The heads of non-secretariat organisations, which are integrated with the secretariat, should functions as the principal advisers to the government in their respective areas. They may retain their present designations but it is not necessary to confer on them a formal *ex officio* secretariat status.

(iii) In other cases, the present distinction between policy making and executive organisations may continue because this distinction is vital for protecting the operational autonomy of the executive organisation in the field.

(iv) Executive functions presently performed by an administrative ministry or department which do not have a close bearing on policy making should be transferred to an appropriate, existing non-secretariat agency or to a new executive organisation specially created for the purpose.

(v) Policy personnel in department and ministries dealing with scientific and technical matters should include persons having relevant specialised experience or expertise.

(B)

(i) In non-staff ministries other than those with broad type of top management, there should be a set up of three 'staff' offices, namely, (a) an office of planning and policy, (b) a chief personnel office, and (c) a finance office. An administrative department with a heavy charge or with functions, which have no close affinity with the work of other departments, may have a separate planning and policy office.

(ii) The office of planning and policy should include the planning cell. This office should continuously be engaged to formulating long-term policies, carrying out policy studies and evolving a series of well-articulated policy statements.

(iii) The chief personnel office in a ministry should serve as a focal point for the formulation and co-ordination of overall personnel policies, initiating measures for promoting personnel development career planning and matters concerning discipline, appeals, and service rules of cadres administered by the ministry.

(iv) Each of the three 'staff' offices should be manned by staff having specialised knowledge and experience.

(v) In addition to the three staff offices each Ministry should have a public relations office or unit.

(vi) The heads of the 'substantive work' wings may deal directly with the chiefs of the 'staff' offices, as also with the secretary and minister on matters of technical or operational policy.

(C)

(i) Distribution of work between the wings of a ministry/administrative department and within the divisions of a secretariat wing should be based on considerations of rationality, manageability of charge and unity of command.

(ii) Today the diarist, after getting back the day's receipts from the Section Officer, passes the receipts to the dealing assistants concerned, after entering them in the diary.

This is emerging, as a consequence of several factors and the organisation has become a many-headed structure. The office of joint secretary has become a regular feature now. It may be mentioned here that the classical administrative opinion in India never extended its supports to this level arguing that no functionary should ordinarily intervene between the Secretary and the Deputy Secretary. The office of Director in the secretariat emerged after the Second Pay Commission – in the 1960s. The chief motivation underlying the creation of a new level, was to remove stagnation of officers. Although superior positions in the ministry are staffed by officers belonging to the IAS, the secretariat, today, suffers from a high degree of departmentalism, and even sectarian thinking.

The secretariat as a concept, does not function in a manner in which it has been stipulated. Its size officious attitude and the style of staffing have all combined to make it an institution in need of radical reforms. Though a policy making body today it dabbles in the type of work which belongs to the executive agencies and this kind of work has been on the increase all these years. This is obviously detrimental to administrative efficiency. The Administrative Reforms Commission, was highly critical of the functioning of the central secretariat. The report says: "The role of Central Secretariat should be to provide initiative and leadership and serve as a Clearing House. It should undertake national planning and research training of planners and trainers, evaluation of programmes and formulation of guidelines are its basic function. Coordination of foreign policy and conduct of centre-state relations should constantly be worked out in central secretariat." The study team found that central secretariat is overinvolved in non-secretariat activities. Suitable and drastic actions are needed to rid the secretariat from this weaknesses that has gathered around it because of poor housekeeping. The non-policy making matters must constitute the responsibility of the executive agencies for which substantial delegation of functions, powers and authority to executive agencies is imperative. Its functioning should be streamlined by getting rid of the dominance of the office. It must function as an officer-oriented administration. Besides, there must be systematic transfer of people between the secretariat and the field to keep it in living contact with field realities. There is no valid reason for paying personnel in the Secretariat at a higher level than those outside. The Secretary of the department carries the designation of 'Secretary to the Government of India.' and most departments of allied nature are bunched together. Home, Defence, Agriculture, Law and Finance Ministries are also organised on the bases of horizontal departmentalisation.

The secretariat is a victim of empire building and is engaged in the performance of work which is either out of its realm or is of an infructuous nature. It is an overgrown institution spoiled by governmental pampering. The secretariat has too many employees in terms of the amount of work.

A secretariat has to concentrate on policy making matter, but because of its sheer size, staffing patterns and styles of functioning today it dabbles in all types of works which essentially belongs to the executive field agencies. This increase of non-secretarial work in the central secretariat has told upon its administrative efficiency and smooth functioning. The ARC report was critical about its encumbrances with non-essential works and over staffing. Commuting upon its unwieldy size the report says "it has lead to occasional blurring of responsibilities and choking of the administrative machinery, which finds excuses for distortions and delays. The outgrowth of personnel has resulted in deterioration in quality. This has inevitably meant increased burden for officers at the higher level". It was supposed to take initiative and leadership and serve as a clearing house for field organisations. Planning and research should have been secretarial functions, but it has failed to provide training to administration and future reforms of administration. The crowd of files and their blocked passages leave no room for consultancy and coordination. The babu-orientation hinders decision making by the seniors and the procedures leave little scope for guidelines and training the trainers. The non-secretarial work of execution being tempting to power hungry senior officials and ministers, the field agencies do not enjoy sufficient delegation of powers. Despite all terms of officer-oriented administration, the lower echelons of hierarchy dominate and dampen living contact with the realities of field administration. Officials in the secretariat feel as if they are a privileged lot of rulers, because of which 'the department' is not viewed as parts of a single machine. A secretary in the secretariat is a secretary to the government and hence allied subjects or departments need some sort of 'bucking together'. Home, defence and agriculture ministries are working on this principle. Horizontal departmentalisation of subjects can be witnessed in the organisation of ministries of finance and law. But most of the developmental ministries seem like victims of 'empire building'. Too many people are doing too much 'non-work' of infractions nature.

The personnel in the secretariat either engage in unnecessary work which leads to the hiring of additional staff, or remain under-worked. The personnel suffer from superiority, even arrogance and vanity vis-à-vis the executive agencies. A systematic transfer of personnel between the secretariat and the field is largely lacking in the secretariat. Lack of adequate delegation to executive agencies results in cumbersome procedures a desire to postpone decisions, to over-consult, to over-coordinate delay in disposals.

The executive organisations can be amalgamated with the secretariat in those areas of work which are of developmental character. Policy bearing agencies have to be identified and merged in the ministerial set up of the secretariat. The policy positions in secretariat should increasingly be given to specialists and technocrats. Decision making in the secretariat should primarily be located at two levels below the minister. Although the babu orientation is giving way to officer-oriented administration, but a lot more has to be done to streamline the systems of level jumping and desk office working. The conventional patterns of dilatory decisional process have to be radically cut down by innovative use of technology and cyber facilities. The decisional levels and decision-making should adopt participating processes and the use of committees has to be made substantial to improve the quality contents of policy decisions. Decentralisation and delegation are laudable principles but the secretariat can induct these principles only by adding diverse points of views to bureaucratic routinisation. The babu bureaucracy which still dominates the scene can be scrapped by creating a new administrative culture of work through weak hierarchy and plural participation with expertise in the central secretariat.

5

Administrative Organisation and Working of Union Ministries

The Constitutional Philosophy and Constitutional Institutions issue in certain procedures of work which condition the working of the administrative systems. Constitutions generally do not talk about public administrations or its bureaucratic working which is generally the result of the infrastructure and administration laws. There is a separate part of the Constitution entitled as services under the Constitution which provides for the constitution of Public Service Commissions at Union and state levels. The administrative relations between Union and state have been outlined as a part of federal structure. Administrative tribunals have been prescribed and a whole lot of quasi-judicial commissions have been created to handle administration of areas which are substantively administrative in their operations. The constitutional philosophy permeates the administration and administrative organisations are working in the framework of rules of law and ministerial responsibility as guiding principles of parliamentary democracy.

The structures, personnel and procedures by which administration works are regulated by administrative laws and rules which represent subordinate legislation approved by the Parliament or its committees. The delegated legislation, which fills up the blanks, gives adequate discretion to administrators that operate in the field at the cutting edge. The administrative organisations have limited jurisdictions which are delimited by the higher laws of the land. The constitutional philosophies of democracy, socialism, secularism and federalism restricts the administration to become arbitrary. The regime of law keeps the check and balance doctrine in operation. The sprit of the Constitution, working under the guardianship of the judiciary inspires administrators who work for popular welfare and social justice. It can be called hallmark of our constitutional framework. In pursuance to this commitment of the founding fathers, a democratic, developmental and decentralised public administration is what the Constitution has enshrined. The following provisions of the Constitution are relevant in this regard:

(1) Representativeness of the administrator which is increasingly visible because of the reservation policy envisaged in the Constitution. Almost 50 per cent of officers or employees of administration of the Union and the state governments at every level represent the weaker and deprived sections of society which contributes to its democratic character. The elitism is being replaced by social merit and the feminisation of public positions may follow quite progressively in a decade or two.

(2) The awareness of human rights and the judicial ensurement of fundamental rights have started forcing the administration to confirm to rule of law. The public officials of colonial era who regarded themselves as a 'breed apart' are being brought in the ambit of common law which treats all citizens alike. The judiciary being the custodian of the Constitution and protector of citizen's rights has been issuing writs and injunctions against senior civil servants to depose before the courts and explain the government position in response to public interest petitions. All sorts of suits against administration or individual administrators are tightening the grip to the advantage of the lay citizen. Judicial activism has expanded this area of judicial control to the extent that citizens can claim compensations and live in dignity by putting the administration in the dock for inhuman indignities, which they have been perpetrating since Mughal times.

(3) The accountability of administration has increased manifold because of the democratic character of its policies. The legislators can control administrative behaviours by asking questions, raising discussion and ventilating public grievances on the floor of the house. The minister and the executives just cannot get away for administrative lapses under legislative supervision. The political leaders in league with corrupt administrators or vice versa feel the impact of this public vigil and its consequences at the grass roots. The organised civil society makes protests and as political leaders become increasingly accountable to their voters, the administrative institutions and civil servants feel the pressure of political change. This control is an effective step towards the democratisation of public administration in India.

(4) Another significant development which has started shaping the working of administration is the rapid proliferation of quasi-judicial, constitutional and extra-constitutional institutions which have taken roots and are reorienting the administrative laws and procedures. The Finance Commission, Election Commission and the Office of Controller and Auditor General of India are statutory bodies whom no wing of administration can afford to ignore. The Planning Commission and its developmental plans add a new dimension to public administration, more specially in the area of Centre-state relations. The National Development Council coordinates the strategic situations of planning which brings a large area of economic administration directly under the supervision of this extra constitutional body. In addition, the Parliament has created a number of statutory commissions like Human Rights Commission, Women's Commission, SC & ST Commission, Minorities Commission and Child Commission to preserve, protect and promote human rights in a developing society. The administrators in these commissions and a host of other regulatory and coordinating bodies are working according to the principle of check and balance. Policing the Police, judging the Judges through media and controlling the controllers of administration is a new phenomenon which has its democratic overtones for the public administration of the polity. New human rights jurisprudence is the contribution of constitutional philosophy and a variety of committees, commissions, boards and bureaus have sprung up, to protect people and groups against arbitrary behaviours of rulers. This parallel sort of administration of these independent bodies adds to the accountability of administration. It also acts as a check on their discretionary powers, confidential operations and unchallengeability of abuse of powers in the milieu of administrative casteism in India. The birth of regulatory bodies in a liberalised open

competitive economy has led to newer policy of debureaucratisation and decentralised functioning of administration.

(5) Amendments 73rd and 74th have made an effective dent in the working of district administration. This area which remained a sole preserve of administrative bureaucracy for half the century since independence has come under the sway of constitutional philosophy and elected leaders at the hustings. The character of district administration, notwithstanding the lukewarm policies of state governments is going to revolutionise the Mughal administration of free India in another decade or two. The dyarchy of regulation and development cannot last long and sooner than later the public administration of rural India will have to usher into an era of democratic functioning in their respective collectorates. This shift from bureaucracy to democracy should metamorphise public administration and its age-old working. It is an impelling force of constitutional structure and the institutions and working of administration will have to change accordingly.

(6) Another noticeably change that democratic structures and philosophies are causing in administrative working can be called the patterns and processes of popular participation in administration. People not only want an accountable administration in negative sense but they are asking for their interactive participation through new administrative structures like Citizens Committees, Mohalla Samitis, representation in decision making bodies and membership of innovative citizen cells in public administration. The right to information and citizen charters are a beginning to dismantle the old colonial structures of secrecy and bureaucracy. It may be somewhat early to envisage action and effective participation in the formulation and implementation of administrative policies of the state. But then there is a growing realisation that administrative system should proceed in this direction. District and police administration are the key area where people's representatives elected or nominated have started making in roads. Over the period, the working of a democratic Constitution should create and stabilise participatory institutions to check the arbitrariness of administration and offer suggestion to improve the quality of public administration at each level.

(7) Free India has witnessed the inauguration of a socialist welfare state through developmental planning and state sponsorship of welfare schemes in varied fields. Millions and trillions of rupees have been funnelled in the developmental pipeline. The results may not be in commensuration to national investment but the discernable change is more than visible. It is a direct impact of constitutional commitment that administration has been asked to share this entrepreneurial responsibility and the challenging task of national reconstruction. The social justice philosophy is being asserted to sensitise the administration and gradually but steadily is coming around the basic issues of social exploitation and cultural indignities to women and weaker sections. The administrative responsibility of government in the exercise of national reconstruction is enormous and till a take off comes the administrative elites have to take care of the tension. Development administration is a constitutional responsibility and working of the administration has varied democratic implications for public administration in India. Some of these implications can be identified as under:

(a) The individual responsibility of each minister holding a portfolio for formulating departmental policies to oversee their implementation and to ensure efficient working of the administrative machinery under his charge;

(b) The supremacy of Parliament over the executive and the right of Parliament to review the working of administrative machinery;
(c) The collective responsibility of the council of ministers to Parliament and the determination of major policies by the cabinet;
(d) The obligation of every civil servant to implement faithfully all policies and decisions of the ministers, even if these be contrary to the advice tendered by him;
(e) The obligation of minister as well as of civil servants to uphold the Constitution and the rule of law;
(f) The observance by civil servants of the principles of political neutrality, impartiality and anonymity; and
(g) The freedom of civil servants to express themselves frankly in tendering advice to their superiors, including ministers.

There is an absolute consensus on these issues and the new generation of political representatives and civil servants, notwithstanding their weakening colonial orientations has started subscribing to the constitutional objectives. The goals of democracy, socialism, secularism, liberalism and nationalism have become clearer and perceivable. Education, legislation, mass media and technologies have helped the rulers and the ruled to march in the desired direction. Institutional framework which was fragile in the initial years has hardened and the infrastructure has proliferated to keep the frame in a tight mould. In other words, the colonial system of running the government through bureaucracy without political leaders is a matter of history now and shall never be revived. The administration may resent the new relationship but the newer generation accepts the collaboration. The political leaders are accepting the compulsions of electoral process and the civil servants realise the relevance of ministerial responsibility. Naturally, this can neither be on the lines of UK or USA. The Indian experience is unique and so different patterns of institutions, and behaviours must emerge in response to contemporary experiences which have very little to do with history. The legacies of freedom struggle will linger and both the political and administrative leaders will cherish them. But the 21st century India will architect a new governance in which political representatives and administrative elites will have a new partnership in the constitutional framework of a techno-nuclear nation.

The Ministries and Departments

The evolution of central secretariat in India during the British period and after the exit of the British government can be studied from three distinct angles, (1) the structural proliferation, (2) the personnel reforms, and (3) the procedural revisions in terms of revised goals. Every constitutional Act, when it introduced political reforms, it brought corresponding administrative changes without much noise. The two World Wars expanded government activities and inducted qualitative changes in the procedural workings of the secretariat. Policies like association of natives and development of self-governing institutions in India expanded and reformed the secretariat on the pattern of White Hall as is evident from the number of ministries and the nature and volume of work, which these ministries handle. A spate of committee reports helped in the expansion and development of ninety years from 1858 to 1947. The names and numbers of departments explain this expansion in their evolutionary perspective.

Departments in the Secretariat

Year	*Names of the Department*
1858	(1) Foreign
	(2) Home
	(3) Financial
	(4) Military
1909	(1) Foreign
	(2) Home
	(3) Military
	(4) Finance
	(5) Public Works
1919	(1) Army
	(2) Foreign and Political
	(3) Finance
	(4) Home
	(5) Legislative
	(6) Education
	(7) Commerce and Industry
	(8) Revenue and Agriculture
	(9) Public Works
1939	(1) Defence
	(2) External Affairs
	(3) Finance
	(4) Home
	(5) Legislative
	(6) Education, Health and Lands
	(7) Commerce
	(8) Labour
	(9) Railways
	(10) Communications

Year	*Names of the Department*
1945	(1) War
	(2) Defence
	(3) External Affairs
	(4) Finance
	(5) Civil Defence
	(6) Home
	(7) Information and Broadcasting
	(8) Legislative
	(9) Commonwealth Relations
	(10 Agriculture
	(11) Education
	(12) Health
	(13) Supply
	(14) Food
	(15) Industries and Civil Supplies
	(16) Commerce
	(17) Labour
	(18) War Transport
	(19) Ports and Air Transport
	(20) Planning and Development
	(21) Railway
1946	(1) War
	(2) External Affairs
	(3) Commonwealth Relations
	(4) Finance
	(5) Home
	(6) Legislative
	(7) Agriculture
	(8) Education
	(9) Commerce
	(10) Labour
	(11) Food
	(12) Industries and Supplies
	(13) Information and Arts
	(14) Ports and Air Transport
	(15) Railways
	(16) War Transports
	(17) Works, Mines and Power
	(18) Health

The advent of freedom witnessed the ascendance of an interim government and partition of the country, which completely reordered the priorities of administrative work. The National government of partitioned India restructured the old departments of the central secretariat and worked with 20 departments before the new Republican Constitution got inaugurated in 1950. The situation between 15th August 1947 to June 1954, witnessed the bunching of departments into ministries as under:

1947 (18 Ministries)	*1954 (20 Ministries)*
(1) Defence	(1) Defence
(2) External Affairs and Commonwealth Relations	(2) External Affairs and Commonwealth Relations
(3) Finance	(3) Finance
(4) Home	(4) Home
(5) States	(5) States
(6) Information and Broadcasting	(6) Information and Broadcasting
(7) Law	(7) Law
(8) Agriculture	(8) Agriculture and Food
(9) Education	(9) Education
(10) Health	(10) Health
(11) Food	(11) Industry and Commerce
(12) Industry and Supplies	(12) Labour
(13) Commerce	(13) Transport
(14) Labour	(14) Railways
(15) Transport	(15) Communications
(16) Railways	(16) Works and Housing
(17) Communication	(17) Production
(18) Works, Mines and Power	(18) Irrigation and Power
	(19) Relief Rehabilitation
	(20) Parliamentary Affairs

The lists indicate that for two new departments of relief and rehabilitation and parliamentary affairs, the old department were given the new nomenclatures with minor adjustments and merger. On the recommendations of Ayyangar Committee the bunching of departments into ministries started and the number departments shot up steadily in the 20th century. Economic development, federal tensions, technological advance, welfare responsibilities, problems of internal security, Atomic energy management and rural development completely changed the scenario. The 20 departments got regrouped into 43 ministries and exclusive departments without ministries. In the 21st century, the policies of liberalisation and globalisation have started making newer demands on the central secretariat. The ARC recommendations have become inadequate and coalition governments need larger and newer ministries with reforms. The enlarged central secretariat on 30th January 2003 was as under:

(1) Ministry of Agriculture
  (i) Department of Agriculture and Cooperation
  (ii) Department of Agricultural Research and Education
  (iii) Department of Animal Husbandry and Dairying
(2) Ministry of Agro and Rural Industries
(3) Ministry of Chemicals and Fertilizers
  (i) Department of Chemicals and Petro-Chemicals
  (ii) Department of Fertilizers
(4) Ministry of Civil Aviation
(5) Ministry of Coal
  (i) Department of Coal
  (ii) Department of Mines
(6) Ministry of Commerce and Industry
  (i) Department of Commerce
  (ii) Department of Industrial Policy and Promotion
(7) Ministry of Communications and Information Technology
  (i) Department of Telecommunications
  (ii) Department of Post
  (iii) Department of Information Technology
(8) Ministry of Defence
  (i) Department of Defence
  (ii) Department of Defence Production and Supplies
(9) Ministry of Disinvestment
(10) Ministry of Environment and Forests
(11) Ministry of External Affairs
(12) Ministry of Finance
  (i) Department of Economic Affairs
  (ii) Department of Expenditure
  (iii) Department of Revenue
  (iv) Department of Company Affairs
(13) Ministry of Consumer Affairs, Food and Public Distribution
  (i) Department of Consumer Affairs
  (ii) Department of Food and Public Distribution
(14) Ministry of Food Processing Industries
(15) Ministry of Health and Family Welfare
  (i) Department of Health
  (ii) Department of Family Welfare
  (iii) Department of Indian Systems of Medicine and Homoeopathy
(16) Ministry of Heavy Industries and Public Enterprises
  (i) Department of Heavy Industries
  (ii) Department of Public Enterprises

(17) Ministry of Home Affairs
- (i) Department of Internal Security
- (ii) Department of States
- (iii) Department of Official Language
- (iv) Department of Home
- (v) Department of Jammu & Kashmir Affairs

(18) Ministry of Human Resource Development
- (i) Department of Elementary Education and Literacy
- (ii) Department of Secondary Education and Higher Education
- (iii) Department of Women and Child Development

(19) Ministry of Information and Broadcasting

(20) Ministry of Labour

(21) Ministry of Law and Justice
- (i) Department of Legal Affairs
- (ii) Legislative Department
- (iii) Department of Justice

(22) Ministry of Mines

(23) Ministry of Non-Conventional Energy Sources

(24) Ministry of Parliamentary Affairs

(25) Ministry of Personnel, Public Grievances and Pensions
- (i) Department of Personnel and Training
- (ii) Department of Administrative Reforms and Public Grievances
- (iii) Department of Pensions and Pensioners' Welfare

(26) Ministry of Petroleum and Natural Gas

(27) Ministry of Planning

(28) Ministry of Power

(29) Ministry of Railways

(30) Ministry of Road Transport and Highways

(31) Ministry of Rural Development
- (i) Department of Rural Development
- (ii) Department of Land Resources
- (iii) Department of Drinking Water Supply

(32) Ministry of Science and Technology
- (i) Department of Science and Technology
- (ii) Department of Scientific and Industrial Research
- (iii) Department of Bio-Technology

(33) Ministry of Small Scale Industries

(34) Ministry of Statistics and Programme Implementation

(35) Ministry of Shipping

(36) Ministry of Steel

(37) Ministry of Textiles
(38) Ministry of Tourism and Culture
 (i) Department of Tourism
 (ii) Department of Culture
(39) Ministry of Tribal Affairs
(40) Ministry of Urban Development and Poverty Alleviation
 (i) Department of Urban Development
 (ii) Department of Urban Employment and Poverty Alleviation
(41) Ministry of Water Resources
(42) Ministry of Social Justice and Empowerment
(43) Ministry of Youth Affairs and Sports
(44) Department of Atomic Energy
(45) Department of Ocean Development
(46) Department of Space
(47) Cabinet Secretariat
(48) President's Secretariat
(49) Prime Minister's Office
(50) Planning Commission
(51) Department of Development of North Eastern Region

A closer analysis of the arrangement indicates that expansion has taken places in the areas of science and technology and welfare tribal as well as urban. The shift from one party rule to coalition ministries is also reflected in the governance of the nation with atomic power. The industrial and commercial ministries have expanded with new emphasis on consumer affairs and food processing The ministry of disinvestment (now abolished) reflects the impact of privatisation policies. The eight departments of atomic energy, ocean development and space and three secretariats of the president, cabinet and PM (office) along with Planning Commission and North-eastern Region Development represent the addition of new department organisations to the central secretariat.

The bunching of departments or their bifurcation and shifting them from one ministry to another is purely a prerogative of the Prime Minister. He with his team of advisers has to do this exercise in terms of workload and allied nature of subjects and their relevance in a particular context. Of course, some ministries are more important than others but mere size is not the criteria. The cabinet ministers, ministers independently in charge, deputy ministers and key portfolios have to be adjusted. The solo department ministries and independent departments without ministries have always been there although the usual pattern is that there are two or three departments. Exceptionally, big ministries have four or even five departments to take care of cognate matters. This facilitates coordination. Politics changes often force bifurcations or amalgamation of departments and innocuous ministries like social welfare, rural development, coal, textiles and company affairs, etc., often face the axe to accommodate individuals. Home, finance, defence and HRD are the key ministries and their ministers are always in the cabinet. To ensure homogeneity, speed and purposeful functioning, the ARC has in its report said that in selecting his colleagues, the Prime Minister should give special attention to considerations of political standing, personal integrity, intellectual ability and capacity for taking decisions and sustained application to work.

Some major recommendations of the ARC with regard to administrative organisation of ministries are:

(1) The strength of the council of ministers should normally be 40. It may be increased in special circumstance but should in no case exceed 45.
(2) The three-tier system in the ministerial set-up, comprising cabinet ministers, ministers of state and deputy ministers may continue. The office of parliamentary secretary, which has now fallen into desuetude, need not be revived.
(3) The Prime Minister should be given institutional support, in the form of a Deputy Prime Minister, for ensuring efficient and effective functioning of the governmental machinery. The Deputy Prime Minister should have the charge, in addition to his own portfolio. The office of the Deputy Prime Minister should be recognised in the Transaction of Business Rules.
(4) The Prime Minister should not ordinarily be incharge of a ministry. His time should mostly be available for guidance, coordination and supervision.
(5) An ad hoc committee of ministers may be set up for investigating (but not deciding) particular issues and reporting to the cabinet or the appropriate cabinet committees, as the case may be.
(6) The official relationship of secretary to the minister should be one of loyalty and of the minister to the secretary one of confidence.
(7) For the reinforcing the principle of collective responsibility, it is essential that (a) the cabinet should be agreed on fundamentals and all important issues are discussed and settled by the cabinet; (b) a minister does not announce a new policy or a major departure from current policy without the approval of the cabinet; and (c) a minister should not ordinarily speak or make announcements on matters not within his portfolio.
(8) Standing committees of Parliament may be set up for reviewing the work of departments grouped in five sectors, namely, social services, economic administration, defence and foreign affairs, food and rural development, and transport.
(9) There should be only two levels of consideration below the minister, namely, (i) under secretary/deputy secretary, and (ii) joint secretary/additional secretary/secretary. Work should be assigned to each of those two levels on the line of 'desk officer' system.
(10) There should be set up in each ministry or major administrative department a policy advisory committee to consider all important issues of long-term policy and to inject thinking inputs from different areas of specialisation into problem-solving.
(11) The Department of Administrative Reforms should confine itself mainly to: (a) studies on administrative reforms of a foundational character, (b) building up O&M expertise in ministries/departments and training the personnel.
(12) A Council on Administrative Reforms be set up to advise the central reforms agency to review progress and induct fresh thinking.

Every time when a new government is formed or is reconstituted in India, the existing ministries are tampered with. It has become not so much a question of choosing ministers for portfolios as of finding portfolios for ministers chosen on regional, communal and other considerations. By a hasty permutation and combination of departments and functions and the addition of executive responsibilities, the required number of ministerial charges is settled.

A smaller cabinet comprising the conventional portfolios of external affairs, home, defence, finance and law, and integrated portfolios of commerce and industry, communications, social service, food and agriculture, each with clearly distinguishable departments in charge of ministers of state supported by deputy ministers needs to be created. Ministries such as industrial development and internal trade, foreign trade and supply cannot function in isolation and should be brought together under the unified control of a single minister. Similarly, railways, transport and shipping, communication and civil aviation should constitute another portfolio. The functions of the ministries such as education, health and labour, should also be combined in one ministry. Food and agriculture might continue as an entity for the time being, but it should interest itself largely with research and co-ordination. These changes should make for a more harmonious relationship between the Union and the states and take the sting out of the demand for a redefinition of union-state relations.

If the state undertakings dispersed in several ministries were to be brought together and placed under an autonomous development board working in close collaboration with the Planning Commission and made accountable to the Prime Minister, assisted by a minister of state, uniformity in employment and procurement policies could be ensured and a national organisation built up for industrial research and designs. A cabinet minister in principle should have a single secretary as his official counterpart. No other arrangement can be conducive to efficiency and economy, In pre-Independence days, each department had a secretary supported by the required number of deputy-secretaries and under-secretaries. But there is hardly a ministry at the centre today, which has a single secretary. In fact, periodic reviews need to be undertaken every fifth year to keep the size out strength of the secretariat in healthy balance and good trim.

Ministry of Home Affairs

Organisational Structure

Presided by the Home Minister of India, it is the nodal ministry, which performs the largest number of key functions of the government. Out of some nine hundred odd functions of total government work, the home ministry performs 165, which is the largest number of functions of heterogeneous nature that effect every citizen and each area of Union government. The former home department now consists of five departments, which have been entrusted to its care. Time and again it has been enlarged and sliced but its nature, as 'Mother Ministry' remains uncharged. All residual matters which do not fall under the jurisdiction of any other ministry are instantly handed over to home ministry as the Residuary Legate. Naturally therefore the administration of subjects like census and elections remain in the jurisdiction of this all encompassing ministry, which is the foster mother of the Government of India since its very inception.

Born in 1843, when the secretariat of the 'Supreme Government' was separated from that of the Government of Bengal, it was organised into six branches: (i) General branch, (ii) Revenue branch, (iii) Marine branch, (iv) Judicial branch, (v) Legislative branch, and (vi) Ecclesiastical branch. It was deliberately conceived to be the residuary legatee for functions of heterogeneous nature. Personnel matters, internal law and order including political matters, jails, police, factories, explosives, petroleum, education, public works, public health, hospitals, municipalities and local boards, etc., constituted the exhaustive list of unrelated subjects which were lived off with time. The following dates need mention in its evolution:

1855 A separate public works department was created by transfer from home department.
1964 A new department of administrative reforms was carved out from home ministry.
1965 Assam Rifles were transferred from external affairs ministry to home ministry.

1970 Personnel and civil services were transferred to the newly created department of personnel.

1973 The department of administrative reform got merged with the department of personnel, then located in cabinet secretariat.

1977 Personnel and administrative reforms shifted back to home ministry.

1985 The two taken out of home ministry and reorganised into a new ministry of personnel, public grievances and pensions.
Subjects pertaining to SC and ST taken away and given to ministry of welfare.

1995 Organised into four departments and a minister of state was given the charge of internal security.

1996 The fifth department of Jammu & Kashmir affairs was added.

In fact, the structure of the Government of India has evolved from chunks of subjects, which have been taken away from the home department to form separate departments. The hiving of two functions of the home ministry and the creation of two new ministries still leaves a vast and varied jurisdiction to the home ministry.

In 1989, the ministry had four departments under it, viz., the department of internal security, the department of home, the department of states, and the department of official language. Now instead of four, it has five departments:

Ministry of Home Affairs: Organisational Structure

Ministry of Home Affairs

MOS

Dy. Minister

MOS

1. Department of Home
2. Department of Internal Security
3. Department of States

Home Secretary

Secretary Official Language

4. Department of Official Language
5. Department of Jammu & Kashmir Affairs

Special Secretaries

Joint Secretaries

Directors

Deputy Secretaries

Under Secretaries

Class III and IV staff

Due to terrorist activities the subject of Jammu & Kashmir was elevated to the status of a department of Jammu & Kashmir affairs in 1994. It was formerly under the charge of the Prime Minister. The former Kashmir division of the ministry was transferred to this newly created department. The home secretary remains the secretary, department of Jammu & Kashmir affairs to facilitate greater co-ordination of policy and handling of Jammu & Kashmir affairs.

In 1993, the legislative assembly of National Capital of Delhi was constituted and a five member National Human Rights Commission has also come into existence. Normally, the ministry is presided by a senior cabinet minister, who is helped by a minister of state and a deputy minister. The ministry is headed by an IAS secretary who by tradition has been a senior secretary. Moreover, there are a number of additional, joint, deputy and under secretaries to assist him. There are a number of directors also. The landmark dates of evolution are:

1971: The home ministry's secretariat consisted of 96 officers of all categories, two secretaries (the number was reduced to one after the transfer of the department of administrative reforms).

1973: One additional secretary, 12 joint secretaries, 29 deputy secretaries and 34 under secretaries were working and the ministry stood divided into 19 divisions with a deputy secretary at the head of each of them.

1974: There were 5 attached and 8 subordinate offices under the ministry.

1985: This number had gone up to 6 and 13 respectively.

1988: There were nearly 3.25 lakh posts under the ministry.

2004: The ministry stands divided into 26 divisions with a deputy secretary at the head of each of them.

2006: There are 7 attached, 8 subordinate, and 3 advisory offices under the ministry.

These 26 divisions of the ministry are:

(1) Administration and O&M Division
(2) Administration Vigilance Division
(3) All India Services Division
(4) Central Secretariat Service Division
(5) Establishment Division
(6) Foreignness and Citizenship Division
(7) Judicial Division
(8) Emergency Help Division
(9) Establishment Officers Division
(10) Police Division
(11) Political Division
(12) State Reorganisation Division-I
(13) State Reorganisation Division-II
(14) Union Territories Division
(15) Union Territories Legislative Division
(16) Official Language Division
(17) Kashmir Division
(18) Welfare Division
(19) Finance and Accounts Division
(20) Public Peace Directorates

(21) Public Division
(22) Public Grievance Division
(23) Training Division
(24) Joint Advisory and Arbitration Division
(25) Secretariat Security Organisation
(26) Resources and Policy Division

Each division is under a deputy secretary. Some divisions like policy, research and welfare divisions have directors also. The Parliamentary Advisory Committees too operate through the officials of these divisions.

The Functions of Home Ministry

The functions, duties and responsibilities of the home ministry are reflected in the organisation of its departments, its attached and subordinate offices, its committees, commissions and executive agencies. Broadly speaking, the home ministry of Union government perform the following functions:

(1) Maintenance of internal security, communal harmony and public peace in the country
(2) Management of Union police agencies and IPS cadre
(3) Modernisation of state police forces
(4) Administration of union territories
(5) Monitoring of union-state relation
(6) Civil defence
(7) Appointments and transfers of High Court judges
(8) Development of Hindi as Official Language
(9) Overseeing of protocol functions, census operations, elections, citizenship immigration, etc.
(10) Combatting insurgency and Kashmir affairs.

The organisation of five departments of the ministry speak of its major responsibilities and the jobs in allied areas They are numerous and expanding in relation to tasks, personnel management and training needs and provide the infrastructure for the state administrations to be efficient and effective at each level. The functional and departmentwise organisation of the Ministry stands as under:

Internal Security Department

There are 21 organisations, which department of the home ministry looks after. Most of them are located in far distant places and supply staff aid and other services for the administration of Union subjects and state governments. The Government of India has changed several acts or statutes for the maintenance of internal security and allied police operations. The Internal Security department looks after the implementation of the following acts:

(1) Arms, Fire Arms, Ammunitions and Explosive Substance Act 1908
(2) Official Secrets Act 1923
(3) Illegal Activities (Prevention) Act 1967
(4) Foreign Aid (Regularisation) Act 1976

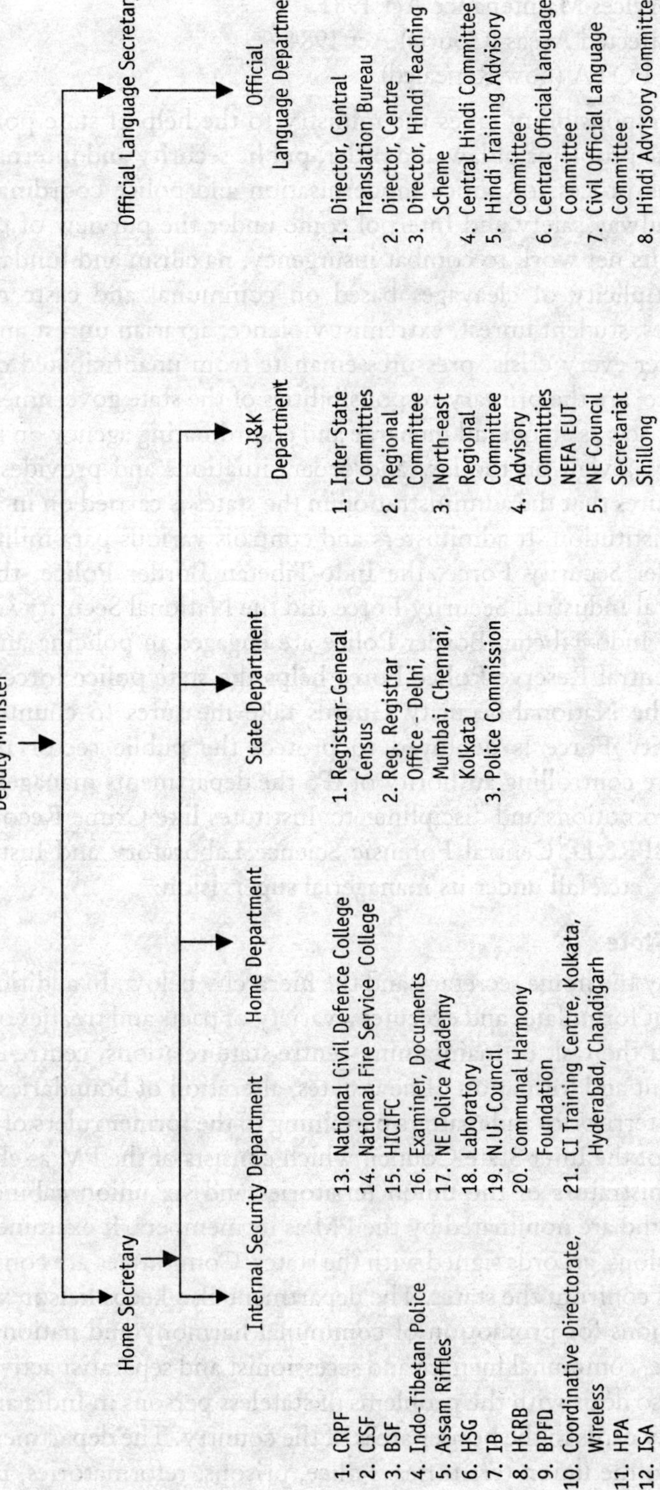
Ministry of Home Affairs
Home Minister
Minister of State
Deputy Minister
Home Secretary
Official Language Secretary
Internal Security Department
Home Department
State Department
J&K Department
Official Language Department
1. CRPF
2. CISF
3. BSF
4. Indo-Tibetan Police
5. Assam Riffles
6. HSG
7. IB
8. HCRB
9. BPFD
10. Coordinative Directorate, Wireless
11. HPA
12. ISA
13. National Civil Defence College
14. National Fire Service College
15. HICIFC
16. Examiner, Documents
17. NE Police Academy
18. Laboratory
19. N.U. Council
20. Communal Harmony Foundation
21. CI Training Centre, Kolkata, Hyderabad, Chandigarh
1. Registrar-General Census
2. Reg. Registrar Office - Delhi, Mumbai, Chennai, Kolkata
3. Police Commission
1. Inter State Committies
2. Regional Committee
3. North-east Regional Committee
4. Advisory Committies NEFA EUT
5. NE Council Secretariat Shillong
1. Director, Central Translation Bureau
2. Director, Centre
3. Director, Hindi Teaching Scheme
4. Central Hindi Committee
5. Hindi Training Advisory Committee
6. Central Official Language Committee
7. Civil Official Language Committee
8. Hindi Advisory Committee

(5) Essential Services Maintenance Act 1981
(6) Terrorist Affected Areas (Courts) Act 1984
(7) TADA and POTA (now Repealed)

This legal responsibility takes the ministry to the help of state police administration, which struggles with the problems of law and order, public security and internal peace and tranquillity in the country. The process of police modernisation and police coordination with organisation of vigilance, jail, railway safety and Interpol come under the purview of the department, which has lately expanded its net work to combat insurgency, naxalism and fundamentalism in the country. There is a multiplicity of cleavages based on communal and caste cleavages, secessionist and terrorist activities, student unrest, extremist violence, agrarian unrest and religious fundamentalist movements. After every crisis, pressures emanate from unanticipated quarters. Although 'public order' and 'police' are the primary responsibilities of the state governments. The ministry of home affairs, however, acts as an overall incharge and co-ordinating agency on matters relating to internal security. It keeps a vigil on the law and order situations and provides assistance to the states if necessary. It ensures that the administration in the states is carried on in accordance with the provisions of the Constitution. It administers and controls various para-military forces like the Assam Rifles, the Border Security Force, the Indo-Tibetan Border Police, the Central Reserve Police Force, the Central Industrial Security Force and the National Security Guards. The Assam Riffles, the BSF and the Indo-Tibetan Border Police are engaged in policing and protecting the northern borders. The Central Reserve Police Force helps the state police forces if large-scale civil disturbances erupt. The National Security Guards take measures to counter terrorism. The Central Industrial Security Force is deployed to protect the public sector undertakings and national airports. As cadre controlling authority of IPS the departments manages matters pertaining to IPS training, pay, promotions and discipline etc. Institutes like Crime Records Bureau, Directorate of Coordination, BPR&D, Central Forensic Science Laboratory and Institute of Criminology and Forensic Science, etc., fall under its managerial supervision.

Department of State

It is controlled by the home secretary and the hierarchy below. In addition to several constitutional responsibilities, it formulates and executes a variety of pacts and treaties on behalf of the ministry. It is entrusted with the task of maintaining centre-state relations, centre-union territories relations. The establishment and formation of new states, alteration of boundaries and names of the existing states and union territories and matters pertaining to the former rulers of princely states. It manages the functioning of the Inter-State Council which consists of the PM as chairman, chief ministers of states and administrators of the union territories and six union cabinet ministers including the home minister who are nominated by the PM as its members. It examines the recommendations of various commissions, accords signed with the states. Committees are constituted to search solutions of problems that confront the states. The department also keeps liaison with the state governments and sends directions for promotion of communal harmony and national integration. Curbing of terrorist violence, communal menace and secessionist and separatist activities fare in the purview of the council. It also deals with the problems of stateless persons in India and has undertaken the task of issuing identity cards in the border areas of the country. The department supervises the extension of Union laws to the union territories. Police, prisons, reformatories, public order and questions relating to public services are looked after by it. Some of the developmental activities like water supply, power, industries, agriculture, fisheries, education, health, social welfare, rural development, tourism and transport and interstate conflicts require the use of its coordinational machinery. Creation of new states and monitoring of welfare schemes in lesser developed areas and states are its major responsibilities.

Department of Home

It is a nodal agency of the ministry for policy administration. Some of its major responsibilities can be enumerated as under:

(1) Issue of notifications for the election of President and Vice President and other Dignitaries
(2) Appointments, leave, transfer and resignation of Governors, judges, etc.
(3) Nomination of members to Rajya Sabha and Lok Sabha (Anglo-Indians)
(4) Citizenship and immigration matters
(5) Declaration of emergency proclamation and formulating arrangements to handle situations under Articles 352, 356 and 358
(6) Administering varied matters such as patents, national anthem and flag, pension of freedom fighters, foreign aid to voluntary associations, awards minorities, census operations, etc.

It handles personnel problems of union territories and is concerned with matters relating to the code of conduct of legislators and ministers and nominations to the Parliament. It obtains the prior approval of the President on the promulgation of ordinances by the Governors and deals with the bills passed by the state legislatures and are further reserved for the consideration of the President. This department deals with matters like grants of pardons, remissions, suspension or commutation of death sentences and petitions for remission of sentences excluding death sentences. Warrant of precedence, formalities to be observed on the death of dignitaries and allowances and relief to be provided to persons who have rendered distinguished service to the nation are also looked after by it.

Department of Official Language

The department was created to implement policy nuances implied in the Official Language Act 1963 (amended in 1967). It issues directions to ensure that the act is implemented in spirit. Its responsibility is to create an infrastructure through training, translations and information centres that Hindi develops as the official language of the Union government by developing bilingualism to begin with. The Central Translation Bureau, the Kendriya Hindi Samiti and the Hindi Salahkar Samitis set up by the various ministries and departments work under its supervision. The cadre management of the Central Secretariat Official Language Service is its function. The official language department implements the provision of the Constitution concerning the official language and the Official Language Act, 1963. It obtains the prior approval of the President of India for authorising the limited use of languages other than English in the proceedings in state High Courts. In addition, it has the nodal responsibility for matters concerning the gradual use of Hindi as the official language of the Union. To coordinate all matters relating to the progressive use of Hindi as the official language of India the department has following agencies under its care:

(1) Director, Central Translation Bureau
(2) Director, Central Hindi Training

(3) Director, Hindi Teaching Scheme
(4) Central Hindi Committee
(5) Hindi Training Advisory Committee
(6) Central Official Language Committee
(7) Hindi Advisory Committee

The Constituent Assembly passed the resolution regarding inclusion of Article 343 by a thin majority. This Article declares, "the official language of the Union shall be Hindi in Devanagri script". Section (2) of that Article, however, says that: "for a period of fifteen years from the commencement of the Constitution, the English language shall continue to be used for all the official purposes of the Union for which it was being used immediately before such commencement". This period has been subsequently extended to an indefinite date. Similarly Section 345 allows the legislature of a state to adopt Hindi or a state language or English as the official language. Most of the states have passed these laws about official language. According to Article 346 the language of communication between one state and another state and between a state and the union will be decided by a mutual agreement of both the states.

Hindi is a language spoken and understood by a majority of the people and is well suited to be the link language. It forms the largest linguistic group and is spoken by 30.4 per cent followed by Telugu (8.6%), Bengali (7.7%), Marathi (7.6%) and Tamil (7%). The upper classes including the middle class intelligentsia, have chosen to accept English as their medium of communication. The unfriendly milieu readers the task of the department all the move difficult. A multi-pronged strategy for the development and spread of Hindi is annually planned by the department and its subordinate offices spread all over the country. The Figures on the following pages outline the administrative structure of official language department of the ministry of home in details.

There are eight regional offices of the department which operate from: (1) Mumbai, (2) Kolkata, (3) Bangalore, (4) Bhopal, (5) Ghaziabad, (6) Guwahati, (7) Cochin, and (8) Delhi. Two magazines entitled *Rajbhasha Bharati* and *Rajbhasha Pushpmala* are published by the department to popularise Hindi and its vocabulary.

Department of Jammu & Kashmir Affairs

The new department was constituted in 1994 because of Prime Minister Rao's policy to combat terrorism on a wider and global scale. Till 1984, Kashmir affairs were with the Prime Minister, but they were reorganised and transferred in 1994 and then again in 1998. Jammu & Kashmir has a special position in the Constitution of India. It has suffered insurgency, aggression and communal violence almost since 1947. Article 371 impels the Union government to take special care of the people of Kashmir who confront cross-border terrorism from Pak occupied part of the state. The home ministry, which is responsible for public peace, civil defence and unity and integrity of the country, strives through this department that special problems of Jammu & Kashmir are taken care of as an integral part of the Indian Union.

The five departments of the home ministry along with hosts of subordinate and attached offices, commissions and advisory committees perform a variety of functions for which the ministry exists as a serving agency. It is a multifunctional ministry and the core and allied functions extend to all the states and union territories during peace and emergency. The functions performed by five departments take care of subjects in the Union List, Concurrent List and administration of the union territories. More than 100 subjects fall in this jurisdiction. All these jobs are accomplished with the aid advise and executive operations of the attached and subordinate offices of the ministry.

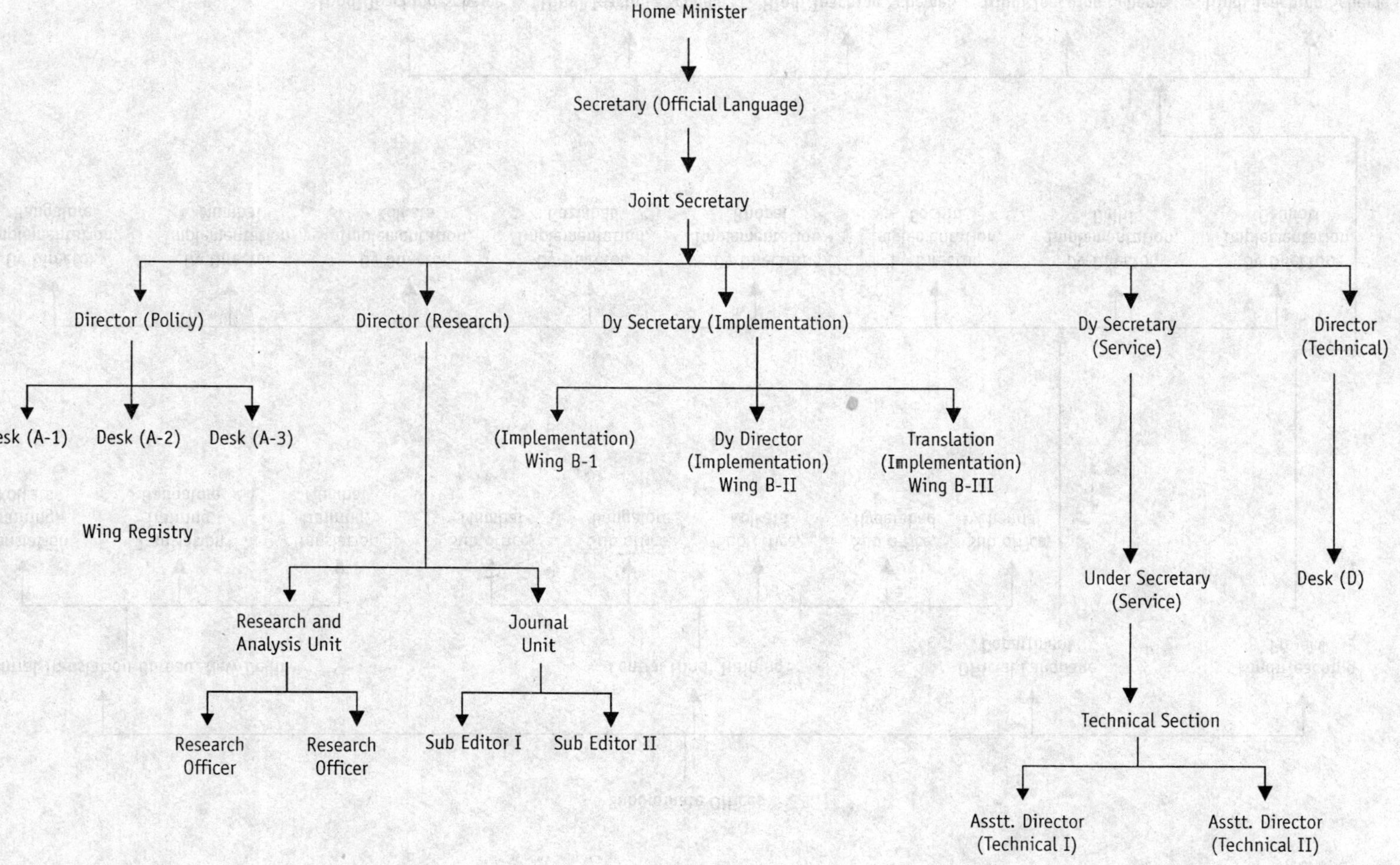
Official Language Department
Home Minister
Secretary (Official Language)
Joint Secretary
Director (Policy)
Director (Research)
Dy Secretary (Implementation)
Dy Secretary (Service)
Director (Technical)
Desk (A-1)
Desk (A-2)
Desk (A-3)
Wing Registry
(Implementation) Wing B-1
Dy Director (Implementation) Wing B-II
Translation (Implementation) Wing B-III
Under Secretary (Service)
Desk (D)
Research and Analysis Unit
Journal Unit
Research Officer
Research Officer
Sub Editor I
Sub Editor II
Technical Section
Asstt. Director (Technical I)
Asstt. Director (Technical II)

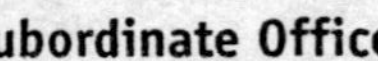

Subordinate Offices

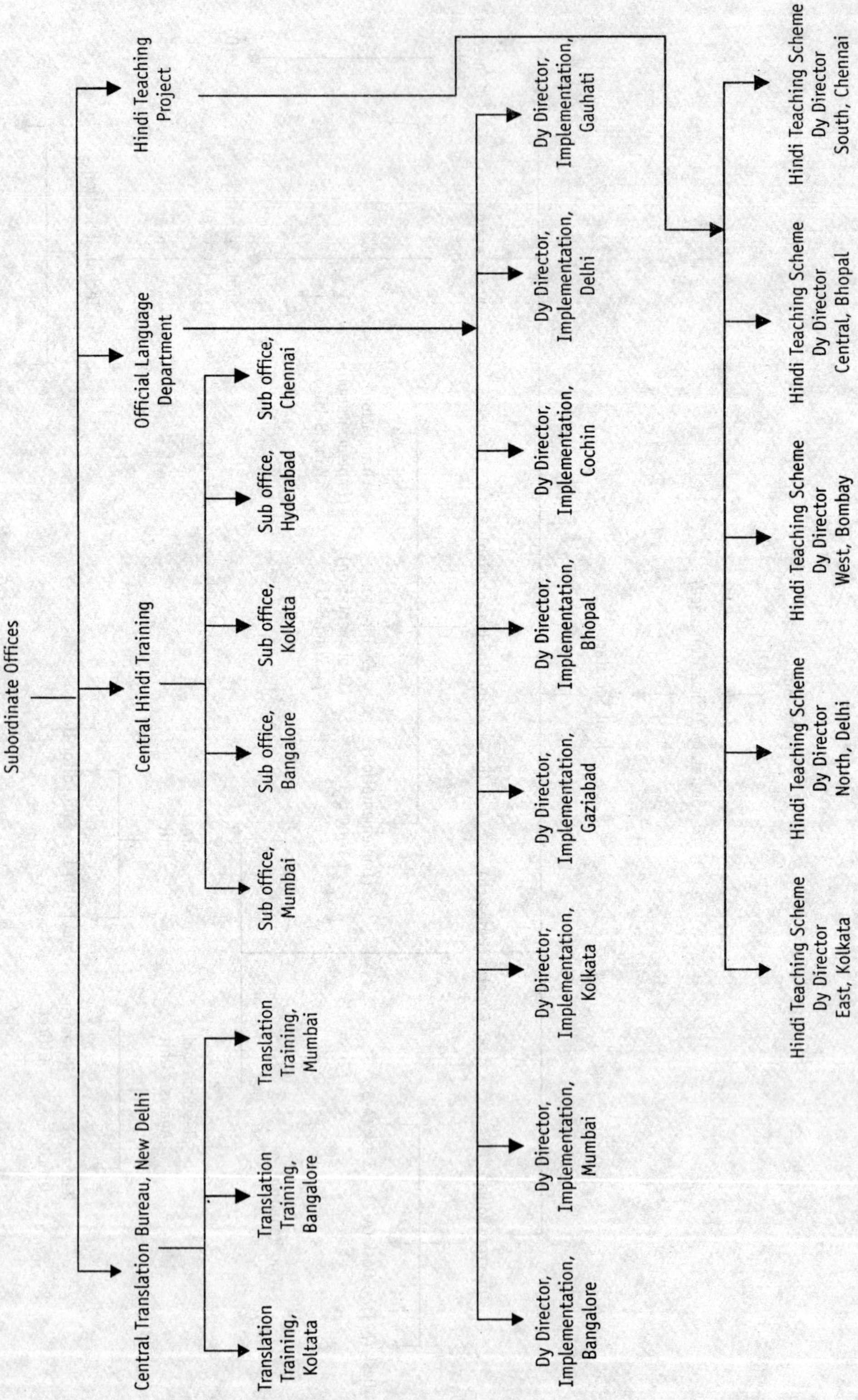

- Subordinate Offices
  - Central Translation Bureau, New Delhi
    - Translation Training, Koltata
    - Translation Training, Bangalore
    - Translation Training, Mumbai
  - Central Hindi Training
    - Sub office, Mumbai
    - Sub office, Bangalore
    - Sub office, Kolkata
    - Sub office, Hyderabad
    - Sub office, Chennai
  - Official Language Department
    - Dy Director, Implementation, Bangalore
    - Dy Director, Implementation, Mumbai
    - Dy Director, Implementation, Kolkata
    - Dy Director, Implementation, Gaziabad
    - Dy Director, Implementation, Bhopal
    - Dy Director, Implementation, Cochin
    - Dy Director, Implementation, Delhi
    - Dy Director, Implementation, Gauhati
  - Hindi Teaching Project
    - Hindi Teaching Scheme Dy Director East, Kolkata
    - Hindi Teaching Scheme Dy Director North, Delhi
    - Hindi Teaching Scheme Dy Director West, Bombay
    - Hindi Teaching Scheme Dy Director Central, Bhopal
    - Hindi Teaching Scheme Dy Director South, Chennai

Attached Offices

Central Intelligence Bureau, New Delhi

It started as a Thugi department in 1887. Its task is to collect intelligence and relevant information about political activities. In 1904, it was renamed as criminal intelligence department to keep a vigil over nationalist and terrorist activities. It acquired its present name and status in 1918. After two years, it was converted into a Bureau and non-political intelligence was also added to its fold. Located in the cabinet secretariat, its activities have expanded into several regional branches. The Delhi director is the Controller of the Bureau operations.

Central Bureau of Investigation, Delhi

It is a very popular organisation called CBI. It was established as an anticorruption agency in 1963 and social agencies doing similar jobs were merged into it. Today, its jurisdiction extends to all grave crimes of political and criminal nature in Union and state governments and also in public sector enterprises of varied nature. It does intelligence of all kinds and its research and investigation network encompasses entire public life. The internal organisation of CBI is quite elaborate to investigate frauds, scandals, scams, interstate criminality and operations of mafias and dons of the underworld. It has earned a fair name and image for its impartial and non-political handling of criminal investigations. It works in close collaboration with Interpol and its achievements have won laurels for the ministry. Recently, it has been given the status of a National Police Station.

L.B.S. National Academy of Administration, Mussoorie

Training academics are attached offices because they aid, assist and do research to make civil servants efficient and effective. The Mussoorie Academy was created in the year 1959 by the amalgamation of Indian Administrative Service Training School, Delhi and IAS Officers College, Shimla. The academy offers base foundational course to new entrants and in service training course for members of senior civil services of the country. Subject teaching apart, teaching of Hindi, computer applications, car driving, etc., is also given as a part of training programme to all India, Central and even state administrators who are invited for specialised courses.

Secretariat Training School, New Delhi

Started in May 1948, this school trains the ministerial staff and level II and III officers of Union government. It offers specialised and technical training in areas like accounts, financial rules and procedures, etc. Some of its training programmes are entry or refresher programmes of short duration.

Office of Registrar General Census, New Delhi

It was established as an attached office in 1951 to conduct census in free India for the first time. The Registrar General Census started operating since June 1953 and organised the new format for the decennial census of the country. It publishes its reports from time to time, non-economic data and information about weaker sections, women and minorities, etc., and are an essential component of census operations. The statewise statistics helps the state governments to formulate plans and policies.

Central Reserve Police, Neemach (MP)

Before independence, it was known as crown's representative police. After independence, it was supposed to work as a reserve police to be made available to the state in hours of crisis and emergencies. The CRPF comes to the issue of State Police Force on need and demand by the state. Emergency like communal riots, insurgency, Naxalite violence, labour unrest, VIP security are combatted by CRPF. The Director General of the Force keeps its battalions in readiness and nowadays they are deployed in conducting elections and insurgencies situations of grave variety.

Border Security Force, New Delhi

After the Indo-Pak War of 1965, the BSF was constituted to guard the borders. The state police was too inadequate to stop cross-border smuggling. Pakistan and Bangladesh borders being too long and volatile required special measures during peace. The BSF Acts 1968 entrusted specific functions of intelligence arrest of illegal immigrants and cross-border crimes on international border. A senior IPS officer acts as Inspector General of Force, which has its head office located in Delhi.

Bureau of Police Research and Development

The BPRD was established in 1970. The main objective of this research organisation is to modernise the police forces of India. The bureau collects data and suggests methods on the basis of police research to deal with newer techniques and technologies of crime prevention. It suggests periodic police research and it runs several police training centres at Kolkata, Hyderabad and Chandigarh. Massive aid for modernisation of weaponry and police equipment is funded by the bureau. It gives national awards for original police research and translation of materials.

Subordinate Offices of the Ministry of Home Affairs

The attached offices generally aid advise and do research, but the subordinate offices are more field-oriented. Although the distinction is not very neat and most of the offices in two categories perform both the sort of functions. The attached offices are generally technical, but the subordinate offices operate in interstate areas, training institutions apart offices dealing with union territories generally fall in this category. The important subordinate offices are:

S.V.P. National Policy Academy, Hyderabad

The academy started as Central Police Training College at Mount Abu in 1948. Later, it was elevated to the status of an academy and transferred to its new campus at Hyderabad. The NPA offers highly specialised professional training to IPS officers of various ranks. The foundational course apart, it has in-service training course like vertical interaction course, integrated training programme and short-term refresher programmes for group 'A' service including IAS, IPS and senior judicial official. A senior IPS officer of DG's rank is the director of the academy and police officers from several countries like Nepal, Sri Lanka, Bangladesh and African countries come to the NPA for police training in specialised areas.

Directorate of Coordination (Police wireless) New Delhi

It was established in 1950. The directorate does coordination function between police radio and communication services. The middle level technical police officers are trained in new techniques to modernise the communication services at state level.

National Fire Service College, Nagpur

Fire services being technical and risky need national effort in fire services modernisation. In 1956, the ministry of home upgraded this college, which was a small institute at Rampur. The latest equipments and firefighting techniques are taught to fire officers who perform a vital role in national security and property protection of the common man.

National Civil Defence College, Nagpur

Civil defence has a double objective. It protects public and civil property and facilitates industrial security. This college at Nagpur was started in 1957. Official and non-officials from NGOs are provided training in disaster management and handling of relief work and emergence situation.

Indo-Tibetan Border Police, New Delhi

It survives from British days and has the responsibility of protecting Indo-Tibetan borders. This border spreads from Ladakh to Lipu Lekh pass via Karakoram hills. The climatic conditions and the sensitive nature of border with China require this special police arrangement. Headed by a DIG, it has 25 battalions, 6 sectors and 3 training institutions. Four battalions of the force specialise in mountain warfare and commando activities. The force is engaged in stopping transborder smuggling. Its commando training is being utilised in VIP security and combatting Naxalite menace.

Regional Registration Office, Chennai

The foreign immigrants to India are registered in 4 regional offices of the home ministry at Delhi, Kolkata, Mumbai and Chennai. The regional offices other than at Chennai are controlled by state governments.

Mobile Civil Emergency Force, New Delhi

It is a new organisation created to help people during emergent situation of violence. Being mobile, it can be activated at a short notice and helps the local police in its routine operations.

Hindi Teaching Scheme – Regional Offices at Delhi, Mumbai, Kolkata and Chennai

The scheme was launched to popularise Hindi and train public services in non-Hindi speaking areas. A presidential order of 1960 makes it obligatory for all government employees below 45 years of age to learn Hindi. The regional offices here trained thousands of employees and the situation has materially changed in Hindi's favour.

Internal Security Academy, Mount Abu

On transfer of National Police Academy to Hyderabad in 1970, the old police school was converted into Internal Security Academy for the CRPF. The NSA organised various training programmes for new probations and senior police officers in areas like insurgency, hijacking, labour unrest and VIP security.

Central Industrial Security Force, New Delhi

The CISF was established in 1969 to provide security guards to vital industrial establishments and monuments of cultural value. Now, the force protects major airports of the country from insurgency hazards. The VIP security and protection of damns and oil refineries have been entrusted to its care and its strength has leaped from 3,000 to 96,000 in 30 years. It is governed by the Parliamentary Statute of 1968 and CISF rules of 1969. Presently, it is guarding the public sector enterprises of the Government of India.

The line between attached and subordinate offices in Government of India ministries has literally been blurred. These offices mushroom as per needs of the times and some disappear leaving the rest to acquire new shapes. But as the functions as ministries expand the scope of activities of these organisations is also expanding specially in the areas of training and technology.

Central Vigilance Commission

As a ministry incharge of the problems of civil services, the home ministry is alive to the mails of corruption in public services. The Southern Committee in its recommendation in 1964 suggested the establishment of this commission, which takes action on the basis of investigations made by CBI. But, it can take up cases and initiate any enquiry suro moto also. The commission submits its annual report to the government and if its recommendations are not heeded, it can invite governments attention by submitting supplementary reports. The position of the CVC is at par with UPSC and legally it is an advisory body, but the governments is bound to respect its advice. Administratively the commission has three branches:

(1) Head office
(2) Technical examination organisation
(3) Departmental enquiry and office of the commission.

The CVC has a cell in every ministry to perform its functions. The vigilance officers of the cells report to the director who coordinates their activities in collaboration with special police establishment. The vigilance officer's duties include:

(1) To mitigate the situations leading to corruption and harassment
(2) To do periodic inspections and raids
(3) To take immediate action in matters of corruption and malpractices

Advisory Bodies

The advisory bodies in the ministry of home are numerous and their functions include technical and non-technical jobs of varied nature.

Central Establishment Board

The board was established to make recommendations for placement of officers of under secretary level and above. The top posts of secretaries, ambassadors and officials of foreign office are outside its preview. The seven members of the board come from:

(1) Ministries (three representatives)
(2) Ministries of economic administrators (two representatives)
(3) Secretary Establishment, Government of India
(4) Cabinet Secretary – Chairman

The CEB is an agency of administrative experts for senior placements, but its recommendations are not sinking on the government.

Emergency Relief Organisation

The Central Advisory Committee for emergency relief performs two functions:

(1) To advise on emergency relief measures to the ERO

(2) To arouse public interest in emergency relief programmes and serve as a bridge between people and the government. The members of the CAC are:
   (i) Home Secretary (chairman)
   (ii) Deputy Secretary
   (iii) Nominee of government
   (iv) Two non-official members

It is a high power body and the chairmanship of home secretary makes it important.

Advisory Committee for Centrally Administered Union Territories

There are three such committees to advice the ministry about:

(1) Andaman and Nicobar Islands
(2) Lakshadweep, Minicoy and Amonideir Islands.
(3) Chandigarh

The advisory committees comprise of elected members, government officials and eminent people of the territory. The committees cover a wide ground and ensure popular participation in administration.

The administration of union territories is a special responsibility of the ministry. Before independence, centrally administered areas were:

(1) Ajmer
(2) Coorg
(3) Delhi
(4) Andaman and Nicobar

The integration of native states changed the situation. Under the new Constitution, they were named as a state. They were 10 in number. In 1950, Cooch Bihar was merged in Bengal and Bilaspur became a part of Himachal Pradesh. Andaman Nicobar continued under State Act 1951. Gradually Ajmer, Bhopal, Vindya Pradesh, Coorg and Conch got merged into Rajasthan, MP, Mysore and Maharashtra respectively. Presently, there are 7 centrally administrated territories, namely: (1) Andaman and Nicobar (2) Chandigarh (3) Dadra and Nagar Haveli (4) Daman and Diu (5) Delhi (6) Lakshadweep (7) Pondicherry. These territories are governed by state Governors who are responsible to the ministry of home affairs. Delhi and Pondicherry have state legislatives and advisory committees to ensure good government in these less developed areas.

The Ministry of Home Affairs is the most important ministry because its functions pertain to the very survival of our nation-state. These basic functions have given birth to several auxiliary functions and ancillary organisations and agencies, which create conditions conducive for national security and preservation of the integrity and unity of the nation. The number of crimes and criminals is escalating with a speed that state governments are increasingly depending upon union police agencies to keep the state together. International disruptive forces render the internal security grave and the home ministry's functions have started overlapping with the functions of ministry of defence and ministry of external affairs. Some of the functions of the home ministry can be summed up as under:

(1) Peace, tranquillity and law and order in the entire country.
(2) Regulation of senior civil services.
(3) Rule making for the creation and maintenance of high positions in administration.
(4) Coordination between Union and states and among states in national interest.
(5) Combatting corruption through various executive agencies and administrative reforms.
(6) Administration of union territories.
(7) Political management like issue of passports, declaration of pestilential rule in states, creation of new states or state upper houses, pardon and reprieve of death sentences, censor of objectiveness publications, etc.

Some of these functions need cordiality between Union and state government. The home ministry organised periodic conferences of governors, speakers, chief secretaries, DGs, etc., to stay in touch with live problems in the field. Electoral system brings a great strain upon the working of home ministry. Various kinds of armed establishment such as BSF, Railway Protection Force, Assam Rifles, Jammu & Kashmir Military, CISF, SPG and National Security Guards are to be kept in trim.

During peace times, these organisations are rigorously trained and when the chips are down they provide the impregnable security cover to the state administration. The intelligence services, the field formations and the training institutes keep the ministry's hand full and it has now launched home guards and civil defence organisations as stand by in case of emergencies. Kashmir, North-East and Naxalite pockets are constant headaches and combatting terrorism has become a principal function of the forces in the field. Civil service reforms need priority because the pressure of democracy, development and technology are forcing the government to have a new patterns of administration to which Indian bureaucracy is gradually being inducted. To bring efficiency and effectiveness to this public security works the following reforms are suggested:

(a) The legal codes, which are too old and out of date, must be scrapped and rewritten. Here amendments make situations worse. For instance, Indian Police Act 1961 and CRPS, IPC and Indian Evidence Act should be re-authored by committee of law experts and popular representatives.
(b) A permanent National Police Commission and State Police Commission must be constituted to monitor continuous reforms in police organisation. The Dharma Veer recommendations should be taken to their logical end as they too have become out of date.
(c) Training being a special function should be made professional. It has to be linked with promotion and punishment so that the reutilisation may yield results. In fact, training enterprise should be liberated from the clutches of senior administrators who treat trainer positions as punishment placements. Knowledge organisation should be the model of the training institutes which should be decentralised at field level.
(d) A Training, Research Reform Cell should be created in the home ministry. This cell should concretise administrative reform proposals on the basis of trainees' ideas and experience. A high level official should watch these feedbacks and suggest specific reforms in training as well as working of the organisation. It is more especially needed in police academies, which are headed by senior policeman not interested in their change.

(e) The union territories have diverse problems. Lakshadweep Islands and Goa are simple incomparable. A new policy is needed to merge Goa, Daman, Pondicherry and Chandigarh in nearby states. If not feasible, a mandate system may be evolved to merge them in neighbouring states. The task may be given to administrative division of the ministry, which should develop these areas and history should not obstruct the mainstream.

(f) The ministry of home is too big and its 26 divisions have expanded with intricate functions. The ministry should have its own internal review mechanism and reorganisation should be attempted every fifth year with the advent of the new government.

(g) The attached and subordinates offices should either be streamlined or abolished. The existing arrangement is anomalous.

Thus, the evolution, organisation, working and functions of the ministry of home indicate that the present structure is too big and too heavy. Perhaps, segmental and continuous reforms can keep the Leviathan functional and responsive to the spirit of 21st century.

Ministry of Finance

Like the home, the ministry of finance is also a huge organisation looking after the financial, fiscal and monitory administration of the country. The parliamentary system of government entrusts this ministry to take legislative authorisation of income and expenditure from the Parliament through budget and to see to it that public expenditure disbursement follows the will of popular representatives. It is an enormous responsibility that influences union-state relations, international and domestic borrowings, monetary situations and taxation policies and welfare activities of the government. In fact, all public activities need finance and every paisa to be raised and spent, has to be accounted for. The ministry not only prepares and executes the Union Budget but also has to undertake exercises in resource mobilisation and economising on expenditure. The entire economy of the nation looks to its financial managers for fiscal reforms, economic development, and financial health aid commercial transactions, which determine the nature and character of government.

The ministry of finance has its origin in the department of finance set up in 1810. The department of finance and union company administration came into existence by bifurcating the public department whose secretary continued to head both the departments till 1816. The workload situation created two separate secretaries for the two departments in 1843. This year the joint secretariat of Bengal government and Government of India were separated and this lead to a change by which revenue branch of the finance department got shifted to the department of home. After the taking over of the colony by the crown in 1858, the finance department passed through following reorganisations:

1860 All matters pertaining to commerce and trade were passed on to finance department.

1905 The commercial and industrial subjects of the finance department were transferred to the newly created department of commerce and industry.

1907 The powers of Central government were devolved to state governments but the finance secretary became more powerful on advise of the Governor-General.

1909 The Morley Minto Reforms reorganised the finance department into seven branches:

(1) General finance
(2) Revenue

(3) Money and banking
(4) Salary and allowances
(5) Public accounts
(6) Military finance
(7) Military accounts

1919 Montford reforms created the Office of Comptroller and Auditor General of India. The public accounts committee made parliamentary control tighter and four separate wings were created under two secretaries. These wings were:
(a) Tax imposition and collection administration,
(b) Questions pertaining to centre province financial relations,
(c) Public and defence expeditions of India, and
(d) Matters pertaining to public debt.

All these matters required the concurrence of Secretary of State for India (SSI) from London and the Haldane Committee justified it in the name of a sound financial system. The committee observed:

It is essential to a sound system of finance that the minister is responsible for raising the revenue should also have a predominant voice in deciding on the amount, and – to some degree – on the character of the expenditure. It has been held that it is only in this way that he can secure the necessary check on the demands that are made upon him, and a proper appreciation of the liabilities to which he is being committed by the policy of his colleagues. If he is to be held responsible for filling the reservoir and maintaining certain depth of water in it, he must also be in a position to regulate the outflow.

1935 Despite of dyarchy in the provinces the SSI continued to control financial matters from London.

1945 After the war, the seven wings of the departments were expanded into nine, viz., (1) revenue, (2) railways, (3) security, (4) communication, (5) general expenditure, (6) public establishment, (7) budget, (8) finance, and (9) planning.

1947 With the achievement of independence in 1947, the finance department was given the new nomenclature of the ministry of finance, which was organised into three major wings: (1) expenditure, (2) economic affairs, and (3) revenue.

1979 The ministry was organised into four departments of (1) expenditure, (2) economic affairs, (3) revenue and insurance, and (4) banking, each department under the charge of a secretary to government.

1985 In March, the ministry was once again organised in three departments, the department of banking having been merged with the department of economic affairs as a separate division.

1990 The ministry comprises three departments, namely, (1) economic affairs, (2) expenditure, and (3) revenue.

Since 1949, the department of economic affairs stands organised into four division, called, (1) External finance, (2) Internal finance, (3) Budget, and (4) Planning. Due to the increase of workload in planning matters, the revenue and expenditure were separated as independent departments. A new department of company law was added to the ministry in 1955. After three years, it was transferred to ministry of commerce and industries. In 1963, it was retransferred to the revenue department of finance ministry. Later in 1964, the insurance department and company law were amalgamated to constitute the fifth department in the Ministry. In 1966, company law was shifted to law department and coordination department was abolished to reduce the number of departments to three. The organisational structure of the ministry in 2000 stands as below:

Organisational Structure of the Ministry of Finance

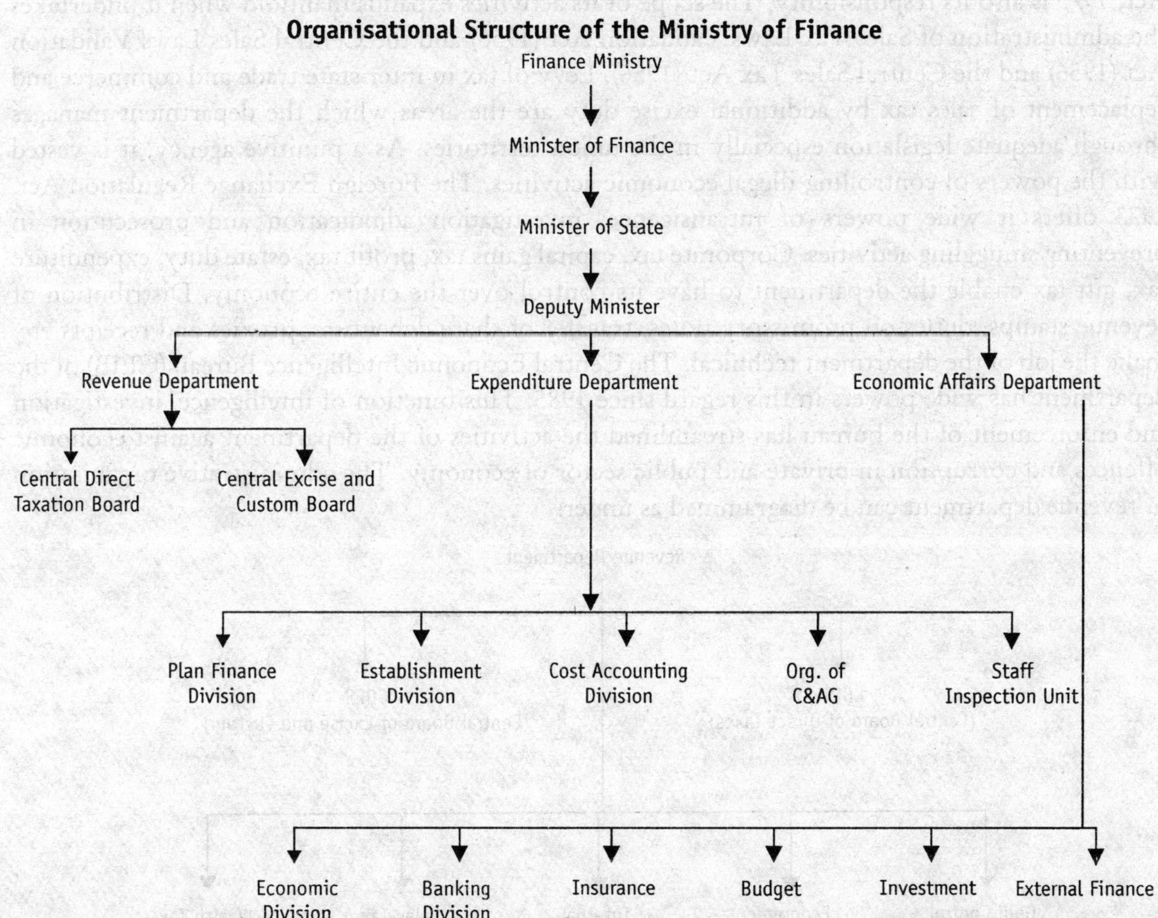

Department of Revenue

This department of the finance ministry administers revenue or income matters which largely pertain to direct and indirect taxes. The two boards, namely, Central Board of Direct Taxes (CBDT) and Central Board of Excise and Customs (CBEC) are the executive agencies through which this income is assessed and realised. The department implements the provisions of four basic acts which are:

(1) Income Tax Act, 1961
(2) Wealth Tax Act, 1957
(3) Estate Duty Act, 1958
(4) Gift Tax Act, 1958

In addition, Gold Control Act, 1963 and administrative affairs of life insurance also fall in its purview. The department has an objective of building a bridge between the tax payer and tax collector. It also handles the problem of tax evasion and tax arrears. It has a preventive role also in controlling cultivation and export of opium and narcotic drugs. Enforcement of the Customs Tariff Act, 1975 is also its responsibility. The scope of its activities expands manifold when it undertakes the administration of Sales Tax Laws Validation Act (1956) and the Central Sales Laws Validation Act (1956) and the Central Sales Tax Act (1956). Levy of tax in inter-state trade and commerce and replacement of sales tax by additional excise duty are the areas which the department manages through adequate legislation especially in the union territories. As a punitive agency, it is vested with the powers of controlling illegal economic activities. The Foreign Exchange Regulation Act, 1973 offers it wide powers of intransigence, investigation adjudication and prosecution in preventing smuggling activities. Corporate tax, capital gains tax, profit tax, estate duty, expenditure tax, gift tax enable the department to have its control over the entire economy. Distribution of revenue stamps, duties on promissory notes, transfer of share debenture, proxies and receipts etc. make the job of the department technical. The Central Economic Intelligence Bureau (CEIB) of the department has wide powers in this regard since 1985. This function of intelligence, investigation and enforcement of the bureau has streamlined the activities of the department against economic offences and corruption in private and public sector of economy. The administrative organisation of revenue department can be diagrammed as under:

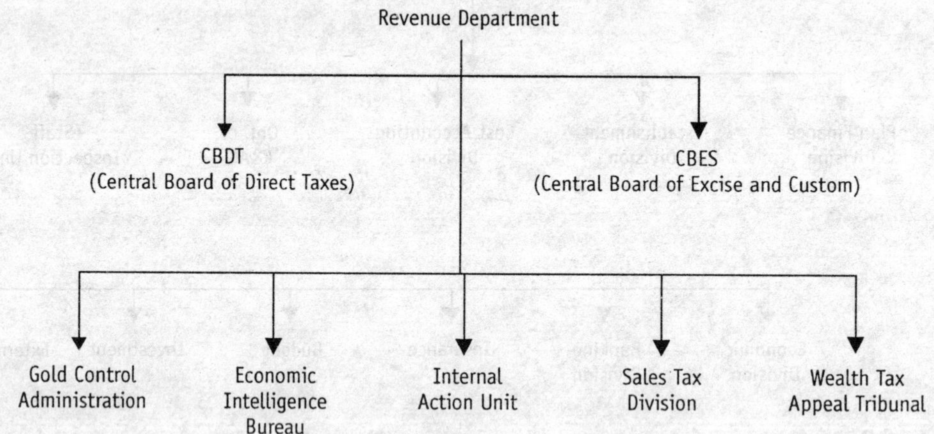

The department is manned by 1 secretary, 17 deputy secretaries, 2 OSDs, 2 directors, 31 under secretaries, 51 section officers and 4 apprentices. All this explains the importance of the department which concentrates on the revenue part of financial administration.

Central Direct Taxation Board

The CDTB was established in the year 1964 under Revenue Board Act, 1963. Assessment and realisation of entire tax income is the board's responsibility. The board has a chairman and 6 members. Eight directorates work under the control of the board. The chart below explains the CDTB organisation:

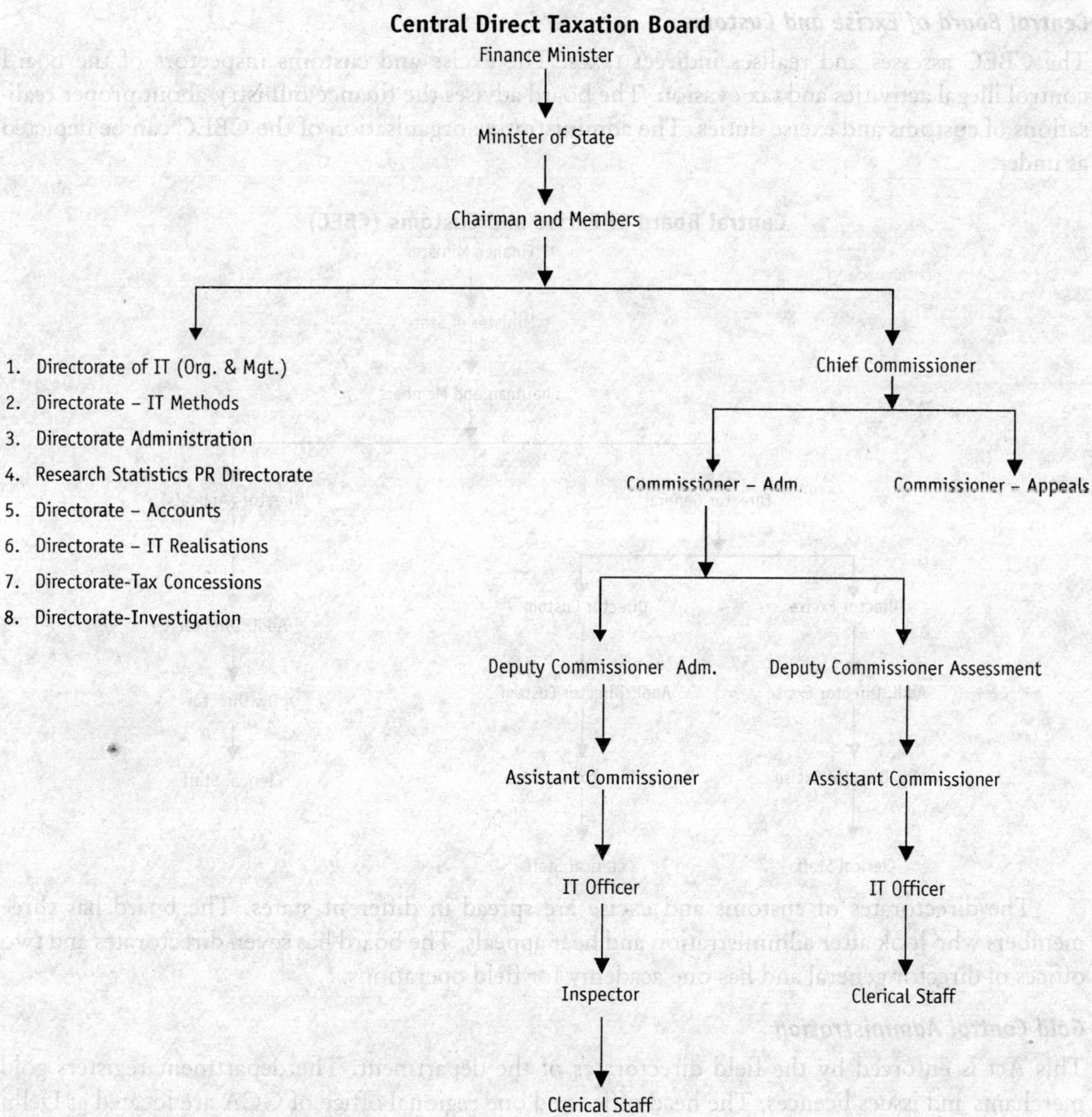

Directorate of Income Tax (Methods)

It is headed by a chief commissioner. He is assisted by two senior officials working as commissioner (administration) and commissioner (appeals). The number of deputy commissioners varies from five to ten depending on their workload. The assistant commissioners and ITO are spread all over the country. The CBDT has five regional offices headed by:

(1) Director General Income Tax (Administration), Delhi.
(2) Director General Income Tax (Training), Nagpur.
(3) Director General Income Tax (Concessions), Kolkata.

Central Board of Excise and Customs

The CBEC assesses and realises indirect taxes. The excise and customs inspectors of the board control illegal activities and tax evasion. The board advises the finance ministry about proper realisations of customs and excise duties. The administrative organisation of the CBEC can be depicted as under:

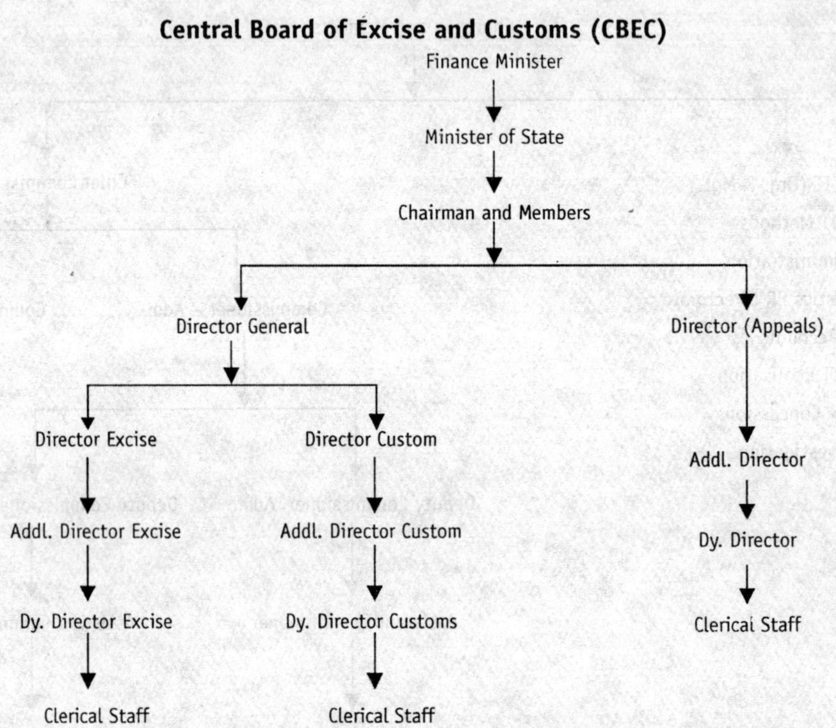

The directorates of customs and excise are spread in different states. The board has three members who look after administration and hear appeals. The board has seven directorates and two offices of director general and has one academy for field operations.

Gold Control Administration

This Act is enforced by the field directorates of the department. The department registers gold merchants and issues licences. The head office and one regional office of GCA are located at Delhi and Mumbai respectively.

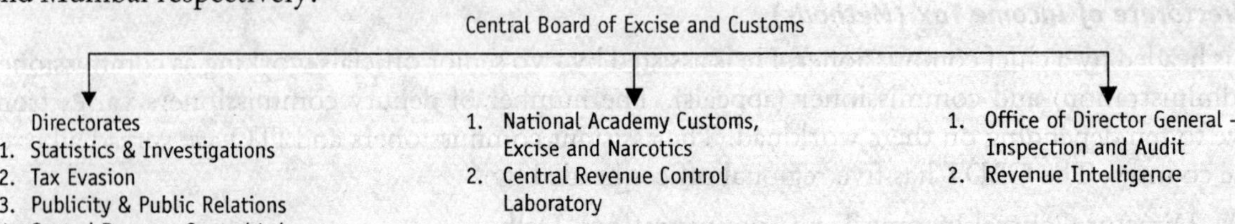

Economic Intelligence Bureau

It was established in 1985. Its main function is to have an eye on economic offences and collect intelligence about black money, smuggling and activities of mafia underworld.

Internal Study Unit

Established in 1985, the unit works to enhance efficiency in revenue collection. It suggests simplification of rules and decentralisation of operations to yield results. It does action research and experiences are pooled together to monitor reforms.

Sales Tax Division

In 1956, the administration of sales tax was handed over to the states. They keep the income but appeals against sales tax assessment, evasion, etc., lie with the revenue department.

Attached Property Appeal Tribunal

The Act was passed in 1976. The Delhi office has regional offices at Chennai, Mumbai, Kolkata and Guwahati. The tribunal hears appeals and decides cores launched by field officers.

Attached Offices of the Department

There are seven attached offices under the revenue department of finance ministry of Government of India.

(1) Department of Insurance, Shimla. It has three functions:
   (a) Administration of Insurance Act, 1861 (revised in 1938).
   (b) Assistance to government in legal matters.
   (c) Advise the insurance councils.

(2) Directorate of Enforcement, New Delhi: It deals with matters of violations under Foreign Exchange Act, 1947.

(3) Directorate of Inspection, Research, Statistics and Publication, New Delhi, established in December 1960. Its functions include:
   (a) Interpretation of policies and control of administration of direct taxes.
   (b) Getting the tax forms printed.
   (c) Publication of all India revenue statistics.

(4) Directorate of Income Tax, Inspection Wing, New Delhi.
   It supervises the work of assistant commissioners of income tax and suggests measures to keep them efficient. It is an old office to which the status of an attached office was given in 1946. It examines reports, does inspection of field units and evaluate the work of officers engaged in revenue collection.

(5) Directorate of Inspection (Income Tax) Investigation Wing, New Delhi.
   The wing was created in 1952. It is responsible to the CBDT. Its job is to investigate complex cases of tax evasion. It does vigilance work and offers technical advise to the board on the basis of inspections, relations and reports from the field. Coordination of remedial measures is also its function.

(6) Directorate of Inspection (Customs and Central Excise), New Delhi.
   It was established in 1939. It advises on methods of social inspection and technical matters. It branched of from the board as an attached office in 1946. Today, it has regional offices at

Allahabad, Kolkata and Hyderabad. The Delhi head office along with regional offices performs following functions:

(a) Inspection of the work of excise and customs collectors
(b) Implement boards' programmes and remove handicaps
(c) Reporting on the feasibility rules and laws
(d) Suggesting measures to improve efficiency
(e) Advising the board on problems of excise and customs collection
(f) Training of departmental functionaries
(g) Any responsibility entrusted by the board

(7) Directorate of Revenue Intelligence, Delhi

Before 1958, it functioned as an unit of central excise and customs directorate. In this year, it was reorganised to do intelligence and detect cases of tax evasion. Today, it launches campaigns, raids and seizure operations on an all India basis on smugglers and black money dealers. It also makes arrangements for training of field collectors for vigilance.

Like attached offices, the revenue department of the finance ministry has seven subordinate offices and their field branches in various cities for revenue collection. These offices are:

(1) Offices of the collectors of customs, Mumbai, Kolkata, Chennai, Vishakhapatnam and Kandla.

The goods that pass through these port cities are inspected, assessed and duties are realised on the items. Efforts are made to arrest the law violators and import exports are controlled in national interest. In addition to the above five, three more offices have been opened at Cochin, Pondicherry and Goa. The custom and excise officers are directly controlled by Central Board of Revenue which has a commissioner for each of these regional offices.

(2) Offices of collectors of central excise, Mumbai, Kolkata, Chennai, Bangalore, New Delhi, Shillong, Hyderabad, Allahabad, Vadodara, Patna, Poona, Nagpur, Cochin, Kanpur, Panji and Pondicherry.

The excise collectors enforce the laws and collect excise income of the government at 16 regional offices through their collectors. The central board supervises their field reparations.

(3) Income Tax Department

The department has 26 units. Each unit works under an income tax commissioner. Its tax net has been expanded in recent years and with the introduction of PAN, the units have been activated to mop up resources. The Nagpur Academy arranges for their training.

(4) Intelligence Branch (Central Excise), New Delhi.

It was organised as a separate office in 1946 and the status of a subordinate office was accorded to it. Its major functions are: (1) collection of data about narcotics and excise figures for the board, (2) collection and analysis of the data, and (3) advising the board in technical matters of importance.

(5) Central Revenues Control Laboratory, New Delhi.

(a) Research work in analytical methods to improve the quality of work in junior laboratories.
(b) Advisory work in chemical matters.

(6) Office of the Narcotics Commissioner, Gwalior.
The office was established in 1950 and its functions include coordination and reform to assist the administration of drugs and narcotics. The international pacts have to be carried out as a part of National Policy.

(7) Directorate of Emergency Risks Insurance Scheme, New Delhi.
The Insurance Act 1962 (Goods and Factories) makes it obligatory on the government to carry out the emergency risks stated in the Act. The cities like Kanpur, Kolkata, Chennai and Mumbai have field offices and the head office at Delhi has been functioning since 1965.

Life Insurance Corporation is a public undertaking of revenue department. In 1956, the Government of India nationalised the insurance industry for the security of the policy-holders. Its objective was to encourage savings and provide security to various sections and classes of society. Another purpose was to develop capital formation for national investment in development projects.

The LIC was born on September 1st 1956 with its headquarters at Mumbai. There are seven regional offices functioning from Kolkata, Chennai, Hyderabad, Mumbai, Delhi, Kanpur and Bhopal. There are more than 100 zonal offices with 2,046 branches all over the country. Today, it has expanded its network to Mauritius, Fizi, UK and in various African countries. The joint ventures of LIC are operational in Nairobi, Kualalampur, Bahrain and Kathmandu. There are six advisory committees functional in its day-to-day working.

(1) Executive Committee (2) Investment Committee (3) Service and Budget Committee (4) Public Relations Committee (5) Regional Advisory Board (6) Employees and Agent Committees.

The LIC as a public sector undertaking is today competing with various private companies and corporations – national as well as international. The policies of privatisation and globalisation have pushed the LIC into global arena with new roles and newer policies of public security.

Department of Public Expenditure

This department controls and supervises the entire expenditure of the union government and handles specified items of work like financial rules and regulations and delegation of financial powers and sanctions. It administers all financial rules, and deals with financial sanctions concerning all the ministries and offices of the union government. It scrutinises the financial and economic implications of legislation and releases grants and loans for the state plans, plan budgets and plan assistance for expenditure on relief measures for natural calamities. The department acts as an administrative authority for the Indian audit and accounts department, the Comptroller General of Accounts. It also serves as the cadre management authority for Group 'A' and Group 'B' officers of the Central Civil Accounts. The junior level central civil accounts staff is trained by this department.

In a broad sense it determines the general principles of government accounting, forms of accounts and framing or revision of rules and manuals. The department prepares the annual and monthly accounts showing the receipts and disbursements for purposes of the Union government under respective heads. The Central Treasury Rules assists the ministries and department in the enforcement of management accounting system which reconciles the cash balance of the Union government with the Reserve Bank, and reserve deposits pertaining to various ministries. To be more specific, department of expenditure looks after the administration of the following subjects or activities:

(1) Staffing of government establishments
(2) Cost accounts and cost investigations
(3) Expenditure proposals of Delhi administration
(4) Indian audit and accounting department
(5) Defence accounts department
(6) Statutory and ad hoc grants to states and legislation
(7) Financial assistance and loans and their implications
(8) Local taxation, state finance, capital budget
(9) Planning and development finance-projects
(10) Bureau of Public Enterprise
(11) Indian Institute of Public Administration

Organisation of Expenditure Department

The department has no subordinate and attached offices and stands organised into seven branches, wings and units. Divisions of these divisions have functional specialisations and work as under:

Establishment Division

Basically, it looks after the administration of rules and regulations. The detailed functions include:

(a) Fixation of salary grades
(b) Fixations of allowances increments, etc.
(c) Cadre review and comparative evaluation
(d) Recommendations of Pay Commission, etc.

The establishment division is responsible for processing of reports for economy in Central government and expenditure, grants-in-aid. The administrative wing looks after personnel management, office administration, vigilance matters and foreign assignments and training of the officers of the department.

Plan Finance Wing

The wing is organised into two divisions:

(1) Plan Finance I division is concerned with all aspects of state finance. They include the assessment of financial resources of five-year and annual plans of states, matters relating to Centre-state financial relations, centrally sponsored schemes and central plan schemes, overdraft regulation scheme, state legislation natural calamities and follow-up action on the recommendations of the Sarkaria Commission and the Finance Commission. The wing monitors the ways and means and resources position of states on a continuing basis and takes action to advise the states. It releases central assistance to states for state plans, hill areas development programmes and relief in natural calamities.

(2) Plan Finance II division deals with matters of central plan which cover the estimates of resources for central plan, allocation of outlays among different ministries of the Central

government, appraisal of plan projects for submission to the Public Investment Board (PIB) or Expenditure Finance Committees (EFC). It works as the secretariat of the PIB and attends to works, relating to wage settlement in public sector undertakings.

Cost Accounts Branch

This branch is a pricing organisation of the government of India. As a repository of expertise in cost and management accountancy, it renders professional assistance to different ministries, committees and other agencies of the Union government. Created in 1978 it advises the department on matter pertaining to ICAS cadre.

Staff Inspection Unit

Born in 1964, the unit has two objectives:

(a) To reduce or retrench the number of employees in terms of efficiency.
(b) To set performance standards and work norms in government offices and institutions substantially or wholly dependent on government grant.

The unit also provides guidance to the internal work study unit and management survey units in various ministries in the area of work measurement and job grading. In addition to work measurement studies, the unit reviews the various reports and offers advice to ministries in the matter.

Comptroller General of Accounts

He functions as an apex accounting authority of the Government of India and exercises the powers of the President under Article 150 for prescribing the form of accounts of the Union and state governments. He frames rules and regulations in the field of accounts and internal audit. The publication of account codes and manuals and issue of periodical instructions and circulars help in the consolidation of accounts. He looks after pensions of the Central government employees and his office has commenced functioning with effect from 1st January, 1990. The functions of this office can be enumerated as under:

(1) To prepare and integrate the monthly accounts of Central government.
(2) To propose appropriation and finance account for annual presentation to Parliament.
(3) To strengthen internal audit system.
(4) To monitor expenditure of civil departments and ministries
(5) To supervise banking and disbursement system of finance
(6) To monitor revenues of customs and excise in an effective manner
(7) To reform accounting and audit for financial control

The CGA arranges for training of officers of the ministry at its regional centres at Kolkata, Chennai and Mumbai. The advent of computer and other cybernetics has added to its functions. The MIS has enlarged the scope and quality of decisions.

Finance Commission Division

This division is concerned with all aspects or implications of the recommendations of the Finance Commission. It continues to function as the secretariat of the Inter-Ministerial Empowered Committees (IMEC). Huge grants of crores of rupees are released to the state governments for every Finance Commission Works. This division is mainly concerned with:

(a) The implementation of recommendations of the Finance Commission.
(b) The preservation of commission's records to help the future commissions.
(c) The examination and trend analysis of receipts and non-plan expenditures of the government.
(d) The study of statistics of state financed projects.

National Institute of Financial Management

This institutions was established as an autonomous body for training and research. The six categories of accounts service of the Union government are imparted professional training which attracts accounts service trainees of countries like Nepal, Sri Lanka and friendly countries of Africa.

The expenditure department is managed by 7 secretaries, 2 additional secretaries, 10 joints secretaries, one director, 25 deputy secretaries, 40 under secretaries, and the junior staff which runs into hundreds. This speaks volumes of its relevance and importance in financial management.

Department of Economic Affairs

It is a large department and covers a wide area of varied activities. It consists of seven main divisions, namely, (1) economic, (2) banking, (3) insurance, (4) budget, (5) investments, (6) external economic management, including commercial banks, (7) term leading institutions, investment regulations, external assistance, production of currency/bank notes and coins of various denominations, postal stationery and postal stamps. It also analyses economic trends and advises the government on matters regarding financial management. Policy changes to accelerate growth, control over inflation banking procedures of public sector banks, and other economic institutions need its guidance. It formulates policies of the insurance companies and prescribes terms and conditions of service, monitoring performance. Department tenders economic advice to the government on important economic policy matters and handles public grievances. It analyses the prevailing economic trends, and appraises economic policies for improved economic performance. Public policy issues in the fields of public finance, money and credit, prices and wages, foreign trade, balance of payments, external assistance and international finance are studied by the department. It works in close cooperation with the Reserve Bank of India, the Planning Commission, the Central Statistical Organisation, the ministry of commerce and the economic and statistical wings of other ministries.

The budget division of the department prepares the budget of the Union Governments as well as of those states which are under President's rule, and their budgets are presented to the Parliament. It recognises stock exchanges and ensures that the transactions in them take place in accordance with rules and laws. Development of capital market and the protection of the investors' interest with faith in the system are its responsibility. The department deals with the aid received by the country from international institutions and the aid given by India to other countries.

The Reserve Bank had liberalised the terms and conditions for housing loans and the National Housing Banks are actively engaged in the development of housing finance in the country. The department deals with cognate matters like internal finance, currency, coins, printing of currency, gold and silver refinery, import and export of gold and silver, fixation of interest rates for the Central government's borrowings and lendings, and accounting and audit procedures. It controls foreign exchange, budgeting, foreign and non-resident Indian investment and foreign exchange resources. Several international institutions such as the International Bank, the European Economic Community, the Commonwealth Fund for Technical Cooperation, the India Consortium and agencies of the UN maintain a close contact through it. The aid given by India to the members of the Colombo Plan, to African countries and investment pattern for Employees' Provident Fund are also handled by the department. Legally speaking, 47 functions of the DEA can be classified into 18 heads as under:

(1) Monetary control
(2) Foreign exchange and budget
(3) Control of source of foreign exchange
(4) Foreign capital investment
(5) Import export of gold ornament
(6) Foreign aid under technical programmes
(7) Administration for foreign aid by India to other countries
(8) Matters relating to plan committees, funds and missions
(9) Banking and money matters
(10) Advise to UN
(11) Budget, loans, savings, accounting and finance
(12) Planning, taxation, state finance, goods and development
(13) Sales Tax Act.
(14) Insurance, LIC
(15) Corporation Acts
(16) Stock exchanges and securities
(17) Joint stock companies
(18) Miscellaneous

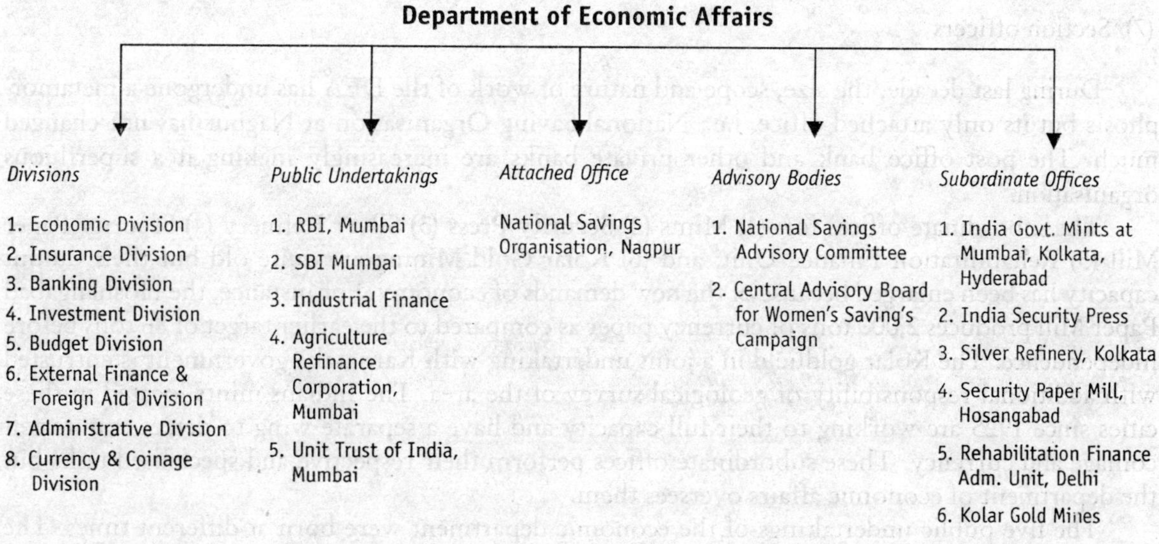

Organisation of DEA

The department of economic affairs has 8 departments, 8 subordinate offices, 1 attached office, 1 public undertaking and 2 advisory bodies.

The eight divisions of the department of economic affairs as diagrammed above point out the nature and scope of economic administration which have a direct bearing on revenue and expenditure of the government. As the names of the divisions are self-explanatory, it appears that this department is engaged in the development of infrastructure to help the banking and insurance industries which have wider repercussions for external finance and investment. A number of Acts exist in these areas and their implementation is the responsibility of different divisions. For instance, if investment division looks after activities like foreign investment, share markets, capital control, NRI investments and India Investment Centre, the budget division administers the Contingency Fund of India, recommendations of the Finance Commissions on implementation of the recommendations of C&AG and review of interest rates on loans, etc. The printing of stamp papers, currency notes, postal stationery by the Indian Security Press are onerous responsibilities and have to be managed by an independent division. Banking and insurance administration are closely linked with foreign trade, debt servicing and foreign exchange management which are under the specific administrative divisions. The secretariat of this large department of the finance ministry has:

(1) Secretary and additional secretary	2
(2) Economic advisers	2
(3) Joint secretaries	6
(4) Deputy secretaries	10
(5) Under secretaries	20
(6) Research officers (S&J)	7
(7) Section officers	52

During last decade, the size, scope and nature of work of the DEA has undergone a metamorphosis but its only attached office, i.e., National Saving Organisation at Nagpur has not changed much. The post office bank and other private banks are increasingly making it a superfluous organisation.

The subordinate offices for: (1) Mints (2) Security Press (3) Silver Refinery (4) Security Paper Mill (5) Rehabilitation Finance Unit, and (6) Kolar Gold Mining are quite old but their output capacity has been enlarged because of the new demands of economy. For instance, the Hoshangabad Paper Mill produces 2,000 tons of currency paper as compared to the earlier target of 86 tons before independence. The Kolar goldfield in a joint undertaking with Karnataka government is entrusted with additional responsibility of geological survey of the area. The Indians mints located in these cities since 1925 are working to their full capacity and have a separate wing to detect counterfeit coinage and currency. These subordinate offices perform their respective and specialised tasks but the department of economic affairs oversees them.

The five public undertakings of the economic department were born at different times. The Reserve Bank of India Act was passed in 1935 but it became a nationalised bank in 1948. It is a Bank of Bankers and its major function is to maintain economic stability in the country. It controls the exchange rates and makes periodic surveys by collecting data about the economy in its international context. The bank has a Governor and it formulates banking policies and coordinates and controls other banks through a central board of directors nominated by the government.

The State Bank of India Act 1955 created the SBI to assist banks in urban and rural towns. It promotes industrial loans and small scale industries through its scheme. The Industrial Finance Corporation was created in 1948 and the object was to provide loans and financial assistance to small companies. It is a corporate undertaking and can extend support to industrial units in backward areas. The three branches operating from Mumbai, Kolkata and Chennai offer loans and assistance to cooperative societies, hotels, and companies engaged in productive activity.

The Agricultural Refinance Corporation was created in 1963 and it refinances land mortgage banks. It works with the Reserve Bank of India with a purpose to give boost to rural banking.

The UTI Act 1963 was enacted to sell units and promote private investment in development projects. The LIC and the SBI gave the seed money but because of recurring crises it lost its image. Now, it has been reorganised for the better security of the unitholder's money. The advisory bodies on national savings and women's savings are functional in varied ways and have mopped up public savings through certification.

Frailties and Reforms

The ministry of finance has been subjected to severe criticism by Dean Paul Appleby and also by Administrative Reforms Commission for its tight and negative control over the purse of the government. It has been condemned for its 'Pennywise and Pound Foolish' approach in financial matters. Some of its structures are getting century old and very little fresh air is permitted by its die hard bureaucrats pursuing negative centralisation. Understandably, financial matters anywhere need special care, but if this ministry does not take the right advise and right path for functional actions, all operations in government slow down to stand still. A deeper look at its administrative organisation reveals that;

(1) Three departments of revenue, expenditure and economic affairs are scientifically organised but inside each department there are obsolescent wings, units and even divisions which need to be pruned and cut to size. The mushroom growth of non-secretariat units in the secretariat organisation is malignant and periodical weeding out is needed in every division and office.

(2) Some of the departmental divisions have became redundant or incongruent with the reorganised administrative system. For instance, insurance and banking, after 1997, need a fresher look in the era of liberalisation. The structures were needed to begin with but the vested interests in bureaucracy do not allow the structures to be dropped. Consequently, overlap and duplication of functions have resulted in non-functioning or obstructive operations of banking and insurance divisions of the ministry.

(3) Linking of planning with financial administration also needs a new look; partly because Planning Commission and public enterprises are passing through a new area of liberalisation and privatisation and partly because the coordinational regulatory activity of the Finance Ministry requires new kind of flat and advisory structure for its acceptability.

(4) The ministry notwithstanding its openness to reform or change remains a ministry to manage national finances and the budget. The globalisation policies have started making a dent. The NRI finance and investment is a mere beginning and imports are to be discouraged and exports need to be promoted for which separate and independent divisions are called for with appropriate infrastructure conducive for development.

(5) The budget function on which the finance ministry concentrates all the year round has to be performed with the aid of cybernetics. Computers have come to stay and a heavy investment

in Management of Information System (MIS) is called for. The ministry has taken the change in an ad hoc manner. It has to modernise its budget division not only in terms of software, but in a big way to prepare a variety of budgets with latest techniques of PPBS and ZBB. The personnel of the ministry should constantly be trained and the units readjusted with the new organs of the ministry.

It is true that finance ministry represents a valuable legacy of the colonial period and has shown resilience in responding to the change since 1991. But the fact remains that its manpower dreads reforms or accepts them with a pinch of salt. Innovations are not welcome because they negatively reduce the authority and generate a fear of debureaucratisation, free economy is a miracle and the shift invites risks and hazards. Matters like portfolio investment, global depository receipts and direct foreign investment are too sensitive to be acceptable to rule oriented bureaucrats. Naturally, the climate of scepticism renders the scenario exciting as well as frustrating. The challenge of change can be met by flexibility for which the ministry of finance should have its own independent permanent reforms cell more powerful than an O&M. It should prepare a blue print of organisational reforms of the ministry for five years and get it processed every quarter under instructions from finance minister and the prime minister of the country.

Ministry of Defence

In the era of global conflicts and cross border terrorist threats, the national security of the country is of supreme importance. Naturally, the defence minister ranks fairly high in protocol and his ministry gets a lion's share of national budget. Moreover, the defence services of the nation – Army, Air and Navy have to be in a state of constant preparedness to meet any unexpected threat to borders from any quarter. Even in the age of privatisation, the defence ministry has to have its own defence production and management through ordnance factories and storage depots. It has to have a huge training and research establishment to keep their men in good trim. The need of modernisation of equipment to handle conflict situation in an atomic world of today has inducted science and technological know how in the organisation of the defence ministry. It is interesting to see the evolution of defence organisation in British India since 1776. The following dates are relevant in this development:

1776 The East India Company created a military department from the public department in their government of the Colony.

1786 The secrecy department was split into three branches including the military branch.

1789 An independent secretary of military department took over from the secretary of foreign affairs.

1833 Secretariat of Bengal government got separated.

1843 Four departments under four secretaries including the military department were created.

1864 The military accounts department of the presidencies were merged in the military department.

1895 The three separate presidency armies got unified into a single Indian Army but four commands were retained for administrative convenience.

1905 The military department was abolished and two new departments were created. (1) Department of military supply under the military member, and (2) Army department under the Commander-in-Chief.

1909 The post of military member was abolished and the C-in-C became Army member with full authority. A military secretary was created in home government to advise the Secretary of State for India.

1938 The department was redesigned as defence department.

1942 During war, the defence department was bifurcated into: (a) War department, and (b) Defence department.

1946 The departments got reunited into a security department.

1947 On the advent of freedom the defence ministry got Commander-in-Chief positions for Army, Navy and Air.

1955 The President of India assumed the role of Supreme Commander under new Constitution and the old post of C-in-C was abolished to redesigned Chiefs of Army staff, Naval staff and Air staff.

1962 A new department known as department of defence production was added to the ministry.

1965 Another department called as department of defence supplies was established for planning and execution of schemes for the substitution of imports requirements for defence purposes.

1995 Three departments of: (1) Defence, (2) Defence production and supplies, and (3) Defence research and development were created.

Thus, the history of the department contributed to specialisation and unification of defence services. The development needs put a pressure on the government to cut on defence expenditure but the wars with Pakistan and China made it imperative to enhance defence budgets for modernisation of defence equipment and infrastructure at the borders.

Organisation of the Ministry

The organisation of the ministry is unique. It has a secretariat, three service headquarters, a number of inter-service agencies and training institutions. It is divided into three departments, i.e., (1) defence, (2) production, and (3) defence supplies. At the apex stands the cabinet minister who is assisted by a minister of state known as the minister of defence production. Each of these departments has its own secretary but the administrative head of the ministry as such is the defence secretary. A special feature of this ministry is that policy decisions on defence matters are taken by a network of committees. The responsibility for national defence rests with the cabinet but important matters concerning defence are handled by the cabinet committee on political affairs. There are a number of committees in the secretariat which ensure coordination of defence strategies. The defence minister is assisted by two committees, namely, (1) the Defence Minister's Committee and (2) the Defence Minister's Production and Supply Committee.

The three departments of defence ministry are partly independent and partly interdependent. Coordination of defence effort and mutual assistance is the strength of defence enterprise yet the specialised activities of army, navy and air force have very little in common. They should appreciate each other's efforts and limitations and do their utmost to produce a collective effort. This philosophy is reflected in the organisational structure of these departments of defence administration, defence production and defence research and development. As on old and traditional structure of the defence ministry works through twenty divisions, which as their name suggests, manage twenty kinds of technical defence activities. These divisions are:

(1) Army division
(2) Navy division

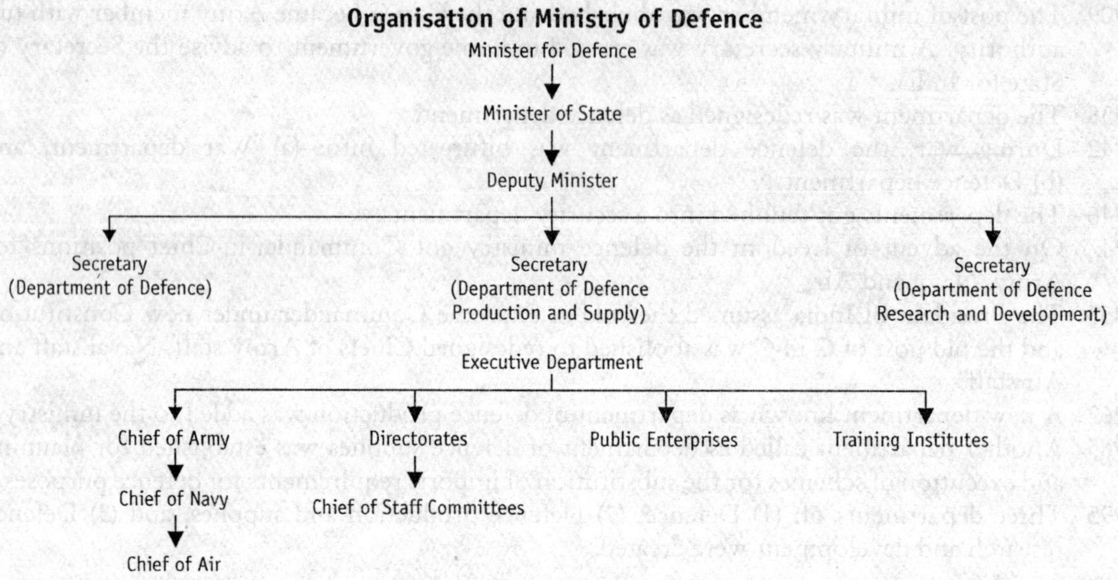

(3) Air Force division
(4) Civilian division
(5) Inter Services Organisation
(6) Defence production and supply division
(7) Defence research division
(8) Coordination division
(9) Protocol and discipline division
(10) Defence budget and finance division
(11) Army pay division
(12) Allowances and pension division
(13) Soldier welfare division
(14) Vigilance and O&M division
(15) Military training division
(16) Defence personnel policy and planning division
(17) Staff duty division
(18) Historical reference division
(19) Medical supply division
(20) Transport, communication and canteen division

Functions

The ministry of defence is a huge national organisation which performs administrative and technical functions during peace and war. All the three wings have similar, common and different kinds of functions which pertain to the following:

(1) Defence of India and every part thereof including preparation, prosecution and effective demobilisation.

(2) The armed forces of the Union, namely, the Army, Navy and Air Force.

(3) The reserves of the Army, Navy and Air Force.
(4) The Territorial Army and the auxiliary Air Force.
(5) The National Cadet Corps.
(6) Works relating to the Army, Navy and Air Force and execution of works relating to defence production organisation.
(7) Military farms organisation.
(8) Canteen Stores Department (India).
(9) Civilian services paid from defence services estimates.
(10) Hydrographic surveys and preparation of navigational charts.
(11) Formation of cantonments, delimitation/excision of cantonment areas and local self-government in such areas.
(12) Acquisition, requisition, custody and relinquishment of land and property for defence purposes.
(13) Matters relating to ex-servicemen including pensioners.

Functions in these areas imply a variety of policies, programmes and administrative operations of line and staff nature. The field formations of three branches have cantonments in their respective commands. The NCC and the territorial army play the standby but the ex-servicemen who gave their best to the organisation remain the responsibility of the ministry. The defence services come to the society for civilian services of varied nature during natural disaster and emergencies. Even the defence production and defence research takes a large part of defence allocations of the nation. All these tasks can be articulated as functions in the following manner:

(1) Protection of national borders.
(2) Defence policy articulation.
(3) Management of land and property for defence purposes.
(4) Administration of cantonments.
(5) Supply and production of war materials.
(6) Research and development for defence modernisation.
(7) Care and welfare of ex-servicemen and their families.
(8) Recruitment and training of the soldiers and officers.
(9) Execution of the defence policies of the government.
(10) Activities conducive for high morale of the defence forces of the nation.

Department of Defence

Headed by a senior secretary, this department looks after policy matters, coordination of defence efforts and management of cantonments and military land and property. It has a big department and its activities spread all over the country for all the three branches of the armed forces. It handles very sensitive questions like national security, civil supply maintenance for the forces, hydrographic surveys and preparation of navigational charts. National Cadet Corps Organisation, territorial army training and rehabilitation of retired soldiers are very big tasks to keep the forces in high morale and good trim. Some of the functions of this department can be listed as under:

(1) Security of the nation.
(2) Enhancement of coordination between civil and military wings.
(3) Decisions pertaining to defence policies and service condition of defence personnel.

(4) Coastal guard organisation, reserve forces and canteens.
(5) Veterinary and farm organisation.
(6) Civilian services of defence establishments.
(7) Management of army lands department.

The department deals with several allied jobs in relation to acquisition, requisition, custody and relinquishment of land and property for defence purposes, formation of cantonments and cantonment boards, house accommodation and control of rents and purchase of foodstuffs for military requirements are managed by it. The defence accounts department and the canteen stores department also fall under its case. The enforcement of Acts, like the Pension Regulations for the Army (1961), and the Navy (Pension) Regulations (1964) and other miscellaneous duties such as civilian services, hydrographic surveys, navigational charts and ex-servicemen's pension, etc., are a responsibility of this department. Its size and varied works render it too big to manage.

Department of Defence Production and Supplies

It came into existence by the merger of defence production department and defence supplies department. It has the defence minister, the minister of defence production, the three service chiefs, the defence secretary, the secretary (defence production), the secretary (defence supplies), the financial adviser (defence), the additional secretary, the director-general of ordnance factories, the director-general of inspection and the chief controller (research and development) who regulate defence production effort in the country and coordinate it with the civil industrial capacity. Reviews of mobilisation for defence production, approval of projects for submission to the cabinet committee on political affairs, directions for the operation of ordnance factories, and taking policy decisions on matters relating to import substitution are some of its major functions. The department supervises production items which are developed by the Defence Research and Development Organisation (DRDO). The implementation of the defence schemes and plans for exclusive defence procurement are continuously worked out by the officers of the armed forces. Defence production, Ordnance Factory Organisation and the directorate of standardisation which handles the work of standardisation of defence equipment and stores are supervised by the department. The development of the aeronautics industry and the export and import of defence goods constitute its vital functions. Export of defence goods like small arms, weapons, spare parts, electronic items and panels of Boeing aircraft reduces defence expenditure and savings are used by the department for the modernisation of the forces.

The following establishments work under this department of the ministry:

(1) *Director General of Ordnance Factories*: It administers, directs and controls numerous ordnance factories engaged in defence production at various centres in the country.
(2) *Director General of Inspection*: It controls the production units by physical inspection. The quality of production and maintenance of stores is its basic responsibility. For this, the D.G. has several defence laboratories which do the testing work as per specifications prescribed.
(3) *Directorate of Planning and Coordination*: It coordinates the work of Defence Production Board, directorate and other ministries engaged in industrial development. It remains in touch with Planning Commission and CSIR.
(4) *Heavy Vehicles Factory, Avadi*: Established in 1968 at Chennai it is engaged in the production of medium tanks.

(5) *Accelerated Freeze Drying Factory, Hareratpur*: It prepares specialised dry food packets for mountain warfare.
(6) *Directorate of Technical Development and Production*: It inspects aeronautical instruments and raw materials of Air Force depots.
(7) *Directorate of Standardisation*: It prepares the standards for defence equipment in consultation with scientific adviser, military experts and research officers of the department.

All these establishments check the quality of defence production and see to it that their qualitative supply is maintained for the field units through store houses and ordnance depots.

Defence Research and Development Organisation (DRDO)

Born in 1958, the organisation called DRDO was created by merging several scientific and technical organisations working for the ministry. In 1980, it was accorded the administrative status of a department to have unified control and supervision over 50 laboratories pursuing research work in defence weaponry and industrial technology for self-sufficiency. The secretary of the department is the scientific adviser of the defence minister. The DRDO prepares designs, programs and proposals for research in defence equipments and missile technology and implements them in a phased manner. It administers laboratories, facilities, ranges, establishments, programmes and projects pertaining to defence research, including the Aeronautics Development Agency. It deals with all matters concerning protection and transfer of technology generated by the activities of the department, certification of the design and air-worthiness of military aircraft and their stores and equipment. The department is the coordinating agency of the ministry of defence and the instruments of accord with foreign governments in regard to acquiring technologies finalised by it. It offers advice to the defence minister, the three chiefs and inter-service organisations regarding the various aspects of weaponry, military operations, surveillance, support and logistics in potential threats of war. The influence of developments in science and technology on national security are periodically assessed and the defence minister is advised accordingly.

In a short span of twenty-five years, the DRDO has made astounding progress and is known for its outstanding achievements like:

(1) Prithvi, Agni, Nag missiles for surface-to-surface launching.
(2) Tanks like Arjun manufactured by swadeshi technology.
(3) Flight simulators for aircraft.
(4) Pilotless target crafts.
(5) Super Computer Pace Plus, and
(6) Medium range weapons and explosives.

All this has revolutionalised the Army's powers to strike and defend. The computer technology of warfare represents an advance and 70 per cent of imports of the defence purchase have been cut down and replaced by indigenous production. This equipment is of high quality and its export is increasingly mounting up to other countries of the world. Matters that are connected with research organisations of foreign countries and inter-governmental agencies, training of Indian scientists and technologists of the department abroad are the concern of the ministry. Financial aid to individuals and institutions for study and training on scientific and technological aspects of national security are funded by this organisation. It also analysis and approves all weapon, systems and technologies which the ministry of defence proposes to acquire.

The department keeps itself in touch with 70 educational establishment, 50 national scientific and industrial centres and 150 private and public enterprises in the country. Some of its functions are:

(1) To keep the defence minister informed about new techno developments in the realm of warfare,
(2) To study and research in areas having a bearing on national security,
(3) To analyse information and available technology in terms of their relevance and utility,
(4) To serve as a nodal agency for import and export of technology,
(5) To administer the affairs of aero development agency,
(6) To act on matters acquired by the ministry under Patent Act 1970 (39),
(7) To purchase land and do construction work on the same,
(8) To prepare designs, plans and programmes in scientific fields, and
(9) To supervise the scientific labs and establishments of the department.

In performing these wide ranging innovate functions, the DRDO and the defence ministry are assisted by several committees, councils and boards. Important of them are:

Appellate Committee on Pensions: It consists of (1) the defence minister, (2) the minister of defence production, (3) the defence secretary, (4) the chief of staff concerned and (5) a few others. The committee provides a final forum for appeal in respect of disability and family pension claims relating to the armed forces personnel.

Defence Research and Development Council: It is a large body consisting of about sixteen members with the defence minister as the chairman. It is responsible for coordinating and directing scientific research relating to defence problems.

Chiefs of Staff Committee: The three-service chiefs meet as a committee which is presided over by the member who has been the longest on the committee. The committee, in turn, is assisted by several sub-committees dealing with specific problems relating to planning, training, and other related activities. The three service chiefs are collectively the professional military advisers to the government on important defence matters. The secretariat for the committee and its sub-committees is provided by military wing of the cabinet secretariat.

Ordnance Production Board: Set up in 1974 this inter-ministerial body has broad financial and policy making power. Its members are: (1) secretary (defence production) as chairman; (2) representatives of the departments of expenditure, economic affairs, defence supplies and industrial development; (3) representatives of the three armed forces and (4) the director general of ordnance factories. The purpose is to bring together in a central authority various governmental functions in respect of ordnance factories so that decisions are taken under joint responsibility and without much delay.

At the apex level, there are two high power committees for the administrative management of the defence ministry. These committees are:

(a) Cabinet Defence Committee, and
(b) Defence Minister's Committee.

Obviously, all defence matters that come before the cabinet for policy analysis and decisioning are whetted out and discussed there at by the cabinet committee consisting of very senior ministers. The second committee is more of an administrative committee which consists of three service chiefs, scientific advisers and senior secretaries. It prepares proposals for cabinet's consideration and later works out detailed programmes for implementation of decisions taken by the cabinet. For matters being sensitive and confidential and need technical, administrative and political inputs, their financial implications are worked out and the past decisions have to be reviewed to inform the PM, the cabinet and the Parliament.

Financial Division

There is a unified financial division for defence budget and defence accounts. The appropriate estimates are prepared in details and are to be sent to expenditure department. Budget making apart, this division handles all sorts of financial sanctions and disbursements in the execution of defence budget. It advises the three service chiefs and their committee.

National Security Council (NSC)

The NSC was established by Prime Minister V.P. Singh on August 24, 1990. The prime minister, home minister, defence minister and finance minister are its permanent members. The first meeting took place on October 5, 1990 but the later political development rendered it dysfunctional. Prime Minister A.B. Bajpai revived it on the recommendations of K.C. Pant Committee. This time it became an extended council with three kinds of agencies.

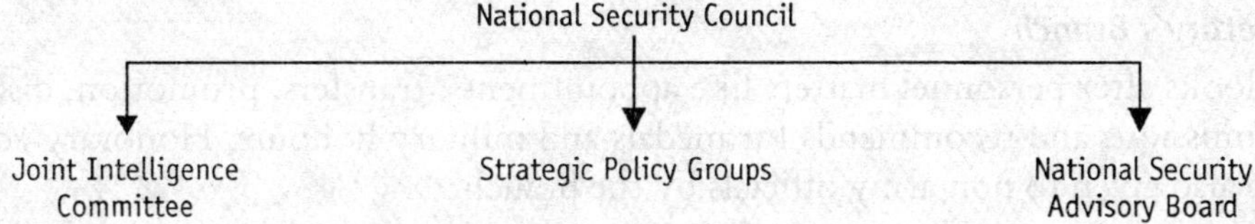

Headed by the PM, it has a variety of members including cabinet ministers, members Planning Commission, cabinet and senior secretaries and chiefs of staff from the three services. Governor, Reserve Bank of India, scientific adviser to the defence minister and secretary atomic energy department and officials from IB and RAW are associated with it. The Advisory Board has representatives from press and NGOs. The post of adviser to NSC is a key post. Much of the work of the council is secret but it helps the cabinet to take policy decisions. The ministry of defence and the joint intelligence service hosts its meetings and keeps the records.

Services Headquarters

Below the president, prime minister and the defence minister, there are three service headquarters of Chiefs of Army, Navy and Air. The service headquarters of each wing have their own internal organisation in the field and work through various kinds of line establishments.

Army

Its headquarter is in Delhi and Chief of Army staff operates with the help of his deputy and several other principal staff officers. The two Deputy Commanders-in-Chief, one Adjutant General, one Quarter Master General, one Master General of Ordnance, one army secretary and one Engineer-in-Chief looks after the administration of land army from Delhi headquarters. The Army headquarter is headed by chief of staff who has following six branches under him to keep the organisation functioning:

General Staff Branch

The branch looks after military activities, training, military surveys, maps, planning and supply services, etc. It controls inter-services communications, coordinates armed core units, purchase weapons as per policy decisions. The two deputy chiefs, thirteen directors, six vice-chiefs and seven deputy chiefs of army staff assist the C-in-C in managing the army headquarters and its technical branches and its commands.

Adjutant General's Branch

It looks after subjects like manpower, recruitment, leave, pay, pension and service conditions, etc. The health and welfare of Jawans fall in its purview.

Quarter Master General's Branch

This branch runs the administration of stores, foodstuffs, oil and fodder, etc. The military farms, military post offices, canteens, fire brigades and other supply services fall in its jurisdiction.

Master General of the Ordnance Branch

It is concerned with the supply and maintenance of equipments, explosives and depots and their reinforcements

Military Secretary's Branch

This branch looks after personnel matters like appointments, transfers, promotion, discipline, etc. It grants commissions and recommends for medals and military honours. Honorary commissions and ranks are also given to non-army officials by the branch.

Engineer-in-Chief Branch

All sorts of engineering services, anti-land mines operations, bomb neutralisation squads and construction works constitute its major responsibilities.

Commands and Areas

The Army headquarter have five commands under it. They are:

(1) Southern Command
(2) Eastern Command
(3) Western Command
(4) Central and Northern Command
(5) Training Command

All the commands have a uniform system of administration in terms of rules and discipline. A senior Lieutenant General is called the General Officer Commanding-in-Chief. The command is divided into areas and sub-areas which are headed by General Officer Commanding (Major General) and Area Commander (Brigadier) respectively. The army has several branches and services located in the area. Some of them include: armoured tanks regiment, army aviation core, signals core, army service core, electrical and mechanical engineers core, army farm service, army education core, intelligence core, army police core, pioneer core, territorial core, army police core, territorial army, defence security core, record office, recruitment organisation, training centres, etc. These cores give an idea of work that goes on in army command areas during peace and war. Indian

Army is an old and national organisation. Its professional nature requires that it should constantly be modernised, trained and kept in high morale.

Navy

The major responsibility of Navy is to protect the coastal interests of the country and protect its property. Its headquarter is in Delhi. The naval headquarter has a Chief of Naval staff who is assisted by four principal staff, Vice Chief of Naval staff, head of personnel and materials in his administration. The work of four principal Naval staff is coordinated by a Naval Secretary. The Chief of Naval staff controls the administration of five parts of the Naval organisation as under:

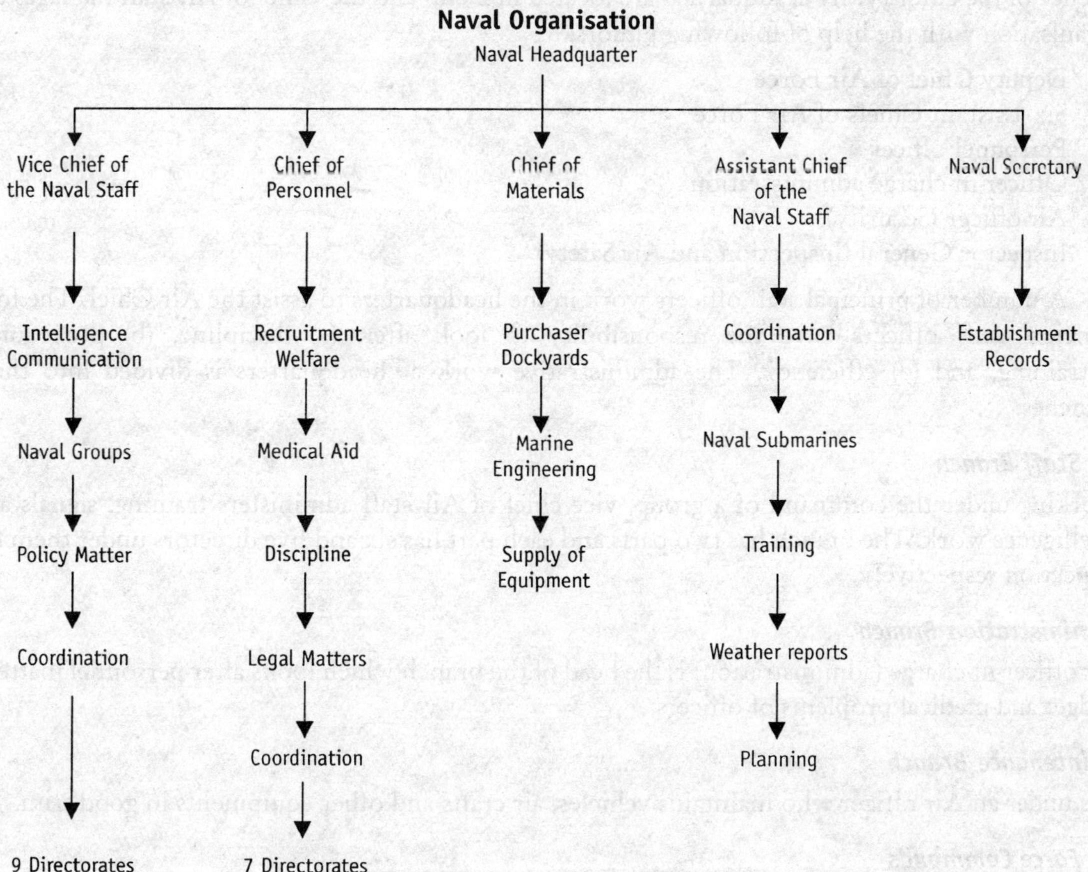

For operational purposes, the chief of naval staff works through three commands called as:

(1) Flag Officer Commanding-in-Chief, Western Naval Command, Mumbai.
(2) Flag Officer Commanding-in-Chief, Eastern Naval Command, Vishakhapatnam.
(3) Commodore Commanding, Southern Naval Area, Cochin.

The Mumbai command takes care of ships in Jamnagar and Lonewala also. The Vishakhapatnam command spreads up to Kolkata, Andaman & Nicobar and Chennai. The Cochin Commodore is responsible for ships in the ports of Goa and around.

Naval Commands

The naval administration is conducted through Mumbai, Vishakhapatnam and Cochin commands. The Flag Officer Commanding-in-Chief in each command is of the rank of vice admiral. The Western and Eastern commands are operational while the Cochin command looks after naval training. The naval establishments are spread in international waters and the commands protect the peninsular borders of India surrounded by the oceans from three sides.

Air Force

Relatively speaking, it is a younger organisation but its supporting services make it vital for the defence of the country. Its headquarters are located in Delhi and the Chief of Air staff manages the organisation with the help of following juniors:

(1) Deputy Chief of Air Force
(2) Six assistant Chiefs of Air Force
(3) Personnel officer
(4) Officer-in-charge administration
(5) Air officer (Security)
(6) Inspector General (Inspection and Air Safety)

A number of principal staff officers work in the headquarters to assist the Air Chief. The four principal staff officers have the responsibility to look after, (a) discipline, (b) procedures, (c) training, and (d) efficiency. The administrative work at headquarters is divided into three branches:

Air Staff Branch

Working under the command of a group, vice chief of Air staff administers training, signals and intelligence work. The branch has two parts and each part has six and five directors under them for inspection respectively.

Administration Branch

Air officer-in-charge (administration) is the head of the branch which looks after personnel matters, budget and medical problems of officers.

Maintenance Branch

It is under an Air officer who maintains vehicles, air crafts and other equipments in good trim.

Air Force Commands

For administrative purposes, the headquarters look after five commands territorially organised. These are operational commands and they control the flying units, fighting planes and signal units. Technical training and aid is provided to the forces in the field. Maintenance of the crafts and explosives, etc., is also the responsibility of the command officers. The commands are:

(1) Western Air Command
(2) South-western Air Command
(3) Central Air Command
(4) Eastern Air Command

There are commissioned posts in all the three branches of defence forces. They are called by different names but there exists a correspondence of commissioned officers in the Army, Navy and Air Force, in terms of status, salary and protocol. The position of commissioned officers and their counter officer posts can be presented as under:

Table 1: Commissioned Posts in Defence Forces

Army	*Navy*	*Air Force*
Field Marshal	Admiral	Air Chief Marshall
General	Vice Admiral	Air Marshall
Lt. General	Rear Admiral	Air Vice-Marshall
Major General	Commodore	Air Commodore
Brigadier	Captain	Group Captain
Colonel	Commander	Wing Commander
Lt. Colonel	Lt. Commander	Squadron Leader
Major	Lieutenant	Flight Lieutenant
Captain	Sub Lieutenant	Flying Officer
Lieutenant		

Parity apart, this kind of classification keeps the three services in a coordinated frame under the President of India, who is Supreme Commander of armed forces of the country. There are a dozen areas in which the three chiefs confer themselves and resolve various administrative conflicts. For this, there exists inter-service organisation which does staff work through eleven such organisations in the following fields:

(1) Office of the Chief Administrative Officer
(2) Directorate General, National Cadet Corps
(3) Military Lands Cantonment Directorate
(4) School of Foreign Languages
(5) Directorate General, Armed Forces Medical Services
(6) Historical sections
(7) Directorates of Public Relations
(8) Armed Forces Film and Photo Division
(9) Services Sports Control Board
(10) Indian Soldier's, Sailors and Airmen's Board
(11) Directorate General of Resettlements

These eleven inter-service organisations create the basic infrastructure and enable the army to concentrate on its professional assignment with commitment. The allied problems like standby forces, military land management are crucial areas. Soldier's welfare is a function which the army can ignore only at its own peril.

No work can be functional, still less efficient without an effective system of specialised training to its land, water and air forces. The Indian army has an excellent tradition and outstanding training institutions for defence personnel spread all over the country. Some of these training establishments are:

(1) Indian Military Academy, Dehradun
(2) National Defence Academy, Khadakvasla
(3) National Defence College, New Delhi
(4) Defence Services Staff College, Wellington
(5) Armed Forces Medical College, Poona
(6) Specialised Training Establishments as shown below:

Table 2: Specialised Training Establishments

Army	*Navy*	*Air Force*
(a) College of Military Engineers, Kirkae (b) The School of Artillery, Devlali (c) The Infantry School, Mhow (d) The Ordnance School, Jabalpur (e) The Mont's Veterinary Centre (f) The School of Physical Training, Pune (g) The Army and Air Transport School, Agra	(a) INS, Bendurnthi (b) Naval Air Centre, Gawda (c) The Engineering College, Lonewela (d) INS, Jamnagar (e) INS, Vishakhapatnam (f) INS, Shimla and Mumbai	(a) The Air Force Flying College, Jodhpur (b) The Air Force Technical College, Jalahali (c) The Air Force Administration College, Coimbatore (d) NCC Officers Training School, Kanjti

In addition, there are many small training centres for varied defence jobs. Some of them are:

(1) Officers Training Academy, Chennai
(2) National Military College, Dehradun
(3) National Unity Foundation, Pune
(4) Naval Academy, Goa
(5) Defence Establishment, Delhi
(6) Institute for Defence Studies and Analyses
(7) Army Transport College, Agra

A variety of training programmes are organised by regimental centres. Ordnance and materials management is taught to new recruits by practical demonstrations.

Public Undertakings

The department of defence production of the defence ministry has eight public undertakings engaged in production of equipments and materials for defence use and modernisation.

(1) Bharat Electronics Limited, Bangalore: It has nine units at Bangalore, Chennai, Hyderabad, Machlipattanam, Pune, Ghaziabad, Kotdwar, Panchkula and Taloja.
(2) Bharat Earth Movers, Bangalore.
(3) Garden Reach Ship Builders and Engineers Limited, Calcutta: It has three departments: (a) Ship section, (b) Engine section, and (c) Engineering section.
(4) Majgaon Docks Limited, Mumbai.
(5) Mixed Metal Corporations Limited, Hyderabad.
(6) Hindustan Aeronautics Limited, Bangalore: It has thirteen units in six states.
(7) Goa Shipyard Limited, Vasco De Gama.
(8) Bharat Dynamics Ltd., Hyderabad.

Most of these undertakings are self-sufficient and working to their maximum capacity. New developments in technology and sensitivity of intelligence makes their work extra important. The department of supplies though merged in defence production, still does this work and continues with the legacies.

A holistic look at the ministry of defence leads to the conclusion that it is a very big ministry and organisationally it is too conventional and bureaucratic. Its training establishments, public undertakings and field formations are by and large attuned to conventional ways of warfare and defence. Although the defence department has defended the country and its borders in several wars against Pakistan and China, but as compared to other defence forces of the developed countries a lot has to be done to modernise the administrative organisation of the defence establishments. Some of the weaknesses of the ministry and reform ideas can be evolved under following points:

(1) The Britisher's organised Indian army with a philosophy of negativism. The cantonment-based army had been insulated from the society it seeks to serve. Today, the army society interface is a need which is felt by both. A positive philosophy requires 'selective conscription' and strengthening of territorial army so that Army may get popular support and its strength is increased by constant cooperation from the people.

(2) Modern warfares are televised and stand computerised for precise strikes. Although the three branches of Indian Army have come a long way in modernising the equipment and weaponry, yet enough more has to be accomplished to catch the Pentagon and latest techniques in the areas of training.

(3) Intelligence and research today have undergone a sea change. The administrative organisation being too bureaucratic underplays the professionals. India does not suffer from the threat of military coup d'état yet the commanders and soldiers need a better deal at the hands of civilians and political representatives.

(4) The development of atomic energy presents Indian Defence Services in a new perspective in post-Pokaran era. The nature of defence and offence both have changed. Foreign policies and diplomacy must provide the basic infrastructure for defence. Obviously, there should be more coordinational and participative structures in the ministry to build consensus on defence policies and their implementation. The rigidity of structures must give way to more flexible units and development agencies in every field.

The defence studies and analysis has done an outstanding work in sensitising the military administration to its professional and administrative needs. There should be self-reforming exercises within the organisation and their targeted time bound implementation can make our defence preparedness better and more effective.

Ministry of Personnel, Public Grievances and Pensions

This ministry has come into existence in March 1985 by a merger of two departments, namely, the Department of Public Services from the Ministry of Home and the Department of Administrative Reforms. Originally, the department of personnel was located in cabinet secretariat. In 1970, the independent department of personnel was created but the 1973 Janta government change shifted it to home ministry, from where now it comes to the new department in 1985. Similarly, the Administrative Reforms work started in 1954 with the establishment of O&M division in the cabinet secretariat, but in 1964, this division was elevated to the status of a Department of Administrative

Reforms in the Ministry of Home. In 1973, it was shifted to personnel department to be located in cabinet secretariat. The Janta government brought it back to the ministry of home. In 1985, the two separate departments of personnel and administrative reforms were joined together to create a new and independent nodal ministry of personnel, public grievances and pensions.

The ministry generally functions under the overall charge of the Prime Minister who is assisted by a minister of state and a deputy minister. The administrative head of the ministry is the secretary (personnel) who is a career civil servant, invariably from the IAS. The junior and middle level positions in the ministry are filled by personnel drawn from different services but the senior policy making posts are monopolised by members of IAS. The staffing pattern is governed by the same criteria as applied to other ministries. Whatever specialisation the official has, he gets it while on his job, on completion of their stipulated term, the functionaries are transferred and new officers join. The junior staff generally receives some training in one of the state-run training institutions, but their morale is rather low owing to a lack of recognition of their expertise and absence of opportunities for promotions.

Created on the recommendation of the Administrative Reforms Commission, the ministry follows a different kind of administrative organisation. There is no separate cabinet minister for the ministry. The PM is the overall in charge and is assisted by a minister of state and a deputy minister. In practice, it is the minister of state who looks after ministry's functions. The secretary as administrative head has three additional secretaries and a host of officers in charge of administration of each of the three departments in which the ministry stands organised. These officers have a number of joint secretaries and several official of supporting staff under them. Like other ministries, it follows the tenure system and most of the senior posts are filled by the members of Indian Administrative Service. However, the junior and middle level posts are manned by members of allied services. In brief, there obtains no expertise or specialised knowledge of personnel matters in the personnel of this ministry.

The organisational chart with functions can be depicted as under:

Ministry of Personnel, Public Grievances and Pensions

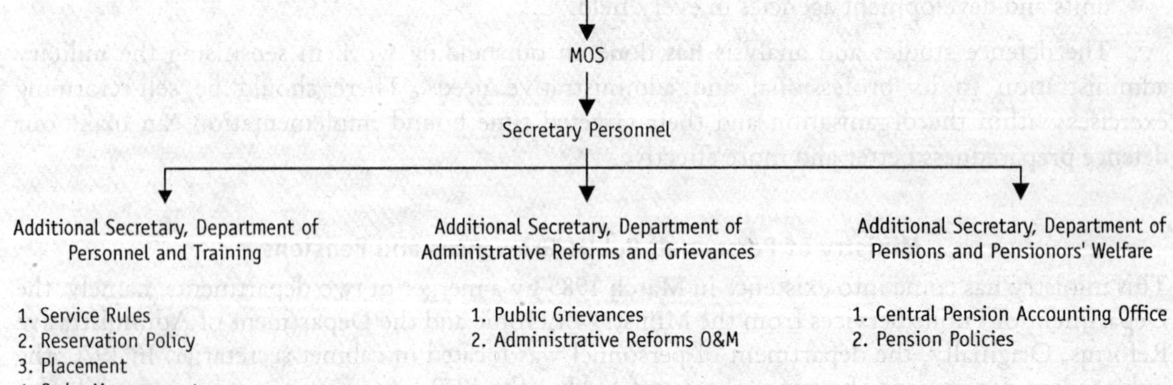

The functions of the ministry are very neatly divided into three specific departments. The personnel and training department coordinates the different aspects of personnel policies and management. Recruitment, placement, training, cadre review and administrative vigilance and its thrust areas and the functional activities extend to a very wide area of policy formulation, programme implementation, and evaluative exercises of varied nature. This involves the placement of officers in the senior and middle management levels, planning for career development and foreign assignments. The tenure deputation of posts in the secretariat from the level of under secretary and above in the ministries of Central government (except the ministries of railways and external affairs) is operational from the panels of names for the posts from under secretary to the joint secretary in the ministries concerned. The Appointments Committee of the Cabinet (ACC) approve these posting at the level of deputy secretary and above. Such an approval is required also for all important, non-secretariat senior appointments to positions of all public sector undertakings, nationalised banks, statutory authorities and government companies and enterprises. Proposals for posts above the level of joint secretary are initiated by the Cabinet Secretary and hundreds of officers are appointed to the levels of under secretary, deputy secretary, director and joint secretary every year. Similarly, career development including foreign assignments as a part of this development is administered by the ministry. The state governments also make individual career plans for their direct recruits. The department selects officials for foreign training assignments on the basis of computerised records. The department selects suitable officers to prepare a panel of experts for three years. A variety of assignments with the United Nations and allied agencies are seconded by the ministry.

The department is responsible for not only the IAS and other cadres in similar services but also for the cadres of section officers and the central secretariat service. The cadre management aims at rationalisation of the cadre structure based on manpower projections. The cadre review exercises work out the structural ratio of various cadres and the threshold profile of the members of the services are compiled to indicate the biannual position. The Cadre Review Committee scrutinises these briefs and communicates its recommendations to the concerned cadre controlling authorities. As a nodal agency the department identifies, formulates and implements a large number of training programmes for officers in priority development sectors. The development of trained manpower and the upgradation of the training potential in state/central institution is the purpose and career based training programmes, and the creation of a greater awareness have revised the course contents of the training programmes. The training of IAS probationers, and the in-service training programmes are a special responsibility of this department. The in-service training for IAS officers consists of one week and three week critical issue based programmes for the senior officers. The department conducts 17 one week training programmes at 11 different national institutions and state training centre in the country.

The officers who have served for 6 to 9 years, 10 to 16 years and 17 to 20 years have to undergo training in programme implement, management concepts, policy planning and analysis in different groups, clubbed in 9, 5 and 4 kinds of programme modules. A large number of training programmes have been sponsored to improve planning and implementation capabilities of senior and middle level officers. The scheme has general programmes and the state level programmes for various categories of public servants.

The department of personnel undertakes coordinate work of various ministries for maintenance of discipline and reduction of corruption in their respective areas of operation. It handles administrative matters which pertain to the Central Bureau of Investigation and the Central Vigilance Commission. The vigilance and anti-corruption measures institute disciplinary proceedings against high level officials. The Central government employees go to CAT in service matters for adjudication of pending cases transferred to it from High Courts and subordinate courts. The department of personnel and training is the administrative department for CAT created in 1985.

A Non-Statutory Voluntary Scheme for compulsory arbitration has been introduce for the Central government employees on the pattern of Whitley Councils of Great Britain. This has been functioning as a Joint Consultative Machinery (JCM) and applies to all the regular employees of the Central government, except the Group-A and Group-B services, UT employees and police personnel. The three-tier machinery of JCM consists of the National Council at the apex body and departmental councils and regional/office councils below. There is a provision for compulsory arbitration in cases of disagreement, either in the National Council or in the departmental council on matters relating to pay, hours of work and leave. A Board of Arbitration also functions under the administrative control of the ministry of labour for the similar purpose. The department of personnel functions as a change agent in the machinery for both the bodies.

The Department of Administrative Reforms and Public Grievances

The department has two specific functions to perform:

(a) It initiates and monitors administrative reforms at micro and macro levels.
(b) It ensures the redressal of citizen's grievances against government organisations.

For this propose, the department conducts research studies and provides management consultancy to various central government ministries, particularly in relation to issues relating to organisational structure, methods and procedures obtained there. The organisation and methods activities include modernisation of government offices through cybernetics, reduction in paper work, records management through computer and minimising level in file disposal.

Most of the ministries in the Government of India have directors of grievances. Each such director has powers to call for papers connected with grievances pending for more than three months and to take decisions. The Department of Administrative Reforms and Public Grievances organises periodic review meetings and the directorate suggests ways and means to handle complaints and provide succour to the aggrieved. The concept, volume and nature of public grievance demand right to information, citizen charters, Janta darbars and sensitisation of administrative officials at every level of hierarchy. The department keeps in touch with relevant people and initiates reforms to lessen public grievances fake or real in a democratic polity.

The Department of Pensions and Pensioners Welfare

Its creation indicates the concern of the government about its employees. The retirees have special problems of geriatric health and old age security, the absence of which may destabilise their security and damage their integrity while in service. The pension schemes and pensioners welfare have several new and unprecedent dimensions in the age of liberalised economy and expanding insurance services. The department coordinates matters related to retirement benefits to employees and ensures a fair deal for safe and happy retirement. The old scheme of pension needs revision in the context of employment to the youth, voluntary retirement schemes and old age pensions to all.

The Ministry of Personnel (Administrative Reforms) Public Grievances and Pensions is a unique experiment in secretariat system. Headed by an additional secretary, it enjoys a high status and takes care of all administrative matters relating to the Union Public Service Commission, Central Bureau of Investigation, Administrative Tribunals and the Indian Institute of Public Administration, the LBS National Academy of Administration (Mussoorie) and the Institute of Secretariat Training, Delhi. The two recruitment agencies, the UPSC and the SSC recruit candidates and conduct open and departmental examinations for various services. Besides these, the Public Enterprises Selection Board recommends appointment to the posts of chief executives, directors and part-time chairmen of central public enterprises. All these three organisations are autonomous and the department of personnel and training is the administrative department for the agencies.

The reservation policy of the Union government is outside the administrative preview of the department. Yet it works out the number of reserved posts in each cadre. Reservation for SC/ST in the civil service is made on the basis of the total number of vacancies occurring in each recruitment year. Backlogs are cleared by special recruitment drives for reserved vacancies. The Central government keeps revising the categories and quantum of OBC quota and provisions for the reservation of ex-servicemen and the physically handicapped. The department implements these rules and functions as a nodal personnel agency which combines personnel reforms with administrative change, public grievance redressal and pensioners welfare.

Ministry of External Affairs

The ministry of external affairs, also called as foreign ministry in common parlance is the administrative organisation that formulates foreign policy and executes the same through its diplomatic offices located all over the world. Naturally it is a ministry with a difference because its activities sensitise several ministries and it has to keep its vigil on what goes on in the entire world. In 1947, with the transfer of power to Indian hands, it was named as 'Ministry of External Affairs and Commonwealth Relations'. In 1949, the appendage Commonwealth Relations was dropped and the new nomenclature 'Ministry of External Affairs' was given which continues till today.

The evolution of the ministry can be traced back to 'The Secret Department' of East India Company. In 1783, it was renamed as foreign department, but no Foreign Secretary was appointed. Three year later, 'The Secret Department' was reorganised into four branches, namely, (a) Secret Politics (b) Secret Military Relations (c) Secret Foreign Affairs, and (d) Secret Reforms. By the close of 18th century, it was again reorganised into two departments, viz., (1) Secret department, and (2) Foreign and Political department.

1833 Charter Act made the secret and military departments responsible to the Government of India.

1843 Foreign department became a regular administrative department after the termination of the mixed secretariat.

1859 Portfolio system was introduced in Governor-General's council but the Governor-General kept the department under his control as crown's representative.

1914 It was christened as foreign and political department with two branches, (1) Political Branch, and (2) Foreign Branch. The first one dealt with princely states while the second one was responsible for foreign relations.

1937 The two branches were elevated to the status of administrative department. The Governor-General being in charge of the department, the matters pertaining to Burma (now Myanmar), Sri Lanka and other British Colonies were handled by a separate department called Commonwealth Department.

1946 The Interim government under Prime Minister and Foreign Minister of free India Pandit Nehru created two departments with common responsibility. They were called: (1) External affairs department, and (2) Commonwealth relation department.

1947 The above two departments were merged into a joint department of foreign and Commonwealth relations.

1948 The task of external publicity was added to its functions.

1949 The appendage Commonwealth relations was dropped and it became the ministry of external affairs.

1964 The post of the Secretary General responsible for coordination among three secretaries was dropped.

1966 A Foreign Service Committee was constituted under N.N. Pillai who recommended that:

(a) The post of Secretary General should be revived and he should be the principal adviser to the foreign minister.
(b) The SG will be responsible for over all coordination among all operations.
(c) The SG will implement policy decision of the ministry.
(d) He will be the senior-most official of Indian foreign services and will be responsible for efficient administration.
(e) He will act as secretary of policy planning and review committee of the ministry.

After Pandit Nehru's demise, the successors did not like to keep the office of Secretary General. Today secretaries, EA-I, EA-II and the Foreign Secretary directly send their files to the foreign minister. The ministry has a big secretariat but its subordinate and attached offices are quite different from their counterparts in other ministries. In fact, the ministry has no attached office in the technical sense and subordinate offices have varieties.

These offices and divisions of the MEA are organised partly on the basis of place and partly on purpose. The purpose functions are managed on a territorial basis so that local and regional problems of the country concerned can be handled with expertise. Moreover the missions, high commissions and legations, which are stationed in different countries as per diplomatic practices under international law, may work effectively on the basis of reciprocity. There is tremendous amount of flexibility in the organisation and changes are indicted as per needs of the country concerned. In the year 1990, there were 14 territorial divisions. The African division looks after 43 African countries; American or the AMS division looks after Canada and the USA; the BM division looks after Bangladesh and Myanmar; East Asia division which is responsible for 6 counties including People's Republic of China, Japan and Republic of Korea (South) and Democratic People's Republic of Korea (North); East Europe (EE) division is in charge of 8 countries including the erstwhile Union of Soviet Socialist Republics. With the break-up of the USSR in late 1991, a new situation has emerged and there has to be a reorganisation of divisions; West Europe (WE) division looks after 26 countries including the UK and the Federal Republic of Germany. With the unification of West and East Germany a new classification has been added. Gulf division looks after 8 countries including Saudi Arabia; Iran, Afghanistan and Pakistan (IAP) division is looking after

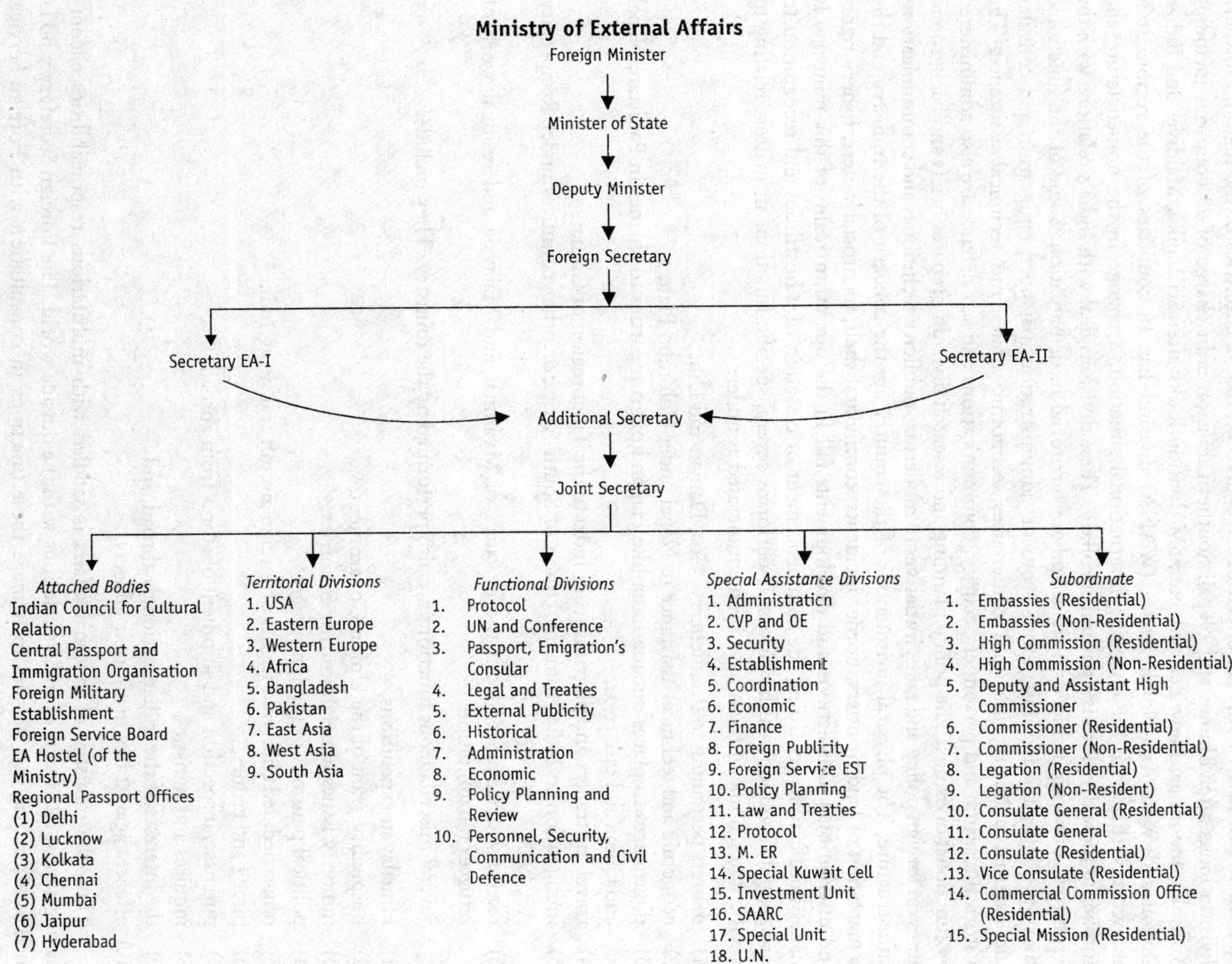
Ministry of External Affairs
Foreign Minister
Minister of State
Deputy Minister
Foreign Secretary
Secretary EA-I
Secretary EA-II
Additional Secretary
Joint Secretary
Attached Bodies
1. Indian Council for Cultural Relation
2. Central Passport and Immigration Organisation
3. Foreign Military Establishment
4. Foreign Service Board
5. EA Hostel (of the Ministry)
6. Regional Passport Offices
(1) Delhi
(2) Lucknow
(3) Kolkata
(4) Chennai
(5) Mumbai
(6) Jaipur
(7) Hyderabad
Territorial Divisions
1. USA
2. Eastern Europe
3. Western Europe
4. Africa
5. Bangladesh
6. Pakistan
7. East Asia
8. West Asia
9. South Asia
Functional Divisions
1. Protocol
2. UN and Conference
3. Passport, Emigration's Consular
4. Legal and Treaties
5. External Publicity
6. Historical
7. Administration
8. Economic
9. Policy Planning and Review
10. Personnel, Security, Communication and Civil Defence
Special Assistance Divisions
1. Administration
2. CVP and OE
3. Security
4. Establishment
5. Coordination
6. Economic
7. Finance
8. Foreign Publicity
9. Foreign Service EST
10. Policy Planning
11. Law and Treaties
12. Protocol
13. M. ER
14. Special Kuwait Cell
15. Investment Unit
16. SAARC
17. Special Unit
18. U.N.
Subordinate
1. Embassies (Residential)
2. Embassies (Non-Residential)
3. High Commission (Residential)
4. High Commission (Non-Residential)
5. Deputy and Assistant High Commissioner
6. Commissioner (Residential)
7. Commissioner (Non-Residential)
8. Legation (Residential)
9. Legation (Non-Resident)
10. Consulate General (Residential)
11. Consulate General
12. Consulate (Residential)
13. Vice Consulate (Residential)
14. Commercial Commission Office (Residential)
15. Special Mission (Residential)

these three countries. Latin American or LAC division has 32 countries of the region; Northern division looks after Bhutan and Nepal; Southern division is in charge of 23 countries including Australia, Indonesia, New Zealand, etc.; SM division looks after Sri Lanka, Maldives and Indian Ocean; and West Asia-North Africa (WANA) division has 16 countries of the region. It is noteworthy that with the changing international situation, a change in the nomenclature and number of these divisions is a natural corollary. These divisions deal with India's relations with the respective countries included in them and are territorial in demarcation. Some of the functional divisions look after administration, protocol, administration, passport, emigration and consular and external publicity, UN and conferences, economic affairs and technical assistance. The historical research and personnel, security, communications and self defence are also administered by functional divisions. The policy planning and research division prepares briefs and background notes on foreign policy and takes initiatives to modernise publicity techniques and communications infrastructure. The physical jurisdictions of the country are the concern of the ministry and the demarcation of land frontiers, border incidents, continental shelf, territorial waters, fishery rights and international jurisdictions and developments fall in the operation realm of this ministry. It makes notifications regarding the commencement or cessation of a hostilities and recognition to foreign and Commonwealth visitors. It performs several specific functions in matters relating to specific states. Some of them have been enumerated as under:

(1) matters pertaining to Pondicherry, Goa, Daman and Diu;
(2) economic and technical assistance to Nepal under Colombo Plan;
(3) pilgrimages to places outside India like Haj and pilgrim parties to shrines in Pakistan, Nepal and China and *vice versa;*
(4) travel for traders and pilgrims from India to the Tibet region of China;
(5) immigration to India from the Union of South Africa or other countries under Reciprocity Act 1943;
(6) recovery of advances from the evacuees of Myanmar and Malaysia and residual work of refugees rehabilitation.

Several miscellaneous functions are also performed by the ministry. They include:

(1) Himalayan expeditions,
(2) hospitality grant of the Union Government.
(3) minority issues in neighbouring countries,
(4) political pensions to foreign refugees,
(5) non-scheduled chartered flights of foreign aircraft transiting India,
(6) piracy and crimes,
(7) purchase, inspection and shipment of stores from abroad,
(8) inquires and statistics,
(9) the interests of the Indian nationals abroad, and
(10) offences against law in allotted subjects.

Thus, the ministry of external affairs is saddled with multifarious responsibilities encompassing almost all aspects of India's relations with the outside world. The Foreign Secretary who is an IFS officer has vast powers to manage these functions in consultation with Foreign Service Board.

The Foreign Service Board

It works under the chairmanship of the Foreign Secretary and other members which include secretary (east), secretary (west) and joint secretary (administration) in the ministry. The secretary in the commerce ministry is also a member. The board tenders advice in postings and transfers of the diplomatic officers other than those of heads, promotions and confirmation in the Indian Foreign Service in consultation with the UPSC; and grant of diplomatic status of officers placed in Indian missions abroad.

Foreign Service Training Institute: The ministry trains its own personnel. Some of its training programme include:

(1) a model professional courses in diplomacy and international relations for IFS probationers,
(2) a refresher course for commercial officials abroad,
(3) a familiarisation programme for resident foreign diplomats,
(4) the basic professional course for IFS (B) personnel,
(5) several training programmes for use of computers for the ministry officials, and
(6) a foreign language training programme for IFS probationers has been launched since 1991. The institute maintains contact with other training institutions both in India and abroad.

The India Council of Cultural Relations: It is an autonomous body established in 1950 with headquarters at New Delhi. It has seven regional offices in different parts of the country. The basic objectives was to establish and strengthen cultural relations and exchanges programmes between India and other countries. It looks after the welfare of foreign students studying in India and granting them scholarships. The council organises programmes and promotes awareness and appreciation of Indian cultural heritage abroad. It has established Indian cultural centres in some foreign countries which maintain libraries; organise lectures, exhibitions, competitions, performance of dance and music, staging of plays, screening of films and publication of news bulletins. Indian music, dance and languages are taught at these centres of the council. The council organises Maulana Abul Kalam Azad Memorial lectures and confers Jawaharlal Nehru Award for International Understanding. It brings out quarterly journals in English, French, Arabic, Hindi and Spanish languages. It also publishes books and maintains a big library of 100,000 volumes to help readers and research scholars. To have an effective and overall assessment of diplomatic missions abroad, an inspectorate was reactivised in 1964. It was headed by an additional secretary but the experiment proved abortive. The functions of MEA can be classified into five kinds:

(1) Conduct of India's relations with foreign.
(2) India's representation in the UN.
(3) Advise to other ministries in dealing with foreign governments and institutions.
(4) Administration of Indian Extradition Act, the Passport Act, the Reciprocity Act, etc.
(5) Work of the ICCR.

This makes the ministry responsible for a variety of detailed activities for which the other ministries solely depend upon it. No comprehensive list of these activities can be drawn. S.R. Maheshwari has culled these activities in the following enumeration:

(1) External affairs.
(2) Relations with foreign states and Commonwealth countries.

(3) All matters affecting foreign diplomatic and consular officers and UN offices and UN specialised agencies in India.
(4) Passports and visas, excluding the grant of visas of endorsements for entry into India, but including the grant of entry permits to South Africans of non-Indian origin under the Reciprocity (South Africa) Rules, 1944 and the grant of entry visas for Sri Lankan nationals except missionaries.
(5) Extradition of criminals and accused persons from India to foreign and Commonwealth countries and vice versa, general administration of the Indian Extradition Act 1903 (XV of 1903), and extra-territoriality.
(6) Preventive detention in India for reasons of state connected with external and Commonwealth affairs.
(7) Repatriation of nationals of foreign and Commonwealth countries from India and deportation and repatriation of Indian nationals in foreign and Commonwealth countries to India.
(8) All emigration under the Indian Emigration Act 1922, from India to overseas countries and the return of emigrants; immigration to India from the Union of South Africa or any other country to which the Reciprocity Act may apply.
(9) All consular functions.
(10) Travel arrangements for traders, muleteers, porters and pilgrims from India to the Tibet region of China and vice versa.
(11) Liaison work connected with the education ministry's cultural scholarship schemes and nomination of private students of Indian origin domiciled abroad to reserved seats in medical and engineering colleges in India.
(12) Matters relating to the state of Nagaland transferred to the home ministry on 19 May, 1972.
(13) Political pensions paid to foreign refugees and descendants of those who rendered services abroad.
(14) Ceremonial matters relating to foreign and Commonwealth visitors and diplomatic and consular representatives.
(15) Matters in respect of Pondicherry, Goa, Daman and Diu, involving relations with France and Portugal.
(16) Relations with states in special treaty relations with India such as Bhutan.
(17) Himalayan expeditions and permission to foreigners to travel beyond the 'Inner Line'.
(18) Coordination and development measures in border areas.
(19) United Nations specialised agencies and other international conference.
(20) Indian Foreign Services.
(21) Indian Foreign Branch 'B'.
(22) External publicity.
(23) Political treaties, agreements and conventions with foreign and Commonwealth countries.
(24) (a) Pilgrimages to places outside India including the administration of the Port Haj Committee Act 1932 and the rules made thereunder and the Indian Pilgrim Ships Rules 1933, and pilgrim parties from India to shrines in Pakistan and vice versa.
(b) Protection and preservation of non-Muslim shrines in Pakistan and Muslim shrines in India in terms of the Pant-Mirza Agreement of 1955.
(25) Abducted persons (recovery and restoration).

(26) Evacuation of non-Muslims from Pakistan to India.
(27) Protection of the rights of minority communities in India and Pakistan (except rehabilitation of Muslim migrants who have returned from East Pakistan to West Bengal under the Nehru-Liaquat Pact; rehabilitation of Muslims internally displaced in West Bengal at the time of communal disturbance on the partition of the country;
(28) Non-Muslim migration from Pakistan and Muslim migration from India.
(29) Recovery of advances granted to the evacuees from Myanmar, Malaya, etc., during the years 1942–47 and residual work relating to refugees given asylum in India during World War II.
(30) Notification regarding commencement of cessation of a state of war.
(31) Foreign jurisdiction.
(32) Piracies and crimes committed on the high seas or in the air, offences against the law of nations committed on land or the high seas or in the air.
(33) Inquiries and statistics for the purposes of any of the subjects allotted to this ministry.
(34) Fees in respect of any of the subjects allotted to this ministry.
(35) Offences against laws with respect to any of the subjects allotted to this ministry.
(36) Hospitality grants of the Government of India.
(37) Demarcation of the land frontiers of India.
(38) Border raids and incidents on the land borders of India.
(39) Diplomatic flight clearances for non-scheduled chartered flights of foreign civil and military aircraft transiting India.
(40) Matters relating to the continental shelf, territorial waters, contiguous zone, the question of fishery rights in the high seas and other questions of international law.
(41) Economic and technical assistance given by India to the Government of Nepal under the Colombo Plan for cooperative economic development.

The ministry has no attached offices. However, there are 140 Missions/posts abroad. The diplomatic and consular missions abroad have a unique status and cannot be called as attached or subordinate offices. The ministry does have two subordinate offices, viz., (1) the Central Passport and Emigration Organisation, New Delhi and (2) the External Affairs Hostel, New Delhi. Several innovative measures were introduced by the Consular, Passport and Visa (CPV) division to rationalise, simplify and further streamline the functioning of the passport offices in India and the consular sections of the Indian missions in foreign countries. There are two dozen regional passport offices in the country.

The Foreign Secretary runs the ministry and administers the foreign office almost single-handedly. He defines national interests almost independently and there is relatively less intervention by political representatives. His coordinating role is of significance. Designated as Secretary General – before 1947, now he is called as Foreign Secretary.

Reforms in the Context of Changing International Scenario

The administrative organisation of MEA by and large continues to be Nehruvian which the foreign policy of India and the post-cold war world have undergone a sea change. The non-alignment of seventies has yielded place to new alignments in the Uni-polar World of 21st century. The scenario is changing so fast that all foreign policies are in doll drums. The disintegrated Soviet Republics are still in a process of adjustment. The US has been reeling after twin tower tragedy and the Iraq War haunts the hawks. The UN confronts a grim struggle for survival and reorganisation as a representative body of world public opinion. The neighbouring countries of India are unstable and the new triangle of India, China and USSR is still a far-fetched reality. The West Asian crises and South Asian instability are newer challenges to which policies of globalisation and liberalisation keep adding dilemmas of new markets and worldwide trans-border terrorism. The drug and weapon trade by smugglers needs new repatriation tactics. MOU on trade and commerce and oil diplomacy have to be administered with caution. Pakistan alone, as a factor in India's foreign policy and diplomacy demands a reorganisation of the ministry in more than one way.

Some of the suggestions offered by ARC and Pillai Committee are relevant even today. Obviously the position of Foreign Secretary needs to be strengthened and the new entrants to IFS have to be kept in high morale. Gone are the days when the service enjoyed extra prestige. Today the open economy and world trade places higher responsibilities and poor compensation to officials living in exile. The smaller countries have been neglected for long and the lack of professionalism in IFS cadre takes a heavy toll of efficiency. Some of the following measures suggested by ARC deserve consideration:

(1) The ministry is too much of a bureaucratic adjunct, overcrowded with divisions. It shall be worthwhile to associate a variety of committees to the administration of the ministry to make it operational for democratic diplomacy of our times.
(2) The ambassadors and high commissioners are selected by the cabinet but a real quality feedback is needed to the panels by the ministry. Presently, it has no mechanism to improve this recruitment to mission positions.
(3) The ministry deals with every department or ministry of government. It shall be administratively more convenient if a regulatory agency or department is created to coordinate these sensitive activities of far reaching consequence in economic matters.
(4) The territorial organisation has its good points and strength, but some regional and continental arrangements can facilitate diplomatic relations at a wider level.
(5) The attached and subordinate offices of the ministry need streamlining. In fact, they should be organised to make globalisation a reality and recap the benefits of worldwide phenomenon called liberation, promotion of joint ventures. Search for markets should be one of the functions of MEA and it should have a division at Delhi and cells in every mission abroad.
(6) With the increase in functions the ministry's organisation should pursue a policy of administrative decentralisation. Professionalism can come to the cadres of IFS if they are rigorously trained and their language proficiency is increased to work for Indian politics, economics and culture in foreign countries.

Thus, the ministry of external affairs is no longer an opaque house. It has to work for the policies of the country including foreign policy. World Peace is our avowed mission but UNO and its specialised agencies need to be strengthened in national and global interests. The narrow technical view of diplomacy has already yielded place to global democratic notions of interstate diplomacy with which the MEA should adjust its bureaucratic organisation in the era of globalisation, liberalisation and atomic wars.

6

Executive Agencies and Commissions

A secretarial system works with a network of executive agencies, authorities boards and commissions which implement the policy at different levels. Some of these bodies are constitutional, others are created by the statues of the Parliament and most of them grow with the expansion of government activities in the public sector. With the advent of liberalisation and globalisation the new area of regulatory agencies and advisory structures has witnessed a proliferation of these bodies in every field of activity in India. It is not possible to define theoretically the specific nature of these agencies yet broad distinctions can be highlighted in their constitution and working. Some of these can be called as misnomers and the so-called corporations and commissions are functioning as boards or bureaus. Similarly, the agencies are undistinguishable from authorities and attached offices are functioning as subordinate or subordinate-cum-attached offices in the field.

The attached offices are closely and directly associated with the ministries or departments in the shaping of policies, as they furnish essential technical data and advice and provide executive direction to the department concerned. They are also responsible for implementing the policies and decisions of the government. The attached office may also be regarded as the repository of technical information in the light of which a policy is formulated and a decision is taken by the concerned ministry. Subordinate offices function as field establishments, which are responsible for the detailed execution of decisions taken by the government. A subordinate office normally functions under an attached office. But, if there is no attached office in a ministry, a subordinate office may function directly under the ministry. There is no clear line of distinction between the two types of offices. However, it may be said that the importance of attached offices is greater and their number is smaller than that of the subordinate officer which are inferior in status.

Bureaus, Boards and Commissions

If an organisation reposes its responsibility in a single official it will be known as a 'bureau' but if it is a group the organisation will be called a 'board' or a commission. A bureau is the principal internal unit of the department. Its head is responsible to and works under the direction of the head of the organisation. Bureaus have homogeneous structure, and perform a single task or a series of related tasks. It is the working unit of administration, and the department is a coordinating device. The well-known examples of bureaus are those of Bureau of Public Enterprise and the Central Bureau of Investigation (CBI) in India. A bureau is more suited for administrative functions and is designed for those services which demand quick decisions and immediate action. The single head enforces better discipline. Police and fire services, prison administration, highway patrol may be placed in this category.

A board is a body of members who are required to act collectively. A 'commission' is also a body of members, but they have two capacities. *First,* the members act collectively like those of a board; and *secondly*, each member also acts individually as head of a distinct branch of the organisation. The common examples are those of a Municipal Board, and a Public Service Commission. The term 'commission' is be used when the body is charged with important regulatory duties to public utility enterprises. Where the duties are primarily administrative or regulatory, they relate to matters other than public utilities. The administrative board is the departmental head for an organisation unit of a government. It is so-called because all the powers to administer reside with it, even though substantial authority may have been delegated to a chief administrative officer.

But board or commission type of organisation is preferred where the principal function consists in exercising discretion on a large scale, and drafting of rules affect private rights. In such cases the judgment of a number of persons is likely to be superior to that of a single individual. The kinds of services for which a board or commission is particularly desirable and useful are: (1) Quasi-judicial and quasi-legislative services such as public utility corporations, which perform/ formulate rules and regulations for determining the rates and conditions of services; and quasi-judicial decisions or judgments on issues effecting public and private rights arising under such rules and regulations; (2) Those services which call for discretionary powers or control, for example, Public Service Commissions; (3) Services where different interests are to be represented, for example, labour conciliation board having representatives of labour, employers and the general public. The Railway Board, Election Commission, and Public Service Commission fall in this category. (4) Operations which need depoliticisation for example, Human Rights Commission.

But there are a number of branches of administration, whose duties fall in both field – administrative and quasi-legislative or quasi-judicial. In such cases, it is better to combine both types of organisations, that is a single officer for administrative work and a board for other works. For example, in a municipality there may be a superintendent of education for administrative work and a board for determining policy and programme. However, as regards the relative jurisdiction of the two there may be two alternatives: (1) to make both the offices independent and coordinate; and (2) to vest all authority in the board and make the administrative officer its executive secretary. Boards and commissions are statutory when they are set up by the Acts of Parliament. It is argued that the board or commission system involves expense, delay and diffusion of responsibility which makes cooperation and coordination more difficult. The single administrator is preferable because it gives a chance of more knowledge, more activity, more responsibility and, more zeal and attention. The decisions of boards are slower, their energy is less and their responsibility is more diffused.

Administration by a board or commission has been commonplace throughout the history of government. These bodies have to take quick decisions for efficient and rapid realisation of that commodity or service for which they have been constituted. This necessitates more autonomy and flexibility in the administration that are possible for departments within a government. This form of organisation is preferred in the interest of administrative integrity in the face of external pressures. The majority of these bodies are neither purely expert committees nor purely representative in nature, but a combination of both these elements, to provide a balance between the specialised requirements and the representative character of a democratic government. The authority to perform quasi functions is safer, if entrusted in plural bodies rather than in a single individual.

A board or commission type of organisation is recommended when public policy has not been fully finalised, and, requires joint discussion and deliberation before its formulation. Since the Second World War, increasing and extensive use has been made of these types of agencies all over the world. In India numerous board, commissions and corporations have been established for performing functions like regulating trade and commerce, transport and communication, conducting examinations, providing public utility services and rendering financial assistance.

These bodies can be classified on the several basis: (a) Nature of Authority: (i) whether a board/commission is purely advisory like the Small Scale Industries Board; (ii) or a board/commission combines policy making and administrative directions, like the Planning Commission; or (iii) whether a board/commission not only makes policy and gives administrative direction but also executes the policies, like the Railway Board or the Atomic Energy Commission. (b) Legal Status: These boards/commissions are provided for in the Constitution itself or set up by the President under his constitutional powers. This category includes commissions like the Finance Commission. (c) Act of Parliament: The boards/commissions may be created by an act of Parliament like the University Grants Commission, the Oil and Natural Gas Commission and could be called statutory boards/commissions. (d) Legal Units: Some boards/commissions are created by a resolution of the Union government and could be termed as attached boards or commissions placed directly under the control of relevant ministries, for example, the All India Handloom Board. (e) Substitute Boards: Similarly a board of commission may be substitute for the ministry or department or an agency under it. The examples of such substitute bodies are the Railway Board, the Posts and Telegraphs Board and the Atomic Energy Commission.

To carry out the executive functions of the government without fear or pressure, the framers of the Constitution have provided for the setting up of independent statutory authorities to deal with specified duties. These may be enumerated as: Attorney General of India, Comptroller and Auditor-General of India, Election Commission, Union Public Service Commission, Finance Commission and the Special Officer for Scheduled Areas, etc.

The commissions mentioned in the Constitution enjoy the greatest amount of autonomy; and are appointed directly by the President of India. They do not come under the general administrative control of ministry in their day-to-day functioning. The statutory boards are put under the general administrative control of the ministry concerned but are free from the regular departmental procedures. The third category of bodies like the Handloom Board, the Handicrafts Board, etc., are created for a specified period of time and their existence depends upon the will of the ministries concerned. They are attached to the ministry and are known as attached boards.

Advisory Bodies, Committees and Councils

Advisory committees are committees (or bodies) attached to the machinery of government – for the purpose of advising the organs of government generally consist of non-officials – individuals or representatives of various interests or public organisations. Since the use of 'non-officials' implies exclusion of 'persons not on the payroll of government' it is argued that the term 'non-officials' does not convey the common connotation.

The term 'bodies' is wider than 'committees' and includes councils as well as conferences. The ordinary concept of the advisory body is a group of experts and representative of the public called into functions, usually on a voluntary basis, as a consultative group and to tender advice in regard to administrative problems and procedures. In its widest sense, the term 'advisory body' is intended to describe anybody appointed with the purpose of advising the government at any level – national and local or any branch of administration.

A notable trend in public administration is the increasing use of advisory bodies relative to the processes of administration. In India, there has grown up in the past few decades, a network of advisory bodies at all levels of government/administration. The methods of government services are largely bureaucratic as their attention is mostly devoted to routine operations, and the various government departments or agencies work, in watertight compartments. So it is necessary that government services maintain intimate contact with private interests affected by their activities. Advisory bodies are the best means through which government agencies can maintain contacts with the public, since they embrace representatives of the private interests and organisations, and representatives of the government. These advisory bodies are an aid to the executive and the legislature in formulating and acting upon governmental legislation as well as budgetary proposals. Many agencies have developed an extensive system of such rules which establish a procedure by which private interests are consulted by the agency, but are not permitted to block action.

A number of advisory bodies are composed mainly of experts, that is, persons possessing special qualifications, training and experience. They may be regarded as expert committees, which are needed because the tasks of modern administration have become increasingly technical and scientific. Thus, the government/administration must have or obtain the services of professional, scientific and technical persons. In case the administration does not have such persons in service, it should seek their advice and cooperation through the instrumentality of advisory bodies. This deficiency can easily be made up by setting up discovery bodies of experts like the panels appointed by the Planning Commission for the purpose.

Field Formations and Feedback Systems

The Central or state governments operate or work through offices which are scattered throughout the country. These functions of the government are performed by hundreds of offices which are situated far away from the capital, into the field. A majority of the operating departments or agencies of the Union and state governments have a large number of field stations at the regional, district and local levels for performing most of their operations under the general direction and control of their respective headquarters organisations. The various activities carried on by these field stations for their organisations constitute what may be termed s 'field service'.

It is highly desirable that the field offices should be classified and graded, so that allotment of funds and staff and other matters of practical administration may be put on a systematic basis. Another very great advantage of classified field stations under a unified system is that employees may easily be transferred from the one to the other. From the administrative point of view even sub-stations are created under field stations. The line of authority in such a case runs from sub-station to station to the headquarters. The field administrative organisation falls under either of the two patterns (1) territorial and functional or (2) unitary and multiple. The first is organised horizontally, the second, vertically but both are organised hierarchically. In the unitary or territorial form the central authority creates regional or area agencies which have overall charge of all the activities of the area.

States in India follow a mixed pattern which includes both area and functional agencies. The revenue department has its independent hierarchy. At the headquarters stands the Boards of Revenue; below it comes division with divisional commissioner as in charge. In India, divisions are divided into districts under the charge of collector and the districts in turn are divided into subdivisions under the charge of sub divisional officers. They are further split into tehsils which are headed by the tehsildars; below the tehsil lies the pargana/revenue circle under the charge of kanungo; and then comes the lowest primary unit, the village whose important official is the patwari. These field units or revenue areas are examples of area administration in India.

The term 'headquarters' implies a central or supervisory officer, usually in the capital. The office which usually gets the approval before taking administrative actions from the headquarters are under the control and direction of the latter. They are called 'field offices'. Thus, field organisations are those which work in the field away from headquarters. In day-to-day administration, the implementation of policies and programmes is the responsibility of the field establishments. The performance of multifarious kinds of activities by the state necessitates the establishment of field offices in all parts of the country. The welfare state has to cater to the needs of its citizens and the field offices perform the tasks. Increase in the regulatory activities of government and technological advances – have played a very important role in the expansion of field organisations. Citizens want services at their door. Also, there is a demand for greater citizen participation in policy formation and execution. Field organisations are inevitable in international relations where a country has to maintain its diplomatic missions abroad.

Coordination at the Field Level

All activities which are interrelated and interdependent need coordination. Taken together they culminate in realisation of planned targets. All the departments are, thus, partners in the joint enterprise of a modern welfare state. Institutionalised efforts are also called for this purpose. The district collector has been the traditional coordinator in the district committed to his charge. The Prefect performs this function in France, and some countries appoint general area officers who provide common staff services to others and function as the convener and coordinator for the area. The authority to establish field offices is vested in the chief executive but the legislature must lay down the service of the activity to be performed by the government. The creation of the local offices is the responsibility of the chief executive.

There should be delegation of authority to the field offices. They should have the power to take decisions. The control by the headquarters should not interference in the day-to-day working of the field offices. This control may permeate below by methods such as:

Permission in advance, budget control, control through review of action and the power to get reports or personal inspections, and strengthening of control over field stations.

Usually differences develop between the headquarters and the field stations. It is also possible that communication is lost and the officials of the headquarter may not be able to appreciate local office problems and difficulties. The harmonious relationship can develop by personal visits by headquarter staff to create a healthy atmosphere – a sense of belonging to a service. Inspection has been a traditional method of fault-finding. The essential elements should be instructing and guiding the person working in the inspected agency, and actually demonstrating on the spot as to how defects have to be rectified and discrepancies reconciled. The rotation of the staff from the field to the headquarter and vice versa helps in developing insights. Field headquarter relationship depends upon an effective communication system which is vital to the successful achievement of agency objectives. The communication should be clear, consistent, uniform, adequate and be addressed in easy, simple language. The field staff should have a feeling that headquarter staff has confidence over their competence and listens to their voice and attaches weight to their arguments. After independence, the developmental expansion of ministries in the Union government has made the neat classification of these executive agencies still more difficult. Yet the following types can be identified:

(1) Attached Office (e.g., central public works department).
(2) Subordinate Office (e.g., Sardar Patel National Police Academy, Hyderabad).
(3) Departmental undertaking (e.g., ordnance factories).
(4) A company registered under the Companies Act (e.g., Hindustan Steel Limited).
(5) A corporation or board set up under a special statute (e.g., Damodar Valley Corporation, Tea Board, etc.).
(6) A society registered under the Societies Registration Act (e.g., Indian Institute of Foreign Trade).

There are also instances of executive agencies functioning as an integral part of the ministry itself, but this is not a widely prevalent practice. The most important forms of executive agencies are the attached office and the subordinate office. In addition, the Constitution of India has created several institutions which fall in the category of constitutional authorities or constitutional bodies. Some of them are:

(1) The Comptroller and Auditor-General of India (Articles 148–151).
(2) The Election Commission (Article 324).
(3) The Union Public Service Commission (Articles 315–323).
(4) The Attorney-General for India (Article 76).
(5) The Special Officer for Scheduled Castes and Scheduled Tribes (Article 338).
(6) The Special Officer for Linguistic Minorities (Article 350 B).
(7) The Finance Commission (Article 280–1).
(8) The Official Language Commission (Article 344).
(9) The Committee of Parliament to Examine the Report of the Language Commission (Article 344(4)).
(10) The State Public Service Commission (Articles 315–23).
(11) The Advocate-General for the state (Article 165).
(12) Administrative Tribunals.

These bodies differ from each other in respect of their functions as well as in matters of composition. They may be classified on the basis of (i) whether they are single-member ones or organised as commissions; (ii) whether they are common to both the Central government and the states or belong to one or the other of these two levels of government; (iii) whether they have been visualised by the Constitution since its inception or have been incorporated subsequently by amendments;

and (iv) whether they are of standing nature, being permanently in session or set up at prescribed intervals. These criteria are not exclusive. Some of these bodies are common to both the levels of government. These are the Comptroller and Auditor-General of India; the Election Commission; and the Finance Commission.

Attached and Subordinate Offices in Union Government

Administrative agencies can be grouped functionally into 'administrative offices' and 'operating or commercial offices'. The first group can be further subdivided into two categories – attached offices and subordinate offices. According to the manual of office procedure these offices are created: "Where the execution of the policies of government requires decentralisation of executive direction and the establishment of field agencies. A ministry has under it subsidiary offices which are also called as attached and subordinate offices. The attached offices are responsible for providing executive direction required in the implementation of the poiicies. They also advice to the ministry on technical aspects of questions. The subordinate offices function as field establishment or as the agencies responsible for the detailed execution of the decisions under the direction of an attached office, or a ministry." Apart from executive agencies, there are advice-tendering agencies, research and training agencies, departmental undertakings, corporations under the company law, corporations and boards under special status, registered societies and non-statutory boards and committees. There is no uniformity in the matter of executive agencies as between different ministries and departments. For instance, the ministry of external affairs has no attached office but has a number of subordinate offices under it. In addition, it has a number of diplomatic and consular offices all over the globe, which have a peculiar and unique status and do not fall in the traditional category of attached or subordinate offices. Similarly, the ministry of human resources and development has no attached office but has numerous of subordinate offices under it. In addition, it has a number of autonomous organisations like the University Grants Commission, National Council of Educational Research and Training and a number of central universities under it. The department of parliamentary affairs, has no attached, subordinate or any other kind of office under it.

The internal organisation of subordinate offices differs from that of ministries and departments. The head of such an office is a technical officer called registrar, director-general, chief engineer, etc. Below him, there are other technical and non-technical officers who help him in his tasks. The proportion of technical to secretarial officers differs from one attached office to the other depending upon the nature of work. The pattern of organisation among attached offices is varied. The status of heads of these offices also differs from that of an additional secretary and their personnel up to the rank of section officers hails from a common cadre with the ministry concerned. Their lowest rungs are known as subordinate offices. They function as field establishments or as agencies responsible for the detailed execution of policy decisions. It functions at the cutting edge of administration especially under an attached office. Though responsible for the execution of policy or decision, it has been accorded a inferior status, and is called 'subordinate'. Being field agencies, they generally have a large component of technical field staff with the usual ministerial staff for administrative work. Unlike attached offices, the subordinate offices have only limited administrative and financial powers, and for most of the major items of work have to approach the attached office or the ministry for sanction. They submit periodical and other reports and returns to the attached office and the administrative ministry concerned. Sometimes the heads of these offices are generally lower as compared to those of equivalent posts in the attached offices. In fact, there is no uniformity in this matter even amongst the subordinate offices themselves.

The relationship between the attached and subordinate offices and the secretariat and non-secretariat organisations raise issues of bifurcation and separation. The manual of office procedure demarcates the spheres of activity of the two categories. The attached offices "are responsible for providing executive direction required in the implementation of the policies laid down by the ministry to which they are attached". In other words, the attached office plays a dual role of directing the subordinate offices below and submitting proposals to the secretariat above. Conversely, a subordinate office is a mere field agency "responsible for the detailed execution of the decisions of the government". In fact, being at the delivering end, its role can be more crucial. In actual practice, no such clear-cut distinction exits between the two categories of offices. The subordinate offices generally function under the direction of the attached offices but they may function directly under the ministry also. This makes confusion worse confounded and a satisfactory definition of 'an attached office' seems unworkable. The only justification for such a distinction may justify lower scales of pay for the ministerial staff in subordinate offices than in attached offices.

The situation of attached and subordinate offices in the ministries of Government of India at the end of 20th century stood as under:

MINISTRY OF AGRICULTURE

Department of Agriculture and Cooperation

Attached Offices

(1) Commission for Agriculture Costs and Prices
(2) Directorate of Economics and Statistics
(3) Directorate of Plant Protection Quarantine and Storage

MINISTRY OF CHEMICALS AND FERTILIZERS

Department of Chemicals and Petrochemicals

Attached Offices

(1) National Institute of Pharmaceutical Education and Research
(2) Institute of Pesticide Formulation Technology
(3) Petrofils Cooperative Limited

MINISTRY OF CIVIL AVIATION AND TOURISM

Department of Civil Aviation

Attached Offices

(1) Director-General of Civil Aviation
(2) Bureau of Civil Aviation Security
(3) Commission of Railway Safety

MINISTRY OF CIVIL SUPPLIES, CONSUMER AFFAIRS AND PUBLIC DISTRIBUTION

Attached Offices

(1) Forward Markets Commission
(2) Directorate of Vanaspati, Vegetable Oil and Fats

(3) Directorate of Weights and Measures
(4) Indian Institute of Legal Metrology
(5) Hindustan Vegetable Oils Corporation Limited
(6) Bureau of Indian Standards
(7) National Consumer Disputes Redressal Commission
(8) National Cooperation Consumer's Federation of Indian Limited
(9) Super Bazar

MINISTRY OF COAL

Attached Offices

(1) Office of the Coal Controller
(2) Office of the Commissioner of Payments

MINISTRY OF COMMERCE

Attached Offices

(1) Director-General of Foreign Trade
(2) Director-General of Commercial Intelligence and Statistics
(3) Offices of the Custodian of Enemy Property

Department of Supply

Attached Offices

(1) Director-General of Supplies and Disposal

MINISTRY OF DEFENCE

Department of Defence

Attached Offices

(1) Army Headquarters
(2) Naval Headquarters
(3) Air Headquarters
(4) Coast Guard Headquarters
(5) Director-General of Defence Estates
(6) National Defence College
(8) Director-General of Armed Forces Medical Services
(9) Director-General of National Cadet Corps
(10) Joint Cipher Bureau
(11) Services Sports Control Board
(12) Directorate of Public Relations
(13) Director-General of Resettlement
(14) College of Defence Management
(15) Army Purchase Organisation
(16) Central Monitoring Organisation

Department of Defence Production and Supplies

(1) Director-General of Ordnance Factories
(2) Director-General of Quality Assurance
(3) Directorate of Technical Development and Production (Air)
(4) Directorate of Standardisation
(5) Directorate of Planning and Coordination
(6) Directorate of Exhibition

Department of Defence Research and Development

(1) Defence Research and Development Organisation

MINISTRY OF ENVIRONMENT AND FORESTS

Department of Environment and Forests

Attached and Subordinate Offices

(1) Ganga Project Directorate
(2) National Afforestation and Eco-Development Board

Subordinate Offices

(1) Botanical Survey of India
(2) Forest Survey of India
(3) Indira Gandhi National Forest Academy
(4) National Zoological Park
(5) Zoological Survey of India
(6) National Museum of National History

MINISTRY OF FINANCE

Department of Revenue

Attached Offices

(1) Enforcement Directorate
(2) Customs, Excise and Gold (Control) Appellate Tribunal
(3) Settlement Commission (Income Tax, Wealth Tax)
(4) Central Economic Intelligence Bureau
(5) Appellate Tribunal for Forfeiture of Property
(6) Authority for Advance Ruling
(7) Central Excise and Customs Collectorates located in different parts of the country

Department of Economic Affairs

Attached Offices

(1) Directorate of Economic Affairs
(2) Indian Security Press
(3) India Government Mint, etc.

Department of Expenditure

(1) Controller General of Accounts
(2) Central Pensions Accounting Office

Department of Company Affairs

The department has a number of Registrars of Companies posted in different parts of the country.

MINISTRY OF FOOD

Department of Food

Attached Offices

(1) Directorate of Sugar

Subordinate Office

There are over 25 subordinate offices

MINISTRY OF FOOD PROCESSING INDUSTRIES

Attached Office

(1) Directorate, F&V Processing

MINISTRY OF HEALTH AND FAMILY WELFARE

Department of Health

Attached Office

(1) Director-General of Health Services
(2) Ninety-seven subordinate offices under DGHS

Subordinate Office

(1) Family Welfare Training and Research Centre

Department of Indian Systems of Medicine and Homeopathy

Subordinate Office

(1) Pharmacopoeia Laboratory for Indian Medicine
(2) Homoeopathic Pharmacopoeia Laboratory

MINISTRY OF HOME AFFAIRS

Department of Internal Security

Attached Offices

(1) Directorate of Intelligence Bureau
(2) Director-General of Central Reserve Police Force
(3) Bureau of Police Research and Development
(4) National Institute of Criminology and Forensic Science
(5) National Crime Records Bureau
(6) Border Security Force

Department of Home

Attached Offices

(1) Office the Registrar-General and Census Commissioner of India.
(2) Office of the Chief Controller of Accounts

Department of States

Attached Offices

(1) Northern Zonal Council
(2) Inter-state Council

MINISTRY OF HUMAN RESOURCE DEVELOPMENT

Department of Education

Subordinate Office

(1) Directorate of Adult Education
(2) Central Hindi Directorate
(3) Commission for Scientific and Technical Terminology
(4) Central Institute of Indian Languages

Department of Culture

Attached Office

(1) Archaeological Survey of India
(2) National Archives of Indian

Subordinate Offices

(1) Anthropological Survey of India
(2) National Museum
(3) National Gallery of Modern Art
(4) National Library
(5) National Research Laboratory of Conservation of Cultural Property
(6) Central Reference Library

MINISTRY OF INDUSTRY

Department of Industrial Policy and Promotion and Industrial Development

Attached Offices

(1) Office of Economic Adviser
(2) Bureau of Industrial Costs and Prices
(3) Office of the Salt Commissioner
(4) Office of the Chief Controller of Accounts

Subordinate Office

(1) Director-General of Patents, Designs and Trade Marks
(2) Office of the Chief Controller of Explosive
(3) Principal Accounts Office

Department of Heavy Industry

Subordinate Office

(1) Commissioner of Payments

Department of Small Scale Industries and Agro and Rural Industries

Attached Offices

(1) Development Commissioner for Small Scale Industries

Department of Heavy Industrial Development and Industrial Policy and Promotion

Subordinate Office

(1) Office of the Chief Controller of Extremes
(2) Office of Controller General of Patents, Designs and Trade Marks

MINISTRY OF INFORMATION AND BROADCASTING

Attached Offices

(1) Principal Information Officer
(2) All India Radio
(3) Doordarshan
(4) Publication Division
(5) Registrar of Newspapers of India
(6) Directorate of Audio and Visual Publicity
(7) Photo Division
(8) Directorate of Field Publicity
(9) Song and Drama Division
(10) Films Division
(11) Research and Reference Division
(12) National Films Archives of India

MINISTRY OF LABOUR

Attached Offices

(1) Director-General of Employment and Training
(2) Office of the Chief Labour Commissioner
(3) Director-General of Factory Advice Service and Labour Institutes
(4) Chief Labour Commissioner (Central)
(5) Labour Bureau

Subordinate Office

(1) Director-General of Labour Welfare and Offices of Welfare Commissioners
(2) Director-General of Mines Safety
(3) Industrial Tribunals-cum-Labour Courts
(4) Board of Arbitration

MINISTRY OF LAW AND JUSTICE

Department of Legal Affairs

Attached Office

(1) Foreign Exchange Regulation Appellate Board (FERA)
(2) Law Commission
(3) Committee for Implementing Legal Aid Schemes

Legislative Department

Subordinate Office

(1) Vidhi Sahitya Prakashan

MINISTRY OF MINES

Attached Office

Nil

Subordinate Offices

(1) Geological Survey of India
(2) Indian Bureau of Mines
(3) Controller of Mining Leases

MINISTRY OF NON-CONVENTIONAL ENERGY SOURCES

The Ministry has eight regional offices located in different part the country to carry out monitoring and inspection of projects and maintain liaison with the concerned state governments and organisations.

MINISTRY OF PARLIAMENTARY AFFAIRS

It has no attached and subordinate office.

Department of Personnel, Public Grievances and Pensions

Attached Offices

(1) Lal Bahadur Shastri National Academy of Administration
(2) Staff Selection Commission
(3) Institute of Secretariat Training and Management

Subordinate Offices

(1) Central Bureau of Investigation.

MINISTRY OF PETROLEUM AND NATURAL GAS

The ministry has no attached or subordinate offices.

MINISTRY OF PLANNING AND PROGRAMME IMPLEMENTATION

Department of Statistics

Attached Offices

(1) Central Statistical Organisation
(2) Computer Centre
(3) Accounts Office

Subordinate Office

(1) National Sample Survey Organisation

Planning Commission

Attached Office

National Information Centre

MINISTRY OF POWER

Attached Offices

(1) Central Electricity Authority
(2) Badarpur Management Contract Cell

Subordinate Offices

(1) Nearly 15 organisations including eight Central Electric Authorities.

MINISTRY OF RAILWAYS

Attached Offices

(1) Research Design and Standards Organisation
Besides, the following four organisations work directly under the Railway Board:
   (1) Railway Recruitment Board
   (2) Railway Rates Tribunal
   (3) Railway Staff College
   (4) Office of the Chief Mining Adviser–Railways

MINISTRY OF RURAL AREAS AND EMPLOYMENT

Department of Rural Development

Attached Office

(1) Directorate of Marketing Inspection

Subordinate Office

It has a large number of subordinate offices.

Department of Rural Employment and Poverty Alleviation

It has no attached or subordinate office.

Department of Wastelands Development

The department has no attached or subordinate office.

MINISTRY OF SCIENCE AND TECHNOLOGY

Department of Science and Technology

Attached Office

Nil

Subordinate Office

(1) Survey of India
(2) National Atlas and Thematic Mapping Organisation
(3) India Meteorological Department

Department of Bio-technology

It has no attached or subordinate office

Department of Scientific and Industrial Research

It has no attached or subordinate office.

MINISTRY OF STEEL

Attached Office

(1) Office of the Department of Commissions for Iron and Steel.

MINISTRY OF SURFACE TRANSPORTS

Attached Office

(1) Boarder Roads Development Organisation

Subordinate Offices

(1) Director-General of Shipping
(2) Director-General of Light Houses and Lightships
(3) Andaman and Lakshadweep Harkons Works
(4) Minor Parts Survey Organisation

MINISTRY OF TEXTILES

Attached Offices

(1) Office of the Development Commissioner for Handlooms
(2) Office of the Development Commissioner for Handicrafts

Subordinate Offices

(1) Office of the Textile Commissioner
(2) Office of the Jute Commissioner

MINISTRY OF TELECOMMUNICATION

Department of Posts

The Department of Posts has no attached office under it. But it has a large number of subordinate offices numbering nearly 25.

Department of Telecommunication

Nil

MINISTRY OF URBAN AFFAIRS AND EMPLOYMENT

Attached Offices

(1) Central Public Works Department
(2) Directorate of Estates
(3) Directorate of Printing
(4) National Buildings Organisation

Subordinate Offices

(1) Controller of Stationery
(2) Controller of Publications
(3) Land and Development Office
(4) Town and Country Planning Organisation

MINISTRY OF WATER RESOURCES

Attached Offices

(1) Central Water Commission
(2) Central Soil and Materials Research Station

Subordinate Offices

(1) Central Ground Water Board
(2) Central Water and Power Research Station
(3) Farakka Barrage Project
(4) Ganga Flood Control Commission

MINISTRY OF WELFARE

The Ministry has under it a number of constitutional commissions as well as subordinate offices. The commissions are: National Minorities, Commissioner for Linguistic Minorities, etc.

Department of Atomic Energy

Attached Offices

(1) Atomic Energy Regulatory Board

Department of Electronics

Attached Office

(1) Standardisation, Testing and Quality Control

Subordinate Offices

The department has 14 subordinate offices comprising 9 electronic test and development centres, 4 regional test laboratories and the centre for Reliability. It has also under it 4 public enterprises and 10 autonomous and registered bodies.

Department of Ocean Development

Attached Offices

(1) Polymetallic Nodules Cell
(2) Sagar Sampada Cell
(3) Antarctica Study Circle.

In development administration, powers should necessarily gravitate towards the attached and subordinate offices. In 1946, there were 31 attached offices in the central government. This number has touched 70 towards the close of the century.

Tottenhaum Report in 1945–46 recommended the abolition of distinction between the two categories of officers. The First Pay Commission (1950) also found such distinction 'artificial' and suggested to regroup them into:

(1) policy making secretarial organisations,
(2) executive and advisory organisations; and
(3) subordinate to the two categories.

The Second Pay Commission (1959) also suggested a functional classification – the criteria being (1) offices furnishing data and advice to head office and executive directions to field agencies; and (2) Policy formulating offices may be designated as attached offices; while offices responsible for the execution should be called subordinate offices. The ARC looked at the problem from secretariat and non-secretariat point of view. However, the attached offices have improved their status almost co-equal to that of the secretariat but subordinate offices continue to languish in their subordinate position.

Legally speaking, the secretariat does policy making and legislative functions and serves as a memory and clearing house preparatory to vital decisions and supervisory executive action. However, development has caused a steady increase in the volume of work at the secretariat level. This has increased the authority, influence and prestige of the secretariat. The executive agencies resent this neglect of their specialist or technical skill. The non-secretariat organisations do not appreciate this criticism of the secretariat. The ARC found that the heads of non-secretariat organisations feel that the secretariat contributes little but delay. They often find this secretariat control frustrating. To them, the secretariat largely acts as a drag on the execution of schemes and programmes by delaying sanctions and insisting on meticulous observance of rules, and procedures. The heads of technical organisations complain of being treated unfairly in that they have to serve under generalist administrators who hardly understand their points of view and their difficulties. There is an attitude of resentment against invidious service distinctions and the unwillingness of the secretariat 'overlords' to delegate authority. The secretariat officers, on the other hand, often complain of lack of responsibility and insufficient regards for rules and procedures on the part of heads of non-secretariat organisations.

The importance of proper relationship between the ministries/departments and heads of executive departments, particularly of attached offices, determines the success of the government policies both in formulation and implementation. The handling of work flow from attached offices to ministries has its bearing on this relationship. Practically every case, is subjected to duplicate handling at the office level and at each place resulting in duplication of staff, waste of manpower and delay in disposal of business. The Llewellyan Smith Committee (1919) highlighted it and a clear line of responsibility of each is insisted upon. The manual of office procedure lays down that officers in both the kinds of organisations should ensure that proposal are formulated after joint consultation at lowest level and should ordinarily be dealt with by the branch officer or the deputy secretary at the secretarial level. However, there exists no uniform pattern of handling cases and ministries have developed their own types of secretariat of organisation to handle work received from their attached offices. At present, there are six varieties of relationships in the union ministries:

(1) *Distinct and separate offices and files of their own*. Consultation between the ministry and the executive department takes place through self-contained communications. The examples are the office of the chief engineer, central public works department in relation to the ministry of works and housing, and the Director-General of All India Radio in relation to the ministry of information and broadcasting.

(2) *Separate offices and separate files*. Under this pattern the head of the executive department is brought in closer contact with the ministry office by investing him with appropriate *ex officio* secretariat status. It represents a compromise between complete separation and complete fusion. The textile commissioner, who is also *ex officio* joint secretary in the ministry of commerce can be cited as an example in point.

(3) *Separate offices but common files*: A single file bureau or records cell is located in the organisation of the executive department. The attached office submits proposals on its own files and refers the papers to the ministry. The proposal is disposed of by the ministry and the file is returned to the executive department. A good example of this single file pattern is the ministry of defence and the Air Force headquarters.

(4) *Common office, common files and a common files bureau*. Here the control of the executive department is total and the ministry's office is merged into the headquarters organisation of the executive department. The common office serves the officers for both the secretariat and the department. There is only one file bureau and all references, whether required by the department or by the secretariat, are dealt by the same dealing person. The physical proximity of the ministry and the attached office is an essential prerequisite for the working of this pattern. The Director-General of Posts and Telegraphs before the constitution of the Posts and Telegraphs Boards worked on this pattern.

(5) *Concurrent jurisdiction*. A senior officer of the ministry holds both the offices, so that he remains responsible for the formulation and execution of the policy with the assistance of the office located in the ministry. In other words, a senior officer of the ministry holds concurrently the office of the head of the executive department with a common office and single file bureau located in the ministry itself under his control. The Director-General of Food (who is the additional secretary in the department of food), and the Director-General of Employment and Training (who is joint secretary in the ministry of labour) is the best example of this system.

(6) *Complete merger*. The ministries and heads of executive departments may be merged as a special case as can be seen in the merger of Railway Board and the Posts and Telegraphs Board.

All these types of organisations represent experiments at bridging the gulf between secretariat and non-secretariat organisations. Devices like giving *ex officio* secretariat status to the heads of executive agencies; introduction of single file system; functional placement of executive agencies in the secretariat without secretariat status are attempts to remove the deficiencies in the existing system. One such attempt has been grant of liberal autonomy to the executive departments by delegation from the secretariat. Since the responsibility of implementation of policies rests with the heads of executive departments, it is worthwhile that they enjoy adequate powers and discretion to act effectively with initiative. All reports on administrative reforms agree to this. Still the act reminds that "while ... some increased delegations have been made in recent years, the overall approach has been one of hesitancy and caution. Delegations are often made piecemeal and with reservations, as if they were a favour and not a normal method of work organisation." The powers delegated to heads of executive agencies lack uniformity and delegation has been ineffective. The executive departments resent 'interference from above' and they do not allow delegated powers to their subordinates.

The abolition of this distinction has been advocated on the lines obtained in British Whitehall and some other countries. The ARC recommended that the distinction be abolished and non-secretariat organisations may be integrated with the administrative departments in the secretariat. The State Commissions have also suggested the substitution of the parallel hierarchies by some sort of composite office. An administrative organisation needs specialisation in administration and deficiency can be made good by specialised assistance to the secretary or to the head of department. The parallel hierarchies cause duplication and specialised functions need to be assigned to a single office to improve the quality of performance only "A composite office can permit more specialisation in separate offices. It shall enhance competence and reduce dependence on 'generalist' ... ."

However, the ARC report (1968) was opposed to *general* abolition of the distinction although the duplication of functions was to be avoided. The Commission found that the work of subordinate offices can be classified into six categories:

(1) Regulatory and allied activities,
(2) Developmental activities,
(3) Education and training,
(4) Survey and research,
(5) Production or supply of a commodity,
(6) Planning and developmental programmes.

Very little has been done to implement these recommendations at the Union and state levels because of political instability and politics of vested interests. All these varieties of arrangements have evolved over decades. Some of the relational patterns are too intricate and function specific that they cannot be called a type. Yet the most important agency, which sustains the autonomy and independence of ministries and department, are the commissions, which are plural as well as functional. The Constitution of India provides for three major commissions viz., the Union Public Service Commission, Finance Commission and the Election Commission. Notwithstanding several constitutional structure and agencies like the office of the C&AG of India, the Planning

Commission of India is one significant inter-structural development which has completed more than five decades of its growth under the aegis of National Development Council of India. A chain of Statutory Commissions like Human Rights Commission, Women's Commission, Minorities Commission, SC and ST Commission and Child Commission of India has stretched their bonds to promote and protect human rights jurisprudence rapidly evolving in the country.

Union Public Service Commission (UPSC)

Constitutions generally do not talk of civil services and their roles. The British Parliamentary System of government evolved a merit-based bureaucracy for which a Royal Public Service Commission was created to ensure fair and independent recruitment in India. After the introduction of Montford Reforms 1919 as more and more Indians were to be associated with the governance of the colony, the civil services were targeted as a field of reform. Hitherto the Civil Service Commission used to conduct competitive examinations in England and not in India. Its chairman and members were appointed by the Secretary of State for India, who according to Macaulay Committee Report (1854) was the guardian of higher civil services of India. The introduction of dyarchy in the provinces and the Queens Royal Proclamation of 1916 necessitated a new look on civil service policy and Lee of Farnham was assigned the task to report on superior civil services in India. The Lee Commission in its report of 1924 made a strong plea for the constitution of an independent, non-political and impartial Public Service Commission to provide a merit-base for the senior services. The Lee report maintained that "to secure an efficient civil service it is essential to protect it from political or personal influence. The position of stability and security is vital to its successful working as an impartial and efficient instrument, by which the government may give effect to its policies. In countries, where this principle has been neglected, and where the 'spoils system' has taken its place, an inefficient and disorganised civil service has been the inevitable result and corruption has been rampant."

The Government of India Act 1919 provided for the establishment of a Public Service Commission. Section 96-C of the said Act prescribed that "The Public Service Commission will consist of not more than five members, of whom one shall be a chairman, appointed by the Secretary of State in council. Each member shall hold office for five years, and may be reappointed. No member shall be removed from office before the expiry of his term of office, except by order of the Secretary of State in council." The commission was given functions of recruitment and control of public services which were to be assigned to it by the Secretary of State in council.

The Lee Report was accepted in 1936 and the Central Public Service Commission got its jurisdiction over all India and higher civil services of the country. Later Simon Commission argued for its advisory role to the government and final authority in matter of recruitment of Public Services. The Government of India Act 1936 accepted the Simon recommendations and Section 264 of the Act rechristened the commission as Federal Public Services Commission of India. The Act specifically mentioned the composition, functions and role of the FPSC in relation to recruitment, promotion, transfers and disciplinary matters. When the Republican Constitution of India was hammered out, Section 264 of the Act was in operation although the 1935 federation could not get inaugurated because of the non-cooperation of native rulers. Article 315 of the Republican Constitution maintains the continuity and provides for "A Union Public Service Commission for the Union and a Public Service Commission for each state."

The composition of the UPSC in terms of its size and conditions of service of the members has been left open to be determined by the President of India, who originally fixed it at six to nine members including the chairman. Article 316 of the Constitution provides "that as nearly as may be, one-half of the members must be persons who have held office for at least ten years under the Government of India". The expression 'as nearly as' cannot be read as equivalent or approximate. The ARC, in its report on personnel administration suggested that the chairman of UPSC should be consulted while making appointments of members of the commission, and even with regard to the appointment of the new chairman. Not less than two-thirds of the members may be drawn from among the chairmen and members of State Public Service Commissions. The President can ask a member to take charge as chairman until the new incumbent assumes office.

This provision of ten year experience has been inserted obviously to guarantee the presence on the commission of officials of sufficient experience. A member holds office for a term of six years or until he attains the age of sixty-five years, whichever is earlier. He or she is not eligible for the same appointment for a second term nor can he undertake employment under the Union or state government. The ban can be interpreted even against honorary posts. The chairman is ineligible for any future employment, but other members can accept the chairmanship of the Union Public Service Commission or of State Public Service Commissions. He can resign earlier or can be removed by the President. Article 317 permits removal or suspension by the President on grounds of misbehaviour, but the matter has to be referred to the Supreme Court for enquiry. The Supreme Court under Article 145 sends its verdict to the President and the latter is bound by this advice. Article 317 elucidates the causes of misbehaviour as under:

(1) Insolvency
(2) Paid employment
(3) Infirmity of body and mind
(4) Interested and participation in profit, benefit or emoluments therefrom.

Independence of the Commission

The founding fathers intended to make the Union Public Service Commission an independent body like the Supreme Court and High Courts. But constitutionally speaking the members of the commission are not on par with the judges. They do not take an oath of office. The judges are appointed by the President under his seal and signatures which is not the case in the appointment of the chairman and members of the commission. The difference is also there in the procedure for removal of members. The CAG and the judges are removed by the President after impeachment by the Parliament. However, the members of the UPSC are removable by the President and, in specific cases, the Supreme Court can be requested to hold an enquiry. The Constitution mentions that the conditions or service cannot be altered to the disadvantage of a serving member. The chairman of the UPSC is ineligible for further employment but a member, can be appointed as chairman of UPSC or of a state public service commission. This provision ensures the independence and impartiality of the members of the commission. They have been deprived of any office with which the executive can tempt them to depart from duty norms. It is a disincentive to younger people because employment has been viewed by the courts as control of the employer over the employee. The Supreme Court has held that the office of the Governor of a state and of a High Court judge are not employments under government. Though appointed by the President, these functionaries hold office under the Constitution without being subordinate to the Government of India. The courts permit the former chairman/member of public service commissions to hold the office of Advocate General or Vice Chancellor as there is no relationship of master and servant. Similarly, the retired members of UPSC can contest elections of the Union Parliament or state legislatures. The functions of UPSC have been enumerated under Article 320 of the Constitution. These functions are:

(1) Conduct of examinations for appointments to the services of the Union.
(2) Assistance in framing and operating schemes of joint recruitment for specialised services for which two or more states request.
(3) Consultation on:
    (a) Matters relating to methods of recruitment of civil (non-military) post;
    (b) Principles to be followed in making appointments, promotions, transfers and suitability of candidates for civil service posts;
    (c) Disciplinary matters affecting a person in a civil capacity;
    (d) Claims and costs of acts done in civil capacity and are to be paid out of the Consolidated Fund of India; and
    (e) Claim for a pension in term of damages in a civil capacity.

Article 321 provides for conferring of additional functions and mentions that "An Act made by Parliament or the legislature of a state as the case may be, may provide for the exercise of additional functions by the Union Public Service Commission or the State Public Service Commission in respect of the services of the Union or the state and also in respect of the services of any local authority or other body corporately constituted." Additional powers may be conferred on the UPSC either by the Parliament or by rules and orders of the executive or by conventions. The Delhi Municipal Corporation Act (1957) is an example in point which provides that selection for superior posts in Delhi Municipal Corporation will be made by UPSC. Similarly grant of extension in services was formerly made after a reference to UPSC but after 1954 it was rescinded. The Commission has been conventionally conducting entrance examinations for recruitment to armed forces, which actually falls outside its purview. The UPSC is a recruitment agency of the Union government and as such its primary and major functions are:

(1) Selection of candidates and recommend them for appointment by the government.
(2) Advise to the government on personnel matters of general nature and in matters involving grievances of individual civil servants.
(3) Protection of the interests of public services by suggesting revision of rules or creation of new services under the Constitution.
(4) Submission of its annual report to Parliament mentioning specific cases wherein the executive dishonoured, avoided or partially diluted its advise to the determent of public interest.

These functions are fairly wide yet they have their prescribed limits. The UPSC has to be consulted and this consultation is mandatory on the issues like methods of recruitment, promotion and transfer to civil services and civil posts. All disciplinary matters, claim settlements or matters which the President likes may be referred to the Commission.

On September 1, 1958 the Government of India made regulations which granted exemption to the government from consultation on matters lying in the purview of Article 320 (3) (a) and (b) of the Constitution. The list of posts and services excluded from the purview of the UPSC after the publication of these regulations is fairly long and the Annual Report (1992–93) of the UPSC enumerates them as under:

Services and posts exempted from UPSC consultation

(1) All civil and criminal judicial posts in union territories under the control of a High Court or a court of a judicial commissioner, other than those included in Item (7).
(2) Posts in the secretariat and personal staff of the President and the Vice-President.
(3) Posts in government hospitality organisation under the ministry of external affairs.
(4) All technical and administrative posts in or under (a) the department of electronics, and (b) Electronics Commission.
(5) Recruitment/Promotion of scientific and technical personnel in the Defence Research and Development Organisation (DRDO) under the ministry of defence.
(6) All Group 'A' and Group 'B' posts in or under the Central Administrative Tribunal.
(7) Posts of computer specialist, programmer (software), programme assistant, technical assistant, editorial consultant, senior research officer, bibliographer (Lexicon), library assistant, reprography assistant and folk art consultant in department of arts for five years.
(8) Scientific posts in the ministry of science and technology, department of ocean development, department on non-conventional energy sources and the department of environment, forests and wild life, as specified in the annexure to the department of personnel and training notification No. 39018/2/86-Estt. B dated 1–4–87 except in respect of appointment to be made thereto by promoting through the DPC.
(9) Group 'B' (non-gazetted) posts of assistants and stenographers Grade 'C' to be filled by direct recruitment through open competitive examination.
(10) Posts of advisors and equivalent in the Planning Commission in the scale of Rs 5,900–8,000 except where they are required to be filled under the senior staffing scheme or those included in any organised services.
(11) Group 'B' non-gazetted posts in the department of telecommunications.
(12) Group 'B' non-gazetted posts under the Andaman and Nicobar Islands and Lakshadweep administration.
(13) Posts/Services to the exclusion of which the Commission agreed under item (2) of the Schedule to the UPSC (Exemption from Consultation) Regulations:
    (i) Posts connected with the Special Border Security Scheme under the ministry of external affairs.
    (ii) Posts in the Central Reserve Police and the Indo-Tibetan Border Force.
    (iii) Posts in the technology mission of oilseeds production under the ministry of agriculture up to March 31, 1991.
    (iv) Posts in the technology mission on drinking water, in rural areas under the department of rural development to September 30, 1990.
    (v) Posts in the High Commission of India, London, and in other Indian missions abroad to which recruitment is made locally by the respective Indian missions.
    (vi) Teaching posts, to be filled by transfer on deputation, under the Lal Bahadur Shastri National Academy of Administration for a period of 2 years.

Schedule-II includes posts which are excluded for purposes of Art. 320(3) (b) of the Constitution. Non-gazetted posts Group 'B' under the ministry of water resources fall in this category.

Recruitment to services is made on the basis of a written examination or of a *viva voce.* In cases of promotions, demotions and transfers, it can only give advice which is not binding. The success at an examination conducted by UPSC does not confer the right to appointment. The Commission only forwards the list of successful candidates to the government, which alone can make appointments. The advice is normally accepted but it is not mandatory. If a department does not agree with the advice given by the Commission, the matter has to be referred to the Appointments Committee of the cabinet.

This legal situation apart there is a tendency in the ministries to bypass the advise of the commission. The proviso to clause (3) of Article 320 is sometimes abused and the government can remove specified posts from the purview of the commission. The President in 1958 enacted in (Exemption from Consultation) Regulations III and class IV appointments under the government. These regulations provide that "It shall not be necessary to consult the commission in regard to the selection for temporary or officiating appointment to a post if (a) the person appointed is not likely to hold the post for a period of more than one year; and (b) it is necessary in the public interest to make the appointment immediately and a reference to the commission will causes undue delay; provided that (i) such appointment shall be reported to the commission as soon as it is made; (ii) if the appointment continues beyond a period of six months, a fresh estimate as to the period for which the person appointed is likely to hold the post shall be made and reported to the commission; and (iii) if such estimate indicates that the person appointed is likely to hold the post for a period of more than one year from the date of appointment, the commission shall immediately be consulted in regard to the filling of the post." It has enabled the government to expedite urgent appointment. The annual reports of the commission have repeatedly been citing instance of governments making temporary or officiating appointments initially for a period of less than one year but continuing them for many years and then seeking concurrence of the commission.

A major complaint against the commission is that its recruitment is subject to long delays. Interval spans extend to more than a year. Then the appointment orders are issued very late by the government. The temporary appointee who is required to leave the post after a long time develops a grievance. In matters where the commission's advice is not binding the position has remained the same as before Independence. The Joint Selection Committee felt that PSCs can be move effective if it is advisory rather than mandatory. The Constituent Assembly and its drafting committee concluded that it will not be advisable to create 'a kingdom within a kingdom'. In matters specified by Article 320, consultation is necessary but acceptance is discretionary. The President of India has made regulations. The commission is not consulted in regard to the selection for appointment to a central service (Class I and Class II). Tenure post in central service and appointments which are likely to last only for a year stand excluded from commission's purview.

Additionally Article 335, mentions that "the claims of the members of the Scheduled Castes and Scheduled Tribes shall be taken into consideration, consistently with the maintenance of efficiency of administration, in the making of appointments to services in connection with the affairs of the Union or a state." The Commission does not advise the government in regard to these matters like its predecessor the Federal Public Services Commission (1935). The proviso to Article 321, dilutes the consultative role of the commission. In fact a liberal use has been made both by Union and state governments. The commission is not consulted with regard to selections of members or chairmans of tribunals or commissions; diplomats; and group C and group D employees who constitute about 90 per cent of the total number of government employees at the centre.

The obligatory consultation of the commission and non-acceptance of advise by the government is regarded as a violation of the spirit of the Constitution. So, the governments consult the commission and then do not accept its advice. A detailed account of the cases in which the government fails to consult or does not accept the advice is sent to the President in its annual report to be laid down before the Parliament. The President places this report before the Parliament with an explanatory memorandum, as to why the advice was not accepted. The two houses consider the report and the memorandum. The government has to justify its action before the Parliament, which has the power of repudiating the government's action. There are very few cases in which this advice is not accepted. The average number being less than two per year. Nevertheless, a discussion on the commission's reports on the floor of the house about non-acceptance of its advice is an in-built safeguard against executive's arbitrariness in civil service appointments.

The UPSC is a recruiting agency and talent hunt is its prime function. For this, it conducts competitive examinations and selects candidates by written examinations, interviews or both. The commission is autonomous in its internal working and advises the government in personal policy matters. The Kothari, Satish Chandra, Hota and Y.K. Alagh Committees have suggested total and revolutionary changes in the system of PSC recruitment of senior civil services in India. The commission is consulted in matters of appointment by transfer or deputation The chairman or a member of the commission presides over the selection committee constituted by each state to fill the promotion quota of 33 per cent posts in all India services every year. The UPSC gives its advise to the President of India in matters where penalties like censure, withholding of increments/promotion, suspension, compulsory retirement, removal or recovery from pay, etc., are involved as a part of punishment. The commission is consulted before the decision to take action against is made but not for a second time if the civil servant submits a petition for review.

The advice of the commission in disciplinary matters is also not final. The government, while taking disciplinary action, has to consult the Central Vigilance Commission and the Administrative Tribunal. If these bodies disagree in the specifics of any action, the government may rescind the decision. Moreover for disciplinary proceedings by the tribunal, the Commission is not consulted, but the decisions of the UPSC are challengeable in a court of law if they violate the rules. The court can examine a composite written and *viva voce* test if marks were not allocated separately under the different heads of test.

There is little or no relationship between the UPSC and State Public Service Commissions. Yet their functions being similar, the Constitution does provide some mobility from state PSC to UPSC. For instance, in making appointments to a State Public Service Commission, the Governor should consult the chairman of the Union Public Service Commission and the chairman of the State Public Service Commission. Not less than two-thirds of the membership of the Union Public Service Commission are drawn from among the chairman and members of the State Public Service Commissions. Conventionally, one of the members of a State Public Service Commission should belong to a different state. A member selected from among government officers should have held office under a state government or the Central government for at least ten years. Members selected from non-official category should have practised at least for ten years in any of the recognised professions like teaching, law, medicine, engineering, science, technology, accountancy or administration.

Now after more than six decades of operation the workload of UPSC has increased in volume and quality. It processes thousands and thousands of cases and individual candidates for selection to various posts. A rough idea of this workload can be assessed from the following statistics computed from an Annual Report of the UPSC (1990):

(1) Direct Recruitment

12	Examinations
6,41,801	Applicants for written examination
5,667	Interviewed
4,527	Recommended for selection

(2) Recruitment by Interviews

1,720	Total posts
1,263	Recruitment completed
17,055	Applications received
16,233	Interviewed
1,487	Recommended for selection

(3) Consideration of cases for Promotion

27,246	Total number of cases
24,385	Cases disposed of
2,861	Balance
3,441	Empanelled

(4) Consideration of cases for Confirmation

4,324	Total number of cases
3,317	Cases disposed of
1,007	Pending

(5) Promotion to All India Services

431	Considered to IAS
129	Recommended to IAS
235	Considered to IPS
96	Recommended to IPS
272	Considered to IFS
72	Recommended to IFS

(6) Miscellaneous Cases

ICS Examination	1995
Candidates for Preliminary Examination	2,83,000
Candidates for Main Examination	9,000
Candidates for Interview	1,990
Candidates Selected	700

The figures explain that the UPSC is engaged in a gigantic operation and the overincreasing numbers indicate the .challenges ahead. There are constitutional limits but the socio-political changes in the Indian scenario has made the commission an object of criticism in performing its role honestly, independently and even judiciously. The Consultation Exemption Regulations (1958) is criticised for its systematic abuse. It may be an operational necessity but it betrays faith in the credibility of the commission. The cases of delayed and deferred appointments need to be reduced to the minimum. The commission is accused of ineffectiveness and its non-partisan character requires strengthening for secrecy and competence. The state PSCs should imbibe the UPSC culture. The confidential method of 'moderation' of actual marks looks untenable although the Satish Chandra Committee found it satisfactory. Similarly several government organisations, including public sector undertakings, are outside the purview of the commission. The A.R.C. Study Team on Public Sector Undertakings (1967) suggested that the UPSC may be given the task of approving the regulations governing recruitment, promotion, selection boards and promotion committees. The commission should not be consulted in the formulation of broad personnel policies and the details of selection and promotion recommending bodies.

These minor criticisms apart, the UPSC has done an excellent job in discharging the responsibilities entrusted to it by the founding fathers of Indian Constitution. While the state counterparts of the commission have lost their prestige, the UPSC maintains a reasonably high and fair image in a political milieu charged with corruption and political jobbery. It is partly because of the leadership but mostly because of the inbuilt checks obtained in the system. The UPSC can and should do better if it develops an internal mechanism for self-evaluation and organisational renewal. Having accepted the merit principle and reservation policy for public services of the country, UPSC should innovate newer methods of recruitment to keep public services efficient and representative.

This further needs structural innovations and massive use of technology and cybernetics to filter merit of millions of candidates who will opt for civil service careers. It is an irony that when Royal Public Service Commission in UK has been downgraded by Foulton and the Federal Service Commission of USA has been disbanded, the situation in India does not seem to have a better alternative. Because of population pressure and the rigidity of stagnant education system in India, PSC reforms are neither feasible new desirable. But the insulation of PSCs from corrupt environment of society and business is an urgent need of the hour. The state PSCs are in a sorry state of affairs. Perhaps some control of UPSC and on the spot training to state members of PSCs can help to make the situation better. The vigilance agencies should be on extra alert where the careers of young persons are at stake. The recruitment of selectors is the real malaise of Indian administration. Of course political recruitment of members of commission is a necessary evil but here too panels of eligible names may be discussed in Rajya Sabha and the press so that back door political entries are minimised. The present system should neither be over burdened nor bypassed. Rather it should be constantly reviewed and updated in response to the mounting challenges and changing needs of the times.

The Finance Commission of India

All federations have double government which implies a relationship between the centre and the federating units. India does not fit in the neat framework of a federal system. Rather it has been called a 'Union' or a quasi-federation of a centralised polity. The 1935 federation envisaged a division of subjects on the basis of three lists which unlike USA, Canada and Australia put the state governments in a subordinate position. The founding fathers of the Republican Constitution had special problems of a disintegrating polity and unevenly developed units after the merger of native states and historically poorer hinter land regions during the colonial rule. The rim land states of the coastline were richer as compared to scarcity-hit provinces of Central India. Naturally a permanent arrangement of distribution of resources was neither possible nor desirable in an unevenly developed polity. Naturally the financial relations between the Union and state governments were outlined in the Constitution but they were left open for continuous five year review by an independent Financial Commission to keep a balanced economic growth in the polity. The imbalance between the expenditure requirements of the Union and state governments gets heightened by the weak capacity of states to raise resources to meet their development requirements. The vertical federal fiscal imbalance, indicates the deficit faced by the states vis-à-vis the surplus experienced by the national government. The horizontal federal fiscal imbalance, indicates the relative financial imbalance between their own revenues and expenditures among the states themselves. The former refers to a fiscal situation wherein the federal government experiences a budgetary deficit, and no automatic mechanism operates to correct this mismatch to bring about fiscal balance in the entire federation. This also implies that deliberate intervention is called for to minimise the latter variety of fiscal imbalance. Horizontal federal fiscal imbalance refers to a fiscal situation of individual constituent states where some states experience budgetary deficits while some other states experience budgetary surplus. There is no automatic mechanism to reduce these budgetary imbalances across the states and hence a deliberate intervention is required to reduce the horizontal federal fiscal imbalance.

The federal fiscal transfers are a common practice in all federations. To meet this constitutional and extra-constitutional provisions are made to provide for financial transfers from the national government to the states governments. In India, these transfers have been institutionalised by creating a Constitutional Finance Commission under Article 280, which is expected to review the financial needs of the states and to recommend the quantum of resources and their *inter-se* distribution among the states every fifth year. Articles 270, 273, 275 and 280 provide for the constitution of this Commission at stated intervals to recommend to the President certain measures relating to the distribution of financial resources between the Union and the states, for instance, the percentage of the net proceeds of income tax which should be assigned by the Union to the state and the manner in which the share to be assigned shall be distributed among the states (Art. 280). The Finance Commission (Miscellaneous Provisions) Act (1951), supplements the provisions of the Constitution. The chairman of Finance Commission has to be a person of 'experience in public affairs'. The other four members are appointed from amongst the following:

(a) A High Court judge or one qualified to be appointed as such;
(b) a person having special knowledge of the finances and accounts of the government;
(c) a person having wide experience in financial matters and administration;
(d) a person having special knowledge of economics.

It is the duty of the commission to make recommendations to the President as to:

(a) the distribution between the Union and the states of the net proceeds of taxes which are to be or may be, divided between them under this chapter and the allocation between the states of the respective shares of such proceeds;
(b) the principles which should govern the grants-in-aid of the revenues of the states out of the Consolidated Fund of India;
(c) and other matter referred to the commission by the President in the interests of sound finance.

In contrast to the Union Public Service Commission where it is specifically indicated that at least 50 per cent of the members should be from the union and or/state services, no reference has been made to the nature of the background of the chairman and members of the Finance Commission in the Constitution. The Finance Commission Act, 1951, prescribes experience in public affairs for the chairman and four categories for the members.

The working of the Finance Commission as an expert body has been reasonably satisfactory. From 30th December 1952, when the First Finance Commission submitted its report to 7th July 2002 when the Eleventh Finance Commission completed its labour there has been hardly any controversy about its reports, except in 1984, when the recommendations of the Eight Commission were not implemented by the Union government on the ground of financial difficulties and the Union government took a position that commissions' recommendation are neither binding nor justifiable. The commission has been headed by eminent public figures and its reports have kept the Indian federal system in a flexible mould of cooperative federalism even in odd times. The following table presents the work of Finance Commission at a glance:

(1) Neogy Commission worked from 30th November 1951 to 30th December 1952 for 13 months on its report.
(2) Santhanam Commission submitted its report in 10 months only on 30th April 1957.
(3) Chanda Commission was constituted on 15th December 1960 and completed its work in one year only.
(4) Rajaram Commission appointed on 8th May 1964 and laboured for 15 months to submit its report on 12th August 1965.
(5) Tyagi Commission took 16½ months to submit its controversial document on 30th June 1965.
(6) Brahmanand Reddy Commission report came on 30th October 1973 after 14 months of labour.
(7) Shelat Commission appointed on 23rd June 1977 after national emergency grappled with hard problems of economy.
(8) Y.B. Chavan Commission 20th June 1982 to 30th April 1984 worked for 20 months with controversial recommendations.
(9) N.K.P. Salve Commission worked for 2½ years.
(10) K.C. Pant Commission appointed on 15th June 1992 worked for 3¼ years.
(11) Khasro Commission (1988–2002) laboured for 2 years.
(12) Rangrajan Commission

The first Neogy Commission recommended that: (a) 55 per cent of the net proceeds of income tax shall be assigned by the Union to the states and that it shall be distributed among the states in the shares prescribed by the commission, (b) The commission laid down the principles for guidance of the Government of India in the matter of making general grants-in-aid to states which require financial assistance and also recommended specific sums to be given to certain states such as West Bengal, Punjab, Assam, during the five years from 1952 to 1957.

The Santhanam and A.K. Chevda reports were accepted and implemented during the Nehru era. The Fifth Finance Commission under Mahaveer Tyagi made radical recommendations in fixing state share of income tax at 75 per cent and raising the Union excise duty share to 20 per cent. The Sixth Commission under Brahamanand Reddy reviewed the debt position of states and suggested measures to bridge the non-plan capital gap. The recommendations of Eighth Commission ran into rough weather and could not get implemented. The recommendations, granting moneys to the states were not implemented by the Government of India on the ground of financial difficulties and late receipt of the commission's report. Obviously, this placed some of the states in financial difficulty and the State of West Bengal raised vehement protest against this unforeseen situation. Responsible authorities in West Bengal threatened litigation but eventually nothing was done presumably because the matter was non-justifiable. Article 280(3) enjoins the Finance Commission to make 'recommendations' to the President and Article 281, asks him to lay the recommendations of the commission before each house of Parliament. The recommendations of the commission are not binding upon the Government of India and they do not give any legal right in favour of the beneficiary states to receive the moneys recommended. Of course, non-implementation can cause grave dislocation in states which might have acted upon the anticipation founded on the commission's report.

The Ninth Finance Commission (1987–1989) under N.K.P. Salve made heroic efforts and submitted two reports, first report for 1989–90 and second report covering the five-year period from 1990-1995. It examined in depth and made far-reaching recommendations including enhancement in the share of the states in income tax and excise duties to 85 per cent. It also suggested a nine point criterion for distribution of this share. The commission recommended that:

(1) 10 per cent of shareable proceeds of income tax should be distributed among the states on the basis of contribution,
(2) 45 per cent on the basis of the per capita income of a state from that of the state with the highest per capita income multiplied by the 1971 population of the state concerned,
(3) 22.5 per cent on the basis of population of the state concerned,
(4) 11.25 per cent on the basis of the composite index of backwardness compiled by the commission, and the remaining
(5) 11.25 per cent on the basis of shareable proceeds unit be distributed among the states on the basis of 1971 population,
(6) 12.5 per cent on the basis of Income Adjusted Total Population (IATP),
(7) 12.5 per cent on the basis of index of backwardness,
(8) 33.5 per cent on the basis of 'distance' of per capita income, and the remaining
(9) 16.5 per cent among the states with deficits, in proportion to deficit of each state to the total of all states' deficits.

Liberal grants-in-aid of revenues to certain states were recommended under Article 275 (1) of the Constitution towards meeting their non-plan revenue gap as assessed by the commission for five years (1990–95). It also recommended the grant to certain states to cover a part of the deficit of Plan Account for the years 1990–95. Regarding debt relief, the commission's recommendations included:

(i) elongation of maturity period of future central loans for state plans from 15 years to 20 years with 50 per cent loans enjoying a grace period of five years;
(ii) consolidation of such loans advanced during 1984–89 and its rescheduling to 15 years with relief in repayments ranging from 5 per cent to 10 per cent;
(iii) write-off of certain central loans;
(iv) moratorium of two years (1990–92) on payment of principal and payment of interest in respect of special loans granted to Punjab.

For financing relief, expenditure the commission recommended replacement of the existing system of margin money by the Calamity Relief Fund for each state to which the Centre should contribute 75 per cent in the form of non-plan grant and the balance of 25 per cent should be contributed by the state government.

The Tenth Finance Commission under K.C. Pant had wide terms of reference. The other members were Debi Prasad Pal, B.P.R. Vithal, C. Rangrajan. M.C. Gupta was the member-secretary of the commission. Several chief ministers, at the meeting of the National Development Council, wanted a say in the formulation of the commission's terms of reference. However, the Centre did not concede this demand, possibly to avoid a precedent. Unlike its predecessor the Tenth Commission was asked:

(i) to take into account the need for not only balancing the revenue budget both at the Centre and the states, but also generating surplus for capital investment and reducing fiscal deficit;
(ii) to examine the resource adequacy to the Centre to meet expenditures on civil administration, defence, border security, debt-servicing and other committed liabilities;
(iii) to consider the issue of capital maintenance expenditure on plan schemes to be completed by March 31, 1995, the norms for fixing specified amount and the manner of monitoring them;
(iv) to consider the requirements of states for modernisation of administration including computerisation of land records;
(v) to take into account the revenue resources of the states for the Five-Year Plan period (1995–2000) on the basis of 1993–94 levels of taxation and potential for raising additional taxes for meeting the non-plan expenditure of the states;
(vi) to suggest changes in the principles governing the distribution of net proceeds of the additional excise duties in any financial year, replacement of the sales tax levied formerly by the state governments and the grants to the states in lieu of the taxes levied under the repealed Railway Passenger Fares Act, 1957;
(vii) to assess the debt position of the states as on March 31, 1994 and suggest corrective measures, keeping in view the financial needs of the Centre; and
(viii) to review the existing scheme of Calamity Relief Fund.

The commission has a decisive impact on the financial relationship between the Centre and the states. The distribution of financial resources under the Constitution is loaded in favour of the Centre. Its sources of revenue are elastic such as income tax, corporation tax, customs duties, excise duties, etc. The Centre has the sole authority to create money by printing notes. It can raise loans both in the country and abroad without any limits. On the contrary, the revenue resources of the states are inelastic; except the sales tax. Most of the developmental functions like education, irrigation, agriculture, health and family planning, cooperation, etc., are entrusted to the states. The state governments have to provide money for Panchayati Raj Institutions and urban bodies. Naturally, therefore, the states are in perpetual deficit. Moreover, the state governments are incompetent and profligate. By and large, they have failed to husband their resources wisely. Aware of these facts the Constitution provides for liberal transfer of financial resources from the Union to the states. The Finance Commission only maintains a national and a regional balance between the backward areas and the developed areas through the instrumentality of correcting these imbalances as a part of Union's responsibility.

The Finance Commission is a constitutional body and has the most crucial job to distribute resources and decide principles for grants in aid to the states over the period spanning half the century. It has depoliticised the political struggles between the Centre and the states. As governments following various party persuasions came to power, the commission has concentrated on objective criterion determination in the allocation and distribution of resources. No state, except some minor protests has disagreed with the awards of the Finance Commission, nor has the Union government tried to bring a partisan approach to its deliberations and decisions. The work is too technical and the commission has reconciled its federal role with the working of democratic institutions at state level. Moreover, it has avoided bitter controversies with the Planning Commission without violating the sovereign character of the Indian Parliament. It is an effective constitutional tool that has shaped an even development of the country, its progressive policies of regional growth and state autonomy.

The Election Commission of India

Adult suffrage can be called the lifeline of a democratic polity. India was introduced to a partially elected council system under the Morley Minto Reforms. From a system of limited, communal and indirect election the country witnessed the expansion of franchise under dyarchical and autonomy reforms in provinces. The bicameral legislature at centre under the Government of India Act 1935 could not be inaugurated because of the failure of the federal experiment, but India and Indians were reasonably familiar with a democratic electoral system when Englishmen decided to leave the country. The Constituent Assembly of India consisted of indirectly elected political representative who were members of provincial assemblies elected on the basis of limited and communal suffrage. The Republican Constitution completed the process by introducing adult suffrage without any distinction of colour, caste, sex or creed. This massive democracy and the largest electorate for a Parliament goes to polls under the superintendence of an election commission about which Article 324 of the Constitution has provided as under:

"The superintendence, direction and control of the electoral rolls for, and the conduct of all elections to Parliament and to the legislature of every state and of elections to the officers of President and Vice-President held under this Constitution, including the appointment of election tribunals for the decision of the doubts and disputes arising out of or in connection with election to Parliament and to the legislatures of the states, shall be vested in a commission."

The provision proposes to centralise the election machinery in the hands of a single commission, to be assisted by regional commissioners, working under the supervision, direction and control of the Election Commission and not under the control of the state Governor. The centralisation of electoral administration was proposed "to prevent injustice which may be done by the provincial governments to the minorities or to the people other than those who belonged to the provinces". The commission is an all-India body having jurisdiction over elections to Parliament, state legislatures, offices of the President and the Vice-President. The reason for not having State Election Commissions to conduct elections in each state was that states have mixed populations who were racially, linguistically or culturally different from the native people. The state government may discriminate against outsiders and deprive them of their franchise. To prevent this kind of injustice being done to any section of the people, a central body was found desirable to conduct free and fair elections from local influences.

According to Constitution, the Election Commission consists of the Chief Election Commissioner and such number of election commissioners, if any, as the President may fix from time to time. The Chief Election Commissioner (CEC) stands at the apex of the hierarchy and other commissioners are appointed by the President subject to the provisions of law enacted by the Parliament. The President appoints them at the behest of the Prime Minister because it is a constitutional necessity under the Parliamentary system of government. The Chief Election Commissioner acts as the chairman of the Commission and his tenure is independent of the executive discretion. He cannot be removed from his office except in the like manner and on the like grounds as a judge of the Supreme Court. To discharge his functions without fear, favour or pressure from the executive or the party in power the security of his tenure has been guaranteed like that of a Judge of the Supreme Court. The Chief Election Commissioner functioned since inception, but in 1989, the President fixed the number of election commissioners (other than Chief Election Commissioner) at two till further orders. The President rescinded his earlier notification and removed the newly appointed commissioners on January 1st 1990. In 1993, the government converted the Election Commission into a three-member body by appointing two more election commissioners. This decision came in the wake of a series of controversial decisions taken by the then Chief Election Commissioner. All political parties demanded that the commission be made a multi-member body because the CEC had suspended all by-elections on the issue of the commission's power over deployment of paramilitary forces and polling personnel.

The President promulgated an ordinance amending the Chief Election Commissioner and other Election Commissioners (Conditions of Service) Act. The amendment provided for 'unanimous' transaction of business, but in case of difference of opinion among the three members the matter was to be decided "according to the opinion of the majority". In *S.S. Dhanao* vs *Union of India*, the Supreme Court held that when an institution like the Election Commission is entrusted with vital functions, it is necessary and desirable that the powers are not exercised by one individual, however all-wise he may be. "It ill conforms to the tenets of democratic rule." The constitutional provision tilted in favour of the Chief Election Commissioner. The Constitution being silent about a single member or a multi-member Election Commission, the CEC acts as its chairman. Under the ordinance, the conditions of services of the commissioners have been placed at par with those of the CEC and Supreme Court judges. They will have a six-year term or serve up to 65 years of age whichever is earlier. Now the ordinance relating to transaction of business of Election Commission provides that the Election Commission may, by unanimous decision, regulate the procedure for transaction of its business as also allocation of its business amongst the Chief Election Commissioner and other election commissioners. All business of the Election Commission shall, as far as possible, be transacted unanimously and if the CEC and other commissioners differ in opinion on any matter, such matters shall be decided according to the opinion of the majority.

The amended conditions of service rules retrospectively (since 1986) entitle the CEC to the salary and other facilities, equivalent to that of a judge of the Supreme Court. The interim order of the Court confirmed the pre-eminent position of the CEC but the final verdict (July 14, 1995) provides the full interpretation of Article 324 of the Constitution whereby the Court has upheld the new legislation providing for the appointment of two commissioners. "The question whether it is necessary to appoint other election commissioners besides the CEC is for the Government to decide and that it is not a justiciable matter".

To assist the Chief Election Commissioner in the performance of his onerous duties there are officers and subordinates like the regional commissioners, deputy election commissioners, secretary, under secretary, research officers, etc. During the first general elections, (1951–52) the President sanctioned four posts of regional election commissioners, and only two were filled in for a limited period of six or seven months and discontinued at the time of second general election. In place of the regional commissioners, a new post of deputy election commissioner was created in the commission. The deputy chief election commissioner is appointed by the President and is usually on deputation. He can be recalled by the Central government at the request of the Chief Election Commissioner any time. The deputation ordinarily extends up to a period of five years subject to extension for a specified period.

At the state or the union territory level there is the Chief Electoral Officer who is a key official in the electoral machinery. He is nominated by the Election Commission in consultation with the state/UT Government. He is usually a senior executive or judicial officer of the state government. He may be a whole time or part time officer, and may be required by the state government to attend other duties also in addition to the election work. He was accorded statutory status in 1956. At the district level the electoral duties are discharged by the district officer or the executive officer in addition to his normal administrative routine. He was accorded statutory status in 1966 through an amendment to the Representation of the People's Act, 1950. The responsibility for the preparation and revision of electoral rolls is vested in an officer called the Electoral Registration Officer. The officers of the status of deputy collectors such as sub divisional officer and executive officers are designated as electoral registration officers. The election in every constituency is supervised by an officer known as the returning officer nominated by the Election Commission in consultation with the government of the state. The same officer can be nominated as returning officer for more than one constituency. He is assisted by one or more assistant returning officers so designated by the Election Commission. The state government sends the list of officials with their designations to the Election Commission which after scrutinising the same formally designates them as such for assembly and parliamentary constituencies. The staff consisting of presiding and polling officers for the actual conduct of the poll is appointed by the district election officer who also appoints a presiding officer for each polling station and such polling officer or officers as are necessary.

Functions and Role

The functions of the Election Commission of India are not enumerated in the Constitution but they imply in the responsibility of conduct and superintendency of election work as prescribed by Parliament under the Peoples Representation Act. Adult suffrage, reservation of seats or constituencies, recognitions of political parties, disqualifications of candidates and the implementation of rules of conduct poll like security deposit, peaceful campaigning, mechanical counting of votes, control over electoral expenses and evil practices in polling, etc., are the innumerable operations that have flowed from the basic responsibility of conducting free, fair, and malpractices proof elections in the country. It is a gigantic operation and its frequency in states or in by-elections needs an electoral administration too complex to be managed by a small commission located in Delhi and using the administrative machinery of the states and central and state police forces of the country. Some of the major functions of the ECI are:

(1) Delimitation, revision and periodic re-demarcation of the constituencies general as well as reserved as directed by the President on the recommendation of the Parliament of India.
(2) Updating and revision of electoral rolls for all elections to ensure fair and free polling and avoid bogus voting.
(3) Recognition of political parties who contest elections at national and regional levels and giving them identity in terms of symbols, etc., to facilitate the mandate of the voters.

(4) Control of the actual conduct of polls through procedures like scrutiny of nomination papers, deposit of fee, campaign ethics, re-poll and counting, etc., in the interest of free and fair elections.

(5) Conduct of administration of election which includes complaints disposal, scrutiny of election expenses, maintenance of poll peace and hearing of election petitions, appeals, etc. It puts a heavy quasi judicial burden on the commission, because the courts are not allowed by the constitution to directly interfere in the conduct of elections. However, the later appeals may go to the courts and the jurisdiction and verdicts or the commission may be challenged.

While performing these functions, the Election Commission of India has spread its tentacles too wide and its election administration at every bend of the electoral process has expanded the powers of the commission. For instance, the practice of sending observers to the constituencies and ordering re-poll on their advice make its role effective and all pervading. To facilitate the process of elections the country has been divided into constituencies. The task of delimiting the constituencies is performed by a Delimitation Commission. The Election Commission has distributed the seats districtwise in each one of the states and directed the Chief Electoral Officers to prepare proposals for the physical demarcation of constituencies according to the prescribed criteria. The association of Parliamentary Advisory Committees with the Delimitation Commission give priority to political considerations. As an outcome of the recommendations of the Election Commission the Parliament enacted the Delimitation Act, 1952. This commission consists of three members, two to be nominated by the President from serving or retired judges of the Supreme Court or High Courts and the Chief Election Commissioner to be an *ex officio* member. A new part (Part-IV A) has been added to the Representation of the People (Amendment) Act, 1951 on registration of political parties. Section 29(A) (now inserted) provides for registration with the commission of associations and bodies of individual citizens of India as political parties for purpose of this Act. Since 1989, a recognised political party has been classified either as a National Party or a State Party under paragraph 7 of the Elections Symbol Order, 1968. The commission has specified certain symbols as reserved and as free. The reserved symbols are only available for candidates sponsored by the recognised political parties and the free symbols are available to other candidates. The commission adjudicates upon disputes with regard to recognition of political parties and rival claims to a particular symbol for purposes of elections. The Supreme Court has held that the commission is a tribunal for purposes of Article 136 while deciding such a controversy.

The nomination papers of the candidates are accepted if found in order, or rejected otherwise. This duty is performed by the returning officer who notifies to all the contesting candidates the date, time and place for the formal scrutiny of nomination papers. The returning officer decides the objections raised. He is also to see whether the requisite requirements of security deposit, election symbol, declaration of assets, election agent, etc., have also been fulfilled. He is empowered to reject the nomination papers if the candidate is not qualified or is disqualified to fill the seat under Articles 84, 102, 173 and 191; or Sections 33 and 34 of the Representation of the People's Act. The commission can order a re-poll for the whole constituency under compulsion of circumstances. Article 324 confers on the Election Commission necessary powers to countermand the poll because of hooliganism and breakdown of law and order at the time of polling or counting of votes within 10 days from the last date of filing the returns. The returning officer submits to the Election Commission a list of all the candidates and their agents. The commission scrutinises the accounts and decides whether the returns are in proper form and whether they have been lodged in time. In case of default, it notifies the candidates or their agents of their disqualification by publishing these in the Official Gazette. The Representation of the People Act was amended in 1988 to authorise the registration of political parties. The amendment has added a new Section (29-A) providing for such registration.

ECI and Electoral Reforms

Electoral reforms is a wide area that falls into the realm of political reforms rather than administrative management of polls. The ECI has a limited role to cleanse poll politics and has almost no role in filtering the better representatives from a society still seeped in caste, class and religious bigotry. It can only ensure a free and fair poll as per rules of the game but if the players and captains are not fielded properly the game cannot be neat and challenging. Still the role of the commission remains crucial and the commission can do its negative job to minimise the foul play and not permitting the poll exercise into a farce or an arena of law-breakers. The Indian electorate during last sixty years has become quite articulate also, for which the election managers can take a legitimate share. It has made "the role of Election Commission of India much more crucial, and its effectiveness much more critical. It is through free and fair elections, based on universal, adult suffrage that complex issues can be resolved in a manner acceptable to all concerned." As things become more complex the rivalries between political parties has become more acute and the Election Commission had to change from a reactive to a proactive organisation, to ensure free and fair elections.

The administration of elections is shared between the Election Commission and the executive government of the day to recruit its legislators. The judiciary has been asked to standby and allow the people to exercise their franchise without fear and favour. It presupposes:

(1) An intelligent and educated electorate with political awareness.
(2) Well organised and ideologically disciplined political parties, having internal democracy.
(3) Consensus about rules, regulations and procedures by which the poll has to be conducted.

The Election Commission comes at the last stage. It can cleanse the system but cannot improve it. But even to cleanse it the administrators in the Election Commission have to be non-partisan, independent, honest and above all committed to democratic ideals of peaceful change. Several reforms have been suggested by outsiders and insiders in this regard.

(1) It has been suggested more than once that the ECI be given a constitution like UPSC and the ECI should become effective and respectable in the eyes of people and the administrators.
(2) Once the commission draws the schedule and declares elections, the political executive should work under the command and control of the Election Commission of India for four weeks.
(3) Justice Tarakunde suggested that the members of ECI should be picked up by a committee consisting of PM, leader of the opposition in the Lok Sabha and the Chief Justice of India. The President should formalise the appointments.
(4) When multi-member commission is being welcomed by all political parties, the chairmanship may be rotated among members each year.
(5) There has been some criticism of a Troika Commission on the basis that there is not enough work and the members may pull the cart in opposite directions. The facts speak that the commission should function like a bureau-judicial organisation on the lines of an Independent

Regulatory Commission. It should act as an arm of the Parliament, a headless head executive organisation functioning as an island of autonomy.

(6) The commission may have state level organisations and if federalised its state units may provide a support structure to panchayati and urban local institutions, which avoidably proliferates election machinery in the states.

The nature of work demands that Election Commission of India should have three kinds of members from among judges, civil servants and former speakers of Parliament. The retired judges of Supreme Court, the former cabinet secretaries and the speakers of Lok Sabha should be eligible and the chairmanship should always go to the judiciary. The commission should have mandatory power and evolve its own rules and regulations for conduct and superintendence of polls. The commission should ensure that inner party democracy becomes a reality in respect of all recognised parties. The commission has already taken first major step to keep the convicts out of the precints of Parliament and state legislatures. The commission must restructure and tighten the law, so that the law-breakers do not reach to the position of lawmakers. Anybody having a grievance against a political party, candidate, minister or official can approach the commission for its redressal. The Election Commission is the only suitable agency for the removal of their electoral grievances and can render the requisite help and guidance in all matters pertaining to elections. The commission has to generate a sense of faith that the people repose in its integrity. It should function independently and come heavily on the political parties indulging in rigging, booth capturing and other malpractices. A restructured and reformed Election Commission should use cybernetics and encourage new kind of electioneering through MIS.

Planning Commission and National Development Council

A Planning Commission on the Soviet model of a GOSPLAN in a liberalised and globalised economy of India seems like a contradiction in terms. But the 42nd Amendment to the Constitution justifies its existence in a socialist economy, which has obviously a different meaning in the Indian context. The western socialists and Karl Marx viewed socialist order as an antithesis of capitalist *Laissez Faire*, while to Pandit Nehru it was more of a doctrine of welfare state through state intervention. Nehru was at best a Fabian, a drawing room socialist, who defined planning as "an integrating process which has an overall view of the general conditions and tries to progress all along the line, with certain priorities". He believed that if economic and social problems are analysed objectively and assessed in terms of well-defined criteria, a course of action for desired results can be mapped out. Planning can be called "a purposive adaptation of resources to socialist ends".

It implies centralised control of economic activities. This has been particularly so in Asia and Africa where colonies provided the raw materials required by industries in the mother country and served as a market for the goods manufactured by the latter. After the attainment of independence, these colonies had to develop their economy with a social objective – which was conspicuously absent in the colonial era. Socialism to Pandit Nehru was a necessary consequence of our political democracy and national unity. It shall not be possible to sustain them, unless we widen the base of our democracy by common sharing of our economic and social development.

The concept of global development demands an induced change through the strategy of planning which can fasten the speed of growth and reduce the gap between the living standards of the developed and developing countries. According to the World Bank view of public administration, open and liberal economies can coexist with modified versions of economic planning. The wave of New Right has already swept the countries of Eastern Europe, Russia and China. England, France and even USA are no longer hostile to the notions of indicative planning or persuasive planning with regulatory measures. A globalised economy in a developing country may be competitive but the core sector might remain wedded to social welfare and extra ordinarily protected by planned and controlled measures of the state. Democracies of UK and France permit their responsible governments to nationalise and denationalise core sectors of their respective economics as per needs of the times. France has a standing Central Planning Commission, while UK keeps revising its notions and strategies of indicative planning. In USA, the Council of Economic Advisor in the Executive Office of the American President prepares long-term economic plans which comes quite close to indicative planning. Even the practice of Program Planning and Budgetary System (PPBS) has created a situation of nucleus planning without using the term 'planned economy' which the devotees of Statue of Liberty abhor. The promoter, facilitator, partner and monitor roles of the states are today accepted by all the states which implicitly concede the utility of planning in national economies.

Evolution

Historically speaking the Karachi session of Indian National Congress (1931) attempted to define the economics and social contents of 'Swarajya', envisioned by Bal Gangadhar Tilak. Nehru and the young Turks belonging to the socialist wing of the Congress were its pioneers. Concurrently the Gandhian model of Sarvodaya Planning was advanced and discussed to evolve appropriate models of planning for India. Later when provincial autonomy was conceded by the Government of India Act, 1935, the Congress Party set up a 'National Planning Committee' under the chairmanship of Pandit Nehru. This committee constituted two subcommittees, one for national planning and the other for administrative machinery for such a plan. Owing to the outbreak of the Second World War and epoch making developments in freedom struggle, these subcommittees could report only in 1948. The Government of India, pressed by the circumstance of war, created a department of planning and development in the year 1946. When Pandit Nehru took over as head and Prime Minister of Interim government, he appointed a Planning Advisory Board in October 1946. One of the terms of reference for this board was to suggest administrative arrangements necessary for carrying out the plan. It was in pursuance of the recommendation of the Advisory Board that the present Planning Commission was born in March 1950 by an administrative order of the government. In the meantime, the Constituent Assembly conclusively debated and ruled out a planning body as a part of the constitutional structure. This prompted Prime Minister Nehru to create the statutory body of which he became the chairman. Besides being the creator he remained its mentor and lent lustre and prestige to the concept of planning and the institution of Planning Commission in India.

The Objectives

The Nehru era of planning which spans from 1950 to 1964 could witness the drafting and implementation of first three Five-Year Plans. Mahalanobis, a noted economist who was later joined by Sukhomoy Chakravarti, D.R. Godgil, Ashok Mehta and many others laid down the foundations of a planned economy which could build the infrastructure for a take-off stage of liberalisation and globalisation. As a dreamer and a visionary, Pandit Nehru visualised planning as a panacea to rid the country from poverty, backwardness, stagnation and traditional systems of production. Naturally, the commission was given an ambitious agenda which slated the following objectives:

(1) Promoting development in agricultural, industrial and other sectors and striving to achieve inter-sectoral development.
(2) Speeding up the development of relatively backward regions and promoting balanced regional development.
(3) Securing an increase in national income.
(4) Accelerating the planned rate of investment to enhance the proportion of actual investment to national income.
(5) Reducing in a progressive manner, incidence of poverty by providing food, work and productivity to the people below the poverty line.
(6) Increasing the quantum of employment for the maximum possible utilisation of manpower.
(7) Modernisation of the economy through effecting shifts, in the sectoral composition of production diversification of activities advancement in technology and institutional innovation.
(8) Mitigating the inequalities of income and wealth and regulating the concentration of economic power.

The Ten Five-Year Plans

To achieve these lofty goals, the entire plan process aimed at mobilising the material and human resources of the nation to bring about an accelerated growth, both of the infrastructure inputs as well as of consumer goods to improve the living conditions of the people. The basic concept was to bring about a balanced growth that would not only remove regional imbalances, but also the imbalance between the rural and urban sectors. The Planning Commission embarked upon the arduous task of formulation and execution of Five-Year Plans.

During last 55 years, this plan process of development has passed through several ups and downs including plan holidays, rolling plans and national emergency of 1975. The chronological order with interludes and interregnums are depicted below:

1.	1951–1956	First Five-Year Plan
2.	1956–1961	Second Five-Year Plan
3.	1961–1966	Third Five-Year Plan
4.	1966–1969	Three Annual Plans
5.	1969–1974	Fourth Five-Year Plan
6.	1974–1979	Fifth Five-Year Plan
7.	1979–1980	Annual Plan
8.	1980–1985	Sixth Five-Year Plan
9.	1985–1990	Seventh Five-Year Plan
10.	1990–1992	Two Annual Plans
11.	1992–1997	Eighth Five-Year Plan
12.	1997–2002	Ninth Five-Year Plan
13.	2002–2007	Tenth Five-Year Plan

The disruptions in the plan process can be seen in the years 1966, 1979 and 1990. Nehru's death in 1964 and Pakistan's aggression in 1965 disrupted the economy beyond repair. The return of Mrs Gandhi to power after Janta experiment and later her assassination created a wedge in the plan process. Similarly the year 1990 was the year of great financial calamity and serious structural adjustments in policies and their macrolevel stabilisation was necessitated by declining balance of payments position and inflation during 1990–91. The Janta government terminated the Fourth Five-Year Plan one year ahead of schedule on March 31, 1978. The experiment of the Rolling Plan was short-lived and was abandoned with the return of Mrs Gandhi to power and the Sixth Plan was launched in 1980.

The last one, a-half-decade since 1990 after the collapse of Soviet Union has radically changed the global scenario and the new policies of liberalisation and privatisation have drastically revised the plan priorities and readjustment of planning process with external capital investments and joint ventures in public sector. The K.C. Pant years of planning were the years of relaxed planning but the BJP government policies of disinvestment and liberalisation put the Planning Commission under freeze. The return of Manmohan Singh government has tried to rehabilitate planning and a restructured Planning Commission under M.S. Ahluwalia is engaged in infusing life and blood in the process of planned development in collaboration with World Bank and international agencies. The new dispensation has to take the following *characteristic features* of Indian planning into account:

(1) Democratic planning, involving popular participation.
(2) Federal planning following the methods of democratic centralism.
(3) Indicative and detailed planning involving all sectors of economy.
(4) Long range, short range and annualised planning taking advantage of previous experiences.
(5) Unlike past the focus can be public, private and mixed sectors.
(6) Scientists, bureaucrats, politicians and social workers have to be involved in planning process.

Dr Rajendra Prasad as chairman of the Constituent Assembly did not accept Dr B.R. Ambedkar's suggestion for a constitutional body for production planning. As a compromise economic and social planning was put at entry 20, List III in the Concurrent List. Now after the 74th Amendment Act 1992, Article 243(W) has been added about powers, authority and responsibilities of municipalities. The same Article 243(ZD) pertains to the creation of district planning committees.

The Administrative Reforms Commission's (ARC) Position

The Administrative Reforms Commission's position is that the Prime Minister in a parliamentary democracy should not be the chairman of an extra-constitutional body because it belittles the stature of the cabinet and violates the principle of parliamentary sovereignty. The Planning Commission in ARC's view should be a professional body and its control by the political leadership should be reduced to the minimum. The Prime Minister, should cease to be its chairman, but he and the Finance Minister should continue to remain closely associated with its working. The ARC did not favour the formal membership but appreciated the imperatives of their close association with the planning process. In the ARC's opinion, the Planning Commission has "added to its functions and personnel and has stepped into the area to the executive authority of the governments by using the umbrella of PM's Chairmanship." No wonder some plan watchers call it a parallel cabinet or a super cabinet. It has diluted the responsibilities of the ministers to the legislature and eventually, to the people below. But then the vital link with the Prime Minister should continue. Copies of the agenda may be sent to him. He may attend the meetings, express his views and participate in the discussions. He may also summon a meeting of the commission, address it and should preside over the meeting if he attends it. In ARC's view, the PM and his cabinet colleagues have contributed little to the deliberations of the Commission. The final decision on the plans is taken by the cabinet and, therefore, the association of only some ministers at the initial stage of formulation may cause complications. The Government of India did not accept the ARC position and decided that the PM and the finance minister will continue to be the chairman and member respectively but the rest of the ministers may or may not be appointed as members. This ambivalent position has become much worse after the acceptance of LPG policies of the government.

The Structure

The administrative organisation of the Planning Commission has been subjected to changes since its inception in 1950. The Prime Minister till to date continues to be a part-time chairman by convention. The following chronological developments deserve mention to appreciate its organisation and working:

1951 A full-time deputy chairman was appointed: A responsible minister of planning was created as spokesman of the commission. Ministers of planning and finance were appointed as *ex officio* members of the commission.

1953 Strength was fixed at three.

1966 Strength increased to five.

1973 Total membership re-fixed at four.

1977 Finance, defence and home ministers were added to the commission as part-time members besides full-time members.

1980 Strength was raised to eight members, including the deputy chairman and five full-time and two part-time members.

1994 Membership stood at thirteen.

1997 Full-time members to be taken as experts in fields of industry, science, economics and administration.

Deputy chairman was given the rank of full cabinet minister and others were accorded the status of minister of state. The organisation structure of the Planning Commission is illustrated in the chart on the following page.

The commission has a member secretary who assists the deputy chairman and division heads in the day-to-day administration of Yojana Bhawan. His functions pertain to the management of the following:

(1) Developmental policy
(2) International economics
(3) Financial resources
(4) Industry and minerals
(5) Perspective planning
(6) Plan coordination
(7) Administration

The secretary has his deputies and assistants. As the work of the commission keeps expanding there are special secretaries on deputation and also a number of specialists and technocrats assisting the work of the technical division.

The Working

The organisational chart indicates that the commission functions like a staff agency receiving inputs from its divisions and their output are refunded into ten areas headed by various members as portfolios. The ministers of Union government are part-timers but the whole time members look

Chart 1

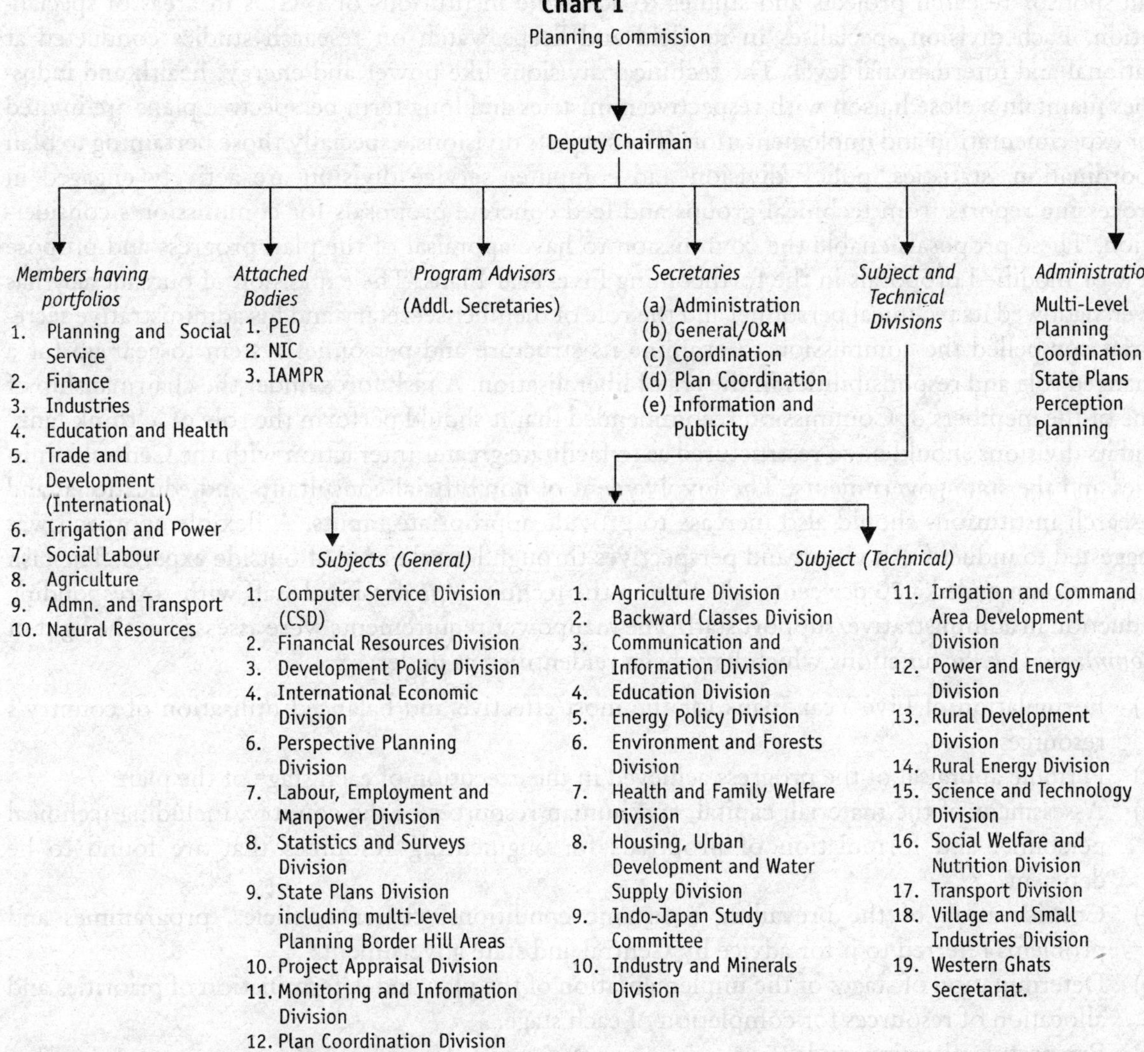

Source: R.K. Arora, *Indian Public Administration.*

after a bunch of subjects of allied nature. As there are 13 members, this division in not fixed and follows the expertise of members. Broadly, the subjects are bunched as under:

(1) Energy, transport, project and programme appraised.
(2) Agriculture and rural development including Panchayati Raj and irrigation.
(3) Science, space, environment and ocean development.
(4) Culture, tourism, labour and small industries.
(5) Health, family planning, youth and nutrition.
(6) Education, social welfare and weather sections.
(7) Technical education, housing, water supply and urban development.

The members supervise the work of 18 technical and 12 general subject division. Their research reports are screened and discussed by various sub-committees of experts. Every division can sponsor research projects and studies to academic institutions or NGOs in areas of specialisation. Each division specialises in its field and keeps watch on research studies conducted at national and international level. The technical divisions like power and energy, health and industries maintain a close liaison with respective ministries and long-term perspective plans are invited for experimentation and implementation. The subjects divisions, especially those pertaining to plan coordination, statistics, policy division and computer service division are actively engaged in processing reports from technical groups and feed concrete proposals for commission's consideration. These proposals enable the commission to have appraisal of the plan progress and propose new or modified proposals in the forthcoming Five-Year Plans. The expansion of bureaucracy has overshadowed its technical personnel and the role of member secretary and his administrative secretariat compelled the commission to examine its structure and personnel system to gear up for a changed role and responsibilities in the era of liberalisation. A task force under the chairmanship of one of the members of Commission recommended that it should perform the role of a 'think tank' and its divisions should be so restructured as to facilitate greater interaction with the Central ministries and the state governments. The involvement of non-official consultants and educational and research institutions should also increase to provide appropriate inputs. A flexible approach was suggested to induct fresh vision and perspectives through lateral entry of outside experts. The task force recommended a 20 per cent reduction in the technical/professional staff with corresponding reduction in administrative/support staff. The manpower requirements were assessed in the light of *Commission's basic* functions which have been reidentified as under:

(1) Formulation of Five-Year Plans for the most effective and balanced utilisation of country's resources.
(2) Periodic appraisal of the progress achieved in the execution of each stage of the plan.
(3) Assessment of the material, capital, and human resources of the country, including technical personnel and formulation of proposals for augmenting resources that are found to be deficient.
(4) Consideration of the prevailing economic conditions, current policies, programmes and problems referred to it for advice by Central and state governments.
(5) Determination of stages of the implementation of the plan and determination of priorities and allocation of resources for completion of each stage.
(6) Perspective planning, and
(7) Determining the nature of the machinery required for the implementation of the plan in all its aspects.

Out of all these functions, the formulation of Five-Year Plans constitutes the key function. This task is too heavy and too complicated that it takes its maximum time and energy to prepare the document. The plan formulation is the basic stage of planning process which commences with the assessment and augmentation of national resources. The Five-Year Plan document has to be designed in great details. Its implementation stages have to be identified and necessary prerequisites are to be provided for annual phasing. The executive machinery for plan implementation has to be created and its periodic appraisals and reviews are to be undertaken by the commission. The commission also offers appropriate advise to Central and state governments so that planning exercise may reach to its fruition.

The Plan Preparation

The process of planning at the central level is "essentially a backward and forward process – an exercise in successive approximation as well as successive coordination". The state of planning at the central level follows the prescribed route:

Preparation of Five-Year Plan

1 Target Fixing
2 Guideline Indicators
3 Approach Paper
4 Draft Plan
5 Plan Format Finalisation
6 Implementation Plan
7 Evaluation Exercise

The commission lays down the tentative and general goals for a long-term development, against the background of broad targets for a Five-Year Plan formulation. The five-year targets are given provisional guidelines by Central Working Groups, created for each sector. The specialists, economists and administrators in the central ministries and the Planning Commission fix targets for their respective sectors, keeping the needs and resources in view. On the basis of the reports of the working groups and the details received from the state governments and union territories, the Planning Commission prepares its approach paper for the Five-Year Plan. It is discussed and approved/modified by the National Development Council. Later the commission prepares and publishes the draft Five-Year Plan which outlines the set of objectives and makes resource-assessment to offer broad indications of the priorities and targets in various sectors. The plan represents a synthesis of the technical, financial, administrative and 'political' imperatives of growth and development. The Five-Year Plan is formally endorsed by the Union cabinet and then presented to the Parliament. The final plan is communicated to the concerned central ministries and state governments. The process of implementation starts with the release of sanctions by the ministry of finance, and at the state level, by the respective departments of finance. Finally, periodical evaluations and appraisals of the plan are undertaken at the levels of the National Development Council, the Planning Commission, central ministries, state governments and the district planning authorities. Readjustments can be made in the plan outlays in the light of these evaluations.

The attached bodies of the Planning Commission represent the proliferation of staff units within its staff agencies. As the work of the commission is of a very specialised and technical nature the staff subunits provide the necessary feedback to help the commission's conclusions. The Programme Evaluation Organisation (PEO), functions under the Planning Commission. It provides feedback on the implementation of various development programmes. Its main functions are:

(1) To evaluate the impact of programmes on the target groups,
(2) To discover assessment of plan programmes against the stated targets,
(3) To examine the adequacy of the delivery mechanism, and
(4) To render technical advice to the state evaluation organisations and impart training.

National Informatics Centre: The NIC is a nodal science and technology organisation of the Government of India, functioning under the commission. It is designed to introduce information technology through some of the following tools in government administration:

(1) Management Support System (MSS),
(2) Model Base (MB) and Knowledge Base (KB), Decision Support Systems (DS),
(3) Development of Databases (DB),
(4) Geographic Information System (GISNIC),
(5) Fileless office concept,
(6) Electronic Mail Service (NIC MAIL),
(7) Multimedia-based IT training and
(8) Tele-information services

Hundred districts through its satellite-based computer communication network "NICNET" and nationwide operational modes, facilitates: (a) the monitoring of key socio-economic projects, (b) online retrieval of data, (c) optimum utilisation of computer resources, (d) emergency communication systems, (e) sharing the new software tools, (f) dissemination of information, and (g) exchange of information.

The Links

The ARC in its detailed report has justified the present state of the Planning Commission as a Non-Statutory Advisory Body, accountable to Parliament for plan performance.

A Digest of Ten Five-Year Plans in India

Plan	*Years*	*Thrust Area*	*Rate of Growth*
First	1951–1956	Agriculture	3.6 per cent growth achieved
Second	1956–1961	Industrialisation	3.9 per cent achieved
Third	1961–1966	Self Reliance	2.3 per cent achieved
Fourth	1969–1974	Growth with Stability	5.5 per cent targeted
Fifth	1974–1979	Alleviation of Poverty	5.5 per cent targeted
Sixth	1980–1985	Basic Structure and Managerial Efficiency	5.2 per cent achieved
Seventh	1985–1990	Modernisation Social Justice Self Justice	5.8 per cent achieved
Annual Plans	1990–1991 1991–1992	Employment and Social Change	
Eighth	1992–1997	Growth with Social Justice Infrastructure	5.6 per cent achieved
Ninth	1997–2002	Savings Domestic Resource Public Enterprise	First 3 years – 4.8 per cent achieved Last 2 years – N.A.
Tenth	2002–2007	Investment Debureaucratisation Reduction in Deficit	6.5 expected

Item 20 of the Concurrent List makes it desirable that the Planning Commission should formulate its plans and implement them successfully and effectively with active cooperation, close collaboration and goodwill of the Union and state governments. The close organisational links have developed through organisational devices which have evolved over the years for this purpose. The Prime Minister as chairman of the commission has provided this link at the highest level. He does not attend all the meetings nor does he attend to its day-to-day business, conducted by the deputy chairman of the commission. The PM is only kept informed of the important decisions taken by the Commission. Copies of agenda and connected papers are sent to him. A number of other ministers have been appointed as the members of the commission. The minister of planning acts as a spokesman of the commission in Parliament. Ashok Mehta combined in him the twin offices of the union minister for planning and the deputy chairman of the commission. In earlier days the Cabinet Secretary used to act as the *ex officio* secretary to the commission. Notwithstanding revival efforts of 1973, the reports of the Estimates Committee forced the government to put an end to this position and appointed a full-time secretary to the commission. Close connection has always existed between the Planning Commission and the Central Statistical Organisation. Professor P.C. Mahalanobis, Honorary Statistical Advisor to the government acted as the *de facto* member of the commission for several years. The deputy chairman of the commission has from the very beginning provided the main working link between the cabinet, the chief ministers and the commission. This link has been particularly effective when he was a cabinet minister also. Today he is a permanent invitee to the meetings of the cabinet and its committees.

Criticism

The functioning and the role of the Planning Commission has been a subject of debates and severe criticism. The ARC moved the ball and found it overstretching its limits and abusing the chairmanship of the Prime Minister. It erodes the responsibility and goes against the spirit of the Constitution. It even dilutes the responsibility of ministers and as a staff organisation it is divorced from operational responsibilities. Flexibility in regard to organisational development has rendered the commission a victim of Parkinson's Law. The staffing strength of the Commission has bludgeoned to disproportionate limits and there is excessive centralisation of functions vis-à-vis central ministries and the state governments. In addition to causing delay, it undermines the policy making responsibility of the department of economic affairs in the ministry. Thus there is a measure of overlapping of functions and the commission has not been able to relate itself to the political and administrative institutions, particularly at the implementation levels.

The commission exercises great influence in determining the relationship between the Centre and the states, in the field of finance. "As the entire plan comes within the purview of the Planning Commission and as the assistance to be given by way of grants or loans is practically dependent on the recommendations of the Planning Commission, it is obvious that a body like the Finance Commission cannot operate in the same field. The main function of the Finance Commission now consists in determining the revenue gap of each state and providing for filling up the gap by a scheme of devolution of funds partly by a distribution of taxes and duties and partly by grants-in-aid."

The critics point out the following specific loopholes in the existing arrangement:

(1) The commission has, in some measure, earned the reputation of being a parallel or super cabinet; but in a parliamentary democracy no authority, advisory or expert, should be allowed to earn such a distinction;
(2) It is no longer a small body of expert advisers, but has degenerated into a department with bureaucratic crowd of promotion seekers;
(3) The overlapping responsibilities bring it into conflict with Finance Commission which is a constitutional body;
(4) The inter-relationship between planning and economic welfare has made the Planning Commission and agency of economic coordination, which is largely a function of the finance minister;
(5) The inclusion of the Prime Minister in the commission has downgraded the position of the Cabinet;
(6) It is a staff organisation that is divorced from operational responsibilities;
(7) It has not manifested the vigour of a truly brains-trust organisation;
(8) The commissions a victim of the Parkinson's Law; the number of persons working in the Planning Commission is more than two thousand;
(9) It has caused a subversion in the federal system by developing a Dole distribution system of grants;
(10) The implementation jurisdictions of Planning Commission violates the executive freedom of executive departments and autonomy of the state governments.

Planning with a Human Face

The policies of liberalisation and privatisation to which India shifted in the nineties created embarrassing situations before the Planning Commission. The public sector enterprises brought a bad name to planned development. The international organisations took over the monitoring of the national economy. P.V. Narsimha Rao invited foreign investments and disinvested started from the ailing units of public sector. The liberalisation of economy rendered the planning process dysfunctional even in the areas like health, education and communication. The lopsided development got a set back in the popular mandate of 2004. The new PM, Manmohan Singh promised development with a human face which ultimately means a new kind of planning by a new sort of Planning Commission. Montek Singh Ahluwalia takes over the Planning Commission and is entrusted with the responsibility of systemic change alongwith new priorities, programmes and strategies of planning. A holistic and integrative approach has to be adopted to preserve the core sector and boost development with improved efficiency and effectivity. The mixed economy will have to follow the path of complementing planning with the private sector.

The National Development Council and Planning Process in India

Notwithstanding the PM's chairmanship of the Planning Commission the federal nature of Indian polity demanded political supervision and overseeing of the planning process in the Commission. The Neogi Advisory Board appointed in 1946 before independence recommended that "a Planning advisory organisation may be constituted," which should include "Representatives of the Provinces, Princely states and other interests to coordinate developmental activities through planning." After the birth of the Planning Commission in 1950 when the draft outline of first

Five-Year Plan was being hammer out, the cabinet secretariat issued a resolution which stated that "In a country of the size of India where the states under the Constitution have full autonomy within their own sphere of duties, it is necessary to have a forum such as a National Development Council at which, from time to time, the Prime Minister of India and the chief ministers of the states can review the working of the plan and of its various aspects."

Consequently the National Development Council was set up by a proposal of the cabinet secretariat of the Government of India in August 1952. It was intended to be a coordinating mechanism and the object was to ensure 'uniformity of approach and unanimity in working', and to soften the rigidities which are incidental to the existence of autonomous states in a federation. The ARC examined the 15-year long working of NDC (1952 to 1967) and suggested concrete functions to determine its role as a planner for economic development of India. These specific functions are:

(1) Assessment of resources required for implementing the plan and to suggest ways and means for raising them.
(2) Review of the working of the plan from time to time and to recommend such measures as are necessary for achieving the aims and targets.
(3) Prescription of guidelines for the formulation of the national plan.
(4) Consideration of the national plan as formulated by the Planning Commission.
(5) Consideration of important questions of social and economic policy affecting development.

Broadly speaking, the purpose of NDC was to secure the active participation and cooperation of the people, improving the efficiency of the administrative services, ensuring the development of the less advanced regions and sections of the community and, build up resources for national development. It was envisaged that the NDC would advise and make recommendations to the Central and state governments. It has been functioning since its inception as a high power consultative body wherein the frame of the Five-Year Plans and the policies, that have to be adopted for tiding over the urgent problems of economy have been discussed and solutions arrived at. Thus, in addition to the plan, the council has concerned itself with problems like food, creation of the State Trading Corporation and land reforms. The council is to act as a kind of bridge between the Union government, the Planning Commission and the state governments. It helps in the coordination not only of policies and programmes but also other matters of national importance. It provides a useful forum for full and free exchange of views and served as an effective device for sharing of responsibility between states and the Union government.

The resolution which created the NDC says: "The council shall meet as often as may be necessary and in any case at least twice a year." Until the end of 1966, it had held twenty-five meetings, each meeting continuing for two days. The council makes its recommendations to both the Central and state governments. The secretary of the Planning Commission acts as the secretary to the council, and the Planning Commission furnishes administrative and other assistance for the work of the council. The agenda of a particular meeting consists of: (i) items suggested by the Planning Commission itself, (ii) items suggested by the central ministers and (iii) items suggested by the state governments. The secretary of the council prepares a memorandum on each item of the agenda which along with papers are circulated. The Prime Minister as chairman of the council addresses the opening meeting of the council.

Administrative Organisation

Ever since its inception (1952), the NDC was designed as an advisory-cum-deliberative body between the Central governments, state governments and members of the Planning Commission. The ARC looked into this composition and suggested reorganisation (1967) which was accepted by the government as under:

(1) The Prime Minister
(2) The Deputy Prime Minister, if any
(3) The Central Ministers of:
  (i) Finance
  (ii) Food and Agriculture
  (iii) Industrial Development and Company Affairs
  (iv) Commerce
  (v) Railways
  (vi) Transport and Shipping
  (vii) Education
  (viii) Labour, Employment and Rehabilitation
  (ix) Home Affairs
  (x) Irrigation and Power
(4) The Chief Ministers of all states
(5) The members of the Planning Commission.

Prime Minister continues to be the chairman of the NDC, while the secretary of the Planning Commission acts as its secretary. The council ordinarily meets twice a year and ordinarily passes no formal resolutions. The practice is to have a complete record of discussions and gather out general trends pinpointing particular conclusions. Decisions are usually unanimous but because of the capture of political power by different political parties in the states, the chief ministers have started demanding greater say and autonomy for the constituent units in our cooperative federalism.

The Committees

Presently, the council comprises of the Prime Minister, all the Union cabinet ministers, chief ministers of all states or their substitutes, representatives of the union territories and the members of the commission. There have been occasions when the Reserve Bank Governor and other experts have been invited to address the meetings. The large membership of the council reduced the utility of the council for discussion as a compact body and so a Standing Committee was established (1954) with only nine chief ministers and a few Union ministers as members. It often seeks the assistance of committees, of ad hoc nature, to which it entrusts the investigation of such problems. In 1955, it formed a Committee on Village and Small Scale Industries. A year later, another *Committee on Pan Projects* was set up with a view to achieving economies consistent with efficiency in the execution of the plan projects. The council has also constituted Committees on Price Control (1960), and on Savings (1961). The 43 meeting of the council (1992–93) constituted the following six committees of the council:

(1) Committee on Population
(2) Committee on Microlevel Planning

(3) Committee on Austerity
(4) Committee on Employment
(5) Committee on Literacy
(6) Committee on Medical Education

Needless to mention that all these areas are vital in national development and for union-state collaboration for better results. Population, education and employment have been topping the agenda for development. Health of the nation and gainful use of physical and human resource need microlevel planning at the level of the district and panchayats below. The membership of the committees comprised chief ministers of various states, union ministers and members of the Planning Commission. Each committee was presided over by a state CM, while a member of the Planning Commission has acted as its member-secretary or convenor. The reports of the committees have helped in the implementation of plans by the Centre and the states and, have offered meaningful inputs for the formulation, implementation and evaluation of schemes and programmes. These committees analyse details for role-effectiveness of the Council.

The Critical Comments

The working of NDC in Nehru and post-Nehru era has invited favourable, unsympathetic and critical reactions from scholars and practitioners of Indian politics and administration. The composition, chairmanship, and decisions and affectivity of committees have been subjects of debate and controversies. The collapse of the Congress ruled states and later the coalitional prime ministers and opposition chief ministers have totally revised the political scenario and the institutional roles of the commission and NDC are being adjusted to changing patterns of liberalised economy and regionalised federalism. The one party dominant era attracted favourable assessments from eminent persons some of whom evaluated NDC's role in the following words:

> The NDC was established as a supreme administrative and advisory body on planning. It lays down policy directives invariably approved by cabinet. Its standing committees have virtually relegated the Planning Commission to the Status of a Research Arm.
>
> —Michael Brecher in Pandit Nehru's Biography

> Among the advisory bodies to the Planning Commission is included the NDC. This is surely incorrect as is clear from its composition. The NDC is a body obviously superior to the Planning Commission. It is indeed to be a policy making body and its recommendations cannot but be regarded as policy decisions and not merely as advisory suggestions.
>
> —H.M. Patel

> The position of the NDC has come to approximate to that of a *Super Cabinet* of the entire Indian Federation, a cabinet, functioning for the Government of India as well as for the governments of all the states.
>
> —K. Santhanam

> The NDC acts arbitrarily in fields which belong to other bodies. The council is incompetent both by law and by the nature of its composition to take high level national decisions.
>
> —A.P. Jain

> The meetings of NDC are not held on a regular basis. The initiative for calling a meeting of the NDC lies with the Planning Commission of which PM is the Chairman. Members cannot compel the

Commission to call a meeting. The government only reports its decision and alternative policies are not presented.

—ARC

The NDC has not been able to act as an effective instrument for developing consensus and commitment to National Policies. Decisions concerning resource allocations between Centre and states have been dominated by the view point of the Centre.

—Sarkaria Commission

The approach to planning regarding the allocation of financial resources has been unilateral in its operation. There was need for greater share for the states in taxes and plan assistance ... and also for market loans and institutional finances.

—Jyoti Basu and CMs from 16 states (1977)

Overlapping of the Planning Commission, the NDC and the cabinet had distorted the constitutional position.

—Ashok Chanda

These sympathetic and not so very sympathetic assessments working of NDC give the impression that as Indian democracy enters into an era of regional federalism, the chief ministers are asserting for their share in the developmental cake. The Gadgil formula of Central assistance to states has been replaced by a new formula in 1990 which proves that the so-called super cabinet does not owe any collective responsibility to prime minister's leadership. The Prime Minister vs. Chief Ministers has already introduced discordant notes and the working of NDC stands torn between centralism and consensus. The uniformity and commonality of planning has to be reconciled with state diversity and regional divergence. The NDC has failed to grow as a forum for informal consultations. The vigorous dissent articulated by Joyti Basu (1977) was a revolt and unless the Union government makes special efforts to come out with an agreed agenda and alternate policies, the cooperation from states may get inhibited. Similarly, the dependence of the NDC on the initiatives of Planning Commission demoralises the chief ministers who feel deprived of the privilege of evaluating the implementation of Five-Year Plans on a continuing basis. The NDC, though works through committee but it has no infrastructure to examine the performance of the planning process on a continuous and periodical bases. The council does not take follow-up action and even as a forum for consultations it operates in a partisan frame which hampers the cooperative spirit of federal collaboration. In other words the NDC of Nehru era needs a transformation in the era of coalitional politics for faster regional development.

Suggestion for a NEDC

The Sarkaria Commission was so much dissatisfied with NDC's performance that it recommended "A new nomenclature viz., National Economic and Development Council (NEDC) to become more effective as a supreme institution for Centre-state planning relations." Invoking Article 263 of the Constitution, the Justice has suggested the creation of a Standing Committee of the NEDC consisting of:

(a) Prime Minister
(b) Finance Minister
(c) Deputy Chairman, Planning Commission
(d) Governor of the Reserve Bank of India
(e) And six chief ministers, one from each zone selected by rotation and consensus.

This revised composition is suggested to restructure NDC to become a more powerful and broad-based constitutional authority. Such a body can evolve a national agenda for holistic growth with emphasis on economic development of the nation. The association of chief ministers will be selective but from all the zones and the Governor of Reserve Bank will be available for expert advise. The current conflicts will get minimised and the domination of Planning Commission members or Union ministers will reasonably cut to size. The constitutional status will add prestige and the extraconstitutional status of the Planning Commission will also get streamlined.

The present criticism that the NDC too is unwieldy in size and is not in continuous session. The Planning Commission provides it secretarial assistance and can over shadow its decisions. All this can be mitigated if the Sarkaria proposal for the NEDC is accepted with reasonable modifications.

Special Bodies

In addition to the NDC, there are several special bodies which assist the Planning Commission to enrich its contents in policy planning. Some of these special bodies are:

(1) PEO – Program Evaluation Organisation
(2) COPP – Committee on Plan Projects
(3) ACIPP – Advisory Committee on Irrigation and Power Projects
(4) CCPC – Coordination Committee for Public Corporation
(5) RPC – Research Programme Committee

The PEO was set up in 1952 to make a systematic and recurring evaluation of the results of community development programmes. It was to point out effective extension methods in the field. The broad purpose was to anticipate the obstacles that were going to emerge in future. The Programme Evaluation Organisation has since its inception functioned as an independent unit but within the framework and general guidance of the Planning Commission. It is, thus, part of the latter but functions as an independent unit. It is headed by a 'Chief,' who is assisted by joint directors, deputy directors, assistant directors and other subordinate staff. The joint directors are specialists in statistics, sociology, agricultural economics and institutional economics. It has its network of organisations in the field and maintains seven regional evaluation offices at Kolkata, Mumbai, Madras, Hyderabad, Lucknow, Jaipur and Chandigarh. A regional evaluation office is headed by a deputy director and has under it a number of project evaluation offices.

The PEO performs a general appraisal of the programmes of the commission and conducts field surveys to assess the impact of programmes on economic and social conditions. The NDC constituted COPP (1956) to explore the possibility of achieving economy in the projects. The committee was expected:

(1) to secure the implementation of suggestions made in reports submitted to the committee on plan projects and to make the results of studies available;
(2) to organise investigation, including inspections in the fields of important projects through specially selected teams;
(3) to promote the development of suitable machinery for continuous efficiency audit in individual projects and in agencies responsible for their execution;
(4) to initiate studies with the object of evolving suitable forms of organisation, methods, standards and techniques for achieving economy and ensuring efficient execution of projects;

(5) to undertake other tasks which the council may propose for the promotion of economy and efficiency in the execution of Five-Year plans.

The COPP consisted of the home minister as its chairman and the ministers for planning and finance and the deputy chairman of Planning Commission as its members. Besides, two chief ministers of states for each category of projects are the nominees of the prime minister attached to the committee. The committee has divided the projects under heads like irrigation and power, public works and buildings, agriculture and communications, industrial enterprises and social services. For each set of projects, the committee works through groups of ministers. Reports of investigation teams are discussed with the chief ministers of states concerned and matters of policy concerning investigation of the projects are considered in meetings of the Standing Committee of the NDC. For instance, the B.R. Mehta team recommended a three-tier organisation of Panchayati Raj in the district and the era of democratic decentralisation could be ushered in.

Advisory Committee on Irrigation and Power Projects (ACIPP)

The Advisory Committee on Irrigation and Power Projects is chaired by the state minister for planning and one member each is taken in this committee from the ministries of finance, irrigation and power and the Central Commission of Power and Board of Irrigation. The main function of the committee is to scrutinise the schemes prepared by the Central or state governments regarding power and irrigation. It examines whether its estimates are complete and technically accurate. Besides, it also verifies whether benefits expected and financial forecasts made are based on hard or not.

Coordination Committee for Public Cooperation (CCPS)

The Coordination Committee for Public Cooperation (1952) was set up with a view to secure maximum cooperation of the people for achieving the targets of Five-Year plans. It gives suggestions to Planning Commission for this purpose and has senior members and strives to maximise popular cooperation in the plan process.

Research Programmes Committee (RPC)

The Research Programmes Committee is a special organisation of the commission which consists of the deputy chairman of the Planning Commission and eminent social scientists. It invites research projects from interested research workers, gives necessary technical guidance and provides with financial assistance.

Additionally, the Planning Commission is also assisted by a number of advisory and associated bodies such as Advisory Committee on Irrigation; Flood Control and Power Projects; Coordination Committee for Public Cooperation; National Advisory Committee on Public Cooperation; Capital Goods Committee; Foreign Agreements Committee, etc. The Reserve Bank of India and the Central Statistical Organisation are also closely associated with the work of Planning Commission. The system of appointing working groups is important in the planning procedure. Several working groups have been set up on resources, agriculture, steel, industrial machinery, community development, fuel, fertilisers, general education, etc. The Commission has developed the practice of consulting representatives of organisations in the private sector such as Federation of Indian Chambers of Commerce and Industry, the Associated Chambers of Commerce of India and All India Manufactures Organisation. Attempts are made to secure the cooperation of the private sector enterprises also in the formulation of the plan.

The Plan Process

The planning process being decentralised and participatory follows three distinct stages, viz., (1) formulation, (2) implementation and (3) evaluation of the plan.

The first stage: The commission prepares a rough draft of schemes and projects in consultation with the union ministries and state governments in the background of the perspective plan. This determines priority; take stock of the available resources; and distribute them among different agencies on a approximate basis. These estimates and projections are then placed before the NDC and the schemes are modified in the light of discussions. They are then sent to the union ministries and state governments in the form of preliminary instructions.

The second stage: Each union ministry and state government prepares its own plans. Detailed instructions are sent from the commission and the state governments to districts to prepare local and village plans within the general framework. For this, the commission consults representatives of different groups in the Parliament and at the end of these exercises, the draft plan is published and thrown open for discussion. The universities, the press, political parties, industry and trade organisations and individuals comment on the draft.

The last stage: At this stage, a prolonged and detailed discussion between the commission and the representatives of state governments and the Central government takes place and some tentative agreements are placed before the cabinet and after its approval sent to the NDC. The plan is then presented to the Parliament and after its approval it is published. The approach paper, the draft plan and the final plan are well-written documents.

The commission is an advisory body and has no executive functions. The task of implementation belongs to union ministries and state governments. Much of the criticism against planning falls in this field and the effective implementation has been the weakest link in the process. Apathy of the people, character of officials, insufficient and ineffective supervision in adequate communication, and lack of criterion of evaluation are responsible for the bottlenecks. Efforts have been made to introduce democratic decentralisation, popular participation and evaluation of work by the commission which makes appraisal through monthly reports, quarterly reviews and the annual progress reports through the advisors and committee on plan projects. There are no attached or subordinate offices under the commission. The Programme Evaluation Organisation, functions only as an independent unit of the Commission. The total investment in the First Five-Year Plan (1951–52) was of the order of only 2000 crores. It have been doubling ever since and today the total investment envisaged stands at the mind-boggling figure. Very many eminent economists, social scientists and administrators have indicted the commission for uneven growth concentration of wealth in few hands and creation of black money in the economy. In many areas of infrastructure even China is ahead of us. A whole new sector of parallel economy has come into existence, in which the affluent sections escape the tax net. Even liberalisation and privatisation policies have not yet made a dent to defreeze the economic stagnation prevailing for decades. The planning process had its ups and downs. Under Nehru it was followed with enthusiasm but Indira Gandhi confronted the phenomenon of Annual Plans. Rajiv Gandhi, had to take resort to large-scale borrowings from foreign and indigenous sources. Chandra Shekhar's government had to pawn the country's gold reserves to get a paltry loan of Rs 400 crores. Rao and his Finance Minister had no alternative except to embark upon a new LPG policy arising out of economic compulsions dictated by the creditors, especially the World Bank and the International Monetary Fund. This shift in policy is a revolutionary roll back leading to the demolition of various forms of controls which makes the economy free and competitive. It has proved somewhat effective and selectively successful. The need for continuous planning and the market mechanism has to coexist and need to be dovetailed. Planning with a human face is necessary to take care of the poor and the downtrodden. The socialistic planning has adversely affected financial discipline and regionalism seems antithetical to planning. India has to be both federal and democratic and the alternative is, to adopt a loose model of planning for democratic development. The process of industrialisation has built an infrastructure for a competitive economy in the country. The long-term growth rate has been satisfactory. The level of capital formation in the economy has risen high. The technology of production in agricultural and industry has improved substantially and the country has developed a strong and diversified technological base. The development in the agricultural and industrial sectors has stimulated a matching expansion and modernisation of the banking, insurance, ports and shipping and commerce sectors. Self-reliance in plans has implied a reduction on the dependence of foreign aid, diversification of domestic production and a consequential reduction on imports of critical commodities. The objective of social justice has been achieved through the twin programmes of improving the living standards of the poorest groups and in reducing the inequalities in asset distribution. Success has been achieved in the field of public investment in irrigation, power, transport, etc., and in basic industries and to some extent in the extension and diversification of educational and health services. India has built large multi-purpose dams, steel plants, and petrochemical refineries, fertiliser complexes, copper and other mineral-based industries, heavy engineering, heavy electrical and cyber net organisation.

India has the third largest pool of highly trained manpower – scientists, technologists and managers. But notwithstanding all this India's economy lacks the capacity to save enough, to meet its growing energy needs and to provide work for all, to meet repayment obligations abroad, and to maintain a high level of investment in development. Currently in India, it is the implementation of plans of development, particularly in the modern business sector, that is continuously creating, positions described as monopolistic. The failure has been the failure to maintain stability and the unchecked increase in prices and population. Planning has not been able to reduce, further accentuation of, inequalities of income and wealth. New regional disparities in economic conditions have emerged and massive poverty, disease, malnutrition, illiteracy and misery continue to persist.

"The outcome of all the Five-Year Plans has been the emergence of two Indias' – one characterised by high-tech and sophisticated industries, advanced in the field of nuclear energy, deployment of satellites in geo-stationary orbit, prosperity and five-star culture and the other as rural traditional India, seeped in poverty, unemployment, hunger, disease and illiteracy. This economic dualism in the country has become more acute and we have urban India with all amenities and rural India with not even safe drinking water."

The Future

India possesses resources of unusual richness. It is visible on all sides – in the endowments of nature, in economic and technological capacities, in potentials for growth, in the quality and wealth of manpower, in the institutions for research and training, in the available pool of talent and experience. Presently, these resources and energies are being somewhat frittered away by lop sided development and a failure to build up a shared national effort. To maintain stability and not to allow inequality to increase through development plans; it should progressively be possible to increase the welfare and egalitarian aspects. The corrective approach will be to equip planning with a viable, integrated set of regulatory and control policy instruments which should include an integrated price policy, an income policy and policies to shifting emphasis, in agriculture to area planning and in industry, to employment and disposal.

The growth models reflecting the experiences of developed world have influenced most of the Indian planners. The inherent characteristics of the Indian economy have been ignored. It has no option but to forge the heavy industry and opt for the Extended Wage Goods Strategy of Development as propounded by economists like Professor C.N. Vakil and P.R. Brahmanand. The Extended Wage Goods Strategy of Development has been evolved to suit the specific economic requirements of large, over-populated and poverty-stricken countries like India. This strategy of development was put forth as an alternative to the Mahalanobis Model of 'heavy industry first'. There can be no satisfactory solution to India's economic problem of growth with welfare and social justice, The vision of Mahatma Gandhi and the humaneness of Jawaharlal Nehru have to be maintained in perspective.

The year 1990 announced the end of a closed economy which is bound to have its repercussions on planning process in India. The new rightism borders on social Darwinism, but the practice of decentralised democratic policy will have to correct its aberrations. "Economic growth with Justice and Development with Human Face" are the new slogans which put planning in the heart of development. The upper affluent class in India has welcomed this first phase of liberalisation and globalisation as an end of centralised, all comprehensive and book based planning. The boom in production and rise in GDP and GNP are regarded as indices of development, but a large number of people below poverty live and still more, deprived of basic facilities of health and education demand social services from the government to have their share in the national sake. From the Soviet Model of Centrist Planned Development to Gandhian Model of Sarvodaya Planning, there is a long road which India will have to traverse to push its teeming millions into a sprawling middle class. This will lead to a quest of Alternative Models of Planning as per needs of the coming decades. In other words, India cannot dispense with its planning apparatus which is more than essential for the establishment of a welfare polity in the country. But then the Nehruvian Planning will not be needed in a vibrant Indian economy, inextricably linked up with globalised versions of liberalism called Manmohanomics. The Planning Commission of India and the National Development Council will have to reformulate their planning strategies and plan priorities afresh perhaps after every national election in the context of the international scenario obtained in coming decades. Regulatory and Indicative Planning will be the basic functions of the Planning Commission and an effective political supervision by the NDC should add meaningful democratic contents to further plan outlays and plan programmes so that open competitiveness may be combined with specific objectives of social justice in a democratic polity.

7

Administration in States: Issues and Perspectives

Unlike the US Constitution, the Indian Constitution is one document which contains the framework of Union and state governments and their relationships during peace and emergencies. Apparently it is a borrowing from the Government of India Act 1935 in which a federal form of government was envisaged for the central government of the Governor General and provincial governments of the Governors along with princes or rulers of native states. While the Constituent Assembly was engaged in hammering out the republican Constitution, the partition was announced and the native rulers were given the options to join India or Pakistan or stay independent. Sardar V.B. Patel, the first Home Minister of free India launched a policy of integration of states in the Indian Union and the Constituent Assembly had to classify states into A, B, C and D categories. The A states were former British Indian provinces under the Governors, while the B states were carved out from the princely map of native India under Rajpramukhs. The C states were small territories or former chief commissioner's provinces, some of which still continue as union territories. A special status was accorded to Andaman and Nicobar Islands as D class state. Thus, when the republican Constitution was adopted on 26th January 1950, India had 9 part A states, 9 part B states, 10 part C states and one part D state. These 29 states were quite uneven in area, population, resources and levels of development. The Freedom Movement arrested the fissiparous tendencies of disintegration, although their manifestation were quite visible in the Nehru Report of 1928 and the Simon Report of 1930. The Congress party stood for reorganisation of states on linguistic basis and the demand was so vehement that a linguistic provinces commission under the chairmanship of S.K. Dar was announced in the Constituent Assembly itself in June 1948. The Dar Commission warned against linguistic chauvinism but the Congress party appointed the JVP (Jawahar, Vallabh Bhai and Pattabhi) Committee to review the Dar report. Andhra Pradesh for Telugu-speaking people was the major demand and the Government of India had to yield to appoint a Justice Fazali Ali State Reorganisation Commission on 29th December, 1953 with H.N. Kunjru and K.M. Panikkar as its members. It was a landmark decision and its report opened a pandora's box. On the basis of revised reports of SRC, a bill was introduced in the Parliament in November 1956 and 14 states and 6 union territories were carved out by redrawing the map of India. Since then, this linguistic map of India have been freely changed in response to political needs, cultural pressures and economic viability of the units. In the year 2005, there were 28 states and 7 union territories in the Indian Union and each constituent state has its own separate government without sovereignty but as mere creatures of the Constitution.

The state governments and his administrations are by and large patterned on the structure and working of Union government in their spheres demarcated by the 7th Schedule and other provisions of the Constitution. For instance states and union territories have different systems of government. Then, Article 370 gives a special status to Jammu & Kashmir with a privilege to have its own state Constitution. Another Article 371 makes special provisions for Andhra Pradesh, Gujarat and Maharashtra, Nagaland and Assam which have special situations under Article 371-A and B respectively. A similar provision exists for Sikkim under Article 371-F.

The working of the Indian Constitution has witnessed a paradoxical situation that when states are weak their role in development has increased by leaps and bounds. On the one hand, the Union government wants to use them as agencies for the execution of plan programmes, on the other hand the Constitutional Amendments 73rd and 74th enjoin upon the states to transfer a part of their functions to local bodies. Thus, law and order and security which is the basic function of any state is with the state administration. The welfare and development administrations are their additional responsibility which they share with the Union government above and local government and people below. Moreover, these state functions become complex when the Union government assigns them additional responsibilities like conduct of elections, census operations, VIP security and special development of hill areas and tribal pockets.

Under the Constitution, the state governments enjoy a judicial status. The dual polity coexists within the framework of state. The political and administrative organisations of the states are somewhat similar to their counterparts, i.e., the Union government. Like President, council of ministers, Parliament and Supreme Court at the Centre, the states have Governor, council of ministers, legislature and a High Court. The state level commissions, President's rule, state secretariat, district administration, Panchayati Raj and local self-administration fall within the constitutional frame of the state administration.

Unlike USA, the states in India have a parliamentary form of government which presupposes a nominal head and a political executive responsible to the elected legislative assembly of the state. The High Courts are a part of single integrated judicial system created by the Constitution and are amenable to the jurisdiction of Supreme Court of India. The secretarial system and the merit-oriented civil services in the states work under a chief secretary, the counterpart of whom does not exist in the central secretariat. The all India services are state based and their junior positions are manned by state public service commission and recruited through their respective public service commissions. Unlike Centre, there are no Planning Commissions in the states but planning boards or planning departments are found in the state secretariats to negotiate about grants-in-aid from the Centre. The directorates function like attached offices in state administration and the field offices in the district and below are comparable with subordinate offices of the Union government. The panchayati and urban local tiers added by 73rd and 74th Amendments are in the process of adjustment with the district administrations and state governments all over the country. This sandwiched position of state administration puts some of its functionaries and organisations under unending controversies about their dual role and predominant loyalties. Some of the issues that often generate debates and confusions in state administration in India pertain to:

(1) The office of the Governor
(2) The role of chief minister
(3) The chief secretary, state services and state secretariat
(4) The directorates and technical services

(5) The coordination of vertical and horizontal planning
(6) The induction of Panchayati Raj in the district administration of states

As the state governments operate on a very wide spectrum of political maturity and economic dynamism their relationships vary with the Centre and also among themselves. The partisan character of the state governments has been catalysing some of these institutions and administrative arrangements. As compared to 1950, the situation has undergone a sea change and consensus has been emerging about these roles and relationships at every level. Yet the novelty of the Indian experiment has no parallel with federal experiences of other countries of the world.

The Governor

The criticality and the dilemma of Governor's position in state government can be summed up in the irreconcilability of parliamentary role of the nominal head with the active role of a federal agent of the Union government. The constitution leaves it open and the UK and USA examples do not lead us anywhere near reconciliation. The judicial and political decisions have complicated the conflicts and as democracy takes roots and federalism shapes cooperative regionalism into coalitions, the Governors find themselves into awkward and even in humiliating position of getting transferred and dismissed by the Union governments. Conversely, the governments of opposition parties in the states find them persona non grata and the chief ministers have been struggling to make them dysfunctional. The conventions do not help and even the court verdicts do not restore the dignity of a gubernatorial office. The Constitution outlines the position, powers, functions, roles and relations of the Governor in more than 20 Articles from 153 to 233 but the actual position invariably depends upon the political configurations obtained in a state or in the country at a particular given point of time. The usual lists of legislative executive, financial and judicial powers are there, but are these powers discretionary or to be exercised in individual judgement is essentially a matter of shifting interpretations. It becomes all the more controversial when Article 356 is invoked and Governors are accused of sabotaging state democracy for partisan ends. Several commissions have delved deep about Governor's eligibility methods of appointment and removal and even his code of conduct but the partisan nature and behaviour of the incumbents persist with the result that partisan and personal equations determine his role rather than the functions enumerated in the Constitution.

The constitutional functions and powers can be summed up as under:

Executive Realm

All executive actions of the government of a state are formally taken in the name of Governor. He can make rules specifying the manner in which the orders and other instruments made executed in his name shall be authenticated. These rules help in convenient transaction of the business of a state government and the allocation among the ministers of the said business. The chief minister and other ministers are appointed by him and they hold office during his pleasant. The Constitution prescribes that a tribal welfare minister in the states of Bihar, Madhya Pradesh and Orissa will be appointed by him. The Advocate-General of the state holds office during the pleasure of the Governor. The state election commissioner, the chairman and members of the State Public Service Commission are appointed by him but can be removed only by the President of India. He can seek any information relating to the administration of the affairs of the state and propose for legislation to the chief minister. He can advise the chief minister to submit for the consideration of the council of ministers matter on which a decision has been taken by a minister. He enjoys a special privilege of recommending to the President the imposition of constitutional emergency in a state. During the period of President's rule in a state, the Governor enjoys extensive powers as an agent of the President.

Legislative Realm

A Governor is an integral part of the state legislature. In this capacity, he has the right of summoning or proroguing the state legislature and dissolving the state legislative assembly. He addresses the state legislature at the commencement of the first session after each general election and the first session of each year and can send messages to the house or houses of the state legislature. He appoints a member of the state's legislative assembly to preside over its proceedings when the offices of both the speaker and the deputy speaker fall vacant. One sixth of the members of the state legislative council are nominated by him from amongst the persons having special knowledge or practical experience in literature, science, art, cooperative movement and social service. He may nominates one member to the state legislative assembly from the Anglo-Indian community. The question of disqualification of members of the state legislature are decided by him in consultation with the Election Commission. He gives his assent to the bills or may withhold assent to a bill or return the bill (if it is not a money bill) for reconsideration of the state legislature. However, if the bill is passed again by the state legislature with or without amendments, a Governor has to give his assent. He can reserve for consideration of President any bill passed by the state legislature which endangers the position of the state High Court. He can also reserve the bill if it is *ultra vires* or opposed to the Directive Principles of State Policy or against the larger interest of the country. The Governor can promulgate ordinances when the state legislatures is not in session. These ordinances must be approved by the state legislature within six weeks of its reassembly. He can also withdraw an ordinance anytime. The reports of the State Finance Commission, the State Public Service Commission and the Comptroller and Auditor-General relating to the accounts of the state are laid before the state legislature on his behalf.

Financial Realm

He sees to it that the Annual Financial Statement (state budget) is laid on the floor of the state legislature. Money Bills can be introduced in the state legislature only with his prior recommendation. No demand for a grant can be made except on his recommendation. He can make advances out of the Contingency Fund of the state to meet any unforeseen expenditure. He also constitutes a Finance Commission after every five years to review the financial position of the panchayats and the municipalities in the state.

Judicial Realm

The Governor can grant pardons, reprieves, respites and remissions of punishment or suspend, remit and commute the sentence of any person of any offence against any law. The pardoning power of the Governor differs from that of the President because the President can pardon death sentence while the Governor cannot. Similarly the President can pardon sentences inflicted by court martial while the Governor cannot. He is consulted by the President while appointing the judges of the concerned High Court of state. He makes appointments, postings and promotions of the district judges in consultation with the High Court. He also appoints persons to judicial posts (other then district judges) and other senior officials in consultation with the state High Court and the State Public Service Commission. As a Chancellor of universities in the state he appoints the Vice-Chancellors also.

The Colonial Mould

Without foreseeing the deeper implications of parliamentary and federal roles of the Governor, the founding fathers of Indian Constitution inadvertently put the State Governor in the colonial mould of a Provincial Head. Following the 1935 pattern, they even envisaged 'discretionary' and 'individual judgement' powers without realising that he will be an Indian citizen, perhaps a political species belonging to a different genus. The 1935 distinction between discretion and individual judgement was that discretionary powers implied the freedom to consult the responsible chief minister or ministers in his discretion but individual judgement powers were those where consultation with CM was essential but to abide by the advise was a matter of individual judgement of the British Governor. Without formally classifying these powers, the Republican Constitution of India vests powers in the federal Governor of state to act in his discretion in the following matters:

(1) Appointing the chief minister when no party has a clear cut majority in the state legislature.
(2) Dissolution of the state legislative assembly if the council of ministers has lost its majority.
(3) Seeking information from the chief minister with regard to the administrative and legislative matters of the state.
(4) Dismissal of the council of ministers when it cannot prove the confidence of the state legislature assembly.
(5) Reservation of a bill for the consideration of the President.
(6) Determining the amount payable by the state of Assam to the autonomous Tribal District Commission as royalty accruing from licenses for mineral exploration.
(7) While exercising his functions as the administrator of an adjoining union territory (in case of additional charge).
(8) Recommendation for the imposition of the President's rule in the state.

These are quite sensitive and wide ranging areas of political discretion which encroach upon the domain of parliamentary responsibility of the cabinet and the chief minister. Even the very selection and dismissal of the chief minister leading to President rule in state cannot be accepted as a prerogative of a nominal head. There have been bitter political fights in this area. Then at the top of it, the Governor has certain special responsibilities to discharge according to the direction issued by the President. In this regard, The Governor, though has to consult the chief minister and the council of ministers but he can finally act in his individual judgement. They are:

(1) Maharashtra: Establishment of separate development boards for Vidarbha and Marathwada.
(2) Gujarat: Establishment of separate development boards for Saurashtra and Kutch.
(3) Nagaland: With respect to law and order in the state for so long as the internal disturbance Naga Hills Tuensang Area continues.
(4) Assam: With respect to the administration of tribal areas.
(5) Manipur: Regarding the administration of the hill areas in the state.
(6) Sikkim: For peace and for ensuring social and economic advancement of the different sectors of the population.
(7) Arunachal Pradesh: With respect to law and order in the state.

The discretionary powers of the Governor encompass all fields and his discretionary decisions cannot be questioned in any court of law. While discharging his special responsibilities as Presidents' emissary he need not even consult the chief minister or his cabinet. Appointment and dismissal of chief ministers or his council of ministers is a discretionary function. Similarly, summoning proroguing and dissolving the state assembly are vital decisions which he can take in his discretion. The powers to give assent to bills or return of bills to house or reservation of bills for reconsideration by the President have far-reaching consequences. His address may be prepared and approved by the cabinet but he has the freedom to edit and even skip lines which run against his political convictions.

The Article 356

Article 356 has been the real apple of discard. Under this provision, the President on receipt of a report from the Governor or otherwise, if he is satisfied that a situation has arisen in which the state government cannot be carried out in accordance with the provisions of the Constitution, he can declare a state of emergency. Such an emergency in states of India has occurred more than dozens of times. The factors which promoted the Governors to feel satisfied about this state were: breakdown of law and order machinery, political instability as a result of defections and paralysis of the parliamentary process. Maladministration, disintegrative movements causing disaffection and loss of public confidence may cause the breakdown. If a party refuses to form the government and prevents the installation of a coalition arrangement leading to political anarchy then the Article 356 may be invoked.

The Way Out

The Article 355 which makes the Union government responsible for peace tranquillity and good government in the country ipso facto implies that emergency under Article 356 can be imposed in the state without consulting the chief minister. It is a discretionary power and the report has to be debated and approved by the union cabinet and the Parliament for its imposition and extension. Once the proclamation is issued by the President, the Governor can assume to himself all or any of the functions of the government of the state other than the High Court and declare that the powers of the legislature of the state shall be exercisable by or under the authority of the Parliament. He can make provisions necessary or desirable for giving effect to the objects of the proclamation. The Bomai judgment of the Supreme Court circumscribes this discretion a little bit by streamlining it. Yet the satisfaction of the Governor is a discretionary pocket which no law can define and still less delimit. In fact the controversy about Governor's position and role hinges around three counts:

(1) The qualifications, eligibility and credentials of the incumbents for this gubernatorial post.
(2) How should they be chosen and by whom to be worthy of this high office?
(3) How should they function under a system of checks and balance so that the office may not be abused for partisan ends.

All the reports and suggestions use the ethical term 'should' which does not ethicise the behaviour of these incumbents. There is a demand in some quarters now that this office of the Governor should be abolished and the Chief Justice of the state High Court may be asked to perform the formal and routine functions, assigned to this office. The office needs several structural changes for which a constitutional amendment will be necessary to save the high office from wanton political attacks and a systematic abuse by the Union government for political ends. Three suggestions in this regard warrant a public debate and national consensus:

(1) The Governor of the state should be an eminent outsider from the other state known for his distinguished service to the nation in some public field of consequence.
(2) He or she should be chosen from a national panel to be prepared by the cabinet secretariat and whetted and updated by the Rajya Sabha after a thorough screening through a parliamentary committee. The cabinet committee may shortlist the names from whom the President may appoint the Governor in consultation with the Prime Minister and the leaders of the opposition. If NDC can be constitutionalised the original panel may also be approved by this federal body also.
(3) The Governor and chief minister should work together but in applying Article 356, the report of the Governor should be discussed with the Chief Justice of the state and a joint report alone should be sent to the Union government for Presidential rule in the state.

These nebulous suggestions need further crystallisation. The purpose is to depoliticise the office and making it acceptable to the state government even when he recommends its dissolution. It is a unique situation and the Congress and BJP both have been guilty of abusing this office and even transferring and dismissing Governors like petty governmental official. The arguments are there on either side but the dignity of the office can be preserved only when eminent and nationally respected people are empanelled through parliamentary weeding out and they exercise their sensitive political powers especially that of suspending the democratic process in the state in consultation with the judiciary and as per norms of rule of law. The gubernational office should either be abolished or held in high esteem by the state government and the people. It is undignified to ask the Governor's resignations on every change in national government at Delhi. The conventions could not evolve because Governors have been active politicians and they have been intervening as agents of Central government. With varied party governments and coalitions the Indian Policy can not afford Nehruvian Governors even in the name of National Unity. The workable alternative is that (a) a panel of names may be suggested by the chief ministers every year. (b) The panel should be whetted by the Rajya Sabha. (c) The Cabinet and PM may suggest those names from which the President should select incumbent as per need of the state.

The Constitution envisages a parliamentary form of government at state level with Governor as the nominal head and chief minister as a real political executive. The former heads the state while the latter is the head of the state government. The positions of the Governor and the chief minister are somewhat analogues to that of the positions of President and Prime Minister in the Union government but there is a marked difference when it comes to relationship between the CM and the PM and the Governor and the President. Political working apart even the Constitution does not envisage President's rule and National Cabinet of the President during normalcy. The Governor and chief minister have no say in the functioning of the Union government but the vice versa is not true when it comes to union-state relations. Article 163 of the Indian Constitution maintains that every state shall have a council of ministers headed by the chief minister to aid and advise the Governor in the exercise of his powers and functions, except the discretionary ones. The chief minister and other ministers are appointed by the Governor on the advise of the chief minister. However, a tribal welfare minister should be appointed in the states of Bihar, Madhya Pradesh and Orissa. The ministers hold office during the pleasure of the Governor and the council of ministers is collectively responsible to the state legislative assembly. A minister who is not a member of the state legislature for a period of six consecutive months shall cease to be a minister.

The Office of Chief Minister

At the state level, the chief minister though selected as leader of the majority party in the state legislature works with his team of ministers under the formal frame of 'Governor's government'. The chief minister and his council of ministers should enjoy the confidence of the state legislature which implies several kinds of relationships of the chief minister with the Governor, the council of ministers and the state legislative assembly.

Constitutionally speaking, the chief minister is the principal channel of communication between the Governor and the council of ministers (Article 167). He makes it imperative for the chief minister to communicate to the Governor all decisions of the council of ministers relating to administration of the affairs of the state and proposals for legislation. He must furnish such information relating to state administration and proposals for legislation as the Governor may call for. If the Governor so requires the chief minister must submit for the consideration of the council of ministers any matter on which a decision has been taken by a minister but which has not been considered by the council as a whole. The chief minister should advise the Governor with regard to the appointment of important officials like Advocate-General, chairman, and members of the State Public Service Commission, State Election Commissioner, etc.

The chief minister enjoys a wide range of powers as head of the council of ministers in the state. The Governor appoints only those persons as ministers who are recommended by the chief minister. He allocates and reshuffles the portfolios among ministers and can ask a minister to resign or advise the Governor to dismiss him in case of serious differences of opinion. The chief minister presides over the meetings of the council of ministers and influences its decisions. He guides, directs, controls and coordinates the activities of his cabinet and can bring about the collapse of the council of ministers by himself resigning from the office. The chief minister is the leader of the legislature. He can recommend the dissolution of the legislative assembly to the Governor anytime and announce the government policies on the floor of the house.

Additionally, the chief minister is the leader of the party in power, leader of the state and the political head of the services. He plays a very crucial role in state administration. However, the discretionary powers of the Governor can reduce to some extent the power, authority, influence, prestige and role of the chief minister in the state administration. During last 50 years of working of state administrations in India, there have been numerous kinds of chief ministers and Governors in Indian states. Their appointments and removals or dismissals have been subjects of bitter controversies during Nehru, Indira and post-Indira periods. The strong and weak CMs apart, the relations of CMs with President, Vice-President and Prime Minister have varied as per exigencies of party situations and perceptions of the Governor. The PMs have been making and unmaking chief ministers and the informal interactions in party forums have determined the actual roles. Confidential correspondence between PM and CM has its own part to play. In addition, the CM has to interact with several central ministers, particularly union ministers of home, finance, education, agriculture, industries and rural development. The quantum of central support which a state gets in the form of financial grants, centrally sponsored schemes and assistance depends on the CM's influence and rapport with the union ministers. The state's representation in the Union cabinet also influences the quantum and quality of support to the state. This relationship of CM with PM and his Union government has extraconstitutional linkages through National Development Council and Planning Commission. The CMs being members of the NDC, are active partners in the determination of planning objectives for development in general and of their states in particular. The NDC meetings provide a CM with a forum to plead the state's case for more grants and increased Central assistance. Similarly, the role of the CM of a state vis-à-vis the Planning Commission determines the size and contents of the state five-year and annual plans which are approved by the Planning Commission. The commission lays down the priorities and state plans have to be adjusted within the national framework. The state plans are discussed in details and the CM justifies the state demands for various schemes or sectors. Thus, he brings funds for the state's socio-economic development from the Union government. He also maintains a close and continuous liaison with the Planning Commission in matters of implementation of the development programmes.

The Cabinet

The chief minister has a council of ministers which might have three kinds of ministers in the state government:

(1) Cabinet ministers with portfolios.
(2) Ministers of state, and
(3) Deputy ministers

The team works according to the principle of collective responsibility and the CM act as a primus inter pares. The council takes policy decisions concerning the government of the state. It also oversees the implementation of these decisions. Each cabinet minister is the head of one or more departments. The ministers are not only the political heads but, being responsible for all actions of the department, assume the overall administrative leadership also. Broadly speaking the cabinet like any of its other counterparts deals with the following matters:

(1) Matters concerning state policy in areas of revenue, expenditure, investment and audit of accounts and proposals for budget and advances from the Contingency Fund.
(2) Matters referred to it under Clause (i) of Article 167 including Governor's address to Vidhan Sabha.
(3) Structural changes in the state administrative system and appointment of chairman and members of Public Service Commission, Board of Revenue, district and session judges, etc.
(4) Matter referred to it by the chief minister including proposals for legislation.
(5) Proposals to refer any matter to the zonal council, pertaining to union-state relations and inter-state relations.
(6) Proposals regarding grant of land for public institutions.
(7) Appeals made by government servants to the Governor against the orders issued by the state government on disciplinary matters.

The council of ministers is also responsible for rendering advice to the Governor on all important administrative matters of the state. The Rules of Business prescribe the cases which have to be placed before the council of ministers and the procedure to be followed in this respect. The office of the CM is headed by a secretary who provides administrative assistance to the CM and maintains confidential documents and other correspondence. He takes follow-up measures on cabinet decisions and apprises the CM about developments in the conduct of assembly business. The staff of the secretariat process files which go to the chief minister. The cabinet also plays a legislative role and all money bills are prepared by the cabinet. All money bills need Governor's prior consent. The increase in delegated legislation has enhanced its powers. The Governor is within his right to withhold assent to drafts of ordinances. Although his inaugural and budget addresses are approved by the council of ministers, the council advises the Governor to summon, prorogue or dissolve the legislative assembly. In doing so he may not accept the Cabinet advice, which is not binding. The ministers answer questions, call attention motions and adjournment motions regarding the functioning of their departments. The parliamentary and federal roles of the Governor will always push him into controversy of the multiparty system obtained in India. When CM and his ministers are political activist the Governor can be a balance wheel and a respectable elder only if he is acceptable to the state government because of his neutrality, anonymity and previous record of public service. Britain does not have Governors and the U.S. Governor is an elected political leader without any federal role. Our Rajya Sabha should be given some special functions to restrain Governors and select them on a much wider criteria than the choice of the PM.

The Multiparty System and Alliance Politics

Thus the CM and his cabinet work in a parliamentary framework on which the federal pattern of Union government stands superimposed. There was a time when Indian polity has one party dominance and the state CMs were running their respective states as per dictates of the PM during Nehru era. But even in that era there were stalwarts like B.C. Roy, Nambudripad, Rajaji and Morarji Bhai who as CMs could never be considered as puppets of the PM. After the rise of non-Congressism in states, CMs like Jyoti Basu, M.G. Ramchandrana, Karunanidhi, Rama Rao and several others were too strong to fall in line to the dictates of the PMs. The situation has radically altered during BJP regime and later coalition era, when CMs started lobbying for the office of the PM. The hung parliaments and legislative assemblies have contributed to the strength as well as to the weakness of the offices of PM and CM. Individual illustrations apart, it is difficult to surmise whether multiparty system or the alliance politics which dominates multi-regional party system will make the PM or CM handmaid of each other. The Constitution does envisage a federal structure and the state CM in future will be dependent on the political winds of Panchayati Raj. Similarly in a huge country of India's size and diversities, the PM may have to draw his sustenance from regional political parties and their leaders who will be chief ministers. Hence, the CM will remain sandwiched between local panchayati democracy and centralised federalism of Union government. The intricate balance will be critical and the opposition politics of India at Union and state levels will be uncomparable with British and American systems for a long time to come. A strong CM can be a prop to democracy and federalism by balancing the powers and position of the PM. Conversely a strong PM may accelerate the pace of development but his weakness will foster cooperative federalism through mutual collaboration. The panchayati politics adds a new dimension to India's democracy and development. The office of the CM must strengthen the office of the PM to reinforce both at all the levels of polity.

The Chief Secretary and State Secretariat

While the Governor and the chief minister enjoy a constitutional status under the Constitution of India, the chief secretary, his secretariat and state services have been created to make the state government function on the pattern of secretariat of the Central government. The state secretarial consists of departments of state government which are headed politically by the ministers and administratively by the secretaries. The chief secretary is the head of the entire state secretariat while a secretary is a head of one or two departments. The secretary is a senior administration officer of generalist variety. The secretary is the secretary to the state government as a whole and not to the individual minister concerned. The number of secretariat departments vary from state to state and may ranges from 15 to 40 departments. The departments which are common to most of the states are:

General Administration	Irrigation and Power	Agriculture	Local Government
Home	Law	Labour and Employment	Excise and Taxation
Finance	Social Welfare	Panchayati Raj	Industries
Jail	Housing	Public Works	Publicity and Information
Revenue	Civil Supplies	Education	Cooperation
Forest	Transport	Planning	Health

The executive department has a top functionary called as head of the department. The health department in the secretariat for instance, is headed by the medical secretary, but the director of health is the head of the department. The latter is subordinate to the former. All secretariat departments do not have 'executive departments'. Some of them like departments of finance, personnel, planning, administrative reforms, law, etc., offer advise. The head of the department may be a specialist and the secretary a generalist but no hard and fast rules exist in this regard. The merger and bifurcation of departments is a prerogative of the cabinet and it is a continuous process as per policy requirements of the government. Public corporations may be attached to the departments and similarly state secretariat may also have a regular department of public enterprises. In addition to the functional departments the state secretariats have staff organisations like CM's secretariat, cabinet secretariat and CS office which act as policy making centres with powers of coordination and control. Right from the British times there exists a uniformity in the organisation and personnel system of the state departments. Usually, a secretary of the department is assisted by a hierarchical team of several junior officials called as: special secretary/additional secretary, joint secretary, deputy secretary, under secretary, and assistant secretary. The office component of the secretariat consists of assistants and clerks called as: superintendent (or Section Officer), assistant superintendents, upper division clerks, lower division clerks, steno-typists and typists, and manual workers.

The secretary heads the department and acts as a principal adviser of the minister on administrative and policy matters. He is personally responsible for the observance of Rules of Business and other activities of his department. He represents his department and can be called a link with other departments of the government. He issues instructions and orders distribution of work among the staff and is responsible for the organisation and efficiency of the department. The additional secretary may function as secretary in relation to subjects allotted to his charge. He is the de facto head and deals directly with the minister. The deputy secretary acts on behalf of the secretary. The under secretary has the responsibility of submitting all relevant materials to his seniors. The deputy secretary functions as one more level of scrutiny. The under secretary initiates actions on all communications and examines the papers under disposal and submits the case to the deputy secretary.

The secretarial officials are subject to tenure system and are appointed for a fixed term. They are drawn from the field and revert to the field after secretariat tenure and most of them belong to generalist services. The state secretariat like any other secretariat is a repository of authority of state government. It serves as a think tank and a coordinating nodal agency. It is essentially a policy processing agency but it does offer advise, directions, guidance to field staff and prescribes procedures of work for the executive units in districts and below. The ARC found that the secretariats are doing non-secretarial functions. The Shiv Charan Mathur Commission tried to identify these specific functions of the state secretariat in Rajasthan. Some of the following categories of functions are usually found in most of the state secretariats:

General Functions

(1) Correspondence with the Government of India and other governments;
(2) Matters involving the framing of new legal enactments or rules or amendments in the existing ones, involving interpretation or relaxation of existing rules of government orders;
(3) Interdepartmental coordination;
(4) All matters of general policy;
(5) Inspection, reports and tour notes, recorded by the heads of departments;
(6) All matters relating to the preparation or adoption of new plan schemes and important modification in the existing schemes;
(7) Review of the progress of plan schemes, both physical and financial;
(8) All-India conferences and important conferences of state level;
(9) Delegation of powers;
(10) Public Accounts Committee, Estimates Committee, assembly and parliamentary questions;
(11) Litigation notices under Section 80, CPC;
(12) Appeals, revisions, etc., within the powers of the state government; and
(13) Territorial changes and changes at headquarters.

Finance Related Functions

(1) All proposals involving new items of expenditure;
(2) Sanction of expenditure from the Contingency Fund;
(3) Scrutiny and approval of development budget, estimates, major appropriation of accounts, surrender of funds, and supplementary grants;
(4) Write-off cases beyond powers of heads of departments and audit objections regarding the offices of heads of departments, etc.;
(5) Financial sanctions not within the competence of the heads of departments.

Service Related Functions

(1) Initial appointment of officers belonging to the state service of infliction of major punishments upon them;
(2) Creation of posts, their extensions and continuance re-employment, resignations, special pay, allowances and pensions not within the powers of the head of department;
(3) Matters relating to senior appointments, promotions, transfers and cases of disciplinary proceedings against gazetted officers;
(4) Approval of service rules and amendments thereto.

State secretariat system unlike the central secretariat system of the Union government works under a chief secretary. The Rules of Business allocate responsibilities through standing orders which are approved by the state cabinets. By and large all states have a uniform pattern and keep reforming it by recommendations of committees and commissions. The state of Orissa attached various state owned corporations to respective secretariat departments and abolished the departments of state public undertakings and corporations. The Maharashtra state made an inquest in the working of its secretariat in 1968 and adopted the desk system and ex offices joint secretary system for the technical officers. State like Punjab, Andhra and Tamil Nadu borrowed several progressive measures from central secretariat. Innovations like group system, cell system, O&M introduction, desk office system, attach system and officer-oriented system were experimented upon to cut on delays and improve the efficiency of the personnel. The State Committees and later the ARC in its report on state administration in 1969 identified these areas of secretariat administration as problems of:

(1) Inordinate delay in decision-making.
(2) Interference of secretariat officials in executive affairs by their non-secretariat activities.
(3) Irrational grouping of subjects in departments.
(4) Lack of field experience of senior offices working under tenure system.
(5) Out datedness of allocation of subjects.
(6) Failure to adapt with the change of new governments in the states.

Thus, the neat separation between policy formulation and policy execution which is so often debated in academic circles is conspicuous by its absence. There is no uniformity of delegation of authority to executive heads of departments. The ARC struggled with it and suggested workable measures. To quote the commission:

(1) "Due to the dominant position of the secretariat, secretariat appointments are considered prestigious. A secretariat posting ensures an officer's stay in the state capital. Moreover, he escapes the pressures and tensions of the field which are enormous in a functioning democracy. A stay in the secretariat assures the official a cosy existence with many social amenities of life. He functions in close proximity to ministers and senior colleagues which helps in winning promotions and better postings. It should change.
(2) There are too many levels and functionaries involved in the secretariat leading to delays in the transaction of public business. The system is falling apart. The cell system can be a good example of innovative reform.
(3) There is the problem of overadministration. The need for a bigger administrative apparatus will be left with the diversification of the functions of the government and the result is the expansion of the secretariat activities. Moreover it is easier to create new positions in the secretariat, as the persons with decision-making authority are all located in the secretariat and the human factors influence the decisions."

The role of bureaucracy in Indian polity is largely determined by the secretariats and their working. The working of the cabinets and field establishments warrant radical change in the organisation of state and central secretariats.

The Chief Secretary

One key civil service position the like of which does not exist in the Union secretariat is the post of chief secretary in the state administration. The office originated in the Central government during the of rule Lord Wellesley in 1799. G.H. Barlow was the first appointed to this office. Later on the office disappeared from the Central government and was adopted by state governments much before the attainment of independence. The chief secretary is the executive head of the state secretariat and is the administrative head of the state administration. He stands at the top of the state administrative hierarchy and his position vis-à-vis other secretaries is more than first among equals. His control extends to all the secretariat departments. He leads, guides and controls the entire administrative apparatus of the state and holds a pivotal, position to performs a variety of roles in the governance of the state. His job is not a professional one and he can be called a part of the process of democratic government wherein he is more than a mere administrator.

Since 1973, the chief secretary was the senior-most civil servant in all the states. Before that, he was considered junior to the financial commissioner in Punjab and members of the Board of Revenue in UP. But in Tamil Nadu, he was the senior-most civil servant. In 1973, this office was standardised on the recommendation of the Administrative Reforms Commission and the post was equated with that of the Secretary to the Government of India, both in status and emoluments. The office of chief secretary has been excluded from the operation of the tenure system. There is no fixed tenure for this post. The Administrative Reforms Commission of India recommended that the tenure of chief secretary should be of three to four years but the recommendation was not accepted and the old system continues.

The chief secretary is picked up by the chief minister of the state who consults the Union government regarding the appointment but this consultation is not binding. Likewise, the CM may consult the cabinet or his ministerial colleagues but the decision is his or her. It is a selection post, which means seniority cum merit criterion is applied in shortlisting and selecting the politically acceptable senior candidate. Usually, three factors are considered: (1) the seniority, (2) the service record, and (3) evaluation of the chief minister. It is difficult to say which factor is decisive, but violating the seniority criterion creates embarrassment, politicisation and demoralisation of civil servants. Moreover in a parliamentary system, if a state government is changed the issue of replacing the chief secretary like that of the Governor has wide ranging implications. A fixed tenure with security may bring a political deadlock and a reshuffle with every political change may destroy the political neutrality of the civil service. The ARC delved deep into the problem and recommended that a chief secretary should have a minimum tenure of three to four years. This suggestion was not accepted and was found non-feasible because a CM may find himself confronting a chief secretary appointed by his predecessor. However, in practice his tenure depends upon his administrative, experience, rapport with change and capacity to take an objective decisions. The functions of chief secretary by and large depend upon the role he opts to play in the working of the state government. There are all sorts of examples of strong and weak chief secretaries playing the alter ego of the chief minister and the fifth wheel in the government. In addition to enormous amount of authority, dignity, status and influence the chief secretary is a sort of administrative chief minister or vice-chief minister (as in Japan) who is linked with every organ of the state government. His functions touch, overlap, strengthen and relate to the following:

(1) Union government
(2) Other state governments
(3) Chief minister of the state
(4) Ministers in the cabinet
(5) Secretaries of the department
(6) Director-General Police
(7) Planning Commission and NDC
(8) Divisional Commissioners
(9) District Collectors
(10) Heads of public enterprises
(11) People
(12) MPs and MLAs
(13) Political parties
(14) Media and press
(15) Civic groups
(16) Panchayati Raj Institutions

These wide ranging activities and operations that skirt around the office of chief secretary render him the centre of gravity, a hub around which the political and administrative machinery rotates. Some of these powers and functions are enumerated in the rules of business, but most of them emanate from conventions and inter-relationships between political institutions and the people. Broadly speaking these functions can be classified as under:

1. Adviser to the CM

The chief secretary acts as the principal advisor to the chief minister on all matters of state administration. The chief minister consults him on all policy issues related to the governance of state. He explains to the chief minister about the administrative implications of the proposals forwarded by the state ministers. He also serves as a link between the chief minister and other secretaries of the state government. This advisory function becomes too broad when the administrative implications of a particular policy make the CM think and revise his policy decisions. As a confidence booster and conscience keeper of the CM, the CS works on policy options in terms of their administrative viability and costs.

2. Secretary to the Cabinet

The chief secretary acts as a secretary to the state cabinet. He is the administrative head of the cabinet secretariat and attends the meeting of the cabinet and its sub-committees. He prepares the agenda for cabinet meetings and keeps records of its proceedings. He takes steps for the implementation of the decisions taken in such meetings. He acts as the *ex officio* secretary to the council of ministers and while acting in this capacity, he may be called as the secretary to the cabinet.

3. Head of State Cabinet Secretariat

The functions of the cabinet secretariat are prescribed by the Rules of Business of each state. But, in broad terms, these functions are: secretarial assistance, implementation of decisions, policy coordination and providing information. The cabinet secretariat works under his overall control and command.

4. Resource Person of State Government

The chief secretary is often asked to express his views on important matters. His information and advice as secretary to the council facilitate political decision-making. His administrative experience, "may sway policy preferences and shift implementational consequences". He plays a supervisory role, as a resource person in tendering advise for final decisions or for their onward transmission to the proper quarters.

5. Head of Civil Services

The chief secretary acts as the head of the state civil services. Important cases pertaining to appointments, transfers and promotion of senior state civil servants go to his desk. He plays an important role in maintaining the morale of the civil services. As a conscience-keeper of all state civil servants he determines vacancies, appointments, transfers, placements, seniority, promotions and retirement of public servants. He is also consulted by the chief minister in amending service rules and making appointments to senior positions. As personnel secretary, he has to ensure that conduct rules are followed and disciplinary actions are taken. The Annual Confidential Reports (ACRs) or Performance Appraisal Reports (PARs) of senior officers of all-India services posted in his state are written by him. He initiates matters involving staff welfare and service conditions of state officials and is overall in charge of training and career management of civil servants of his state.

6. Coordinator of Civil Service Efforts

The chief secretary ensures inter departmental coordination. He advises the secretaries on inter departmental difficulties. He is the chairman of coordination committees which are set up for resolving inter departmental disputes. He presides over the meetings of the department secretaries and divisional commissioners, district collectors and the heads of departments of district administration to effect coordination. This coordination in state administration has to be between Centre and state, between administrations of various states, and between various levels of hierarchy in the state administration itself.

The Union ministries, the Planning Commission, the NDC and cabinet secretariat of the Central government operate through the office of the chief secretary. He is the formal channel of communication and informal network of consultative agencies which operate through his office. The Chief Secretaries Conference, the zonal councils and interstate council provide him forums for inter- and intrastate level coordination. He is an effective link to resolve interstate disputes relating to boundaries or river waters as an adviser to the CM. He is also the chairman of the Planning and Development Coordination Committees. To provide effective coordination at regional and district levels he calls conferences of senior officials like divisional commissioners, district collectors, heads of the departments and superintendents of police every year.

7. Head of Secretariat Departments

The chief secretary may also act as an administrative head of some secretariat departments. His position varies from state to state but in most of the states, the general administration department, personnel department, planning department and administrative reforms department are kept by the chief secretary under his direct charge. The general administration department in the state secretariat is usually under the chief minister who is concerned with sensitive matters affecting the entire business of the state government. The Administrative Reforms Commission recommended that the personnel department in all the states should be directly headed by the chief secretary. In times of crises like flood, drought, communal disturbances and others, the chief secretary plays a significant role by providing guidance and leadership to field officers and agencies engaged in relief operations. He chairs all such committees which take high level policy decisions during crisis situations. In fact, he acts as the disaster manager and virtually represents the state government for all the officers concerned with relief operations.

8. Residual Legatee

The chief secretary also acts as the residual legatee, that is, he looks after all those matters which do not fall within the purview of other secretaries. He acts as secretary, by rotation, of the zonal council of which the state concerned is a member and exercises general supervision and control over the entire state secretariat. The administrative control over the secretariat building, the staff attached to the ministers, the central record branch, the secretariat library, the conservancy and watch and ward staff of the secretariat departments vests in him. He is the principal channel of communication between his government and the Central government and other state governments and in this capacity plays a significant role in the administration of law and order and planning. He attends the annually held chief secretaries conference presided over by the Cabinet Secretary of the Union government and acts as a spokesperson of the state government. As the chief advisor to the Governor when President's rule is imposed in the state and if the Central advisors are not appointed he runs the administration. The CS attends the meetings of the National Development Council. In some states the chief secretary looks after the Administrative Reforms Department and monitors administrative reforms. He functions as the secretary, general administration and provides necessary facilities to departments and officers. Functions like looking after the visits of dignitaries to the state, chairing of expert bodies which decides matters of awarding honours and distinctions fall in the purview of GAD which also looks after matters relating to compensation to ex-rulers and freedom fighters. He is authorised to initiate changes in Rules of Business. Cases concerning grants-in-aid to NGOs are routed through him to the CM. Similarly, matters of housing accommodation and government buildings and circuit house fall under his general jurisdiction. These responsibilities of the chief secretary affect all the departments and therefore, become significant and even decisive. Lately the office has been criticised for its over politicisation and several competent seniors have been ignored in the name of seniority-suitability selection process by political leaders of various categories. It opens a flood gate of manipulations, in-service rivalries and political manipulations of administrative seniors. It is unfortunate that a chief secretary is known as chief minister's man and becomes persona non-grata on change of the incumbent of the office of CM. Perhaps association of a High Court Judge in the selection process can be of some help. Those superceded in the selection of CS post should compulsorily be sent on deputation rather than to languish disgruntled and demoralise their colleagues.

To improve the functioning of the chief secretary's office, the ARC has made several recommendations. The commission said: "The secretarial organisation needs coordination and discipline. This can be done by strengthening the position of the chief secretary who is to function as the chief coordinator under the chief minister. Being the captain of the team of secretaries to the government, the chief secretary should be a senior person of outstanding ability. He should not only command respect and confidence of all the services in the state but also enjoy good reputation at the Centre so that he can deal with the secretaries to the Union government on equal terms." In

ARC's view "The selection of the chief secretary should be made with great care. He should usually be the senior-most fit person who by virtue of his ability, experience, integrity and impartiality commands the respect and confidence of all officers. The chief secretary should be the senior-most person, due regard being paid to merit. He should have a minimum tenure of 3 to 4 years. He should be relieved of routine and non-essential work and, where necessary, given proportionate staff assistance to enable him to ensure quick implementation of cabinet decisions and effective co-ordination in the policies and programmes of the state government."

The State Chief Secretary and the Union Cabinet Secretary Compared

The two functionaries are often compared because of their seniority positions and key roles which they play in their respective administrations. In fact the comparison is invidious because the post of Cabinet Secretary in the state is always held by a very junior functionary while the office of the chief secretary does not exist at Delhi. The committee of secretaries (COS) has been taking care of coordinational activities in central secretariat. The Cabinet Secretary in Union government is the senior-most civil servant of the country, but his functions and roles have little to do with the Union ministries. He leads his cabinet secretariat which is a special and distinct organisation, separate from the central secretariat. Hence it can be maintained that there is no office in the Union government which can be equated to that of the chief secretary in the state. To some extent, the Cabinet Secretary can be called the counterpart of chief secretary but the functions performed and the roles assumed by the chief secretary in the state administration are so vast, varied and wide that they are shared at the Central level, by the Cabinet Secretary, the personnel secretary, the home secretary and the finance secretary. Still the comparison can be attempted on the basis of similarities.

(1) Both the functionaries are chief advisors to their respective chief executives.
(2) Both of them are chief coordinators of their respective administrations.
(3) Both are secretaries to their respective cabinets at both the levels.
(4) Both are administrative heads of their respective cabinet secretariats.
(5) Both the offices originated at the Central level because of their functional relevance
(6) Both supervise the implementation of the decisions of their respective cabinets
(7) Both are heads of their respective civil services.

But then the differences between the two are genuine and deep.

(1) The powers and functions of chief secretary are much more than that of the Cabinet Secretary.
(2) The former is the administrative head of the state secretariat, while the latter is not the administrative head of the central secretariat.
(3) The chief secretary is the chief of state secretaries, while the Cabinet Secretary is not the chief of central secretaries but only a primus interprets or first among equals.
(4) The chief secretary is the Residual Legatee at the state level, while the Cabinet Secretary does not perform this legal function at the Centre. At the central level it is performed by the Principal Secretary to the Prime Minister who is the administrative head of the PM office. Some departments of the state secretariat are under the direct charge of the chief secretary who does not head, the state cabinet secretariat.

State Public Services

The Indian Constitution ensures merit-based bureaucracy through the institution of state public service commissions. Articles 309, 310 and 311 provide legal safeguards and the right to equality ensures protection against discrimination on the basis of colour, caste, sex or creed. The parliamentary system of government at state level expects the state public services to be neutral and accountable to the political executive under the doctrine of ministerial responsibility. There are two kinds of public services in the state (1) the All India Services borne of the cadres of the state, and (2) state public services of various categories and classes including the technical services.

The service conditions of three all India services are governed by the rules made by Union government. But while serving under a state government, they fall under the administrative control of the state government. Their postings, transfers and other ancillary matters are under the control of the state government which can even impose minor penalties after consultation with the Union Public Service Commission. Major penalties are imposed only by the Central government. The service is constituted of fixed cadres for each state dividend into senior posts under the state government as under:

(1) Senior posts under the Central government filled by the deputation of officers borne on the state cadre,
(2) A deputation of officers borne on the state cadre,
(3) A deputation reserve meant to cover appointments to posts outside the prescribed cadre, and
(4) A leave reserve, a training reserve and junior posts.

There is a separate cadre for union territories. Depending upon requirements, a central deputation quota is provided in each variety of the all India service. In addition to direct recruitment to these services, there is a provision for recruitment by promotions or selection from amongst members of the state services. Appointments to the Indian Administrative Service by promotion and selection are not to exceed 25 per cent of the numbers of senior duty posts borne on the cadre and not more than 15 per cent of the post available for promotion and selection may be filled by selection (the percentage has now been raised to 33.5%). Promotion vacancies are filled by the Central government on the basis of a select list of members of the state civil service who have served as deputy collectors and who are considered fit for promotion in consultation with the Union Public Service Commission. A similar provision exists for promotion in the Indian police service.

The state services are the services and posts, the recruitment to and conditions of which are regulated by the Acts of the appropriate state legislature or by rules made by the Governor of the state (Article 309). The state government exercises powers to make rules providing for the making of first appointment, method of appointment, number and character of posts and conditions of service in respect of the state and subordinate services. The state services consist of such services as the state government may, from time to time, declare. The state service covers the whole field of administration in the middle grades. The numbers vary from state to state depending on size, population and work.

There are four classes in state services on the pattern of central services. Class I, II, III and IV are classified on the basis of rank classification. The generalist and specialist nature of the state services bears a parallelism with central services. The recruitment, promotion and training of state level services have no special problem except the fact that senior state officials are dissatisfied with their promotional quota in the IAS and IPS. The OBC reservation categories vary from state to state and where the posts are to be filled partly by direct recruitment and partly by promotion, there is lot of litigation with regard to interpretation of rules.

Article 320 (3) of the Constitution empower the State Public Service Commission to advise the state government in all matters relating to methods of recruitment to civil services and for civil posts. Service under government is not a matter of contract but tenure, subject to the pleasure of the Governor/President. However, the doctrine of pleasure operates under certain limitations. Article 311 states that "no member of the civil service shall be dismissed or removed by an authority subordinate to that by which he was appointed, and no such person ... shall be dismissed or removed or reduced in rank except after an enquiry in which he has been informed of the charges against him and given a reasonable opportunity of being heard in respect of those charges and where it is proposed, after such enquiry, to impose on him any such penalty, until he has been given a reasonable opportunity of making representation on the penalty proposed."

Every state has public service training institutes or academies to provide foundational, professional and refresher training to its officials. In some of the states, there are special training institutions to train different kinds of services. Some of them are:

(1) The Gopalbandhu Institute of Administration, Bhubaneshwar (Orissa);
(2) Administrative College, Mumbai (Maharashtra);
(3) Administrative Staff College, Guwahati (Assam);
(4) Administrative Training Institute, Mysore (Karnataka);
(5) Administrative Training Institute, Ranchi (Jharkhand);
(6) Directorate of Training, Union Territory Civil Services, New Delhi;
(7) Gujarat Institute of Training in Administration, Ahmedabad (Gujarat);
(8) Lal Bahadur Shastri Institute of Public Administration, Bhopal (Madhya Pradesh);
(9) Police Training College, Sagar (Madhya Pradesh);
(10) Officers' Training School, Nainital (Uttranchal);
(11) Secretariat Training School, Trivandrum (Kerala).

All the states do not have their own training institutions. They take the advantage of training in the institutions maintained by other states. Some states take the advantage of the central training institutions or autonomous/private training institutions partly or fully. The number of such institutions runs into dozens.

The training for the state services is largely modelled according to training programmes for IAS and IPS probationers. There is a need to train the trainers. The trainers, the trainees, the syllabi, the training methods, evaluation, incentivisation and linkage with promotion, all need to be streamlined. Most of the training programmes lack creativity receptivity and effectivity with the result that training assignments are viewed as punishment postings by the field officers. The Union government has come in a big way to augment training facilities and extend them to state officials and their institutions. More recently the Panchayati Raj training has become a more urgent need for officials and non-officials in the states. The union training academies are jointly involved in clearing the backlog and devising new and relevant programmes to make Panchayati Raj institutions viable and workable.

The Directorates and Technical Services

Directorates are found both in the Union and state governments. Literally it means the office of the director, which is analogous to the attached office of the Union government. But in state administration it is a line agency which controls the field units also. A secretariat is a staff agency while a directorate is regarded as a line agency. In other words a secretariat is concerned with policy making while a directorate is concerned with policy execution as an executive arms of state government. The directorates translate into action the policies which are framed by the state secretariat. They are also known as executive departments as distinct from the secretariat departments. Except few cases, each secretariat department has a corresponding executive department. The executive department "is an administrative unit, separate from the secretariat, which reaches its apex usually in a single officer like the Director General of Police or the Chief Conservator of Forests; outside the secretariat." Such a head of department is usually concerned with a single secretary to government and a single minister, for his orders and the funds. In general, each administrative department of the secretariat has a corresponding executive department in the field. But some secretariat departments like law have no field agency.

The directorates are as a rule located outside the secretariat. They constitute distinct organisational entities headed by director who is assisted by additional directors, joint directors, deputy directors and assistant directors. However, the head of a directorate (i.e., executive department or executive agency) may also be known by various names viz., Commissioner, Director-General, Inspector-General, Registrar, Controller, Chief Engineer, Chief Conservator, and so on. The following table contains the names of directorates or executive departments and their heads:

	Directorate or Executive Department	*Designations of the Heads*		*Directorate or Executive Department*	*Designations of the Heads*
1.	Agriculture Directorate	Director	9.	Jail Department	Inspector General
2.	Animal Husbandry	Director	10.	Labour Department	Commissioner
3.	Cooperative Department	Registrar	11.	Police Department	Director General
4.	Education Department	Director	12.	Sales Tax Department	Commissioner
5.	Excise Department	Commissioner	13.	Printing and Stationery Department	Controller
6.	Forest Department	Chief Conservator			
7.	Housing Department	Commissioner	14.	Employment Directorate	Director
8.	Irrigation Department	Chief Engineer (Irrigation)	15.	Industries Department	Director

Heads of the departments are officers who are in overall charge of the actual administration of specific services or administration and execution of projects. There are also heads of departments who are responsible for the collection of taxes and administration of laws relating to taxation. The state government exercises control over the working of heads of departments through 'administrative departments' of the secretariat. The work relating to the initiation and formulation of policies of the government requires decentralisation of executive directions and the establishment of field agencies. Hence for the most part of the substantive work of the state secretariat, there exist executive departments, varying in size and powers to provide executive directions in implementation. These executive departments advise the secretariat departments on technical aspects of questions. Below them are field agencies responsible for a detailed execution of the programmes. The generalist secretaries are the administrative advisers while the heads of departments are their executive instruments working as the 'ears and eyes' of the ministries respectively. The major functions of a state directorate are:

(1) To provide technical advice to the ministers.
(2) To exercise disciplinary powers over the subordinate officers as per rules.
(3) To inspect implementation of work by the departmental district staff.
(4) To make all appointments, confirmations, postings, transfers and promotions of officers within the prescribed limits and approved rules.

(5) To render advise to the State Public Service Commission regarding promotions and disciplinary actions.
(6) To allocate grants and make budget reappropriations.
(7) To carry out departmental research and experiment programmes to improve the efficiency of the department.
(8) To organise in-service training programmes for departmental officers.
(9) To accord sanction to the officers for the attendance of conferences.
(10) To prepare the budget of the department.

The number and size of heads of departments depend upon the number of important subjects administered by the state. The heads of the departments are usually called directors or commissioners. They are assisted by additional directors, joint directors, deputy directors and assistant directors. Most of the departments have divisional headquarters. Each division is under a joint director or a deputy director. A head of department may have officers-in-charge at regional or district levels. There is in every district a representative of almost each department. Supervision over departmental activities in districts is done by the regional officer, though overall superintendence vests in the principal head of office. The collector/deputy commissioner of the district is kept in touch with these activities by the district level officials. A 'Head of Office' may exercise, some of the specified financial and administrative powers also. The officers or the heads of departments are generally patterned in the same way as the secretariat. The office staff is generally drawn from the department which includes the specialists and the technicians. The departments are generally headed by technical officers with varying designations. The following list illustrates the variety of directorates in a state administration:

Name of the Executive Agency	*Designation of the Head*
Accounts of Treasuries Directorate	Director of Accounts and Treasuries
Agricultural Department	Director of Agriculture
Animal Husbandry Department	Director of Animal Husbandry
Archives of Historical Documents Department	Director of Archives and Historical Documents
Ayurved Directorate	Director of Ayurved
Buildings and Communications Department (Executive)	Chief Engineer (Buildings and Communications)
Charity Organisation	Charity Commissioner
Cooperative Department	Registrar of Cooperative Societies
Dairy Development Department	Dairy Development Commissioner
Education/Public Instruction Directorate/Department	Director of Education/Public Instruction
Employment Directorate	Director of Employment
Excise Department	Director of Excise/Excise Commissioner
Fisheries Department	Director of Fisheries
Food and Civil Supplies Department	Director of Food and Civil Supplies/Supply Commissioner
Forest Department	Chief Conservator of Forests
Geology and Mining Department	Director of Geology and Mining
Government Printing and Stationery Directorate	Director of Government Printing and Stationery
Housing Department	Housing Commissioner
Industries Directorate	Director of Industries/Industries Commissioner

Cont'd...

Cont'd...

Information and Publicity	Director of Information and Publicity
Irrigation and Power Department (Executive)	Chief Engineer (Irrigation)
Jail Department	Inspector-General of Prisons
Judicial Department	Advocate General, Registrar of High Court
Land Record Office	Director of Land Records
Language Directorate	Director of Languages
Labour Department	Labour Commissioner
Medical Service Department	Director of Medical Services/Surgeon-General
Motor Vehicles and Transport Department	Director of Transport
Planning and Development Department	Development Commissioner
Police Department	Inspector-General of Police or Director General
Registration Department	Registrar/Registrar-General
Public Health Department	Director of Public Health
Sales Tax Department	Sales Tax Commissioner
Settlement Office	Settlement Commissioner
Social and Harijan Welfare Directorate	Director of Social and Harijan Welfare
Technical Education Department	Director of Technical Education
Tourism Directorate	Director of Tourism
Town Planning Department	Director of Town Planning

Source: Avasthi and Avasthi, *Indian Administration*.

The table indicates that the executive agencies do not have a common designation system for their heads. Then wide differences exist between the emoluments, position and roles of the heads of departments. This uniformity in the relationship between the secretariat and the executive departments does not exist. In theory the departments are free in their internal working but as subordinate agencies they have to submit periodic or ad hoc reports to their superiors. Inspections of these offices are conducted by secretariat officers and there exist disparities in rank and remuneration of the heads of executive departments and the secretaries. The relationship in state administration poses problems. A clear-cut demarcation of functions should leave policy matters with the secretariat and the field agencies should execute under the overall supervision of the former.

Special Agencies

In addition to directorate, there is a variety of special agencies which help the state administration in performing its varied tasks. The Advocate General, the Board of Revenue (or financial commissioners in Punjab, Haryana, Himachal and Jammu & Kashmir) the state public service commissions, the state vigilance commissions, the Lok Ayukatas and a variety of public corporations exist to assist the planners and implementers of public policy. As the Planning Commission is an extraconstitutional body its counterparts do not exist in the states. But then almost all the Indian states have a planning department or a board which is headed either by the chief minister or by a cabinet minister. The CM and through him, the cabinet approves all planning decisions. The chief secretary heads the planning department but in some states, the planning secretary also looks after the administration of the planning. The directorate of evaluation, and the directorate of district gazetteers are located in planning departments in states. The plan cycle involves the formulation of the annual and the Five-Year Plans and their constant evaluation and monitoring. Several coordination committees take collective decisions in matters pertaining to inter-department developmental projects for the benefit of political masters.

Planning Machinery in the State

The functions of State Planning Boards were outlined by the ARC which maintained that they should: (1) determine plan priorities of the state within the framework of the priorities of the national plan; (2) make an assessment of the state resources and formulate plans for the most effective and balanced utilisation of those resources; (3) assist district authorities in formulating their development plans within the spheres in which such planning is considered useful and feasible and to coordinate these plans with the state plan; (4) identify factors which tend to retard economic and social development of the state and determine conditions to be established for successful execution of the plans; and (5) review the progress of implementation of the plan and measures as the review may indicate. The board's secretariat should normally have four units – one dealing with agriculture and irrigation, the second with power, industry and transport, the third with social services, and the fourth with evaluation. Planning cells should be constituted in the development department of the state governments.

The ARC recommended for the setting up of planning boards to complement and supplement the existing planning machinery in the states. They are generally headed by the chief ministers and planning minister and the finance minister are their members. The chief secretary and senior secretaries are members of these board with other experts. The boards are mainly concerned with perspective planning, plan formulation and plan evaluation. The planning departments provide secretarial assistance to these boards. They strengthen the planning process through inputs of information and analysis but they will have to go a long way to become counterparts of the Planning Commission at the state level. A number of state governments of the opposition parties, have been complaining about the dominance of the Central government through the National Development Council and the Planning Commission. The states complain that the Planning Commission determines the total size of the state plan and, even the sectoral plans, including individual schemes are approved by it. The Central assistance is more in the form of loans than of grants and, while allocating grants, the needs of the weaker states are not given due weightage. The earmarking of resources by the Planning Commission, reduces the autonomy of the states and "plan the process of formulation, scrutiny and finalisation of state plans, introduces unitariness in administration. The bureaucratic structures and the all India services monopolise plan administration and the state governments stand as beggars at the gates of Planning Commission. The need for federalisation of Planning Commission is opposed on the ground that it will create a parallel economic government. But, then the state planning boards in state administration have proved to be ineffective and irrelevant.

Panchayati Raj and District Planning

One great event that should revolutionise the character of state administration is the induction of Panchayati Raj in the district administration of the country. The 73rd and 74th Amendments establish the network of local self-government institutions and endow them with powers of local and district level planning. Initial difficulties or teething troubles apart, these institutions will take away some of the functions of the state and district administrations. In all the states of the country development work has been transferred to the newly created local bodies and their elected representatives. This takes away a large share of district governance from the state administration.

Amendment 74th (243-ZD) lays down that a District Planning Committee (DPC) shall be constituted in each district to consolidate the plans prepared by the panchayats and the municipalities in the district concerned and to prepare a draft development plan for the district as a whole. Not less than four-fifths of the total number of members of a DPC are elected by and from amongst the elected members of the panchayats at the districts level and of the municipalities in the district in proportion to the ratio between the population of the rural areas and of the urban areas in a given district. Article 243-ZD also prescribes that "while preparing the draft development plan, a DPC will keep in view: matters of common interest between the panchayats and municipalities such as planning, sharing of water and other physical and natural resources, development of infrastructure and environmental conservations; and the extent of availability of financial and non-financial resources." The chairperson of DPC forwards the development plan to the state government, which coordinates the district plans and integrate them with the sectoral plans. Thus, the 74th Constitutional Amendment Act has conceived of the Planning Committees as constitutional authorities and representative structures of the district population. The DPC should facilitate integration of planning for urban and rural areas. The specialists, experts, government representatives, public men will work out plans with special reference to spatial planning. Efforts are being made to allocate natural resources between the panchayats and municipalities for an integrated development of the rural infrastructure. A consultative process in the drafting of district plans and schemes will be attempted to integrate the district and state plans. Similarly a Metropolitan Planning Committee (MPC) for every metropolitan area prepares a draft development plan falling in its jurisdiction. A metropolitan area has municipalities as well as panchayats and the two get representation in the MPC. The Constitution lays down that not less than two-thirds of the members of an MPC should be elected by and from amongst the elected members of the municipalities and the chairpersons of the panchayats in proportion to the ratio between the population of the municipalities and that of the panchayats in that area. This whole exercise of lining district development with state plan projects is in a state of gestation. The district bureaucracy which has a huge vested interest in rural development is struggling to impress upon the state and Union government that panchayati institutions are ill-equipped to undertake planning exercise which needs coordination and support of funds from both the governments. The state administration is hard pressed from both the ends. The Union government and its agencies stress upon the accountability of the state administration, while panchayati institutions are new entrants and their representative character wants to assert and plead for autonomy in the area of development administration.

Parliamentary democracy in a three-tier federal system of India is a unique and unprecedented experiment which has special problems in store for the middle tier. The six areas discussed above emanate from the paradoxical demands of centralised development and decentralised democracy. The Governor is a federal agent presiding over the parliamentary apparatus of chief ministers government. These two political functionaries who guide the destinies of state administration will continue to have their ding-dong battles in the name of federalism v/s democracy. The ultimate consensus must lead to an equilibrium between national interest and regional autonomy. The Governor will have to appreciate the demands of state people represented by the chief minister and conversely the latter must understand and realise that a perennial conflict with Union government will be suicidal. This may be projected as a centralisation vs decentralisation debate in Indian polity and the state administration which represents the operational aspects of state politics must conform to the norms of the Constitution which professes a decentralised democracy in an iron clad nation-state of India. The office of the chief secretary and executive field directors present specific administrative problems which are different from those obtained in Union government. The secretariat system and the merit bureaucracy and its operations are quite similar at two levels but the chief secretary represents an administrative centralisation which is not the characteristic feature of Union administration. The field directorates or executive offices in states work under the command of a generalist secretary and his boss the chief secretary. Efficiency and discipline being the quest the office of the chief secretary has emerged as administrative vice chief minister of the state. This development has overshadowed the specialist services and the concept of attached office directorate has been reduced to subordinate offices of the department. Hence there is an increasing demand for administrative decentralisation in the field with more and more powers to specialists and technocrats, while the chief secretary continues to personify centralisation to deal with the monolith which the Central government represents in India.

The tribulations of the middle-level state tier are manifestly visible in the development administration of plans and projects which the state bureaucracy has been implementing in the district and below. Half a century of this planned development has been a mixed success and the state administration deservingly wants to take credit of this change in the countryside through union funds and initiatives. Now this planning from below has developed its panchayati side and the state administration has not only to share but transfer development from the office of the collector. The new patterns are emerging but the state level has tensions of snatching grants from the Centre and then reluctantly conceding the same to the panchayati bodies. The pressure from both ends renders it into a hung administration. The Union government has monopolised planning and the panchayati institutions do not deserve autonomy is the usual alibis. But then the size and diversities of the country demand that extreme centralisation and reluctant decentralisation may continue at both the ends. The middle tier of state should judiciously combine planned development with decentralised democracy. This hyphen role of state administration is yet to be visualised at the top and at the grassroots. The framers of the Indian Constitution were primarily concerned with the structure and nature of the Union government. Its prototype miniatures were envisaged for the state without much considered thought of relationships and dynamics of technological development. During Nehru era federalism stood arrested by nationalist aspiration of democracy without any infrastructure of development. The Indira phase represents the regional tensions and after 1994 the new era of LPG policies threaten to redefine the basic concepts of democracy, development and federalism. The Constitution has responded to all these changes but state level changes have been marginal. The 73rd and 74th Amendment introduce radical changes and they should go a long way to redefine the relationships of a three-tier democratic federalism. As people develop political consciousness about their rights and the urge for equitable development gains momentum the state administration will have to come out from its traditional frame of policy implementation. The issues in state administration are not mere operational, but the entire state administration has to be a partner with Union government above and panchayati institutions below.

8

District Administration and Decentralised Governance: From Dyarchy to Self-Government

Prime Minister (late) Narsimha Rao will be remembered for his epoch making achievement of the year 1992 when he constitutionalised Panchayati Raj and urban local bodies by 73rd and 74th Amendments to the Constitution of India. It was something heroic on his part to add this third tier to Indian federalism which besides being unprecedented in world history has added an extra-decentralised dimension governance to a highly centralised polity. This democratic decentralisation or introduction of a three-tier arrangement of Panchayati Raj institutions in the districts of the country along with a district administration of the collector is a unique experiment wherein the administrative bureaucracy of civil servants and the popular democracy of elected representatives are working out a new model of district governance, somewhat uniform yet highly diversified in different states of the country. Unlike USA or Germany, the federal model of Indian polity has been engaged in evolving a cooperative federation of centralised variety. The introduction of Panchayati Raj and urban local bodies has added newer tensions which put the state and district administrations under conflicting pressures from above as well as from below.

Local self-government being a subject in the State List, is being given a final shape by the state governments which are ruled by different political parties – national as well as regional in character. The Central government has proceeded with great caution and the two amendments are only to introduce uniformity in the pattern within which local varieties of the model will evolve. But then the district administration all over India being non-political has a uniform system of government since the Mughal and the British times. The amalguzars and subedars of the sarkars, whom the Company government converted into the office of the collector and the Republican Constitution of India left untouched and unscratched continues to be the 'Representative of the state government'. The 11th Schedule of 29 subjects empowers the Panchayati Raj institutions to take care of these developmental subjects without violating the functional jurisdiction of the collector. Moreover, a collaborative jurisdiction with separate funds have been provided to work out this "Regulatory and developmental dyarchy in the district in such a way during transition that district administration understands that their days are numbered and the panchayati leaders should feel that they have to deserve before they desire to stake their claims to political power."

The Rationale for Dyarchy

The situation is strikingly similar and somewhat comparable to dyarchical reforms of Montford Scheme of 1919. There the state government was bisected into reserved and transferred halves. The reserved subjects were key area for which the Indian ministers were found unsuitable to govern. The transferred half consisted of developmental subjects of popular welfare and responsible Indian ministers were asked to learn by running this transferred half of state government. Today the same dyarchy has been revived. The collectorate and its officials are administering the key areas like law and order, criminal justice, irrigation, electricity and revenue management while the panchayati subjects which are mostly spending subjects without revenue have been assigned to panchayati leaders to prove their worth and learn in running the affairs of the government. Curiously enough, the arguments advanced for this dyarchical arrangement in the district are almost the same which the colonial masters gave in 1919 for the province and in 1935 for the country.

(1) The people are uninformed, untrained and far below the mark to run self-governing institutions.
(2) The instalments of self-government offer increasing opportunities to learn under a parental command.
(3) The key subjects like home, finance, jails, security are too sensitive to be handed over to Indians or to villagers now.

Today, the urban born so-called elites are finding the rural folks too incompetent to manage their own affairs. The bureaucratic presence is being defended on the ground that collector's office alongwith other technical extension officers will train panchayati leaders in self-government. The village leaders, especially women and representatives of weaker sections are making a chaos in the name of social justice and state officers of police and revenue are better qualified to supervise and make them worthy of self-government.

The national leaders, including the Father of the Nation and Pandit Nehru called it a national affront and a colonial conspiracy to argue with this kind of imperial logic of Whiteman's Burden. Mahatmaji gave a clarion call to his elected Congress leaders to resign and the much-maligned dyarchy failed in 1921 before it was experimented upon. Ignoring this classical fact of modern Indian history, the state governments and their bureaucrats are keeping panchayati institutions in bondage and argue for the continuance of the collector with the same logic that rural India is a backward India and urban educated Indians are the successors of British Raj and they will determine when should rural people be liberated from the yoke of urban colonialism.

The District Administration

This dyarchy in the district is a combination of district administration of the past and locally managed areas of administration of future. The Indian states are the reorganised units of British Indian provinces or the new states created by Sardar Vallabh Bhai Patel. They are too big to be managed from one state centre, hence right from the Mughal times the field administration has followed territorial and functional patterns. The British rulers reorganised these area units horizontally as well as vertically, but in both cases they remained hierarchical. In the unitary or territorial form, the central authority creates regional or area agencies which have an overall charge of all the activities of the area. The heads of other specialised units at that level are his subordinates. In a multiple or functional form of organisation, the different divisions of the headquarters have their corresponding field establishments and there is no coordinating or integrating authority at the area level.

The French Prefecturate Approach

Finding a total absence of local bodies in India, the English rulers thought of borrowing the French model of prefecturate and the collector was designed as an Indian prefect with long arms and long fingers and the vice versa. A mixed pattern of area and functional agencies was created. Revenue administration was combined with magisterial executive and residual functions and territorial offices emerged. The Board of Revenue was for the province and below it came the division with divisional commissioner in charge. It is not true of all states. The division is divided into districts under the charge of a collector/deputy commissioner. Districts in turn are divided into sub divisions under the charge of subdivisional officers. These are further split into tehsils/talukas which are headed by the tehsildars. Below the tehsil lies the Pargana/revenue circle under the charge of revenue inspector or kanungo; and then comes the lowest primary unit, namely, the village whose important official is the patwari or lekhpal or now a gram sevak.

The village, the paragana, the tehsil or taluka or Zila are the various levels of revenue administration coming from the times of Todarmal and Akbar. The functionaries are known by varied names. The English ruler gave a semblance of uniformity to the offices of collector (district), subdivisional officer (SDO) in subdivisions and Tehsildar at the level of tehsil or block. Each state has its own variation of these functionaries. Land revenue codes of various states provide for the division of a district into subdivision with a subdivisional officer as its head. Similarly, the criminal procedure code authorises the government to divide a district into subdivisions for purpose of criminal administration with a sub divisional magistrate in charge. Most of the states have created a common subdivision for both revenue and criminal administration with a common officer as the head known as the subdivisional officer and the subdivisional magistrate. Like Collector the subdivisional officer also is an all-purpose revenue, magisterial and executive officer in the subdivision. He is a territorial officer like collector in the district and tehsildar in the tehsil, where he functions as the chief executive officer and representative of government. After the advent of Panchayati Raj, the SDO and the BDO functions as ex-officio members of the panchayat samiti without a right to vote. The samiti is superheaded by an officer called the block development officer who is a leader of the team of development officers. He is a key figure in the development administration of India and enjoys a position of significance which is next to that of the district officer. The BDO is a career civil servant under the employment of the state government and is responsible for the development administration in the block.

The SDO exercises control over field offices through his visits to gram panchayats and tehsil headquarters. His main functions are to control and supervise the subordinate magistracy, labour problems, grant and cancellation of licences etc. He is a sort of an area administrator. The BDO is the secretary and the chief executive officer of the panchayat samiti who is expected to be guided by the DO. This mixture of revenue and panchayati hierarchies is headed by the district collector, who even today is the head of the administration in the colonial mould.

The Legacy

The office of the collector looks like a significant legacy of the British Raj. It has passed through many vicissitudes of history and the company and crown governments relied upon this functionary for revenue as well as administration. Some of the following landmarks deserve mention:

1772	The office was created and abolished in 1773 – recreated in 1786.
1787	Magisterial powers were given to function as DM.
1793	Cornwallis code separated judicial and magisterial function in Bengal.
1843	Deputy collectors and deputy magistrates were created.
1857–1914	(a) A fiscal representative, (b) a treasurer of local funds, and (c) a DM for law and order with powers of superintendence over police and management of jails.
1857–1919	A little Napoleon, all purpose officer and an embodiment of Imperial government.
1919	Dyarchy strengthened the position.
1930	Simon supported a strong collector.
1937	Failure of provincial autonomy enhanced powers.

When Britishers left in 1947, India was ruled by collectors who were all powerful rulers. Historians like Woodruff and O'Malley may quote examples of their humanitarian gestures during epidemics or disasters but by and large they were the enemies of national movement and did their worst to thwart the non-violent protests of the Mahatma.

The Ziladhish: Functions and Role

The Constituent Assembly did not discuss the arrangement of district administration and the collector and his bureaucracy got a lease of life in free India also. During the period from 1950 to 1993 the image of the British DM was totally lost and an Indian feudal counterpart took over the office by discouraging panchayati experiment. The urban trained Indian civil servant consolidated his position and the political masters were tamed by developing a perverse nexus of power. In place of working with people the philosophy of ruling over the people in the name of their popular apathy miseducated the popular leaders and a myth of indispensability was perpetrated. The political leaders developed an inferiority complex and the undesirable ones made a gang of freebooters to loot the countryside. Absence of democratic institutions along with huge developmental spoils without any popular accountability made the collector the kingpin and they became 'Ziladhish' of medieval variety. The functions did not change but increased to the extent that today there is very little which he shares with other agencies. Before independence his duties consisted of collection of revenue, maintenance of law and order, direction to development plans, disaster management, redressal of citizen grievances and other regulatory duties. Today, each one of these functions has enlarged in its components and ramifications. It is impossible to enumerate his actual functions but the important ones can be categorised as under:

(1) As a Revenue Collector

The collector is the head of district administration and as such he is an appointing and punishing authority for the ministerial and junior servants of the collectorate and the tehsil staff. He functions as a controlling, drawing and disbursing officer of the district. Annual budget estimates for the district in respect of revenue buildings are prepared by him and he has responsibility for the maintenance of government buildings under the charge of the revenue department. He is in charge of the treasury and the district stamp office and is responsible for verification of the security of government treasury. He is the chief protocol officer of the district and holds interviews with the members of the public and other officials. He serves as the principal agency of government in matters of general administration in the district and is the chairman/president of various local institutions and government committees at the district level.

The most significant task assigned to a collector is *the assessment and collection of land revenues.* Timely collection is necessary otherwise other measures become necessary to enforce collection. Dues such as irrigation dues, income tax dues, agricultural dues, canal dues, taqavi loans, excise, etc., have to be collected by his office. Excise duties on commodities such as liquor, drugs, petrol, etc., are levied by the district excise officer, who works under him. Assessing the amount of relief and distribution of loans in case of drought and famine, and also their recovery is collector's responsibility. He has to acquire land for development projects, housing schemes, slum clearance, etc. The district treasury functions under his supervision. Economic offences have added to his burdens. In fact, no development can take place unless the collector maintains peace and tranquillity in his district.

(2) As a District Magistrate and Disaster Manager

The district administration consists of the police, the judiciary and the jails. The superintendent of police as head of district police force works in collaboration with the District Magistrate. In metropolitan cities, the responsibility for law and order vests with the police commissioner. Article 50 of the Constitution has separated the judiciary from the executive and the judicial proceedings have become the responsibility of the district and Session's Judge under the supervision of the High Court. The collector can still hear cases under the 'preventive' section of the Code of Criminal Procedure and exercises his authority in case of disorders in his district. He supervises the subordinate magistracy, and posts magistrates during festivals and elections etc. Implementation of Trade Mark Act, Sugar Factories Control Act, Entertainment Tax Act, Press Act, etc. are still with him although the separation of judiciary has brought a sharp decline in his authority.

As a district magistrate he visits the jail from time to time and ensures expeditious disposal of cases of undertrials. Questions like grant of classes to prisoners, premature release of prisoners, release on parole, mercy petitions of prisoners, etc., are decided by him. He *organises rescue operations*, take steps to check epidemics, and call for the army for help and supply food items during emergency. He has powers under the Defence of India Rules and he enforces civil defence measures for the protection of vital installations, along with other cognate matters.

(3) As an Implementor of Government Schemes

In fact Collection of land revenue and other government dues were the basic functions for which the office was created. From this flows the distribution of taccavi loans, their recovery, assessment of losses to crops and relief measures. All matters relating to land records, administration of *nazul* land, land acquisition work, enforcement of Stamp Act, management of government estates and payment of rehabilitation grant, hearing revenue appeals are made under his orders. He takes relief measures in case of scarcity conditions, flood, water logging and excessive rains. Sanctioning land revenue assignment, payment of zamindari abolition, compensation and rehabilitation grants and assessment are his routine function. He promulgates orders for public peace and disposes of *petitions of government*. He submits his annual criminal report to government at intervals. Labour problems and strikes, etc., enforcement of entertainment tax, enforcement of press laws constitute his official duties. Functions like appointment and punishment of village chowkidars, and payments under the Workmen's Compensation Act, take much of his time. Grant and cancellations of many kind of licences and recommendations of schemes for the development of forests are some of his major functions.

The collector is the returning officer for parliamentary and vidhan sabha elections. As a district census officer, he is responsible for the conduct of census operations once in ten years. His other functions include the treasury grant of old-age pensions, preparation of district gazetteers, grant of house-building loans and protection of ancient monuments. In some states he is also the district registrar of cooperative societies. He is the *supervising authority over municipalities in the district*. The special responsibilities in regard to civil supplies is also responsible for such work as the national savings or the state loans floated from time to time. Contributions to the National Defence Fund are made through his office. In addition, he is the *chairman of a number of official committees* such as the Soldiers and Sailors Welfare Fund, Staff Welfare Committee, Public Grievances Committee, Planning Committee, etc. In short, the duties and functions of the collectors are enormous and they leave many things unsaid. Paradoxically the current shift in emphasis on developmental functions has not diminished the importance of regulatory functions. The other side of development has added to the functions of the already over-worked collector. With his regulatory and developmental duties, the he has *to work with NGOs*. Then, there are frequent visits by experts and the VIPs. The celebration of days, weeks and fortnights jubilees and centenaries need his initiative. Much of his time and energy are spent in meeting district politicians and village leaders and listening to their grievances, demands and 'advices'. He is also increasingly in demand for functions outside the strict official beat.

(4) As a Staff Official for Development

In fact a textbook approach to collector's functions is a matter of colonial days. Because the laws have not changed much so the revenue, magisterial and general administrative functions remain unaltered. But in practice a number of new participants have entered into the decision making apparatus of the collectorate. So the role suffers from the overload and inter agency conflicts are more visible even in routine functions like revenue collection and law and order maintenance. The separation of judiciary weaken the collector as a ruler and now Panchayati Raj leaders asking for their share in development administration have made him a functionary without much power but with all legal responsibilities.

From a line official role he is being transformed into a staff official. In fact he spends more time on staff functions of supervision control, coordination and integration of schemes and plans, building up personnel, eliciting cooperation and participation of the people. He has to be more and more on the spot. The Administrative Reforms Commission believed that the collector's tour should be utilised for enquiring into public grievances and taking remedial action. Besides in a number of development programmes he should play an advisor and work like a leader in development activity. The departmental agencies should implement their programme of development in consultation with the collector.

(5) As Chairman of DRDA

The *ex officio* chairmanship of the District Rural Development Agency posits the collector face to face with the district level officials who are responsible for the implementation of schemes. Then this role of the collector in rural development can be evaluated in terms of his position in the zila parishad. The Panchayati Raj bodies need his support. The office is undergoing a sea change and the elected representatives have shattered many myth including that of the 'steel frame'. The collector, rural development agencies, the police, revenue officers, the judiciary – all of whom have to function as a team but the plurality has disturbed the unity of purpose and singularity of approach. He has less time for development administration and his role is declining as the chief executive officer. The two amendments of 1993 and 1994 are indicative of this diminishing role in development administration. Even his revenue functions are being transferred to panchayats. Despite the recent measures to reduce the responsibilities of the district collector, this key functionary of Indian administration continues to suffer from overwork of multiple responsibilities that go with the change. However he has to reach his midway in the midst of conflicting pressures of continuity and change.

(6) As Coordinator of Technical Departments

Although the collector under the Company rule was purely a revenue officer with magisterial functions., the reforms of 1919 and 1935 introduced a variety of technical departments resulting in the multiplicity of command. The central role changed into a coordination function which the collector continues to perform even today. This gave birth to the dichotomy of regulatory and developmental administrations at the level of the district. The technical officers heading specialised agencies were called as extension officers and they are supervised by their respective regional or state level officers. Some of these departments in the state administration are:

Name of Department	*Designation of the District Head*
Agriculture	District Agriculture Officer/Assistant Director of Agriculture
Backward Classes/Harijan Welfare	Backward Classes Welfare Officer/Harijan Welfare Officer
Cooperation	Assistant/Deputy Registrar of Cooperative Societies
Education	District Education Officer/Inspector of Schools
Employment	District Employment Officer
Excise	District Excise Officer/Superintendent of Excise
Forest	Divisional/District Forest Officer
Health and Family Planning	District Health Officer
Industries	District Industries Officer/Assistant Director of Industries
Jails	Superintendent of Jails
Judiciary	District and Session Judge
Labour	Assistant Labour Commissioner/District Labour Officer
Medical	District Medical Officer/Civil Surgeon
Panchayats/Panchayats and Social Services	District Panchayat Officer
Planning	District Planning Officer
Police	Superintendent of Police
Publicity/Information	District Publicity Officer/Assistant Director of Publicity
Public Works	Executive Engineer
Registration and Revenue	Collector

Source: Avasthi and Avasthi, *Indian Administration.*

These technical departments and their officers though a part of district level field administration but they are not the hierarchical subordinates of the collector. But the working of centuries has created a traditional image and a customary inter linkage of functions because of which coordination vs. control problems have risen in their varied manifestations. The generalist specialist controversy and the bitterness that surrounds it, force the collector to be a mere leader than a controller. The police officials like SP and DIGs have challenged the collector's evaluation of police performance under Indian Police Act in the law courts. The collector is not acceptable as a controlling link between the police range or a commissionarate in some states. The Panchayati Raj Institutions are systematically eroding the omnipotent image of a sole government representatives. Naturally varying patterns of relationship between the collector and the technical heads of the departments have emerged. The technical heads of state departments do not want interference of the collector. They have their independent ministers in-charge and they find the collector, a generalist, increasingly irrelevant in taking work from technical field officers. Then regional officers of technical departments object to collector's role which encroaches upon their specialised areas of administration. Even the (primus inter pares) first among equals role is more a matter of courtesy because the technical officers are senior in age and experience and the young collectors are generally persona-non-grata to these field officers who are doctors, engineers, agronomists, forest officers and superintendent of jails.

Most of the executive departments have regional offices interposed between the state headquarters and the district organisation. However, the territorial jurisdictions of regional offices of departments are not co-terminus. This renders coordination difficult. The number of departments with regional offices is increasing and their officials supervise the work of the officers at the district and sub-district levels. They act as evaluation agency in the field. The ARC suggested that supervisory work, size of the set up and need of intermediate level should be the criteria to create a regional office.

Broadly speaking, the executive departments at the state headquarters are organised in departments which have regional offices under them above the district. Some departments are organised on both area and functional bases. Departments like revenue have their regional offices at the division under the commissioner; police with its range under the Inspector-General of Police; forest with its circle under the Conservator of Forests; Public Works Department with its circle under the Superintending Engineer. The registrar of cooperative societies may be a head of the department. There is no uniformity in these matters between different states and even in the same state there is little uniformity between various executive departments. The growth of corporate sector, NGOs and panchayati institutions are shaking this field set-up in more than one way.

The Divisional Commissioner: A Fifth Wheel

In this chain of supervisory area administration, the revenue administration of the collector has been superimposed by a divisional commissioner. A division is an administrative area between the district and the state government comprising 3 to 6 districts, the number varying from state to state and from division to division within a state itself. The officer-in-charge of this area is called the commissioner who is a senior member of the Indian Administrative Service. The post was first created in 1829 when the then Bengal government established an intermediate authority between the collector and the headquarters administration in the form of commissioners of divisions. The appointment of commissioners in the subsequently acquired provinces of Punjab, Burma, Oudh and the Central Province followed in due course. Before independence, every province in India except Madras had divisional commissioners. He was primarily a revenue official and heard appeals in revenue cases from subordinate authorities.

The divisional commissioners have been called the Fifth Wheel of the car. He has little direct contact with the people. It is a promotion post for the senior members of the civil service. The

Royal Commission for Decentralisation, 1907 recommended its retention. The issue, however continued to crop up again and again, particularly at the time of constitutional reforms of 1919, 1935, and 1947. After independence, the state governments merely tinkered with traditional revenue set-up and the states of Maharashtra, Rajasthan, and Gujarat abolished the posts of divisional commissioners but later revived them. Assam too experimented with the abolition and later restitution of the post. In Uttar Pradesh, the offices of commissioners were reduced and their functions and powers were drastically cut down.

The commissioners have been described as a 'superfluous layer in the hierarchy' and 'a mere post office' whose abolition has been asked on grounds of economy. Γhe government also feels the need to examine the utility of the institution in the context of Panchayati Raj experiment changed set-up. This office looks like a symbol of colonialism and people want to demolish it as a strong-holds of bureaucracy.

Its retention is justified on administrative ground. The commissioners serve as a valuable link in the chain of administration between districts and the state headquarters. Even Simon Commission (1930) held that the tradition of official administration in India is against the creation of large central establishments; The commissioner as a regional coordinating authority for technical departments is a useful link to help, guide and advise the collectors in his division. His advice to headquarters is also likely to be more mature and comprehensive than that of the collector. As the 'area' representative of the state government he is 'government' in the division. The Decentralisation Commission's (1907–09) maintained the same view when it said that "In a country like India, it is specially important to prevent any system of government by professional experts ... . It is a distinct weakness in an oriental country that there should be no local officer to whom the people can go with general grievances, and that they should come to regard the government as a mere collection of scattered and independent departments." The Administrative Reforms Commission Study Team on State Level Administration also concluded "that it is necessary to have this post for regional coordination. But the commission disagreed with its own Study Team and observed that there should not be any intermediate level of administration between the district and the government".

The commissioners have judicial powers to hear appeals in revenue matters from district officers in various rent, revenue and tenancy matters. Statutory powers have been conferred by acts and administrative orders in the fields of police, land acquisition, local government transport and other allied matters. He enjoys the district magistrate's responsibility in the areas of maintenance of law and order and jail administration. Along with collector he has special powers during crisis and emergency. He keeps a vigil on developmental activities going on in the districts of his division. His supervisory and coordinative roles include an overall supervision of general administration, law and order, land reforms, land management, food and relief administration and activities in the division of all departments/directorates and implementation of plans and non-plan development schemes. The law enumerates the duties of the commissioner as under "Inspection of district, subdivisional and tehsil offices; consolidation of various statistics for the division; disbursement of some grants; a large number of reports and returns in the division sent to government or the Board of Revenue, special reports including confidential reports; grant of certain types of licences for the fire arms; the sanction of certain rewards; allocation of village police and the assessment of the cost of additional police; inspection of jails and chairmanship of revision boards; general supervision over excise department; chairman of regional transport authorities; recommendations for filing government appeals; certain routine duties with regard to revenue buildings; control over certain forests; writing off of losses and stamp; etc., temporary establishments in revenue offices; general supervision over collection of land revenue; canal dues and other dues".

Whatever may be the legal position this 'Fifth Wheel' in the automobile is presently criticised for his controlling role of Panchayati Raj institutions. The prefecturate of the collector is gradually shifting to the office of the regional commissioner. It is probably to reconcile the post of the district collector with the Panchayati Raj set up. But the bureaucratic control over local institutions may continue so the commissionerships are being strengthened. A more senior generalist bureaucrat in commissioner's office will serve the double bureaucratic purpose, i.e., (1) keeping the technical officers under command, and (2) getting the panchayati institutions dissolved at will for a period of six months. This bureaucratic strategy of continuing the present system, but pushing it one step higher will buy more time for postponing the democratic and technological revolution in the countryside. Howsoever senior the bureaucratic position may be, it cannot replace the authority of the state level technocrat. Similarly the French argument of keeping a bureaucratic supervisor over the mayors is untenable in the mass democracy of India. The administration cannot ascend up. It will have to descend down and if people's representatives are the sovereign, the senior bureaucratic commissioner's should not over awe them by threats of supercession temporary interventions.

Rural Self-Government of Panchayati Raj

The establishment of a military state by the Mughals was the end of the rural system of local communities about which Sir Charles Metcalfe wrote that they contributed more than any other cause to the preservation of the people of India through all the revolutions and changes which they have suffered. From Akbar to Aurangzeb, the empire maintained a district administration without any local bodies. The English rulers found the countryside blank and a French model of perfecturate of a collector was their natural response. With their commercial establishments at port cities and in the rim land belt, the Board of Directors of the company thought of urban local bodies first and created corporation in Madras (1688) Calcutta (1722) and Bombay (1793). The British collector found the rural countryside non-conducive for local reforms. It was as late as the year 1864 that Lord Lawrence brought a resolution in the Governor General's Executive Council about Indian peoples capability to run their own local affairs. Lord Mayo (1870) in a resolution adopted decentralisation with respect to sanitation and public works. In 1871 and 1874, new municipal Acts were passed providing for elective municipal bodies. But the most important step came in 1882 when the famous Ripon Resolution of Local Self-Government, became the basis of local self-government in India. But after Ripon's governor-generalship local self-government did not receive much encouragement. In 1915, the Government of India resolved to reform local bodies and the declaration of 1917 assured a progressive realisation of responsible government in India. Under dyarchy, the provincial governments exhibited some progress of local reforms. The provincial autonomy enshrined in the Government of India Act, 1935 marked by a significant move in the direction of democratising local bodies and strengthening them. There were variations in the nomenclatures of different institutions in different provinces.

Like the guilty men of partition, the founding fathers of the Constitution have been called the betrayer of Mahatma's dream of autonomous village republics. They systematically avoided the basic provisions for a gramrajya or a 'Ramrajya' and like the Royal Proclamation of 1917, only promised to put rural India "on the road to self-government by developing self-governing institutions in instalments". The local bodies were made the creatures of state legislatures without any independent and separate status of their own. Entry fifth in the Seventh Schedule included "local government, that is to say, the constitution of municipal corporations, improvement trusts, district boards, mining settlement authorities and other local authorities for the purpose of local self-government or village administration". The Article 40 of the Constitution on Directive Principles of State Policy got away by enjoining upon the state to "take steps to organise village panchayats and endow them with such powers and authority as may be necessary to enable them to function as units of local government".

Pandit Nehru unlike Gandhi had a different philosophy and vision of rural development. He resolved to launch community development projects in the countryside through a special ministry of CD and through an ongoing thrusts of Five-Year Plans to be formulated by the Planning Commission. In pursuance of the Directive Principles of State Policy for a new social order, ways and means were explored and the Fiscal Commission of 1949 recommended the launching of a national extension service for the entire country. The Planning Commission in the First Five-Year Plan made a proposal for setting up a rural extension service for securing integrated development. Community development was described as the method and rural extension as the agency through which the transformation of the social and economic life of villages was to be attempted. Thus, the community development programme which was launched on October 2, 1952 aimed at: (a) all round development of the people in rural areas, and (b) people's participation in these programmes of rural reconstruction.

The Experience of Community Development

The experience of community development experiment through bureaucracy of the district produced mixed results. The Planning Commission came forward in a big way and the entire concept of community development and the administration of the programme were entrusted to a newly created agency called the community projects administration, located in the Planning Commission. This agency was raised to the status of a separate and independent ministry of community development in 1956. The same year the ministry was merged into the ministry of food and agriculture and continued there till 1974. The main functions of the department of community development were to lay down policy relating to this programme and formulate the plan of expenditure to be incurred in the blocks. The picture differed from state to state and block development and district development became controversial areas in administrative policy. The CD Ministry and its Secretary Mukerjee maintained that "community development was a roaring success and extension scheme should continue". At this time came the report of Balwant Rai Mehta Committee on the working of plan projects and programmes in the states. This 1957 report not only strongly refuted the claim of bureaucracy but maintained its following position in very strong words:

> So long we do not discover and create representative and democratic institution which will supply the local interest, supervision and care necessary to ensure that expenditure of money upon local objects conforming with the needs and wishes of the locality and invest it with adequate powers and assign to it appropriate finances, we will never be able to evoke local interest and excite local initiative in the field of development.

With these words, the Mehta Committee wrote the Magna Carta of rural folks of India who were to have a three-tier structure of local bodies at village, block and district levels under the scheme of democratic decentralisation. The Mehta Committee conceived the middle tier of panchayat samiti as an executive body and zila parishad as a coordinating and supervisory body with district collector as chairman of the zila parishad. All planning and development activities were to be entrusted to the elected representatives. The major recommendations of Balwant Rai can be summed up as under:

(a) A three-tier system of Panchayati Raj from the village to the district level with multi-level linkages be created. The institutions envisaged were zila parishad at the district level, panchayat samiti at the block level and gram panchayat at the village level.
(b) There should be a genuine transfer of power of these institutions.
(c) Adequate resources should be transferred to these bodies.
(d) All developmental schemes at these levels should be channelled through these PR institutions.
(e) The system of Panchayati Raj should facilitate further devolution and disposal of power, responsibilities and resources in the future.

Year	*Panchayats*	*Panchayat Samitis*	*Zila Parishads*
In 1975	2,19,892	3,863	210
In 1990	2,20,000	5,300	351
In 1992	2,26,108	5,736	457
In 2005	2,31,815	6,087	537

The National Development Council accepted these recommendations in January 1959 and desired flexible patterns to grow as per needs of the states. The credit goes to B.R. Mehta for legitimising the system and presenting a concrete and viable alternative to develop popular participation in development administration. The panchayati institutions were to groom rural leadership and could bring rural people to the main stream of national life. Given the opportunity, these institutions were going to develop democratic traditions and help in revitalising self-confidence and responsible citizenship in rural areas. The state governments were to initiate and monitor this change and the three-tier system acquired different institutional forms in the states of Rajasthan, Andhra Pradesh, Karnataka and Maharashtra. This phenomenal growth of PRI in the country since 1975 to 2005 speaks volumes about the dynamism of rural people of India.

The B.R. Mehta report entrusted three specific roles to Panchayati Raj bodies:

(1) To work as unit of rural local government.
(2) To serve as an instrument of community development.
(3) To act as an agency of state governments.

The experiment being unprecedented evoked a wide variety of patterns about (1) the core unit of development, (2) association of the collector, and (3) the area and size of the panchayat samiti. The Maharashtra Model made the president of zila parishad a virtual chief minister of the district, while the Rajasthan and the Karnataka models made block as the core unit and kept zila parishads as supervisory and coordinating units.

In Maharashtra, Gujarat, West Bengal and Karnataka the collector was kept out of the zila parishad while in Uttar Pradesh and Bihar, he was entitled to attend the meetings of the panchayat samiti and its standing committees but without a right to vote. In Assam, Punjab, and Rajasthan, the collector was a non-voting member of the zila parishad. In Tamil Nadu, he was the chairman of District Development Council as well as of the zila parishad and in Andhra Pradesh he was not only the member of the zila parishad but the chairman of all the standing committees.

From One Mehta to Other Mehta

The three-tier experiment of Panchayati Raj bodies encouraged research in this area and a number of committees skirted their findings around the block and district models in operation. Some of the study teams and committees appointed to examine the functioning of Panchayati Raj between 1960 to 1976 were the following:

1960	Rao Committee on Rationalisation of Panchayat Statistics
1961	Mishra Committee on Panchayat Cooperation
1961	Iswaran Committee on Panchayati Raj Administration
1962	Rajgopal Committee on Naya Panchayat
1963	Diwakar Committee on Position of Gram Sabha in PR Movement
1963	R. Krishanaya Committee on Budgeting and Accounting Procedures of PR Institutions
1963	K. Santhanam Committee on PR Finance
1965	K. Santhnan Committee on PR Election
1965	Khanna Committee on Audit and Accounts
1966	G. Ramchandran Committee on PR Training Centres
1969	Ramnathan Committee on Basic Land Reform and PRI
1972	Ramkrishanaya working group on Five-Year Plan on CD and PRI
1976	Daya Chaubey Committee on CD and Panchayati Raj

These committees helped in evolving the reform model on the basis of field experience of PR institutions. Meanwhile, the government at Centre got involved into a series of crises and Prime Minister Indira Gandhi having carved out a Bangladesh found herself trapped in National Emergency in 1975. The panchayati experiment was put on the sack burner and the post-emergency Janta government in 1977 drafted a second Mehta (this time Ashok Mehta) to do the surgery of ailing panchayati institutions which were mostly in a state of suspended animation. The Janta coalition wanted to explore the possibilities of reviving and strengthening Panchayati Raj and Ashok Mehta a veteran socialist and former Deputy Chairman of Planning Commission submitted his report in 1978.

This Ashok Mehta Committee prefaced its report containing 132 recommendations leading to a new approach towards Panchayati Raj. This new approach was to view Panchayati Raj as 'Government' in its own right at the grass-roots level. The report said, "the formulation of structural functions and the utilisation of financial, administrative and human resources in Panchayati Raj institutions should in our opinion be determined on the emerging financial necessity of management of rural developments." The Ashok Mehta Committee recommended:

(1) A two-tier structure of Panchayati Raj in place of the Balwant Rai Structure of three tiers. The district body to be the executive and the block or taluka bodies as viable operational units with a population of 15,000 to 20,000.
(2) The Nyaya Panchayats to be presided by a qualified judge and function as a separate unit.
(3) Open participation of political parties in Panchayati Raj affairs by contesting election on a party basis with reserved constituencies for Scheduled Castes and Scheduled Tribes and minimum of two reserved seats for women. The Panchayati Raj elections should be conducted

by the Chief Election Officer of the state in consultation with the Chief Election Commissioner.

(4) The zila parishad should be responsible for planning at the district level with compulsory powers of taxation to reduce their dependence on the state government.

(5) There should be an independent authority to carry out 'Social Audit' of the funds to check whether funds allocated for weaker sections are actually spent on them. A Social Justice Committee in each zila parishad should ensure that Panchayati Raj bodies function for the welfare of the weaker groups.

(6) The state government must not supersede Panchayati Raj institution on partisan grounds. If necessary there should be elections within six months.

(7) A minister for Panchayati Raj should hold charge of the Panchayati Raj department to look after the enactment of Panchayati Raj legislation; elections to Panchayati Raj institutions; promotion of audit of Panchayati Raj accounts; review of Panchayati Raj activities for report to the state legislature; and promotion of camp training of elected members of Panchayati Raj.

(8) Development functions should be transferred to the zila parishads and all development staff should work under the elected district body.

(9) The collector would continue to exercise the regulatory, revenue and other functions assigned by the state government.

(10) The voluntary agencies should mobilise people's support for Panchayati Raj and should be strengthened and encouraged to supplement the efforts of the Panchayati Raj institutions.

The chief ministers at their conference at New Delhi in May 1979 considered the committee's report and prepared a set of guidelines to draft a model bill. But the collapse of the Janta government at the centre put an end to further progress in this direction. Though the recommendations of the committee were not accepted by the Union government due to change in the ruling party still, some of these did exercise varying influence upon the working of Panchayati Raj. The states of Karnataka and Andhra Pradesh took special interest and a fair trial was given to Ashok Mehta model envisaged in the above recommendations.

From Rajiv to Rao

The period from 1978–1990 was the most tumultuous period when India was rocked by political turbulence, instability and assassinations of two prime ministers in succession. The political landscape changed drastically and Prime Minister Rajiv Gandhi was advised to revive Panchayati Raj institutions to take care of the non-Congress ruled states which were threatening to destabilise his sympathy vote bank. The C.H. Hanumantha Rao report came on District Planning in 1984. The Rao Committee suggested:

(1) Decentralised planning at district level.

(2) Separate district planning bodies under collector.

(3) Panchayati bodies should be associated with collector as coordinator.

(4) Development move function of Panchayati Raj rather than that of district administration.

Another significant area probed in the year 1985 was rural development and poverty alleviation. The Planning Commission appointed G.V.K. Rao Committee which examined the bureaucratisation of development administration. The Rao Committee recommended:

(1) District as the unit of planning.
(2) Planning of rural development by PRI.
(3) Decentralised planning by transfer of state planning functions.
(4) District development commissioner to be the chief executive.
(5) Regular elections of Panchayati Raj bodies.

While these explorations were going on Prime Minister was forced by political circumstances to revitalise democracy and development through Panchayati Raj. The CAARD (Committee on Administrative Arrangement for Rural Development) report or GVR Rao report paved the way for another committee for which Rajiv Gandhi selected L.M. Singhvi to be the chairman. Singhvi Committee of 1986 heralded the era of constitutionalisation of panchayati institutions. The Singhvi Committee recommended:

(1) A new chapter should be added in the Constitution to give Panchayati Raj an inviolable identity through regular fore and fair elections.
(2) Naya Panchayats for a cluster of villages.
(3) Gram Sabhas as embodiments of direct democracy.
(4) More financial resources for Panchayats.
(5) Judicial tribunals for election disputes or punishments like dissolution, etc.

The 64th Constitutional Amendment Bill incorporated the recommendations of Singhvi Committee. It was passed by Lok Sabha in August 1989 but the Rajya Sabha could not muster up the special majority. In fact, its provisions were later modified and put into the 73rd Amendment of 1992. The basic provisions of 64th Amendment were:

(1) it should be mandatory for all states to set up PRIs,
(2) the tenure of all panchayats would be five years and if dissolved before time, fresh elections should be held within six months,
(3) all seats (except a few meant for the representatives of other institutions) to be filled through direct elections,
(4) their elections should be conducted by the Chief Election Commissioner,
(5) due reservation of seats to be made for SC/ST and women in all PR bodies,
(6) PRIs to be entrusted with an increased range of functions such as minor irrigation, soil conservation, bio-gas, health, benefits to SC/ST, etc.,
(7) planning and budgeting systems be introduced in an appropriate manner at the panchayat level (Rajiv Gandhi emphasised this idea),
(8) the accounts of PRIs be audited by the Comptroller and Auditor-General of India.
(9) a separate commission be set up to review the finance of the PRIs, and
(10) the state legislature may authorise panchayats to levy taxes, duties, tolls and fees,

After Rajiv Gandhi's assassination, Prime Minister V.P. Singh continued the dialogue with the chief ministers. His cabinet formulated the 74th Amendment but it got delayed on account of the Congress Party coming to power under (late) P.V. Narsimha Rao as the New Prime Minister. This time it was presented as 73rd Amendment which Lok Sabha passed on December 6th, 1992 and Rajya Sabha on December 23rd, 1992. Seventeen state legislatures ratified it and the amendment could see the light of the day on April 24th 1993 on receiving presidential assent four days later.

Thus, a glorious and epoch making chapter was added by the 73rd and 74th Amendments. It fulfilled the gap which the Constituent Assembly left in the draft Constitution by being silent about district government at the grass roots.

The 73rd Constitutional Amendment, 1992

The Amendment Act has added part IX to the Constitution of India entitled as 'Panchayats'. The part consists of provisions from Article 243 to 243-0. A new schedule called as Eleventh Schedule lists 29 functional items that panchayats are supposed to deal with under Article 243-G. The basic provisions of the Act are divisible into compulsory provisions and voluntary arrangements. The provisions which the state statutes will have to provide for are:

(1) creation of a State Elections Commission to conduct elections to PRIs,
(2) in order to review the financial position of the PRIs, each state to set up a State Finance Commission for five years.
(3) tenure of PRIs fixed at five years and, if dissolved earlier, fresh elections to be held within six months,
(4) creation of a three-tier Panchayati Raj structure at the zila, block and village levels,
(5) the minimum age for contesting elections to PRIs to be 18 years,
(6) reservation for women in panchayats (chairman and members) up to one-third seats,
(7) reservation of seats for SC/ST in panchayats (chairman and members) in proportion to their population,
(8) indirect elections to the post of chairman at the intermediate and apex tiers,
(9) all posts at all levels (with two exceptions) to be filled by direct elections, and
(10) organisation of gram sabhas,

As local self-government is an item in the State List, the state governments have been given a reasonable discretion to take decisions in the following areas. These voluntary provisions vary from state to state:

(1) voting rights to MPs and MLAs in these bodies,
(2) reservation for backward classes,
(3) financial powers,
(4) autonomy of the panchayats, and
(5) devolution of powers to perform functions of the Eleventh Schedule and planning.

The Eleventh Schedule of the Act enumerates 29 subjects which fall in the purview of the panchayats. The Act has refrained from putting those into the Seventh Schedule of three lists for the simple reason that states are free to determine the Panchayati Raj activities and adjust this Eleventh Schedule as per situations and resources. The Schedule is quiet flexible and exhaustive. The PRI can make rules, regulations and administer them by creating services and charging tax, cess, octroi, etc., in lieu of these functional services. The Tenth Finance Commission suggested grants-in-aid for the local bodies from state exchequers to supplement their efforts. The panchayati institutions can take policy decisions in the areas like land reform, ecology preservation, rural industries and farming. The PR institutions have been accepted as the implementing agency of the state governments. The Eleventh Schedule lists the following 29 subjects:

Eleventh Schedule

(1) Agriculture including agricultural extension.
(2) Land improvement, implementation of land reforms, land consolidation and soil conservation.
(3) Minor irrigation, water management and watershed development.
(4) Animal husbandry, dairying and poultry.
(5) Fisheries.
(6) Social forestry and farm forestry.
(7) Minor forest produce.
(8) Small scale industries, including food-processing industries.
(9) Khadi, village and cottage industries.
(10) Rural housing.
(11) Drinking water.
(12) Fuel and fodder.
(13) Roads, culverts, bridges, ferries, waterways and other means of communication.
(14) Rural electrification, including distribution of electricity.
(15) Non-conventional energy sources.
(16) Poverty alleviation programme.
(17) Education including primary and secondary schools.
(18) Technical training and vocational education.
(19) Adult and non-formal education.
(20) Libraries.
(21) Cultural activities.
(22) Markets and fairs.
(23) Health and sanitation, including hospitals, primary health centres and dispensaries.
(24) Family welfare.
(25) Women and child development.
(26) Social welfare, including welfare of the handicapped and mentally retarded.
(27) Welfare of the weaker sections, and in particular, of the Scheduled Castes and the Scheduled Tribes.
(28) Public distribution system.
(29) Maintenance of community assets.

The pre-1992 situation about PRIs was chaotic. Most of the states did not bother about any uniform pattern. The partisan character of the state governments viewed Panchayati Raj politics in terms of their support structures or destabilising factors. In either case, they were apprehensive of Union governments intervention or opposition parties taking over Panchayati Raj bodies. The votaries of Panchayati Raj were states like Andhra Pradesh, Karnataka, Gujarat and Kerala. While other states like Rajasthan, West Bengal, Uttar Pradesh and Punjab became lukewarm and less enthusiastic about panchayat elections. States like Bihar, Haryana, Orissa and Jammu and Kashmir viewed the change with scepticism. Hence the Union government has to proceed with caution and the amendment was designed to develop and keep the consensus in basic areas of panchayati governance. The salient features of the 73rd Amendment can be presented as under:

The Gram Sabha

The act provides that a gram sabha will consist of persons registered in the electoral rolls of a village within the area of a panchayat at the village level. Thus, it is a village assembly consisting of all the registered voters in the area of the panchayat. It exercises such powers and performs such functions at the village level as the legislature of a state determines. The Balwant Rai Mehta Committee made no formal mention of the gram sabha but the gram sabha was existing as a statutory body in almost all the states. In states like Bihar, Orissa and Rajasthan, all the adult residents of a village or a group of villages are its members. The membership of a gram sabha ranges from 250 to 5,000 and it meets twice in a year. The sabha elects from among its members an executive committee and the sarpanch presides over the meetings. The budget, plans and programmes, audit reports and progress reports of panchayats are placed before this popular body. The Sadiq Ali Committee which reported about gram sabhas in Rajasthan in 1964, pointed out the following weaknesses in their working.

(1) Poor attendance, particularly of women.
(2) Absence of secretarial assistance, and
(3) Its meetings were not duly publicised.
(4) The illiteracy of villagers.
(5) The sarpanch avoided calling a meeting for fear of being questioned.
(6) Meetings were held during the harvest season.

The apathy and non-attendance of villagers in gram sabha meeting has been a major issue of criticism of PRIs. The Rajasthan state constituted G.L. Vyas Committee in 1973 to rectify this dysfunctionalism of the grass roots institution. The Vyas Committee suggested:

(1) Compulsory attendance for the sarpanch in meetings.
(2) Statutory recognition of gram sabha.
(3) The tehsildar, the naib tehsildaar and the village school teachers should encourage villagers to ask questions.
(4) The time of meetings to be May-June and January-December.
(5) Compulsory attendance of the patwari and VLW.

The activisation of gram sabha is a problem in all the states. Officials attribute it to the apathy of rural folks while villagers complain that meetings are manipulated and decisions are neither publically arrived at nor accountability is fixed. The 73rd Amendment has addressed itself to this ailment and has provided the following for activisation of this core institution.

(1) Public problems of the village will be discussed and beneficiaries of welfare programmes would be identified.
(2) The panchayat secretary will be the secretary of the sabha also.
(3) Two compulsory meetings otherwise the sarpanch will be asked to quit.
(4) The quorum of meetings will be one-tenth of the total.
(5) Assistance to panchayat in the execution of rural development schemes.
(6) Vigilance committee of the sabha will keep an eye on the panchayats.
(7) The budget and programmes of the panchayat will keep the suggestions of the sabha in view.
(8) A constitutional status to gram sabhas.

All this has improved the situation considerably. The research indicates that it is not the apathy, but the feeling that their will is being ignored, makes them absent in the meetings. Now as

National Rural Employment Guarantee Programme comes into operation, the panchayat/gram sabha secretary can not afford to take grama sabha meetings lightly. The community has to identify and certify the list of beneficiaries and this will generate sustained interest in the working of the gram sabha. Government aid for national disasters like floods, famine, quakes, etc., need rural support and people increasingly realised the relevance and importance of grama sabha participation.

The Three-Tier System

The Union government has prescribed a uniform three-tier system of panchayati institutions for a period of five years. The B.R. Mehta model remains the basic frame and the Act defined the institutions as under:

(1) Panchayat means an institution (by whatever name called) of self-government for rural areas.
(2) Village means a village specified by the governor by public notification to be a village for the purpose, and includes a group of villages so specified.
(3) Intermediate level means a level between the village and district levels specified by the governor's public notification for this purpose.
(4) District means a district in a state.

Thus, the Act brings about uniformity in the structure of Panchayati Raj throughout the country. However a state having a population not exceeding 20 lakhs may not constitute panchayats at the intermediate level. All the panchayati institutions are to be elected on the basis on adult suffrage but the chairpersons at all the three levels should be elected indirectly by and from among the elected members. But the state legislatures are free to revise this indirect election pattern.

The Act provides for the reservation of seats for Scheduled Castes and Scheduled Tribes in every panchayat (i.e., at all the three levels) in proportion of their population to the total population in the panchayat area. Further, the state legislature provides for the reservation of offices of chairpersons in the panchayat at the village or any other level for the SCs and STs. It further provides for the reservation of not less than one-third of the total number of seats for women (including the number of seats reserved for women belonging the SCs and STs). Further, not less than one-third of the total number of offices of chairpersons in the panchayats at each level are to be reserved for women.

The Act also authorises the legislature of a state to make any provision for reservation of seats in any panchayat or offices of chairperson in the panchayat at any level in favour of backward classes. The term of office is five years but a panchayat can be dissolved before the completion of its term. Further fresh election to constitute a panchayat should be completed (i) before the expiry of its duration of five years; or (ii) in case of dissolution before the expiry of a period of six months from the date of its dissolution. The Amendment Act prescribes the qualifications and disqualifications of members subject to revision by state legislatures. The Act says that person shall be disqualified for being chosen as for being a member of panchayat if he is so disqualified (i) under any law for the time being in force for the purposes of elections to the legislature of the state concerned, or (ii) under any law made by the state legislature. However, no person shall be disqualified on the ground that he is less than 25 years of age if he has attained the age of 21 years. All questions of disqualifications are referred to such authority as the state legislature determines.

The Two Commissions

The Parliament knew it for sure that elections will be the real arena of discord and problems may lead to crises and an early collapse of the system. The Act envisions an election commission in every state to ensure free and fair panchayati elections periodically. It was quite a challenging job to get elections conducted at the grass-roots level. The Election Commission of India could not be involved in it but a similar and uniform model on the lines of Election Commission of India should be workable over a period of time. The amendment is extra conscious of the sensitivities of the states and to keep them in good humour even the powers and the functions of these institutions have been envisaged in a vague manner with enough leeway for the state legislations to fill up the blank functions and powers.

The state legislature may endow the panchayats, with such authority as may be necessary to enable them to function as institutions of self-government. Such a scheme may maintain provisions for the devolution of powers and responsibilities upon panchayats at the appropriate level with respect to: (i) the preparation of plans; and (ii) the implementation of schemes for economic development and social justice as may be entrusted to them, including those in relation to the 29 matters listed in the Eleventh Schedule.

The state legislature may: (i) authorise a panchayat to levy, collect and appropriate taxes, duties, tolls and fees; (ii) assign to a panchayat taxes, duties, tolls and fees levied and collected by the state government; (iii) provide for making grants-in-aid to the panchayats from the Consolidated Fund of the state; and (iv) provide for constitution of funds for crediting all moneys of the panchayats.

The reformers were quite sanguine to the fact that states will be unenthusiastic to endow panchayati institutions with adequate resources and the experiment may crash in the want of funds. Political partisaness apart the development work in rural areas may keep these institutions starving for a long time and the local leadership may get exhausted and frustrated in the process of procuring resources. The Constitution provides for a finance commission for distribution of resources between the Centre and states. Here the resources were to be distributed between states and panchayati institutions with a possibility of federal grants-in-aid system. So the amendment makes a statutory provision for the state Finance Commission.

The governor of a state shall, after every five years, constitute a Finance Commission to review the financial position of the panchayats. It shall make the following recommendations to the governor:

(1) The principles which should govern:
   - The distribution between the state and the panchayats of the net proceeds of the taxes, duties, tolls and fees levied by the state.
   - The determination of taxes, duties, tolls and fees which may be assigned to the panchayats.
   - The grant-in-aid to the panchayats from the Consolidated Fund of the state.

(2) The measures needed to improve the financial position of the panchayats.

(3) Any other matter referred to the Finance Commission by the governor in the interests of sound finance of the panchayats.

The state legislature may provide for the composition of the commission, the required qualifications of the members and the manner of their selection. The governor shall place the recommendations of the commission along with the action taken report before the state legislature. The Central Finance Commissioner shall also suggest the measures to augment the Consolidated Fund of a state to supplement the resources of the panchayats in the states. The state legislature has to make provisions with respect to the maintenance of accounts by the panchayats and the auditing of such accounts. The 73rd Amendment applies on union territories also, subject to exceptions specified by the President of India. But it does not apply to the states of Nagaland, Meghalaya, Mizoram and Jammu & Kashmir for their special status and tribal council situations already in existence.

The Panchayat Tier

Although almost all states of the Indian Union have passed necessary Panchayat Acts, still the suggestion of ARC of having one panchayat for one village of about 2,000 residents is far from being implemented. Adult suffrage with social justice reservations is a great step forward yet the wide variety of patterns in the spectrum raise many eyebrows. The reservation of women in some states and disqualifying panchayat leaders on the birth of a third child or absence of supercession dissolution rules stand in the working of panchayats in their initial years of gestation. Some of these frailties are obvious and can be identified as under:

(1) An unhealthy electoral environment.
(2) Lack of proper state guidance specially that of the revenue and police authorities.
(3) Sarpanchs and especially husbands of female Sarpanchs dominate.
(4) Rules and procedures.
(5) Slow action against defaulters.
(6) Weak secretarial assistance.
(7) Poor financial resources.

The need, therefore, is to augment the resources and establish 'Gram Sachivalayas' as suggested by Shiv Charan Mathur panel of Administrative Reforms in Rajasthan. The district secretariats will give PRI a distinct identity and clarity of rules and procedures will make the institutions affective.

The Panchayat Samiti Tier

The panchayat samiti or the block level institution has been in great debate in the two Mehta Reports. As a key functionary, the BDO has been the centre of controversies. The variations in power role and even in nomenclature demanded a consensus. In pre-1994 situation, the panchayat samiti was known as:

(1) Mandal Panchayat in Karnataka
(2) Janpad Panchayat in Madhya Pradesh
(3) Panchayat Sangh in Tamil Nadu
(4) Taluka Panchayat in Gujarat
(5) Anchal Samiti in Arunachal Pradesh
(6) Kshetriya Samiti in J&K

The ARC suggested that the area of the block should be coterminous with that of a tehsil or a sub-division. The 73rd Amendment has introduced the necessary uniformity. The panchayat samiti today has two kinds of functions:

(1) Primary functions such as, drainage, roads, primary health centres and primary schools, cultural activities and health services, and
(2) Developmental functions which may include execution of development programmes, seeds and fertilizers distribution, conservation of soil, credit for agricultural purposes, irrigation facilities, forests, cattle and fodder improvement, cottage and small scale industries, etc.

To discharge these functions, the panchayat samiti can seek people's cooperation through functional committees. The BDO who is equivalent to the position of a SDO serves as the executive secretary of the samiti administration. The samiti can levy taxes, but the scarcity of resources is a perennial grievance.

The Zila Parishad Tier

Like panchayat samiti, the institution of zila parishad had variation as strong and weak zila parishads. Some status accepted it as the major unit of rural development. Others like Haryana, Madhya Pradesh and Orissa have underrated its importance and have even tried to abolish it. The names of the institution explain the nature of the models.

(1) Assam Mahakama Parishad
(2) Tamil Nadu District Development Council
(3) Andhra Pradesh Zila Praja Parishad
(4) Gujarat District Panchayat

Ending the diversity in composition which caused variations in roles, the new dispensation makes it a directly elected body of the people with a tenure of five years. Its functions and roles have been delineated by the act in specific terms. According to the statute, the zila parishads will:

(1) advise state government on matters relating to development in the district,
(2) coordinate development plans prepared by the panchayat samitis,
(3) coordinate the work of panchayat samitis, and
(4) advise the state government on the allocation of work to Panchayati Raj institutions.
(5) examine and approve the budget of panchayat samitis,
(6) distribute funds to various panchayat samitis,
(7) issue directions to panchayat samitis for efficient performance of their duties,
(8) inform the divisional commissioner and the district collector about irregularities in PRIs,

The chairman of the ZP, called as Zila Pramukh is an indirectly elected functionary but happens to be a member of the parishad. He is accountable to the zila parishad which can remove him by a vote of no-confidence. It is around this pivot, that the future pattern of Panchayati Raj will revolve in the states. The role of the collector vis-à-vis zila parishad is the key issue and his relationship with the District Rural Development Agency (DRDA) has already heralded the change. The Administrative Reforms Commission, in its report on state administration has recommended that "the developmental function should be transferred from the collector to the zila parishad and a whole-time senior officer be appointed as the chief executive officer of the zila parishad. This officer be designated as the district development officer and he should exercise supervisory control over the district level officers of various development departments and the technical and non-technical staff of the zila parishad. The district development officer should work under the leadership and guidance of the zila pramukh." The 73rd Amendment enables the legislatures of the states to endow panchayat bodies with the powers and responsibility to prepare plans for economic development and social justice. It will cause a steady increase in the developmental powers and functions of this apex body.

The Services without a Sachivalaya

The existing personnel system in Panchayati Raj administration is a mixed and open one which can be called a transitional arrangement till regular cadres of PR bodies are recruited by some qualified recruiting agency. The state officials who are working on deputation or whose services have been loaned cannot run the autonomous local government institutions and what has happened thus far is a story of continuous conflict between strong bureaucracy and weak democracy. The district collector and his team of SDOs or BDOs has to be kept out of the Panchayati Raj institution because their very presence as managers of development or captains of extensions officers team or administrative secretaries of elected bodies destroys the very spirit of democratic decentralisation. The experience of practically all the states of the country denotes that state level officers have their prejudices and even a petty village level worker treats the panchayat as a pocket borough for his depredations. Secretarial assistance or some sort of a gram sachivalaya is a necessity and the deputation arrangement should soon has to replaced by a regular cadre of Panchayati Raj administrators at every level. Naturally, the state level civil servants do not like this change and the solution lies in asking the State Public Service Commissions to screen state official for final absorption in Panchayati Raj service cadres – senior as well as junior.

The Financial Management of Panchayats

Presently the financial administration of all PR bodies is also run by state official on deputation. The VLW, the BDO and the secretary, zila parishads are acting as finance officers responsible for maintaining accounts books, records and registrars. The ARC anticipated a situation when panchayati institutions will be financially autonomous and viable. An independent system of panchayati accounting and panchayati audit is a precondition to run the system. The half-heartedness of state officials and lack of political will on the part of state leaders have created an anomalous situation because of which the inbuilt control of state officials over PRIs has rendered them ineffective. The present arrangement of personnel and budget management cannot be tenable and all kinds of controls through state bureaucracy have to be replaced by a new system of accountability and democratic working.

The institutional, administrative, financial and technical control of state government over Panchayati Raj bodies is inimical to the spirit of the 73rd Amendment. Even coordination by state authorities or institution will be far from the intention of the reformers. Like the 1919 dyarchy, the reserved half of district government is making a bid to foil the democratic working of the transferred half in the name of coordination through structural arrangements and common work procedures.

The Gestation Period

It is too early to evaluate the working of Panchayati Raj in India. A decade is hardly a time to appreciate the potentialities of the institutions suffering from teething troubles. The legacies of community development administration are not healthy. The district administration presents the entire experiment with a jaundiced eye. The prejudices have been rationalised to the extent that failures have been declared much before the launching of the reform. Research indicates that state level political leaders are the real villains of peace. They talk from housetops about the inevitability of decentralisation, but are extremely suspicious and nervous in parting with power. They see the erosion of their roots in panchayati elections. Once these institutions get roots the parachuting of state and national leaders will become difficult. So they keep talking about district development councils and the alibis that go with district developmental planning. The 73rd Amendment offers a big opportunity to create the third tier of parliamentary government in India's Federal Scheme, but the obstacles in place of being removed are being created by:

(1) MPs and MLAs of the states,
(2) Cabinet ministers in the states,
(3) Civil servants at each level, and
(4) Village leaders of caste, class and community who see threat to their established position in the change.

The Frailties of the System

Although panchayati elections in almost all the states have been a phenomenal operation and PR institutions have settled down to normal working without adequate resources and much-needed infrastructure. Still, the problem areas of the frail structure and their working can be identified as under:

(1) Poor local leadership based on narrow sectarian considerations of caste without much vision and far sight. The social justice class arising from reservations of varieties tends to push the real deserving outside the pale of power in the rat race for scrumbles.
(2) Financial crunch, partly because of the lack of state support and partly because of unwillingness of newly elected leaders to tax their voters.
(3) Women leadership through reservation at the grass-roots level, where their husbands and kins play a pernicious role because of the male dominant joint family system.
(4) Apathy of district administration to prove their indispensability and convince the common villager that their own local leaders are no match to urban educated outsiders.
(5) Partisan character of local elections which are neither factional nor programme based. The electoral system of higher bodies has criminalised local politics and politicised the petty crime.
(6) The malpractices in panchayat working go unpunished because of the lack of procedures and arbitrary punishment system has become operative in the discretionary pockets in the absence of traditions and clear-cut rules.
(7) Practically all the schemes of development and social welfare are routed to panchayati institutions through the district administration. It makes the former a second fiddle and the legitimacy of panchayati institutions has suffered in the process.
(8) In spite of all provisions of constitutional amendments, the states have been authorised to transfer powers, finance and responsibilities to the panchayats. The constitutional amendment leaves everything to the self-thinking of the states. But, the bitter truth is that the indifferent attitude of the states has been responsible for not giving a chance to develop democracy at the local level.

Therefore, the success of the constitutional amendment depends on the fact that how far the Centre and the states inspired by the public spirits, implement honestly the provisions.

(9) It is still feared that as the narrow politics of the vote has made the biggest democratic institutions of the country useless and bonded to rule, least the Panchayati Raj institutions should meet the same fate.

(10) Some critics are of the opinion that the new panchayat system is the same weak effort as was done to revive the panchayats by adding one directive to the Principle Directives of the Constitution. As per the 73rd Constitutional Amendment, the states have framed different rules to implement it. These provisions, perhaps, would make it obligatory for the states to hold panchayat elections and the economic basis of the panchayats would comparatively be more clear but these provisions would not give a much needed lease of life to the panchayats.

(11) There is no provision to establish "Nyaya Panchayats" or "Gram Nyayalayas" in the amendment. Giving concessions as per differences of the local groups of the state, the constitution and the jurisdiction of these village courts should have been clarified.

The Innovative Approach for 2020

The cumulative impact of all this has rendered the PRIs lame and defunct. They are begging for their due before the officials of the state. The coalition experiments at the Centre and the different political parties ruling the states, have created problems of hung legislatures, wherein panchayati pockets are seen with suspicion and scepticism. In the meantime, the rural world is metamorphosing under the impact of liberalisation and globalisation. The literacy rate has touched an all time high and connectivity revolution of mobile phones and computer internet is the rural market of the future. The mass media has already made in roads and the rural urban distinctions are disappearing fast in terms of development facilitations. The vested interests in *status quo* cannot fight this inevitability of change. But its speed can be accelerated if Panchayati Raj institutions are revamped with a vision. Innovative bold approach to rural governance can rebuild a 'Developed India' by 2020, if the following amendments or reforms are expedited in the panchayati experiment:

(1) The federal government initiates a massive programme of central aid to three selected districts from each state every year on a rational basis merging the MP and MLA funds in the federal aid programmes. If it is done, the scenario will be visibly changed by 2020.

(2) All district development planning is handed over to zila parishad committee co-opting experts and local participants which should involve private sector philanthropists and entrepreneurs to take up individual projects on BOOT or BOLT basis under the coordinational supervision of zila parishads. The district administration should totally be withdrawn from development projects.

(3) The financial resource allocation, though a responsibility of state finance commission, but it should be linked with National Finance Commission and one of the expert members from the National Finance Commission should take care of the quantum of grants-in-aid from the state.

(4) The state development service for PRIs should soon be constituted and the 'Gram Sachivalaya' on the pattern of state secretariat be created at district level to formulate and implement policies of zila parishads with a feedback from below.

(5) An office called as Panchayati Lokpal may be created in each state to hear complaints and ensure an objective implementation of rules and regulations including the suspension and supercession of elected bodies of Panchayati Raj. If it is deemed as expensive, the district and sessions judges may perform this job as an additional charge.

(6) A Gram Nayalaya as recommended in the Desai report of Law Commission may be established at panchayat samiti headquarters to take care of panchayati litigation with a right to appeal to the district and session judge and the High Court.
(7) Panchayati training programmes should be organised at district level and below. Trainers may go to panchayat headquarters and the state should look after 'Trainers' Training' and 'Research and Reform' on the basis of feedback reports from the trainees. Practical aspects of training on the spot should be emphasised.
(8) The state government along with experts from Union government should evaluate the achievements of PR institutions every fifth year after elections and instalmentally transfer more and more regulatory functions from the district administration.
(9) The experiment of district development committee with collector as secretary should be tried in those border areas where integrated development of the district includes the efforts of rural and urban local bodies.

Towards Panchayat Parliamentarianism

Needless to mention that panchayati experiments needs goodwill, courage and optimism on the part of all involved. In 1950, India did not deserve democracy but given the opportunity the countrymen have proved worthy of it. Rural India needs a second war of Indian independence against her own urban elites. The policies of liberalisation and privatisation have started creating the rural infrastructure. Now, there are only three alternatives left for rural governance:

(1) A district level three-tier of panchayati parliamentary democracy with a zila pramukh as a sort of district CM, alongwith a cabinet but without a governor. The modalities may differ and change with the passage of time.
(2) A merger model of district administration in Panchayati Raj governance in coming fifteen years as was envisaged in Digvijay Singh Model for Madhya Pradesh.
(3) Continuation of dyarchy and parallelism of regulatory and develop mental governments with clearer demarcations of jurisdictions.

A serious effort in this direction was made in 1999 when the Congress government of Chief Minister Digvijay Singh took the initiative and made a declaration for the adoption of district government in Madhya Pradesh. From district administration to district government was hailed as a big leap and a detailed legal plan of action was announced to introduce district government by expanding the District Committee System of 74th Amendment. It assigned a new role to the collector and one cabinet minister in charge of the district government to take the district government closer to the people. Originating from the Kanha Plan, the concept was debated at various levels and the institutional shape was envisaged through extended delegation of tasks, powers and responsibilities to the district committees and various kinds of sub-committees in different spheres of administrative activities at the level of the district and below. The idea was to make the dyarchy workable and push the transitional charge towards a positive institutionalisation of democracy at the grass roots. The Digvijay Singh Model as it is called, clarified relationships and exhibited confidence in the capability of the people, whose problems were to be resolved without shuttling between district headquarters and the state secretariat in the capital. The midway approach tried to satisfy all by reconciling the conflicting claims of panchayati leaders, district level bureaucracy and the people down below the line at the grass roots. The purpose was to create conditions conducive for change and the scheme was launched with usual fanfare and honest commitment. But then, it was a political decision and each political party viewed the entire transitional arrangement in terms of its own perspective and political spoils. The BJP government of Uma Bharti felt terribly concerned and even alarmed. She decided to abrogate. The Act and the whole talk of district government vanished with a whimper. The change of district government has to have political repercussions, but the political leaders of all political parties have to sit down to workout details under the leadership of the Union government.

The dyarchy that is being practised today is faulty in principle, faulty in planning and faulty in practice. It is unnatural, artificial and betrays confidence in people. At best it can be justified as a transitional measure, because the rural folks, who can take decisions about development cannot be called incompetent to control their policyless and the revenue administration of the collectorate. The second alternative of merging the district administration into panchayati democracy is being debated and several modalities are emerging. The collector can be the chief secretary of the district ruling set up. The elected political leaders may be trained for some time but the district bureaucracy should know it for sure that their days are numbered. There is no point in lengthening the travails of transition and creating bad blood or bitterness in the process. The parliamentary system of the third lowest tier should not be a copy of the central or state tiers. It will be a grass roots democracy with a difference at the district and then again at block and village levels. From gram sabha to Lok Sabha was a Jai Prakash model and Indianising India's rural democracy requires an optimistic dent in the district system. Debureaucratising rural governance and vesting popular representatives with power to shape their own destiny by 2020 will be the triumph of the second war of Indian Independence which aims to liberate rural India and replace district bureaucracy by parliamentary democracy.

Urban Local Self-Government in the District

The Patliputra of Mauryan age may be a romantic lore of Indian history but urbanisation as a phenomenon of social and political living is a legacy of the British Raj. Having settled down at sea ports, the East India Company unconsciously developed the rim land and the port towns for their sea faring commercial ventures. Calcutta, Madras and Bombay were the direct outcome of this policy. The spells of urbanisation and later industrialisation gave birth to urban centre, like Ahmedabad, Surat, Bhadonch, Coimbatore, Madurai and Paradweep. After independence, almost 30 per cent of country's population has migrated to big cities like Kanpur, Chandigarh, Bangalore, Hyderabad, Jaipur, Lucknow, Ranchi and Bhopal. The former cities have become metropolitan towns and new megalopolises are developing around as satellite metro centres of Delhi, Mumbai and Chennai. These urban centres are a part of the district system of government, yet their distinctiveness exits because of population, modes of employment, need of community services and facilitation infrastructures. They are absolutely different from the rural areas. Traditionally, a village has been defined as:

(1) A cluster of houses with a population of 10,000 or less.
(2) A social habitation where most of the people make their living by producing from the farms.

The Blurring Divide

In fact, an urban area is marked by the state government under law. Traditionally it is a poor place where most of the people live like a village family, sharing a common culture and traditional life patterns. As the concept of rural development alleviates rural poverty and means of communication provide connectivity and mobility, the rural urban divide is becoming blurred and untenable. The big and sprawling villages are emerging as towns and perhaps after a decade or two, the town culture will take over the rural culture. To arrest this mass migration from Agraria to Industria is one of the biggest challenges of development. The transitional phase is being cut short by programmes of mass literacy, rural electrification and women's empowerment. Naturally, the divide will remain for some time and a further divide may follow between metro cities and urban centres. The legacy of the British Raj in this field will provide the base but a new urban India in contrast to a panchayati rural India will develop on different lines.

The Historical Perspective

The 74th Amendment Act, 1992 represents the culmination of efforts that were going on in British India since 1687. The company and later on the Crown's government made some abortive attempts to streamline the urban system as it obtained under their rule. The following landmarks deserve mention:

1687 The Madras Corporation was born
1726 The Calcutta and Bombay Corporation were created
1870 Lord Mayo's resolution visualised financial devolution to local institutions
1882 Lord Ripon, the father of local staff government gave the Magna Carta of local self-government
1909 Hobhouse Commission on decentralisation brought local bodies in the limelight
1919 Local bodies were handed over to a responsible Indian minister under the dyarchical reforms in the provinces
1924 The British government got the Cantonment Act passed by central legislature
1935 Local self-government declared as a provincial subject under provincial autonomy

All this could not help urban local bodies to get their due. Except in metropolitan towns of Madras, Bombay and Calcutta, the municipalities and other urban local bodies were only notional in their working. The Constituent Assembly did not show any concern to local problems – rural as well as urban. It was as late as 1985 that the ministry of urban development was created. Even today, the defence ministry and home ministry are the nodal agencies that deal with cantonment boards, and the urban bodies in union territories respectively. Some of the landmarks of post-independence era reflect the casual concerns of Union government which appointed the following committees and commissions to examine urban local problems:

(1) Wittal Local Finance Enquiry Committee 1951
(2) John Mathai Taxation Enquiry Commission 1954
(3) Ahmad Committee on the Training of Municipal Employees 1965
(4) Jain Committee on Rural-Urban Relationship 1966
(5) Zakaria Committee of Ministers on Augmentation of Financial Resources of Urban bodies 1968
(6) Committee on Service Conditions of Municipal Employees 1968
(7) Gajpati Committee on Budgetary Reforms in Municipal Administration 1974
(8) Sahay Study Group on Constitution, Powers and Laws of Urban Local Bodies and Corporations 1982
(9) Correa National Commission on Urbanisation 1988

Today, legally speaking when India's urban population stands in the neighbourhood of 35 crores, i.e., around 33 per cent and above it is obligatory on every government to manage this transformation from rural to urban settlements. Several task forces on planning and development of towns and cities (1975), strategies of urban development (1982) and housing and urban development (1983) have made their recommendations. The concern of these study groups in varied areas has resulted in the creation of National Commission on Urbanisation (NCU). The commission examines issue and problems pertaining to urban management, spatial planning, resource allocation, urban housing, conservation, urban poverty, legal frameworks and information systems. The commission has recommended that: every town with a population of more than 50,000 be provided with an urban community development department, for the processing of development programmes. A National Urbanisation Council should be set up to formulate and implement urbanisation policies. For this the Ministry of Urban Development will have to be restructured and made a nodal ministry. An Indian Council for Citizen's Action can encourage citizens through voluntary effort. Consequently, the Ministry of Urban Development was set up in the Union government and urban development was shifted to the ministry of works and housing which was later renamed as the ministry of works, housing and urban development. Urban development was again shifted to the ministry of planning, works, housing and urban development in 1967 and a separate Ministry of Urban Development started functioning under a cabinet minister of Union government since 1985.

The 65th Amendment systematised the urban local reforms but it was lost in the Rajya Sabha. However, the basic provisions enshrined in this amendment were taken up by Narsimha Rao Government in 1992. The two houses of the Parliament and the requisite number of vidhan sabhas approved it and the President of India gave his assent to this 74th Constitutional Amendment Act of 1992 and it was placed on the statute book on June 1st 1993.

74th Amendment Act of 1992

This Act has added Part IX-A to the Constitution of India. It is entitled as 'The Municipalities' and has inserted provisions from Articles 243-P to 243-ZG. In addition, the Act has also added Twelfth Schedule to the Constitution. It contains 18 functional items of municipalities listed under Article 243-W. It gives constitutional status to the municipalities and has brought them under the purview of judicial review. In other words, the state governments are under a constitutional obligation to add this new system of municipalities in accordance with the provisions of the Act. The Act aims at revitalising and strengthening the urban governments so that they may function as effective units of local government.

The Municipal Government

The Act provides for the constitution of three kinds of municipalities in every state:

(1) Nagar panchayats for areas in transition from a rural area to an urban area.
(2) Municipal councils for smaller urban areas.
(3) Municipal corporation for larger urban areas.

A transitional area, a smaller urban area or a larger urban area means such areas as the governor may specify by public notification for this purpose with regard to (1) population density, (2) revenue and (3) percentage of employment in non-agricultural activities.

All the members of a municipality are elected directly by the people of the municipal area. For this purpose, each municipal area is divided into territorial constituencies to be known as wards. The state legislature provides the manner of election of the chairperson of a municipality. It may also provide the representation of persons having special knowledge or experience in municipal administration, the members of the Lok Sabha, the state legislative assembly, the Rajya Sabha and state legislative council and the chairpersons of committees. Ward committees shall be constituted consisting of one or more wards, within the territorial area of a municipality having population of three lakhs or more. The state legislature may make provision with respect to the composition and the territorial area of a wards committee and the manner in which the seats in a ward committee should be filled. It may also make provisions for the constitution of committees in addition to the wards committees.

The reservation of seats for the Scheduled Castes and the Scheduled Tribes in every municipality in proportion of their population to the total population in the municipal area has been provided by the statute. It also provides for the reservation of not less than one-third of the total number of seats for women including the number of seats reserved for women belonging to the SCs and the STs. The state legislature may provide for the manner of offices of chairpersons in the municipalities for the SCs, the STs and the women. It may also make any provision for the reservation of seats in any municipality or offices of chairpersons in municipalities in favour of backward classes. The term of office for every municipality is 5 years. However, it can be dissolved before the completion of its term. The fresh election to constitute a municipality have to be completed (i) before the expiry of its duration of five years; or (ii) in case of dissolution, before the expiry of a period of six months from the date of its dissolution. A person shall be disqualified for being chosen as or for being a member of a municipality if he is so disqualified under any law for the time being in force for the purposes of elections to the legislature of the state concerned; or under any law made by the state legislature. However, no person shall be disqualified on the ground of age if he has attained the age of 21 years. All questions of disqualifications shall be referred to such authority as the state legislature may determine.

The Election Commission of the state shall have the power of superintendence, direction and control of the preparation of electoral rolls and the conduct of all elections to the municipalities. The state legislature has been vested with the power to endow the municipalities with authority as may be necessary to enable them to function as institutions of self-government. The scheme may contain provisions for the devolution of powers and responsibilities with respect to the preparation of plans for development and social justice; and implementation of schemes, regarding 18 matters listed in the Twelfth Schedule. The state legislature can authorise a municipality to levy, collect and appropriate taxes, duties, tolls and fees, levied and collected by them or by the state government. It may provide for making grants-in-aid to the municipalities from the Consolidated Fund of the state; and provide for constitution of funds for crediting all moneys of the municipalities.

The Finance Commission with a term of five years is constituted by each state to review the financial position of panchayats and municipalities. It makes recommendations to the Governor about the principles which should govern the distribution between the state and the municipalities, the net proceeds of the taxes, duties, tolls and fees levied by the state, the determine of the taxes, duties, tolls and fees which may be assigned to the municipalities and the grants-in-aid to the municipalities from the Consolidated Fund of the state. The commission may recommend other matters referred by the Governor in the interests of sound finance of municipalities. The Central Finance Commission may also suggest the measures needed to augment the Consolidated Fund of a state to supplement the resources on the basis of the recommendations made by the Finance Commission of the state. The state legislature makes provisions with respect to the maintenance of accounts and the auditing of such accounts. The Act does not apply to the Scheduled Area and Tribal Areas (Article 244) and does not affect the functions and powers of the Darjeeling Gorkha Hill Council of West Bengal. The President may extend the provinces to union territories with exceptions.

Every state has to constitute a District Planning Committee to consolidate the plans prepared by panchayats and municipalities in the district, and to prepare a draft development plan for the district as a whole. The state legislature may make provision about the composition of such committees; and the manner of election of their members. The functions of these committees in relation to district planning is determined by the legislature of the states. Four-fifths of the members of a District Planning Committee are elected by the elected members of the district panchayats and municipalities in the district from amongst themselves. The representation of these members in the committee is in proportion to the ratio between the rural and urban population of the district. The DPC in preparing the Draft Development Plan, gives regard to matters of common interest between the panchayats and the municipalities' spatial planning; sharing of water and natural resources; development of infrastructure and environment conservation.

The plan so prepared by the DPC is sent to the state government by the chairperson of the committee. The Act also provides for the establishment of a Metropolitan Planning Committee to prepare a draft development plan. The metropolitan area should have a population of 10 lakhs or more encompassing one or more districts and/or two or more municipalities or panchayats as contiguous area. The state legislature may make provisions with respect to composition and representation in these committees and also their functions in relation to planning and coordination for metropolitan areas. The Act lays down that two-thirds of the members of a metropolitan planning committee have to be elected by the elected members of the municipalities and chairpersons of the panchayats in the metropolitan area from amongst themselves. The 74th Amendment states that the Metropolitan Planning Committee shall prepare a draft development plan for the area as a whole. Not less than two-thirds of the members of such committees are elected by and from amongst the elected members of the municipalities and chairpersons of the panchayats in the municipalities and the panchayats in that area. There were 23 metropolitan agglomerations in the country in 1993. The Draft Development Plan, takes account of local plans in the metropolitan area and the matters of common interest, hire spatial plans, water and resource, development, infrastructure and environmental conservation. The overall objectives and priorities set by the Government of India and the state government are organised in view of resources available.

Like the Eleventh Panchayati Raj Schedule, the 74th Amendment contains the Twelfth Schedule of municipal functions which are 18 in number. These basic urban functions are:

(1) Urban planning including town planning
(2) Regulation of land use and construction of buildings
(3) Planning for economic and social development
(4) Roads and bridges
(5) Water supply for domestic, industrial and commercial purposes
(6) Public health, sanitation, conservancy and solid waste management

(7) Fire services
(8) Urban forestry protection of the environment and promotion of ecological aspects
(9) Safeguarding the interests of weaker sections of society including the handicapped and mentally retarded
(10) Slum improvement and upgradation
(11) Urban poverty alleviation
(12) Provision of urban amenities and facilities such as parks, gardens, playgrounds
(13) Promotion of cultural, educational and aesthetic aspects
(14) Burials and burial grounds, cremations grounds and electric crematoriums
(15) Cattle ponds, prevention of cruelty to animals
(16) Vital statistics including registration of births and deaths
(17) Public amenities including street lighting, parking lots, bus stops and public conveniences
(18) Regulation of slaughter houses and tanneries.

The Variety of Urban Local Institution

A look on the items of the schedule indicates that the Act has taken care of a wide variety of subjects and areas where municipal planning and services will be needed in future. It preserves the existing structure of urban local bodies and has further provided for unifunctional local institutions for experimentation in big cities. The Act creates eight kinds of these urban local bodies for urban areas in states:

(1) Municipal Corporation
(2) Municipality
(3) Notified Area Committee
(4) Town Area Committee
(5) Cantonment Board
(6) Township
(7) Port Trust
(8) Special Purpose Agency

Municipal Corporations

The areas for different types of urban bodies are specified by the governor of the state on four counts:

(1) the number of residents,
(2) density of the population,
(3) revenue generated by the local body, and
(4) percentage of employment in non-agricultural activities.

A municipal corporation has a statutory status and is created by an Act of the state legislature or of the Parliament in case of a union territory. An act may exclusively set up a single corporation as the Madras City Corporation Act (1951). The other model is obtained in the U.P. Mahanagar Palika Adhiniyam, (1959) which was a general act for all the five KAVAL (Kanpur, Agra, Varanasi, Allahabad and Lucknow) cities. It exercises only those functions which are assigned to it by the state government. Headed by a Mayor its legislative and the executive wings are separate. The standing committees constitute the deliberative wing which takes decisions. The commissioner has the executive authority to enforcing these decisions.

Municipality

The municipalities are established for the administration of towns and smaller cities. Like the corporations, they are also set up in the states by the acts of the concerned state legislatures and in the union territory by the acts of Parliament of India. They are also known by other names like municipal council, municipal committee, municipal board, city municipality and the like.

Like a municipal corporation, a municipality also has three authorities namely the council, the standing committee and the chief executive officer. The composition of the council including the reservation of seats for SCs, STs and women is governed by the 74th Constitutional Amendment Act. The council is the deliberative and legislative wing of the municipality. The council is headed by a president/chairman who is assisted by a vice president/vice chairman. Like the mayor of a municipal corporation he plays a significant role and is the pivot of the municipal administration. The standing committees are created to facilitate the working of the council. They deal with public works, taxation, health and finance. The chief executive officer is appointed by the state government and is responsible for day to day administration.

Notified Area Committee

(1) A notified area committee is created for the administration of fast developing industrial towns, and (2) towns which do not yet fulfil all the conditions necessary for the constitution of a municipality, but which are otherwise considered important by the state government. Since it is established by a notification in the gazette it is called as notified area committee. It functions within the framework of the State Municipal Act but only those provisions of the Act apply to it which are notified in the government gazette. It may also be entrusted to exercise powers under any other act. Its powers are almost equivalent to those of a municipality. But unlike the municipality, all the members of a notified area committee including the chairman are nominated by the state government. Thus, it is neither an elected body nor a statutory body.

Town Area Committee

A town area committee is set up for the administration of a small town. It is a semi-municipal authority and is entrusted with a limited number of civic functions like drainage, roads, street lighting, conservancy. It is created by a separate act of a state legislature. Its composition, functions and other matters are governed by the same act. It may be wholly elected or wholly nominated by the state government or partly elected and partly nominated. The Rural-Urban Relationship Committee (1963–66) headed by A.P. Jain recommended that small town area committees should be merged with the Panchayati Raj Institutions to avoid multiplicity. MP and Haryana have done accordingly but UP still has a large number of them in the state.

Township

The steel plants at Rourkela, Bhilai and Jamshedpur, Bharat Heavy Electricals Limited near Bhopal and Hindustan Aeronautics near Bangalore have housing colonies for the staff and workers. The townships of Jugsalai and Adityapur near Jamshedpur are the examples of townships which are administered by the municipal corporation or council within whose boundary they fall. The corporation or council usually appoints a town administrator, who is assisted by technicians. The townships are planned and facilities like water, electricity, roads, drainage, markets, parks, etc. are provided. The expenditure on these services is shared by the industry located in the township.

Cantonment Board

A cantonment board offers municipal administration to civilian population in the cantonment area. It is a delimited area where the military forces are permanently stationed. The cantonment board are created under the Cantonment Act of 1924, enacted by the Central government. It works under the administrative control of the Defence Ministry of the Central government. Thus, unlike other types of urban local bodies a cantonment board is created and administered by the Central government. There are scores of cantonment boards in the country. They are grouped into three classes; Class I: Civilian population is more than 10,000; Class II: Civilian population is between 2,500 and 10,000; Class III: Civilian population is less than 2,500.

A cantonment board consists of partly elected and partly nominated members. The elected members hold office for a term of three years while the nominated members (i.e., *ex officio* members) continue so long as they hold the office in that station. The military officer commanding the station is the ex-officio president of the board and presides over its meetings. The vice-president of the board is elected by the elected members from amongst themselves for a term of three years. The Class I cantonment board consists of: a military officer commanding, an executive engineer, a health officer, a nominated first class magistrate, four military officers of the station, and seven members elected by the people of the cantonment area.

The functions performed by a cantonment board are similar to those of a municipality. These are statutorily categorised into obligatory functions and discretionary functions. The sources of income include both, tax revenue and non-tax revenue. The executive officer of the cantonment board is appointed by the President of India. He implements all the resolution and decisions of the board and its committees.

Port Trust

The port trusts are established in the port areas like Mumbai, Chennai, etc. for two purposes: one to manage and protect the ports; and two to provide civil amenities. A port trust is created by an Act of Parliament. It consists of both elected and nominated members. Its chairman is an official. Its civic functions are more or less similar to those of a municipality.

Special Purpose Agency

The municipal corporations, municipalities, notified area committees, town area committees, cantonment boards, townships and port trusts are area-based multipurpose agencies. The state government has the right to set up certain agencies to undertake designated activities or specific functions which legitimately belong to the domain of municipal corporations or municipalities or other local urban governments. These are function-based and not area-based. They are known as 'single purpose' or 'uni-purpose' or 'special purpose' agencies of 'functional' local bodies. Some such bodies are:

(1) Housing Boards
(2) Electricity Supply Boards
(3) Town Improvement Trusts
(4) City Transport Boards, and so on
(5) Water Supply and Sewerage Boards
(6) Pollution Control Boards
(7) Urban Development Authorities

These local bodies are established as statutory bodies by an act of state legislature or as departments by an executive resolution. They function as autonomous bodies and deal with the functions allotted to them independently of the local urban government, that is, municipal corporations or municipalities. They are not subordinate agencies of the local municipal bodies.

Nagar Panchayats

The Act also provides for setting up of nagar panchayats. They are constituted for a transitional phase and are basically rural in character. Hopefully they will develop urban characteristics over a period of time. Hence, this urban local body is supported to perform both rural and urban functions.

The Municipal Personnel

The 74 Amendment does not prescribe any pattern or the constitution of a new standing cadre for municipal services in urban areas. So different states have regulated the existing system which follows three specific types of personnel management: *Separate Personnel System* wherein each local body appoints, administers, and controls its own personnel. They are not transferable to other local bodies. It is the most widely prevalent system. This system upholds the principle of local autonomy and promotes undivided loyalty. In *Unified Personnel System* the state government appoints, administer and control the municipal personnel. In other words, statewide services (cadres) are created for all the urban bodies in the state. They are transferable between the local bodies in the state. This system is prevalent in Andhra Pradesh, Tamil Nadu, Uttar Pradesh, Rajasthan, Madhya Pradesh. Under the *Integrated Personnel System* the personnel of the state government and those of the local bodies form part of the same service. The municipal officials are the members of the state services and are transferable not only between the local bodies in the state but also between local bodies and departments of state government. Thus, there is no distinction between local civil services and state civil services. This ystem is prevalent in states like Orissa, Bihar, Karnataka, Punjab, and Haryana.

In most of the states senior positions – both administrative and technical, are filled by senior officers of the state service. Some may belong to the municipal service or may be deputed from other services to the local bodies. Under the mixed system certain posts are directly recruited on the basis of examinations conducted by Public Services Commission or the Municipal Service Selection Board. Certain posts are filled by promotion, for which, a selection committies may be set up. The lower grade officers are deputed by the state government to these bodies. The lower grade personnel and safai karamcharis are directly recruited by the urban bodies according to procedures specified.

Training is an urgent necessity to broaden the horizons of the municipal personnel and make them more responsive. There are five major training institutes in the country which are engaged in training at the induction level and in-service training in areas relating to municipal management, taxation, finance, functional areas, urban services, planning, housing, poverty alleviation, etc. These institutes are:

(1) All-India Institute of Local Self-Government (Bombay) constituted in 1927. It is a private registered society.
(2) Centre for Urban and Environmental Studies (New Delhi) set up in 1967 on the recommendation of Nur-ud-Din Ahmed Committee on Training of Municipal Employees (1963–1965)

(3) Regional Centres for Urban and Environmental Studies (Kolkata, Lucknow, Hyderabad and Mumbai) set up in 1968 on the recommendation of Nur-ud-Din Ahmed Committee on Training of Municipal Employees (1963–1965)
(4) National Institute of Urban Affairs, established in 1976
(5) Human Settlement Management Institute, established in 1985

The officers deputed to the urban bodies from the All India or the state services draw their pay in the scale in which they work. The officials of provincial municipal service, draw their salary according to fixed pay scales. Officers deputed by the Central and state governments continue under the disciplinary control of their respective governments and this also applies to officers of state municipal service.

Central Council of Local Government

The Central Council of Local Government was established in 1954 under Article 263 of the Constitution by an order of the President of India. Originally, it was known as the Central Council of Local Self-Government. However, the term 'self-government' was dropped and replaced by the term 'government' in the 1980s. Till 1958, it dealt with, urban as well as rural local governments, but after 1958 it has been dealing with matters of urban local government only. The council is an advisory body and consists of the minister for urban development in Union government and minister of local self-government in the states.

The State Control

Although, the Act ensures more autonomy than the pre-1992 situation, but the actual relationship of control over urban local bodies has not changed substantively except in case of corporations. The state director of local bodies and the department of local government in every state have not taken much initiative for devolution of powers or relaxation of control in this regard. This state control which is legislative, administrative, judicial and financial keeps urban municipal government quite subservient units of local administration rather than functioning as institutes of local self-government. As creatures of state laws the statues and notification prescribe their composition and functioning. The minister is accountable to state legislative for their lapses and they can be superceded or dissolved for a period of six months. The judiciary under the Indian Constitution is the guardian of citizen's rights and various kinds of writs can be issued to keep the local administration within their bounds.

The state governments approve municipal budget (except that of the corporation). Even the modified local tax structure needs government's prior approval and later ratification. The loans, borrowings and grants-in-aid even when monitored and regulated by state finance commission, the procedures regarding resources mobilisation and public expenditure confer little autonomy on the elected bodies. The accounting and audit system of the examiner of local fund accounts of the state exercises and financial control in a tight mould.

Worse still is the day-to-day administrative control in field operations. During the British days, this control was too tight and even after the 74th Constitutional Amendment Act it has not ended. There is no uniform single pattern of this administrative control of state, but it normally manifests in the following ways:

(1) Approval of bye-laws and rules framed by the municipal bodies and annulment of their resolutions.

(2) Inspections and direction to urban bodies.
(3) Submission of periodic reports to the state government.
(4) Appeal against arbitrary behaviour of the municipal body to the state government.
(5) The default power of the state governments to get local work done at local body's cost.
(6) Dissolution of the local body for a period of six months.
(7) Appointment, transfers, conditions of service and disciplinary action against municipal officials.

The 74th Amendment makes a material differences about the powers of supercession and dissolution of a local body. It states that in case of pre-mature dissolution:

(1) The state government will give to the municipality a reasonable opportunity for being heard
(2) Elections for constituting a new municipality will have to be completed within a period of six months
(3) A municipality so constituted after dissolution will continue only for the remainder of the period for which the dissolved municipality would have continued.

Now the state legislatures do not have the power to make amendments in any law which can result in supersession or dissolution of any municipality, before the expiration of its normal term of five years. It is a security against arbitrary action by the state government.

The Weak Resources

Urban local government have been pampers and beggars since their very inception. The reasons are not difficult to discover. The state governments are reluctant to part with the share which they think they shall not dole out to the undermining. Secondly, the local institutions refuse to tax their people because of the fear that irritated voters will throw them out in the next elections. The 1992 Act identified four specific sources of income of the urban local bodies in India as under:

- Grants-in-aid
- Loans
- Non-tax revenue
- Local taxation

Apparently, there are inbuilt limitations of these resources. The state governments, which are themselves in a state of insolvency insist on ad hoc and discretionary grants and the scientific principles of aid even when available or not acceptable. The loan proposals needs to be cleared by the Reserve Bank of India and heavy rate of interest and fixed time periods discourage it. Taxation income and non tax revenue through fees and fines are fluctuating assessment, realisation, seepage, erosion, cost of tax administration, corruption are varied reasons because of which the so-called municipal income, besides being meagre, degenerates into a source of popular extortion and exploitation by petty local functionaries. The account code, the audit system and procedural checks are too traditional to improve matters even in the age of computer. The new arrangement leaves much to be desired and the financial crunch continues to effect adversely the very nature of democratic decentralisation at the grass roots.

The Mounting Chaos

Like Panchayati Raj rural bodies, the state of affairs in urban municipal government are no better. Here the situation is worsening because the rural influx in town and cities is increasingly converted them in ghettos. The metro cities are bulging and their administration pertaining to civil amenities like water, sanitation, upkeep of roads, transport, housing, etc., is getting unmanageable with the result that crime syndicates and vice dens have made life unsafe and horrifying. Most of these problems emanate from ill planning but the dynamism of city management itself presents unprecedented problem of urban development and urban renewal in the context of space, ecology, urbanisation and science technology. Some of these problems of poor local management can be identified as under:

(1) Unplanned expansion without much care of master plans of development. The urban bodies have failed in their primary duty to check complications created by rapid urbanisation. The growth of slums, shortage of houses and traffic congestion pollutes the cities every where.

(2) Exclusive state control on traditional lines without adequate freedom and autonomy to operate in a decentralised manner.

(3) The administration of local taxes is ineffective. The urban authorities do not possess the required infrastructure to mobilise resources, take independent investment decisions and exercise a high degree of self-discipline. The system of accounting, as prescribed is not followed which leads to embezzlement, leakages and extensive under-assessment. The funds borrowed at a high rate of interest lie unutilised and action is not taken on the audit report on time.

(4) Urban life of anomie and a social living causes low level of popular participation and even apathy among people for their local institution.

(5) Acute shortage of space, funds and local services especially in the areas of housing, transport, education, health and entertainment because of which citizens are forced to commute from distant places and accept a dehumanised social existence.

(6) Poor local leadership without regular and frequent elections with the result that undesirable people are in the seats of power without reasonable accountability to the voter. The elected bodies are ineffective and the committee system has become dysfunctional.

(7) The municipal employees and officials are an immensely disgruntled lot, indisciplined and untrained to serve the people. The municipal bodies have failed to attract qualified and competent personnel. Gujarat made systematic efforts with financial assistance from the World Bank but without much success. Frequent strikes, corruption, favouralism, inefficiency, harassment of people characterise the local services.

(8) Although urban pockets suffer from a deeper malaise of economic exploitation and social discrimination, there is no government pressure to protect weaker sections of urban society. Women are more vulnerable to crime and the alcoholic culture of the city dominates. There is a constant outcry from the public as well as the government. The most basic necessity, water is not supplied properly, drainage facilities do not cover the entire city, unplanned colonies and slums develop fast, menace of stray cattle on the roads continues, traffic is hazardous, roads are not properly maintained and unsafe buildings are allowed to continue to exist despite the obvious threat to the inmates.

(9) Urban government increasingly need professional services of experts. In the name of democratic working, these services in metro or big cities are poorly managed and insanitary conditions threaten disease. Lack of rapid transit system gives nightmares. Single purpose local bodies have created a multiplicity of local units with overlapping jurisdictions. A multiplicity of agencies engaged in urban administration invariably leads to problems of co-ordination.

(10) The growth of unplanned sub-urban colonies around the city are breeding life patterns which are neither rural nor urban. The rich or affluent sections have moved to the sub-urban with their establishments in the downtown. The core city is dying and in the want of urban renewal the exodus from rural areas has rendered the old city into a mass slum without amenities. The growth of population and industries presents an unprecedented challenge of ecological degradation and pollution of water, air and land. The federal initiative in wenting and the states are too weak to come to the rescue of towns and metros. Due to an acute lack of civic consciousness, public participation in urban bodies has been negligible. Most of the city population was once rural but even now it looks at the city merely as a place to earn a livelihood without any civic involvement.

Looking Forward

Of course, there are no instant or short range solutions of urban problems. What is needed is constant awareness and timely strategy to combat the problems as and when they arrive. The 74th Act only offers a structure which should evolve plans, programmes and strategies to catalyse conditions of urban growth and human development. Some of the following measures can help:

(1) *The District Planning Committee* (DPC) and *the Metropolitan Planning Committee* (MPC) should meet more often and draw 'Master Plans' at regional, district and city levels. The Mega Plans, the Metro Plans and the Master Plans should be prepared with professional experts advise in a time bound manner and their coordination should be monitored on a quarterly basis by the union ministry. This exercise has to be given top priority and Parliament should be appraised about the decisions, accomplishments and handicaps. The zonal councils and other federal agencies should keep discussing these plans which should operate as under:
   - Mega plan (for regions) 100 years
   - Metro plan (for selected cities with a population of 20 lakhs and above) 50 years
   - Master plan (for emerging cities having a population of 10 lakhs to 25 lakhs) 25 years

   The councils should identify and map out the cities or metros of future. These plans should be in a state of constant revision as per availability of funds.

(2) With this *centralised planning* the municipal government *should decentralise* its operations in wards through various committees in collaboration with NGOs and agencies of the private/corporate sector. The municipal institutions should provide the core structure and nuclear services to which private contributions be made to improve the quality of sanitation, primary schooling, food services, transport facilities, etc. The concept of good governance needs to be operationalised in municipal bureaucracy and contract system needs to be encouraged on BOOT and BOLT basis.

(3) *State control over local bodies has to be minimal.* The 74 Amendments has strived to take away the state's right to punish local agencies by permanently superceding or dissolving them. Fresh election is a better solution and public accountability with increased awareness can improve functioning rather than state administrators inspecting or giving provisional or final approvals. Rules in this regard should be so framed that citizens can take resource to legal action and fair compensation.

(4) In the area of *finance*, the urban institution should be encouraged to collect service charges or municipalisation of local services. Bus services, hotels, entertainment centres may be owned by

local body or may be managed as a joint venture with corporate houses. The tax income should not be overemphasised. Indirect tax should be collected at source and people should pay in lieu of services like phone calls, cyber cafes, tolls on highways and toiletries at petrol pumps. The single function services may pay a part of their income to municipality and the Central and state governments should adopt some selective towns and cities for development rather paying grants-in-aids.

(5) A large part of local budget is spent on training ventures which do not yield results in commensurate to their investments. The training should be only in professional practical fields and the official should be weeded out if they get poor grades for performance in private training institutions. Each state can have one year diploma course in its state level training institute and the employee should serve the local body for minimum five years with some promotional incentive.

(6) The present system of registration and *grant giving to NGO* should be abandoned and a NGO should be eligible for 20 per cent of its budget grant as aid with an annual liability to submit audited accounts. Those NGOs who do not hold regular elections or are monopolised by individuals should be denied state grants. The share of state grants may increase in proportion to matching funds available in the budget of the NGO.

(7) The urban leadership has failed to inspire confidence among the people and once elected, they hardly visit their wards to learn about the gravity of the problems in their constituencies. Moreover the urban bodies do not have a proper public relations machinery, through which the achievements of the urban bodies can be communicated to the people. To ensure active participation of citizens. Senior groups, Neighbourhood Committees, or Citizens Committees may be set up to mitigate inconvenience in obtaining civic amenities. The exhausted people find it futile to look up to the urban bodies for any succour.

The present system has very few alternatives because the root problems exist at state and union levels. The population, industrial health and education policies of the union and state governments determine exodus and immigration patterns. The city government is a victim of ill-planning at higher levels. But this does not mean that the local government at city and metro levels cannot mitigate people's sufferings. Efficient and effective management has its role. It needs democratic direction but the availability of technological services or cybernetic facilities can be a long way to improve the quality of urban local services. The collaboration with private sector has shown results and the experiment should constantly be revised and improved in the light of newer experiences in the field.

From Dyarchy to Self-Government

The dyarchy in the districts of India is a transitional arrangement and shall ultimately yield a new pattern of local government quasi-rural and quasi-urban for a few decades. The twin revolutions of democratical change and technological facilitations have started knocking at the gates of rural and urban worlds of India. The divide is neither neat nor will it last in the present form. The panchayati democracy will revolutionise the bureaucratic governance of the district but the cities will advance towards international patterns of living with technological facilities. The democratic elections and democratic leaders of PRI will be groomed by the new system to create a self-governing rural polity wherein people will be more awakened and less and less poor. Because of population pressure on the farm sector India may never have the American spectacle of rich farmers concentrating in mechanised farming and flushing out the surplus chunk to a dozen metro or magloconglo morations. But then, towns of various sizes will grow within the district system of governance. These cities, towns and metros will experience the travails of technological and information revolutions. Twenty-first century is viewed as a Century of Asia wherein Japan, China and India will be partners in a venture of unprecedented consequence. The prophets of doom will have to admit that a more awakened and more affluent people will reproduce at a lower rate and once the rural population touches the minimum level of semi-urbanisation with extraordinary mobility the rural-urban divide will get blurred. The management patterns of local governments will cease to be rural and urban. Economic development and technological advances will eradicate social justice. Once women come somewhere near equality with newer spousal values of family, the Indian citizens around 2050 will not tolerate pseudo democratic or bureau-democratic alibis in their governance.

Hence, the three-tier parliamentary democracy is a wider vision of 22nd century India. The problem is not the direction but that of the speed. The Englishman in 1919 gave dyarchy with the hope that people will become more and more deserving and in 1950 the people were accepted as equal participants in parliamentary system at Centre and in the states. In 1993, this new dyarchical structure has been enacted for rural India and enforced at three levels of village, block and district. Apparently, the self-government in rural India seems like an advanced concept but two to three generations will make it a reality with universal education and mechanised farming. From dyarchy to self-government may acquire varied forms and even setbacks will come as was the case with Digvijay Singh Model of District Government. The imbalance between rural and urban India is a historical legacy and connectivity and communication revolutions are forcing the rulers at national and regional levels to accept parliamentary patterns at lower levels also. The so-called obstacles need a mind set, a dynamic leadership of initiative and vision. Once the take off comes and the speed becomes a little faster the transitional dyarchy will yield place to parliamentary institutions and their working will be more than welcome at the lower levels of district and below. Neighbourhoods will die and even sub-urban living will have local variations. Liberalisation, privatisation and globalisation, if they continue as policies for another 50 years the Euro-urban culture will develop and the techno-change will bring pressures on so-called rural democracy. This may bring a situation when urban centre of local government may need manager patterns of governments. The speed of change in India is so fast that past is no indicator of the future. Moreover democracy and technology cannot be reversed or wished away. The managers of dyarchy in the district should read the writings on the wall and accelerate the change to be in line with the developed countries of the world by the year 2020.

9

Civil Services in India

Public administration of a country has to be manned by public services which can be called civil services also if they constitute a professional body of officials – permanent, paid and skilled. This great body of men and women that the government has for its daily contacts with the rank and file in the country performs varied functions. It is a civil army of functionaries necessary for the realisation of the purposes for which government exists. Public service denotes a wider canvas and can encompass employees of public corporation and local bodies, while civil service in British sense is quite restrictive and excludes judges. All civil servants are public servants but the opposite is not necessarily acceptable to all students of personnel administration. Starting from man management to personnel administration, the studies in this area have come to human resource development (HRD). The narrow objectives of Weberian bureaucracy are being replaced by democratic participatory models of public service, wherein efficiency has given way to effectiveness or long-term result orientation for good governance.

The ancient Indian or medieval Mughal models of civil service were outrightly rejected by the British who initiated a new model of merit bureaucracy for their senior civil services in the colony. But this Weberian model has to be combined with a guardian and patronage bureaucracy which at lower levels was bound to degenerate into a cast bureaucracy of M. Marx's classification. The English rulers for sure knew the limitations of their model, but this was the 'least bad' for a colony which was too vast and had diverse groups without any national system of education. So the Indian Civil Service was gradually evolved from 1858 to 1947 on the base which the East India Company rulers built on the Mughal structure to extract colonial revenue along with some civilisational characters of liberalism. Started as covenanted and uncovenanted services of the company, the public services in later era became imperial/central provincial and subordinate services. The idea of 1935 Federation concretised the concept of all India services which happens to be unique characteristics of Indian civil service system. The 1909 and 1919 Constitutional Reforms articulated several innovations in the structure and working of civil services in India and the secretary of state for India continued to be a guardian of civil servants till the end of the British Raj. The salient features of Indian civil service system during these 90 years of Crown's rule can be identified as under:

(1) A three-tier service system, namely, (a) All India Services (b) Functional Central Services, and (c) Provincial Services.

(2) Generalist services to function as a support structure for the nascent parliamentary institutions of self-government.

(3) Elitist public services to ensure merit, efficiency and above all loyalty of the senior civil servants to the Raj.
(4) Political neutrality of meritorious civil servants, working anonymously and independently for the colonial power in the midst of a nationalist freedom struggle.
(5) Unaccountability to the people of India, who were not their sovereign masters. Public welfare was a secondary function, development works were conspicuous by their absence and the professed objective was association of Indians rather than serving the teeming minions.

Independence has radically and totally revised the philosophy, structure and objectives of civil service in India. It is a common sense clichés that civil services cannot rule free India. Today they will have to work with people's representatives. Their role in development and planned economy has to be varied and critical and they will have to be representative, accountable and professional. Their size has expanded and learning from British and American experiences they seems like an apology of the past. The political system has democratised itself but the administrative response to this change is still slow and halting. On the other hand, the pressure of work and the revolution of rising expectations have pushed the civil services into defensive. They accept their new tasks and roles but find themselves structurally and behaviourally handicapped to move faster. The following statistical facts speak volumes about the scenario that has materially changed all over the world:

1. The average annual increase of civil servants – 5.75 per cent
2. The total number of civil servant in UK

1797	16,000
1994	700,000

3. The total number of civil servants in USA

1789	300
1939	100,000

4. The total number of Central government employees in India

1948	14,45,050
1957	17,73,570
1971	29,82,000
1991	41,60,000

5. The total number of gazetted employees in 1994 – 1,40,000, i.e., 3.5 per cent
6. The total number of non-gazetted employees in 1994 – 34,00,000, i.e., 96 per cent
7. The total number of women employees in 1991 – 2,89,000, i.e., 7.58 per cent

Out of these 41.60 lakh employees (1991):

(a) The Railways employees were 16.5 lakh, i.e., 43.41 per cent.
(b) The Post and Telegraph employees were 5.2 lakh, i.e., 13.8 per cent.
(c) The Defence Services employees and others were 9.6 lakh, i.e., 23.07 per cent.

Even the classwise recruitment of public servants in class I, II, III and IV in 1971 and the corresponding increase in 1991 was striking.

(in lakhs)

		1971	1991
1.	Class I	0.34	0.89
2.	Class II	0.46	2.50
3.	Class III	15.45	16.50
4.	Class IV	13.47	17.50
	Total	29.62	38.60

Similarly this rise of two decades (1971–1991) in groups of employees can be seen as under:

(in lakhs)

Groups	*1971*	*1991*
1. Administrators	0.5	0.7
2. Technical Professionals	6.4	6.9
3. Clerks	17.9	18.5
4. Productive Workers	20.5	23.9

The Third Pay Commission classified the posts into group A, B, C and D and the Fourth Pay Commission supplied the pay basis for this classification. The A and B category personnel is called 'officer' which includes generalists as well as specialists. In 1984, out of every one hundred employees of Union government, 35 were D group employees, 61 were group C clerks and remaining four were in group A or group B kind of officers. Class III and class IV posts taken together accounted for 97.2 per cent of the total staff. Class I and class II posts formed about 1.2 and 1.6 per cent respectively of the total in 1971 as against 0.6 and 1.1 per cent respectively in 1957. The increase in the number of class I, class II and class III posts in all Central government departments taken together was 99.4 per cent, 73.5 per cent and 48.0 per cent respectively in 1984 over 1971. The additional posts at higher levels were thus created at a much faster rate than at lower levels. This resulted in progressively increasing share of the higher level posts in total employment. Of the total of 68,000 class I posts, as many as 31,825 were encadred in various organised services other than the three All India Services. The organised services showed a marked increase: the class I services including All India Services were 49 in 1984 as against 30 in 1971. Engineering personnel numbered about 10,000, i.e., 15 per cent of the total class I posts. The government no longer employs only generalists and clerks but it is increasingly employing specialists like scientists, doctors, engineers, psychiatrists, agronomists, meteorologists, economists, statisticians, jurists and educationists. According to the Third Central Pay Commission Report (1973), the technical and professional (engineers, doctors, scientists, etc.) services group of officials constituted 6.4 per cent of the total number of Central government employees. Their number increased and in 1984 the technical and professional personnel, such as engineers, doctors, scientists, etc., totalled 3,73,493 constituting 9.9 per cent of the entire public service population in the Central government. This expansion is an addition to that which has taken places in the autonomous scientific organisations financed by the government, such as the Council of Scientific and Industrial Research and Indian Council of Agricultural Research. The table explains the expansion:

		1946	1971
1.	Doctors	1948	6268
2.	Economists and Statisticians	1547	12238
3.	Teacher	1948	16576
4.	Scientific and Technological Personnel	1012	31983

The Changing Scenario

The ARC study team on personnel administration discovered, "The growth of the administrative apparatus, both in size and complexity has been the most notable feature of the contemporary administrative scene. Old units have expanded and numerous new units have been added in all tiers of government at the Centre, in the states, at local government levels and in quasi-government bodies. In March 1966, the entire public sector employed a total work force of 93.64 lakh people; or, in other words, one member of every tenth family in India found employment under government". Subsequently the ARC report on the machinery of the Government of India expressed concern about this growth and was shocked that there was "a disinclination among quite a number of ministers to welcome frank and impartial advice from the secretary or his aids and an inclination to judge him by his willingness to do what they wish him to do. This has also bred a tendency to attempt to anticipate the minister's wishes and proffer their advice accordingly". A further development of this trend has been the growing politicisation of civil servants, which came to surface during the years of Emergency. The ministers tend to make the officials their scapegoats for acts of omission and commission in their charge. This has adversely affected the morale of honest civil servants.

The traditional concept of civil servant in a parliamentary democracy has been that of the neutralist anonymous servant of the minister who should be constitutionally bound by convention to make his experience, judgement, and departmental knowledge confidentially available to his political master irrespective of his party affiliations. He was to accept and put into effect the minister's decisions. This neutrally of civil service implies: public confidence in the freedom of the civil service from political bias; minister's confidence in loyalty of civil servants; high morale based on confidence that promotions will come from merit alone. The role of the senior civil servants is to advise the political masters and to perform managerial functions. The administrator is required to defend the decisions which the minister has taken, because he participates in policy making process. Moreover, administration provides social services and is expected to promote development of human potential. A century ago the tasks of government were passive and regulatory but today they amount to a much pro active and positive engagement in human affairs.

The heart of administration according to Appleby is the management of programmes designed to serve general welfare. It is becoming increasingly involved in planning and measuring results, reviewing procedures and quantifying different courses of action. Today the administrator convasses support for governmental policies and seeks people's participation in the execution of these policies. The civil servant has to take initiative, evoke popular support and enthusiasm in their implementation. The political direction brings obligation of political accountability. The need for expert participation in plan formulation and implementation has been recognised in the planning process of India. The ARC found that public expectations have gone up and when they are either not fulfilled or ill-fulfilled, they resort to criticism of administration and exercise pressure. The people are unaware of the difficulties of administration and criticism of civil servants on the floors of the legislatures is frequent. The exasperated civil servants seek escape by evading responsibility. The political interference in administration is increasing and the government servant works in a political atmosphere; which adversely affects the morale of the public officials especially during period of political instability. In the changed context of India, it is not enough for the civil servant to be efficient, competent, anonymous, neutral and to possess managerial capacity and integrity but he must be a specialist and a professional with commitment to national goals. The old Trevelyan-Macaulay philosophy of the civil service which believed in the omni competence of the generalists is being challenged seriously even in Britain and the Fulton Committee (1968) has recommended professionalisation of civil service which should include skill in the job and adequate knowledge of the subject.

The Administrative Reforms Commission has called these specialised services as 'functional services' which are charged with a technical function for which a pre-entry vocational education is required, e.g., the engineering services and also services like the accounts, income tax and others for which no pre-entry vocational education is needed. According to ARC view each function needs specially trained and competent personnel who should, normally, specialise and stay within a particular career. The commission has argued that even a generalist service like the Indian Administrative Service should be regarded as a functional service, and its area should consist of "land revenue administration exercise of magisterial functions and regulatory work in the states in fields other than those looked after by other functional services". The traditional concept of anonymity and neutrality of the civil servant is also changing fast in the existing context. The commission warned that "to identify 'good management' in the civil service with indifference to the objects of management and unconcern with the social consequences of politics renders public administration barren and unimaginative". The role of civil services in the changing context of India is being identified as under:

(1) Protector and promoters of democratic working of the polity.
(2) Coordinator and regulator of new liberal policies in the context of globalisation and privatisation.
(3) Adviser in policy formulation.
(4) Executor of public policy laid down by the Parliament.
(5) Implementers of developmental programmes of public welfare and economic growth.
(6) Guardian of weaker sections in the ensurement of social justice policy.
(7) Defender and promoters of human rights.

These new roles cannot be fulfilled by a Weberian bureaucratic model of civil service which has developed inflation in cadres at all levels. The generalist model still refuses to concede parity and even functional autonomy to technical or specialist services. The merit basis of the model has been diluted by the policy of reservation of posts and sons of soil theory insisting for informal reservations. The senior positions have been removed from the preview of public service commissions and the selection posts are being created at top to bypass seniority of civil servants. The collapse of the Weber model demands a radical revision of Taylor model of hierarchical efficiency.

The Constitution of India under Articles 310, 311 and 312 lays down certain conditions of services whereby: (1) right type of efficient and honest incumbents may be recruited for public service (2) these civil servants have to live under a regime of discipline and it has been ensured that (3) they remain answerable before the courts of law. The President and Governor can make rules from time to time for their regulation subject to the judicial scrutiny of the courts. The tenure of public service (Article 310) and recruitment through independent Public Service Commission (Article 315) are two distinct features that characterise the Indian Civil Service System. India has inherited these features from UK where public service is at the pleasure of the Crown. Our Constitution also declares that anybody who holds a post (civil or military) under the Union or a state holds his office during the pleasure of the President or the Governor, as the case may be [Article 310 (1)]. It further implies that any government employee may be dismissed at any time and on any ground, without giving reason to any cause of action for wrongful dismissal, except where the dismissal is in contravention of the constitutional safeguards.

Discipline and Punishments

This right of the government to dismiss a government servant at its pleasure cannot be fettered by any contract if so contract made to this effect would be void. This rule is, however, subject to one exception specified in Article 310(2) namely that where government is obliged to secure the services of technical personnel or specialists, not belonging to the regular services. This pleasure has certain exceptions and limitations. The Indian Constitution lays down specific procedures as to how their service may be terminated. The Supreme Court judges, the Auditor General, the High Court judges and the Chief Election Commissioner shall not be removed from their offices except in the manner laid down in Articles 124, 148, 218, 324 respectively. These offices constitute exceptions to the general rule of tenure 'during pleasure' of government servants. Similarly, two procedural safeguards are provided for the security of tenure of 'civil' servants as distinguished from military personnel, namely, that:

(1) A civil servant shall not be dismissed or removed by any authority subordinate to that by which he was appointed. The object of this provision [Article 311(1)] is to save a public servant from the caprices of officers of inferior rank.
(2) The other security which is guaranteed by the Constitution is that no dismissal, removal or reduction in rank shall be ordered against a civil servant unless he has been given a reasonable opportunity of being heard in respect of the charges brought against him.

The authority must: (i) frame specific charges, (ii) intimate charges to the government servant concerned, (iii) give him an opportunity to answer charges, (iv) after considering his answers, take its decision, and (v) the rules of natural justice should be observed in coming to the finding against the accused. But no inquiry need be held where the employee is given sufficient opportunity to explain his conduct but he does not wilfully avail himself of that opportunity. This would not, however, apply where he fails to attend the inquiry owing to default of the government in allowing him subsistence allowance. The inquiry must be held and the opportunity to be heard must be given if the employee is a member of a civil service of the Union or an all India service or a civil service of a state or holds a civil post under the Union or a state and such an employee is sought to be dismissed, removed or reduced in rank. A person 'dismissed' is ineligible for re-employment under the government, but no such disqualification is attached to a person 'removed'. The elements which are common to dismissal and removal are that both the penalties are awarded on the ground that the conduct of the public servant is blameworthy or deficient in some respect and the situations entail penal consequences, such as the forfeiture of the right to salary, allowance or pension already acquired for past services. Termination in terms of the conditions of service is permissible if the conditions are not inconsistent with the provision of the Constitution. The department rules permit fixing an age for superannuation or compulsory retirement and enforcement thereof. Reduction in rank means the degradation in rank or directed by way of penalty. It involves reduction in the physical sense, meaning demotion by way of penalty. The government servant is reduced to a lower post or to a lower pay scale. Even reduction to a lower pay scale implies a reduction in rank, causing a loss of seniority in the gradation list of his substantive rank. About the penal nature of reduction, the judiciary applies the test of 'right to rank', in the same manner as 'right to post'. A government servant has a right to rank, hence the reduction from that rank is deemed as penalty. Thus, an officer who holds a permanent post in a substantive capacity, cannot be transferred to a lower post. But a person promoted to a higher post on an officiating basis, can be reverted to his substantive post. But even here the reversion order will amount to reduction in rank if it entails penal consequences.

The 42nd Constitution Amendment Act, 1976 pertaining to adjudication of disputes relating to the recruitment and conditions of service places it in the Administrative Tribunal for the Union or of states. According to this Administrative Tribunal Act, 1985 (as amended in 1986), the Central Administrative Tribunal adjudicates disputes and complaints with respect to the 'recruitment and conditions of service of persons appointed to public services and posts in connection with the affairs of the Union' except members of the defence forces, officers of the Supreme Court or High Courts and members of the secretarial staff of Parliament, or of legislatures of states. Excluding these categories, any public servant of' the Union who is aggrieved, in the matter of his appointment, removal or reduction in rank or the like, shall have to be contended with administrative justice by a tribunal instead of by a court of law. The only court to which the aggrieved person might run, as a last resort, is the Supreme Court. The decisions of the Administrative Tribunal can, therefore, be challenged only before the Supreme Court and the High Courts are not competent to interfere. The chapter entitled "Services under the Constitution" provides about setting up of All India Services and Public Service Commission at the Centre and in each state. This lays down the basic structure of civil service, which the Acts of Parliament and state legislatures administer. The Constituent Assembly debated the role of civil services in free India and Sardar Patel had a tough time in defending for whom the freedom fighter had little respect. In 1946, there were 10 all India services, 22 central services and a number of provincial services along with a jungle of public services in princely states. The European officers were given three options: (a) to return home on proportional pension, (b) to serve India, and (c) to choose Pakistan. The Muslim officers and the Hindu civil servants were adjusted but out of 1157 ICS British officers in the year 1947, 608 preferred to return home. After partition, this number dwindled to 451 and those who opted to serve India were just 33. By the year 1950 when Sardar Patel, completed the 'Integration Exercise', the problems of public services integration in newly formed B class states and merged states in the border provinces as well as reorganisation of services at par in big states like Mysore, Hyderabad, Travancore, Cochin, etc., became so complex that it took a decade to normalise. The structure of Provincial Services was recast to get linked with the all India services. Similarly, Princely services were categorised at par with state services and got merged and integrated in state services in terms of status and emoluments. It was a Herculean task of administrative reorganisation in general and civil service integration in particular. The All India Service Act was passed in the year 1951 and the Central and state services got reorganised by respective acts of the Parliament and state legislatures. The civil services in India were grouped under central services and state services, but the all India services were to serve both. Today there exist three all India services and 59 central services with varying pay scales. According to the Fifth Pay Commission the total strength of Central government employees was 38.76 lakhs in 1994 with a bulk of these employees belong to group D.

The All India Services are:

(1) Indian Administrative Service
(2) Indian Police Service
(3) Indian Forest Service

The rules and regulations that govern the conditions of these services are determined by the following acts of Indian Parliament:

(1) The Indian Administrative Service (Recruitment) Rules, 1954
(2) The Indian Administrative Service (Regulation of Seniority) Rules, 1954
(3) All India Services (Conduct) Rules, 1954 and 1968
(4) All India Services (Discipline and Appeal) Rules, 1954 and 1969
(5) All India Services (Leave) Rules, 1955
(6) All India Services (Provident Fund) Rules, 1955, and
(7) All India Services (Study Leave) Regulations, 1960

The central services are functional services governed by their respective cadre managing ministers and departments of the Government of India. It is also true that these central services are more all India than All India Services in their operations because they do not belong to any state. The Third Pay Commission grouped them into A, B, C and D categories, out of which 34 and 25 central services belong to Group A and B as under:

Central Services, Group A: These 34 services include Indian Foreign Service, Indian Äudit and Accounts Service, Indian Postal Service, Indian Post and Telegraphs Traffic Service, Indian Meteorological Service, Indian Revenue Service (Customs, Central Excise and Income Tax branches), Indian Frontier Administrative Service, Indian Statistical Service, Indian Economic Service, Central Engineering Service, Central Electrical Engineering Service, Central Engineering Services, Central Secretariat Service, Indian Information Service, Overseas Communication Service, Railway Inspectorate Services, Telegraph Engineering Service, Railway Personnel Service, etc.

Recruitment to all these services is made by UPSC:

Central Services, Group B: These 25 services include Central Secretariat Service (Section Officers Grade 2), Central Secretariat Service (Grade IV), Central Secretariat Stenographers Service, Grade I, Central Secretariat Stenographers Service (combined), Labour Officers Service, Group B, Central Health Service, Group B, Postal Superintendents Service, Group B, Post Masters Service, Telegraph Engineering and Wireless Service, Group B, Telegraph Traffic Service, Group B, Central Excise Service, Group B, Customs Appraisers Service, (Principal and Head Appraisers), Customs Appraisers Service, Group B, (Appraisers, Chief Inspectors and Inspectors), Income Tax Service, Group B, Geological Survey of India, Group B, Botanical Survey of India, Group B, Zoological Survey of India, Group B, Central Electrical Engineering Service, Group B, Central Engineering Service Group B, and Indian Salt Service, Group B.

Recruitment to these posts is also made by UPSC:

Central Services, Group C: They are a non-gazetted class category and include, Central Secretariat Clerical Service and Post and Telegraph Accounts Service. The Staff/Selection Commission makes recruitment to the group C services. The Commission is responsible for conducting competitive examinations for the posts of clerks, stenographers, senior accountants and inspectors. The day-to-day administration of these services rests with the individual ministries under which the posts exist. The ministry of personnel, public grievances and pensions and the ministry of finance are responsible for the management of all these services.

Central Services, Group D: This category consists of peons, gardeners, janitors, sweepers, etc. Their services are needed in all the departments.

The group C central services are non-gazetted class service and among others it includes (1) Central Secretariat Service, and (2) Post and Telegraph Accounts Service. In fact in ministries below A and B class gazetted officers are manned by junior functionaries to provide secretarial services of various kinds. The accounts service of post and telegraph service has a history and accounts keeping being too complex, this C class service has a distinctive character.

Central Secretariat Service

The Central Secretariat Service was created under the Central Secretariat Service (Reorganisation and Reinforcement) Scheme in 1948. Later the cadre of assistant secretary was abolished, and the service continued with four grades of under secretary class I, section officer class I, section officer class II non-gazetted, assistant class II non-gazetted. Grade III was created primarily as a kind of training post for direct recruits. The scheme allowed a free interchange of positions among the section officers of the two grades. The Second Pay Commission amalgamated the two grades into a continuous class II grade. There is also the addition of a new grade called the selection grade comprising deputy secretaries and above. The members of the Central Secretariat Service nowadays are appointed as directors and joint secretaries and their number is increasing. Deputy secretaries in the central secretariat service have been put in the select list for director's grade while deputy secretaries have been included in the select list for the post of joint secretaries. The selection grade joint secretaries are equivalent to the director and deputy secretary in the ministry while Grade I officers are at par with under secretary, section officer's grade and assistant's grade.

For the purpose of promotion to selection grade, a select list of officers of grade I is prepared. Similarly, appointment to grade I is made by promotion on the basis of merit of permanent officers of the section officer's grade having atleast ten years' service. Appointment to the section officer's grade is made partly by direct recruitment and partly by promotion. One-third of vacancies are normally filled through direct recruitment, the remaining by promoting assistants with eight years' minimum service, and by holding annually a limited departmental competitive examination. Assistants are appointed directly and through promotion in the ration of 3:1.

Evolution

The evolution of Indian Civil Services can be traced back to Company rule when the first classification was attempted as: (a) covenanted, and (b) uncovenanted public services A committee of the Halisbury College used to recruit officials through the institution of board of directors. It was the age of free booting, spoils system and patronage appointments.

In 1854, the Macaulay Committee on Indian Civil Services broadly created an Indian Civil Service for British graduates between 18 to 23 years. Competitive examinations were recommended for entry to constitute a 'Merit oriented career service which can bring loyalist, neutral and anonymous public servants to govern a colony of India's size'. In 1858, when Crown took over, the

Secretary of State for India became the guardian of Indian Civil Services and three issues emerged for discussion.

(1) What should be the age for ICS?
(2) Should executive and judicial services be separated?
(3) What kind of Indians should be associated with civil services and at what level?

From 1856 to 1885, the covenanted civil services were reorganised as a privileged services while uncovenanted civil services were informally earmarked for Anglo-Indians and Parsis. There was a marked difference in the two varieties, the latter being non-British and mostly for provincial administration. From 1886 to 1923, three Imperial Commissions were established to give a shape to the civil service system which inter alias recommended:

(1) Aichism Commission (1886)
  (i) Statutory civil services were abolished.
  (ii) Provincial civil services were started.
  (iii) The old covenanted and uncovenanted services were renamed as Imperial and Provincial Services.
(2) Islington Commission (1917)
  (i) Work-based organisation of services into first, second and third class services was recognised.
  (ii) The London based examinations were to be terminated.
  (iii) The new recruits were classified as:
    (a) Selected in London.
    (b) Selected in Europe.
    (c) Selected in India.
(3) Lee of Farnham Commission (1923)
  (i) Recommended political control over provincial civil services in the transferred field of dyarchy.
  (ii) All services were to be classified.
  (iii) A public service commission was to be established for recruitment to central and quasi-judicial services.
  (iv) Association of Indians was to be increased cadre-wise.
  (v) Better pay package and service conditions were to be created.

While Lee Commission was seized with the problem, the All India Services positions were allotted as under:

Name of Services	*Sanctioned Strength*	*Actual Number of Posts*
ICS	1,350	1,290
IP	732	739
IFS	399	348
IES	421	345
IAS	157	109
IVS	54	38
IFES	18	17
IMS	420	373
IES	728	716
Total	4,279	3,975

To increase participation of Indians in Imperial Services of the colony the Lee Commission recommended the following formula:

Services	*Indians (per cent)*	*European (per cent)*	*Promotion quota (per cent)*
ICS	40	40	20
IP	30	50	20
IFS	75	25	–
IES	45	33	22
IIS	40	40	20

Only those services or departments which were under the supreme government were named as central services. Railways, taxation, customs and excise and accounts and audit services, which were not a part of imperial services fell in this category. Several imperial services which had come to stay were given a nomenclature along with provincial services like Bombay Provincial Services and Madras Provincial Services, etc. After Montford Reforms the position in 1920 stood as under:

Name of All India Service	*Year of Establishment*
IFS	1862
IES	1892
IVS	1892
IMS	1897
IP	1905
IES	1906
ICS	1907

By 1935, when the Federal Public Service Commission and provincial PSCs were to recruit candidates it was quite clear that:

(1) Functional services should collect revenue and maintain peace to serve colonial interests, and
(2) The all India, central and provincial services should operate in an imperial way to meet the political and federal needs of the colony.

This situation continued till 1947 and when Englishmen left, there were 10 all India and 22 central services in the country.

All India Services

Legacies apart the All India Services in India even today represent a "steel frame which English Prime Minister Loyd George called impregnable for the safety and continuance of British rule in India". Notwithstanding radical and epoch making changes, the steel frame still performs the basic tasks of:

(1) Maintenance of law and order.
(2) Regulation of public services for national survival and development.
(3) National unification and nation building.
(4) Managing the federal polity through centralised union-state relations.

To these basic tasks a number of new responsibilities have been added such as:

(1) Social justice policy and welfare programme implementation.
(2) Induction of science technology and modernisation of administration.
(3) Institution building and support to democratic process.
(4) Regulation of liberalised and globalised economy of the country.

Although, there are three All India Services, Article 312 (1) of the Indian Constitution says that, if the Rajya Sabha declares by a resolution, supported by not less than two-thirds of the members present and voting, that it is necessary or expedient in the national interest to do so, Parliament may, by law provide for the creation of one or more of all India services – common to the Union and the states. In 1951, the Parliament enacted the All India Services Act. Article 314 of the Indian Constitution, provides for safeguards and privileges of the ICS officers who were appointed by the British Crown. In 1955, the State Reorganisation Commission recommended the creation of the Indian Service of Engineers, the Indian Forest Service (IFS) and the Indian Medical and Health Service. In 1961, the Rajya Sabha passed a resolution for the creation of the Indian Service of Engineers (Irrigation, Power, Buildings and Roads), the Indian Forest Service and the Indian Medical and Health Service and the All India Service Act, 1951 was amended. Though the Indian Forest Service was created on 1 July 1966, the other services could not see the light of the day. Article 312(1), (3) and (4) refer to Indian Judicial Service which when created would not include any post inferior to that of a district judge.

The All India Services are common to both the Central and state governments. Persons appointed to this service are allotted to different state cadres. The concept of these services is based on tenure system. Prior to 1947, there was no separate cadre for the central secretariat. Its officers were drawn from the provinces to whom the various all India services were attached. Such officers went back to their original provinces after a fixed stint of services in the central secretariat.

Thus, the All India Services like which no other public service functions in any federation of the world, has following distinguishing characteristics:

(1) They are recruited and trained by the union government like other central services and are then placed on the cadres of the state governments.
(2) Their recruitment, promotion and service conditions rules are made by union ministry of personnel (for IAS), ministry of home (for IPS) and ministry of environment (for IFS).
(3) The officers of the All India Services are borne on the cadres of states (preferably not the home state of the incumbent) but they keep moving to union ministries and agencies under tenure system.
(4) The pay, allowances and pension of these officers are paid from the respective state exchequers except for the period when they are on deputation to the Union government.
(5) The incumbents are under the disciplinary control of the state governments but the Union government has to be informed in case of suspension, arrest or inquiry.

This federal nature of this historic service contributes to the centralised functioning of Indian polity. Moreover, the dilution of merit through reservation policy and the sons of soil neglect in these services cause resentment. Still their relevance, rationale and utility are defended with vigour.

Arguments For

(1) The direct recruits to All India Services work away from their home-states and bring objectivity and impartiality to their jobs.
(2) They serve the Central as well as the state governments. While working at the Centre they gain grass roots experience of the district and while working at the state they take a wider view of reality, redesign state policy in tune with national needs.

(3) Their national perspective and interaction with international institutions facilitate a wider perspective and improves the quality of policy and decisional systems.
(4) During Presidential Rule in the states these officers act as representatives of Union governments and smoothen the transition.
(5) Their intellectual calibre is substantially high and coming from varied educational backgrounds, they bring in elements of rationality and innovation into the conduct of official business.
(6) These services build bridges between those two integral levels of the federal system.
(7) These services cherish a national vision and perspective and are important bulwarks against parochial and regional thinking. The members of these services act as instruments of national integration.
(8) The constitutional safeguards of security of service enable the officers of All India Services to give independent advice to their state political leaders.

To make them more effective even Justice Sarkaria Commission (1983–87) has recommended that:

(1) Three more new All India Services for health, education and engineering be created.
(2) A pool system of services for industry agriculture and cooperative may be helpful.
(3) An advisory council for the management of All India Service with Cabinet Secretary as chairman should be established.
(4) The state governments should be dissuaded to control and discipline all India services officers.
(5) A period of minimum service under Union government with new rules for promotee officers be enacted to ensure their dual role.
(6) Selection, training, placement, promotion policies of the services should be improved further, and
(7) Greater specialisation should be inducted in place of generalism in these services so that they may play the role which the Constitution assigns to them in parliamentary democracy and national development.

Still the other side of the coin has raised controversies of strong bureaucracy in a weak democracy. The logic of British neutrality and generalism in public services does not hold much water in the Indian context of a populist democracy. Even Dean Paul Appleby as early as 1954 found them "becoming a new class or caste, elitist in nature, a closed group resisting entry into its fold of others ever conscious of protecting its members anywhere and everywhere and the tendency to grab. The service not only denied entry of others but was even on the look out for grabbing new posts and positions like those of vice chancellors and registrars in the universities, headship of public undertakings and postings to plum posts abroad." Moreover, the service, on the whole, developed western culture and way of living. Yet this service has been retained because it helps the cause of national integration which is being promoted by strong means other than bureaucracy. The all India services are cashing the glamour of history without having illustrious members to their fold. Today their merit does not inspire a mission of nation building but the petty fights of loaves and fishes have rendered them as glorified positions of mere employment with privileges and amenities. They are an anachronism in a democracy and the caste class character of these services brings their so-called Weberianism to disrepute and abuse. Condemned as 'New Brahmins of India' belonging to an Indian Avtar Service the incumbents are losing. Their merit-legitimacy are 'Bureaucratising democratic politics by teaching the elected ministers to play collectors'. All sections of Indian society blame popular representatives for corruption and mismanagement but the all India services as their principal adviser cannot get away from the charge, that they have their share in the spoils.

Arguments Against

(1) The term 'All India' is a misnomer because for all intent purposes they are state services, less all-India than Railway or Income Tax Services.

(2) The tenure system has its negative overtones because the government at two level operates in different fields and unwanted state officials are pushed to Centre from where they do not return.

(3) The generalist nature of IAS has worked to the detriment of technical services and development of science and technology. Even the flight of talent abroad can be explained in the dominance of this service.

(4) As an elitist public service proud of its so-called talent, its incumbents are alienated and arrogant fighting among themselves or with their political bosses.

(5) Its political neutrality and independence is a myth and the political affiliations are so obvious when elections are declared and new governments assume office.

(6) The superiority and alienation of public service are a drag on democracy and people in the countryside cannot even discuss a glimpse of freedom when they see collectors and superintendents of police as VIPs with police guards on their gates.

(7) The dominant position of all India services has rendered the Central and state services inferior and the flow of talent has become hierarchical, consequently police, income tax, railways and communication services get the residue.

(8) The state services and their associations feel that they are bossed over by younger officials who are neither better nor different. Their promotion chances stand blocked because they cannot make lateral entries into the All India Services except by seniority and that too in very few cases.

The All India Services are incompatible with a federal system of government because they restrict state autonomy in several ways. States which are backward in the field of higher education tend to go un-represented or under represented in recruitment competition. The control over the service is dual and the Union government has the ultimate word in disciplinary matters. The loyalties of the services are divided and they tend to look up more to the Union for the protection of their interests which makes them suspect in the eyes of the state governments. Joint control has become impossible because different parties control the Centre and the states. The layering of the services is horizontal with little or no movement from the subordinate level to the middle level and superior services. The numbers of the all India services are far too few and they adversely effect the quality of the work of state services. The top levels of the services have generally tended to follow their political bosses. By and large, the all India services have collectively shown little enthusiasm for improvement in their standards of efficiency. They have also not been very receptive to new ideas and innovations. The preoccupation of the services with their careers, has militated against their achieving the level of efficiency. The adoption of the eighteen languages of the Eighth

Schedule of the Constitution as alternate media in the competitive examination for recruitment can only lead to the break-up of the unity of the service. The wide disparity between them and other public services breeds a sense of superiority in one and spirit of envy in the others. The exclusiveness and the casteist spirit of the All India Services and the treatment of other public services, even All India Technical Services by the generalist civil services has been the subject of bitter complaint. The widespread discontent among the technical services and their plea to be constituted, as all India services at par with the administrative services are largely the result of the attitude of the generalist administrative services towards them.

The creation of a hierarchy of rural local self-governing institutions, and the vast expansion in public employment have brought quantitative rather than a qualitative changes since independence. They have markedly added to the financial burdens. The greatest need in the state is to have highly qualified staff in the technical fields like engineering, agriculture, medical and veterinary services, small scale industries, higher education, economics and statistics. The general administrators are no substitute for these experts in specialist areas.

Although, the Indian Police Service and Indian Forest Service are not totally generalist, but Indian Administrative Service, in spite of several reorganisations remain a hundred per cent generalist service in cameralist sense. Kothari Report having allowed the doctors, engineers and agronomists to compete for this generalist service, opened it to the technocrat or the specialist but the fact remains that the specialist engineer can become agriculture secretary and a medical graduate after a decade or so may adorn the finance secretaryship in the government. The controversy has generated enough heat, hostility and extended arguments while it is essentially a battle for plan posts and domination. From Foulton to ARC, the reports meticulously argue for their cause but the fight remains a political confrontation of trade unions, the devils quoting scriptures to prove legitimacy of their historical control or future dominance.

Neither Lord Maculay used the term 'generalist' nor Foulton implied a scientist administrator by the term 'specialist'. The European tradition of cameralism precedes generalism which comes close to Plato philosopher king, or pursuit of excellence wherein knowledge leads to a life of virtue. But ARC uses this term for a general-purpose service like IAS, whose members serve on varied posts in different functional areas. In contrast, the specialists work in their specific fields of specialisation. ARC identified these services as 'Functional Services', which have a technical function for which a pre-entry vocational training was required and specialised post entry training helped in grooming excellence. The references of civil services of UK, Canada, Russia or France do not serve any purpose because they never had any elitist or feudal public service as a colony of a foreign power. India inherited the generalist tradition of ICS, but if these illustrious predecessors like Metcalf or Woodruft who ruled India are made development officers or communication advisor or medical and agriculture directors today, they will be the first to resign and shall refuse to control their technical colleagues whose specialities they should respect. The post-war era of science and technology is simply incomparable with the kind of administration and society found all over the world yet the debate goes on to brain wash politicians and administrators. In the Indian parlance, a generalist administrator is one who:

(1) Works in that or those branches of administration for which he did not have any formal training at the university.

(2) Is extraordinarily brilliant and wants to pursue excellence through devoted pursuits.

(3) Learns from field experience only and has the capacity to transfer his talent to any task assigned.
(4) Can work with political representatives and advise them in policy making much against their vested interests.
(5) Can coordinate the implementation of policies and work with people by his liberal outlook and catholicity of education.
(6) Can lead a life of virtue and perfect integrity because of his intellectual enlightenment and academic disposition.

In contrast to this, a specialist in Indian administration means a public servant who possess a professional or service degree and opts for a bureaucratic career in administration. As developmental activities expand in governmental field the doctors, engineers, agronomists, scientific researchers, chemists, botanist, horticulturists and foresters have flooded the government service. These technical services are attracting talent and are engaged in field activities of economic development and social welfare. The Foulton Committee in UK regretted that this welcome phenomenon is not well received by generalist administrators and the specialist class are not given full responsibility and opportunities nor the corresponding authority. The debate is dubbed as puerile, yet the case for both needs to be understood and appreciated in the context of Indian democracy and development.

Arguments in Favour of Generalism

(1) In a parliamentary democracy, the doctrine of ministerial responsibility make administration responsible to Parliament and a generalist policy adviser alone fits on this pattern.
(2) The cameralist generalist administrator is a better coordinator which is the heart of administration at secretariat level.
(3) The generalist can afford to be detached to his own department and can take a long range and holistic of sustainable public policy.
(4) As a mediator, arbiter and implementer the generalist is capable to cultivate the virtue of discipline of logic for reasonable success of functions.
(5) His intellectual disposition and mental brilliance has a social relevance and if genuine, he is bound to have honesty and integrity.

The qualities of head make the qualities of heart and a generalist scholarly person can afford to be appreciative of differing points of view of different political leaders in a democracy.

But this does not mean that specialist do not have or cannot cultivate these virtues by training.

The Case for Specialism

(1) If democracy needs a policy adviser of calibre, development implies a kind of policy input which no generalist is capable to offer.
(2) Administration of science and technology is the key area and its creative policies can change the shape of future society. So if generalism was past, specialism is the future of administrative and humanity.
(3) All arguments comparing the capabilities of two are prejudiced and based on false premises of organisational behaviour.

(4) The disparity in pay packets, promotional avenues and power status has demoralised scientists, causing a disastrous brain drain.
(5) Merit is equitably distributed in all services and those who pursue science as a career should be an object of envy for all IAS officers.
(6) The specialist technocrats like Bhabha, Kothari, Chilliah, Swaminathan, Sethena, Pitroda whenever given opportunity worked wonders in administration which falsifies the monopolistic claims of the generalists.
(7) Placing specialists in subordinate offices or directorates in states is highly insulting and a waste of their talent.

The false dichotomy and its perpetuation by vested interests has lowered the political ethics of the nation. The sheer and vulgar fight for privileged positions represents the scrumble for power so apparently visible to all.

The Irritants

(1) The generalists dominate the areas of development finance and technology.
(2) Generalists tend to undervalue the advice of specialists.
(3) The mobility of specialists is relatively restricted in interorganisational sense.
(4) Top policy positions are denied to specialists.
(5) The generalists treat the specialists as 'subordinates' in place of colleagues.
(6) The specialists have less proximity to the political masters as compared to the generalists.
(7) Promotion channels for specialists are not as fast as those of generalists.
(8) The work of specialists is assessed by generalists who lack technical competence and work experience to evaluate.
(9) Pay and service conditions of specialists are less attractive than those of the generalists.
(10) The proposals of the senior level specialists are questioned and turned down by 'amateur' generalists.

When all this is being recognised at all levels, the political system does not respond to this anomalous situation of civil service history. Pakistan had a similar legacy but a President, (late) Z.A. Bhutto showed courage and statesmanship to make a new experiment in August, 1973. This fundamental change in the structure of former ICS of Pakistan is worth emulation.

The Unified Civil Service of Pakistan

(1) All classes among the public personnel have been abolished and replaced by a unified grading structure; a peon at the bottom, and a secretary or departmental head at the top. In all, a unified 22-grade pay scale has been introduced, thus doing away with the more than 600 salary scales which were in operation.
(2) All the services and cadres have been merged into a unified grading structure with equality of opportunity for all who enter the service at any state-based on the required professional and specialised competence necessary for each job.
(3) There is provision for lateral entry to government services.
(4) The unified structure of the civil service enables promotions to higher posts throughout the range of the public service and for horizontal movements from one cadre to another including the movement of technical personnel to the cadre of general management.
(5) The correct grading of each post is determined by job evaluation.

This Pakistan Civil Services Reform of 1973 makes a historical landmark in the administrative annals of the Indian subcontinent. A radically new public personnel system has been designed and put into operation in Pakistan. It has enabled engineers, doctors, scientists and other technical specialist staff to be drawn into the stream of higher management from which they were barred thus far. As the direct result of these reforms, the road to top management opened up to all scientific and technical personnel. Bangladesh too has adopted a unified civil service while Indians keep calling it 'Radicalism misplaced'. The reform process in India still skirts around ideas like:

(1) Closer interaction between minister and specialists,
(2) Joint hierarchy,
(3) Parallel hierarchies,
(4) Integrated unified hierarchy, and
(5) Separate hierarchies with party.

The Eight Kinds of Functional IAS

All these reforms are suggested as palliatives – a midway which may not dislodge the single generalist service from the position of power dominance and its proximity to centre of political power. The ARC tried to catch the bull by the horn and suggested that a functional field must be carved out for the IAS. This could consist of land reforms, administration, exercise of magisterial functions and regulatory work in the states in the fields other than those looked after by other functional services. The senior managerial positions should be manned from the functional services and non-functional personnel should be inducted through a mid-career competitive examination. These new incumbents should obtain technical knowledge and work experience. The eight areas of specialisation are:

(1) Economic Administration
(2) Industrial Administration
(3) Agriculture and Rural Development Administration
(4) Social and Educational Administration
(5) Personnel Administration
(6) Financial Administration
(7) Defence Administration and Internal Security
(8) Planning

Placement in these areas will be made on the basis of qualifications and previous background of the incumbent. The ARC suggested that the competitive examinations should include a written test, an interview and an assessment of the candidate's previous record. The test, besides being academic should evaluate:

(1) communication skill,
(2) clarity of thought,
(3) management ability,
(4) power of analysis, and
(5) comprehension of current affairs.

The test should not put the generalist and the specialist to any disadvantage. The ARC believed that it would promote functional specialisation but the recommendation was pigeon holed by a committee of secretaries constituted by the government. Functionalisation as a precondition for professionalisation was a radical dent which aimed to reduce generalist hegemony of a particular service.

The Pay Commissions Palliatives

Several other workable solutions have been spelled out by the Pay Commissions without disturbing the existing structure. Some of them are:

(1) Pay parity and equalisation of service conditions and benefits including promotional avenues in their respective cadres.
(2) Unified hierarchies under single heads with a unified grading structure as suggested by Foulton Committee in Britain.
(3) Joint training programmes for senior officials in generalist and specialist hierarchies.
(4) The policy making positions should be open for both the kinds of officials and they should have an equal and open access to the minister or the executive to present his point of view.
(5) Specialised mid-career training to generalists in functional specialists and to specialists in generalised administration.

All these alternatives are nowhere close to the objectives which ARC had as its reform package. In practice, the ethos will breed bitterness because of the casteist attitudes of civil services, which just cannot be changed by mere wishing away, or using the word 'should'. Attitudinal changes do not come through training. They are rather reinforced as cold wars on training campuses which are headed by generalists. The structural changes generate attitudinal changes and the vice versa seems like a strategy to postpone basic reforms which sometime when become inevitable are killed through piecemeal reform strategies.

The net result of all this has been the Kothari recommendations which allowed the specialists like doctors and engineers to enter into generalist All India Service by offering medical and engineering subjects in recruitment examination. It has made things worse and when Satish Chandra was asked to review the situation after a decade in 1989, he found that engineers are flooding the police and administrative services in the name of a so-called merit through an examination. The Satish Chandra Committee found it correct that doctors and engineers compete for the higher civil services. They should be free to take their chances alongwith graduates in other disciplines and their performance in All India and Central Services has been satisfactory.

This generalist specialist controversy in Indian administration has been overplayed and its results have been disastrous for democracy as well as development. Professionalism is the future of all public services and Foulton or no Foulton on the truth has to be admitted. Much of the past has lost its meaning in India. The princely rulers and feudal lords had their justifications in their times but a 21st century India has to look to the future. As the system of man education in India is out of joints and problems of regionalism, social justice, gender parity and panchayati development rock the political system, the best products of liberal education cannot hold the fort. The coming decades of liberalisation and globalisation will not only take an advise of merit but push the failed administrators into pits of corruption playing second fiddle to the political rulers. Well groomed knowledgeable strong proportionate is the only way out to build strong bulwarks of bureaucracy against the degenerating politics of social system.

The civil service structure in India has four levels:

(1) All India services
(2) Central services
(3) State services
(4) Local or municipal services

The All India Services are only three and they have three categories:

(1) Super timescale,
(2) Senior scale, and
(3) Junior scale.

The Central services are functional in group A and group B. Group C services are recruited by the selection commission while group D are recruited by respective ministries and departments.

The state services have their dozens of cadres and categories as senior and subordinate services. They administer state subjects and are recruited by state public service commissions established under statutory provisions of Indian Constitution. The state services work under the overall control of All India Services and a small quota of services from these services is promoted to All India Service as per rules made in this regard.

The local and municipal service in all the states is in a state of unorganised chaos. Some states have constituted local services; most of them are working with borrowed state or all India personnel on deputation. The panchayati services are yet to be constituted in general special fields of functional activities.

The Recruitment

The entire cadre strength of All India Service officers is recruited in the services through:

(1) direct recruitment through combined competitive examination,
(2) promotion from members of the state services.
(3) special selections, from among certain gazetted posts under the state governments and or from among the released Emergency Commissioned Officers and Short Service Commissioned Officers, through a limited competitive examination.

The All India Services Act of 1951 specifies that senior positions, not exceeding 33.33 per cent in IAS and IPS will be filled by promotion of officers employed in Senior State Services. Every state has to constitute a Special Selection Committee for this purpose. In practice, this committee is chaired by a member of UPSC with Chief Secretary, DG (Police) and some others as members.

The bulk of the IAS and IPS officers are recruited through open competitive examinations conducted by the UPSC. The selection to the senior posts is geared to the task of locating the likely administrator who has awareness and potential to perform with competence. This Maculay system, besides being dysfunctional was found out of date and inadequate to run the administration of a maturing democracy in 1970. The reform process has its upshot in:

(1) Kothari Committee Report,
(2) Satish Chandra Committee Report,
(3) Yogendra Alagh Committee Report, and
(4) Hota Committee Report (under consideration of government).

The recommendations of these committees on recruitment policy and selection methods have almost revolutionised the system. The Kothari recommendations, which widened the scope of recruitment examinations on the lines of 'Talent Search' tests in science, injected a capsule revolution by allowing regional language media and bilingual (Hindi/English) pattern of question papers. The Satish Chandra Committee which reviewed the implementation of Kothari reforms was by and large satisfied with the change although many of its merit protecting recommendations were not accepted by the Union government in 1990. The second decimal review made by Yogendra Alagh and further re-examined by Hota intends to lower down the age of entry and educational qualification to higher secondary without optional papers and all compulsory papers stressing upon rural development, computer science and human rights in Indian polity. If these reports are accepted by the government, the real and discernable changes will follow. Competitive examination system will be more reliable and the evils of Indian education and annual examinations will be eliminated without modernisation. As the detailed report is still awaited, one can compare the position of pre-Kothari and post-Satish Chandra era in the processes of recruitment reforms.

The Pre-Kothari Situation

Only one combined competitive examination for direct recruitment to IAS/IPS and central services class I and class II used to be conducted by UPSC. The age limit was 21–26 years, with relaxation for SC/ST candidates. The scheme of examination had three categories for different services,

(1) *Category I*: IAS and Indian Foreign Services,
(2) *Category II*: IPS and class II Police Services of union territories and
(3) *Category III*: Central Services class I and class II.

Candidates used to take three attempts for each of the three categories. The scheme of examination consisted of: a written examination in three compulsory subjects, two optional subjects in category II, and three optional subjects in the rest along with an interview of varying weightages. The maximum marks in all totalled at 1,750 for the IAS and 1,050 for the IPS.

The Post-Kothari Era

The UPSC in its meeting on 19th January 1974 resolved to constitute a committee of the following to suggest reforms in recruitment system through the commission.

(1) Prof D.S. Kothari – Chairman
(2) Mr Bhagwan Sahai
(3) Prof Sukhmoy Chakravorty
(4) Mr B. Parthsarthi
(5) Dr Motilal Dhar
(6) Prof M.V. Mathur

The terms of reference given to this committee were to consider:

(1) The desirability of single unified competitive examination in place of current three examinations for IAS and class I and other services.
(2) The adequacy of personality test in said examinations.
(3) The required changes in the optional papers and subjects.
(4) The number of chances to be allowed to the candidates.
(5) The measures to be taken to implement the use of languages as media mentioned in the 8th Schedule.

(6) The system of review of syllabi for the examination.
(7) Ways and means for a system of recruitment in class I and II central services.
(8) The criterion of short listing of candidates for examination and viva voce.
(9) Any special system of recruitment for scientific and technical posts.
(10) Any other cognate matter.

The Committee took two years and its chairman who was a renowned physicist and a great protagonist of Hindi and common man could evoke a national consensus on several vexed questions. The Kothari Committee recommended:

(1) There should be two examinations for higher civil services – the preliminary and the main. The first should be qualifying and objective type while the main should be a written test and interview.
(2) The preliminary examination will have two papers (i) general studies (150 marks) and (ii) one optional subject (300 marks).
(3) The main examination will have eight subjects of 300 marks each. The first two papers (Indian Language and English) formed part of a qualifying examination of senior secondary standard and the marks secured in these papers will not be added to the total score which will be 1,800.
(4) Interviews by five to six interview boards of the UPSC will be of 250 marks. The merit list will be worked out on the basis of aggregate marks in the main examination (1800 marks) and interview test (250 marks) totalling 2,050 marks.
(5) The age limit will be 21–26 years but the Government of India changed it from 21 to 28 years.
(6) Candidates will be given two attempts for civil service examination in both the general and the SC/ST categories but the government relaxed it to three attempts to the general candidates, and no restriction on the number of attempts for the SC/ST candidates, within prescribed age limit.
(7) The candidates will have the option to answer the general studies and optional papers (other than language and literature papers) either in English or in any of the language of the Eighth Schedule of the Constitution.
(8) The minimum educational qualification would be a university degree. Candidates holding technical degree in medical and engineering, etc., will also be eligible to take these examinations.

One of the recommendations of Kothari Committee not accepted by the government was the third level test called post-Training Test. The LBS Academy at Mussoorie was to conduct it and its marks were to be added to the main examination performance. It was rejected on the ground that it will downgrade the status of UPSC and necessitate a reorganisation of National Training Academy.

The Satish Chandra Review

In 1989, UGC Chairman, Satish Chandra was asked by the UPSC to review and evaluate the system of selection introduced by Prof D.S. Kothari Committee. The Committee examined the issue in the light of the objectives and addressed itself to following questions:

(1) Whether the preliminary examination is manageable to net in larger numbers?
(2) Whether main examination has generated a healthy competition among candidates?
(3) Whether there is any bias in favour of any optional subject or group of subjects?

(4) Whether intellectual attributes and faculties are being tested properly?
(5) Whether social traits and mental alertness of candidates being tested properly?

The major recommendations of Satish Chandra can be summed as under:

(1) The combined civil service examination should be for 12 services only. These services should include Indian Administrative Services, Indian Foreign Service, Indian Police Service, Indian Audit and Accounts Service, Indian Income Tax Service (class I), Indian Customs and Central Excise Service, Indian Defence Accounts Service, Indian Railway Accounts Service, Indian Postal Service, Indian Posts and Telegraphs Accounts and Finance Service, and Indian Civil Accounts Service. The seven central group A services and eight central group B services should be de-linked from the combined civil service examination. This suggestion was not accepted.
(2) The age limit of 21–26 years for general candidates, with relaxation of five years of age for members of the SC and ST should continue. It was not accepted.
(3) The general candidates and the SC/ST candidates may have three and six number of attempts. This suggestion too, was not accepted.
(4) There should be a system of negative marking for the wrong answers in the preliminary objective test.
(5) The candidate who qualify in the main examination and appear in the interview test should be admitted directly to the main examination of the following year. This recommendation was also not accepted.
(6) An essay paper of 250 marks in English or in any of the Indian languages should be introduced but the scripts should be evaluated by two independent examiners and the mean of the two scores be awarded. In pursuance of this recommendation the essay paper of 200 marks was introduced in 1993.
(7) The interview marks should be increased from 250 to 300. This was accepted and implemented with the 1993 examination.
(8) The subjects of French, German, Russian and Chinese should be dropped from language and literature group (It was not accepted by the UPSC). Education, electronics and telecommunication engineering, and medical sciences should be added to optional subjects. This suggestion was partially implemented and the first medical sciences examination was conducted in the year 1994.
(9) Group discussions not psycho tests should be introduced as an integral component of the interview test. The interview test should have group discussion preceding the individual interview.
(10) Doctors and engineers should continue to be eligible for the civil services examination and their allotment should be done on the basis of the rank in the merit list and the preference for the services they choose.
(11) Minimum qualifying marks for the interview test should not be there.
(12) English or any of the Indian languages should continue as medium of evaluation. It is fair and ensures justice.

Satish Chandra found that a large number of successful candidates come from villages or small towns. The number of first divisioners and women candidates has also increased. A significant percentage of the first generation students, from the poor and deprived sections of society, have successfully competed in an intellectually tough competitive examination. A sizeable number of general, and most of the Scheduled Castes and Scheduled Tribes candidates hail from low-income groups. The Committee found that substantial number of candidates belonging to SC came upto general standards, but the successful candidates of ST are somewhat poorer in quality. The Committee suggested faculty development and infrastructural facilities at the Shastri Academy and Police Academy, revision of training syllabi, adequate publicity for civil service examinations and more coaching centres.

Kothari and Satish Chandra as architects of new recruitment system have totally revised the pre-1979 system. The Alagh and Hota reports may update it further. After two-and-a-half decades of experience this pattern of civil service examination stands as under in the opening years of 21st century.

Civil Services Examination

The age limit for IAS and IPS in the year 2007 was 21–28 years and the upper age limit is relaxable for the SC/ST candidates up to 36 years. The eligible candidate has to be: (1) a citizen of India and (2) a graduate of any of the universities professional or technical recognised by the government. The competitive examination is conducted in two phases: (1) the preliminary (objective type) and (2) the main examinations (short and long questions).

The Screening Test

The marks obtained in this screening test make the candidates eligible for admission to the main examination but they are not counted for determining the final order of merit. Paper I of General Studies covering a wide area of varied disciplines carries 150 marks. The second paper on one specialised subject from a list of optional subjects is of 300 marks. Thus the two papers make a total of 450 marks.

The question papers in the preliminary examination are of the objective type set in English and Hindi. The course contents of the syllabi for the optional subjects are of BA (Hons) level. Each paper is of 2 hour duration and those clearing this examination appear for the main examination. This number vary from year to year, along with the number of vacancies and the level of cut-off marks in the preliminary examination. The principle of 50 per cent reservation for SC, ST and Other Backward Classes has been introduced. It may be further readjusted in the light of shifts in reservation policy monitored by the Supreme Court and suggestions offered by V. Moily Committee.

The Second Examination

The number of candidates allowed to appear the main examination is twelve to thirteen times of the total number of vacancies in a particular year falling vacant. There are nine papers in all. The four papers in two optional subjects constitute 1200 maximum marks. The two papers in general studies carry 300 marks each and make another 600 marks. The two language papers in English and any Indian language are also of 600 marks. But the essay paper in any Indian language consists of 200 marks only. Thus, the total maximum marks for the written examination are 1200 + 600 + 300 + 300 + 200 = 2600. To this 300 marks of interview are added and the candidates who finally make their way to civil services examinations are ranked on the basis of 2900 marks.

The language papers are of secondary level and are only for the qualifying. Indian languages paper is not compulsory for candidates from northeastern states. Candidates can answer papers in any of the languages of the Constitution or in English. The question papers are also set in Hindi and English. Candidates scoring minimum qualifying marks in the written examination are called for interview as per rules of the Commission.

The Viva Voce Test

The number of candidates for interview are double the number of the vacancies to be filled every year. The interview does not have minimum qualifying marks. The marks of the written and interview of the main examination determine the ranks. The overall position in the examination and the preferences given determine allotment for the various services. These rankings can get modified, following the foundational course examination which is conducted by LBS Training Academy at Mussoorie.

All sorts of survey and research evaluations are made by UPSC in its annual reports or on the basis of data published in these reports. It is obvious that more and more candidates are appearing partly because they have been thrown open to first generation candidates with Hindi medium. The unreliability of tests encourages all sorts of eligible to take these examinations to add to their social prestige. The divisions awarded by universities have become meaningless and the success ratios of students from Patna, JNU and Chandigarh are somewhat similar. Similarly, if History and Public Administration are more popular as subjects it also explains their incomparability with subjects like Physics or English literature. The high success ratio of engineering graduates since 1990 further explains the injusticiability of these examinations. The 50 per cent reservation of seats for SC, ST and OBC explodes the myth of prestigious campuses and all sorts of coaching institutions have mushroomed in metropolitan cities to groom merit on commercial basis. The UPSC has been hijacked and the guess paper industry of campuses and their stereotype teachers have reduced the system into a routine for Bazaar success.

A competitive examination in the socio-educational milieu of India is bound to have its disfunctionalities. The policy of reservation, relaxation in age limit, choice and evaluation standards in optional papers spell have defeated the purpose workable merit against subjectivity and diverse opinions about ideas and facts. Most of the experts see this unreliability and undependendability as under:

> In civil service viva examinations, it was discovered that for the same candidates, but by different boards, differences of as many as 92 and 70 marks were shown in extreme cases, with the average of 37 marks on the basis of 300 being the maximum marks. The marks awarded by individual examiners varied even more than the common results obtained by the board collectively. One candidate put first by one board was put twentieth by another.
>
> —Herman Finer, *An Enquiry by International Institute of Examinations*

> The criteria by which personnel are selected by the Public Service Commissions are not up-to-date, and examining and appraising techniques are far from modern. Selection tends to be by one type of person, which naturally perpetuates its own type. Selection is too much in terms of academic records and appraisals by experienced academic examiners, too little in terms of many other considerations, highly important in public administration, too little attention in selection is given to any but the most subjective and incidental attention to capacity for growth.
>
> —Dean Paul Appleby

> There are also often complaints about the low standard of some of the papers set for optional subjects, and it is felt that candidates taking those subjects have an unfair advantage. This is inevitable from time

> to time, but in order to give as equal a chance as possible, that part of the examination which is common to all candidates must form a larger proportion of the whole than at present, enabling relative merit to be more properly judged.
>
> —A.D. Gorwala

The importance of psychological tests must be realised and they must gradually replace the viva voice. A fifteen minutes conversation with laymen, although possessing the wide experience of the Public Service Commission, can be no substitute for an expert psychological examination designed to give a scientific insight into the candidate's mental and emotional make-up. Naturally, a civil service competitive examination should take extra and special precautions to ensure fair evaluation and merit protection in the midst of reservation policies, age relaxation and choosing optionals with varied syllabi from university studies.

Civil Service Training in India

Training is a learning process and howsoever narrowly defined the concept implies mental receptively and wilful acceptance of undertaking the exercise. The modern theories of learning make little difference between education and training and the so-called emphasis on theory and practice has also disappeared in the age of technology and info revolution. The historical perspectives on training during the colonial era do not lead us anywhere and those who advocate combining the two are in fact saying that training should be built on an educational base of the employee. Mere literacy does not generate learning although it adds to capability for learning. Then mere learning without work causes a deeper ambivalence because the social milieu discourages the trained people to experiment or perseveres against odds as public servants. As mass education in India tells upon the quality of educational contents, the delitisation of education has eroded its value base. The so-called degree holders without deep basing of values through primary socialisation take training as a ritual and despite of newer researches and enormous funding, the public servants in India at all levels treat it to be a ritual. The ethos of illiteracy does not respect a learned servant as much as he respects, obeys a powerful senior without any merit. This tradition of ruling the society of illiterates has changed very little and young brilliant officers leave university careers to join the power game of status and privilege. This culture of power, in preference to knowledge and freedom, makes the civil service czars knowledge proof and training programmes are taken as "Holiday at the government expense" or "a travelling spree with family for a change". Cynical it may appear but in a society where education has sunk low, training is bound to be a second rate enterprise. It is good to establish knowledge corridors or training universities, but the problem is to inspire the power drunk trainee and that too, by a trainer who himself thinks his trainer position as a punishment post. Still the optimist will live to hope against hopes that first rate training institutions exist in India and they can be improved, no matter public servants take advantage of their libraries and learning materials.

Training can be called adult education or continuous education. It is to make the 'able' 'suitable' and still more suitable as he climbs the hierarchical ladder. The army does sit in a more systematic effective way because soldiers can be shaped in committed ignorance more easily than civilians who should cherish civilisational values of excellence and descent. The East India Company rulers took training of civil servants seriously because they had to operate in an alien land without knowing the language and customs of the natives. Warren Hastings trained them in official

Persian language with roots in European studies. The training of Indian Babu's was a must to dispose of office papers; still Philip Woodruff maintains that they learnt only what would fit them for the unprofitable duty of mere copying clerks. Annoyed by the incompetence of untrained who were mismanaging and bungling, the Viceroy Wellesley (1760–1842) worked on his dream mission and succeeded in establishing the Fort William College in 1800 which was more of a college than a training institute. It was a milestone in a country without any chain of universities or even high schools. Patterned on the models of British universities Clergy Provost and Vice Provost organised: (1) European, and (2) Oriental studies on a liberal canvas to induct their colonial free boaters into a regimen of colonial governance.

The experiment being a mixed success, the company moved to Haileybury where the training operations of this college continued till 1858. Training in Oriental and European studies could not enable British civilians to avert the mutiny and the recommendations of Lord Maculay Committee completed the chapter without any tangible alternative.

The Maculay Report proposed two year training in history, geography, jurisprudence, commerce and Oriental language to the British civilian officials in the age group between 18 to 25 years. Training to English rulers bordered on education. The span was two years and the pattern of teaching was as obtained at Oxford, Cambridge, Dublin and London. The field trainings were supplementary with district collectors. Lord Ishington in 1912 recommended the extension of training period to three years and training of inter-provincial trainers. The World War II again gave a big jolt and a Dehradoon training camp got started in India in 1941.

The post-independence period witnessed the proliferation in numbers of civil servants and an urgent need to disorient and reorient them into new roles. The democratic working and developmental exercise through successive Five-Year Plans required a massive effort to make the civil servants suitable to size up the challenge. Consequently:

(1) A variety of national and state level training institutes were created for training civil servants in functional specialities.
(2) Training programmes were redesigned with new course contents and newer teaching methods to make training effective.
(3) Huge funds were allocated to Union government, state government and corporate sectors to equip the personnel for the establishment of a socialist welfare state in India.
(4) Training policy and its implementation has been made the responsibility of training division of Union government to keep liaison and perform coordination of training programmes at state level and below.
(5) A variety of autonomous training institutes have been promoted to make experiments and provide an ecology of learning in prominent forms alongwith collaboration of their international counterparts.

The members of three all India services are recruited by the Central government, trained under the directions of the Central government and allotted to various union territories and states by the Central government immediately after the training period. They develop a espirit *de corps* and structural homogeneity creates a sort of administrative unity in a federal framework. The Central services, the personnel of which man Central government professional or technical departments function all over the country. The state governments have their own services for their functional areas. A large number of personnel is employed by public undertakings and other semi-government organisations. The all India, central and state services are functionally classified into two broad categories, the 'generalist' and 'specialist'. They can be further sub-grouped as 'professional' and 'technical'. The civil service training system in India overstresses the training of generalist and professional services, and the technical services depend upon their formal university education. The differentiations characterise the training system and the training institutions function at the national, regional, state and local levels. The ministry of personnel, public grievances and pensions administer training programmes. The training division sponsors and coordinates these programmes. Some of which pertain to management of information systems, organisation development and other techno-administrative matters. Efforts are being made to make civil service training attractive, creative and effective.

The Central government training institutions, like National Academy of Administration at Mussoorie and the Institute of Secretariat Training and Management directly work under the home ministry and organises in-service and refresher programmes for officers of the government. International courses on management techniques for officers of developing countries are also organised.

Several institutes like Institutes of Management and the Administrative Staff College Hyderabad and Bangalore are 'autonomous' institutions registered as societies. The Indian Institute of Public Administration (IIPA), New Delhi was set up on the recommendation of Dean Appleby in 1953. It concentrates on training programmes for officers of the Government of India and public undertakings. A nine-month long Advanced Professional Programme in Public Administration (APPA) for senior officers is a unique experiment. The Administrative Staff College at Hyderabad (1957) and numerous autonomous and national training institutions, organise training programmes for public sector undertakings. Similarly there are regional centres for municipal training. The training institutions like the Indian Institute of Mass Communication, New Delhi, National Institute of Cooperative Management, Pune, and National Institute for Training in Industrial Engineering, Bombay work with training institutions, spread all over the country. The National Institute of Bank Management, the Banker's Training College, Bombay, the Reserve Bank of India, the State Bank of India, the United Commercial Bank, the Punjab National Bank and the Bank of Baroda, run their respective training institutions for refresher courses. Hindustan Steel, Bharat Heavy Electricals Ltd., Life Insurance Corporation of India and the air corporations have also launched career development programmes. The states do not have uniform patterns of training. Diversity and varying levels of development cause problems in training institutions of the states. The state government departments are trying to create new structures of administrative training to the middle and subordinate level of their officers.

It is almost impossible to draw a list of civil service training institutions at national-state-local levels. Many of them have mushroomed with prescribed intakes and without much result or responsibility. Prime Minister Rajiv Gandhi was the only political leader who was somewhat serious about training policy and he offered special incentives and facilities like computer, internet, etc., because of which the training vision extended a little bit. His premature exit took the system back to its ritualism and enough noise is heard about new programmes and facilitations but by and large the dent is not visible. Still others will hold that, but, for the training institutions the public services would have relapsed into mediaeval attitudes and political leaders would have not established their legitimacy. The quality of training may be a subject of debate but civil servants have to undergo:

(1) Foundational training,
(2) Professional training,
(3) Field training,
(4) In-service training, and
(5) Refresher courses of varieties.

This fact keeps them on toes and somewhat up-to-date with an additional advantage of change, mobility and dynamism. Most of the training institutes are conducting courses in public administration. Quite a few of them have been created principally and primarily for training. There are some institutes (like Institute of Applied Manpower Research) which see training as a device to accord themselves legitimacy and respectability. Regardless of the precise mix of activities, a list of these training organisations as prepared by S.R. Maheshwari is appended below:

(1) Lal Bahadur Shastri National Academy of Administration, Mussoorie.
(2) National Police Academy, Hyderabad.
(3) National Institute of Health Administration and Education, Delhi.
(4) National Institute of Rural Development, Hyderabad.
(5) National Institute for Training in Industrial Engineering, Bombay.
(6) Institute of Local Self-Government, Mumbai (non-government).
(7) Indian Institute of Mass Communication, New Delhi.
(8) Indian Audit and Accounts Staff Training College, Shimla.
(9) Indian Institute of Foreign Trade, New Delhi.
(10) Indian Institute of Public Administration, New Delhi (quasi-governmental).
(11) Institute of Secretariat Training and Management (formerly Secretariat Training School), New Delhi.
(12) Institute of Applied Manpower Research, New Delhi.
(13) Indian Revenue Service (Income Tax) Staff College, Nagpur.
(14) Administrative Staff College of India, Hyderabad (autonomous).
(15) Administrative Staff College for Educational Planners and Administrators, New Delhi.
(16) Central Emergency Relief Training Institute, Nagpur.
(17) Family Planning Training and Research Centre, New Delhi.
(18) Customs and Central Excise Training School, New Delhi.
(19) Institute of Rural Development.
(20) Small Industries Extension Training Institute, Hyderabad.
(21) Railway Staff College, Baroda.
(22) Management Development Institute, Gurgaon.
(23) Vaikunth Mehta National Institute of Cooperative Management, Poona.
(24) Regional Centres for Training in Municipal Administration in four cities.

In addition, there are a host of training centres of state governments. The policies of liberalisation and globalisation have given unprecedented impetus to training enterprise in public and corporate sectors. Even the training programmes for babu bureaucracy are also on the increase.

Training for all India services today is a special responsibility of LBS National Academy of Administration, Mussoorie (for IAS), S.V.B. Patel National Police Academy, Hyderabad (for IPS) and National Forest Research Institute, Dehradun (for IFS). The post-entry training of new recruits to the all India services and a variety of in-service specialised and mixed training programmes are conducted by the two national academies for their senior officials. The induction training which was formally imparted at Metcalfe house was designed as a three-level training for the probationers which by and large through with (several changes) continues even today. These stages are:

- Foundational training,
- Institutional or professional training, and
- Distinct or field training.

Foundation Training

It is common to All India and Senior Central Services and is the responsibility of LBS Academy which conducts a combined training programme of 16 weeks for new recruits under a common roof. The purpose of the course is to provide basic foundation, i.e., understanding the socio-political milieu and its impact on administrative skill and professional values. It is very broad kind of liberal educational experience which must enable the young officers to identify their roles and prepare themselves mentally for the challenge ahead. Moreover, it is to foster spirit de corps and share the national ethos with their compares in different services from different parts of the country. The course contents are too wide and too rich to keep the probationers engaged as whole-time students. They include the following:

(1) Constitution of India, political ideologies, the political system, and foreign policy;
(2) Indian economy, industrial population and food polices;
(3) Social change, social policy and voluntary organisations;
(4) Financial administration and audit;
(5) History, culture, fine arts, and allied aspects;
(6) Civil and criminal justice and administrative tribunals;
(7) Communication technology and computers;
(8) Management, motivation, decision-making, MIS, O&M; and
(9) Administrative accountability, responsibility, ethics and integrity.

The IPS probationers are given a similar training at Sardar Vallabhbhai Patel National Police Academy (Hyderabad). The in-service training includes foundational and professional courses. The foundational course is of sixteen weeks for the probationers of central services group A. The professional course for IPS probationers has a duration of eleven and a half months with eight months' practical training in states in between called as sandwich training.

In 1989, an experiment was made to conduct this foundational training programme at four places, i.e., in Mussoorie, Hyderabad, Nagpur and Baroda academies. The course contents were common but teaching and examination patterns differed because of which the examination assessment created complications of determining the seniority of probationers. So under present arrangement, the foundational training of IAS and IPS probationers is being imparted only at Mussoorie, while that of Central services is conducted by other institutions.

The IAS probationers are attached to districts for practical work. They also undergo secretariat training with special emphasis on the study of languages. The recruits to the IA&AS are sent to the Indian Audit and Accounts Staff Training College at Shimla where they are trained in their professional work. At the end of the training they have to pass a departmental examination before being posted as assistant accounts officer in the office of the Accountant-General in some state. Similarly, the recruits to the Indian Revenue Service are sent to the Indian Revenue Service (Income Tax) Staff College at Nagpur. The recruits to the Railway Service (IRAS) go to the Railway Staff College

Baroda and their professional training programme is of two years' duration. This training is practical and has a direct bearing on the work of the trainees. At the end of each course, there is a written examination and the marks are added to the marks of the UPSC examination. This determines the probationer's rank in the service. The examination is conducted in areas like, Management and Behavioural Sciences, Constitution of India, Economics for Administration, History, Culture and Law.

The teaching methods in all these courses comprise lectures, tutorials, syndicate exercises and case studies. After the completion of the course, the probationers of the other services' go for institutional training to their respective training institutions but the probationers of the IAS continue to stay at Mussoorie Academy for their institutional training and final placement.

Institutional and Field Training for IAS and IPS

This training primarily stresses upon legal framework and uprises the trainees about civil, criminal and revenue laws. The rules, regulations and functional duties are taught to appreciate the working of field agencies at the level of district and below. The out of state trainees are administered primary lessons in regional language of the state concerned. Before 1969 this training was completed at a stretch before the final phase of the district training. After ARC recommendation it has been calendered into two phases – The first spell of five months acquaints the probationer with work scenario of the state assigned to him. Here he identifies problems and discovers solutions. The second spell takes him to district where he confronts grass roots problems and administrative ethos of rural culture. The total period of 53 weeks devoted to this institutional and district training is planned by the collector and a member of the training faculty of National Academy, Mussoorie. This training is sandwiched between institutional training of state and district training in the field. Hence, the name sandwich training for which a joint calender is prepared and specific attachments are given to the probationers to interact with a variety of state level and district level functionaries. The purpose is to become familiar with posts and persons and develop insights into the state and district administrations through 'On the Spot Interactions'. The state administrators coordinate training programmes which include visits, discussions, paper writing and informal get together. The calender of this institutional and field training is somewhat uniform in all the states. The time is spanned as under:

S.No.	*Duration*	*Attachments with*	*Focus*
1.	7 days	Tehsil	Revenue work
2.	7 days	VLW and BDO	Panchayati Raj
3.	14 days	Zila Parishad	Development
4.	7 days	Sub Division Officer	Land management
5.	Two days	S.P.	Familiarisation
6.	14 days	District Judge and other agencies	Coordination
7.	7 days	DRDA	Development projects
8.	Two days	Police Station	Public grievance
9.	Two days	Municipality	Urban issues
10.	28 days	Independent charge as BDO	Practical work
11.	28 days	Independent charge as Tehsildar	Land records
12.	7 days	As Settlement Officer	Land settlement
13.	21 days	Institutional Training at state institute	Theory
14.	28 days	Institutional Training	Practical work
15.	Three days	Debriefing	Experiences
16.	Twenty-eight weeks	Independent ADM	Decision making

Having spent their time in respective states the probationers return to Mussoorie and complete the rest of the second phase of training in the light of field experience of the district and the state. The sandwich training experience has to be integrated with the theoretical knowledge. Problem oriented issues are discussed with faculty and in group discussion for a period of three months.

Then comes the final examination and the marks obtained in this examination and the foundational course examination at the academy are added up to determine the final ranking of the probationers in the batch. The successful completion of this probation period gives the trainees confirmation in the cadre and they proceed to their allotted states which hand over their orders of placement.

The Sandwich Training for IPS

The Kohli Committee recommended the new nomenclature, (i.e., National Police Academy) in place of former CPTC at Mount Abu. It suggested a yearlong professional training for IPS probationers. The Gore Committee on police training enriched the course contents wherein the field training comes between two phases of institutional training for the IPS. The revised pattern for practical training of IPS probationers was for a sandwich course which was enforced by the Central government in 1986. The National Police Commission (1977) endorsed the suggestions of the Gore Committee and suggested that this training should span for first five years of service and alternate between the National Police Academy and training on the job. The sandwich course for the IPS probationers, is of 96 weeks and the institutional training, in both the phases, is imparted by National Policy Academy, Hyderabad. Practical training is the responsibility of the cadre-states. The 96 weeks training generally follows this calender:

Sandwich Field Training for IPS Probationers

S.No.	*Duration*	*Attachment with*	*Focus*
1.	41 weeks (Tour – 2 weeks)	NPA, Hyderabad Phase I	Police craft
2.	28 days	Central School for Weapons and Tactics	Weaponary use
3.	21 days	Army Unit	Familiarisation
4.	10 days	Joining Time	
5.	6 weeks	State Police Academy and Rural Police Station	Field problems
6.	8 weeks	SP office	File management
7.	14 days	Revenue Inspector	Revenue offences
8.	7 days	A.P.P.	Prosecution work
9.	14 days	District Police H.Q.	Police grievances
10.	14 days	Dy. S.P.	Orientation
11.	7 days	Armed Police Battalion	Familiarisation
12.	12 weeks	Independent Charge of a Police Station	Field experience
13.	10 days	Joining Time	
14.	12 weeks	Institutional Training at NPA, Hyderabad	Experience sharing
	96 weeks		

Phase I

After completion of the foundational course the institutional training for IPS commences at NPA Hyderabad. The academy curriculum includes subjects on: policing and police administration along with penology texts to develop insights in crime prevention and crime records management. Investigation of crime and prosecution, forensic help constitute the technical components. Maintenance of public peace and order, traffic control, security of foreigners/crowds and unlawful assemblies are also taught to have an appraisal of one's personality, character and moral values in police administration. The probationers have to pass several qualifying tests in subjects like map reading and wireless communication. Hindi and or regional languages are also taught at the academy campus. Physical training, weapon use, swimming, field craft and driving are taught in the second phase. Subjects like rural development and elementary Hindi or regional language are arranged as a part of orientation. Handling of bombs and explosives provide exposure through films and live demonstrations. Hereafter the trainees proceed for an advanced weapons training course at the CSWT, Indore and an attachment with the Army. Later on they join their respective states for a 34 week training in the field.

The field training has varied attachments of different durations. The State Police Training College, the District Superintendent of Police, the district headquarters, police stations and State Public Prosecutor induct the young trainee into police profession. After this the probationer takes independent charge of a police station, and the regular incumbent is removed. The Dy S.P. accompanies the probationer when he spends two weeks with the Armed Police Battalion. Later he proceeds to NPA, Hyderabad for Phase II of his institutional training.

Phase II

It spans for a period of 3 months wherein subjects like police supervision, management techniques, human behaviour and police problems are taught by experts. The outdoor work includes ceremonial drill, unarmed combat, *yoga,* and other exercises. At the end, a written examination is conducted which includes evaluation of indoor and outdoor work. The minimum pass marks gives eligibility and the probationers can clear the final examination in two attempts. The marks of the final assessment and final examination are added for the determination of probationer's seniority in his cadre.

In-Service Training

In-service training of public servant is stressed to keep the public servants up-to-date and improve their knowledge and skill as per needs of the changed society. It is given to all officials, irrespective of their cadres and categories to re-examine their concepts and values and reorient their functional attitudes. It gives an opportunity to intercept and combine learning with field experience. It further links field problems and experiences with techno facilities available at all walks of life. Naturally, it is conducive to long-range administrative reforms.

Since 1985, the ministry of personnel, public grievances and pension has created facilities for refresher courses for senior, junior and middle level officers to be in touch with recent developments in allied areas. Then there are in-service programme of longer duration for officers with:

(1) Six to nine years of experience
(2) Ten to sixteen years of service
(3) Seventeen to twenty years of service

The number of these courses is increasing and they are organised at various locations and central service officers and senior IAS officers attend these programmes with benefit. The course contents of this kind of training normally include: administrative environment, organisational behaviour and centre-state relations. International trade management control systems, industrial policy, planning and development and environmental management are emphasised as core areas. Social welfare, rural and urban development, HRD evaluation are highlighted for discussion with senior officials. Public policy analysis, project management, use of computers to restructure Indian economy and its impact are taught as regular subjects. The management of state enterprises, energy development, along with problems like terrorism and violence management are posed to stir the stereotype thoughts of senior officials. This liberal approach to training fits into the generalist character of the service. It makes them aware of varied responsibilities at the Central and the state levels. Both the National Academies at Mussoorie and Hyderabad run such courses. The Mussoorie Academy organises a six-week refresher course for officers of the seniority of 10 to 15 years. Hyderabad training courses include:

(i) Management Course (four weeks) for IPS officers for 6 to 10 years of service and SPS officers on the select list of IPS;
(ii) Management Course (four weeks) for IPS officers having 11 to 16 years of service;
(iii) Management Course (two weeks) for IPS officers with 17 to 20 years of service;
(iv) Vertical Interaction Course (one week) for IPS officers (SP to DGP);
(v) Training Administrators Course (four weeks) for SPs;
(vi) Training of Trainers Course (four weeks each in two phases) for DSPs; and
(vii) Vertically Integrated Training Programme (one week) for IAS officers (Sub-Collector to Cabinet Secretary) on the specific theme of terrorism and violence.

The Academy also conducts short-term specialised courses such as one week course on Women in Bureaucracy and two week course for the probationers of Indian Customs and Central Excise (Group A) Service. The non- or semi-government organisations like the Indian Institute of Public Administration, New Delhi and the Administrative Staff College, Hyderabad have taken a lead in designing new courses.

Indian Institute of Public Administration (IIPA), New Delhi: Dean Paul Appleby's in his Survey of Indian Administration (1953) recommended the creation of IIPA. The Ford Foundation funded the institute in early years to model it on the lines of Littauer Centre at Harvard and the Maxwell School at Syracuse. The school developed as an educational-cum-training centre to bring the academic and the administrative officers in close contact. The Management Development Programmes are sponsored by the personnel ministry for senior or middle level officers drawn from various state governments and public sector units. A course on Criminal Justice Administration-I has been sponsored by the personnel ministry for senior officers of state governments. In addition, the institute organises workshops on computer application, personnel inventory, financial accounting, project management, etc. The training of forest tribal interface for officers of the Indian Forest Service is sponsored by the ministry of environment and forests. The IIPA has been doing good work in the field of training of Union and state officers and has entered into a new area of social welfare. A nine month Advanced Professional Programme (APPA) is a prestigious training programme of the Institute for mid-career development and is attended by senior officers of all the varied services joint secretaries to the Government of India and officers at the middle level. The APPA focuses attention on:

(1) Foundational areas
(2) Management subjects
(3) Administrative Environment and
(4) Elective Areas Group for Specialisation.

The trainee officers hail from various states and are of different services and seniority. They interact with each other on theoretical and practical aspects of public management over a year, and gain insights into administrative processes in a variety of political settings. The officers prepare dissertations and record their observations and experiences about administrative situations in the field. These dissertations provide a rich feedback to their respective department for policy planning and academic research.

The training programmes sponsored by international institutions at IIPA act as motivators to enhance job satisfaction and improve vision of senior level trainees. The candidates are selected for foreign training by the institute and the exposure is helpful. Utilisation of these trained officers is made to improve human resource potential of the cadres.

Administrative Staff College, Hyderabad: The college was established in 1957 on the recommendation of the All-India Council of Technical Education. It is patterned on the Administrative Staff College at Henley in Britain. The college aims at bringing together senior administrators, the private sector and public sector officials for an interface to exchange ideas and experiences to assume higher responsibilities. "... The college provides a course of studies which investigates the principles and techniques of organisation and administration in civil life and gives them an opportunity of examining different administrative practices to prepare them for still higher responsibilities in future."

Institute of Secretariat Training and Management, New Delhi: Established in 1948, the old Central Secretariat Training School was given this new name in 1971. It is a training institution for the lower levels of civil servants like section officers, assistants and upper and lower division clerks. The courses include organisation and methods, office procedure, financial rules, and regulations. After completion of their training these junior officials are posted to different ministries for practical training. The institute also conducts refresher courses as mid-career training programmes for the employees when they are close to promotional positions.

National Institute of Rural Development, Hyderabad: The subject of public administration developed from the study of local self-government as it was the primary school of British democracy. The All India Institute of local self-government was created in 1927 as a non-government organisation it has rendered an invaluable service to the cause of local self-government in training, research and reform. Though local government falls in the spheres of the states, the Union government has promoted research and training. The institute runs foundational and professional courses of various sorts.

Refresher Courses

The objectives of refresher courses can be listed as (1) broadening the mental horizon, (2) providing of new skills and knowledge, (3) exchange of ideas and improving the standards of performance and organisational efficiency. This in-service training is imparted at various central and state training institutes. Some of them invite mixed groups of officers from all over the country. Specialised in-service training to personnel of various ranks in the form of short-term and long-term refresher courses are compulsory for officers as a part of their career planning. Some of them relate to field training. Various national and state academies of training organise executive development programmes such as annual refresher courses, courses for special areas, general short term courses, management programmes and promotional courses including advanced ones. In 1980 vertical interaction training programmes were started to help the senior and the middle-level officers to interact with their colleagues and juniors in other states. These courses are useful in developing awareness of inter-level problems and orientations. Seminars for senior officers focus upon operational problems faced by the officers in the field. Several in-service courses for the officers invite overseas officers in various age groups. The training wing of the Academy organises training programmes for trainers posted at training institutions in the country. Vertical interaction courses and international training programmes sponsor officers for training experience in Japan, UK and Australia.

Frailties of Civil Service Training

The weakness of training programmes have been examined by various committees at all levels. They can be catalogued as under:

(1) Notwithstanding repeated reiterations, there is no clarity about training policy issues in specific training programmes which need to be constantly revised from the point of view formulation and operationalisation.

(2) The Academic Boards of Training Academies do not meet periodically, the syllabi is not updated and the overlap between course contents makes the exercise insipid and unacademic.

(3) The training faculty is ill-equipped and trainer assignment is regarded as a punishment post. The officials who went to administrative vocations because of their power orientations refuse to learn and convert the entire exercise into primary school information feeding.

(4) The senior officers invited for interaction are extra cautious of their status and come ill-prepared to do a job for which their credentials are dubious.

(5) The teaching methods continue to be traditional and newer methods do not get adequate response, specially by senior trainees of short term courses who have given up the habit of reading, writing and even speaking.

(6) Most of the trainees lack enthusiasm and avoid assignment by showing their indispensibility in the field.

(7) Training exercise is unlinked with promotion policy and does not motivate the officials who get transferred on return. This proves the irrelevance of the experience.

(8) Training evaluations are subjective, perfunctory and not credible. The trainees who take the assignments seriously are not adequately rewarded.

(9) Teaching materials in Hindi do not exist in libraries and reference books remain unused because of linguistic deficiency and over engagements.

(10) The cost of training is not commensurate to its return and like all other academic institutions in the country it is in a state of neglect decline and ritualistic rhetoric.

The induction training of probationers has not cut much ice. The latter in its theoretical aspects does make an attempt to include subjects which have a relevance to job performance but the syllabus does not include topics on management and social change. Topical subjects like economic literalism, public sector disinvestment, cyber crimes, social tensions, terrorism are dealt superficially. The sandwich pattern does help in breaking the monotony of theoretical learning but the district training does not motivate to get a feel of environment and practical conditions on the ground.

Training activities of institutes in the field have expanded beyond management. The participants feel that training has low utility and their training needs have not been identified. Training methodology does not experiment and executives do not get enough from classroom lectures. Methods like case studies, programmed learning, management games and seminars do not evoke participation. In-service training is not linked to mid-career developments and the failure to make the job assignment conform to training makes the exercise repulsive. Evaluation of training performance is perfunctory and foreign service training scarcely lends any benefit to the officials on return. Unlike defence services, training in the civilian sector is a peripheral phenomenon in administration. Commitment and competence are lacking to accord a place of primacy to training enterprise.

Suggestions for Reforms

This civil service training structure, though elaborate needs to be strengthened and moulded into a more effective instrument of intervention in socio-economic change and administrative development. This reform process to make civil service training effective and purposeful is a long drawn out effort that requires consistency, insights, courage and imagination. These reforms are needed in course contents, faculty specialisation, rigorous evaluation and promotional rewards. Some of these reforms can be listed as under:

(1) The formulation of a comprehensive training policy,
(2) preparation of perspective and long-term training plans,
(3) setting up of a National Training Commission and state level training boards for effecting coordination among training institutions,
(4) development of professional training faculty,
(5) integration of training with the total public administrative system,
(6) rectification in the imbalance in the training system,
(7) stress on a sounder system of evaluation, and
(8) giving due importance to the training of lower level Babus.

Most of these weaknesses and reform needs of civil service training are well known to the trainers, trainees and training administrators. But like educational reforms in India everybody finds himself too weak or too irrelevant to reform civil service training. The committee's reports keep suggesting but the trainers and the trained like teachers and students everywhere have a low morale to get involved into it. The three significant features of a civil service training have to be:

(1) Receptivity,
(2) Creativity, and
(3) Effectivity.

The administrative culture of India destroys all the three features of learning in the name of discipline. The hierarchy rules the roost and the creative juniors are taught to conform rather than to suggest. Even new ideas are seen hierarchically and they are shunned if they originate at lower levels. Some of the state institutes are headed by power hungry bureaucrats who do not even eat from a similar menu plate in lunches and dinners of junior trainees. The course contents are seen in terms of high school modules and the external trainers from departments get their lectures prepared from textbooks and read out their addresses. Like a religious discourse non-confirmation is punished rather than appreciated. New tools are possessed only to utilise modernisation budgets but the trainees who have lost proficiency of English language neither use library facilities not read and write in the absence of linkage between training performance and career advancement. Nobody is interested in creating learning materials and the rush of short-term courses do not even motivate average trainee to even visit the libraries. The administrators at senior and junior levels live in two different worlds and the charm between the two levels of administrations makes the training exercise quite irrelevant and wastefully dysfunctional.

The Civil Service Reforms in India

The Quest for a Model

Ever since Dean Paul Applaby submitted his report on administrative reforms in India in 1952 the quest for a new civil service model has been a subject of debate, dialogue and discussion. Individual researchers, veteran civil servants, political representatives, pay commissions and various reform committee in their comments and suggestions have argued for civil service reforms, basic as well as supplemental. The ARC probed the entire issue in depth and even Sarkaria Commission suggested more all India services with fixed and longer tenures at the central secretariat. The state governments had made their sporadic attempts and today the whole issues of merit recruitment is being reviewed with the advent of New Panchayati Raj and Urban Municipal Services. All these exercises throw some light on the dark areas suggesting better deal for the civil servants. But then most of these reports end up lamenting the decline of integrity, neutrality and motivation of public servants who are increasingly engaged in corruption and malpractices. The lower functionaries remain alienated and impervious to all civil service reforms and when the chips are down only a corrupt patwari and a ruthless thanedar seem like running the show at the heisting.

Obviously, the reform exercise is segmental and when the senior leadership should have improved the system the budging number of the juniors continue to play their mediaeval game of ruling the teeming millions. The senior officers have been rendered and apathetic and they watch the field spoils as big brothers of a costist family. The 'Babu Raj' remains incorrigible and the desk officers also tend to become dignified babus. The procedure articulations do not change and Weber and Taylor remain the guiding spirit of the monolith. At the cutting edge, these petty functionaries play the little Napoleons and very conveniently pass on the once to elected representative who apparently look more corrupt and power drunk. All seminars on civil service reforms end up by saying "People get a system they deserve". "Let people be more deserving." But the issue is how can people be more deserving when administration thrives and has a vested interest in the apathy of the undeserving people. So the inevitability of gradualness is paraded as a watchword of reforms and every generation feels comfortable in postponing the nucleus reforms specially the ones, which in their perception destabilise their positions. The reformers do not want to commit suicide and the paradox continues. "Those who can reform the system they do not want these reforms and those who want reforms they cannot induct reforms in the stagnant system and hence the rhetoric."

For the first time, a dim light is visible at the end of the tunnel when policies of liberalisation and globalisation have coined the phrases like 'downsizing' and 'debureaucratisation'. If meaningfully contended these two concepts can effectively remove the malignancy. The government is not an employment giving agency from the taxpayers money and if unwanted public servants are not endowed with bureaucratic powers of harassment and extortion the people will feel relieved and the parasite babus and chaprasi who were employed by colonial masters to have increasing association of natives will be productively engaged in improving the economy of the nation. The private sector cannot afford avoidable burden on its budget and a competitive government has soon discovered that a monopoly rule is the babu raj which has kept the country in backwaters. Whatever may be the 'Human Face' arguments, the size of group C and group D employees should drastically be curtailed and 'downsizing' will automatically debureaucratise. It will induct senior public servants into a global culture of work and a feudal bureaucracy will learn to live and work like civilised people in other parts of the globe. This one reform which is opposed in the name of 'humanism' or compassion will ensure human values of equality and dignity of man and work. India has delayed this reform without bothering that compassion and merit go ill together. If the babu and chaprasis services have to be reformed the answer lies in:

(1) Part-time hourly employment without cadres.
(2) Contractual arrangement of job performance in offices.
    This reform has the advantage of:
    (a) Engaging the women workforce which has to combine job with family responsibilities for several productive years of female life.
    (b) Stopping abuse of D class workers in personal domestic work by senior officials.
    (c) Ensuring more income to workers who will be free to work at several places.
    (d) Developing a work culture of self-help, individual dignity and efficiency with diversified jobs.
    (e) Eliminating present-day conflicts of trade unionism, litigation and strike that put innocent citizens to ransom.

The ill-educated and trained clerical or chaprasi services can be procured when needed, but they can never be developed as lifetime career for a decent living. Sooner we downsize, better becomes the base for senior civil service reforms.

The structure scope, nature and service conditions of all India services evoke a lot of heat among reformers. With the passage of time there seems to be a consensus that these services should continue, but their present structure and role has caused heart burning jealousies and bitterness among state services, specialist services and the functional services of the Union government. Moreover their generalist nature, promotional prospects, reservation quotas, state basing and tenure arrangements are being criticised in view of the colonial change in the country. Of course arguments are there on either side of the fence, but a rational personnel policy must take into account of the following:

(1) There should be more all India services. Sarkaria Commission talked of six, Administrative Reforms Commission prescribed eight. Now All India Judicial Service is on the anvil and the number can touch a dozen. Leaving it to Rajya Sabha resolution simply means the government of the day should identify these dozen areas for another 50 years and all India services may be

created in all these area with absolute parity of pay and principles of their incumbents. The ARC suggestion has rationale and with more all India services the talent will flow to all areas of service and hegemony of one service over other will diminish. This democratisation of talent spread will keep all the senior services in high morale and a national recruitment will justify their edge on the state services. The Pakistani model of integrated civil service, though quite different can be tagged with all India services model in a variety of ways.

Now the second question. Should these all India services be directly recruited from the market, or through promotee quota of recruitment or by some mixed model as in the present. These three models are called:

(1) Establishment of an Indian Union Service
(2) Noronha Model of promotee services
(3) Extension of the existing three services into a dozen services

To end the present day diversity it is suggested that an unified civil service for the Centre known as the Indian Union Service may be created. Recruitment to this service should be made by a common competitive examination under the auspices of the UPSC which should publish a list of required number of recommended candidates. At present such candidates are grouped under various services and then sent for foundational training at various academies. All such selected probationers, should be awarded a stipend during the period of common training. Thereafter, these probationers should be tested by written and oral examinations, as at present. In addition, methods must be devised to test their aptitudes, equipment and preferences. After such tests, successful probationers should be allotted to different central services and sent to various training institutions for specialised training, including field training for two years. This system should be a definite improvement upon the existing system. Quite contrast to it Noronha, the retired Chief Secretary of Madhya Pradesh sometime back advanced a revised model of recruitment for all India services. Noronha, a protagonist of state service interests has desired that open market recruitment shall be limited to the most junior level of the state civil service. After working for three years at this level, the successful candidates will have two chances at the limited competitive examination for the senior level of the state civil service, the level of deputy collectors. After eight years, deputy collectors throughout the country will compete for entry to the senior scale of the IAS, there being no recruitment in the junior scale. The successful candidates will constitute the IAS and open market recruitment will be abolished. IAS officers will be posted to their parent states unless state needs more officers than that can be provided by the successful candidates from that state. Noronha also pleaded for uniform pay scales for all India services. "His position is that ... different pay scales for the different all-India services are totally unjustified. The qualifications are the same and the responsibilities are equally onerous". This model reminds of the old Madras presidency system of direct recruitment only at the lowest rung of the administrative ladder and filling up all other posts up to the level of deputy collectors and their selection grades by promotion. What Noronha did was to amend this scheme by providing for direct recruitment through a closed competitive examination to the senior posts of the senior scale of the IAS, totally abolishing the junior scale of the cadre. Noronha sent his scheme when he was acting as adviser to the Punjab government, to the home ministry at New Delhi but the ministry just pigeonholed it.

If the extension of the existing system has to be experimented upon, the government will have to classify and take a bold stand on the following issues:

(1) Three categories of reservation: (a) SC and ST (b) OBC and women, and (c) Poor minorities and handicapped.
(2) Statewise reservation of posts for the sons of the soil.
(3) Special 6 to 12 months additional academic training programme for incumbents in the reservation category.

The merit recruitment of all India service is often exaggerated. Merit is more than a mental faculty and if it is to issue in the ethical value of human character no examination and viva voce test can ensure meritorious public life through mere recruitment. So, integrity and effectivity of public service demand that unmeritorious should be weeded out. But this is not easy or workable through subjective annual confidential reports. The ARC recommended a mid-career examination which appalled the senior public servants because they cannot face merit screening and the annual confidential report system suits to the incompetent and flattery loving at the cost of public welfare. Moreover, there is a rat race for promotions and they are being demanded on the basis of seniority or so-called merit. The pyramid being too vertical, than is an inflation in all cadres at top and ex-cadre positions of additional secretarians, OSDs and special advisers have been created to accommodate officials for whom the posts do not exist. It began with the guidelines issued by the Union government in 1978. A series of cadre reviews have demonstrated that the civil services are trying to outbloat each other. A large number of super-time scale posts were added in IAS/IPS. This proliferation has taken place both at the central and state government levels. Some states have half-a-dozen officers in the rank of chief secretary with varying designations, nearly eight inspectors-general of police. In consequences, new posts have been created like Director-General of Police, Engineer-in-Chief, Principal Secretary, and so on. One of the motives behind this inflation has been to "improve the promotion chances in various services".

A similar proliferation has been going on in the defence services. This has led to devaluation of promotions. The status of the official hardly improves and there is no added authority like personal staff, housing, staff cars and office space have not kept pace with the explosion in senior ranks. It has adversely affected the quality of the cadre. The overstaffing and the mad rush for promotions has bred the undesirable trait of 'careerism' which is replacing professionalism by Cannibalism in civil service.

To arrest careerism and adhocism at senior ranks, it is suggested that there should be a high power Civil Service Board to perform the following functions:

(1) Protection of merit and equal opportunities to all who have spent a lifetime in the civil service.
(2) Placements, promotions and transfers of senior civil servants in national interest.
(3) Determination of positions to be filled through lateral entries and specifications of qualifications, experience and suitability/contractual entries.

It will take away some of the functions and powers of personal ministry but the Board may be placed in the ministry like the UPSC. The Board may have specialised wings for position classification, promotions after training and inter ministry administrative transfers. The board should be headed by a retired judge of the Supreme Court and its members should be civil servants, defence officers, retired PSC members, expert academicians and senior journalist. Functioning on the lines of UPSC (though outside the constitution), the Civil Service Board take care of promotee recruitment, linkage of professional training with senior civil service placements, determination of transfer policy and matters of position classification and lateral entry. This will ensure objectivity in cadre management and cadre review will be taken up by expert panel of the board in place of brother bureaucrats. The Board may prescribe different kinds of selected tests for mid-career reviews and merit entry may be followed by merit protection and ensurement of equal opportunity which executive ministries are handicapped to promote.

An allied area that needs probe is the constant review of discipline rulers. Of course, the Parliament as a sovereign body enacts the rules but the minister of personnel has to be advised by this independent board which should not be a mere bureaucratic adjunct. The Board may prepare an annual calendar for promotional committee meetings, training courses and transfer panels ministrywise and the committee of secretaries may help the Board to work out an annual planning and implementation of personnel policy in a phased and systematic manner.

The Pay Commission has done a good job in reviewing pay packets and other benefits to public servants. As these functions are vital and often cause collective bargaining, efforts should be made to expand the scope of work of the Pay Commission. It should specifically earmark and revise the ancillary benefits and facilities to which a public servant should be entitled while holding a particular job. The cost of the benefits should be identified and Parliament should be informed by the minister how much each position costs to the public exchequer and how much comparability exists with other services like defence, judiciary, science, technology and medical, etc. This exercise by Pay Commission will protect the moral of the senior civil service. Moreover, the nation has a right to know through an independent and honest body like Pay Commission, how much public service costs to the nation and whether this cost is in commensurate to their need or expertise. Whether civil service in India is underpaid or overpaid must evoke a national dialogue which the Pay Commission report should initiate.

The basic Civil Service Reform in India has to originate from position classification. The Third Pay Commission classification as groups A, B, C and D is too hierarchical. Once, group C and group D services are decaderised and made part-time on daily or hourly basis, the A and B groups can be merged or at least meaningfully linked in terms of promotions. The central services should be reduced in numbers and a management pool can take care of their professionalism. The ARC examined the problem at length and their suggestions holds much water even today. The ministry of personnel can examine the feasibility of these suggestions. The report says "the basis of position classification is the individual positions in the machinery of public administration, and each position represents certain well-defined duties and responsibilities". What is needed is that each position should be given a detailed job description mentioning as accurately as possible the nature of duties associated with each position. The next step will be prescription of qualification for each position corresponding to its duties. Then should follow the fixation of pay scales for each position. Attempt should be made to fix equal pay for equal work. Positions carrying same scales of pay should then be placed in different grades which should be reasonable in number. A start can be made with the class I post under the Centre and those to be manned by all India services officers in the states. All these posts should be evaluated and assigned, in half a dozen common pay scales, each representing a grade. These grades may be divided into three levels, namely, junior, middle and the senior. Naturally, a democratic administration should have lesser number of levels and layers with less and less disparity in pay packets and qualification. The right to equality and dignity of individual notions of human rights jurisprudence militate against wide differences of ability, pay and privileges. So, nine grades and those levels seems like a workable compromise for another few decades.

The 180-Degree Appraisal

Performance appraisal of junior employers by senior officers was introduced at a time when junior were too low and too inefficient in hierarchy and the purpose was to discipline them. A democratic government cannot be run on the assumption that a senior know much more and is more honest because he was recruited on the basis of so-called merit and reservations. The very idea of confidentiality is a matter of debate because secrecy does not inspire honesty, rather it is conducive to conspiracy. No one individual howsoever wonderful can judge the performance of an individual in its totality. It is after all a working hypothesis. Even when human computerised it does not cease to be subjective. Demning rightly argues for its abolition because the juniors deserve to be treated as colleagues. Even when they are deficient they should be heard or sent for training. The corporate world is increasingly taking to 180-degree appraisal which means an official should be judged by:

(1) His immediate senior
(2) His remote senior
(3) His juniors
(4) His client group or citizens effected
(5) His own self
(6) His colleagues in the organisation

The weightage to all these assessments may not be equal. It may unleash a very complex process and 'out of turn' promotions may become impossible. Demning suggest that the incumbent falling low should be heard by a group and uphold his position by producing facts. The specific appraisals may be computerised and duly graded and a total picture should emerge in place of the one sided picture of a chance senior who himself might have been adjudged as sub-standard by his senior. The 180 per cent appraisal may be difficult but it can be experimented upon for A class posts with the help of external panels. It presupposes that each employee be given at the time of his joining the job a detailed and definite list of functions and duties he has to perform along with this job description. He should also be handed over a document showing what is expected of him and the concrete basis on which he shall be judged and his performance evaluated. The officers should also know the exact criteria for earning promotion and should also be encouraged to give his own annual assessment of his work, particularly what he regards his achievements of the year. The more objective and quantified the criteria, the more acceptable they should be. Above all, there should be created an environment in which it is accepted that government service is not a right but a duty. Annual increments, crossing of efficiency bars, earning promotions, winning prizes and awards have to be related to achievements of the employee. An effective performance appraisal needs that each position-holder in government service is evaluated objectively. He should have faith in the system and confidence in the senior evaluator. The criteria of evaluation should be mutually agreed upon; and the exercise should be taken seriously. True that seniority is quantitatively measurable and minimises controversy, but the distrust built up an atmosphere of confrontation and the evaluators play safe in giving vague remarks. This exercise is done casually without any serious intent. The annual confidential reports often lead to litigation and bad blood. M. Veerappa Moily should discover a new system of appraisal which should be more objective and command an all-round support and acceptance.

Civil service training needs radical reforms like educational reforms in India. Mere funds, more programmes and newer methods yield only marginal results. A new training policy has to evolve and it should be based on the following principles:

(1) No training for non-gazetted public servants. Only on the spot orientations should be enough.
(2) Post-entry probationary training should be exhaustive and determine the seniority of the trainee recruits.
(3) Mid-career training should be followed by an examination linking eligibility with promotions.
(4) Short-term refresher courses should be remedial and should generally be for those who are deficient.

These training programmes should be calendarised by a National Training Commission of the personnel department. The chairman of this training commission should be a former vice-chancellor of proven merit and members should come from civil service, defence services, journalism and industry. They should have panels to draw syllabi of various programmes and revise and update them every year in March. The management of training through this commission should be time bound and training evaluations should be prepared coursewise, subjectwise and traineewise. The Commission should give full autonomy to the training campuses to teach and the faculty should be free to grade and decide pass standards. The Commission should have three administrative writs:

(1) To conduct training programmes,
(2) To undertake research with the help of senior and brilliant trainees, and
(3) To suggest specific and concrete reforms every year with all sorts of follow up measures.

The probationer training, the promotee training and the remedial training should be seen as distinct categories. The first as a part of recruitment, the second as a part of promotional recruitment and the third as a part of merit protection policy. Nobody should be penalised for poor performance but the training institutes and their faculty must review individual cases and organise supplementary programmes to keep recruitment merit oriented. In other words, the training programmes should make the probationer realise that his university merit is not the civil service of a public servant. Training is a part of merit selection and the training commission should have the status of a Public Service Commission. If these are constitutional problems, the training commission may be created within the constitutional jurisdiction of Union/State Public Service Commission.

The promotee training in recruitment alone should conduct it with honesty and efficiency. The duration, the faculty, the examination, the practical work will have to be planned and the training commission should declare the eligible pass lists like the UPSC declaring the initial recruitment. It will weed out the undesirable, who cannot be dropped by individual seniors due to variety of practical considerations.

The remedial training will be in the continuation of the present system. The only difference will be the deficient public servants and the areas in which they need professional equipment. The individual training institutes will further judge the course the composition and decide about duration, mixed nature of training and the require faculty in terms of professional inputs. They will be watched and their monthly feedback will be sent by the institute to the National Commission for Training.

The present ineffective and routinisation of training can be rectified by linking it with confirmation, promotion and eligibility. The love for knowledge is not an adequate incentive for power seeking bureaucrats. The investment in training remains unproductive unless vested with power and return benefits to the trainees. The three kinds of training can make public servants serious and they will take the exercise seriously to improve their job prospects for which the governments spend millions.

Thus, Indian Civil Service from recruitment to retirement needs an overhaul. It has outlived its relevance partly because the colonial purpose is over and the new generation of citizens in free India are abusing its so-called merit elitism and colonial alienation. The reform efforts stay cosmetic and the nucleus changed is blocked in the name of transitional challenges which have taken more than half of the century. In the meanwhile, the society has changed and the political institutions have required a fragile democratic character. The civil servants have very successfully passed on the buck of failure to political masters who were bound to be unrepresentative and corruption proves. The politicisation of civil service has been an area of honest debate in the initial years of change. The challenge of 21st century is to save the political masters from the inbuilt evils of elitisation or bureaucratic ruling justified in the name of backwardness of people. De-elitisation of civil service is the care reform for which a democratic polity should endeavour. New institutions alone will change bureaucratic behaviour.

10

Police Administration and Criminal Justice System in India

The developing polities have endemic problems of security, survival and violence, which can be viewed as 'other side of development'. Development threatens social equilibrium and disorders and urban anomie leads to crime, vice and conflicts of varied nature. Police as an instrument of law and order and status quo is increasingly being asked to participate in political development and supplement the processes of change and growth. Naturally the administrations of police and judiciary which were formerly called as 'Regulatory Administrations' today stand conjoined with development administration of social welfare and economic growth. The latter should minimise violent crimes and discriminatory exploitation of the weak. The police and judiciary have been rather slow or even hesitant to accept this positivist philosophy of democratic transformation. Consequently, the segmental crises in the area of so-called regulatory administration have led to: (1) crisis of obsolescence, (2) crisis of incongruence, and (3) crisis of innovation to understand the malaise and the kind of reforms that need initiation. Let us screen the police organisation and the judicial system of India and their complex interlinkages vis-à-vis the Indian society.

When the East India Company took the reins of administration from the Mughals, the law and order situation in the empire was at a low ebb. Depicting the prevailing anarchic conditions, Sir Thomas Munro wrote: "A very large population of the *Taliaris* (or police officers) are either themselves robbers or employ them and many of them are murderers." The police organisation conniving at crimes and harbouring offenders in return for a share of the booty was a veritable challenge to the ingenuity of the foreign traders. Of course, they had their own interest in imperialistic exploits, yet the problems of internal security and protection of their commercial establishments on an alien soil invited their best attention.

The 1861 Police Reform

The mutiny of 1857 shook the very roots of the administration of law and order in India. The diversity and inadequacy of the police machine to deal with the increasing problems of violence and disorder made the imperial government realise the urgency of a unified and reorganised police system for the entire country. The heavy expenditure involved in maintaining a military-like police to prevent disorder and a civil police to detect disaffection in advance during the days of 1857 upheaval and after compelled the government to appoint an All India Police Commission in 1860 to look into the problems of police administration, and to suggest ways and means for an increase in police efficiency and to reduce excessive expenditure involved in maintaining the police force. The terms of reference of the Commission also included a quest for uniformity in the police system as it obtained in British India.

The Police Commission in its historic report recommended:

(1) The abolition of the military police as a separate organisation;
(2) The constitution of a single homogeneous police force of civil constabulary for the performance of all police duties;
(3) A police system on provincial basis with an Inspector General of Police as the head of the provincial police organisation;
(4) A district-based police system in which each of the district police establishments was to be headed by an SP, who was to function under the general control and supervision of the DM;
(5) Two senior police functionaries – the IGP and the SP – who have to be citizens of European origin;
(6) A subordinate police force which was to consist of inspectors, head constables, sergeants and constables;
(7) The commissioners of divisions who were not to wield additional police powers;
(8) The continuance of DMs supervision of the district police organisation but not beyond the level;
(9) The abolition of military police; and
(10) The retention of village police, which though inefficient and corrupt, was to be continued as a halfway house for its usefulness in the Indian context.

The major recommendations of the Commission were incorporated into a Bill, which was more or less on the lines of Madras Act of 1859. Later on, it was passed into a law as Act V of 1861. The basic structure of police organisation as provided in the act has withstood the ravages of time and forms the corner stone of the police administration in India till today. This Indian Police Act and the basic law codes that determine the nature, scope and limits of police jobs present the Indian police organisation as a line organisation which should seek assistance of and render help to various administrative agencies in the maintenance of law and order and prevention of crime and vice in society. Police organisation thus got linked up with several other departments and agencies like magistracy, jails, hospitals, courts, transport and communications (including the Indian Railways) and the like. Finally, the police administration in its wider ramifications became a support administration for the defence services of the nation which in turn has to come to its rescue if the emergency problems of internal security render the police dysfunctional.

The police reforms of 1860 remained a matter of debate and controversy for the rest of the century. In Bombay, the post of the police commissioner which was created in 1855 was abolished in 1860. This led to the creation of the office of the IGP in 1885, but a large amount of power of discretion and control remained inoperative. In United Provinces, the commissioner was made the *ex officio* deputy IGP with wide powers in police personnel matters. In Punjab, the same system operated with a new development that the DIG of police was gradually rendered into a nominal professional adviser to the divisional commissioner, who was also the *ex officio* DIG in status. Thus, the reforms of 1860 did not alter the situation materially and the total scheme remained in abeyance for one reason or the other in various provinces of the country.

Indian Police Commission (1902–1903)

Another significant landmark in the history of the Indian police during the British period is the appointment of the Second All-India Police Commission which came on the turn of the 19th century. The preceding Commission and the subsequent Police Act of 1861 were obviously deficient in several aspects and respects. Inefficiency and corruption in the ranks of police force were woefully rampant and the personnel recruited in the organisation continued to be untrained and ill-equipped for the job. To streamline this rumbling structure a thorough probe became necessary. The Governor-General in Council with the approval of the Secretary of the State for India appointed the Second All-India Police Commission in the year 1902 to study the state of police organisation in different provinces of the country and to make the police force effective in the changing context of Indian politics. It was the first attempt of its own kind to screen and revamp police administration in its entirety. Some of the major recommendations offered by the body were:

(1) A criminal investigation department was to be established in each province with a Dy IGP as its administrative head.
(2) The province as a unit of administration was to be divided into several ranges and each such range was to be controlled and commanded by a DIG of police.
(3) The office of the SP of the district was to be strengthened and a Dy SP was to be appointed to assist the SP.
(4) A separate and independent police organisation to be known as Railway Police Force was also to be constituted.
(5) The divisional commissioner/collector will have supervision over police administration to strike a balance between civil guidance and professional autonomy.
(6) The police circles within a district were to be under a sub-Inspector who will be different from their former counterparts, namely, the *Darogas*, the *Thanedars* and the *Kotwals.*
(7) The pay and other remunerative benefits of the police officers were to be raised quite substantially.
(8) An armed police force was to be constituted at the headquarter of each district to serve as a reserve police force.
(9) The institution of the village headman was to continue to perform rural police duties through the deployment of village watchman.

A critical look at the police reforms of 1902 would indicate that they were purposefully planned to strengthen the district police and thereby to make it serve as a powerful bulwark for the sustenance of the gigantic structure of the empire. Naturally, they ignored some of the very vital aspects of reforms like Indianisation of the police force or decentralisation of the organisation. The weakness of the Commission's report was highlighted by Maharaja Nameshwar Singh of Darbhanga, the only Indian member of this Commission, who in his dissenting note wrote:

> We require Englishmen as well as Indians in the higher ranks of the police in the interest of good administration ... . A uniform method of admission is best calculated to secure these objects ... to create a separate grade for Indians would not adequately secure the twofold object, namely, to bring the police administration more in touch with the people and to secure a class of self-relying and capable Indian officers.

He broadly agreed with his British colleagues in the Commission but made out the following points in his note of dissent:

(1) The policy of speedy Indianisation of the senior ranks in the Indian police organisation should be given a fair trial.
(2) The discriminatory treatment of Indian Dy SPs in comparison to their European counterparts (assistant superintendents) should be stopped without further delay.
(3) The policy of recruitment by open competition in the ranks of police organisation to provide fair opportunities to Indian youngman of talent and promise to serve their motherland was to be accepted and encouraged in a positive manner.
(4) The control of district police authorities must not be vested in the hands of European DMs or collectors, who viewed the police organisation as a tool to further English imperial interests.

The history of the Indian police during the first half of the 19th century is a history of status quo. The Englishmen labouriously built the police machine and very meticulously tended its organisation to suit to the colonial needs of the Imperial government. For decades, the police had to strive to attain the status of a district and independent departmental organisation. Yet by way of an overall assessment of the legacies of the British Raj, one may agree with J.C. Curry who maintains:

> To the self-governing India of the future, the Indian police force is not the least of the gifts which Britain has to offer and it can only augur ill for the future, if those who claim to speak of modern and of some progress fail to realise how much it mews to India to have such a weapon made ready at hand.

During the freedom struggle, the Indian masses saw treason in the professional loyalty of the honest policeman. Taking advantage of mass illiteracy, deep-rooted tradition of autocratic rule and widespread poverty, the English rulers in particular, designed a police force through which they could use the natives to counterpoise the natives. The low prestige of a garrulous police force did not bother them much so long as they were prepared to use wanton force on the bidding of their alien masters to keep them in power. The result has been that police administration in India has been much maligned on the one hand and has sunk deep in the cesspool of stagnation and decay on the other. The Indian rulers continue to exploit it even after independence and the masses hate it much more for the simple reason that it has neither changed nor improved. The dawn of independence unleashed a new tendency which is symbolised by the fact that the rulers and even the ruled have quite often joined hands in simultaneous denunciation of the police. The former debunk the police to cover their own misdeeds while the latter would treat them as sold agents of the ruling class.

The growth of administration in general and police administration in particular during the last decades in the wake of rapid rise in crime statistics and public disorders can be attributed to the growth of urbanisation and other compulsions of democracy. As a result of this, a great amount of structural proliferation can be witnessed in the organisation of police, general and especially in the emergence of specialised agencies at the Centre. Some of these CPO are: Central Reserve Police Force (CRPF), BSF, Special Police Establishment (SPE) the Intelligence Bureau (IB), CBI, CPF, ITBP, BP&RD, SPG and NSG. A spate of reform have renovated these organisations and changed the functions of these units in the light of the new needs and techniques available today.

The Dharam Veer Police Commission (1978–80) assisted by extremely able policemen like Rustamji, Narsimhan and N.S. Saxena laboured for almost three years and notwithstanding a very limited term of reference attempted a thorough inquest and produced a dozen reports with several dozens of valuable recommendations. The Commission took advantages of the labours of state level study teams and voluminous reports of Wankhede Commission in Maharashtra, A.P. Jain Commission in Uttar Pradesh, Justice Khosla Commission in Delhi and similar bodies in Bihar and Bengal. It was a thorough exercise in administrative research and the reports bear an imprint of collective wisdom and empirical insights into the operation of Indian police. The later governments have taken to the implementation of some of the recommendation of NPC in a piecemeal manner and the twenty first century police reformers may hopefully reshape the organisation.

But the legacies of British Raj continue to be dilemmas of sorts for Indian Police which D.H. Bailey has summed up as under:

(1) Philosophy and negativism
(2) State-based system
(3) Armed and unarmed constabulary
(4) Horizontal stratification
(5) Muscle-oriented police force
(6) Magisterial supremacy over police

Free India has witnessed all kinds of administrative reforms and violent agitations for their initiation. Most of the states have evinced interest in police organisations and appointed high-level commissions. The reports of these commissions have identified deep-seated maladies which demand radical overhaul in the structure and working of police administration. All these commissions have recommended better conditions of service for the constabulary, specialised training programmes, independence of police from the magistracy in the administration of law and order, modernisation of police equipment, steps for bringing about cordial relations between the police and the public and basic reforms in all-India codes like Criminal Procedure Code of India, the Indian Penal Code and the Indian Evidence Act. The Commissions have also made a spirited plea for a citizen police force. They have welcomed the role of Union government as a coordinator of police administrations in the states. But then, notwithstanding all these suggestions, literally very little has been accomplished in terms of reforms and improvement of police administration since independence, which more or less, stands where it was in 1861.

Police administration in India on the dawn of 21st century continues to confront the two major questions of Bayley, viz., (1) Is the Indian police system capable of coping effectively with the basic tasks of police responsibilities? and (2) Is the present system of Indian police is compatible with a democratic polity as it was with a colonial regime? The answers to these questions are obviously in the negative. Naturally, the people, the politicians, the civilian bureaucrats and the policemen should put a concerted effort and have a fresh look on the organisation and its framework in terms of its potentialities and limitations. It is true that the challenges confronting the police are numerous as well as enormous but then, in their wider ramifications, they are not a challenge to a segment of administrative organisation but to the political system itself. The survival and growth of democratic institutions require a well-ordered polity which does imply a critical role for the police. Who these policemen are? What do they do? And how do they accomplish what they are assigned to do, these are the basic issues to which we need to address ourselves. Do police personnel represent all the strata of society? Are they capable of throwing up and working with new leadership? Do they participate in and influence policy decisions? What are their priorities in law enforcement? Do they really enforce law? Where is the locus of their initiative? Are they secretive or open? Do they act impartially? How do they behave with the common man? These are some of the open questions which need the attention of social scientists. If the police administration fails in performing its basic jobs, the future of democratic institutions may be in jeopardy. The policeman can contribute to the erosion of faith in popular government and conversely, he can provide a sustenance to the ongoing system of Indian democracy. The dichotomy between regulatory and development administrations is not only superficial but also disastrous. Obviously, all investments in police administration or reforms in policing are an indirect input in political development. The Indian society should learn it the rational way.

I

Union Policing

Technically speaking, there is no independent department of police at the central level, but the union ministry of home affairs certainly performs numerous police functions, though it shall be erroneous to call it a ministry for police affairs. The Union Parliament, which have exclusive and paramount jurisdiction on central and concurrent subjects respectively, does not directly legislate on police affairs but the Constitution admits of a large amount of legislative discretion and executive accountability in regard to police administration both at the Union and state levels to the sovereign Parliament of the country. The indirect but dominant role of the Central government in police administration of the country, which is symbolised by the Union Parliament and the union ministry of home affairs, manifests itself as follows:

Union Government's Role in Police Administration

Parliament	*Ministry of Home Affairs*
1. Law-making on subjects in the Union and the Concurrent Lists.	1. Administration of All-India Statutes.
2. Amendments in Basic Police Acts.	2. Administration of Union Territories.
3. Special measures during emergencies.	3. Personnel Management of the IPS.
4. Police coordination.	
5. Supply and control of arms and equipment.	
6. Operations of Home Guards and Civil Defence.	
7. Operations through a network of staff agencies and auxiliary units of CPOS.	

Article 246 of Schedule VII of the Constitution enumerates police as a subject in the State List, but then it simultaneously includes a long list of allied and quasi-police subjects in the Union List also. Accordingly, the administration of subjects like all India services, CBI, preventive detention, arms, ammunition, explosives, extradition, passports and a host of similar others is the sole responsibility of the Central government. Naturally, the administration of these subjects has a direct and critical bearing on the police administration which in strict constitutional sense falls within the state jurisdiction. The problems become still more intricate and complex when one goes through the subjects enumerated in the Concurrent List, which includes subjects like criminal law, criminal procedure, maintenance of public order, evidence, trade in essential goods and even price control. The administrative activities, pertaining to these subjects generally fall in the domain of die police activity and if the Union Parliament decide to legislate on any of these subjects, the state governments have to accept, adjust and act accordingly. Similarly, the power to amend some of the basic police statutes like the Indian Police Act 1861, the Indian Penal Code 1860, the Code of Criminal Procedure 1861, the Code of Civil Procedure 1859 and the Hindu and Islamic laws operative in the Indian Union lies with the Parliament. One of the Directive Principles of State Policy of the Constitution also urges upon the governments at the Union and state levels to evolve a Uniform Civil Code in the country.

The Central government wields the power to direct the state governments to ensure full compliance of the laws passed by the Union Parliament. There are already several Central Acts which control and guide performance of police functions throughout the country. The acts lay down and condition the pattern of police organisation and procedures of its working at length. They also outline in general the duties, powers, rights and the privileges of the police and prescribe its relationship with the magistracy. However, the state legislatures are competent to amend these acts but they cannot modify their underlying principles. The three basic acts are:

(1) The Indian Penal Code;
(2) The Code of Criminal Procedure; and
(3) The Indian Evidence Act.

These acts have their jurisdictions all over the country. They govern the procedure followed in the administration of criminal justice. The state police administrations, irrespective of their nature, have to operate within the prescribed framework of these statutes.

The ministry of home affairs is also directly responsible for the maintenance and administration of police forces in the union territories which are directly administered on behalf of the President of India through civil administrators. All of them are administered under different acts of the Union Parliament. The administrative agencies of these territories are specially manned by regular cadres recruited for the purpose.

Another important function of the ministry relates to personnel aspects of police administration in India, particularly with regard to the personnel belonging to the IPS. The ministry lays down general conditions of service, its rights and duties, pay and pensions and conditions governing other assignments and deputations. It also exercises control through rules and regulations which directly impinge upon implementation of these service conditions.

The Centre's role is critically important because it largely determines the standard of police efficiency and also saves a large amount of foreign exchange, as the home ministry arranges for the manufacture of indigenous arms and equipments. Since 1957, it has also started advancing crores of rupees for modernisation and also as annual loans to the state governments for the construction of living quarters for the non-gazetted police officials of the states. The ministry maintains civil defence services in readiness in selected places to be pressed into service for training and other ad hoc purposes. There are mobile civil emergency forces at Delhi and Kolkata which are expected to assist the police organisation of these areas in rescue operations. The home ministry also ensures an adequate supply of arms and ammunition to the state home guards and provides special facilities for the training of instructors in civil defence with active cooperation of the National Rifles Association of India.

These auxiliary police agencies of the Union government have not only increased in number, but the nature and scope of their police work have also undergone a change in the context of democracy and federalism. Some of these Central Police Organisations (CPOs) are purely staff agencies. Others are functioning as reserve units with line operations while yet others have mixed functions and overlapping jurisdictions in concurrent fields. The chart below can present this classification as under:

Central Police Organisations

Staff Units	*Mixed Units*	*Line Units*
1. Central Forensic Institutes	1. CIB	1. CRPF
(a) CFI and IB	2. CBI	2. BSF
(b) Serologist Office	3. SPE	3. The Assam Rifles
(c) Central Fingerprint Bureau	4. CVC	4. CRPF
(d) Central Detective Training School	5. CISF	
(e) Central Institute of Criminology and Forensic Science	6. India Reserve	
(f) Examiner of Questioned Documents	7. National Security Guards	
(g) Masters of Mints	8. SPG	
(h) Master, India Security Printing	9. RAF	
(i) Inspector of Explosives		
2. Sardar Vallabhbhai Patel Police Academy		
3. Internal Security Academy		
4. Directorate of Police Wireless		

Staff Units

A descriptive profile of staff units popularly known as CPOs is outlined below:

(1) Central Forensic Institutes: The organisation has three major units at Kolkata. They are:
 (i) The Central Forensic Science Laboratory;
 (ii) The Central Detective Training School; and
 (iii) The Central Finger Print Bureau.
  (a) Central Forensic Science Laboratory
  (b) Serologist to the Government of India
  (c) The Central Finger Print Bureau
  (d) The Central Detective Training School
  (e) Examiner of Questioned Documents
  (f) The Masters of the Mints
  (g) The Master, India Security Printing
  (h) The Inspector of Explosives

(2) Sardar Vallabhbhai Patel Police Academy

(3) The Directorate of Police Wireless

Mixed Units

(1) Central Intelligence Bureau (CIB)
(2) Central Bureau of Investigation (CBI)
(3) Special Police Establishment (SPE)

Line Agencies

We now turn to a description of the more important line agencies:

(1) The Central Reserve Police (CRPF)
(2) Border Security Force (BSF)
(3) The Assam Rifles
(4) The Railway Protection Force (RPF)
(5) Central Industrial Security Force (CISF)
(6) India Reserves
(7) Indo-Tibetan Border Police (ITBP)
(8) National Crime Records Bureau (NCRB)
(9) Bureau of Police Research and Development (BPR&D)
(10) Development of Riot/Plastic Pellets
(11) Modification of 303 rifles for firing plastic pellets
(12) Vajra-Anti Riot Vehicle with T.S. Shell Launchers
(13) Shock Batons
(14) Mechanised Bullet Proof Bunker
(15) Anti-Explosion Material for Petrol Tanks of Vehicles
(16) Bullet Proof Jackets/Steel
(17) Pollution Masks
(18) Mobile Kitchen
(19) Portrait Building System
(20) Water Cannon Mounted Vehicle
(21) Training Division
(22) Research Division
(23) Forensic Science
(24) National Institute of Criminology and Forensic Science (NICFS)

India is a federal polity with a strong centre. The classical theory of federalism has been diluted and adapted to the dominant needs of a centralised polity. Obviously, the law and order administration in general and the police administration of the country in particular, also bear a distinct imprint of centralising tendencies of the federation, which in fact, has received approbation at the hands of ARC. The role of the dominant centre in a federal polity of Indian variety may be a matter of debate but police administration conditioned by discipline and organisational patterns of military variety accepts the role of the Central government as part and parcel of the system. The existing arrangement is also defensible on the ground that the state governments have freedom to maintain police organisations in their respective areas, though the Government of India plays a leadership role in evolving uniform patterns of administrative structure of police under its overall supervision and coordinating command.

II

State Police Organisation

The police organisation in Indian states is primarily governed by the Police Act of 1861, which was based on the recommendations of the Police Commission of 1860. Section 4 of this statute lays down the principles, on which the organisation of the police force rests till today. The section inter alia states:

> The administration of the police throughout a general police district (now called states) shall be vested in an officer to be styled the Inspector General of Police and in such Deputy Inspectors General and Assistant Inspectors General as the State government shall deem fit.

Organisationally, the police system in India represents a queer amalgam of the Hindu, Mughal and British traditions and institutions. Conventionally, the field formations were typically mediaeval, over which the Englishmen grafted a quasi-sophisticated system of district police. As the district was the hub of revenue activity in rural India, the district police gradually became a significant organisation. The demands of national movement along with vast topography and the absence of communication network yielded a lot of local colour to the ground root organisation.

At the state level, the police largely performs staff functions and some marginal exceptions apart, has a remarkably uniform and standardised patterns of organisation and working. As a line

Police Organisation in the States

Director General of Police
↓
Additional DGPs
↓
Inspector General of Police DIG

IGP/Addl./Deputy/
Asstt. IGP
(at State Police
Headquarters)
Commissioner of Police
(in big cities only)
↓
1. Dy. Commissioner
2. Asstt. Commissioner
3. Inspectors
4. Sub-Inspectors

Special Functions
1. Headquarters
2. Administration
3. Welfare
4. Armed Force
5. Training and Rules
6. Radio Network
7. Anti-Dacoity Operations
8. Railways

SP
1. District Police
2. Reserve Police Lines
3. Crime Bureau
4. Special Branch
5. Traffic Police

Range
1. SP/Addl. SP (Distt.)
2. Dy. SP/ASP(Sub. Div.)
3. Circle Inspector (Police Circle)
4. ASI Outpost
5. Head Const. Chowki, and
6. Constable Beat House

CID
1. Crime Branch
2. Special Branch
3. M.O.B.
4. Criminal Intelligence
5. Scientific Secretary. (in some states)
1. Anti-Corruption
2. Police Radio
3. Legal Sections
4. Railways

Asstt. IGP Rly. Police
(in some states only)
↓
1. SP Rly. Police (in most of the States)
2. Railway Police Subdivisions
3. Railway Police Circles
4. Railway Police Stations
5. Railway Police Out Posts

agency, it is primarily district-based and district-oriented. The state level officials are too far from the scene of activity to matter and be effective as line officers in the police department. At the state level, the role of the police officers even in the line hierarchy gets transformed in staff functions, which they have to perform at three distinct levels as follows:

(1) Staff functions in the Union government and its auxiliary agencies;
(2) Staff functions in relation to home department of the state government; and
(3) Staff-cum-line functions in relation to the line officials in the districts.

The police administration at the state level consists of two organisational wings: (i) the civil and (ii) the professional.

The Director General of Police

The Police Act, 1861 formally made the DGP responsible for the administration of the police of the state or place or any part of the state or place in which the act has been put into operation. The primary functions of the DG of Police of the state are:

(1) to serve as a principal adviser to his state government in all matters pertaining to police administration of the state. In this capacity, he can suggest matters and measures for policy formulation and policy planning to the home minister or the chief minister and the chief secretary of his state through the home commissioner.
(2) to act as an administrative head of the state police organisation and to execute the policy decisions under the directives of the State government. He commands the line operations from the top and supervises implementation of the policy in consultation with those who formulate the same.
(3) to keep his own house in order and also to keep it going in terms of detailed routine work. He is responsible for internal economy and all those steps which are necessary for the efficient handling of the security services in the state.

The office of the DG of Police is the highest and the most significant office in the realm of police administration in the state. It provides a vital link between the government and its police organisation. He periodically supplies statistical data and intelligence regarding crime to the government for purposes of police assessment from a long-range angle. He also furnishes relevant information to the state and Union governments with regard to political situation, industrial troubles, communal tensions, agrarian unrest, student violence and foreign espionage in the state, offers his expert advice on these matters and suggests how to deal with them. He can also initiate anticipatory action by deployment of police forces and directing them to the needs of the situation. He uses his police force for the service of the community during natural calamities like accidents, fires, floods, earthquakes and famines. He has other special responsibilities also like providing security to very important persons, national leaders and foreign dignitaries within the state. He controls political disorders during election time and is expected to take remedial measures as advised by the Government of India.

Police Administration at Range Level

With the introduction of the new positions of the DG and additional DGs of police in states, the inspector general of police have become staff officers to look after functional responsibilities of specialised nature. Each state has several IGPs at its capital headquarters, looking after professional tasks like police training, police computers, anti-corruption, intelligence, police modernisation and police welfare, etc. In these areas, they may be helped by additional inspector general of police, which every state has for staff aid to the DGP and the ADGPs as the case may be. The IGP has a number of DIGs each heading the administration of a police range. Some of them look after administration and working of specialised branches like intelligence, CID, armed police, police training, anti-corruption and the like at the state headquarters. Each police range normally comprises 4 to 6 administrative districts, depending upon the size and importance of the district concerned.

The area and population variables provide differing criteria in the delimitation of the boundaries and the number of districts in a range varies from 2 to 8 in the small and large states of Kerala and Uttar Pradesh respectively. The range which coordinates the administration of the district police at the intermediary level constitutes middle tier in the administrative hierarchy, which is higher than that of the district but lower to the state. These functions and duties of the DIG present him in a double role as staff adviser to the DGP or IGP and as a line commander of the range, controlling the administration of police districts under him. In the latter category, his functions include operational control over the working of the organisation through personnel management and budgetary execution. He is a delegator, a coordinator and a controller and much of his role depends upon the way he conducts himself with his seniors.

The Organisational Profiles

The chart broadly outlines the organisational system of the state police as it obtains in different states of the country at the levels of the DGP, ADGP, IGP and the DIG. The CID and the specialised wings functions as staff-cum-line agencies. The Police Commissioner System, which is operative in the metropolitan towns, has its own administrative hierarchy in which the commissioner stands somewhere between the DGP and the IGP. He has a team of colleagues and subordinates, who operate territorially as well as functionally under him.

Each state determines the hierarchy of these branch organisations according to its size and the volume of work it has to handle. The CID and the anti-corruption departments are generally headed by senior police officers of IGP or DIG rank but the organisations like special armed police, training colleges, mounted police and police wireless are placed under the command of senior SPs. Most of the states generally have four specialised branches, viz., (1) The CID; (2) The anti-corruption department; (3) The railway police; and (4) The PAC. Some of the states also maintain mounted and women police forces. The Central government have urged upon the states to build an organisation of home guards as a part of the state police under senior police officers. A closer view of the various branches of the professional wings lists them as under:

(1) The CID
(2) The special branch

Thus, the professional wing of the state police works under the overall command and supervision of the DGP of the state. He has a couple of special, additional director general of police to aid and advise him at the police headquarters. They may also administer some of the specialised police functions like anti-corruption, vigilance, civil defence training and traffic, etc., at the state level. The DGP is the chief of the state police and the Police Act assigns specific responsibilities to him in the areas of police policy formulation and line operation involved in the execution of the policy. He is the chief personnel officer of his department and has wide powers and discretions with regard to financial management and disciplinary matters in his organisation. As an administrative leader of his team, he functions through a number of deputy inspector general of police working on territorial or functional basis. The DIG in charge of a police range supervises the work of 4 to 6 administrative district, which constitutes the intermediary level in the administrative hierarchy, just below the state and above the district. The functional DIGs at the state level take care of auxiliary units such as the CID, the intelligence department, the railway police, the police training institutions, the police headquarters and the armed battalions at the state level. There is no uniform pattern about the number and work of the DIGs in various states of the Union. The DIG range exercises a general supervision over the work of the district superintendents of police and the latter look to him for advise, guidance, leadership and coordination of police work in the range. As in charge of the specialised branch like CID, intelligence, anti-corruption, traffic, railway and armed police forces the DIG has his own independent hierarchy and functional network, depending upon the nature and scope of his operations. For instance, the DIG, CID, has a horizontal organisation to which MOB, finger print bureau, forensic laboratories of the state and dog squads are attached as subordinate offices. The Police Training Institutions in states have their quasi-autonomous organisations and are generally headed by IG of Police. The Railway Police Organisation follows the district and state system of jurisdiction in different states. This jurisdiction conforms to the railway

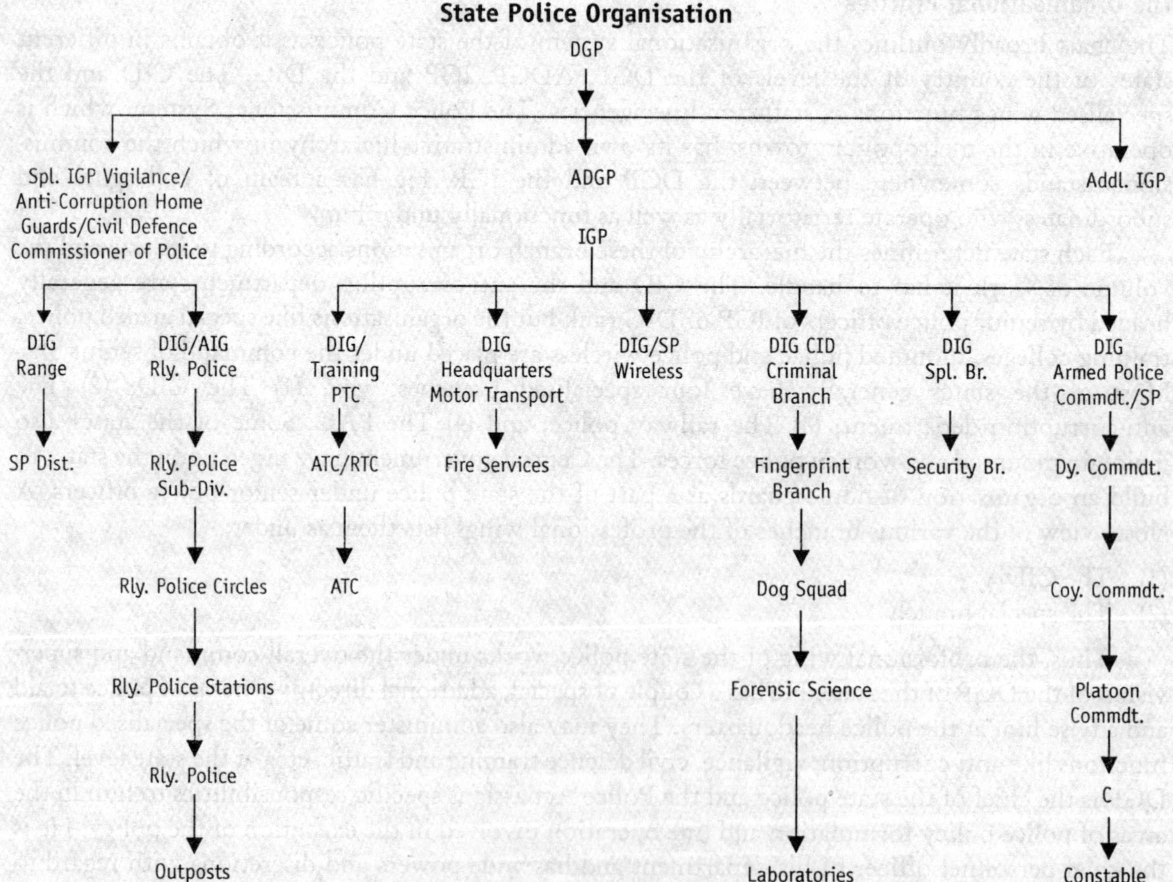

limits, extending between outer signals and the running trains. The functions of the railway police are similar in all the states and it functions as an island of police administration within the larger ocean of police administration of the state. The exchange of personnel between civil and railway police at each level brings home the complementary nature of the railway police organisation. The state armed police force represents the continuation of military police and the crown representative police of pre-independence days. It is called by different names in different states; PAC in UP and Rajasthan, Special Armed Police in Madhya Pradesh, Military Police in Bihar, Assam Rifles in Assam and Malabar Police in Tamil Nadu. They are in the nature of reserves at the disposal of the DGP, who can deploy them on the requisition of the DIG of the range. As a reserve striking force, they are employed in special situations or on security duties in sensitive areas. The organisation of the traffic police at the state level police administration is a phenomenon emerging in the wake of increasing urbanisation. At the state level, the function of the traffic police fall mostly within the arena of staff duties, such as planning, road research, coordination of district level efforts and advise to the DGP in matters pertaining to movement of heavy vehicles and road safety in the cities. The wings of women police and mounted police represent welcome additions to the state police organisations in view of the changing nature and techniques of crime, vice and public disorder in free India. The organisation of home guards has been sponsored and financed by the Union government as an auxiliary unit of the state police administration in most of the states. These functional agencies can be listed as under:

(1) The Crime Branch
(2) The Railway Police
(3) State Armed Police Force
(4) Traffic Police
(5) Women Police
(6) Mounted Police
(7) The Home Guards
(8) State Police Training Academies

The Metropolitan Police

The office of the Commissioner of Metropolitan Police combines the functions of a state DGP, an IGP and the DM of a town, in Kolkata particularly, the police acts give the organisation a local colour. The major characteristics of the metropolitan police organisation are independent from the control of the magistracy and functional nature of the police organisation. Such an organisation specially suits the big cities where the chunks of urban population are concentrated in congested areas, big industrial establishment are haphazardly dispersed, a special kind of floating population keeps on moving from the suburbs and the hinterland to the city and back and the city dwellers, besides being critical of police performance, are highly indifferent to their social obligations. The unhelpful attitude of the city public underlines the necessity of a highly specialised and refracted police organisation which may be pressed into service with speed, efficiency and effectivity in difficult and trying situations of urban ecological setting. During British days, the organisations of the state police and the commissioner, tended to be aloof from one another. After independence the conditions of service have been made uniform and a greater exchange of personnel and a closer cooperation's in handling police problems have been brought about. The ARC has recommended a wider application of this experiment than what obtains at the moment.

Thus, the police organisation at the state level has a wide and complex network of specialised branches. Operating above the level of a district, it controls, coordinates and supervises the work of its field agencies, which are concerned with the execution of policy. It also provides a link between the political and the administrative echelons of the machinery for law and order at the state level. It is here that critical decisions about the problems of regulatory administration are taken, which in turn are pumped into the political mechanism of the government as advice and are systematically processed and formulated into regular policy propositions. Later, they are transmitted to the line below through their initiators for purposes of implementation. In addition to the basic administrative duties of planning, staffing, coordinating, directing, controlling and budgeting, the state police organisation operates through a network of staff agencies. Each of these agencies provides a special kind of police service to the district administration with marginal variations. The state level organisations of police administration in India function under a unified command of the Director General, who through his IGPs and DIGs supervises the work of his district SPs and their juniors below the line. The police headquarters of the state, have staff units like CID, anti-corruption department, railway police, reserved armed police and home guards, which have their district units within or outside the regular police organisation. The DGP and his aids procure information from the line units and through the specialised agencies of the police. The office of the DGP studies the information and keeps the home department appraised with its evaluations and the home commissioner in turn conveys to the DGP the current thinking of the government. The office of the DGP again works out administrative details of the policies in terms of a blueprint of clear-cut operations and follow-up actions. The policy sub-decisions of die state level organisations are shared by and with his colleagues in the head office and subordinates down below the line. The line officials concretise these actions at each level. Thus, the state level police organisation at the state headquarters has to perform the following roles in relation to the state government and the people:

(1) To collect relevant information or data for feeding into policy decisions;
(2) To advice the political masters in the areas of critical decision-making;
(3) To supervise, coordinate, direct and control the line agencies and keep a check on the implementation of details through procedural tracks;
(4) To keep a network of staff-cum-line agencies functioning as clearing house and to conduct the administration of special police services through these specialised agencies;
(5) To arrange for the training of state police personnel, especially the Dy SPs and SIs who form the linchpin of the entire edifice of police organisation at the state level; and
(6) To assist the Union government in discharging its constitutional responsibilities in the maintenance of peace and tranquillity in the entire country or any part thereof during peace time as well as during emergency.

The foregoing profile of roles presents the state level police administration in a dual capacity: it performs the line and the staff functions. Some of the staff agencies operate from the headquarters of the state and may or may not have field organisations with a unity of command through their district headquarters. The line functions of the state level police administration include implementation of policies pertaining to law and order and detection and investigation of crimes with the help of district units, which operate through a wide network of rural police stations. The state DGP/IGP command, control, supervise and coordinate implementation of policies. The advisory role of the specialised agencies like CID, anti-corruption department, training institutes, forensic directorates is equally significant and the office of the DGP has to filter a mass of information that goes under the routine chores of exchange of reports, returns, proposals, estimates, letters and special briefs.

With the thrust of social change the areas of police activity are expanding and the responsibilities of the state level police administration are tending to multiply manifold. As time passes, political forces at the grass-root level will unleash greater challenges of disorder and political instability. Similarly, the new foci of crime and tension will be generated in the wake of relative affluence and erosion of ethico-religious values in society. The pace of increasing urbanisation in the country will also continue to build up additional strains on the police administration, which has remained, by and large, unchanged over the last hundred and fifty years. As a shock-absorber of social tension and political upheavals, the state level police administration in India has to be receptive to the dynamics of modernisation to adapt to the demands of change.

III

District Police Organisation

The police administration is built around police districts. Each police range comprises of four or more police districts, which coincide with the boundaries of the revenue districts. Organisationally, the district is further subdivided into police circles and police stations. The police circles are placed under the control of circle inspectors while the police stations are administratively managed by the SIs of police, which are known by several names in vernacular in different states. Some police stations also have their police outposts or *chowkis* within their territorial jurisdiction, which are usually under the charge of head constables or assistant SIs of police depending on the importance of the place where an outpost is located.

For organisational purposes, a police station is the smallest field unit of police administration. Several states have abolished police inspectors in the wake of administrative reorganisation. The SP who heads the district police office, also coordinates the functions of the heads of the district police lines, district crime bureau, district special branch, district traffic branch and the district prosecution branch. The volume of work which depends upon the size and special demographic characteristics of the district, generally determines the size of police network and the functions of the SP. As a police chief, he has to work in close liaison and collaboration with his administrative seniors at the range and state headquarters. The organisational chart given on the next page depicts the chain of command as it obtains in the police organisation of a typical district.

District Headquarters and the Office of the SP

The district police organisation constitutes the hub of the Indian police system. On an average, an Indian district covers about 3,600 sq miles and a population of over a million and a quarter people. In addition to providing administrative services, the district headquarters have a large jail and store-houses for clothing equipment, arms and ammunition. Constables for the district are recruited and partly trained here. Armed police and sometimes, mounted police also have their reserve lines or barracks there. The CID organisation operates from its headquarters. Adequate discretion has been vested in the police authorities at this level and this facilitates a happy mediation between general directives and adjustment to specific circumstances.

The district police organisation is represented by its chief, the SP. He is always a member of the IPS and wields a great amount of power and prestige in the district. Working under the overall supervision of the DM, he looks after the problems of law and order and that of the administration of crime and vice in the district. As the chief intelligence officer of the district, he collects information from the lower levels and communicates his assessment of the same to his superiors of the district police personnel system and looks after the service conditions of the junior police employees working under his charge. He is directly responsible for their efficiency, morale and discipline as policemen. In districts which territorially include big cities, the SPs have additional and special responsibilities such as regulation and control of traffic, collection of special intelligence and handling of political and communal conflicts of violent nature.

The district or the state police organisation controls the network of police stations spread all over the country. The superintendent of police, who presides over this organisation, is the key functionary through whom the state government operates and the police stations below look to him for command, guidance and action. Hierarchically speaking, the district police in most of the states stand organised into police subdivisions and police circles, which comprise a cluster of police stations. The additional or deputy superintendents of police look after the work of police subdivisions, while the circle inspectors deal with the supervisory work of police stations falling within their respective circles. A number of staff agencies such as crime bureau, special branch and special investigating agency, etc., stand converged into the office of the district SP, who, in turn, operates through a network of line units, such as police stations, special squads, prosecuting branch, traffic police and reserve police.

The SP is empowered to take all sorts of preventive measures, if a breach of peace is apprehended in the district. To avoid untoward situations, he may advice the collector to issue prohibitory orders and even to clamp curfew, if the situation so warrants. In the event of actual breach of peace, he is expected to make adequate police arrangements to cope with the situation. Crowd-control during fairs and religious festivals are his special concerns. If agitations are launched by political parties or other militant groups, the SP is required to take special precautions consistent with the susceptibilities of special groups. Holi, Diwali, Bakra-Id, VIP visits, election campaigns and political meetings, etc., are some of the special occasions when mass congregations threaten to violate public order and as such their management constitutes special responsibilities of the SP.

Deliberate violation of laws is a crime and even where it does not disturb public peace or security in an immediate sense, it has to be detected and plugged in time in the larger public interests. The SP of a district has special responsibility in this regard. He controls the incidence of crime in his district through: (a) effective patrol by his fleet; (b) investigation of grave crimes and making and receiving special reports about these cases; and (c) administrative supervision over his subordinates who keep constant vigilance, take preventive measures. and maintain up-to-date records of criminals in the district. The function entails a number of subsidiary duties. The SP has to call for reports, supervise in person and visit the scenes of crime soon after their occurrence. This is a major traditional function and the victims involved in these crimes after go to the SP as aggrieved parties in appeal.

The SP also supervises the operations of crime and special branches of his CID. He sends periodic information to the DIG (Intelligence) at regular intervals. He also acts as a line agency on

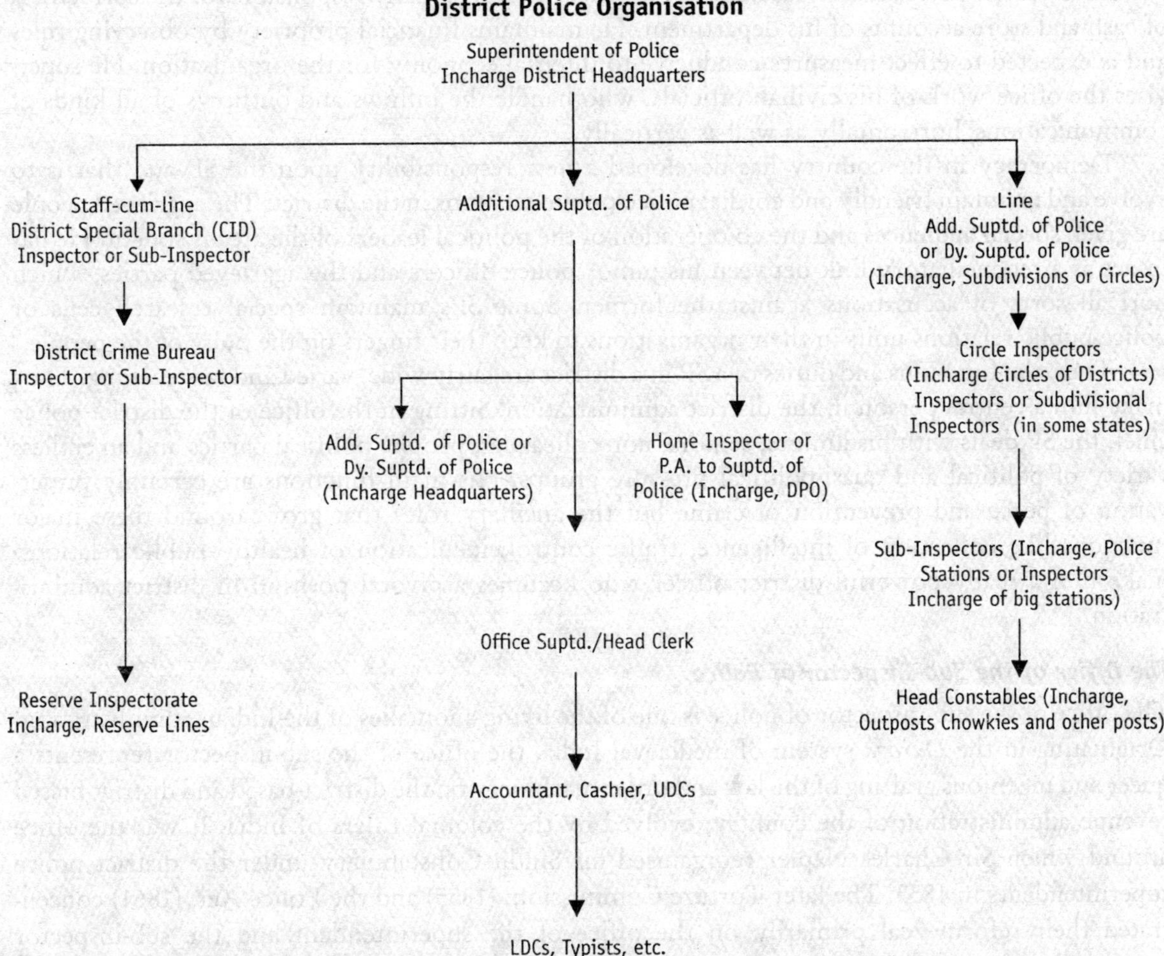

behalf of the state organisation of the CID, which, in turn, may ask him to undertake certain special kinds of intelligence operations on the request of Union agencies like CBI or CIB or SPE. The civil, the political and the senior police officials of the government have to be kept constantly informed about the incriminating activities of the saboteurs of peace and enemies of the state.

The functions of the SP further include various kinds of organisational and personnel responsibilities at the district level. He has to maintain an adequate supply of vehicles, arms, communications, equipments and other accessories like uniforms, etc., in a good shape. He inspects police stations within the jurisdictional limits of his district and provides for necessary physical conditions to keep his men working in a satisfactory state of morale and motivation. As a captain of his team, the SP has a critical say in the policies pertaining to recruitment, promotion, training programmes and disciplinary matters. He evaluates the performance of his administrative subordinates and takes disciplinary actions as and where needed. To effect discipline in the force he attends parades, gives personal interviews and recommends cases for promotion, punishment and transfers to his seniors. He organises sports, tournaments, annual get-together and special meets to keep his district force in high spirits. He undertakes police welfare projects and provides incentives to his juniors for better performance. As head of the office, he is personally responsible for the correctness of cash and store accounts of his department. He maintains financial propriety by observing rules and is expected to effect measures conducive to internal economy for the organisation. He supervises the office work of his civilian officials, who handle the inflows and outflows of all kinds of communications, horizontally as well as vertically.

Democracy in the country has developed a new responsibility upon the SP and that is to evolve and maintain friendly and cordial police-public relations in the district. The aggrieved people are given special audiences and the co-operation of the political leaders of the area is sought. He has to act as a reconciliatory link between his junior police officers and the aggrieved parties, which hurl all sorts of accusations against the former. Some SPs maintain special research cells or police-public relations units in their organisations to keep their fingers on the pulse of the people.

Thus, the functions and duties of a SP in a district are fairly wide, varied and far-reaching. They make him a central person in the district administration. Sitting in the office of the district police chief, the SP deals with his juniors, seniors, non-colleagues, people, political parties and an endless variety of political and quasi-political pressure groups. His main functions are certainly preservation of peace and prevention of crime but the ancillary roles that grow around these major functions like collection of intelligence, traffic control, inculcation of healthy public relations, make him a really powerful district officer who occupies a pivotal position in district administration.

The Office of the Sub-Inspector of Police

The office of the sub-inspector of police is one of the living anomalies of the Indian administration. Originating in the *Daroga* system of mediaeval India, the office of the sub-inspector represents a queer and ingenious grafting of the law and order machinery on the district-based and district-biased revenue administration of the country, evolved by the colonial rulers of India. It was the office around which Sir Charles Napier reorganised his Sindh Constabulary under the district police superintendents in 1853. The later Torture Commission, (1855) and the Police Act, (1861) concentrated their reform zeal primarily on the office of the superintendent and the sub-inspector continued to be a petty functionary with enormous powers and Herculean responsibilities. The Police Commission of 1902 also lamented a great deal about the organisational contradictions and personnel policy loose-ends at all the levels below the superintendent of police but very little concrete or reformatory action could emerge in the background of the history of the national movement. This one potent factor has kept the Indian police insulated and relatively stagnant for almost the entire 20th century. It has contributed a great deal to the omnipotence and omnipresence of the sub-inspector in the realm of the law and order administration. Being the lowest responsible functionary on the spot, he has been handling the sociology of crime and the politics of mass violence and quasi non-violence with a lot of discretion in the absence of a communication revolution. Although independence has radically altered the politics, the economics and the sociology of the country, yet the fact remains that, notwithstanding a few ritualistic exhortations in the periodic reports of the State Police Commissions, nothing basic or serious has been attempted or even conceived of to rationalise his position, powers, duties and relationships in the emerging pattern of administration in the states and at the Centre. Mass education, adult suffrage, parliamentary system of government, Panchayati Raj, urban patterns of living, liberation of women, labour unionism, communal tensions and increasing youth violence have all added to his predicate meats, but still very much like a Casablanca instinctively trained to obey his seniors, he stands on the burning docks of social upheaval with literally very little mental and professional equipment to combat with. His recruitment and training have rendered him into a pathetic picture of apparent muscle, mentally insecure and psychologically timid and starving. He is efficient but he does not care what the social and economic costs involved are. Having nothing but crude and blatant power to exhibit and constantly surrounded by all sorts of criminals, delinquents, neurotics and abnormal, he finds his mental equipment and intellect-cultivation too fragile to stand to the strain. No wonder the psychic needs of his personality tend to make him arrogant and even a slavish flatterer to his seniors. Worse still are the varieties, which become escapists and take an apathetic view of things with mysterious dispositions.

The recruitment and training of sub-inspectors and the constabulary are not only out of tune in themselves but are not relevantly and gainfully linked with the purpose of the organisation and the new philosophy of the profession. Only skills are being imparted and in the absence of norms and attitude they are working the other way round. The neglect of the problems of performance evaluation, incentivisation and follow up programmes do not redound to the credit of the training institutions. The trainers of the equitation and musketry age not only need retraining but bring the problems of gerontocracy or generation gap into play. This breeds professional casteism and generates low morale among those who are yet to launch upon their lifetime careers. Obviously, an ill-equipped recruit militarily trained and brain-washed into the professional skills and physical discipline of the profession by his hierarchical seniors can hardly grow into a dynamic police officer whom the changing police scene in India so sadly needs and so badly demands.

The Police Station

'A police station', by definition, "is a place or post generally or specially declared as such by the state government and includes local area specified by the state government on this behalf". It is a primary administrative unit of police investigation which receives and registers information and complaints about cognisable offences. The jurisdiction of a police station is often changed or recognised by the state government on the recommendations of the DGP, DIG range and the district collector. The average area of a police station in India is about 200 sq miles, covering about one hundred villages or so and with a population of approximately 1,00,000 persons.

However, the jurisdiction of a police station in northern states tends to be larger than what it is in the southern states. The density of population also makes a difference, so much so that while in West Bengal an average police station stretches to 122.4 sq miles of territory inhabiting 106,000 people, in the State of Rajasthan the corresponding figures about a 3 police station are 27 sq miles of territory and 4,210 people only. Normally the personnel of a police station consists of one SI, one head constable and fifteen constables. Functionally speaking, the police stations in Indian states are generally of five types:

(1) The Rural Police Station
(2) The Town Police Station
(3) The Sub-urban Police Station
(4) The Metropolitan Police Station
(5) The Railway Police Station

A police station under law is a unit of police activity in terms of total lice functions. Its three-tier hierarchy is headed by a SI, who along with a team of ASIs, head constables and constables looks after police jobs in the area. He is also called as SHO or the officer-in-charge of police station. He has numerous duties and immense responsibilities in the field of police administration. In fact, he is a multipurpose man and the police laws require demanding services from him. His duties and functions are prescribed and enumerated in the police acts and other statutes but additionally he has a number of other informal and discretionary jobs to perform besides his assigned duties. Some of his major duties as a station house officer can be enumerated as follows:

(1) Pertaining to law and order
(2) Duties pertaining to prevention and control of crime and vice
(3) Duties pertaining to detection of crime
(4) Duties pertaining to intelligence
(5) Duties pertaining to legal matters
(6) Duties pertaining to traffic, public assemblies and processions
(7) Duties pertaining to tours and beat in the areas
(8) Duties pertaining to police prosecution
(9) Duties pertaining to police station management

The SHO enjoys a fairly large discretion in operating various administrative procedures which the police law entails and the civil law warrants. He maintain a host of legal books, report registers and manuals as required under the procedural laws. Some of these important records in a typical police station are:

(1) FIR Book
(2) Case Diaries
(3) Charge sheets
(4) Final reports
(5) Bail bonds
(6) Search lists
(7) Seizure lists
(8) Register of non-FIR cases
(9) Register of unnatural death cases
(10) Inquest reports, especially of the murder cases

All these basic documents contain fairly detailed information about the 'crime profiles' of the area and have to be filled in daily as well as periodically in addition to the above, the SHO is especially charged with the responsibility of maintenance of several other kinds of useful police records which among others, include:

(1) A General Diary
(2) A Crime Register
(3) A Conviction Register
(4) History Sheets and Surveillance Register
(5) Village Information Sheet
(6) The Crime Map
(7) The Bad Character Rolls

(8) The Crime Index
(9) Statistics
(10) Property Register
(11) Summon and Warrant Registers
(12) Absconders Register

In addition to the above, there are other registers which are to be maintained in connection with the administration of Arms Act of 1959. These registers are: (1) Arms Licence Register and (2) Arms Deposit Register. Then, there are other administrative records and legal documents such as:

(1) Buildings Register
(2) Government Property Register
(3) Cash-Book
(4) Accounts Duty Roster
(5) Correspondence Registers
(6) Village Rosters
(7) Jurisdictional Lists

The titles of the police station records are self-explanatory and indicate what all these registers contain. Through these registers the police station keeps an up-to-date record of information about public order, grave crimes, useful intelligence and measures taken by the administration in the past and the present. They also indicate the future course of police action. The SI of police signs all these documents in person and he and his juniors are personally responsible for the safe custody of significant records.

The Constabulary

Constables are the lowest link in the organisational hierarchy of police administration of a district. As they belong to civil police, they are not armed except on special occasions. When on duty, they wear prescribed uniforms. They are recruited straightaway from the masses and mostly belong to rural sections of society. The educational qualifications and equipment of the constables are very low. They generally do odd jobs of manual nature and merely execute such orders which entail little discretion and decision-making. In India, the largest number of police personnel belongs to the rank of constables. His duties and functions, though very significant, are not recognised as basic to police administration by the government and society. Actually, the post of a police constable in India is analogous to that of a *chaparasi* or a class IV servant. Some of the routine functions of a police constable are:

(1) To perform such guard and escort duties as are assigned to him by his seniors from time to time. (He acts as a sentry at the police station and guards prisoners in the lock-up, the treasure chests, the *malkhana* and all the property of the police station.)
(2) To patrol the area of his beat during night and to regulate traffic during day, depending upon the nature and volume of work at his police station.
(3) To regulate processions and assemblies, to suppress public disturbances, to enforce orders for search and seizures and to execute summons and warrants as routine duties. (These duties assume importance during emergencies.)

(4) To serve as orderlies and peons in police stations and police offices. They are often employed to do non-police jobs of routine and manual nature inside police stations and in the offices.
(5) To accompany and assist senior police officials in investigational work with regard to crime and on occasions such as those of post-mortem examination, police funerals and hospital operations of the convicts, undertrial and police custody.

These functions place police constables at the back and call of the seniors who lay down programmes of action for them. The quasi-military nature of the police organisation does not allow the constable to have advisory or staff functions. Whether they guard public property or serve water to their seniors in the office or even act in the midst of a tumultuous crowd, they always execute laws or rules in a mechanical fashion and never forget to take orders from their seniors before they are really up and doing. They are petty officials and their duties and functions, howsoever decisive for the efficiency and image of the cops, are deliberately devoid of responsibility, discretion and individual judgement. They represent and symbolise the law and are even called 'the limbs of law'. Yet, they are neither participants nor decision-makers in the administration of law and order of the country.

The System of Rural Policing

The Indian Police Commission 1902 recommended a system of village police which continued for the rest of the period of British regime in India. The village police in a district has two distinct parts, namely, the village watchman and die village voluntary organisations.

The commissions appointed by different state governments in India have strongly condemned the structure and working of village watchmen. However, the Indian Police Commission of 1902 found it relevant and useful in a particular given context of history and rural sociology. The principle of village responsibility for policing which the commission advanced and advocated would yield the following characteristics of the *chowkidari* system:

(1) The village, recognised as a unit for revenue and general administration should have a police watchman for the village.
(2) The village police officer, i.e., the SHO, should not be the master or superior of the headman.
(3) The village headman should be a multi-purpose person and must concentrate on one village only.
(4) The district police may control his failures of duty in a limited manner and for all practical purposes he should be answerable to the civilian head of the district or to his subordinates.
(5) The post of the village headman should be stipendiary and may be, as far as possible, hereditary and he should only be a part-time government servant.

Thus, the police organisation at the district level has a wide and complex mixed duties pertaining to the registration and investigation of crimes, patrolling, surveillance, services of processes, collection of intelligence, arrest of criminals, searches and seizures of property and other detective and preventive measures are undertaken by the police stations located in the field. The big city police stations are called 'kotwalis' and are generally put under the charge of inspectors. Normally, a sub-inspector heads the administration of an urban as well as rural police station. He is assigned a varying number of sub-inspectors, assistant sub-inspectors, head constables and constables to do the job of policing. The actual number of these functionaries depends upon the size of the police station and the nature of work or crime a police station has to handle. The character and organisation of urban and rural police stations are almost identical and they follow similar procedures of police work in all the states of the Union. As a repository of information about the area, the police stations maintain daily diaries, cases diaries, FIR registers, crime registers, cashbooks, *malkhana* registers and history sheet records. Together they present the profile of crime and criminals, which obviously differ from state to state, area to area and station to station.

Panchayati Raj, as a developmental mechanism has unleashed all kind of new variables and tensions in the politico-economic system of rural India. It has thrown up new leadership and new threats of public disorder and crimes which the old police-machine finds increasingly difficult to cope with. Thirdly, the pace of social change and gradual modernisation of traditional ways of living are not only eroding the structure of social values but have also introduced quasi rural patterns of community living in medium-class towns. The mixed situation, marking transition from rural to peri-urban community living, devolves special responsibilities upon the guardians of law and order who find the police organisation in the district too ill-equipped and stagnant to deal with pressures of change.

The changing context presents a bewildering picture of the district police organisation in which an SP is too high and too far away from the actual scene of police operations and an SI is too inadequately qualified and ill-trained to handle growing complex situations of changing India. The illiterate policeman at the lowest rung of the organisational ladder is fast becoming an anachronism even for the rural police and if the democratic system continues to move with speed, the organisation and officials of the police station will be too frail and too inadequate to live up to their minimal duties. In sum, it can be stated that the structure and mechanism of district police administration has been too static to face the dynamism of change. The lower rungs of the hierarchy are neither recruited from amongst the qualified strata nor are they empowered to do jobs according to the changing needs of the community. There is overcentralisation in organisation and working and the entire organisation is saddled with multitudinous and multipurpose functions. The old structures have yielded little room for specialisation and stratification and still less, for innovation and reform. The organisational functioning of the police has been adversely affected by compulsions of political awakening and new socio-cultural ethos of the post-independence era. The need for decentralisation and autonomous flat structures at state and district level police administration is increasingly being realised and a thorough overhaul and radical re-organisation of the police machine, at all levels of hierarchy, especially at the district is more than overdue.

V

The Challenges Ahead

A close look at the police organisation will reveal that most of its problems emanate from history, the legacies of which make it stagnant, disjointed, outmoded and even dysfunctional. Tom between three lists of the VII Schedule, the task of policing remains shared, muddled and is an overlapping responsibility between the Union and the state governments. The Union home ministry, though not directly responsible for police jobs, virtually functions as the union ministry for police, entrusted with the responsibility of maintaining peace, security and order in the country. This robs the state police departments of their initiative in reorganising the police administration, so much so that the basic Police Act of 1861 and the three All-India Penal Codes, namely, the Criminal

Procedure Code of India, the Code of Civil Procedure and the Indian Evidence Act, remain more or less unchanged since the days of the Indian mutiny. The society has outgrown the police organisation and the state governments, despite their best intentions, have not succeeded in revamping their police structure. The reports of numerous State Police Commissions is an exercise in futility and clearly denote that state police administration has sunk deep into stagnation, from which the Union government alone can pull it out.

Organisationally the three-tier structure of the state, district and police stations seems quite sound and feasible in consonance with the police philosophy and working conditions obtained in the rural area, but the physical conditions, actually available in terms of buildings, furniture, telephone, conveyance, office records, *malkhanas,* police lock-ups, living quarters at the outposts and the police stations are absolutely far from satisfactory. The mounting needs of policing have resulted in the phenomenal expansion and upgrading of police stations, which the state police budgets cannot afford to cope with. The expectations of the common man from his police station have gone very high and the newly recruited police officers also find it demeaning to live and work under sub-human conditions.

From the personnel point of view, the state police administration has a real pathological case to look into. When practically every police department of the state has exploded in terms of numbers and enhanced responsibilities, there is relatively very meagre effort to work out the personnel needs and job chartings of the policemen. The senior police officials complain, and perhaps very rightly too, about the inadequacy of numbers commensurate with the prescribed strengths of their outposts, police stations and special agencies in the department. Worse still is the non-availability of proportionate senior positions in the hierarchy, which forces most of the state police employees to retire without having anything to look forward to by way of reasonable promotions, not even at reasonable intervals. Notwithstanding stray efforts here and there, the police personnel reforms in most of the states have eluded implementation on account of the non-bargaining capacity of the disciplined forces. There is an enormous amount of ill-matching of jobs, persons and emoluments in key positions of the hierarchy. The two offices of the DIG and the Dy SP in the state police hierarchy need a special position classification. They occupy dignified positions, but the incumbents usually complain against the anachronistic situations in which they are placed vis-à-vis their immediate juniors, i.e., the SP and the SI. They have relatively little functions to perform and can very conveniently be bypassed by their juniors in the range and in the district. The training of the IPS officers assigned to the states is a responsibility of the Union government but police training of the state police officials, juniors as well as seniors, leaves much to be desired. There is an obvious emphasis on muscle-building and reading Blue Books, which should have their place but should not be pursued at the cost of mind and liberal orientation of the police officers. The state police training colleges generally do not attract the right kind and the training enterprise, being unlinked with future posting and promotions, as in the army, does not merit attention and involvement of the police officials at various levels of state hierarchy.

Recently, the Union government has initiated steps for the modernisation of police forces in the states. Funds have been earmarked for the modernisation of fleets, wireless equipments, forensic aids, training experiments and housing facilities for the personnel. When all this can be called a welcome beginning, it has hardly touched the fringe of the problem.

Lastly, a reference may be made to the most ticklish and sensitive problem of dyarchy in the administration of law and order in the district. The collector-SP relationship, as postulated in the Police Act, has acquired all sorts of pro-DM overtones in the process of history. Logical rationale apart, it is a problem surcharged with professional bias and status equations in the district administration. The justificational dyarchy of the colonial days in the administration of law and order makes little sense, especially when the two functionaries belong to two all-India services of a coordinate nature. The presence of DM in emergency situations of law and order may have some incidental benefits for the district administration but it certainly betrays a lack of confidence in the senior officials of police, who resent the primacy of the DM in a domain which exclusively belongs to the police.

The problems of Indian police are either too obvious or too subtle to be comprehended by a layman. The common sense clichés about constraints and hazards of police work and miserably unconducive conditions of police service hardly deserve any advocacy by police watchers. Similarly, a cursory look at the voluminous reports of various State Police Commissions pointedly demonstrate that there is no dearth of creative ideas and even empirical research about police reforms. Yet the fact that the organisation of the Indian police remains a thoroughly stagnant organisation, governed by the century old Police Act of 1861 and the statutes of post-mutiny era, demands an explanation from all those who want to demystify this opaque phenomenon of status quoism of police in free India. Again, the reasons are not far to seek and the most of the reasons for not allowing the obvious to happen in the professional, political and socio-cultural arenas of public life in India. The functional constraints of the police profession warrant a cautious and slow moving approach, which when spelled out in operational terms, finds a very low priority for police reforms. Moreover, the police being a buffer or a shock-absorber of social change permits the political rulers of the democratic system to consolidate and legitimise their power positions and naturally, they cannot afford to take risk in the field of policing at their own peril. In addition to this, the socio-cultural systems in the developing world treat their police forces with callous apathy and animated hostility because of which the police profession does not get its due share of attention and credit for stability and development at the hands of popular representatives in the democratic foray. The vested interests in society and in the political system generally tend to join hands in maligning the police and frustrate change and growth: by exploiting the functional nature of the police job and the disciplined character of its uniform. The non-police authors of police reform find it very convenient to keep the police unchanged. Here is an organisation which cannot militantly negotiate as a bargain counter, but, if kept as it is, in its historical role of colonial past, can perpetrate an imperial fallacy that the maintenance of order is synonymous with the preservation of law of the land. In a democracy where this law and the law-makers change too frequently and several kinds of disorders reflect and measure the pace and goals of social change, the professional universe of the policemen is riddled with political problems, which he can neither own nor suffer. The concept of police as a 'limb of law' in a society, wedded to 'rule of law' expects this executive arm of the government to be depoliticised. Conversely, the police organisation cannot be left to its own also, because the job of policing requires political direction and discretionary interpretations, subject to the overall control of the judiciary of the country. The dilemmas and challenges are innumerable and some of them can be listed as under:

(1) The Ubiquitous infrastructure
(2) Explosion of police tasks
(3) Dysfunctionalism of rural police
(4) Anomalous personnel system
(5) The colossal ignorance of either side
(6) The fragility of the equipment
(7) The paradox of para militaryism
(8) Non-development to policing

Thus, the dilemmas of police profession have social, political and professional overtones. Its operational problems are getting aggravated in the want of a new philosophy, more professionalised equipment, better developmental resources and a managerial approach so very essential to handle the dilemmas, the gaps and the conflicts that beset the organisation. When some of these and allied problems are inherent in the nature and scope of the police job, several others and perhaps the more critical ones, have sprung up from the inevitable thrusts of democratic awakening and developmental urge of the teeming millions, ignited by the mounting pressures of modernisation.

A scientific appraisal of the Indian police for 21st century needs a fresh look on the organisation and profession of police in the revised context of a democratic polity and developing society in India. The National Police Commission and several study teams at the Union and state levels have worked out quite objectively to sort out some of these problems to suggest a way out from the present impasse. A futuristic look at the organisation of the Indian police and the concept and image of police and policeman in the twenty-first century are the real terms of reference for meaningful reforms. As most of the problems of police organisation spring from the four centralised structure of coercion and its lack of precise accountability, the remedy lies in decentralisation and introducing a check and balance doctrine to avoid abuse and excesses.

The Reform Agenda

It can be detailed around the following:

(1) The autonomous police organisation
(2) Separation of police for law and police for order
(3) Panchayati police for villages
(4) Renovation of armed police
(5) The Graduate constabulary
(6) The parity of all India services
(7) A package of liberal service conditions
(8) Better trained personnel and modern weaponary
(9) Massive use of cybernetics

But again, when these liberal conditions of service and compensation need top priority, no promotion or even key placement in the field should be assigned to a police official without a creditable completion of a specialised training programme. Like the defence services of the country, the training and promotions should be interlinked and the police training of specialised jobs should be insisted upon as a pre-requisite for ascending the hierarchy. This will foster discipline and motivate policemen to learn their own jobs with skill and profit.

It is not fair to single out policemen for levelling of certain kinds of charges like corruption, political servility and apathy to public job. Actually, these are a part of the administrative culture of India and a policeman is as much immune and susceptible to them as any other public servant in any other department. Police job makes him more vulnerable to scandals. The human clay in any organisation can improve only by inducting structural changes and then recruiting the best and preserving them to be so by keeping them knowledgeable and self-respecting. Obviously, it envelopes the gamut of entire personnel administration more especially where the nature of rigorous discipline does not allow the availability of democratic protests and bargain counters.

Thus, an overview of the spectrum in which a stagnant organisation of police confronts a dynamic society posed for development calls for the appraisal of Indian Police in relation to its infrastructure, i.e., the society and the polity. The police as an agency of law and order can do very little to renovate or rebuild this infrastructure. But conversely, it can sabotage all efforts for police reform, and increased police capabilities. Piecemeal changes in police organisation of India may be welcome, but they are bound to be overwhelmed by the gushing waters of change. The community is not prepared to accept even the changed police in its new image. Similarly, the reformed police will be too hesitant to launch its eventful career with a bunch and even with a note of pessimism. But, the vicious circle has to be cut at some point and a new policeman has to be groomed, whether the society and polity respond to the call of the new experiment or not. A fair image of the organisation helps it to be effective, but the organisation cannot give up efforts for effectiveness just because the image is far from fair or satisfactory. The experiment with new police philosophy and consequent police reform along with mass popular education in police predicaments has to be a simultaneous exercise and in either case it will have to be a lesson in forgetting, past and building a foreseeable future. The police profession cannot be absolutely divorced from the politics of the day, nor can its problems be tackled in isolation from the interpretative versions of political polity laid down by the executive and the legislature. The critical issue of separating the police from the non-police will always hang fire in a democratic system of government, where every outgoing government will assert to be with it. It is a rule of the game that the opposition should accuse the police for its so-called excesses and jealous loyalty to the political masters, vested with powers to help and harm the policemen even when they are in the bounds of law.

The police tasks, when they are expanding quite rapidly, can still be defined as: (a) enforcement of law and (b) maintenance of order. All other functions, new as well as old, can be covered by the terms like ‘plugging the breach of law’ and ‘arresting public disorder’, which also flow from the violations or non-enforcement of public law. In case of the former, i.e., the enforcement of law, what the police needs is a managerial approach and a highly articulate ‘management grid’ to attack upon the conventional violators of law like thieves, burglars, robbers, gangsters, immoral traffickers, smugglers and habitual offenders of the hard core variety. In the latter case, i.e., maintenance of public order, mere professional or managerial competence will not do, though it will be extremely useful. Here a very effective and competent system of specialised police will pay dividends. But what is more important is the availability of a new ‘accountability-structure’ of police which may inspire popular confidence and dispel mass apprehensions. This accountability structure has to be different from the present buffer, i.e., the district magistrate and the post-mortem dissection in the form of judicial enquiries. The district magistrate and the High Court judges may prove a check and bring the facts of the case of police failure before the people, but they have failed to deter the repetition of the occurrences. The effective check on police misuse or policemen transgressing limits has to be developed in organisation of the police itself. Similarly, some other plural democratic organisation like the National Security Council or All-India Police Commission can also safeguard the interests of the citizens and the policemen alike. The present atmosphere of change and growth in India requires that a continuous reform input is needed to reorganise the system, without causing a big dislocation in the total system of police administration of the state.

(1) The state police administration should increasingly experiment with the police commissioner system prevalent in big cities of the country.
(2) The pace of modernisation of the state police set-up may be enhanced. Modernisation in terms of physical facilities and equipments may ultimately lead to specialisation in police tasks and training of policemen.
(3) The staff units in the state police administration may be given an honoured place.
(4) The expenditure on armed police may increasingly be reduced and the state police budgets can be so reorganised as to have more and more of senior positions to make the district police officer-oriented, rather than constabulary-oriented.
(5) The offices of the SP and SI may be reorganised in terms of their routine workload, legal responsibilities, protocol duties and job hazards.
(6) The junior state police functionaries may be specially trained in public relations and special efforts may be made to cultivate various sections of public to project a new image of the police profession in the society.

After independence, three things have happened, which need special mention in the context of the district police administration in India. *First*, the introduction of mass education and quantitative expansion of schools and college have brought a large chunk of rural population within the fold of mass awareness and political awakening in the countryside. These young men and their friends refuse to accept the police in its old image and naturally a constant and serious challenge of attitudinal change confronts the police administration right at the grass-root level. *Secondly*, the introduction of Panchayati Raj as a developmental mechanism has unleashed all kinds of new variables and tensions in the politico-economic system of rural India. It has thrown up new leadership and new threats of public disorder and crimes which the old police-machine finds increasingly difficult to cope with. *Thirdly*, the pace of social change and gradual modernisation of traditional ways of living are not only eroding the structure of social values but have also introduced quasi-rural patterns of community living in medium-class towns. The mixed situation, marking transition from rural to peri-urban community living, devolves special responsibilities upon the guardians of law and order who find the police organisation in the district too ill-equipped and stagnant to deal with pressures of change.

Thus, the state police administration, which, by and large, represents the historical legacies of the colonial days needs fresh thinking, systematic reorganisation and vigorous reform effort to live up to the challenge of change and growth, popularly known as development, in modern India. The organisation as such has a very sound base and the traditions of the discipline, loyalty, legal competence and firmness have nurtured it towards the desired end. The uniformity of the pattern in most of the states of the Union makes it doubly relevant in the present day context of national integrity and national discipline. The real trouble lies in its colonial orientations of negativism, simplicity, secondary status and generalism. In free India, the people, the civilians and the political masters have been callously apathetic to the problems of the police reform. As a state subject, it has suffered neglect and a raw deal at the hands of our planners. Being a disciplined organisation, it could not develop its bargain counters in the democratic system. On the contrary, its functional nature has been responsible for incurring the wrath of all sections of society. Naturally, its case for reform has been lost by default. The foul image of the profession and the service conditions obtained in the state and all-India police services have attracted the second best, which, in turn, has told quite heavily upon the ethics of the profession. The lower level police officials have further exploited the situation and have rendered the organisation and its personnel insulated and incorrigible for reform. The emerging situation in the country today entrusts very heavy responsibilities on the police administrations of the states. The traditional system is obviously ill-equipped to stand to the strains of the situation. The remedy lies in creative thinking inside the state level police administration and on the part of police leadership to take up the challenge of the new political and administrative philosophies of democracy, socialism, secularism and nationalism, so pertinently reiterated in the revisions of the Constitution of India.

VI

Criminal Justice System

Criminal justice process in a democratic society professing the system of rule of law confronts two competing system of values, the tension which accounts for the dilemmas observable in the administration of criminal justice in the country. One such system of values which can be called the crime control model is based on the proposition that the repression of all criminal conduct is the most important function to be performed by the criminal justice process. A government in order to operate successfully in the area of crime control must produce a high rate of apprehension and conviction. It claims that in its ultimate analysis the criminal process in society is a positive guarantor of social freedom and to achieve this, the crime control agencies should focus their primary attention to the efficiency with which the criminal justice process operates to screen suspects, determine guilt and secure appropriate dispositions of persons convicted of crime. The other value system which competes with this crime control value model may be called 'Due process model' which attempts to present formidable impediments to carrying the accused further along in the process. If the former resembles an assembly line, the latter looks like an obstacle race. It insists on the prevention and elimination of mistakes to the extent possible. The due process or civil liberties model does not accept reliability and efficiency as polar opposites. According to this view the system is reliable because it is efficient and any over-commitment to efficiency may jeopardise the reliability of the system itself. Let us examine the deeper value premises of the two systems, the compromise of which through a criminal process can yield criminal justice in a democratic society.

The protagonists of crime control values argue that if the laws go unenforced or if it is widely perceived that there is high percentage of failure to apprehend and convict in the criminal process, then a general disregard for legal controls tends to develop. The law-abiding citizens become victims of unjustifiable invasions. Naturally, speed and finality become the essence of justice. To ensure this the criminal justice process should be seen as a screening process in which each successive stage pre-arrest investigation, arrest, post-arrest investigation, preparation for trial, trial, conviction and disposition should involve a series of routinised operations and their success should be measured by their tendency to pass the case along a successful conclusion. All this involves administrative expertise and the screening process operationed by the police and prosecution should be accepted as a reliable indicator at probable guilt. The dominant goal of repressing crime demand a special weight on the quality of administrative fact-finding and can be achieved through highly summary processes without any great loss of efficiency. This model finds the conspicuous features of the adjudicative process little useful and wants to minimise it because it is unlikely to produce a more reliable fact-finding situation than the one precedes by the expert administrative process that precedes it and is capable of.

To a lay observer the criminal justice process may look mere mundane and routinised, but it has very different meanings to different kinds of people. Every group or agency views it from its own vantage point and naturally these points of views can never be similar and still less identical. There is a point of view of the criminal defendant himself and his family. They will always feel aggrieved and find the system excessively hard on them, even when they know that the suspect is guilty of breach of law. Then secondly, the victim has his point of view.

A criminal justice system in an apparatus society uses to enforce the standards of conduct necessary to protect individuals and society. It operates by apprehending, prosecuting, convicting and sentencing those members of society, who violate the basic rules of social living. This action by the criminal justice agencies against law-breakers serves these distinct purposes beyond the immediate punitive one:

(1) It removes dangerous people from the society, who pose a violent threat to its very survival.
(2) It deters others from criminal behaviour which in general creates conditions conducive for social living.
(3) It offers society an opportunity to transform law-breakers or anti-social individuals into law-abiding citizens of future.

The parliamentary and presidential systems of Western democracy both subscribe to these basic objectives of criminal justice administration. Actually, where the breach is significant in the extent and the form of protections the respective systems offer to individuals in the process of determining guilt and imposing punishment. The Indian system being an experiment in mixed political democracy has to combine the efficiency and effectiveness of the British system, with the civil liberties concept of American justice process.

All criminal justice systems in democratic world have three separately organised parts: the police, the courts, and the prison and corrections. Each agency has its distinct tasks to perform. However, these tasks are by no means independent of each other. What each one does and how it does, materially effect the quality of work done by other agencies in the criminal justice system. The courts can deal only with those whom the police arrests. The job of correction can be done only with those who are delivered to the agency by the orders of the courts. How successfully the correction reforms convicts in a jail or outside determines later police efforts and influences the sentencing policies of the courts with regard to repeaters. Police activities are generally subject to court scrutiny, resulting in strictures, which go a long way to shape police behaviour in future. So reforming or reorganising any part or procedure of the criminal justice system will entail a corresponding change in other parts and procedures of administration. Moreover, the method by which the criminal justice system deals with individual cases represents a continuum. They are not random actions, but proceed with an orderly progression of events, some of which like arrest and trial may be visible, but some others of even greater importance may occur outside the public view.

The criminal justice process in all societies has been under serious interrogation and criticism in the recent decades. Even its best protagonists admit that the process has far much outgrown the system and has developed ailments that need to be cured. Its critic maintain that the criminal justice system even in the West was never designed to take care of the violent ills that seem to take over the technological societies in menacing manner. The notions of 'innocence' and 'culpability' remain at the heart of the system, which is expected to deal with ingenious criminal and that too in mounting numbers. The rise in crime waves in all societies of the world throw the criminal justice process out of gear and the huge piles of caseloads, awaiting processing by tired judges and busy lawyers strike at the very notion of justice, about which very wise pronouncements were made long back, "Justice delayed is justice denied" and "Justice hurried is Justice buried".

The criminal justice process cannot do both, but as situation stands in terms of mounting crime, sinking budgets, increasing disorganisation and spreading disenchantment and sinking credibility, 'delays' have to be cut down without undermining the reliability of the system. The baby cannot be thrown away with the bath water, but the bath water has to be cleaned if the baby has to have his bath. In the Indian context, some of these aberrations of the criminal justice process can be identified as:

(1) An inbuilt and favourable class prejudice in the criminal law to put the weak and the poor in a disadvantageous position.
(2) A distrusted and demoralised police unenthusiastic about its work, because of the frustrating process.
(3) The open and competing system of Elitist Bar without much professionalism and little interest in defending the liberty of the poor and the weak.
(4) A traditional court system, unmindful to the needs of social justice in a changing social order.
(5) A neglected and harrowing system of jail with practically little awareness about the needs of J-reform and rehabilitation.

Inordinate delays, prohibitive expenditures, procedure orientations, corrupt administrative bureaucracy, over-stress on adjudication, harassment and exploitation of the victim by the agencies of criminal justice are some of the well known and off quoted maladies of the criminal justice process in India. Common sense apart, studies point out a number of complex variables resulting in the malignant growth of structures subverting the process. The court bureaucrats, the lawyers, the judges and even the defendants want to procrastinate. Cases proceed at a leisurely pace on appeal from one bench or court to another. The vested interest thrives and keep quoting legal scriptures. The poor victim, who still sees the agencies of criminal justice quite reverentially, prefers to suffer in silence than to invoke the costly luxury of a le process. The criminal elements which are becoming increasingly affluent and powerful in the developing society of India are naturally happy with the *status quo*. But if the criminal justice process wants to be fair and just, it must revise its legal philosophy, reform its police, reorganise the Bar and the bench and rebuild its prisons right from the scratch.

Criminal Justice Agencies

The present day criminal justice system in India is a queer amalgam of Mughal and British systems based on the mediaeval and modern notions of individual's life, dignity and person. Immediately after the Sepoy Revolt of 1857, the Englishmen decided to enact the three base Blue Books of Indian Penology, i.e., CrPC, IPC and the Indian Evidence Act. All of them were authored in the post-Mutiny era. The Indian Police Act of 1861 also represents this psychological dilemma of rulers, who on the one hand were inspired by the noble philosophy of liberalism but on the other hand were confronted with the stark problems of running a colonial administration. The compromises symbolised a heroic task and as such most of the delicate things had to be left to chance and conventional evolution. Later, the history of the freedom struggle did not level enough scope for administrative experimentation. The law was placed in a conservative iron world and the socio-cultural ethos of rural India gradually shaped the police system and the legal and extra-legal procedures of the Bar and the bench in their present form.

Except a few minor and need-based amendments, the bulk of the 'Penological Books' in India remain where they were in 1861. The Law Commission of India itself being a conservative body, staffed with lawyers tends to have developed a vested interest in *status quo*. Moreover, the facts reveal that more cumbersome and complicated procedures have been prescribed in the name of legal reforms in the justice system. 'The parliamentary committees have been weak and ineffective and even the basic laws which stand as items on the Union List of the Constitution have been taken up by the Indian Parliament in an ad hoc and piecemeal manner. The Constitution as the higher law of the land swears by the 'Dignity of die individual' but the lower laws of the land stay incongruent with these laudable professions.

The Indian Police Act 1861 is an anti-diluvian coercive structure of authority and not withstanding a plethora of reports by state and National Police Commissions and the basic structure of Indian Police is highly centralised, quasi-political and non-specialised. The constabulary at lower levels is rustics, muscle-oriented, power hungry and exploitative. The procedures of police work are based on organisational behaviours of their seniors. The petty police functionaries, who write FIRs conduct field investigations and prepare legal documents for prosecution. They are too low to understand the high social responsibility involved in the discharge of their quasi-legal professional dudes. Their training in law tends to prepare them to communicate only with the *vakils* and the judges and that too at the cost of the victim and the society.

The present system of legal education in Indian universities leaves enough to be desired. The fast deteriorating academic standards apart, the ethics of the new generation of advocates has a real challenge in the growth of inflationary economy and respect commanding materialistic values of Indian society. Naturally, the Bar being a free trade in legal aid is liable to develop its own black market, more easily accessible to the neo-rich or the anti-social elements in Indian society.

The professional competition at the Bar has become intense and as a historical ally of politics, the nuances of the latter tend to infiltrate more conveniently in die Bar room. Like most other professions, success has become the criterion of competence and eminence in the legal professions also. Consequently, the competent and the quite honest specialist is at a great disadvantage. This deplorable fact of vanishing species from the Bar-rooms obstructs the processes of administration of criminality in the four walls of the temple of justice.

To write about the India judiciary is itself a great threat to the liberty of the citizen. Recently, Justice K. Aiyer has spoken and written a good deal and pointed out loopholes in the policies and practices of the Indian courts with regard to bails, parole, evidences, witnesses, cross-examinations and sentencing policies of Indian judges. The rigid and procedure-oriented approach emanated from the accusitional philosophy of Anglo-Saxon Justice and has contributed to the evolution of certain kinds of judicial behaviours. The sensitivity, insularity, legal training and the professed political neutrality of the judiciary have resulted in the conditioning of a particular kind of criminal justice system with which the policemen, the vakils and even the medical jurists have acculturated themselves in their perverse interests. Empirically, it has resulted in the accumulation of huge arrears of court cases, inordinate delays in disposals, blatant perjury relaxed polices of bails and parole, cooked evidences, concocted witnesses and a kind of intellectual apathy towards the social responsibility of the judiciary. The criminal reform and the deterrence of crime being watchwords, victimology still seems to be a new democratic area, alien to Indian judicial thinking.

Here again the colonial class system operates. The recent studies done by criminologists establish that Indian jails have grown into new crime factories producing hardened criminals. The horrendous state and horrifying stories of prison management hardly need any documentation. Reform and rehabilitation of criminals are more or less rhetoric for academic seminars. The organisation is outdated. The untrained personnel are callous and have low morale. The budgets are meagre and the jail manuals drafted in the 19th century are handling criminals of the 21st century. People have little awareness and the social norm has been against all softness and experimentation with the convicts.

The Relay Race

The criminal justice administration in any society is after all a relay race. The lawmakers guarantee the basic security of person to the citizen. The police apprehends and brings the law-violator to book. The Bar helps the free citizen to preserve his freedom and the bench imparts justice by inflicting punishment on the guilty and protection to the innocent. The prisons house the criminals and strive to reform and rehabilitate them. If one partner in the race is sluggish or non-co-operative the entire system is bound to collapse. As always the failures of the organismic system will be attributed to segmental break-downs but this is no gratification to say that police organisation is better than prison organisation or judiciary is more honest than the police in India. The totality of the administrative organism has developed social change that the maladies have to be diagnosed and prescriptions attempted.

Most of the maladies of the criminal justice administration in India primarily originate from the accusational philosophy of justice which the institutional milieu of a developing society can ill-afford in the present context of democracy. The Constitution guarantees the fundamental rights, dignity of the individual, and independence and separation of judiciary from the executive but leaves police, prisons and penology to the policies and predicaments of democratic politics. The infrastructure of the Bar, the nature of organised crime and the politics of vested interests have articulated themselves so strongly during the last century that every partial remedy proposed leads to a deeper organic malady of desperate variety. The educated elites have so much stakes in the criminal justice system of the country that apparently when they keep the bogey of penal reforms alive, they continue to work for the preservation and strengthening of status quo. Meanwhile, the segmental crises have depended and the compartmental problems in each realm, which seem exclusive, have become overwhelming.

Indian people in general do not understand the niceties of law. They have by and large failed to generate democratic pressures on their lawmakers to initiate nucleus change in the area of criminal justice. Even the basic policy pronouncements and purposive revisions of legal enactments do not seem anywhere on the anvil. The control over executive is too ad hoc and ineffective to bring the latter face-to-face with the realities of criminal justice system. The occasional criticism of police or opposition invectives on judicial failings have yielded some laudable pronouncements, binding no one to nothing. There has been little co-ordination between the Law Commission, the Parliamentary Committees, the state legislature and the National Parliament. They have not been in a position to develop a national consensus on major issues that bedevil the criminal justice administration of the country. This explains that the legislatures in India are functionally dominated by the luminaries of the legal profession. They have by and large shown apathy to social change and to innovations in the systems of police and law courts which represent their primary vocational pursuits even as politicians.

The executive in free India even during Nehru days of stability and competence was obsessed with the problems of development. It has remained lukewarm to commit itself of the basic change of policy in the area of regulatory administration. Rather, it has apprehended avoidable dangers to the democratic system by being harsh with vested 'interests' operating in the field of criminal justice in India. The police machine in free India has been politically over-used and in turn it has also over mastered the art of circumventing procedures of criminal justice administration in league with its political masters. The police constabulary which was historically trained to attain non-goals has abused its craft and skills to pursue anti-goals within the framework of these system. Overwork, foul image, poor service conditions, muscle building and legal training have encouraged the policemen to dupe the judiciary through their quasi-judicial police work of crime investigation which is regarded as an executive job in India. The prison reforms have attracted attention but neither the legislature nor the executive could assign them the priority they deserved. Manned by petty people of low vision, the prison in India is an alienated place with little legal inputs for change, and rehabilitation. Actually, the most difficult reform has been left to the care of the most reluctant with almost little initiative in policy making and no discretionary funds for innovation.

While playing its historical role quite admirably the judiciary in India has gradually and inadvertently become the prisoner of the Bar. The Bar-Bench relationship, being what it is, has robbed the latter from being dynamic, purposive and time-bound in imparting justice. The professional competence and legal training of judges have generated a very special kind of judicial behaviour too insensitive to social change and popular criticism. It is fairly conditioned by the Anglo-Saxon norms of law and procedures of justice which create 'End means dichotomy'. The Bar which has a role in fretting facts and showing light to the Bench has cashed upon the police judiciary conflicts in India. It has over sanctified the procedures of evidence, witnesses, bails, cross-examinations appeals, exhibits and court rulings to the extent that the system has sunk in perjury and ossified justice has become a purchasable commodity of Benthamite description. The learned counsels represent the capitalism of intellect, exploiting the illiterates and the ignorants in the country. The rich and the powerful classes have their natural allies in the Bar with the result that there exists a favourable tilt in the frame of law for the so-called respectable citizens, who appear as witnesses and sureties against the interests of the poor – the weak and the innocent. The age old procedures followed in court trials in India are so humiliating that no self-respecting citizen will like to compromise the dignity of his person as a willing wish. The raped women is expected to risk scandalisation because the law presumes that all suspected rapist respect women, unless proved otherwise in the court of a magistrate and that too in the presence of *vakils*, cross-examining the victim in lieu of fabulous fees, advanced by the socially decent criminals.

The Indian society by and large hates court going and accepts *vakils* as a catastrophe. Yet, paradoxically enough the lawyers have been the most venerable and flourishing people in India. The society respects their role in democratic politics and has been relatively more lenient to the perversions of the Bar as compared to the evil doings of police and politicians. The popular inertia has obstructed the procedures of criminal justice. Highly educated people do not come forward to cooperate as witnesses. They avoid police and courts partly because of the harassing images of the latter but still more because the concept of participatory justice was never tried in a colony. The rich and the powerful classes alone were acceptable to the British rulers and conventionally they remained simultaneously participants in crime and criminal justice administration of the country.

Thus, free India inherited a legacy of British penology, colonial police and alienated judiciary which she has allowed to coexist and work with her parliamentary institutions based on adult suffrage. Naturally, this inconvenient partnership has developed into a strange bed-fellow relationship. The legislatures condemn the police for crime resurgence, the police with tongue in their cheeks hold the judiciary responsible for letting off the criminals, whom they round up at great risk. The judiciary bemoans the lack of up-dating of laws and the Parliament which alone can do it in a democracy lashes out against the lapses of all these at all levels. The common man thinks that the politicians have pushed the country into a blind alley. He vociferously denounces the criminalisation of politics and politicisation of crime in India. But, the politician also pleads his helplessness in die democratic system, which is genuine to his prolonged survival as a representative. Thus the vicious circle indulges in a nefarious game, e.g., of passing the Buck. The segmental crises keep cumulating into a systemic 'crisis of crises'. The remedy also lies in an organic cure and concerted effort for which even the thought processes have not yet been generated. Here are a few suggestions to size up the chaos.

VI

The Agenda for Reform

The ministry of law and justice should be reorganised as a policy coordinating mechanism with an independent division of criminal justice. This division may have four wings each looking after: (1) Penology, (2) Police, (3) Judiciary, and (4) Prisons. The ministry may have a research bureau as one of its attached offices. The minister of justice must initiate the new shift in philosophy and policy which may issue in a policy statement to be approved by the Parliament. Victimology as a new focus of national policy towards criminal justice must stir a national dialogue through press and research studies. Once this policy and its administrative and legal implications are thrashed out, it should result in basic segmental reforms which each wing of the union ministry of justice should implement as well as coordinate. A democratic consensus for a major reform in regulatory administration is a pre-requisite for this and this can be arrived at through a dialogue, research and debate on various issues by all sections of Indian society. The ministry must listen and respect the views of non-legal professions and prepare a blue print of penological, administrative, procedural and other allied reforms, which need to be processed in due phases at the national and state levels.

To attain this long range but vital objective-orientation in criminal justice administration, the penology wing of the ministry of justice should undertake the historic task of 'reauthoring' (not mere amending) the three basic Acts, i.e., CrPC, IPC and the Indian Evidence Act. This task should not be entrusted to legal experts, who have positive vested interests and biased perspectives. The post-mutiny penology or the concepts of crime and procedures of judicial administration cannot be revised by persons of law, who have been trained into it and have ceased to question its 'Raison d'etre' in the new context. For example, why should crimes in India be classified as 'cognisable' and non-cognisable? Which crimes need to be bailable and non-bailable? What is a grievous hurt? Who is a rapist and who is raped? These issues need the awareness of changed Indian sociology which should be reflected in the Blue Books. Mere amendments in colonial laws create a queer situation and complicate them for the benefit of the legal profession. Crime control cannot be a concern of the Bar and the Bench. Hence, the job of reauthoring the basic Acts may be entrusted to a National Penological Commission, which should have a majority of its members from the press, the politics, the academics, the women's organisations, the weaker sections and the trade unions. The labours of this Penological Commission should be whetted by a parliamentary committee of justice and the final drafts of the new may be discussed and approved by the NDC which should keep the national consensus in view through prolonged national debates.

Acceptance of a penology in obedience to a new philosophy will entail a new police organisation to enforce law and arrest crime. If police is be accepted as a partner in the relay race for criminal justice then die present organisation of the Indian police may be divided into: (1) Police for law, and (2) Police for order. The former, which is popularly known as Civil Police has to be given a quasi-judicial status, something on the lines of the French 'Police Judiciale'. The investigation process of crime has to be given the sanctity of judicial work, which independent and judicious police officers alone should pursue to help the senior judge in the discharge of their dudes. Once the other part of armed police is separated and left to the care of political masters, the investigation and prosecution work of 'Law-Police' may be put under the charge of a prosecution director-general and the prosecution directors, somewhat on the lines of the Comptroller and the Auditor General of India at the Centre and the Accountant Generals in the states. Further details of this independent and quasi-judicial organisation can be worked out through continuous research and experiment. This autonomous organisation of judicial police will enjoy respectability and cooperation of fellow judges. The present situation of distrust will go and the police and the judiciary together will fight for the victim against the onslaught of rich and the strong. Fudging of evidence in cases will not be needed and mercenary witnesses on easy money will not be allowed to make a mockery of justice. The police partnership in place of present confrontation in judicial work will engender higher sense of professional ethics and public accountability of police and the courts.

In a democratic society not much can be done to restrict the freedom of the Bar which is supposed to play the defender of the rights of the citizens. But then, defenders themselves should not exploit the society in the name of defence. Something has to be done to strengthen the moral fibre and professional calibre of the members of the learned profession. Black market in spare or essential commodities in a developing society, black deals in open market of talent or professional services need to be banned. The present state of the legal profession, being far from satisfactory, warrants the following reforms:

(a) The LLB degree of Indian universities like other professional degrees in medicine and engineering should be awarded on completion of a five year study course. The Bar Council should disaffiliate sub-standard colleges and universities. Only youngster of merit and proven integrity should be allowed to enter the law schools of the country.

(b) The Supreme Court and the High Courts should hold annual entrance examinations for their respective Bars. The present practice of allowing entry into the legal profession under the shadow of some established veteran should be discontinued. This second screening will bring the real professionals and as in Japan the black gown of the counsel will be an object of envy and respect in society.

(c) The law should not permit free contracts in legal trade. The cases may be classified as A, B, C and D and the fee scales may be prescribed as minimum and maximum. The advocates should be allowed to charge per appearance or hour-wise professional attendance fees from their clients rather than the present system of case fees and status system of the junior and senior counsels.

(d) The malpractices in the legal profession may be well defined by the law and gradually the voluntary associations may be encouraged to sue their lawyers, for perjury. It will enhance the social responsibility of the legal profession.

(e) Of course, to point out problems and limitations of the bench in the criminal justice system is fraught with misgivings. But, a judiciary in a democracy has to learn to work, in the midst of popular noise all-around. No institution, howsoever high, has a right to silence this dissent, especially when it represents what the court purports to defend. In a democratic system, there cannot be a concept of authority without corresponding responsibility. The bench cannot afford to enjoy a fair image by silencing popular criticism in the name of contempt of courts. The social responsibility of the judges has to be seen in terms of an effective democratic accountability of the bench. A public and open dialogue on judicial behaviour and relationships can help in operationalising this responsibility and accountability in democratic terms. To ensure it, it will be worthwhile and advisable that:

    (1) Judges continue to enjoy the security of tenure and constitutional protection in the discharge of their judicial duties. They should stay untransferred and their service conditions should be lucrative enough to command respectability from the executive and the society. Actually, the present system of independent judiciary should not only continue but should be strengthened in much more independence and competence to do a trying job that involves professional skills, moral integrity and physical hazards of varied nature.

    (2) But when all these privileges and honours seem justified, no court in a democratic system can afford to avoid popular criticism and indulge in 'contempt of the citizen'. Press, political parties and parliaments are the instruments to contain judiciary. Judicial pronouncements also need screening by non-judicial experts and even if motives are imputed in the process the judiciary should take it in the stride. It should command not demand popular resect.

(3) To make conditions conducive for the functioning of a democratic judiciary, it is worth a public debate whether judges should be recruited from the Bar or the judicial career on die bench should not be kept open for lateral entries to members of the Bar. The images and styles of functioning of the two being totally different, a learned *vakil* on the judicial bench is an anachronism. His past hovers over his new career and the previous associations run counter to his new image of infallibility. To enhance professionalism among judges an all-India Judicial Service (IJS) may be constituted. The meritorious ones, desirous for careers on the Bench 'only' should compete and the junior, senior and selection level cadres may be created at district, state and Union levels. The vakils may enter only at the junior level by competitive examination to be conducted by the Supreme Court. The age relaxation may be 35 years, but no High Court and Supreme Court judge should be picked up from among the affluent or successful advocates. Those who love freedom, money and legal acumen should stay in the Bar. But those who wish to enjoy social respect, judicial creativity and independence against all allurements must adom the chairs on the Bench. The retired judges should be attached to the law schools of the universities and should in no case be allowed to appear as *vakils* or part-time politicians for making a living.

Lastly, the prison system in India needs a comprehensive national legislation. The states have no funds or inputs to come in a big way. The federal legislation of a concurrent variety should reorganise the structure and create National or Federal Prisons. A Union agency may be created to supervise and provide administrative funding to the prison organisation in the states. The national, state and district level prisons should be envisaged on a uniform basis and a variety of prison cells may be structured inside the four walls of the state prisons. Inter-district and inter-state transfers of inmates may be tried to keep the jail administration dynamic. The personnel engaged in prison administration may have several cadres of prison service like jail police service, jails inmate reform service and jail health service, etc. Specialists as well as generalists of promise and commitment may be trained in various kind or training institutions of correction, mental health, vocational learning and man-management. A legislative committee of the state Vidhan Sabha and the of the National Parliament should examine the annual reports on state prisons and these committees should visit these prison-houses for study and suggest suitable reforms or legislative enactments for administrative improvements. Participative management may be tried in prison administration and a massive research effort should be launched to identify local problems and experiment with solutions of viable nature. The press should play the watch-dog and the voluntary agencies engaged in correctional and rehabilitation work may be encouraged as a part of a coordinated phased plan of action in the field.

Indian society in the 20th century has traversed a long democratic path. Some of these democratic processes are just irreversible. The regulatory administration of revenue, law and order and justice has remained quite impervious to these democratic changes in the name of continuity and stability in society. The criminal justice administration and its agencies had done a good job in colonial India. The personnel in these institutions suffers from a nostalgia and dreads change. The political masters being too busy in their game of developmental spoils have left them unchanged in their enlightened political self-interest. But the staticism of these institutions has been overwhelmed by the gusts of democratic social change. The institutional conflicts have paralysed the system and self defeating procedures find it difficult to continue in the garb of administrative confidentiality. Deference, class interest and conventional rule of law have become outdated foci in criminal justice administration. Victimology as a new approach to criminal justice system offers new concepts in the light of which conventional procedures like FIR, evidence-collection, witness arrangement, bail granting, cross-examination system and sentencing policies need purposive operationalisation. Procedures though important cannot be the goals of a system. The end means synthesis has to be worked out in terms of the ends. The criminal justice administration in India is one area where the politics of vested interests has perverted the means by taking advantage of history, professional expertise and popular ignorance. It is high time when legislators, policemen, learned persons of law and administrators of prison houses in India should pool their experiences to put their respective houses in order. The spirit of democracy and the need for social audit should permeate the functioning of all and each one of these institutions. The political masters should realise and accomplish this before it is too late to salvage the criminal justice system from being sabotaged by its own defenders.

11

Accountability and Democratic Administration in the New Millennium

Politics in India was thoroughly democraticised in 1950 when the republican Constitution of the country conferred adult suffrage upon the citizens of India without any distinction of colour, caste, sex or creed. It was an unprecedented revolution unknown to Hindu, Mughal and British periods of Indian history. Fundamental rights apart, a government by the people was legitimately recognised as a government for the people. This kind of democratic politics was bound to have its inevitable implications and repercussions on the India administration which could or should never be based on the poll mandate of the people. The British experience of elected political representatives and merit-recruited bureaucrats had little or no parallelism because the colonial administration was not only elitist and alienated but was anti-people. The democratic political process in British India was an arrested one and was experimented with the result that the administration before 1947 was running politics which today has to be the opposite. The working of the Constitution for more than half a century has revolutionised Indian politics in terms of its mass base, developmental thrusts and social justice orientations. The corresponding democratic revolution in Indian administration has not been possible for the simple reason that the administrative elites in India do not find Indian masses capable to rule themselves. The example of Europe and USA do not help here because the administrative phenomenon is unique and refuses to be democratic in the absence of a clearer consensus about 'Democracy in Administration'. The minister-civil servant relations are discussed in a colonial frame as if bureaucracy is a corrective and politicians have to learn under the parental command. The dyarchy of the collector and the zila pramukh in Panchayati Raj reminds the provincial dyarchy of 1919, which was highly humiliating to national pride. The Constituent Assembly debated the lofty ideas of liberty, equality and justice for weeks, but hesitated to prescribe a district democracy in 1950. A little tinkering about all India services and public service commissions were regarded as 'good enough' and the colonial administration kept on running the democratic show by maintaining that 'People get a government they deserve'. This situation of Indian democracy has developed a 'native colonialism' of elitist Indians, who have bureaucratised politics. The ministers and the MPs in free India have imitated the British collector rather than the vice versa. Democratic administration even as a theoretical concept has been shunned in the interest of efficiency and secrecy in government. The concept of public welfare was defined bureaucratically and stability and developments became obsessions to the extent that a three-tier democracy at the district level looks like a second war of Indian independence and that too without a Mahatma.

Democratic Administration Conceptualised

Conceptually, a democratic administration seems like a contradiction in terms 'People's Government' may be a rhetoric but popular administration at best can be an administration without corruption and public grievances. Very many well-meant administrators would call it a democratic administration if it conforms to laws, rules and procedures. Weberian efficiency and Taylor's optimisation of results have been called as decisive ingredients of the democratic nature of administration. The debate may lead to attuning of the bureaucratic enterprise to the democratic ethos of the polity. All democratic systems of parliamentary or presidential or a combination of the two need public administration as a support structure of governance. If adult suffrage gives representativeness and accountability to democratic politics, should a merit-based administration also strive to be representative and responsible? Can openness, transparency and responsiveness of administration ensure its representative an accountable character? If human rights are the essence of democracy, should politics guarantee them to the citizens through an enlightened vigilance of administrative machinery or through an elected leadership against the intransigence of power-hungry civil service manned by brilliant sons of the soil? The midway has to be discovered by reinventing the government in developing countries, where strong administration should induct social democracy to attain a correspondence with political democracy. The Indian Constitution and Indian Polity followed this philosophy till 1991 and the 21st century opens with a bang asking for a full throated democracy at all walks of public life. This end of the endless transition is a metamorphosis and democratic administration is being asked for and is emphatically asserted as an 'end of native colonialism', which was not a fact in European experience.

In 1991, Prime Minister Narsimha Rao announced the dawn of a new era popularly known as LPG (liberalisation, privatisation and globalisation). This triple penetration in the political economy of India is often called a shift to the 'New Right' which like new lift has its varied shades and country specific components. Because of the end of the cold war and disintegration of the Soviet Union in 1989 it has replaced the word 'good government' by a more amorphous term called as 'good governance'. A variety of contents like competitive collaboration, citizen friendliness, innovative enterprise, transparency and responsiveness are being poured into this new concept, which represents a judicious mix of LPG. The Second Minnowbrook Conference (1988) on Public Administration accepted it as a phenomenon of institutional pluralism, which should manage public affairs in the interest of public good and social welfare. Several scholars have called this LPG administration as a World Bank view of public administration which talks of deregulation, de-bureaucratisation and disinvestment from public enterprise. The collapse of the Soviet system proved that the old rule-bound, rigid, conservative, cautious, slow and unresponsive bureaucratic systems was archaic. The winds of change should affect the structures, processes, orientations and behaviour patterns of the government system throughout the world. At the cross-national plane, the emergence of a post-industrial, knowledge-based, global economy has created new opportunities for governments at all levels to respond to these realities. The governments has to be 'reinvented' and made more entrepreneurial and 'run like a business'. This require discarding of old structures and willingness to take real initiatives. A 'catalytic government' should inspire, guide and help society, entrepreneurs and the people. The empowered community ought to become 'competitive' and facilitating with the private sector and the agencies of government.

To quote Osborne and Gaeblar, the rule-driven public organisations should be transformed into a mission-driven government whose public servants pursue organisational mission with newer techniques. Public organisations should introduce quality management in their services. A climate of continuing innovation and reform can modernise the public sector with result orientations. The consumer friendly organisations should explore avenues of revenue generation and profit maximisation. It should be proactive rather than only reactive and 'curative'. Teamwork should replace the outworn Weberian hierarchy. A balance between markets and the community can be tried with popular participation. All these theoretical musing for the reinvention of government have a western or a capitalistic perspective on which the Indian administrators have to superimpose a human face. The politico-economic conditions that prevail in India demand it. A number of countries in the West and socialist systems of China and USSR have taken to the path of liberalisation, privatisation and globalisation but the Indian response has been halting because of the contextual constraints. The mixed economy model is still regarded as the ideal path for economic transformation. The reforms with a 'human face' envisage packages which include greater resource mobilisation through fiscal adjustments, better investments and less spending. It places greater reliance on the market mechanism. Reduction of price controls, subsidies and trading and banking reforms are suggested to have a free flow of capital, technology and services for production relationship between domestic and foreign industries. The policy of delicensing, increased disinvestment and closer of sick industries has to be pursued with vigour. Similarly, exchange rate adjustment through devaluation and control of money supply need to be rationalised.

Broadly speaking, all this is associated with the concept of 'good governance' which includes politics as well as administration. In India, the long-term administrative implications of this democratic governance are far-reaching and profound. With decisional power going to the grass roots, the transformation will force the civil servants to accept the hegemony of political masters. The job of decentralised governance under Panchayati Raj dispensation would create a situation that will modify behaviours and attitudes. The bureaucracy which has been apathetic and resistant to the strengthening of the voluntary sector will have to develop faith in the people and facilitate situations for the endeavours of non-government sector.

This need and demand for democratic administration is being voiced in the context of increasing liberalisation, privatisation and globalisation of politics and economy in India. The 'negativism' of regulatory administration is being reshaped into 'positivism' of competitive collaborativeness at national and international levels. The old institutions of control, vigilance, grievance redressal are increasingly and incrementally being revised and strengthened to make conditions conducive for human rights, clear environment, and technology friendly along with enhanced social responsibility of the business. Naturally a new democratic administration for 21st century in India is being envisaged to optimise the results of the policies of liberalisation, privatisation and globalisation.

Democratic Liberalism in Administration

Democracy in any society or under any system primarily concerns with the basics of self-government and self-development. Its political growth in terms of institutions may stress upon adult suffrage but in practice it implies liberalism, individualism and human rights. In the context of democratic administration in India, one way to identify these democratic characteristics or components is to evaluate the availability of:

(1) Representativeness of public administration.
(2) Accountability of public administrators to people of India.
(3) Human rights and status of citizen's grievances against administration.
(4) Rule of law and integrity in public service.
(5) Participatory administration with involvement of community leaders in shaping and implementing the quality of administrative policies.

Representativeness of Administration in India

Direct Representation of people in administration is neither workable nor desirable. Popularity is the criterion of representatives in political elections but administration being merit based has to be elitist and is regarded as a legal structure created to supplement or correct and modify the political processes monitored by people's representatives. But an elitist, alienated and extra legal administration may destroy the very spirit of democracy, more so in countries like India with colonial legacies. The Constitution of India and the reform policies pursued by successive democratic governments have strived to de-elitise public servants and make them a part of the Indian ethos. The colonial bureaucrats who imitated the foreign rulers have become extinct, although civilians as commoners are still not visible on the horizon. To make administrators representative of the masses, the following measures have gone a long way to deelitise the civil servants:

(a) Fifty per cent reservation of seats in all cadres of government services to brilliant youngsters from SC, ST and OBC has been guaranteed. To these various kinds of formal reservations, several other kinds of informal reservations are being added in the name of social justice for women, poor sections of society, minorities and backward states of the country. Polemics apart, this phenomenon has totally and quite substantially revised the 'manning policy' of administration with its consequent populist orientations at every level.
(b) Still more serious has been the Kothari Committee reform according to which merit of new entrants in public services is screened at various stages and that too through examinations in English, Hindi and mother tongue media. Unlike his predecessor, the average student in India today dreams of a civil service career and can successfully compete for it with his competitors from public schools who still use English as their medium of expression.
(c) During the British days, the viva voce examinations were decisive and merit was subjectively defined by recruiters in the imperial traditions of a 'sahib'. Today, the viva continues but its weightage has become nominal with the result that the entry of middle-class boys and girls has visibly changed the nature and shade of public services in India.
(d) To make administration and administrators representative, the government has launched a variety of training programmes at every level. It is incessantly being dinned in the ears of public servants that they are no longer rulers and must learn to work under popular representatives. This has mellowed down their bureaucratic arrogance and there is a perceptible change of attitude and behaviour which makes Indian administration much more representative than before.

The colonial history, which created a big hiatus between the elite and the masses in India generates debates like minister, civil service relations which are unheard of in developed countries of the west. The Indian administration which has been a preserve of the privileged English knowing elite finds the elected leaders of the masses as ill-equipped to run the country. But as democracy advances the masses are getting enlightened and the privileged elites are getting deelitised and the commoners are forcing their entry into the so-called steal frame. This representativeness of Indian administration is a real transformation and notwithstanding the controversies like strong bureaucracy versus weak democracy, a golden mean is being arrived at by improving the quality of representatives in politics as well as in administration.

Ministerial Accountability of Administration

In a democratic system, there cannot be any authority without accountability. The executive officials of the government have to be answerable to the legislature under the doctrine of ministerial responsibility. The cabinet is responsible to the house and all government functionaries owe their authority to the majesty of law of which judiciary is the guardian. The executive responsibility of administration, legislative surveillance, judicial review, audit, control, financial advisory system in ministries, are some of the mechanics in the system of accountability. In practice, these are reinforced and supplemented by the mass media, political parties, interest groups, electoral processes, and several kinds of watchdog organisations existing in the society. A minister in India is accountable to the Lok Sabha for his actions or lack of them – as well as for those of the civil servants serving in the ministry under his stewardship. The civil servants are protected by the principle of anonymity. The Parliament holds the minister responsible even if the latter has no knowledge of former's misdeeds. The minister's responsibility to Parliament without any qualification or modification is the essence of ministerial responsibility. The minister takes the entire responsibility when questioned in the Parliament. He must protect and defend him and must acknowledge the mistakes and accept the responsibility, although he is not personally involved. The erring civil servant gets blamed by his minister although here too the minister continues to be accountable to the Parliament and the civil servant enjoys his neutrality and anonymity.

Illustrations from administrations of UK and India are a pointer in that direction that this ministerial responsibility is only conventional and cannot be pushed to legal exactitudes. It works within limits of common sense and Prime Minister is the final arbiter when matters come to a pass. As the minister is responsible to the legislature for actions of the civil servants, the latter must obviously be held accountable to this. For this, the civil servants must know well their minister's objectives and faithfully project them in whatever they do. They must observe in all their official transactions with citizens, the due process of law and the laws of natural justice. They must remain alive to the sensitivities of the legislature and must abjure from doing things which might embarrass the minister. They must be responsive to the larger public opinion. This accountability is ensured and made specific by a complex system of organisational and procedural devices. The need for a law of torts and social audit and time bound explanation can strengthen this framework of accountability. Besides periodic reviews and evaluations, which constitute an integral part of the proposed framework, the results of such exercises are fed back into the system. This political accountability of the administration is further reinforced by a more precise system of administrative accountability in carrying out the specific legal responsibilities assigned or assumed by the public servants in day-to-day administration. The misuse or abuse of authority on the part of administrative services may assume various forms such as overriding or circumventing the law; violation of established procedures and channels; dishonesty or lack of integrity; gross inefficiency or incompetence;

nepotism; unethical conduct; and above all, encroachment on rights and freedoms of citizens. Hierarchically the administrators are accountable for the abuse or misuse of this authority to their respective seniors, but a democratic administration has to be vertically and horizontally controlled by several other agencies to stay accountable to the people at large. This democratic accountability is ensured through a variety of controls namely:

(1) Executive control over administration,
(2) Legislative control over administration,
(3) Judicial control over administration, and
(4) Popular control of civil society.

Executive Control over Administration

The executive control of administration in a democracy is positive as well as negative. Its contents consist of supervising, advising, inspecting, and if necessary, punishing the delinquent. It manifests through (i) ministerial control, (ii) administrative control, (iii) seniors in the hierarchy, and (iv) control over expenditure and audit. The personnel management control of staff agencies and practice of professional ethics and self-regulation also exercise this executive part of democratic accountability. Each minister is individually in charge of a portfolio consisting of one or more departments. He controls the actions of civil servants under him so that they may help him in implementing his policies. The secretary is the head of the department. The field offices work under the direction and control of the secretariat. The headquarters' administration controls the field agencies through procedures like (a) prior approval of projects; (b) promulgation of service standards; (c) budgetary limitation upon operations; and (d) approval of key appointments and (e) audit, inspection and investigation.

The finance ministry of the Government of India exercises budgetary control over administration. It follows a prescribed procedure of maintaining records, examining returns and prepares accounts for review by the C&AG. The control of the finance ministry over public expenditure is exercised in:

(i) approval of policies and programmes,
(ii) acceptance of provisions in the budget estimates, and
(iii) prior sanction to incurring of expenditure.

This control is exercised through the instrumentalities like rules of business, a system of internal financial advisers and internal audit. The rules of business provide that no department can issue orders involving abandonment of revenue or incurring of any expenditure for which no provision has been made in the budget. Grant of land or assignment of revenue and creation of grades of posts or the strength of a service require previous consent.

Public servant cannot spend out of the public funds unless the expenditure has been sanctioned by the competent authority and falls within the limit of the appropriations granted by Parliament every year. The finance ministry sends its own officers to each ministry (except the railways and defence ministries), who exercise control over expenditure through scrutiny of the legality, accuracy, and propriety of expenditure. They also advise the departmental heads upon the financial implications of their schemes and furnish reports to the ministry. The financial adviser makes necessary accounting arrangements within the administrative ministry. Since 1962 the secretary has been authorised to overrule the adviser without the matter being reported to any outside authority.

Personnel Control

The Estimates Committee and the Administrative Reforms Commission emphasised the need for the establishment of a central personnel agency in India. Created in 1970, the ministry of personnel regulates matters of general applicability to all services for the maintenance of common standards of recruitment and training. Principles governing seniority, promotion, conduct and discipline and staffing of senior posts are the responsibilities of this department. It is responsible for the creation of new all India services, rules and regulations and all matters relating to personnel policies and review of career management. Inter-ministry cadres, including career planning; personnel management agencies; research; and allocation of personnel contribute to its executive control through personnel management. The other agencies concerned with personnel matters are the ministry of finance and the Union Public Service Commission. The former is responsible for personnel matters having financial implications. Its staff inspection unit conducts periodical reviews for fixing staff standards, work norms and staff strength. The Union Public Service Commission deals with matters connected with the various examinations and recruitment to various posts through it. The Planning Commission though an advisory body takes initiatives in suggesting reforms in personnel matters which go a long way to extend executive control over administration.

Professional ethics of public servants provides an internal check on their self-regulatory activities. In India, the civil service code enjoins upon the public servants to declare their assets and swear allegiance to the values of the Constitution. It recognises loyalty and fairness of public service, as a part of democratic credo. The self-regulatory activities of public servants represent an ethical code, to inspire them to their duties. Thus, a democratic administration has to be controlled internally as well as externally. This control is detailed, specific and penal. The administrators are taken to task and are forced to follow internal rules, subject to external suspension. It prevents arbitrariness and keeps the system rule bound and democratically accountable to the political executive, who in turn has to be answerable to the Parliament.

Legislative Accountability of Administration

Both presidential and parliamentary democracies control their administrative systems through legislatures directly as well as indirectly. In USA, the Congress and its committees participate in administrative decisioning, oversees administrative activities, conducts congressional investigations and provides remedial measure including confirmation or rejection of top administrative appointments. Unlike USA, the parliaments in UK and India have ministers on the floor of the house to initiate measures, answer questions, defend administrative operations or policies and take responsibility for administrative performance. This control of parliaments over administration is exercised in great details through question hours, debates, parliamentary motions, budgetary approval and committee investigations.

Democratic administrations are amenable to parliamentary scrutiny, supervision and accountability in varied ways. As a sovereign body, the Parliament enjoys the right:

(1) To know or attract attention to misuse or abuse of authority and to ventilate the grievances of the citizens. It is usually done through: (a) starred or unstarred questions, (b) zero hour discussions, (c) adjournment motions, (d) motions or resolutions in public interest, (e) short notice motions followed by thirty minute and two hour discussions, and (f) calling attention notice

for classifications or explanation. All these legislative devices enable the popular representatives to interrogate the executive and question the propriety of administrative actions. These tools of legislative accountability keep the administrators on their toes and the responsible ministers explain, defend and improve the administration under their charge.

(2) Debates, discussions and votes on: (a) address by the president, (b) censor motion against the government, (c) various kinds of reports presented to Parliament, and (d) annual budget of the government.

These parliamentary debates are not a formality. The government takes the Parliament into confidence and apprises the latter about its achievements and predicaments. A democratic administration needs to be sensitised in popular aspirations which are reflected in parliament's concerns and approval or condemnation of governmental policies. The members may raise general or specific issues mentioned in the presidential address, finance minister's budget speech or reports presented on the floor of the house. This legislative accountability of the executive in actual practice tends to be the legislative answerability of the administration through its minister as a member of the Parliament.

(3) Parliamentary Committee Investigations: They are the most effective tool of parliaments detailed and systematic control over administrative policies and decisions. The three parliamentary committees of Indian Parliament have established conventions and are known for their role in controlling public expenditure. They are:
   (a) Public Accounts Committee,
   (b) Estimates Committee, and
   (c) Committee on Public Enterprise.

Created in the year 1922, the Public Accounts Committee has 22 members, 15 from the lower and 7 from the upper house on the basis of proportional representation every year. Article 308 of the rules of procedure and conduct of business in Lok Sabha lays down its functions as:

(1) Examination of accounts showing the appropriation of sums granted by the Parliament for the expenditure and the annual finance account and such other accounts laid before the house as the committee may think fit. It does so by examining the annual report of the Comptroller and Auditor-General submitted to Parliament.
(2) Examination of the statement that shows the income and expenditure of state corporations, manufacturing schemes, and projects together with the balance sheets and statements of profit and loss accounts which the President may have required to be prepared, are prepared under the provisions of the rules.
(3) Scrutiny of income and expenditure of autonomous and semi-autonomous bodies, the audit of which may be conducted by the Comptroller and Auditor-General either under the direction of the President or by a statue of Parliament.
(4) Consideration of report of the Comptroller and Auditor-General in cases where the President may have required him to conduct an audit of any receipts or to examine the accounts of stores and stocks.
(5) Examination of whether any money has been spent on any service during a financial year in excess of the amount granted by the house for that purpose. It examines the report which the Comptroller and Auditor-General submits every year to the President, who causes it to be laid before the Lok Sabha which in turn refers it to this committee. The Committee scrutinises this

report with the assistance of the Comptroller and Auditor-General who is not a member of the committee but attends the meetings on invitation and intervenes to clarify points and generally assists the committee.

The Estimates Committee constituted in 1921 scrutinises the new proposals included in the budget. Its 30 members are elected from Lok Sabha by a system of proportional representation. The Committee suggests alternative policies in order to bring about efficiency and economy in administration and examine whether the money is well laid out within the limits of the policy implied in the estimates. The Estimate Committee suggests the form in which the estimates should be presented to Parliament. It does not exercise its functions in relation to such public undertakings as are allotted to the Committee on Public Undertakings by the rules of procedure or by the Speaker. The fundamental objectives of the Committee are economy, efficiency in administration and ensuring that money is well laid out. The Committee may point out the defects causing waste and give reasons for change in the policy for the consideration of the House.

The Indian Parliament has several other committees like Committee on Public Assurances, which reports on the extent to which such assurances have been implemented, within the minimum time necessary for the purpose. The Minister for Parliamentary Affairs takes special interest in the implementation of assurances. The Committee on the Welfare of Scheduled Castes and Scheduled Tribes reports on the actions taken by the Union government on the measures proposed by the committee. The Committee on Subordinate Legislation has 15 nominated members from Lok Sabha. Under Rule 70 (1977), it is provided that bill involving proposals for the delegation of legislative power will be accompanied by a memorandum explaining such proposals and drawing attention to their scope and character.

The Committee examines each order and reports:

(1) whether it is in accord with the general objects of the Constitution or the Act pertaining to which it has been made;
(2) whether it contains matter which in the opinion of the Committee should more properly be dealt within an Act of parliament;
(3) whether the Act contains imposition of any tax;
(4) whether it directly or indirectly bars the jurisdiction of the courts; or
(5) whether it gives retrospective effect to any of the provisions regarding which the Constitution or the Act does not expressly give any such power.

The Committee scrutinises which the executive legislation delegated involves expenditure from the Consolidated Fund of India or the public revenues, whether it appears to make some unusual or unexpected use of the powers conferred by the Constitution or the Act under which it is made; there appears to have been unjustifiable delay in its publication or in laying it before Parliament.

This legislative control through parliamentary committees is well established and can be called positive as well as negative. Similarly it is direct as well as indirect. Examples of positive control are: sanctioning of new taxation proposals and new items of expenditure; ratifying treaties and appointments; issuing framework of policy, examining performance of executive and administrative agencies through various committees. Negative control can be exercised through refusal of demands for grants; not passing government bills, resolution and other proposals; passing adjournment motions.

Consultative Committees of Parliament

To extend this legislative influence of Parliament over executive activity, especially that of bureaucracy, the Indian Parliament set up consultative committees in 1952. They are also known as department related standing committees of Indian Parliament. They are neither statutory nor constitutional but are just informal and have proliferated to all-important ministries of Government of India. Unlike the British practice, the Indian Parliament has constituted 19 committees, 6 chaired by the members of Rajya Sabha and 13 by the members of Lok Sabha. Each consultative committee has 45 members, 30 from Lok Sabha and 15 from Rajya Sabha. These 19 committees with 45 members each practically provide opportunity to every Member of Parliament to get involved in the process of legislative scrutiny of all the ministries of government. These committees consider demands for grants of concerned minister's report to the house. They examine bills, consider annual reports of ministries and examine policy documents to be presented to the Parliament. This practice brings Indian Parliament close to American Congress where the Senate and house committees grill the executive and keep it on its toes. The committees make parliamentary control effective and the administration feels really accountable. The civilians are called to appear and have regular interface with the MPs. There is more time available to go into details, call for the documents and to report about the same to the Parliament.

The 19 committees of Parliament cover the following ministries noted against them:

	Committee	Ministries
1.	Committee on External Affairs	External Affairs
2.	Committee on Defence	Defence
3.	Committee on Finance	Finance, Planning Programme Implementation
4.	Committee on Industry	Industry, Steel, Mines
5.	Committee on Home Affairs	Home Affairs, Law, Justice and Company Affairs, Personnel
6.	Committee on Agriculture	Agriculture, Water Resources, Food Processing
7.	Committee on Science and Technology, Environment and Forests	Science and Technology, Electronics, Space, Ocean Development, Bio-technology, Environment and Forest
8.	Committee on Communication	Information and Broadcasting, Communications
9.	Committee on Commerce	Commerce, Textiles
10.	Committee on Human Resource Development	Human Resource Development, Health and Family Planning
11.	Committee on Energy	Coal, Non-conventional Energy Sources, Power, Atomic Energy
12.	Committee on Petroleum and Chemicals	Petrochemicals, Fertilizers
13.	Committee on Transport and Tourism	Civil Aviation, Surface Transport, Tourism
14.	Committee on Urban and Rural Development	Urban Development, Rural Development
15.	Committee on Labour and Welfare	Labour, Welfare
16.	Committee on Railways	Railways
17.	Committee on Food, Civil Supplies and Public Distribution	Food, Civil Supplies, Consumer Affairs and Public Distribution
18.	Committee on Internal Security	Home and External Affairs
19.	Committee on Social Justice	Women, Children and Minorities

The legislative accountability of administration in India combines the British and American practices. The British tools of parliamentary control restrain the administration and the US-type Congressional committees facilitate parliamentary participation in policy administration at higher levels of bureaucracy and intensive parliamentary functioning in addition to its overall control.

Parliament has responded to this need to consider demands for grants of minister and various kinds of bills, important policies, annual reports of ministries, their implementation and other matters referred by the speaker are examined, discussed and recommended for decisions. The democratic nature of the parliamentary control over administration makes it broad, indirect, partisan and issue-based, but it has the advantage of keeping administrators sensitised, transparent and responsible. The critics maintain that this control is too wild uniformed and extremely democratising to innocent civil servant. But then neither can it be abandoned nor even curtailed if democratic administration has to have roots in a society where imperial traditions make administration secretive, power-oriented and feudal. Several remedies like press conference, media reporting, role of the speaker, right to reply of the aggrieved or even televising the legislative debates are suggested to make it healthy. As democracy matures in India, the peoples representatives will realise the risks and hazards inbuilt in this parliamentary privilege and civil servants will also learn to work under popular gaze of social audit. The right to information is the beginning and the midway between legislative supervision and administration awareness will pave the way for democratic accountability of public administration.

Judicial Control over Administration in India

The Indian Constitution introduces judicial review in the parliamentary model of a written Constitution in India. Unlike UK, Indian judiciary has a wider jurisdiction and has come up to judicial activism which is also called as 'Third Chamber Judiciary in USA'. Legal and sophisticated details apart, the Indian judicial system has been assigned the following roles by the founding fathers.

(a) It should act as a guardian of the Constitution by preserving, protecting and defending the basic structure of the Constitution.

(b) It should play the custodian of citizen's fundamental rights and promote the dignity of the individual by creating conditions conducive for the implementation of Directive Principles of State Policy.

(c) It should dispense justice social, economic and political and resolve litigational conflicts through a judicious system of appeals of public administration by:
   (1) Encouraging public interest litigation (PIL).
   (2) Relaxating its juristic procedures through suo motto cognitions.
   (3) Building broad constructions of public law through liberal interpretations especially in the area of social justice and environment protection.
   (4) Forcing executive to compensate the victims of administrative arbitrariness through liberal provisions of victimology.
   (5) Widening the horizons of constitutional law through liberal democratic interpretations of the text to inspire popular faith in the rule of law system against administrative secrecy, privileges and discretion.

Although judicial control by its very nature has limits and is too narrow to probe into the specifics of administrative laws. The Indian judiciary has struggled against its slow moving, juristic and expensive procedures that run counter to the concept of natural justice. The new human rights jurisprudence and social justice through social legislation have enabled the Indian law courts to extend their sphere and effectivity against executive's arbitrary preserves of feudalism or pockets of new despotism.

This role of judiciary which it has incrementally expanded under the doctrine of judicial activism during last fifty years has restricted the discretion and arbitrariness of the executive and administrative agencies. It has safeguarded the rights and liberty of the citizen and helped in redressing the grievances of citizens. It has mitigated corruption in government and administration by declaring *ultra vires* the acts of the government and administration if and when they exceed their jurisdictions.

The judicial remedies provided under right to constitutional remedies with specific provisions of writs and injunctions have enabled the courts to put administration to task for their actions if they do not suffer from lack of jurisdiction or errors of law and fact finding. The faulty procedures adopted by administration and abuse of official discretion can be challenged in law courts. The Constitution under Article 300 provides that the Union government or a state government can be sued as a juristic person subject to legislation by the appropriate legislatures. The judicial protection available to Indian citizens provides: (1) public remedies by the prosecution of public officers and private officers; (2) private remedies through civil and criminal courts against the government and public officers; and (3) extraordinary remedies like various kinds of writs. The superior courts have sufficient authority to protect the fundamental rights. Article 32(1) guarantees the right to move the Supreme Court by appropriate proceedings for the enforcement of fundamental rights. The court has a concurrent, original as well as appellate jurisdiction in all such cases. For the quick enforcement of these rights, Article 32 (2) empowers the Supreme Court to issue directions or orders or writs like Heabus Corpus, Mandamus, Prohibition, Certiorari and Quo Warranto. Article 226 confers similar authority of issuing writs upon High Courts within their respective jurisdictions.

To democratise administration and administrators, the Indian judiciary is a great bulwark and has lived up to the common citizens' expectations. It has strengthened democratic accountability. Since independence there is a marked trend to supplement ordinary courts with a system of administrative tribunals. Both the Union Parliament and the state legislatives have passed laws creating such tribunals, for example, Income-tax Appellate Tribunal, Railway Rates Tribunal, Industrial Relations Tribunal, Wage Board, and Consumer Courts, etc. The 42nd Amendment has empowered the 'appropriate legislature' to provide for adjudication or trial by tribunals of disputes where legislature has the power to legislate. The 44th Amendment of 1978 modified the jurisdiction but the tribunals like CAT continue to provide relief against tyranny of procedures and delay in the delivery of justice.

Popular Control of Civil Society

The executive legislative and judicial controls over administration are primarily institutional and have their limitations. A mature democracy aims to make administrators directly amenable to people or public opinion. It implies popular initiative, popular criticism and popular participation by average citizen as well as by enlightened citizenry. It is an advanced concept obtained only in small Benelux or Scandinavian countries of Europe. In India, it can be activated and be achieved in a limited manner. Nonetheless, the experiment is worthwhile to arouse public interest in public administration. This notion of popular accountability of administration in an indirect democracy is often conceived as participation of civil society in the working of public administration. In fact, it is an attempt to rid administration from evil and corrupt practices and exercise vigilance through popular community institutions. Some of the attempts made in this area of effective popular control of community over administration in India are:

(1) Effective use of administrative agencies like anti-corruption departments. CBI, CVC and courts with support of the community.
(2) Experiment with the institutions of Lok Ayukts and Lok Pal (to be created to correct administration through popular initiative and cooperation).
(3) Investigative journalism and media exposure to keep administration on the track and to provide structure to judicial courts to rectify the failings of administration.
(4) Establishment of NGOs to promote public interest and protect fundamental human rights through PIL and participatory system of committees.

Thus, accountability administration in order to conform to the spirit of democracy requires the availability of rule of law and human rights in a society where administration will have to work with people rather than for the people with an elitist act of superiority. The Indian Constitution guarantees six fundamental rights and on this, we have superimposed the concept of human rights with Human Rights Commissions at the Centre and in the states. The rule of law doctrine of Dicey is inbuilt in the parliamentary institutionalisation and judicial review practices obtained in India. The two can be called the new pillars of democratic administration which are yet to be strengthened in the democratic polity engaged in a democratisation experiment by more than one billion people.

Rule of Law and Integrity in Public Service

Rule of Law according to the British Jurist Dicey in common parlance implies that:
(1) Nobody can be punished unless proved guilty.
(2) The language of law is the language of equals.
(3) The rights precede and do not follow the Constitution.

In the British context, it simply means a theory of natural rights which guarantees rights to liberty and equality. It is a convention in the unwritten Constitution which reiterates that "rights are enforced because they are rights. They are not rights because they are enforced". The Indian Constitution partially accepts it because it claims to guarantee fundamental freedoms. There can be very many basic or substantive differences in the British and Indian concepts, but the jurists will agree that in the rule of law situation nobody can be above the law (except the British Crown). The executive and the public administrators are the creatures of law and the petty discretions permitted in the law do not permit the lawmakers to operate as law breakers. Even the interpretative freedom of rules and regulations cannot be twisted to the detriment of the people. The distortions and perversions of law are downright crimes punishable under the procedures established by law. The rule of law doctrine does not permit discriminatory behaviour and administration, which is expected to implement the laws faithfully and honestly should not indulge in illegal activities of violative nature. The democratic administration should conform to rule of law in the sense that laws are honoured by the administrators to inspire confidence, faith and respect for law by the common citizen of the country.

The Indian administration professes to practice rule of law under the overall supremacy of the judiciary. But the level of integrity and prevalence of corrupt practices in administration compel the executive to maintain a vigilance machinery to keep its civil servants honest, transparent and wedded to high ethical values of personal and public conduct.

The Santhanam Committee report accepted rule of law violation as corruption and defined it as "Failure to take action in the performance of duty by a government servant for personal advantage". It is a deviant behaviour because the loss of integrity results in violation of rights of citizens that harms public good. Rule of law in Indian democracy stands to democratise its administration which can broadly be outlined as under:

(1) The majesticity of law is to be respected by one and all without any discrimination of colour, caste, sex and creed.
(2) The wilful violations of law will be punished and administrative corruption will be brought to book by legal mechanism of the government.
(3) Integrity in public services will be strengthened through law and codes of conduct.

Democracy cannot be a government of individuals and still less a system of so-called elitist merit. It has been called a leveller, where everybody counts for one and nobody counts for more than one. This concept of Weberian bureaucracy has to be adjusted with democratic politics in such a manner that the supremacy of law is duly protected and those who violate law or use public power for private ends are given exemplary punishments. Apart from dishonesty, the laws in India are violated to advance personal interests at the cost of public good by exploitation of administrator's official position. Deviation from moral standards or lack of integrity takes various shapes in the form of corruption, patronage and undue influence. Corruption is a deliberate and intentional exploitation of one's position, status or resources, directly or indirectly, for personal aggrandisement in terms of material gain or enhancement of power, prestige or influence beyond what is legitimate or sanctioned by commonly accepted norms. It is extravagant expenditure of public money, providing employment to relatives or friends by those in power through patronage.

Unlike rule of law countries of the West, corruption-based violation of laws in India has a wider implication in Indian administration. It boils down to misuse, abuse or even non-use of official position or authority for ulterior motives. In general sense even inefficiency can be called corruption but in common parlance it implies money changing hands in anticipation of favours. It is situational, and in countries like India there are different norms for judging an individual's personal and official lives. Corruption may cause scandals and the magnitude of corruption and the frequency of its occurrence may take several forms. The political and administrative corruption, though interrelated are analytically and operationally different. Several Western scholars have found it functional in development administration, but certainly, it militates against the practice of rule of law, i.e., democracy.

The IPC (1860) defined corruption as the acceptance of any gratification whatever, other than legal remuneration as a motive or reward for doing or forbearing to do any official act or for showing or forbearing to show favour or disfavour to any person, or rendering or attempting to render any service or disservice to any person.

The Prevention of Corruption Act 1947 narrowed the requirements of proving motives behind corruption. The Gorwala Report (1955) paved the way for Santhanam Committee on prevention of corruption. The Committee consisting of four other MPs and two senior officers (1962) identified the following areas and suggested preventive measures for the malaise:

(1) Special precaution should be taken while making appointments and promotions.
(2) Permits, licences and contracts should be granted only to those individuals and companies who are recognised and registered with the government
(3) All civil servants, legislators and ministers should declare their private assets.

(4) Simplification of government laws, rules and work procedures be undertaken so that civil servants may not indulge in corrupt practices.
(5) Letters and files should be disposed of within a specified period.
(6) Information regarding donations to political parties should be made public.
(7) Adequate pay and facilities should be provided to public officials to avoid temptations.
(8) Government servant should not work in private commercial and industrial firms after retirement.
(9) Special police establishments should be strengthened with more powers.
(10) A vigilance commission should be constituted in the Central government.
(11) Article 311 of the Constitution be amended to expedite legal action in matters involving corruption.

The Santhanam Committee made special recommendations for preventing corruption in departments such as income tax, civil supplies, central PWD, central excise, customs, etc. The committee made 137 recommendations, out of which 106 were accepted by the government. Consequently, the Indian Penal Code was amended to expand its scope and the Special Police Establishment was strengthened and Article 311 of the Indian Constitution was also amended in 1976.

This awareness of the malady and the desire to combat the menace resulted into three kinds of efforts to rid the administrative system for enhancement of democratic efficiency.

(1) The vigilance machinery was reorganised and strengthened at all levels,
(2) A review of rules giving protection to public servants was undertaken, and
(3) Efforts to standardise rules and codes of service conduct for public servants were made to ensure integrity in the civil service of the country.

Central Vigilance Commission (CVC)

In pursuance to Santhanam recommendations of 1964, the Central Vigilance Commission was created. It is a one-man commission and the commissioner has one secretary, five directors, three under secretaries and a small office staff at Delhi. Eleven commissioners of departmental engineers (CDI) handle complaints from respective spheres. One chief technical examiner, eight technical examiners and six assistant technical examiners constitute the technical wing which probes the cases of maladministration. The protection of integrity in administration being the major task of the CVC, it performs the following functions:

(1) Exercising a general check and supervision over vigilance and anti-corruption work in ministries, public sector undertakings and call for reports/returns.
(2) Conducting an independent technical examination from the vigilance angle of works undertaken by Central government organisations.
(3) Undertaking inquiry into transactions in which a public servant (in Central government, organisations) is suspected or alleged to have acted in a corrupt manner through the CBI or the CVOs of the respective organisations.
(4) Tendering independent advice in disciplinary cases having a vigilance angle at different stages of investigation, inquiry, appeal and review.
(5) Advising the appropriate authorities to modify the existing procedures in the Central government to mitigate the scope for misconduct.

On receiving complaint, the CVC can entrust the matter for enquiry by ministry or department concerned. It may ask the CBI to probe the matter and furnish relevant records. The director, Central Bureau of Investigation will forward the final report of his investigation to the ministry of home affairs through the CVC, if sanction for such prosecution is required under any law to be issued in the name of the Parliament. Recently, the CBI has been accorded the status of a national police station.

The Commission has laid down procedures to be followed by the administrative ministries/departments. The jurisdiction of the Commission extends to all employees of the Central government and its organisations. It advises on individual vigilance cases only in regard to senior higher-level personnel. The role of the Central Vigilance Commission is advisory, but as per the government resolution, the CVC enjoys the same measure of independence and autonomy as the UPSC of India. The ministers and Member of Parliament are outside the purview of the CVC's jurisdiction. The CVC sends its annual report to the ministry of personnel to be tabled on the floor of the both houses of Parliament.

The vigilancc organisations in every ministry stays in touch with the CVC who coordinates the work with chief vigilance officers. While the primary responsibility for the maintenance of probity, integrity and efficiency in each organisation continues to rest in the secretary of the ministry or the head of the department, an officer in each ministry/department has been designated as chief vigilance officer and entrusted with vigilance work. The chief vigilance officer is responsible for coordinating and guiding the activities of other vigilance officers in the attached and subordinate offices and other organisations with which his ministry/department is concerned.

CBI and SPE

The Central Bureau of Investigation (CBI) was established in 1963 as an attached office of the ministry of home affairs. It prepares and implements programmes of vigilance and anti-corruption. It collects and collates information on corruption cases with the help of governmental as well as non-governmental agencies. The Bureau has six divisions. The Special Police Establishment (SPE), merged with it now, acts as its investigation and anti-corruption division. The other five divisions are: (1) Technical, (2) Crime, (3) Records, (4) Research, and (5) Legal Administration. Today, it functions as a national police station.

The enlarged functions of the Bureau cover investigations of the National Central Bureau for India under the International Criminal Police Organisation (Interpol) as also the Central Forensic Laboratory. The Bureau indexes criminals and Interpol notices are also circulated to various enforcement agencies in the country. The SPE Division of the Bureau is the principal investigating agency of the Central government. Big cases of fraud, cheating and embezzlement by organised gangs having inter-state or international ramification fall in its jurisdiction. The Bureau derives its power to investigate offences from the SPE Act Delhi.

Vigilance Machinery in the States

The anti-corruption machinery at state level does not follow a uniform structural pattern. Some states have state vigilance commissions (SVC), while others have anti-corruption bureaus within the police administration. The state vigilance commissions are patterned like the Central Vigilance Commissions. A state vigilance commissioner enjoys the status of a High Court Judge. In conducting investigations, the SVC is assisted by the special police establishment.

The states not having vigilance commissions, have well-organised anti-corruption departments with differing extents of autonomy. A few states have raised their anti-corruption departments (ACD) into bureaus. They enjoy functional autonomy and their officials come on deputation from the police departments of the states. The directors of ACD or bureau chiefs though attached to home departments generally report to the chief minister. The political supervision of this agency tells upon the image and efficiency of the bureau.

The SVC owes its existence to an executive resolution and its role is advisory in nature. But, it is not subordinate to any other department in the exercise of its powers. Its jurisdiction extends to matters within the executive power of the state concerned excluding cases of political corruption. Broadly speaking, the SVC is empowered to undertake inquiry into transactions in which a public servant is suspected or alleged to have acted in a corrupt manner. The SVC initiate reviews of procedure and practices of administration and collects statistics and other information. At the level of the district, there are district vigilance officers and the network is streamlined by annual conferences prescribed by the CVC.

The Administrative Reforms Commission (1966) examined the whole issue of vigilance along with citizen's grievances and recommended a two-tier machinery of Lokpal and Lok Ayukta. The commission was of the view that they should be demonstrably independent and impartial and their investigations and proceedings should be conducted in private and should be informal in character. The appointment of these functionaries should as far as possible be non-political and their status should compare with the highest judicial functionaries in the country. The incumbents should deal with matters in the discretionary field involving acts of injustice, corruption of favouritism and their proceedings should not be subject to judicial interference. They should deal with cases of political corruption with powers of initiating action against corruption-suspected ministers and MPs. The Lokpal should have his own independent investigating and prosecuting agency without having to depend on the CBI and should have legal powers to prosecute an accused minister in specially designated courts after a prima facie is established against him by the Lokpal's own inquiry. The minister found guilty must compulsorily resign after filling of the charge sheet in the trial court. The CVC should be re-designated as the Central Lok Ayukta and he should be appropriately linked to the Lokpal by making provisions of sharing or having common officers, staff, investigating and prosecuting agencies. He alone should have the powers to finally decide on initiation of disciplinary action or prosecution against any public servant after a prima facie case is established by his own enquiry.

Integrity and Code of Conduct

Vigilance efforts apart, the Government of India has made several positive efforts to keep its civil servants in the state of honesty and integrity which is a condition precedent for accountable administration pursuing rule of law. The Article 311 of the Constitution as amended in 1976, lays down security of public servants. The concept of reasonable opportunity of being heard causes procedural bottlenecks. The over-security of civil servants is a strong cause of their misconduct. The rules require permission of the government which reserves the right to withdraw enquires and prosecutions at any stage. The civil service fraternity which often gangs up and effective actions are lost in the observance of prior permissions. These colonial provisions militate against the accountability of civil servant in a democratic administration which the republican Constitution ensures.

A public servant in a democracy has to be a guardian of public morals. He is entrusted with higher responsibilities of a public office and there are temptations and allurements which may pervert his ethical values and high integrity of civil behaviours. Apparently, the governments make rules and codes to keep their officials in good conduct. Some of these codes have their origin in the behavioural framework of British Civil Services. The Nolan Committee on standards of public life suggested a seven point ethical code of:

(1) selflessness,
(2) objectivity,
(3) integrity,
(4) objectivity,
(5) openness,
(6) honesty, and
(7) accountability of leadership.

The holders of public office should decide on public matters solely in public interest. In carrying out public business, the decisions must be made on merit and the holders of public office have a duty to declare any private interest relating to their public duties. After independence, the Government of India updated the conduct rules to protect integrity in the civil services of the country.

Five separate basic documents provide this framework for the conduct of administrators:

(1) All India Services (Conduct) Rules, 1968
(2) All India Services (Discipline and Appeal) Rules, 1969
(3) Central Civil Services (Conduct) Rules, 1964
(4) Central Civil Services (Classification, Control and Appeal) Rules, 1965
(5) Railway Servants (Conduct) Rules, 1966

To foster integrity and promote honesty in administrative operations most of these rules relate to:

(1) Private trade and employment
(2) Credit and solvency
(3) Loans of gazetted officers
(4) Post-retirement employment
(5) Houses and valuable property
(6) Receiving of gifts
(7) Investments in property and speculation
(8) Subscriptions by public servants

The Santhanam Committee has specifically urged upon the government to ensure that their public servants give an undertaking to the effect that they will not use their offices to secure employment for their family members. They should not make investments which are likely to embarrass or influence the discharge of their duties. A democratic administration has to be clean and clear and it should appear to be cleaner so that people feel inspired and administrative get motivated in the higher tasks of public service. Efforts to arrest corruption and bind public servants to lead a life of austerity and discipline contribute to the enhancement of people's faith in democratic working. In an emerging society of India's diversity it is a gigantic task which the democratic government has taken to itself.

Human Rights and Evolving Jurisprudence

A right is not a claim or demand but something which is not wrong. Natural Rights Theory as propounded by Johu Locke calls rights as pre-political which were available to man in his state of nature. These three human rights of life, liberty and estate were ensured to individuals by virtue of the ethical code of mutuality and moral order. The legal theory of later era found them implicit in the constitutional jurisprudence of the democratic polity. The libertarian and social welfare protagonists of 'rights' argued that the rationale of being right lies in the ethical nature of man. Hence, democratic liberal idealists like T.H. Green have to declare them as "outer conditions for the inner development of man". A democracy must ensure liberty and create conditions conducive for the enjoyment of right to life and liberty for the citizens at large. Rights may be prior to Constitution or a consequence of constitutionalisation, the fact remains that their availability and enlargement is another name of democracy.

The Indian Constitution in its Chapter Third envisaged seven fundamental rights with several Directive Principles for the establishment of a welfare polity in India. The 44th Amendment reduced them to six and accepted right to property as a mere legal (not fundamental) right of the citizen. Similarly, several directives have been accepted as fundamental in the governance of the country. The right to information, primary education and pollution free environment have come on the periphery of fundamental rights. As democracy matures in India, the judiciary is increasingly insisting on the development of human rights jurisprudence and the legal implementation of social legislation for the attainment of human rights in India. The administration has been legally bound to respect human rights and take steps to prevent their violations. Although, there cannot be an agreed list of universal human rights, but the Commission on Human Rights duly constituted in 1946 under the chairmanship of Mrs Roosevelt prepared a Draft Declaration which was submitted to the General Assembly by the United Nations in September, 1948. The declaration was adopted as a common standard of achievement for all peoples and all nations. It has been described as the 'Magna Carta' of mankind. In 30 articles, it sums up the civil, political and religious liberties men have struggled for so long. Later on, some 60 human rights treaties and declarations were negotiated at the UN on the Universal Declaration. In 1954, the Commission on Human Rights submitted two covenants to the General Assembly. The first covenant reaffirmed political and civil rights and the second was concerned with economic, social and cultural rights. The General Assembly adopted them by a resolution in 1966. By another resolution, it also recognised the subject status of the individual by permitting him to petition to the Committee on Human Rights against his own state. These covenants came into force in 1976. The universal declaration has now been accepted by virtually all states and even the erstwhile European Communist states have accepted it formally in the Helsinki Act of 1975.

The fundamental rights, jurisprudence in India promoted awareness of human rights. The commissions for SC and ST, minorities and women have been created and they are gradually becoming effective and functional.

Human Rights Commission

The Human Rights Commission Act, 1993 established the National Human Rights Commission. A human rights cell was also created in the home ministry. States have been advised to set-up human rights cells or Commissions to monitor and follow-up cases of alleged human rights violations by the law enforcement agencies. The President of India promulgated an ordinance to this effect in 1993. The ordinance defines the human rights as "the rights relating to life, liberty, equality and dignity of the individual guaranteed by the Constitution of India". The Human Rights Act, extends to the whole of India including the State of Jammu & Kashmir in matters relatable to any of the entries enumerated in List I or List III in the Seventh Schedule to the Constitution. The NHRC has eight members:

(1) Chairperson who has been a Chief Justice of the Supreme Court
(2) One member, who is or has been the judge of the Supreme Court
(3) One member who is or has been the Chief Justice of a High Court
(4) Two to five members to be appointed from amongst persons having knowledge of or practical experience in making matters relating to human rights.

The chairpersons of the National Commission for Minorities, the National Commission for SC and ST and the National Commission for Women are deemed members of the Commission for the discharge of its functions. The Secretary General is the executive officer of the Commission. The members of the commission are appointed by the President on the recommendations of a committee which consists of the prime minister, the speaker of the Lok Sabha, the home minister, the leader of the opposition in the Lok Sabha and the deputy chairman of the Rajya Sabha. The chairperson or any other member can be removed from office if adjudged as insolvent or infirm or of unsound mind or convicted and sentenced to imprisonment involving moral turpitude. The term of the members and chairperson is five years or the age of 70 years whichever is earlier with ineligibility for future re-employment.

The Commission regulates its own procedure. Its actions and proceedings cannot be questioned and the terms and conditions of service cannot be altered to the disadvantage of the members. The NHRC has a Secretary General of the rank of secretary to the government and a Director-General of Police to supervise the operations of its investigating staff. Section 12 of the Act empowers the Commission to undertake the following functions:

(1) To intervene in any proceeding involving allegation of violation of human rights pending before a court with its approval;
(2) To visit any jail or any other institution under intimation to the state government, where persons are detained or lodged for purposes of treatment, reformation or protection to study the living conditions of the inmates;
(3) To study treaties and other international instruments on human rights and make recommendations for their effective implementation;
(4) To enquire into in a petition presented by a victim or any person on his own behalf with compliant of violation of human rights or abatement thereof and negligence in the prevention of such violation by a public servant;
(5) To review the factors including acts of terrorism that inhabit the enjoyment of human rights and recommend remedial measures;
(6) To review the safeguards for the protection of human rights and recommend measures for their effective implementation;
(7) To spread human rights literacy and promote awareness of the safeguards for the protection of the human rights through publications, media, seminars or other available means; and

(8) To encourage the efforts of non-government organisations and institutions working in the field of human rights;
(9) To undertake and promote research in the field of human rights;
(10) To perform such other functions as it may consider necessary for the promotion of human rights.

The Commission has a sprawling jurisdiction of making inquiries and conducting investigations under the Code of Civil Procedure 1908 (5 of 1908) which include summoning and enforcing the attendance of witnesses and examining them on oath; discovery and production of any document; and receiving evidence on affidavits. The Commission can requisition any public record or copy thereof from any court or office; issue notice for the examination of witness or documents or any other matter which may be prescribed. The Commission have power to require any person under law to furnish information on matters as may be useful for, or relevant to the subject matter of the enquiry. The Commission is deemed to be a civil court and when any offence is committed in the view or presence of the Commission, the commission may, after recording the facts and the statement of the accused forward the case to a magistrate. Proceedings before the Commission are deemed as judicial proceeding within the meaning of Sections 193 and 228 and for purposes of Section 196, of the Indian Penal Code. The Commission can summon and enforce attendance of any person and examine him. Evidence before the Commission is governed by Section 15 of Indian Evidence Act. The reports submitted to Commission are verified for commission's satisfaction.

The Commission may take the following steps upon the completion of an inquiry held under this Act:

(1) Recommend to the concerned government the initiation of proceedings for prosecution against the concerned person or persons.
(2) Recommend to the concerned authority for the grant of immediate interim relief to the victim or the members of his family.
(3) Send a copy of its inquiry report and recommendations to the concerned government with comments, including the action taken in a months time.
(4) Furnish a copy of the inquiry report to the petitioner or his representative.
(5) Approach the Supreme Court or the High Court for directions, orders or writs which the court may deem necessary.

The NCHR follows a different procedure where members of armed forces are involved. It may seek a report from the Central government and may, either not proceed with the complaint or make its recommendation to that government. The Central government has to inform the Commission of the action taken on the recommendations within three months. The Commission also provides a copy of the report to the petitioner. The Commission submits an annual report to the Central government and to the state government concerned and may at anytime submit special report on any matter which is of such urgency that it should not be deferred till submission of the annual report. These reports of the Commission are laid before each house of Parliament or the state legislature respectively along with a memorandum of action taken on the recommendations of the Commission and the reasons for non-acceptance of the recommendations, if any.

The HRC in states broadly follows the national pattern. The state government may, with the concurrence of the Chief Justice of the High Court specify for each district a court of session to be a Human Rights Court to try the said offences. The Commission has expanded its scope to cover socio-economic issues of wider national concern. It has recommended the adoption of appropriate legislation on compulsory primary education, and resources for the same. This enhanced responsibility needs the cooperation of judiciary at lower levels to make human rights meaningful and available to the accused in custody. The legal services should protect the accused against third degree methods followed by police. The NHRC should engage in promoting human rights culture among police officers and doctors. There is need to have emphasis on professional honesty and to scrap draconian laws which violate human rights. The NHRC should engage its own prosecutors and legal staff to proceed against violators without need of previous sanction of the government.

Redressal of Citizen's Grievances

Democratic administration in its essence has to address itself to people's welfare. The common citizen does not have a feel of democratic governance unless the administration is responsive, responsible and transparent. Even the most populist policies when they come to the cutting edge do not provide succour but harass and torture people as if they are being governed by native colonial masters. Elections or laws made by representatives of the people do not satisfy the citizen, but he accepts that administration should attend to his problems with a smile. Human rights and dignity of the individual are loud sounding euphuisms. The lay citizen has his grievances against the administration and even when these grievances are fake or phoney or even exaggerated he has a basic right of their redressal. The Baranbas Study of Delhi found that corruption though a major grievance, is still much low as compared to apathy, embarrassment, delay and harassment, leading to exploitation and abuse of office by the administrators. Corruption, indifference, and insensitiveness on the part of public servants do frequently cause harm and hardship to lay citizens. These grievances of citizens can be general: "against the government, its acts and policies and may be common to all or any section of the community. The Individual grievances are found where the citizens, as individuals, have complaints against the executive organs of government, i.e., the permanent services. The individual grievances in a democratic set up look widespread and poignant. The citizen is within his right to expect that the public servants are honest, responsive, and fair in the discharge of their duties in administration".

The scope of administrative activity includes diverse functions such as issues of licences of public distribution of commodities, welfare services and social services like banking and insurance and registration of private property. These orders are passed by the officials at all levels. There is a vast field of administrative discretion in which administrative authority may act arbitrarily and the injured citizen may not obtain redressal.

The traditional instrument of control over executive power and discretion have been legislative overseeing and judicial review. Our Constitution has incorporated fundamental rights of the citizen which are justiciable. In addition, there exist institutions like Janta Darbar, complaint boxes and paper clipping for the ventilation and redress of grievances in the form of approach to administrative authorities at different levels in their original, appellate, revisional or supervisory jurisdiction. The legislative overseeing does not redress individual grievances arising in the course of day-to-day administration. Similarly, justice through courts is expensive and dilatory. The various administrative tiers and hierarchies have proved inadequate for the purpose.

To streamline the existing governmental machinery for redressal, a commissioner for public grievances was appointed in 1966. Complaint cells have also been set up in the ministries to handle grievances. At present, a separate Department of Administrative Reforms and Public Grievances exists in the Ministry of Personnel, Public Grievances and Pensions to attend to citizen grievances.

The Lokpal and Lokayuktas

The Santhanam Committee recommended the setting up of an institution more or less on the pattern of the parliamentary commissioner in New Zealand. The ARC debated the issue and recommended two special institutions for the redressal of citizens' grievances. There should be one authority dealing with complaints against the administrative acts of ministers or secretaries at the Centre and in the states. There should be another authority in each state and at the Centre for dealing with complaints against the administrative acts of other officials. All these authorities should be independent of the executive as well as the legislature and the judiciary. The first one was to be called the Lokpal and the second one Lok Ayukta. The Lokpal Bill has not been passed even after decades of hope and frustration in spite and despite of loud professions of successive union governments. The Lok Ayukta experiment in some of the states though tried half heartedly has been a dismal failure. The state governments kept institution too weak to take roots and because of the lack of political will, financial resources and adequate investigation machinery, the Lok Ayuktas in states have almost given up their battle till the Union Parliament comes out with a Lok Pal Bill as a model for the states. The Union government could not pilot the Lok Pal Bill under the Congress, the Janta, Rajiv Gandhi and A.B. Bajpai governments for one reason or the other. There is a wide divergence of opinion about the scope, nature, investigation machinery, appeal systems and status of the Lok Pal. The Sompal Committee gave some suggestions but the consensus is far from emerging. Some think that it should be a welcome step to put the suspects in the dock if people have evidence, while others maintain that it will be a duplication of several other machineries like CVC, CBI or a High Court. The Janta government in 1977 designed the bill with three features, namely, (1) the Prime Minister, other central ministers, members of Parliament, chief ministers and other ministers of states and state legislators fell within the jurisdiction of the Lokpal; (2) public servants, as against public men, were excluded from such purview as a separate vigilance organisation was already in existence to deal with misconduct by them; and (3) the Lokpal was given his own administrative machinery to carry out investigations and was vested with the powers of a civil court for the purpose. The Bill endeavoured to make the Lokpal as independent, impartial and prestigious as possible. He was to be appointed by the President after consultation with the Chief Justice of India, the chairman of the Rajya Sabha and the speaker of the Lok Sabha. His term was fixed at five years. V.P. Singh and Rajeev Gandhi tried to extend its scope and revised the provisions with five features, namely:

(1) Lok Pal will be a plural body with a chairman and two members from among the retired and/or serving judges of the Supreme Court;
(2) It will have an independent administrative set-up for investigation;
(3) The Lokpal will have full authority to investigate any matter concerning the misconduct and corruption of all public officials including the Prime Minister;
(4) The government will not take away any matter under the consideration of the Lokpal from his jurisdiction and hand it over to another investigating agency under the Commission of Inquiry Act without the consent of the Lokpal; and

(5) The Lokpal will send a consolidated report of its actions during the year to the President who will place it with his comments before both the houses within 90 days of submission of the report.

The BJP government was sharply divided about its scope and status as a recommendatory body. In the meantime, Lok Ayuktas were created in states and their dismal record further dampened the enthusiasm of the governments about an 'Ombudsman' in the political culture of India. Yet, the modalities are being explored to make it a workable and effective institution.

Redressal of Grievances of Public Servants

The civil servants in India are regarded as a privileged lot for the simple reason that they enjoy security of tenure and the Constitution guarantees them 'equal pay for equal work' through the machinery of pay commissions. Salary apart their perks and fringe benefits formally as well as informally go much beyond the prescribed pay packages. There are all sorts of benefits, like leave, medical reimbursement, housing, vehicles, pension, gratuity, free telephones, hard duty allowances, foreign travel, free children's education and innumerable fringe benefits which were given by the British rulers to treat them a breed apart. Then there are invisible benefits like status, traditional or customary facilities, abuse of office and obliging friends and relatives which cannot be worked out in monetary terms. All this was conceded by the alien rulers to win native loyalty and keep them in elitist living so that they may rule with legitimate comforts and care. The civil service has not only preserved these extra privileges but has raised a bogy that they are underpaid.

Now they are demanding equal benefits in public sector undertakings and in the secretariats at par with the private sector managers. The technique has worked well while their calibre and moral fibre has gone considerably low because of varied factors which they know but do not accept. The trade union movement in the junior cadres of service has been playing havoc and the dividing line between essential and non-essential services has literally blurred. The right to freedom, including protests without arms had caused militancy and even petty grievances are violently expressed much at the cost of human rights of citizens. The social justice movement apart, the junior employees are fighting against the arbitrary policies towards their service in the name of grievances. The senior officials including members of the all India services are discontented and airing their grievances genuine or fake against the people and their elected representatives. People complaint of corruption, senior civilians complain of political interference of leaders and junior employees talk of exploitation. The rule of law is the casualty and grievance redressal mechanism are being suggested to solve the reasonable problems of the civil servants in an effective manner.

Machinery for Consultation and Arbitration

The redressal of reasonable grievances of public servants is important because if they are not attended to in time they may lead to hostility, disputes, non-work and long range bitterness, damaging the very notion of public service. The Constitution of India provides for judicial review and the disciplinary rules if abused, the civil servant can seek judicial redressal. But this being dilatory, expensive and procedure based new methods of adjudication have been suggested by the Constitution itself. The all India services normally use this channel in case of gross misuse of administrative laws by the ministers. But for group A and group B services, the Government of India introduced a scheme in 1966 for joint consultation and arbitration for the Central government employees on the lines of the Whitley Councils in the United Kingdom. This is a non-statutory and voluntary scheme. The main objectives of the joint consultative machinery (JCM) are to promote harmonious relations between the government and its employees; to secure the maximum cooperation between them; and to increase the efficiency of the public services through a collaborative endeavour to narrow the area of unresolved differences. The scheme applies to all the Central government employees except the groups A and B services, employees in industrial establishments, union territories and police personnel.

(a) The scheme provides for a three-tier machinery: (1) the National Council as the apex body, (2) Departmental councils at the level of individual ministries/departments, and (3) Regional office/councils to deal mainly with the local problems. An important feature of the JCM scheme is the provision for compulsory arbitration in cases of disagreement between the official and the staff sides on matters relating to pay and allowances, weekly hours of work and leave of a class or grade of employees.

(b) A Board of Arbitration (BOA) under the administrative control of the ministry of labour has been set up with a chairman, and two other members. The awards of the BOA are binding on both sides except in cases in which the government proposes to modify the award. In the latter case, the government has to place the award before the Parliament explaining the reason for modifying or rejecting the award. Matters determined by the government in accordance with the recommendations of a Commission of Inquiry are not subject to arbitration for a period of five years from the date of recommendation. Orders issued by the government in pursuance of the recommendations of the BOA are operative for three years.

(c) In cases of disagreement, issues which are not covered under the dispensation for compulsory arbitration can be referred to a committee of three ministers, if the staff side makes a request for this. Whenever, there is a dispute between the official side and the staff in regard to the eligibility for arbitration, the issue is referred to the Attorney General of India for his opinion. The National Council has been holding meetings since the inception of the scheme. Besides the formal meetings, its standing committees also meet from time to time.

(d) Efforts have been made to set up departmental councils in ministries/departments and to set up office council in various offices.

The administrative tribunals have become a part of the constitutional machinery of the country. As a system of adjudication their number is on the increase. Administrative tribunals determine the questions of a judicial or quasi-judicial nature of an administrative agency or department. Like a regular court, administrative bodies hear the parties, shift evidence, pronounce decision in cases where legal rights or duties are involved. Administrative adjudication is a process by which administrative agencies settle issues arising in the course of their work when legal rights are in question. They represent authorities outside the ordinary court system which interpret and apply the laws when acts of public administration are attacked in formal suits or by other established methods. The agencies for administrative adjudication usually comprise the minister; the head of the department; a ministerial tribunal; a special committee or commission like independent regulatory commissions; specialised courts of law; single member tribunal or a composite tribunal. The legislative output being enormous gives rise to more litigations, and more restrictions on the liberty of the individual. In a welfare state, the infringement of authority on the common man is infinitely great. Disputes occur between individuals and authority.

The administrative tribunals are becoming popular and are fast proliferating in all countries. The Chief Administrative Tribunals in England are the Railways and Canal Commissioners, the Railway Rates Tribunals and the London Building Tribunal. The Chief Federal Administrative Tribunals in the United States are the Federal Trade Commission, the Interstate Commerce Commission and the Court of Customs and Patent Appeals. In India, their growth has been rather haphazard and they have come into existence as or when required. Over 3,000 such courts exist in India. Income Tax Appellate Tribunals, Railway Rates Tribunals, Labour Courts, Industrial Tribunals, National Tribunals, Wage Boards, Election Tribunals, Rent Tribunals are some of the examples of such tribunals.

The Centre Administrative Tribunal (CAT)

The Administrative Reforms Commission (1966–70) recommended the setting up of civil service tribunals in India to function as final appellate authorities in respect of orders inflicting the major punishments of dismissal, removal from service and reduction in rank. The Supreme Court in its judgement in 1980 observed that civil servants should not waste time in fighting battles in ordinary courts and suggested the establishment of such tribunals. Article 323A of the Constitution provides for the setting up of administrative tribunals for adjudication of disputes in matters pertaining to recruitment and conditions of services of persons employed in public services. Parliament passed a law to establish administrative tribunals in India. The Act visualises a Central Administrative Tribunal (CAT) for the Centre and state administrative tribunal for a particular state. It enjoys the status and power of High Court. In disposing of cases, it follows the principles and norms of natural justice. Appeals against its orders lie only with the Supreme Court of India. The aggrieved person may appear before it personally. It is a multi-member body whose members are drawn from judicial and administrative streams so as to give it the benefit of expertise legal as well as administrative fields. The administrative tribunals deal exclusively with service litigation and are free from the formalities of legal technicalities. The Central Administrative Tribunal (1985) has regular benches operating at the principal seats of High Courts. These benches also hold circuit sittings at other seats of High Courts. CAT consists of:

- One Chairman
- Sixteen Vice-chairman
- Nine Members (administrative and judicial).

The chairman and vice-chairman hold office for 5 years or till the age of 65, whichever is earlier, whereas members enjoy a term of 5 years or continue up to 62 years. They are ineligible for reappointment after retirement. Most of the states have established their administrative tribunals under the Administrative Tribunals Act. But only a few organisations have been brought within the jurisdiction of the CAT. The CAT has strived to achieve speedy justice to the litigants to a considerable extent, despite many constraints faced by it. To assist the tribunal in achieving its goals, the necessary support is provided by the personnel ministry at the Centre. The tribunal has proved its worth and effectiveness against odds.

An administrative tribunal exercising ajudicatory powers differs from ordinary judicial court in the following respects:

(1) Legal counsel may not be needed in matters requiring adjustment;
(2) A degree of informality which suits to the nature of issues involved;

(3) Formal rules of evidence may not be observed;
(4) Decisions may be reached by expert in the subject matter as well as in the law;
(5) Differences in the constitution and procedure; and
(6) Facts may be developed by question and answer and conclusion reached without delay.

The factors that have given rise to the delegated legislation are at the root of the development of administrative tribunal expansion of governmental activities, concept of welfare state, and increased interference with the lives of the citizens. There is an apparent desire to escape from a purely legalistic approach. The procedure of the regular courts is dilatory and cumbersome. An alternative machinery of cheap and speedy justice through tribunals is a response to popular need. The administrative tribunals are vested with the powers to move of their own accord in detecting, investigating and punishing the violation of laws. The adjudicatory functions of the Indian administration encompasses: departmental proceedings against government servants; adjudicatory; powers of revenue authorities; election tribunals; tribunal for land acquisition proceedings; tribunal for industrial labour; adjudicatory powers of transport authorities; and adjudicatory powers of regulatory authorities.

Administrative justice through administrative tribunal is cheaper. In cases lawyers may or may not appear. No court fees are to be paid, no solicitors are to be instructed, no counsel is to be briefed, no affidavits are to be sworn. It is speedy. Oral hearings are dispensed with Intricate trial procedures may be abandoned. Rules of evidence are conspicuously absent and the proceedings are broadly characterised by informality and simplicity. The administrative tribunals perform their functions with flexibility. They are not bound by their previous decisions or precedents of other authorities. Nor are they handicapped in their tasks by judicial precedents and rule of law. Summary procedure is advantage of administrative adjudication. The critics like Lord Hewart calls administrative adjudication as 'organised lawlessness'. Dicey considers it violative to the rule of law, i.e., equality before law, supremacy of law and due procedure of law. It militates against the principles of natural justice. The right to appeal from the decisions of these courts is either very limited or is non-existent. The opportunity for judicial review is restricted. Provision of oral hearing is not there. Even the statements of reasons are not given. These tribunals are not manned by people of judicial training and experience. Summary trials do not take into account precedents. Such courts do not observe uniform procedures. Sometimes appeals to the ordinary court of law is not permitted. It is an inescapable modern democratic society can ignore it only at its own peril.

Some safeguards against administrative adjudication can help as a support structure to judiciary. The adjudicator of dispute should be persons different from those who are involved in a dispute against the individual or group of individuals. The appointment of the members and the chairman should not vest solely with the minister concerned. The Franks Committee in UK recommended that the tribunals be insulated from departmental influence. A council or tribunals in India may comprise judges, both existing and retired, lawyers, academicians and reputed persons in other walks of life. Such a council should be consulted in matters concerning composition and procedures of administrative tribunals. Code of judicial procedure for administrative tribunals should be devised and enforced in view of the prevailing varying procedures of administrative adjudication in India. To quote Lord Justice Denning, "If the tribunals are to command the confidence of the people they must give reasons". Some of the administrative tribunals permit appeal straightway to the court of law; some, however, seek to altogether ban judicial review by making decisions final;

and still a few others keep regular courts out by allowing appeal to a higher administrative authority. Thus, the right to judicial review on points of law must remain unimpaired.

Indian Whitleyism

Whitleyism in England is credited to have effectively cut down on the incidence of strikes. The ARC recommended a similar pattern of staff councils in every department or ministry. The local, regional and National Whitley Councils with senior, junior employees and political representatives have made serious efforts to resolve employee problems through participation and mutual understanding. In India or anywhere, the civil servants grievances are not comparable with that of labourer or industrial workers. Naturally, effective measures are needed to arrest growing trade unionism among junior employees. It is not only a negative problem of handling grievances, but a positive perspective too, that should create a climate of cooperation and mutual trust. Civil servant has a special role in society and public service is not mere employment as was the case during colonial days. Some long rainy measures are needed along with an effective grievance redressal machinery to size up the problem. Some of these measures can be:

(1) Keeping the size of bureaucracy within limits through policies of debureaucratisation or liberalisation so that huge establishments of junior employees may not develop trade union militancy.

(2) A happy balance to strike discipline and high morale of public servants can build climate of trust and cooperation. It is again a dynamic situation and has to be constantly reviewed and monitored on a continuous basis.

(3) In addition, a reasonable pay packet and service conditions conducive for efficiency is a precondition to keep the meritorious in a state of human resource development. The Pay Commission reviews it and disciplinary rules are continuously revised in the context of new philosophies of human rights, social justice and gender parity.

With these preconditions, an effective grievance redressal machinery can be effective. The departmental council can play the forum to open up and discuss the complaints or grievances the employees have. The redressal presupposes effective ventilation and a feeling of being heard. It is a long time process often frustrating but pays results if understood and practised with conviction. The administrative tribunals in India are still in a stage of infancy. They enjoy the faith of employees and are within their reach. Being quasi-judicial they can use various methods of negotiation, arbitration and adjudication. Collective bargaining of trade unions can be practised through departmental council mechanism and tribunals can add a justiciable dimensions to grievance redressal attained by mutual consultations and participatory debates.

In India, a huge number of civil servants in C and D groups have still not accepted the philosophy of mutual give and take. The B group of services has an ambivalent position. The senior junior positions breed hostility and enforcement of discipline leads to militancy of trade unionism. The policy of liberalisation, privatisation and the judicious use of departmental councils and administrative tribunals brings a ray of hope which should mitigate grievance situations and resolve the conflicts that arise from standing grievances of the employees.

Popular Participation

People's participation as a positive concept requires the administration to be receptive to popular suggestions and constructive criticism of the administration. Grievance redressal is necessary but people's participation through citizen committees, civic groups and NGOs can go a long way to make public administration democratic. After all, civil society is the best judge and social audit is the best method of letting the administration know where did it go wrong and how can a vigilant public come to its support. The civic cooperation by enlightened and public-spirited citizens is a great asset on which administrative efforts can be built to yield desired results. Indian administration has of late started launching campaigns of taking administration to villages or towns so that an open interface can sensitise the administrators and educate the people about the limitations of administration. The feedback which people give to their representatives at the time of elections can be of a continuous nature if administrators organise camps, sit with people, listen to their grievances and do their best right on the spot. The people may be ignorant or even hostile to begin with but a continuous interaction with the representatives of NGOs, civic groups, organised associations and respectable citizens in the community not only improves the linkage but renders the administration vulnerable to reform. Indian administration at Panchayati Raj and district levels has made the beginning and the participatory exercise should improve the quality of administration at grass root level.

The methods of popular control and people's participation in administration have increased through press and media, political parties, citizen committees, pressure groups and above all through elections. Civil servants are harassed by people through public agitations and demand for transfers. This citizen participation has been used for support as well as for control by the rulers or lawmakers. It has been direct, indirect, formal and informal having its bearings on administrative operations. The effectiveness of this participation has been dependent upon the degree of seriousness, the participant body or the desire of public administrators to delegate functions and consult the body.

Citizens' participation in administration has been in policy and programme planning and their implementation and involvement in the processes of administration. It demands certain preconditions like lightened political leaders, integrity of civil servants and well-informed and cooperative general public. The barriers in this process have been identified as people's ignorance, role of middlemen, delays and unhelpful attitude of corrupt officials, urban-rural perceptions and all sorts of discriminations obtained in Indian society. The government response has been halting, still several reforms measures like human relations training, positive evaluations, simplification of work procedures and creation of numerous institutional devices have been taken up with change perceptions on either side. On the positive side, the Consumer Protection Act, 1986 has established Central and state consumer protection councils and the district forums for redressal of public grievances.

The Central Consumer Protection Council came into being in 1987 and consists of 150 members with multi-sectional representation. The chairman of the central council is the minister-in-charge of consumer affairs and the secretary in the department is the member-secretary of the central council. The objectives of the council are the citizens to protect against marketing of goods which are hazardous to life and property and to inform him about the quality, quantity, potency, purity, standard and price of goods so as to protect the consumer against unfair trade practices. The citizens has the right to be assured wherever possible, access to a variety of goods at competitive prices and his consumer interests should receive due consideration at appropriate forums. The right to seek redressal against unfair trade practices or unscrupulous exploitation is consumers' fundamental right for which he has right to consumer education. The state consumer protection councils are playing a vital role in creating consumer awareness and in the development of consumer movement in their states.

Privatisation of Public Administration in India

The Second Minnowbrook Conference 1988, revised the definition of the term 'public' and made a plea to look beyond bureaucracy by reinventing government. The World Bank promoted the concept as new rightism and a new wave of Perestroika or Glasnost took over the world in the name of LPG, the collapse of the Soviet state in 1989 discredited the state monopoly system and India also entered into an era of privatisation of its economy and public policy which is also called as Manmohanomics. It is essentially a policy of gradual privatisation with a human face. It has following planks:

(1) Slow and gradual evolution of an open and liberal economy without licence permit Inspector Raj of the past.
(2) Progressive disinvestment from public sector enterprises, specially the sick which private entrepreneur can salvage.
(3) Increased debureaucratisation of public administration by downsizing civil service and removal of avoidable procedural bottlenecks.
(4) Experimentation with mixed model of administration to develop a competitive economy with innovation.
(5) Collaboration of administration with private companies, corporations and foreign subsidiaries to develop the infrastructure of development especially in the areas of education, health and communications.

The last decade has witnessed a phenomenal change in the private and public administrations of the country. The mixed models apart, there is an introspection and common areas of mutual gain are expanding to the ultimate benefit of the people. Understandably, development requires massive resources and the private sector, domestic and foreign can come forward to do the basics which a closed economic system cannot afford. But, the other side of the coin requires the government to play the guardian and protect the citizen against competitive onslaught of private exploitation and profiteering by manipulation of markets. This cautious approach demands that public administration should:

(1) Regulate not control the socio-economic order in the long-range public interest.
(2) Catalyse, facilitate, innovate and borrow the efficiency patterns from private entrepreneurs.
(3) Ask its public administrators to devise e-governance and citizen friendly administration, which in the lack of a better term called 'good governance'.
(4) Compete, collaborate and serve as a support structure for the private administration to undertake social welfare consistent with reasonable profits.

These principles will take time in shaping business ethics and public morality in both the administrations. What private entrepreneur calls profit and what is called 'corruption' in common parlance in the government both exploit the common citizens. The new public administration should trust and help the private managers to enhance national earnings and savings for investment. But the businessmen also have to demonstrate their social responsibility to the community.

Integrity in both the administrations being low and dubious, the transitional years might give an ambivalent relationship between the two. But this distinction between private and public administration which democracy and technology are obliterating in the field of development opens a new dialogue for a new ethical partnership in coming years.

The Narsimha Rao and Atal Bihari Bajpai governments in India encouraged this pattern by selling public sector units to private business houses. Import-Export policies were liberalised and private investment was encouraged in telecom, health and insurance sectors. Air transport was opened for competitive ventures and universities, colleges and institutes are being established in the private sector to meet the challenge of training for change. Banks in the private sectors have been allowed to operate at global level and government has either withdrawn or reduced its equity shares from enterprises in sectors like energy, electricity and oil. Liberal housing loans have been floated to give a boost to employment market and outsourcing is being encouraged to capture world markets. The social welfare programmes of government have acquired a back seat and mega-projects of highways and waterways are in the pipeline to cover rural areas for development.

The debate about the adequacy and rationality of this policy brings pressure from left parties but privatisation of public administration continues in the following pattern with shifting emphasis on government role:

(1) The key areas of Indian economy like oil, agriculture, railways and defence production remain in the monopoly public sector while hotels, telephones, insurance, airlines, tourism, hospitals and universities and entertainment industries are progressively being handed over to the private entrepreneurs.

(2) To protect and promote public good regulatory authorities and consumer councils have been established so that private administration may remain within the bounds of public morality and uniform operations.

(3) This regulation of government may not degenerate into control and interference. For this, new institutions of private-public collaboration are being created on the pattern of independent regulatory commissions of USA so that capitalistic freedom of private business may not push the public administration to the abandonment of its ultimate social responsibility.

This good governance through liberalisation and privatisation adds another dimension popularly known as globalisation to the changing pattern of public administration in India.

Administrative Implications of Globalisation

Globalisation as a phenomenon implies a process of reducing barriers between countries and of encouraging closer economic, social, political interaction which could vastly increase the ability of the people everywhere to improve their living standards by sharing knowledge and the fruits of human labour across the barriers. It promotes specialisation, the theory of comparative advantage and increased production and productivity. It also helps to remove world poverty through trade and the trickle down effect. Its parameters indicate reduction of trade barriers so as to permit free flow of goods and services and of capital and technology among nation-states. It should create an environment in which free movement of labour should take place in different countries of world. Economic liberalisation can be macro or micro and national or sub-national. The macro-liberalisation is known as globalisation while the micro variety of it is known as liberalisation per se or as the composite of liberalisation and privatisation. Hence, liberalisation of economy as a whole, both domestic and global could be more meaningfully termed as liberalisation, privatisation and globalisation, or LPG. Several events of the fateful decade (1980–90) have led to the enthronement of LPG as the ideological anchor of the 21st century. Some of the factors responsible for these phenomenal changes of unprecedented magnitude are:

(1) Collapse of the Soviet Union;
(2) Ascendance of neo-liberalism and proliferation of multinational corporations;
(3) Internet revolution and cyber technologies;
(4) Collapse of Third World and monoculturism;
(5) Emergence of global macro-economics and WTO;
(6) Politico-economic transformations in Eastern Europe;
(7) Growing clout of IMF and the World Bank; and
(8) New version of Cold War.

The rapid progress in science and technology has transformed the pace of transportation and communication. It has also increased productivity manifold. Therefore, distances has been reduced, people and ideas are travelling all over the world very fast, breaking national, cultural and language barriers. People of the world are coming nearer. This process of unification of breaking down of barriers is not only economic, but political, social and cultural also. Globalisation implies the unification of people's cultures, nations and continents through interaction in various fields. Factors like rising population, global warming, depletion of the ozone layer, diseases like AIDS and natural calamities like flood, earthquake and famine have emerged as unifying forces. Interdependence of the world is essential not only for prosperity but also for preservation. The Twin Tower tragedy of September 11, 2001 in the United States have shown that no country howsoever prosperous, technologically advanced, self-reliant and protected by natural frontiers cannot remain safe. This calls for an ethical principle in governance today. Unipolar globalisation represents an offensive phenomenon of the developed countries of north. They wish to establish a global hegemony by hood winking the underdeveloped south. It cannot be called an ideologically neutral event. Ideology as corporate capitalism makes the culture West centric in general and US centric in particular. This globalisation is heavily loaded in favour of America on account of the unipolar nature of present globalisation process. It is called as anti-public and anti-poor. It is leading to de-legitimisation and marginalisation of public administration and the tradition of welfare state. It is creating inequalities between and among the nations and classes ... its mission and goal are the end of democracy by way of centralisation of power, resources and authority in the hands of MNCs, TNCs, World Bank, IMF, WTO and the like which are not accountable to people. A number of forces like the global environment movement, local pressure groups; NGOs; professional and scientific networks of social scientists, and demographers are working for a multi-polar global order. In addition, the tide of international terrorism challenges the military and economic might of US. The anti-unipolar forces are engaging in the wake of constructing a global civil society. But the real threat lies in vulnerability in implementation of economic policies and preparedness of key administrators to adopt the imperatives of globalisation. The limits have to be identified and the components of the policy and responsibilities of bureaucrats are to be properly articulated to handle the implications of this globalised scenario.

The challenges of globalisation with worldwide trend of liberalisation asks Indian administrators to unlearn what they have learnt all through their career. The role reversal expects the public servant to be an entrepreneur in place of a controller of the free enterprise. A new holistic approach is being demanded to take the world along to serve the national interests. This reassessment of role and functions in an open and sprawling economy of India expects from her public administrators to strike a balance between participation and accountability, competition and duplication, customer and citizen, public interest and market tests and old and new laws to be discarded and accepted. Globalisation offers tilting opportunities of corruption to an already corrupt administration but paradoxically it expects the administration to be quick, efficient and effective. The administration has to practice self-restraint and state action must minimise 'satiation' which is another term for 'debureaucratisation'. In simple words, the practice of Indian administrative culture in relation with other countries of the world is a great handicap and the challenge is to democratise it to bring it in correspondence with the administrative culture of other democratic countries of world which expect and demand rule boundedness, efficiency and a corruption free response of public administration.

For this, the Indian civil servants have to develop specialised knowledge and skills to have effects of the policy measures being advocated by multilateral agencies, developed countries and multinationals. They have to indigenise policies to suit local needs to overcome national problems ... the civil servants have to promote efficiency and effectiveness not only in public services but also within government as an indication of responsibility and accountability. Competitiveness and productivity have to be increased. The civil servants have to create an enabling environment for citizens, establish law and order, ensure stability, and provide efficient essential services. For this civil society and polity have to be empowered. There has to be change in mindset of civil servants and they should learn to question traditional values like hierarchy, rules and regulations, permanence and stability of government organisations. Downsizing, reducing fiscal deficit, expenditure control and privatising public enterprises are only means to achieve efficiency and improve effectiveness for economic development as a globalisation phenomenon. It needs a supportive environment, with the interweaving of sophisticated technology, skill diffusion, social ethics and values and a state structure. In a world in which efficiency is measured through productivity, capacity for innovativeness and technology absorption, the challenge of integration of specialists has to be taken up through coordination of interdependent decisions. To cope with the challenges of uncertainty and competitiveness, the quality of management has to undergo a metamorphic change with an entrepreneurial drive. Although the impact of globalisation on public administration and the vice versa is difficult to be predicted in a complex world of interdependent nations and the vanishing national borders, nearing the end of ideology (if not of history). Yet, the shrinkage process of the global village makes it obvious that Indian administrators of future will have to grapple with the following administrative challenges of 21st century:

(1) Management of ecological degradation and arrest of pollution of oceans ozone sphere and radioactive wastes.
(2) Management of technology and change through e-governance and information revolution.

Management of Global Ecology

Ecological preservation is one of the major concerns which globalisation highlights in mutual interests of the developed and developing countries of the world. Every activity of man comes under the purview of environment. "Environment administration is a concept of managing human affairs in a way that biological health, diversity and ecological balance is preserved." In other words, it is a process of carrying out activities which are concerned with protection and enhancement of the quality of the environment. According to the Brundtland Report, "the idea of sustainable development reaches far beyond environmental protection, as it means a process of change in which exploitation of resources, direction of investments, orientation of technological development, and institutional changes are made consistent with future as well as present needs. It is not a fixed state of harmony but rather a balanced and adaptive process of change. The idea of sustainable development requires a careful consideration of sustainable threshold levels for both economic and environmental systems. This eco-system of the world has been degraded by arms race, global warming, radioactive wastes and over mulching of natural resources by the so-called developed countries of the west". To this, the poorer and weaker nations have also made their contribution through population boom, inappropriate application of technology, malnourished children and urban ghettos without facilities for a civilised living. Natural resources of land, air and water have been used recklessly and the planet is becoming a risky place for survival. The environmental problems in India arise from underdevelopment and have negative effect upon the processes of world trade, tourism, foreign investment, forestry and wild life and river pollution through industrial wastes and dirty human settlements.

Administration of Technology and E-Governance

The Government of India has taken several initiatives by forming a National Task Force for IT and implementing its recommendations. It has also passed a Cyber Law, which is the best and the most comprehensive legislation. Information Technology Act, 2000 has been passed by the government which has also enacted the Semi-conductor Integrated Circuits Layout-Design Act, 2000. The ministry of IT has taken up a project to set up community information centres in 486 blocks in the northeast and Sikkim as a part of the Prime Minister's Agenda for the socio-economic development of the region. The ministry of IT has developed a common action plan to promote IT in India. The advent of new information and communication technologies have made electronic governance a tool to enhance relationships of government to government, government to citizens, citizen to government, and government to private and other sectors. The ministry has a Centre for E-Governance and has a well-organised bilingual website, both in Hindi and English. Working groups on IT for masses have provided the basic infrastructure and is taking keen interest in expanding IT revolution in the country.

To push the process of globalised administration, the government has been encouraging software development and hardware manufacturing in the country. Each ministry allocates between two to three per cent of its budget on IT promotion. It has integrated IT with domestic software industry with e-governance through Hindi and regional languages. This has resulted in better citizen government interface through information and communication technologies in general and the internet in particular to design public services from citizen's point of view. In Andhra Pradesh, the IT application through service centres has gone to the extent that Hyderabad is called a cyber city and Bangalore has come close to become the silicon valley of India.

E-governance and Information Technology: The induction of E-governance has started yielding results. The technological innovations are eliminating the dysfunctional procedures in administration. Globalisation has been a workable phenomenon because of E-G and IT and conversely the latter have inaugurated the era of globalised economy and world trade. The Indian administration has to catch up with this technological revolution so that it can create conditions conducive for world markets and foreign investments.

Electronic government has been called an alternative government which implies a government any time and anywhere. In fact, it is a system of delivery of government services and information to the public by using electronics means. These technologies can enable the government to transform its relations with its other wings, citizens, and business. Such an exercise leads to better delivery of government services to citizens, improved interactions with business and industry, citizen empowerment through access to information and a more efficient government management. The resulting benefits can be lesser corruption, increased transparency, greater convenience, revenue growth, and cost reductions. Thus, with emerging information and communication technologies, it is possible to locate service centres closer to the public. But then, as it happens with all new technologies the technological growth is yet to be absorbed in the organisational behaviour of the administration. The creation of database, computer use in banks, internet in secretariats and strict administration or election system or import export documentation have to go a long way to harness their full results. A re-engineering approach is called for to have a better assimilation of technology in the administrative system. It promises to increase efficiency, time-boundedness, cost effectivity, transparency and demolition of discretion and arbitrariness which have been a bone of Indian administration.

People are being replaced by technology and the organisation is able to downsize, which is the process of reducing the number of people, unite knot and do away with regulational and procedural cobwebs, reduce time and increase customer satisfaction. The breakdown of hierarchy in administration and increase in coordinating activity have made coordination better and cheaper. The IT which enabled computers and telecommunication to coverage has revolutionised the working environment of public administration throughout the world and India is in a position to globalise her economy and administration with these electronic tools. The words, pictures known as signals have come to take the form of electrical pulses on a wire. The information processing systems are based on digital computers. It takes information like a basic resource essential for individuals and organisation to survive and succeed in society. Development is closely related to social change and information has an important role in bringing about both.

It has a profound impact on country's economy and the quality of human life. The IT revolution is of much greater significance than the Industrial Revolution. It has opened up new possibilities of economic and social transformation from which developed and developing nations can potentially benefit. That is why governments around the world, at all levels have woken up to the potential of IT in a variety of functions and activities. There is enthusiasm over the furious proliferation of inventions, innovations and equipment. High-speed wireless networks enable faster connectivity to millions of devices,. location sensing has become child's play, devices recognise speech and even gestures and computers hold in their entrails devices possessing artificial intelligence. People are routinely keeping tabs on everything in and around their lives.

Indian IT professionals have delivered high quality solutions and have also emerged as a successful breed of entrepreneurs of the new millennium in the Silicon Valley in America. This has given a sense of pride to Indians, both residents and non-residents, as being second to none in this highly competitive knowledge-based industry, which holds key to future globalisation of economy and development of India as part of the world at large. Thus, globalisation through IT and

E-governance links and integrates the world. The administrators in India have to facilitate and hasten it so that Indian economy can be pulled out from the morass of stagnation.

Towards a New Techno-Global Order

Indian administration in the era of LPG is creatively engaged in responding to the unprecedented changes in Indian and world history. A liberal democratic polity has come to stay and colonial legacies are being given up to democratise administration of a liberalised society and economy. Representative and responsible public administration is being strived upon in preference to a Taylor made Weberian administration which must respect rule of law and human rights. Popular participatory mechanisms are being evolved so that people may work with administration. Transparent open and sensitive administrative models are being devised so that the government by the people may have an administration for the people. This kind of liberal administration for a liberalised polity has to have an Indian variant which can neither be absolutely European nor partially colonial. Continuous and innovative efforts to reform the structures, behaviours and relationships in Indian administration are on and as democracy takes roots and advances towards a technological and knowledge society, the administrators in India will have to forget about their guardianship role and security of working in the steel frame. No one ideal model of democratic administration can be hazarded for a fast changing society, but this model has to be indigenous and less and less Weberian. The representative meritocracy is a contradiction in terms and an indirectly responsible neutral bureaucracy of British model will have to be replaced by a sensitive bureaucracy without elite orientations. The administrative structures have to be open and more and more susceptible to people's aspirations. The humanist orientation to administration should put human rights in the centre and people will have the right to information and social audit to make public administration liberal in a liberalised society of liberalisation era.

Democracy stands for a limited constitutional government. The public administration in this political system will have to evolve a system of checks and balances. Administration will have discretion but their discretionary powers have to be checkmated by a new system of transparency and accountability. Naturally the legislative, judicial and still more administrative controls have to be tightened through institutions like CBI, CVC, Lokpal and a host of state level agencies along with special commissions for the ensurement of human rights, women's rights, minority rights and rights of the weak and deprived. Some of these institutions have acquired teeth, others are in the process of getting roots. These negative and positive institutional measures are sensitising administrators into their democratic responsibilities which ultimately means 'good governance'.

Experiments in Good Governance

As an experiment it will cause fading away of controls and deregulation of economy. But this will not make the bureaucracy weak or ineffectual. Rather it will confer upon it greater moral responsibility to see that the new system takes root and functions without undue intervention. The bureaucracy may compete against powerful business houses. Naturally the role of state will get reduced but it cannot end. The state will regulate the free market. This role will increase in modernising technology and promoting its application in the public system to develop the infrastructure. Empowering people will push administration to develop a positive and helpful attitude towards people to facilitate good governance at all levels.

In the realms of policy making, the specialist and the technocrat will emerge as a decision-maker and the generalist culture will decline. It would necessitate the opening of top policy positions to specialists to facilitate greater role of professionals in the policy administration. The lateral entry into the civil service will be common. It will demand an officer-oriented system in policy departments. Similarly, the top-heavy secretariats of governments will be downsized to broad-base creativity of the policy process. The culture of decentralisation and delegation will pervade the administrative system and the rules and procedures would need relaxation. The controls will give way to supervision. Even the audit procedure would need revision. The accountability of the administrative system will be adjusted with social audit and accountability will stem from a sense of ethical responsibility and social responsibility of business. The HRD will have to be based on a rigorous mechanism of manpower planning, proven and potential merit and competence of entrants through training. The professional competence will reorient attitudes and influence value patterns on a continuous basis.

The era of privatisation in India will demand de-monopolisation of public sector except in core areas of economy, and collaboration of private enterprise in socio economic sectors like education, health insurance, communication and banking. But then, the welfare administration responsibility of the state will not decline. The social responsibility of business will increasingly demand, but the public servants will have non-economic incentives like dedication to public service, national pride, organisational loyalty, dignity, social recognition and professional commitment. The work ethics in public and private administrations may not be similar but the two administrations should compete in serving public good and mitigating corruption based exploitation of the common man. The greed-based corruption has thrived faster than need-based corruption in India. Globalisation and liberalisation have made governments alert to the need for keeping and exhibiting a 'clean' image in the international community. A high-corruption level in government dissuade international investors, and hence combatting crime will be a special responsibility of governments in developing countries. For this, initiatives will have to begin from people's groups and NGOs. The pervasive character of corruption and the belief that corruption is rampant in all Indian society deter the emergence of organisations which can claim to be transparently clean in the perception of people. The centres of morality and integrity have to maintain their existence in a world of dwindling ethics. A number of citizens' groups are working in the area of civil liberties and human rights in India but comparatively there is little private effort to improve moral standards of public life. Combatting corruption is not a perceptible priority of the governments. Rather, it has been accepted as a corollary of development, an inevitable symptom of growth and an insurmountable necessary evil. The illegitimate gratification to public servants emanate from the affluent segments of the private sector. While there is a popular condemnation of those who get corrupted but very little is said of those who really corrupt others. Reinforcement of social responsibility of business and industry has to stress upon the core moral maximum. At the higher level, a system of instituting regulatory commissions or boards on any pattern is the need of the hour. The existing regulatory institutions should safeguard and increase their effectiveness. Newer institutions are needed in critical areas like power, telecommunication, air transport, etc., to promote an open-door policy for international investment. The average productivity of an Indian worker is much lower than that of an average Chinese or Japanese worker because of work culture obtained in India. Indiscipline, perpetuated by laxity in controls, and the attitude of employee unions have nibbled the vitals of Indian administration. The trade unions have to look at their duties towards their organisation, society and the nation in the newly dawned era of LPG.

Globalisation is the logic of 21st century which will be shaped by techno connectivity and info revolution. World markets are bound to be integrated and international investments will cease to be colonial with the vanishing of the nation-state. The region-state will create continental states, continental currencies and continental law of ecology penetration and cyber piracy. Public administration in India will have to be environment conscious and the administrators will have to be eco-friendly. The administration of technology will be international and its innovativeness will yield rich dividends to the national societies and the global community as a whole. Globalisation will cause mass migrations, more and more NRIs and their more frequent visits and investments in home countries. The world-class technology will reach to far of corners of Indian villages where outsourcing might be mutually advantageous to both the partners in the shared markets of globalisation. Reinventing government is a long-range process and good governance through multi institutionalism in plural societies will come only with the decline of hard-core cultural nationalism. Europe has entered into this new era of economic regionalism. Africa and Asia will follow with the advent of middle class affluence and world wide global mobility. USA and Canada may take more time but the cultural plurality of American society will make it different from the America of 20th century. In this scenario, India will take less time than others to be on the forefront of globalism. The Indian administration which has deep moorings in the past will soon get transformed into an administrative system of future. This future will orient, condition and dictate the shape of Indian administration in the era of liberalisation, privatisation and globalisation, which again will be a springboard for a 'Brave New World' of peace, progress, and plenty.

12

Fiscal Administration and Budgetary System in India

Economic administration, financial administration and fiscal administration are used as interchangeable terms by the layman, but to a serious student of public administration the nuances in each case are specific and complex. The economic administration is the management of the economy which includes tools of production, factors behind distribution, determinants of exchange and patterns of consumption in a given society with its international ramifications. The financial administration is more specific and limited with special emphasis on commerce, trade and private public transactions. The budgetary or fiscal administration is still more specific wherein the management of revenue collection and expenditure of public money in terms of government treasury transactions falls for public accountability. The plan administration, the public undertaking management and monetary administration of Reserve Bank of India may touch the fringe areas of all the three kinds of administration. As the governmental functions expand and explode, the neat boundaries get blurred and the border areas of public and private administration determine which is in a flux because of experiments like performance budgeting, Programme Planning and Budgetary System (PPBS) and zero base budgeting. The new budgetary theories, varied patterns of control and audit of public expenditure and still more innovative measures of resource mobilisation by the governments characterise the fiscal administration of democratic states, committed to developmental taxation of popular welfare.

Budgetary Theories

The classical theory of budgeting advocated surplus budget when governmental spending was meagre and remained confined to negative functions of a police state. Both the revenues and expenditures were listed as few items on the budget and the difference of surplus revenue was called 'surplus budgeting'. After Second World War, when the developed countries took to balanced budgetary theory, the developing countries of so-called Third World started advocating the theory of deficit budgets for development. Meynard Kynes, a great protagonist of deficit financing finds it a useful tool of economic buoyancy and financial discipline. The poor countries cannot wait for long to have requisite investments from their meagre savings. The welfare agenda of these newly independent states of Asia and Africa can neither be cut short nor postponed in want of resources. So in addition to taxation and savings, they have taken to public borrowings, external assistance and deficit financing to mobilise resources for funding of development projects and infrastructure building through public enterprises. As the development drama unfolded its dimensions, the sheer size and sequential complications rendered the deficit financing exercise inevitable. The Western world viewing deficit financing in a wider sense includes all government expenditures which are financed through public borrowings such as commercial banks or individual corporations. Deficit financing in India does not include borrowing from people and commercial banks. They are called as 'market borrowing' which includes borrowing from the Reserve Bank of India, withdrawal of part accumulated cash balances and the issuing of fresh currency by the government. In other words, deficit financing reflects direct increase in money supply to take care of budget deficit because RBI borrowings imply issuing of currency notes on transfer of government securities to the bank. This creation of money, technically speaking, gives birth to various concepts of deficit financing. The Government of India recognises five kinds of deficit financing, namely:

(1) budget deficit,
(2) revenue deficit,
(3) primary deficit,
(4) fiscal deficit, and
(5) monetised deficit.

Each concept when practised has overlapping impact on the growth of economy as a whole.

If revenue expenditure of the government exceeds the total revenue receipts, which include tax and non-tax revenues, it is called revenue deficit. Here expenditures also include unproductive expenditures like expenditure on defence, police, judiciary, subsidies and interest payments which do not create or accumulate assets. The budget deficit is worked out on the basis of budget estimates wherein total expenditure is more than the total receipts of the government in a particular budget year. Here, the total receipts and total expenditures include revenue as well as capital figures on both the sides. In 1985, the Government of India accepted S.M. Chakravarty report on the Working of Monetary System in India and defined fiscal deficit as budgetary deficit plus market borrowing, plus varied other liabilities of the government so it includes the total borrowing requirements from internal and external sources. On account of colossal increase in deficit financing, some economists tend to view it as a "non-interest deficit which indicates the primary deficit as fiscal deficit minus interest amount paid by the government". Similarly, the term 'monetised' deficit is used for the phenomenon of increase in net RBI credit to the Government of India. In other words, monetised deficit represents financing by borrowings from Reserve Bank of India.

The review of deficit figures in India, howsoever staggering does not cause panic when developmental deficit is distinguished from other kinds of deficits, caused by unproductive wars and recession in the economy. Deficit financing to finance war operations through taxation and borrowings do not suffice to meet the cost of war. Hence, the governments have no alternative except to create new money by printing more currency. Deficit financing in Germany brought a large quantity of money in circulation in the economy. This increased monetary income and demand for goods. Such a situation results in inflation due to absence of corresponding increase in supply of goods which creates disaster. In 1930, USA confronted with a situation of great depression and massive unemployment. J.M. Keynes has suggested the logic of deficit financing to fight cyclical depressions in capitalist countries and to eliminate mass unemployment. He feels that employment depends on the propensity for consumption. To overcome this, he suggests deficit financing to finance public works projects. This increases the purchasing power of people and results in effective demand for goods.

Keynes called it a 'multiplier effect'. In this way, the economy can be revived and lifted from depression through deficit financing. In India, deficits economy of financing has been resorted to generate resources to finance investment and accelerate the process of economic development. It has helped rapid formation of capital for economic growth breaking bottlenecks and structural rigidities in the economy to increase productivity. It has provided stimulus to economic development by financing investment, employment and output in the economy. However, it has a negative effect also in inflationary rise in prices of goods and services. It is because the deficit financing increases the supply of money in the economy without a corresponding increase in the supply of goods and services. This inflationary character of deficit financing changes the pattern of investment by people and results in forced savings. The adverse affects on balance of payments, increases economic inequalities and increases credit creation by banks. It is a transitional situation and as development adds to the capacity of the people and the nation the debt situation can ease and income and employment situations get stabilised.

Placed as we are, we cannot slow down development nor can we put the present generation under unbearable pressures of inflationary costs. So, the midway impels the quest of safe limits of borrowing and public debt. The capital formation has to grow through deficit financing but inflation should not repel people from being involved in developmental endeavours. The economists are engaged in identifying the safe limit and expanding its parameters. Surplus money by higher taxation and increased loans is being mopped up. The quantity of money and the extent of the rate of growth are being reconciled. The newly created money is being used for productive purposes. Short gestation period projects increase the supply of goods and check price rise. India is making efforts to transfer non-monetised sector into monetised sector. Distribution of goods through rationing is only for BPL people. The import of capital equipment was encouraged and people have cooperated in the implementation of policies for reducing price effect of deficit financing for capital formation. The LPG policies of the government have increased production in private sector and credit creation policies have been integrated with deficit financing.

The Debt Trap

Deficit economies nowadays mostly survive on public debt which is a net additive of governmental borrowing and public loans. The resources like land revenue, urban taxation and public undertaking earnings are too inadequate to keep the economy development-oriented. Foreign aid has shrunk to negligible proportions. Only a variety of loans are available because of the credit and debt servicing capacity of the nations. These loans or borrowings for developmental investments are made available by the bankers, financial institutions and the people. They represent the form of promises by the treasury to pay to the holders of these promises a principal sum and interest on the principal. They are a sort of withdrawal made in return for the government's promise to repay at a future date and to pay interest at the interim. To pay the money back is an obligation on the part of the government. The debt incurred by the government in mobilising resources in the form of loans has very many varieties. For instance, they may be redeemable and unredeemable. The redeemable debts have to be paid off at a specified date while the irredeemable debts have no time limit. But in latter case, the interest has to be paid and hence they are called as perpetual debts in contrast to the former category which makes them terminable. Similarly, internal debts are borrowed from individuals, business houses and financial institution inside the country. Loans floated by foreign governments and institutions fall in the category of external debts. A distinction between productive and unproductive debts is made by calling them active debts for revenue yielding purposes and dead weight debts incurred in funding wars or managing natural disasters. Generally, public debts are voluntary in nature because they are against securities and people are free to subscribe. Compulsory loan are taken in extraordinary situations to curb inflation. Another variety of debt called as funded debts is a long-term borrowing payable after a year, while unfunded debts are payable within a year. The funded debts create permanent assets but unfunded short-term debts are floating debts and they include treasury bills and advances from central bank, etc. If debts add up to unmanageability the nation falls in a *debt trap*. To avoid this, debt servicing must make payment of interest and repayment of instalments of debts inside and outside the country.

The debt trap is caused by unbearable and non-repayable debt burden on a country. It can be a direct money burden or indirect money burden. Similarly, it can be classified into direct real and indirect real burdens. The government collects taxes from the people to pay interest and repay the principal amounts to the creditors. This results in the transfer of purchasing power from poor people to the rich people. The increased economic inequalities also have an adverse effect on the capacity of the people to work and save which results in the decline of the productive capacity of people. The imposition of additional taxes to repay the external debt also adds to indirect real burden on the country. The payment of interest results in the transfer of purchasing power from one section to another. All money payments, paid by taxpayers and the amounts received by the bondholders, cancel out. The external debt also imposes direct money burden and the purchasing power is transferred from citizens to foreigners. The size of the debt also adds to the direct money burden of debt. Indirect money burden is increased by the productive spending of the government which creates demand for commodities and services. This imposes an additional burden on the community due to rise in prices. The size of external debt also imposes an indirect money burden because the debtor country's interest payment causes a decline of the economic welfare of the community.

One effective way of managing debt repayment is called debit redemption. The repayment of public debts can be made in varied ways, like interest payments, terminable annuities, currency expansion or outright repudiation of the set. Some other methods include refunding conversion sinking funds, capital levy and surplus balances of payments. The incurred expenditures or old debts can be replaced by new debts and the money burden is accumulated due to the postponement of debt repayment through refunding. The government may repay a part of the debt every year by issuing terminable annuities. The government can convert old loans into new loans and reduce its interest payments. Unlike refunding, conversion involves changes in terms of loan including rate of interest. Debt redemption fund also called as sinking funds involves the creation and the gradual accumulation of a separate fund by the government every year from its revenues to repay the debt. The government may take recourse to new taxes and raise money for the repayment of old debts by transferring the resources from taxpayers to the bondholders. A special 'redemption levy' or capital levy may lead to heavy taxation on the property and wealth of individuals; levied once for all the clearance of the debt. The surplus budget may leave the government with some money which can be used for the clearance of debts. The repayment of external debt requires a surplus balance of payments (BOPs). Hence, the government should accumulate the necessary foreign exchange by creating export surplus and by reducing imports. As a last resort, the government may print more currency to repay the debts which causes inflation and destroys the value of fixed money claims. The international law being chaotic, some governments may refuse to pay interest or principal or both. The government may ignore the obligation to repay the loans taken by it.

The Bougettee

Government is finance in practice. All the aspects of financial administration and budgeting raise the most sensitive issues of public policy. In 1773, when Walpole opened his Bougettee (the Bag) to present his financial plan of the year, it was called 'opening the budget'. Since then, democratic governments have shaped and reshaped this tool of management which is also called as a tool of coordination and control. Prime Minister Gladstone speaking on the floor of Commons once remarked "A budget is not an exercise in arithmetic but it is a horoscope of a nation that indicates trends of future economy. In fact, budget is a financial document presented to legislature for its sanction. This legislative authorisation of budget entitles the government to raise revenue and spend the allocation of sums as desired. As a policy document, it reflects the priorities of a government in power and a democratic government exercises its managerial control through the instrumentality of the budget." So, a budget is often called:

(1) A statement of revenue and expenditure.
(2) A tool of legislative control over executive.
(3) A policy document.
(4) A tool of management, coordination and control.

The budget ensures the financial and legal accountability of the executive to the legislature and accountability of subordinates to superiors in administrative hierarchy. It is an instrument of social and economic policy to serve the functions of allocation, distribution and stabilisation which facilitate efficient execution of the functions and services of government. The budget is a tool of administrative management and coordination. It unifies the various activities of the government departments into a single whole. As a plan of financing government operations, several forms of budgetary devices have been evolved which help the executive and the legislature to translate people's will into specific policies and projects for execution. Some of these budgetary systems are:

(1) Line Item Budgeting (LIB)
(2) Performance Budgeting (PB)
(3) Programme Planning and Budgetary System (PPBS)
(4) Zero Base Budgeting (ZBB)
(5) Sun Set Budgeting

The line item budgeting was a traditional way of putting allocations under specific items. It had nothing to do with the purpose of the budget but the amount granted by the legislature on a specific item was to be spent on that item only. The objective was to prevent wastage, overspending and misuse of money granted by the legislature to the executive. The itemwise classification facilitated maximum control of public expenditure. The object of line item budgeting was the accountability of funds, which ensured legality and regularity of expenditure. Each year, the Parliament reviewed the figures without revising items but enhancing incremental allocations.

The new systems like PB and PPBS were suggested by Hoover Commission in the context of presidential system of government in US. The ZBB of P.A. Phyrr owes its origin to private sector but has become popular in countries of the developing world. Similarly, sunset way of looking at budget is a reform which has gone a long way to cut on waste and unwanted expansion of public activities.

Budgets of governments can be classified on four basis:

(1) Organisation
(2) Functions
(3) Nature
(4) Special purpose

There are elaborate administrative and political organisations of finance ministry, cabinet committee and parliamentary procedures that formulate, enact and execute government budgets. Similarly, budget can be seen in terms of functions they perform, the kinds of clienteles they effect or offer benefits. Special needs are taken care of by revised estimates, supplementary budgets or vote on accounts, etc. The expansion of state activity makes the budget heavier in terms of outlays and billion, trillion rupees are earmarked for welfare which is a reflection of ideological commitment of ruling governments of a country. In this sense, the beneficiaries and victims of budgetary change are varied sections of society, which need to evolve consensus. Generally, the government budget effects the following:

(1) Prices of goods and services
(2) Inflationary levels and production
(3) Capital formation and investment
(4) Property relations in society
(5) Planning and speed of planned development
(6) Electoral system
(7) Production, distribution, exchange and consumption

Naturally, special care of details should be made to make the budget conform to sound principles of management and democratic working. Some of these principles have been identified as under:

(1) The estimated revenue and estimated expenditure should match to produce a balanced budget.
(2) The legislature should grant money to the executive for one financial year. If the granted money is not spent by the end of the financial year, then the balance would expire and should be returned to the treasury. This is called rule of lapse.
(3) All transactions of receipts and expenditure of the government should be fully and separately shown in the budget otherwise it will reduce legislative control over finances due to incomplete accounts.
(4) The current financial transactions of the government should be distinguished from the transactions of a capital nature and the two must be shown in two separate parts: (i) the revenue budget, and (ii) the capital budget.
(5) The form of budgetary estimates should correspond to the form of accounts such as major head, subhead and detailed head.
(6) The government should incorporate all its revenues and expenditure in a single budget to reveal the overall financial position of the government as a whole, that is, overall surplus or deficit.
(7) The budgetary estimates should be as exact as possible because overestimating leads to excessive taxation and underestimating may cause ineffective execution of the budget.

(8) The expenditure and revenue estimates of budget should be prepared on the basis of what is expected to be actually spent or received during the financial year. It is in contrast to 'Revenue Budgeting' wherein estimates are prepared on a demand and liability basis, regardless of whether they are actually realised or incurred in that financial year.

These principles lead to other relevant principles called as clarity, unity, periodicity variety and purity. In simple words, a budget should be a comprehensive document containing specific policy details or estimates, easy to execute and easier to enforce accounting and audit of these transactions for parliamentary scrutiny.

The fiscal administration of the government through the instrumentality of budget can be divided into two parts:

(a) Preparation and enactment of the budget, and
(b) Execution and audit of the budget.

Each stage can be further sub-divided into:

(a) Formulation of the budget by finance minister, and
(b) Passing of the budget by the Parliament.

The execution part can be examined as:

(a) Revenue collection and expenditure control, and
(b) Accounts keeping and audit.

There are a number of agencies involved in the total process and each stage of budget making and budget execution generates processes which make parliamentary control over public finances real and effective. Then these processes, stages and agencies are different in parliamentary and presidential forms of government for the simple reason that in parliamentary system like that of India the finance minister, the cabinet and the prime minister pilot, monitor and defend the budget on the floors of the two houses which is not the case in the presidential system of USA. The agencies that prepare and get the budget enacted and passed are:

(1) The Administrative Ministries and Departments
(2) The Finance Ministry
(3) The Cabinet
(4) The Planning Commission
(5) The Comptroller of Accounts and C&AG
(6) The Parliament

In the executive part of the budget, all these agencies play their roles and when the finance ministry exercises control over the purse, the Parliament asserts its detailed control through the independent agency of the C&AG and various committees of the Parliament, constituted for scrutiny and review of public expenditure.

Although India and UK follow parliamentary procedures of budgetary administration, yet there are discernable differences in the budgetary systems of the two countries. Unlike UK, India has:

(1) Two budgets, i.e., general budget and the railway budget.
(2) There is no committee of the whole house which discuss the budget as 'committee in supply' and 'committees on ways and means', in a non partisan manner.

(3) The practice of finance minister's speech preceding budget discussions is the other way round in UK where the Chancellor of Exchequer sums up the debate and does not influence the decisions of the house.

The railway budget was separated from the central budget in 1921 on the recommendation of Acworth Committee. Although the commencement of budget year for both the budgets is April 1st of the year.

Preparation of the Budget

It is an executive exercise which the administrative ministry and finance ministry undertake in collaboration with the cabinet and its committees. The budget formulation means preparation of two bills, viz., the Finance Bill (Revenues) and the Appropriation Bill (Expenditure). The drafting of these two bills requires all sorts of statistical facts from drawing and disbursing officers of the ministries. The ministries collect these facts from their subordinate and attached officers around the format of a performa which the finance ministry circulates to all administrative ministries in August every year. The heads in consultation with their finance officers (FOs) and financial advisors (FAs) supply this required information in response to the performa which seeks five kinds of specific figures in the following format:

Heads and subheads of appropriation	Actuals of the previous year	Expenditure of the current year	Revised estimates of the current year	Estimates of the next year	Details of increase and deficits

This information from the ministry presents the past, present and future patterns of revenue and expenditures of the ministry. The actuals sanctioned, revised and future projections explain how the ministry looks at its own functions and their financial allocations. The head of the department, after receiving the estimates from the drawing officers, scrutinises and consolidates them for the entire department and submits them to the administrative ministry. The administrative ministry further scrutinises the estimates in the light of its general policy and consolidates them for the whole ministry and submits them to the budget division of the department of economic affairs of the ministry of finance.

Role of the Finance Ministry

The ministry of finance is charged with the responsibility of raising the resources for the overall expenditure of the Government of India and to see to the desirability of the demands of other departments, taking into consideration the interest of taxpayers. The taxpayer cannot be left to the spending departments. His interests require a careful consideration of each item of public expenditure in its relation to other items and to the available resources of the state. A vigilant supervision of some authority not directly concerned in the expenditure needs to be involved. The ministry of finance acts as an 'extended arm' of the Parliament and ensures that the wishes of the Parliament are fulfilled by the executive. It watches the progress of expenditure and the obligations which the different departments are incurring and gives timely warning if that expenditure or obligations are outrunning the revenue or engaging the nation too deeply in future years. To discharge these obligations, the finance ministry performs the following function in relation to budget making:

(1) Consolidation of budget estimates on the basis of classification.
(2) Detailed scrutiny of the estimates including standing charges.

(3) Collection and collation of figures to be arranged into Finance Bill and Appropriate Bill.
(4) Review of standing charges, on going schemes and new projects included in the budget.
(5) Resolution of differences with the advice of the cabinet.
(6) Coordination of estimates with the allocations in Five-Year Plans with the consultation of Planning Commission.
(7) Preparation of economic classification of budget and other documents including the speech of the finance minister.

Based on the estimated expenditure, the finance ministry prepares the estimates of revenue in consultation with the Central Board of Direct Taxes and the Central Board of Indirect Taxes. It is also assisted in this work by the income tax department and the central excise and customs department. The economic classification of the budget in India usually follows the following pattern:

(1) Capital formation through budgetary resources.
(2) Various levels of budgetary receipts and appropriations.
(3) Resource mobilisation by Central government.
(4) Savings of the Central government.
(5) Total expenditure of the Central government.
(6) Final expenditure of the Central government.

The finance ministry scrutinises all proposals emanating from the spending departments in so far as they have financial implications. This enables the ministry to have control over the formulation of policies of other departments. Generally the scrutiny exercised by the ministry of finance is "very broad in nature ... and is more concerned with the overall financial implications of the proposal and its impact on the expenditure". Thus, every proposal or policy having financial implications has to be scrutinised by the finance ministry and the cabinet attaches weight to the opinion of the ministry. After all the proposals have been received from the spending ministries, it proceeds to determine priorities of the schemes and suggests economies where possible, taking into account the standing and continuing charges. Its main concern is to obtain "proper balance of expenditure between services, so that greater value could be obtained for the total expenditure by reducing the money spent on the service and increasing expenditure on another". To secure a uniform standard in the measurement of the financial sacrifice involved in the activities of all departments, "the general criteria adopted" in the selection of new proposals are:

(1) Whether the costs of individual items is reasonable?
(2) Have all parties interested been consulted?
(3) Is the new expenditure necessary or desirable?
(4) Is the ministry competent to propose such an expenditure?
(5) Does the proposal merit an expenditure from Public funds?
(6) Will the financial arrangements be desirable and economical?

It is on the answers given to these questions that the ministry of finance formulates its decisions. The importance of its control lay in seeking justification for every proposal from the departments proposing it. This control helps to make the departments careful in what they put forward. Equipped with these answers, the ministry of finance proceeds to review the total estimates in the light of likely revenue for the year. It can suggest reduction or as technically known 'cuts' if it finds the estimates too high or 'inflated'. It may also reject proposals which its scrutiny may reveal as technically 'unsound'. While preparing the Finance and Appropriation bills, the ministry has to keep several constitutional requirements in mind. First of all, there is a non-votable part of the budget called as charge on the Consolidated Fund of India. This money has to be provided in the Appropriation Bill and the finance ministry has to provide the expenditure 'charged' and the expenditure 'made' from the Consolidated Fund of India. The charged expenditure is non-votable by the Parliament, that is, it can only be discussed by the Parliament, while the other type has to be voted by the Parliament. The list of the charged expenditure includes:

(1) The emoluments and allowances of the President and other expenditure relating to his office.
(2) The salaries and allowances of the chairman and the deputy chairman of the council of states and the speaker and the deputy speaker of the House of People.
(3) The salaries, allowances and pensions of the judges of Supreme Court.
(4) The pensions of the judges of High Court which exercises jurisdiction in relation to any area included in the Indian territory.
(5) The salary, allowances and pension of the Comptroller and Auditor-General of India.
(6) The salaries, allowances and pensions of the chairman and members of the Union Public Service Commission.
(7) The administrative expenses of the Supreme Court, the office of the Comptroller and Auditor-General of India and the Union Public Service Commission including the salaries, allowances and pensions of the persons serving in these offices.
(8) The debt charges for which the Government of India is liable including interest, sinking fund charges and redemption charges and other expenditure relating to the raising of loans and the service and redemption of debt.
(9) Any sum required to satisfy any judgement, decree or award of any court or arbitral tribunal.
(10) Any other expenditure declared by the Parliament to be so charged.

The Government of India can neither collect nor spend any money without the authorisation of Parliament. Naturally, the passage or approval of budget estimates has to be ensured by the government and further ratification by the President of India is also needed. For this, the Constitution of India has laid down an elaborate procedure in Articles from 112 to 117 which are reproduced below:

(1) The President shall in respect of every financial year cause to be laid before both the Houses of Parliament a statement of the estimated receipts and expenditure of the Government of India for that year. This is known as 'Annual Financial Statement' (Article 112).
(2) No demand for a grant shall be made except on the recommendation of the President (Article 113).
(3) No money shall be withdrawn from the Consolidated Fund of India except appropriation made by law (Article 114).
(4) No Money Bill imposing tax shall be introduced in the Parliament except on the recommendation of the President, and such a bill shall not be introduced in Rajya Sabha (Article 117).
(5) No tax shall be levied or collected except by authority of law (Article 265).
(6) Parliament can reduce or abolish a tax but cannot increase it.
(7) The Constitution has also defined the relative roles or position of both the houses of Parliament with regard to the enactment of the budget (i.e., the Annual Financial Statement) in the following way:

(a) A Money Bill or Finance Bill dealing with taxation cannot be introduced in the Rajya Sabha, it must be introduced only in the Lok Sabha.
(b) The Rajya Sabha has no power to vote on the demand for grants; it is the exclusive privilege of the Lok Sabha.
(c) The Rajya Sabha should return the Money Bill (or Finance Bill) to the Lok Sabha within fourteen days. The Lok Sabha can either accept or reject the recommendations made by Rajya Sabha in this regard.

(8) The estimates of expenditure embodied in the budget shall show separately the expenditure charged on the Consolidated Fund of India and the expenditure made from the Consolidated Fund of India (Article 112).
(9) The budget shall distinguish expenditure on revenue account from other expenditure (Article 112).
(10) The expenditure charged on the Consolidated Fund of India shall not be submitted to the vote of Parliament. However, it can be discussed by the Parliament (Article 113).

Generally, a financial bill may be considered as any bill which relates to revenue or expenditure. However, the Constitution of India uses the term in the technical sense and prefers the term, Money Bill which, in turn, has been defined under Article 110. A bill is deemed to be a Money Bill if it contains only provisions dealing with the imposition, abolition, remission, alteration or regulation of any tax; and the regulation of borrowing of money or giving of any guarantee by the Government of India, or the amendment of the law with respect to any government financial obligations; the bills relating to operation of the Consolidated Fund or the Contingency Fund of India; the appropriation of moneys out of the Consolidated Fund of India, or the declaring of any expenditure as charged and the receipt of money on account of the Consolidated Fund of India or the Public Accounts of India generally belong to the category of a Money Bill which requires the certification of the speaker.

Article 109 of the Constitution lays down that a Money Bill shall not be introduced in the Rajya Sabha. After a Money Bill has been passed by the Lok Sabha, it is transmitted to the Rajya Sabha for its recommendations. In turn, the Rajya Sabha, within a period of fourteen days of its receipt of the bill, should return the bill, with its recommendations to the Lok Sabha, which may accept or reject all or any of the recommendation of the Rajya Sabha. In case any of the recommendations is accepted, the Money Bill shall be deemed to have been passed by both Houses with the said amendment. On the other hand, if no such recommendation is accepted by the Lok Sabha, the Money Bill is deemed to have been passed by both Houses in the form in which it was originally passed by the Lok Sabha. If a Money Bill, passed by the Lok Sabha and transmitted to the Rajya Sabha for its recommendations, is not returned to the former within a period of fourteen days, it is deemed to have been passed by the Rajya Sabha. Thus, in matters of Money Bills, the primacy and supremacy of the Lok Sabha stands established.

Under Article 111 of the Constitution, the President can withhold assent to a 'non-money' bill passed by the Lok Sabha and he may return such a bill to the House for reconsideration, and, if it is passed again by the House, with or without the amendments suggested by the President, and is sent to him for assent, the President cannot withhold assent to it. This discretion of withholding assent or suggesting amendments has been denied to the President by the Constitution, in respect of Money Bills.

All this implies that Money Bill cannot be initiated in the Rajya Sabha but it can recommend amendments to Lok Sabha which may or may not be accepted. There are money matters which do not deal exclusively with matters outside the purview of Article 110. They too cannot be introduced in Rajya Sabha except on the recommendation of the President. The Rajya Sabha can amend or reject such a Financial Bill subject to the limitation that an amendment other than for reduction or abolition of a tax cannot be moved in either House without the President's recommendation. In the case of the second kind of Financial Bills, which involve expenditure from the Consolidated Fund, either House has powers to reject or amend it; but, it requires the President's recommendation before it can be *considered* (as against before it can be introduced).

According to Article 114 of the Constitution, when the demand for grants has been voted for, the Appropriation Bill authorises the withdrawal of the funds from the Consolidated Fund of India, as regards both the votable and the charged items. The bill includes all those items which have already been included in the demands for grants of individual ministries and is a replica of the statement of those amounts, which had earlier been approved by the Parliament. No amendments can be proposed to this bill because that would amount to altering the once decided amount of a grant. The Appropriation Bill provides an occasion for a full-fledged discussion on subjects chosen by the various parties in the House.

The Budget in Cabinet

The cabinet gives its final approval to the Finance Bill and Appropriation Bill to be presented in the Parliament. Before this, the draft bills are debated and discussed to finalise the quantum of deficit and the state of loans and borrowing along with taxation proposals. The policy decisions are concretised in terms of budget allocations and adjustments are made accordingly. The finance minister convinces his colleagues about the desirability of cuts and enhancements. Some estimates are revised on the basis of percentage changes necessitated by policy or plan allocation revisions. The budget is a secret document and leakage can cause disaster to the economy. Hence, Prime Minister has a special responsibility to get the differences resolved and prepare the basic documents for parliamentary approval.

The Budget in Parliament

It is also called as 'enactments of budget' which means converting the two bills into acts. The passage in Parliament has five stages:

(1) Presentation of budget
(2) General discussion
(3) Voting on demands for grants
(4) Passing of Appropriation Bill
(5) Passing of Finance Bill

Article 112 of the Constitution enjoins upon the President of India to get the budget presented before both of the houses of Parliament. Being a Money Bill, it has to be presented to the Lok Sabha first and must classify the charge on the Consolidated Fund and expenditure on the Consolidated Fund of India separately. There is a prescribed legislative procedure in each house and the Rajya Sabha should not delay it for more than fourteen days. The Consolidated Fund, Contingency Fund and public account transactions are updated to appraise the Parliament which operates the

Consolidated Fund at the President's disposal and takes stock of public account assets and liabilities without voting on them. The budget in India had to pass through three readings without any committee stage. The first reading is called the presentation of the budget which includes the following documents:

(1) The economic survey report,
(2) Economic classification of the budget,
(3) Annual reports of the ministries,
(4) An explanatory memorandum on the budget,
(5) An Appropriation Bill, and
(6) A Finance Bill containing the taxation proposals.

The presentation of the budget to the Lok Sabha is in two or more parts, and each part ends within the manner as if it were the budget. Accordingly, the budget is presented as Railway Budget and as General Budget. The introduction of Railway Budget precedes that of the General Budget. While the former is presented to the Lok Sabha by the railway minister in the third week of February, the latter is presented to the Lok Sabha by the finance minister on the last working day of February. The finance minister presents the General Budget with a speech known as the 'budget speech'. At the end of the budget speech in the Lok Sabha, the budget is laid before the Rajya Sabha which can only discuss it and has no power to vote on the demand for grants.

The general discussion on budget takes place during budget session. It lasts for three to four days. During this stage, the Lok Sabha can discuss the budget as a whole or on any question of principle involved therein but no motion is moved or submitted for the vote of the House. The finance minister has a right of reply at the end of the discussion. After the general discussion on budget, the Lok Sabha takes up voting of demands for grants. They are presented ministrywise and a demand becomes a grant after it has been voted. The voting of demands for grants is the exclusive privilege of the Lok Sabha and not of Rajya Sabha. The voting is confined to the votable part of the budget but the expenditure charged on the Consolidated Fund of India can only be discussed. The General Budget has totally 109 demands (103 for civil expenditure and 6 for defence expenditure), the Railway Budget has 32 demands. Each demand is voted separately by the Lok Sabha. During this stage, the members of Parliament can discuss the details of the budget. They can also move to reduce any demand for grant. But increase or upward revisions of estimates are not permissible. The members who propose reduction of grant bring three kinds of cut motions which are either withdrawn or dropped because their passing will be tantamount to a vote of no confidence in the government. Still to attract the attention of the government, the cut motions are moved to bring a moral pressure on the executive. These cut motions are:

(1) *Token Cut Motion:* It expresses a specific grievance which is within the sphere of responsibility of the government. It states that the amount of the demand be reduced by Rs 100. On the 26th day, the Speaker puts all the remaining demands to vote and disposes them whether they have been discussed by the members or not. This is called as 'Guillotine closer'.
(2) *Policy Cut Motion* shows disapproval of the policy underlying a demand. It states that the amount of the demand be reduced to Re 1.
(3) *Economy Cut Motion* asks for economy in the proposed expenditure. It states that the amount of the demand be reduced by a specified amount which may be either a lump sum reduction or omission or reduction of an item in the demand.

Article 113 and 114 provide for the presentation of various kinds of demands for grants by the Parliament. Some of them are:

(1) Vote on credit
(2) Vote on accounts
(3) Vote on exceptional grants
(4) Supplementary grants
(5) Excess grants
(6) Token grants

In addition to the budget, various other kinds of grants are made by the Parliament under extraordinary or special circumstances. When the amount authorised by the Parliament through the Appropriation Act for a particular service for the current financial year is found to be insufficient for the purposes of that year supplementary grants are sanctioned by the Parliament. Similarly, when a need has arisen during the current financial year for additional expenditure upon some new service not contemplated in the budget, Parliament may consider additional grants. Excess grants are given when money has been spent on any service during a financial year in excess of the amount granted for that service in the budget for that year. It is voted by the Lok Sabha after the financial year. Only if approval by the Public Accounts Committee to meet an unexpected demand upon resources and if the account is huge or of indefinite character, the vote on credit is resorted to like a blank cheque given to the executive by the Lok Sabha. For special purposes that form no part of the current service of any financial year, exceptional grants can be made. Parliament makes token grants available if funds to meet the proposed expenditure on a new service are available by reappropriation. A demand for the grant of a token sum (of Re 1) is submitted to the vote of the Lok Sabha and if assented, funds follow. Supplementary, additional, excess and exceptional grants and vote of credit are regulated by the same procedure which is applicable in the case of a regular budget.

The Appropriation Bill and Finance Bill after debate are put to vote on the floor of the Parliament sequentially. The Appropriation Bill comes first and then the Finance Bill has to make revenue provisions for the stipulated expenditure sanctioned by the Parliament. No amendment can be proposed to the Appropriation Bill in either house of the Parliament which will have the effect of varying the amount or altering the destination of any grant voted. The Appropriation Bill becomes the Appropriation Act after it is assented to by the President. This Act authorises the payments from the Consolidated Fund of India. If the government needs money to carry on its normal activities after 31st March, the Constitution authorises the Lok Sabha to make grant in advance in respect to the estimated expenditure for a part of the financial year, pending the enactment of the Appropriation Bill. This 'Vote on Account' is passed after general discussion on budget and is generally granted for two months for an amount equivalent to one-sixth of the total estimation.

The Finance Bill when passed legalises the income side of the budget. According to Provisional Collection of Taxes Act 1931, the Finance Bill in India has to be passed within 75 days. The bill gives effect to supplementary financial proposals for any period. It is a money bill for procedural purposes and unlike the Appropriation Bill the members can move amendments to reject or reduce a tax in a prescribed manner. The proposals for new taxation require a previous consent of the President before presentation. The procedures for Railway Budget and Central Budget are identical.

The Execution of the Budget

Execution of budget means raising the revenue and controlling the spending of government departments in such a manner that they remain within bounds of the budget or desires of the Parliament. The various agencies responsible for this execution task are:

(1) Administrative ministry
(2) Finance ministry
(3) Comptroller and Auditor-General of India
(4) Parliament and its committees

After the budget has been passed, the responsibility for the control of expenditure from thereon lies on the administrative ministry and each head of the department who is aided and advised by an internal financial adviser, a representative of the ministry of finance in the discharge of his responsibilities. During the execution of the budget, it is the responsibility of the ministry of finance to ensure that the amounts are spent properly and economically. It has also to see that the achievement is in accordance with the plans included in the budget of the other departments. Prior consultation of the ministry of finance is sought whenever any department wants to spend on schemes whose estimate exceeds a particular limit. This is technically known as 'expenditure sanction'. Similarly, prior approval of the finance ministry is essential before amounts can be transferred from one sub-head to another, technically known as 're-appropriation'. Besides, the ministry of finance, through its financial adviser, conducts financial reviews after every quarter in order to know the progress of expenditure. This enables the ministry to get a review of the performance of other departments in monetary terms. It also helps the ministry of finance to forecast next year's budget. The other matters arise in various specified fields of expenditure such as grants-in-aid, write-off of losses, waiving of recoveries, contracts, inspection of establishment of other ministries through staff inspection unit. The control exercised by the ministry of finance helps in promotion of a financial discipline in the country. In almost all fields where risk is involved in spending huge amounts, the shadow of the ministry of finance is present though it minimises the effect of financial delegation of powers.

Collection of Revenue

The execution of the Finance Bill, i.e., revenue side of the budget requires three kinds of activities which again involve various administrative agencies. These activities are:

(1) Collection of money as receipts,
(2) Custody of public funds collected, and
(3) Disbursement of funds according to the procedure.

Finance ministry exercises overall control and supervision over the machinery charged with the collection of taxes through the Central Board of Direct Taxes and the Central Board of Excise and Customs. The department of revenue administers details. The Reserve Bank of India, the State Bank of India, the district treasuries and the sub-treasuries are engaged in the custody and distribution of funds. The Constitution of India provides for the custody of public funds of the central government:

(1) Consolidated Fund of India (Article 266)
(2) Public Account of India (Article 266)
(3) Contingency Fund of India (Article 267)

All receipts are credited and all payments are debited to CFI. Revenues received by the Government of India; loans raised by the government by the issue of treasury bills, loans or ways and means of advances; and moneys received by the government in repayment of loans contribute the consolidated fund of India. All authorised payments of the Government of India are made out of this fund and no money can be appropriated, issued or drawn from this fund except in accordance with a parliamentary law. All public moneys (other than those which are credited to the Consolidated Fund of India) received by or on behalf of the Government of India are credited to the Public Account of India. This includes provident fund deposits, judicial deposits, savings bank deposits, departmental deposits, remittances, etc. This account is operated by executive action and payments are mostly in the nature of banking transactions.

The Constitution authorises the Parliament to establish a 'Contingency Fund of India' into which are paid sums as may be determined by the law. The Parliament has enacted the Contingency Fund of India Act in 1950 and it is placed at the disposal of the President, who makes advances out of it to meet unforeseen expenditure. To collect revenue as desired by the budget, the finance ministry has devised machinery for tax administration and determination of procedure. Assessment of tax, that is, preparation of a list of persons liable to pay tax and determining the amount to be paid by them is conducted on annual basis. Objections and appeals are heard and realisation of the amount due from the various assesses is put into the treasury. Realisation of arrears and dealing with the defaulters is a part of administration.

Control Over Public Expenditure

It is also called 'Execution of Budget' which means implementation of the Appropriation Bill by the various ministries under the supervision of the ministry of finance. The finance ministry is the central financial agency of the union government and has the overall responsibility regarding expenditure of public funds. Because of the concentration of fiscal authority the ministry enjoys tight control over the purse. There are prescribed rules of procedures and the competent officials are entitled to disburse money in prescribed limits. Notwithstanding some delegational freedom, the Finance Ministry controls the administrative ministries through some of the following methods:

(1) It sanctions expenditure, subject to powers delegated to spending ministries.
(2) It gives acceptance of provision in budget estimates.
(3) It prescribes a financial code for internal audit system of the ministries.
(4) It approves policies and programmes in principle.
(5) It offers financial advice through integrated financial advisor.
(6) It permits re-appropriation of grants.

The Integrated Financial Advisors

To play this role effectively and efficiently, the finance ministry has a network of controlling officers. The head of the departments is the chief disbursing officer who withdraws funds on receiving financial sanction from the competent authorities. The rules elaborate the powers pf drawing and disbursing officers in each ministry. The accounting section of the administrative machinery operates the payments and maintains accounts books for further audit. Re-appropriation requires the formal approval of the finance ministry or the administrative ministry/department. Re-appropriation is permissible within the same grant only and is not permissible from charged items of expenditures. Expenditure on a new service not provided for in the budget does not fall in re-appropriation category. It is not allowed between different grants voted by the Lok Sabha. Similarly, expenditure which are not sanctioned by the Lok Sabha and involve outlays in the future financial year or are between the revenue and the capital parts of the budget cannot be revised through executive act of re-appropriation. A scheme of integrated financial advisors is working in all the ministries of the central government since 1975. The Integrated Financial Advisors in the ministries are of the rank of joint secretary or additional secretary. They are selected jointly by the administrative ministry and finance ministry and their confidential reports are written jointly by both the ministries. The IFA is under the dual control of both the ministries and also answerable to both. He assists the administrative ministry in the exercise of enhanced delegated financial powers and his advice can be overruled by the secretary of the ministry. But outside the scope of delegated powers, he functions under the general direction of the finance ministry and has direct access to the finance secretary. Some of the functions of IFA include preparation of budget, scrutiny of projects and programmes for the approval of finance ministry and post-budget vigilance. The formulation of performance budget of the ministry and monitoring of the progress of schemes through assistance to the secretary in discharge of his responsibility as the chief accounting authority of the Ministry is the duty of the finance advisor.

Parliamentary Control

There is a prescribed procedure by which the Finance Bill and the Appropriation Bill are presented, debated and passed. The Parliament being sovereign gives grants to the executive, which makes demands. These demands can be of varieties like the demands for grants, supplementary grants, additional grants, etc. The estimates of expenditure, other than those specified for the Consolidated Fund of India, are presented to the Lok Sabha in the form of demands for grants. The Lok Sabha has the power to assent to or to reject, any demand, or to assent to any demand, subject to a reduction of the amount specified. After the conclusion of the general debate on the budget, the demands for grants of various ministries are presented to the Lok Sabha. Formerly, all demands were introduced by the finance minister; but, now, they are formally introduced by the ministers of the concerned departments. These demands are not presented to the Rajya Sabha, though a general debate on the budget takes place there too.

A vote on account is a grant approved by the Parliament in advance of the detailed examination of various demands presented to it. Since legislative programmes proceed on schedule and cannot be hurried, merely to enable the executive to get its grants exactly at the beginning of the new financial year, the executive is given an advance grant to meet its temporary and other running expenditure until the demands are voted by the legislature. The idea is that no governmental activity should be held up for want of funds. Such grants are passed, after a detailed discussion in the House, since no money can be taken without the sanction of the legislature. It again gives a chance to discuss matters of policy, to ventilate grievances and to propose cut motions. In practice, however, the approval of such grants in the Parliament has been a smooth affair on almost all occasions.

The Constitution provides that the Parliament may make a grant for meeting an unexpected demand upon the nation's resources, when, on account of the magnitude or the indefinite character of the service, the demand cannot be stated with the details ordinarily given in the annual financial statement. An Appropriation Act is again essential for passing such a grant. It is intended to meet specific purposes, such as for meeting war needs. The process of reappropriation consists in appropriating from one head, where there is saving, to another where there may be need for more expenditure. It is a process wherein the total amount of the grant remains the same but, there are internal transfers and shifts which change the composition of the demand.

Another related technique of control is through token grants. They are variations of supplementary grants and are submitted when the proposed expenditure is not within the ambit of the demand already approved, but, can be met from the savings within that demand. Thus, this demand also does not involve any additional expenditure.

The control of the ministry of finance is essentially executive and bureaucratic. The sovereign Parliament which authorises the executive government to spend public funds has the right to know and correct the observations that can take place in the form of misspending, misappropriation and improper utilisation of public funds. To have this independent and expert control, the Constitution under Article 148 has created a watchdog which acts as a friend, philosopher and guide of the Parliament. The office of the Comptroller and Auditor-General of India, which was created as early as 1757 by Lord Canning had the purpose of introducing rigour and uniformity in the accounting and audit systems of accounts. The Government of India Act 1935 accorded it the status of a judge of Federal Court, which the republican Constitution maintains by mentioning that "C&AG will be appointed by the President of India for a period of six years or up to the age of 65 years whichever is earlier". He can be removed from office in like manner and on like grounds as in the case of a judge of the Supreme Court. This makes him ineligible for reappointment in any office of profit. His independence has been guaranteed by the Constitution and removal is possible only by an order of the President passed after an address by each house of Parliament supported by a majority of the total membership of the house and by a majority of not less than two-thirds of the members of the house present and voting on the ground of proved misbehaviour or incapacity. His salary and service conditions also cannot be varied to his disadvantages after he is appointed and he is not eligible for further office under the Government of India or of any state, after he leaves office.

The scope of activity domain of the C&AG is quite comprehensive and wide. Before 1976, he was the chief accounts officer as well as the Auditor-General of India. The 1976 reform has separated the two functions and today he is the chief auditor of accounts. His original functions included, prescription of forms of accounts, performance of duties in relation to accounts and reporting to President/Governors on the accounts of the union and states. Accounting in modern parlance means keeping of systematic record of transaction to protect handling of funds and facilitate adjustments of expenditure. It is an aid to audit and reveals financial conditions for reporting to higher authorities. Accounting as a system classifies and summarises transactions for determination of fidelity and to keep the budgetary expenditure within limits for purposes of future policy making. Audit on the other hand is "an examination of the accounts to discover and report to the legislature the unauthorised, illegal or irregular expenditures and unsound financial practices on the part of administration. It is a process of ascertaining whether the administration has spent or is spending its funds in accordance with the terms of the legislative instrument which appropriated the money".

The C&AG heads the Indian audit and account department. He is assisted by two deputy C&AGs of India, one of whom is the chairman of Audit Board. There are five additional deputy C&AGs controlling assistant comptrollers, director-general, principal directors, directors and deputy directors. The states have their respective offices of accountant general with corresponding powers and functions. The C&AG Activity Report 1991–92 presents the organisational set-up as follows:

Organisational Set-up of Comptroller and Auditor General of India: Organisational Setup

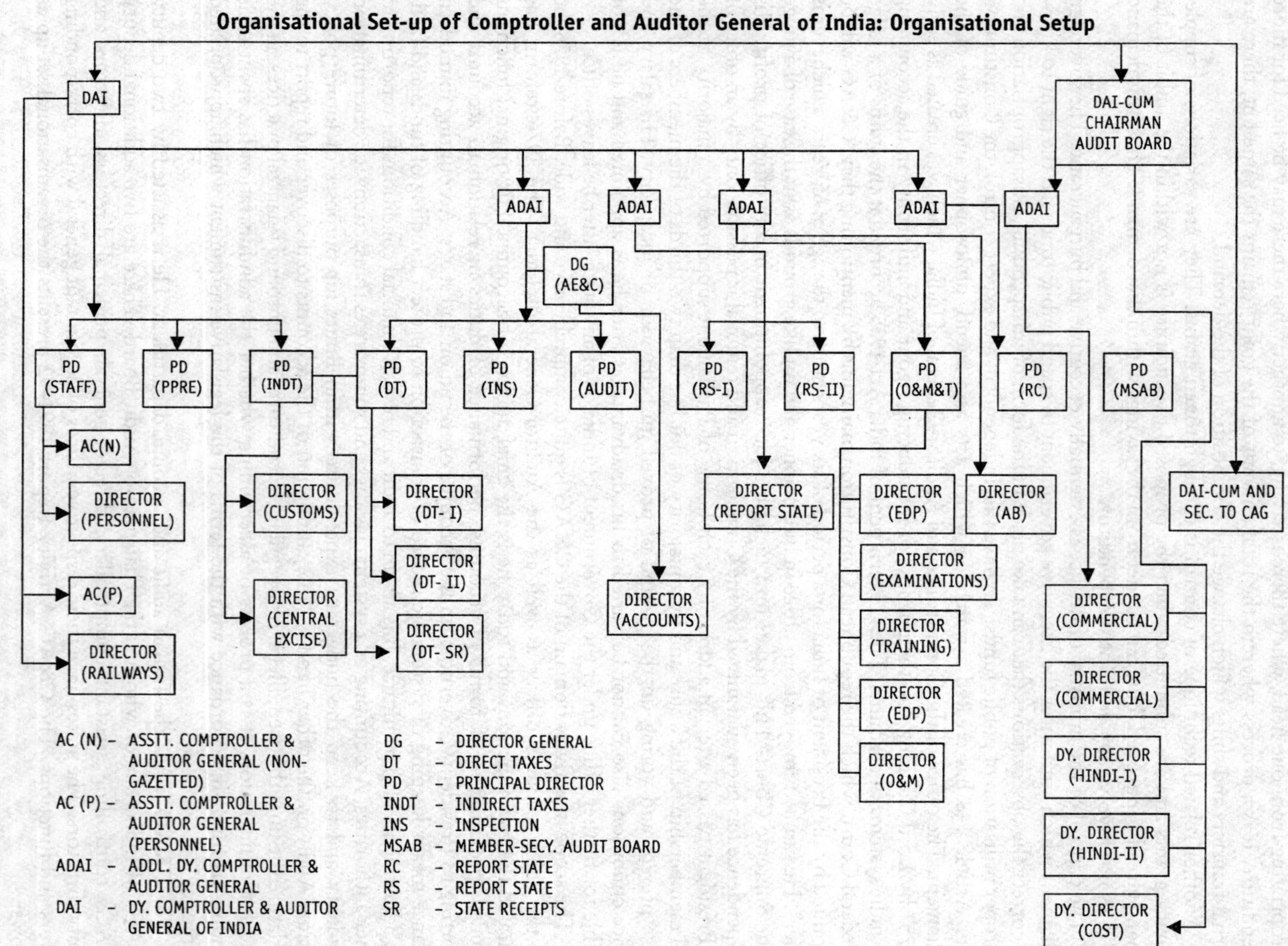

Source: CAG Activity Report, 1991–92 in Arora, *Indian Public Administration.*

The pre-1971 situation pertaining to accounts functions was:

(1) Preparation of annual accounts,
(2) Maintenance of accounts,
(3) Submission of annual report to the President,
(4) Offering assistance in the preparation of accounts,
(5) Providing relevant information.

Similarly, in the area of audit the C&AG has been auditing:

(1) The accounts of central and state governments and union territories,
(2) Reporting upon all expenditure from contingency fund and public accounts,
(3) Reporting on all trading, profit and loss accounts of union and state departments, and
(4) Reporting on the receipt of expenditure of bodies substantially financed from government revenues, government companies and selective public corporations after 1971.

For this, it has a wide field network of offices and training centres to equip its staff for audit efficiency. The functional chart of IAAD as appearing in C&AG activity report 1992–93 is reproduced on the following page.

1976 and After

There is a long history behind the demand of separation of accounts from audit. The combination of two functions was condemned as a public of British rule in India. The Inchcape Committee (1923), the Muddiman Committee (1924) and the Simon Commission (1929) and later on a series of estimates committee report including the former C&AG Ashok Chanda stood for the much needed separation and independence on the following grounds:

(1) The separation will increase the independence of audit.
(2) The separation makes the spending departments not to exceed appropriations sanctioned by the Parliament.
(3) The system had inherent danger of frauds and embezzlements in appropriate combine and executive function in the quasi-parliamentary function.
(4) It will increase the efficiency of audit department and it will concentrate on audit functions only.
(5) It placed the C&AG in a embarrassing position and was against the practice of modern governments.
(6) The use of accounting in decision-making and financial management will improve efficiency.
(7) The accounting responsibilities to departments will improve the system of accounting.
(8) It will facilitate close budgeting and shall make more effective formulation of revised estimates.

The Comptroller and Auditor-General Act, 1976 promoted the government to take two decisions:

(1) To launch a scheme for separation of accounts from audit, and
(2) To transfer employees working in IAAD with the help of advisory committee.

In 1971, the Comptroller and Auditor-General's (duties, powers and conditions of service) Act was passed. In June 1975, the Government of India approved a scheme of departmentalisation of accounts in a phased manner in all the central ministries and departments. It was completed by

Functional Chart of IAAD Office of the Comptroller and Auditor-General of India

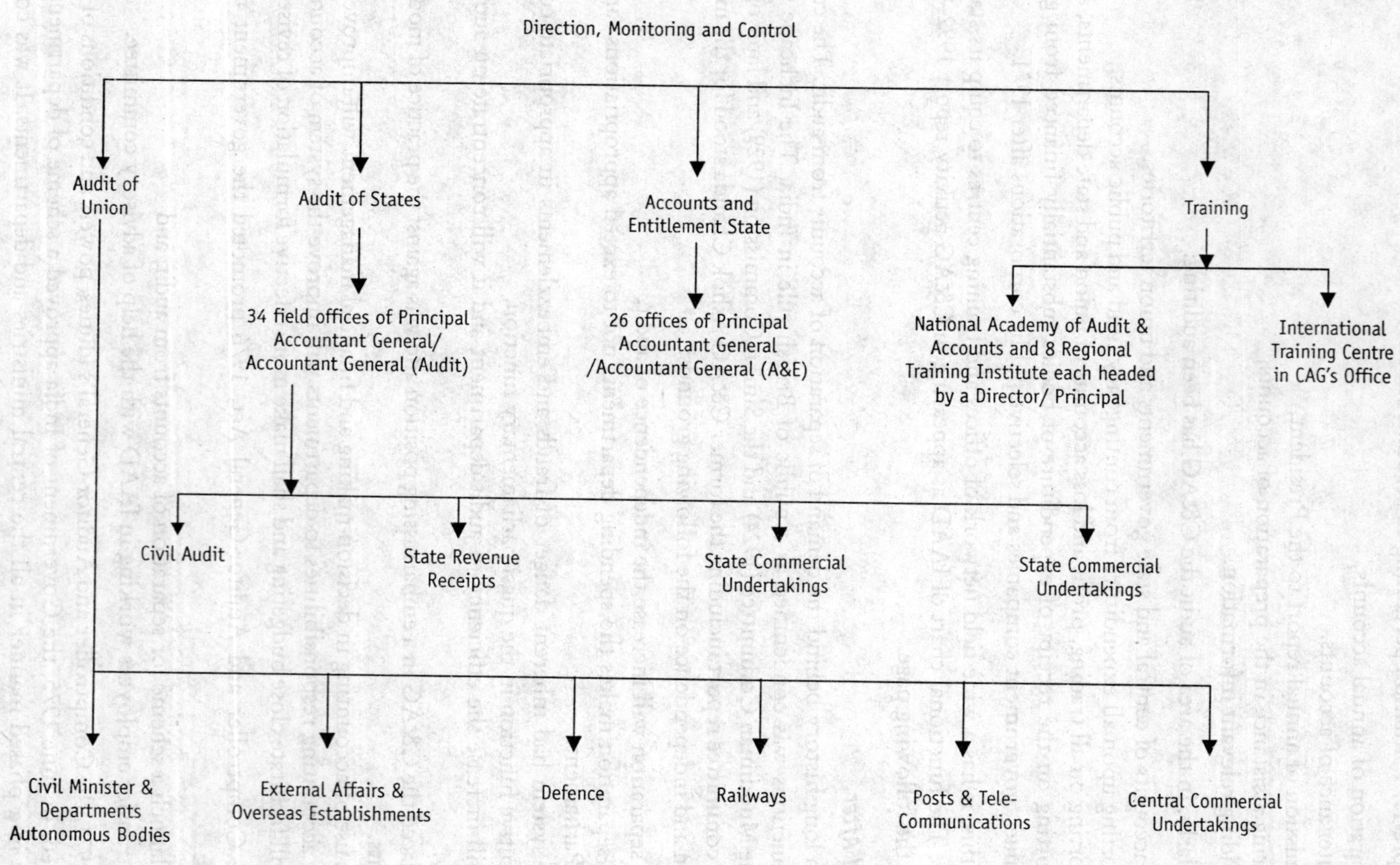

Source: CAG. Activity Report, 1992–93, p. 6 in Arora, *Indian Public Administration.*

October, 1976. Thus, in 1976 the Central government separated accounting from the audit, and since that year the C&AG of India has been relieved of the responsibility for compiling of the accounts of the Central government, and is concerned with the audit of accounts only. This separation of accounts from audit was completed in three phases effective from 1 April, 1976 (covering three ministries of the central government). 1 July, 1976 (covering nine more ministries); and 1 October, 1976 (covering the remaining ministries). As a result, there is now departmentalisation of accounts in the Central government and the administrative departments have assumed full responsibility for making payments and their accounting.

Departmentalisation of Accounts

This new scheme of departmentalisation of accounts envisaged that:

(1) The Comptroller and Auditor-General of India will be relieved of the responsibility of the compilation and maintenance of accounts and will be concerned with auditing only. However, he continues to be responsible for the compilation and maintenance of accounts of the states which have not separated accounts from audit.

(2) The secretary of the ministry will be designated as the chief accounting authority for all the transactions of the ministry as well as its attached and subordinate offices. He will be responsible for the monthly accounts with the assistance of the integrated financial advisor of the ministry.

(3) The administrative departments will assume responsibility for making payments and their accounting.

(4) The integrated financial advisor will be the head of the payment and accounting organisation of the ministry on behalf of the chief accounting authority (i.e., secretary of the ministry). He will look after formulation of the budget of the ministry and its departments and control of expenditure. He will arrange payments sanctioned by the ministry and will prepares the consolidation of the accounts of the ministry as a whole. Preparation of appropriation accounts for the grants controlled by the ministry and introduction of system of management suited to the functional requirements will be evolved by him. He will make internal audit of payments and accounts to ensure accuracy of accounts and efficiency of operations. The integrated financial advisor will be assisted by principal accounts officers, the heads of pay and accounts offices, the chief controller of accounts, and the controller of accounts.

The New Office of the CGA

A new office of the Controller General of Accounts (CGA) has been created as a part of the department of expenditure of the ministry of finance. He administers matters relating to the departmentalisation of accounts of the Central government. Since 1976, the CGA is the technical authority who heads the new accounting set-up of Central government. He is responsible for prescribing the form of accounts and framing rules and regulations in the area of accounts. Internal audit, publication of accounts codes and manuals and cadre management of civil accounts personnel is CGA's responsibility. He makes monthly and annual consolidation of accounts of the Central government. Under Article 283 of the Constitution, the CGA will deal with the custody and other aspects of Consolidated Fund, Contingency Fund and moneys credited to the Public Accounts. He will also prepare a condensed form of the appropriation accounts and finance accounts of the

Central government. These, after getting audited by the Comptroller and Auditor-General of India, are placed before the Parliament by the President. The appropriation accounts compare the actual expenditure under various grants with the amount of voted grants as specified in the Appropriation Act passed by the Parliament. The finance accounts must show (under the respective heads) the annual receipts and disbursements for the purposes of the Central government. According to Article 150 of the Constitution, the form of the accounts of the Central and state governments is prescribed by the President of India on the advice of the Comptroller and Auditor-General of India. The form of budget corresponds to the form of accounts. The existing accounting practice could not meet the requirements of performance budgeting. Consequently, a revised accounting structure was introduced in 1974 by the Central government to serve the objectives of management and the need of financial control and accountability. To ensure this revised scheme, a five tier classification of accounts as sectoral head, major head, minor head, sub head, and detailed head has been adopted. This sectoral classification further sub-divided the functions of government into three sectors: general services (with six sub-sectors), social and community services and economic services (with seven sub-sectors). In addition, there is a fourth sector, namely, grants-in-aid and contributions. The major head of account denotes a function of government while the minor head is assigned to a programme. The sub head denotes the scheme covered by a programme and the detailed head represents the expenditure on the scheme in terms of inputs. The 'object head' (i.e., the object level of classification) has been retained and placed under the last tier. It provides itemwise control over expenditure. The approval of the Comptroller and Auditor-General of India is required for any change in the major head.

Under the new system, the secretary, as the chief accounting authority, has a total and overall responsibility for the efficient working of the payment and accounting set-up. The payment functions have been taken over by the ministries themselves and are discharged by their own pay and accounts officers. The cash transactions of the government are being handled by the Reserve Bank of India, State Bank of India and its subsidiaries and by other public sector banks. It is expected that the departmentalisation of accounts will enable the ministries to watch the flow of expenditure regularly and take effective connective action wherever necessary. It will facilitate the settlement of all claims directly by the departments by cheques. The large variations from the budgeted allocation which were very common till 1976, are expected to disappear under the new system of separation. It will also help in proper maintenance of provident fund accounts and prompt settlement of claims. This will speed up the compilation of accounts. The accounts of the ministries and departments are to be compiled within 25 days after the close of the month.

Even when the Act of 1971 envisages separation, the C&AG under the Constitution has not been totally relieved of his accountant's responsibility. The new dispensation expects the C&AG to perform his constitutional obligations. These powers and duties relating to accounting envisaged under the new Act are as under:

(1) Article 150 of the Constitution empowers the Comptroller and Auditor-General with the approval of the President to prescribe the form in which the accounts of the union and the states are to be kept.
(2) The Act empowers C&AG for preparing accounts every year showing the annual receipts and disbursement of the union and each state. These accounts are designated as 'Finance Accounts'.

(3) He is responsible for keeping of accounts of the union and of each state other than accounts relating to defence and railways and accounts relating to transactions in UK.
(4) C&AG has also to submit report annually to each government in respect of accounts kept by him. 'Appropriation Accounts', i.e., accounts pertaining to expenditure are brought into account during the financial year to the several items specified in the Schedule to appropriate Acts passed in accordance with the provisions of Articles 114 and 204 of the Constitution. In fact, the form of these accounts is determined by the Comptroller and Auditor-General in consultation with government concerned.

Under the second phase, another group of eight ministries was covered. The departmentalisation of accounts has been completed in October 1976 and the revenue, accounting work has also been taken over from April 1, 1977.

All this implies that the C&AG has been relieved of work but not of his final responsibility. The ministry has taken over the executive responsibility of accounts but the audit work does need his supervision and an overall control and approval of changes in the accounting system of the country.

The C&AG as an Auditor

In spite and despite of 1976 change, Articles 148 and 149 of the Constitution remain unchanged. They enjoin upon the C&AG to play a guardian of public purse and control the entire financial system in a uniform manner. The amended version of the C&AG Act 1971 and 1976 expects the C&AG to ascertain whether moneys shown in the accounts as having been disbursed were legally available for and applicable to the service or the purpose to which they have been applied or charged, and whether the expenditure conforms to the authority which governs it. In addition to this legal and regulatory audit, the C&AG can also conduct the propriety audit, that is, he can look into the wisdom, faithfulness and economy of government expenditure and comment on the wastefulness and extravagance of such expenditure. However, unlike the legal and regulatory audit, which is obligatory on the part of the C&AG, the propriety audit is discretionary.

The C&AG is responsible to the Parliament and as such he is a Comptroller as well as an Auditor-General. But unlike UK, the executive can draw money from public exchequer without the approval of C&AG. The new role, which is somewhat vague and overlapping makes him more of a Auditor-General. The 1971 Act expects the C&AG to audit:

(1) All stores and stock of all government departments.
(2) All receipts and expenditure from the Consolidated Fund of India and of the states and union territories.
(3) All transactions relating to the Contingency Funds and Public Accounts.
(4) Accounts of all government companies under the Indian Companies Act, 1956.
(5) All accounts and balance sheets and subsidiary accounts kept in any department.
(6) All accounts of Central government corporations who's acts provide for audit by the C&AG.
(7) All accounts of authorities substantially funded from the Consolidated Fund.
(8) Accounts of any authority, even though not substantially funded by the government, at either the request of the Governor/President or at the C&AG's own initiative.

Audit implies the scrutiny of accounts and examine whether money has been spent according to law and procedures without violating norms of propriety and ethics. These pattern of audit is known as Regulatory Audit, Performance Audit and Propriety Audit including the three E-audit (efficiency, economy and effectively). As an Auditor-General, the C&AG is concerned with the legality, varsity and propriety of public spending. His office visits the ministries and makes a physical check on accounts books to ensure whether:

(1) Sanction has been accorded by the competent authority;
(2) The expenditure has been covered by sanction;
(3) The purpose for the grant was fulfilled;
(4) The expenditure conforms to statutory enactments, rules and regulations;
(5) The programmes involving investments are being run economically;
(6) The demand is supported by a voucher and the payee has acknowledged the payment;
(7) Due regard to principles of financial propriety has been given and
(8) The public sector units are yielding expected results.

This audit control is not only a negative check on accounts or transactions in a ministry or department, but it implies the interpretation of rules and procedure in the name of efficiency, economy and effectiveness leading to propriety. The variety of audit which C&AG does in India can be classified as:

(1) Audit of expenditure
(2) Audit of stocks and stores
(3) Audit of appropriations
(4) Audit of classifications
(5) Audit of authority
(6) Audit of propriety
(7) Audit of efficiency
(8) Audit of autonomous bodies
(9) Audit of public undertakings
(10) Audit of accounting

The Administrative Reforms Commission found these categories confusing and overlapping. It suggested four stages or categories to cover several varieties in a single process. The commission suggested:

(1) *Regulatory Audit*: This is one of the conventional forms of audit in government which seeks to ensure that various rules and regulations whether statutory or administrative are fully adhered to by government agencies.
(2) *Appropriation Audit*: Its object is to ascertain whether the money spent by the government has been applied to the purposes and within the limits set by the grants and appropriation authorised by parliament; the expenditure in excess of the provision is regarded as unauthorised until regularised by Parliament.
(3) *Propriety Audit*: It includes within its scope an examination of the propriety of executive actions even when their legality is not in question. It is generally recognised now that this type of audit which looks beyond the formal procedure of the expenditure to its wisdom, faithfulness, and economy is of equal, if not greater importance.

(4) *Efficiency Audit*: The extension of audit beyond the scrutiny of individual transactions in search of fraud, waste or extravagance, to an examination of the efficiency with which the agency or authority under audit is discharging its financial responsibilities. It entrusts to an external agency the appraisal of efficiency of government agencies – a function which can be regarded as their own internal responsibility.

Appropriation and regularity audit are the statutory duties of the Comptroller and Auditor-General who examines these two aspects of government transactions. The propriety and efficiency audits are discretionary in nature. The Comptroller and Auditor-General determines whether and to what extent he should extend his audit into these areas.

The role of C&AG as an auditor has been criticised by Dean Paul Appleby to the extent that he finds the office irrelevant and even harmful. His ruthless criticism of Indian audit blames the C&AG as a primary course of a widespread and paralysing unwillingness to decide and to act. Dean Appleby maintains "Auditors do not know and cannot be expected to know very much about good administration; their prestige is the highest with those who do not know much about administration". In his judgement "auditing is necessary but is a highly pedestrian function with a narrow perspective and very limited usefulness. The Comptroller's reports are mere substitutions of hindsight for the kind of judgement possible and necessary and proper at the time of action". The Dean questions: "What special competence for appraising objectives and appraising administrative performance in general has the Comptroller and Auditor-General? What is cabinet for, what is prime minister for, what is Parliament for, what are the individual ministers for, what is secretariat for, and what is a bureaucracy for?" He concludes, "Nothing could be more calculated to stop the plan in its tracks to undermine responsible government and to establish government of by and for auditors." This indictment of the Comptroller and Auditor-General of India is total and unqualified. In a democracy of India's size based on audit suffrage the role of audit cannot be dismissed as mere post-mortem work. He may be 'flogging a dead horse' but the Public Accounts Committee and Parliament cannot control public expenditure unless an independent expert agency comes to their rescue. The C&AG office may be an inheritance from colonial rule, but should be know much about good administration. Ashok Chanda, who himself has been a C&AG has stated the balanced position as under:

> In all recognised democracies audit is not just tolerated as a necessary evil, but is looked upon as a valued ally which brings to notice procedural and technical irregularities and lapses on the part of individuals whether they be errors of judgement, negligence or acts and intents of dishonesty. The complementary roles of audit and administration are accepted as axiomatic being essential for toning up the machinery of government.

True that audit discourages government officials from taking decisions and leads to shifting of responsibilities. The overall impact is negative because the procedures create an impression that it deliberately presents administration in bad light. Ashok Chanda further adds, "to steer clear between ignoring trifles and unintelligent literal interpretation is a difficult task of the auditor". The officers who have "nothing to do with the irregularities" have to recreate the sequence of events and defend their retired seniors when grilled before the Public Accounts Committee and the C&AG. It looks irritating and cruel to the witnesses and gives the impression that their bonafides are being questioned". Even full facts are not supplied to audit and the Public Accounts Committee have to ask for them. Audit is essential as an instrument of parliamentary and financial control and the C&AG was created to see to it that the expenses voted by Parliament are well utilised. The C&AG protects public funds and as a Parliamentary watch dog his criticism should be taken in the stride.

Control Through Parliamentary Committees

Parliament is a huge body with sovereign powers. Hence, it has to operate through its committee and the review of their reports from time to time. In the realm of these, parliamentary committees are specific and are vested with responsibilities of scrutiny of public expenditure, economy in public spending and controlling the irregularities and waste in the management of public enterprises. These committees are:

(1) The Public Accounts Committee
(2) The Estimates Committee
(3) The Committee on Public Undertakings
(4) The Standing Committee

The Public Accounts Committee in India was first created in 1923 at the Centre under Montford Reforms (1919). The departments of the central government were for the first time asked to justify their expenditure in details. Though, this body was not a real parliamentary committee, the finance minister was its chairman and the department of finance provided the secretariat of the committee. The Constitution makes no mention of the PAC but the Parliament derives its power to constitute such committees from Article 118 (i) of the Constitution. Originally, it consisted of 15 members, all from the Lok Sabha, but in 1953, the number was increased to 22 to provide representation to the Rajya Sabha. This inclusion marks a departure from the British practice. Pandit Nehru justified it by saying that "The association of the nominees of the Rajya Sabha with PAC was necessary because the Committee was purely investigatory and since under Article 151 (i) of the Constitution, public accounts and audit reports were to be presented to both Houses; it was open to the Rajya Sabha to appoint its own committee, but instead of two, it would be desirable if only one committee was appointed." The members of the committee are elected by the Parliament every year from amongst its members according to the principle of proportional representation by means of single transferable vote. Like Britain, a distinguished member of the opposition is invariably elected as Chairman of the Public Accounts Committee. Though the committee is elected annually, there is convention that there should be two-year term of membership to ensure continuity.

Though the chairman of the committee is appointed by the speaker, the rules provide that where the deputy speaker himself is a member of the committee, he will act as its chairman. The quorum for a meeting is four members and the chairman has a casting vote in case of a tie. The Lok Sabha rules also prohibit a minister from being chosen as a member of the PAC. Each major party is represented on the committee in proportion to its strength in the Lok Sabha and the Rajya Sabha. All shades of opinion are brought to bear on the working of the committee. Yet, no party affiliations are brought into the discussions and scrutiny of the transactions of the government are considered objectively. The one year tenure of the committee is found to short and it is suggested that this term should be coextensive with the term of the Lok Sabha and one-third of the members should retire annually. This suggestion has not been accepted but as a matter of convention, most of the members of the PAC are re-elected for a second term. This ensures continuity in its composition and approach. The function of the Committee as embodied in the rules of procedure and conduct of business is to satisfy itself that the money shown in the accounts books as having been disbursed were legally available for and applicable to the service or purpose to which they have applied or charged. The expenditure conforms to the authority which governs it. That every re-appropriation has been made in accordance with the provision made in this behalf under rules framed by competent authority.

The basic functions and duties of PAC are:

(1) To examine, in the light of the report of the Comptroller and Auditor-General, the statement of accounts showing the income and expenditure of state corporations, trading and manufacturing schemes and projects;
(2) To examine the statement of accounts showing the income and expenditure of autonomous bodies the audit of which may be conducted by the Comptroller and Auditor-General of India, either under the directions of the President or by a statute of parliament; and
(3) To consider the report of the Comptroller and Auditor-General, in case, where the President may have required him to conduct an audit of a receipt or to examine the accounts of stores and stocks.

The report of the Comptroller and Auditor-General constitutes the basis to ascertain whether the money granted by the Parliament has been spent by the government within the scope of the demands. The examination of the committee extends beyond the formalities of the expenditure. Legality, veracity and economy constitute the base on which the report of the Comptroller and Auditor-General of India is drawn out. The report is taken up ministrywise. The secretaries are obliged to appear as witnesses to explain the points raised in the audit. The C&AG remains the guiding spirit and he suggests the lines on which the committee should conduct its examination. He identifies the questions which need clarification from the official witnesses. The relation between him and the committee is close and intimate because he is the "acting hand of the committee, its guide, philosopher and friend". The effectiveness of the committee is largely determined by the thoroughness with which the audit examination has been conducted; likewise the value of audit criticism depends on the support it receives from the committee. Not only are the functions of these two authorities interrelated but there is a measure even of interdependence in their relations. This is emphasised by the fact that, by far, the bulk of the committee's inquiries are concerned with points which the Auditor-General raises.

The committee examines the report of the Comptroller and Auditor-General to find out that the money voted by Parliament has been utilised by the government 'within the scope of the demand'. It means the public expenditure has not exceeded the appropriations and the grant has been utilised for the purpose for which it was sanctioned by Parliament. The nature of items of expenditure compiled against a demand justify their being so compiled. The committee also reviews the form and details in which the estimates are composed and goes into the technical accounting procedure, to find its adequacy to control departmental extravagance. The committee may send for persons, papers, and records. The conclusions of the committee are submitted to Parliament in the form of a report. To enable intensive examination, the committee may take resort to the practices of consulting study groups, such as obtained in defence, railway departments. The Comptroller and Auditor-General submits interim reports to this committee. A convention has evolved that the recommendations of the committee are accepted by the government. Most of the issues are settled through mutual discussion and PAC probe relates to transactions completed and to damage done. It conducts a post-mortem examination of the public accounts yet its findings are of value as guidance and warning. The guidelines prepared by UK PAC are followed by the Indian PAC in its working. The committee must take up the question whether the money spent for a particular purpose has been fruitfully spent or not. The Committee should understand the intention and mind of the Parliament and express their judgement and discretion. It has to ensure that principles of economy have been followed and must maintain a high standard of public morality in financial matters. The committee members can argue, discuss and dissent but the moment consensus is reached, every member must support it.

The notes explaining the various excesses or savings mentioned under each head are sent within a period of two months. The committee selects a few important items for detailed examination for which a 'Key of the Audit Report' is circulated to the members and to concerned ministries by the Lok Sabha secretariat. The official representatives appear before the committee as witnesses to explain their position. The secretaries in India represent the administration and place the administrative point of view. The meetings of PAC are private and the government representatives come to give evidence. The examination of witnesses is initiated by the chairman, who stands briefed by the C&AG. The PAC is not concerned with the internal administration of the ministries or departments. Much time during the examination of witnesses is spent by the members in obtaining information on the organisation of departments. The committee does not function as a reprimanding authority because it does not name the delinquent and is not allowed to be mentioned. The committee tries to know whether adequate action was taken and on that basis it pronounces judgement regarding the adequacy of an action. To get information witnesses may be pushed in tight corner. But these meetings of the PAC are not held in a camera. A record of the proceedings is maintained, but not published. Documents of secret nature are submitted only to the chairman, and he has to preserve the secrecy. The report is prepared by the Lok Sabha secretariat under the guidance of the chairman and the advice of the C&AG. The C&AG makes factual verification and after his approval, it is presented to the Lok Sabha. Here ends the cycle of annual financial activity. The report of the Public Accounts Committee contain the committee's view and findings on the accounts of different departments. It only points out the misuse of public funds and offers remedies for preventing misuse in future. The sub-committees of the PAC can assist the PAC, if detailed investigation become necessary. Each sub-committee consists of four to six members, including the chairman. The C&AG assists these sub-committees and all the reports are considered as a whole in the final report. The interim report of the C&AG to PAC is submitted to avoid the charge that the scrutiny has become old and out of date.

The reports of PAC are published and scandals and irregularities reach the MPs, who discuss them when the reports are put before the Parliament. The reports are accepted and their recommendations are implemented. The committee may reconsider its advice in the light of the reasons given by the government. The contentions matters are sorted out through discussions between the PAC and the relevant department. Responsibility for taking action is the duty of the concerned ministry which keeps an eye on the implementation of recommendations. The ministry sends a response to the PAC on action taken in due course of time.

This action-taken report of the PAC presents highlights of the original report and the recommendations which have been accepted by the Government. The action-taken report contains recommendations which the committee does not wish to pursue and also those recommendations which the committee does not accept and makes a reiteration. Recommendations/observations in respect of which the government has furnished interim replies also form part of conclusions and recommendations. The findings of the committee and its periodical reports are compiled by the C&AG into Abstracts which serve as case laws in respect of financial matters as a guide to the departments. The examination of accounts is treated as a matter of national interest and not of party politics. The association of the members of the opposition assures MPs, that the government spending is going to be scrutinised with no special tenderness. The PAC has been suggesting reforms in the governmental procedures and has stressed adhering to the norms of economy and efficiency. It has been suggesting the separation of accounts from audit and introduction of a proper scheme of accounting and financial control. The Public Accounts Committee has a quasi-judicial role to play and questions those who have been responsible for undesirable deals. Its warnings cannot be ignored easily. The administration does pay attention to its recommendations and it trains the official and politician in responsiveness to public opinion and constructive criticism. The PAC creates a sense of fear in the civil servant which has a deterrent effect on his activities. The reports may not extensively debated in the Parliament but they are useful to those who like to use them. The PAC reports can shake a department out of its complacency or may administer a rude shock. The committee ensures discipline and acts as a check against slackness, negligence, arbitrariness and other defaults on the part of executive.

The Public Accounts Committee does not interfere in the internal administration of departments. It does not concern itself with matters of policy. There is no obligation on the part of the executive to adopt the reports of the committee. Questions may be reserved for reconsideration by the committee in the next session. If an inquiry is to be carried out, it is done at the instance and demand of the C&AG. The C&AG is a source of strength and helps the committee in its deliberations. He may be a source of weakness too, for the weakness of his audit. The PAC is sometimes accused that the delayed presentation of reports reduce their utility. Ad hoc enquiries and reports can enhance the value of the committee's work. The irregularities and losses to the public exchequer come to the notice of the Parliament late. There is scope for expediting the reports of the C&AG and also the reports made by the committee. There is very little discussion on the reports in the House. Besides focusing attention on the shortcomings in the working of government departments, the acceptance of the PAC recommendations by the Central government represents the strength of Indian political system. The fear of scrutiny is a great check on negligence and wasteful public expenditure.

The Estimates Committee

The expenditure has to be within the grants passed by the Parliament for the purpose. But, a detailed examination of the estimates should also secure possible economy in the execution of public accounts. This is done by the Estimates Committee of the Parliament. Joh Mathai suggested the creation of Estimates Committee as a standing committee in 1953, and it is set-up every year from amongst the members of the Lok Sabha by a system of proportional representation and single transferable vote. It consists of 30 members, all belonging to the Lok Sabha. The chairman is appointed by the speaker and if deputy speaker happens to be a member of the committee he automatically becomes the chairman. No minister can be appointed in the Estimates Committee. The committee is renewed every year but one-third of its members retire every year. Conventionally they are re-elected year after year. The Estimates Committee suggests 'economies' in expenditure, and is called a 'Continuous Economy Committee'. The Estimates Committee ensures that minimum expenditure is incurred within rules. The functions of the committee are:

(1) To examine whether the money is well laid out within the limits of the policy implied in the estimates;
(2) To report what economies, improvements, efficiency or reforms, underlay the estimates prepared in policy planning;
(3) To suggest the form of estimates for presentation to the parliament; and
(4) To suggest alternative policies to bring efficiency and economy in administration.

The Estimates Committee suggests possible economies and if it finds that a particular policy is not leading to the expected results or is leading to waste, it brings to the notice of the Lok Sabha about the change. It prepares its plan of work for the year and may constitute sub-committees to examine matters. The reports of these sub-committees are deemed to be the reports of the whole committee. The committee may send for papers, persons, and records and its study-groups can undertake on-the-spot study of the projects under examination. A copy of the report is sent to the ministry in advance for verifications, and then it is submitted to the Lok Sabha. There is no formal debate on the reports of the Estimates Committee which usually contain recommendations for improving the presentation of the estimates. The committee has suggested valuable administrative and financial reforms besides acting as a 'Standing Economy Committee'.

The Estimates Committee in India is not organised on party lines and can present a better picture of economy and efficiency in administration. The control exercised by the committee has advantages. It is judicial in approach which combines the people's approach and prevents the executive from being apprehensive. The Estimates Committee offers a training ground for the legislators to influence policies and thereby it serves as a link between the people and the government. The Committee has justified its existence by discharging its functions successfully. "The Committee's emphasis on review of the policies of government and of the structure of the departmental organisation has substantially altered the character and purpose of the committee. Instead of a fact-finding body, it is converting itself into fault-finding mechanism. With its floating membership it can hardly be sufficiently familiar with the details of administrative processes and problems to be able to suggest fruitful lines of administrative reform. The Committee is arrogating to itself a role which constitutionally belongs to the House of the People. The recommendations of the Committee on matters of administrative reorganisation, reconstitution of departments and redistribution of functions have hardly any practical utility."

The Standing Finance Committee of 1921 constituted under the Government of India Act, 1919 still determines its operations. It is the House in miniature as it represents the parties and groups in the Lok Sabha more or less in proportion to their representation in the House. Considering its importance, the Speaker of the Lok Sabha takes due interest in its working.

The estimates of public undertakings are outside its purview. It follows a selective approach and makes a selection of a few ministries, and a few subjects in some ministries to be examined during the year. The committee concentrates on a few ministries and also on only a few selected subjects within a ministry or a group of ministries. The committee reviews the estimates only after they have been presented to the House. It keeps reporting to the House as the work proceeds. It has no role in the framing of estimates and in the voting of demands in the Parliament. It cannot disallow any expenditure. As an advisory body, it examines estimates after they are passed and suggests economies.

The estimates committee examines the classification and form of accounts presented to the Lok Sabha. The secretariat of the committee examines the estimates and ensures that the classification of the items under 'charged and voted' are proper. The rules prescribe the form in which the ministries furnish material under nine headings. The information pertains to the organisation, volume of work, schemes or projects undertaken, expenditure incurred, reasons for variations, and report by the ministry concerned. The questions are framed by the Estimate Committee on the basis of the information and responses of the questionnaires issued by the committee. A detailed scrutiny is undertaken on-the-spot, witnesses are examined as in the Public Accounts Committee. The officials and non-officials experts participate in the proceedings and help each other to understand their respective problems. The oral and written evidences result in tentative guideline on the basis of which, the secretariat prepares the report. The report is sent to the concerned ministry for confidential verification of factual details. Each report contains recommendations for improving the organisation, for securing economy, and for providing guidance in the presentation of the estimates. The minister gathers support on general proposition on political grounds and the recommendations are given acceptance by the government. The committee sees whether the recommendations are adhered to or not, and the ministry has to send replies from time to time. The estimates committee also prepares a follow-up report showing the implementation status of the recommendations. Members of the Lok Sabha may question the government about non-compliance of the recommendations. The committee suggestions act as guidelines for regulating expenditure. The committee not only suggests economy, but initiates reforms in the overall budgetary practices. The reports create awareness and have educational value. In addition to regular reports, ad hoc reports, horizontal reports, survey reports of the committee deal with procedural matters in financial administration. The Estimates Committee is an expert body of non-experts. The C&AG does not participate in its deliberations. Due to the vast expansion of governmental activity, the committee has to selects three to five ministries and only a few selected areas in a session.

The impact of the Committee on the thinking of the government is substantial and "If the House is not free to use it as it wishes, it deprives itself of the most natural means of obtaining information and advice". It functions in a quasi-judicial atmosphere, and yet, the final effect is not that of pronouncing a verdict. It also has a positive impact on civil servants and the fear of public exposure keeps them alert. It is a training ground for the members of the House. The reports educate the public on the functioning and performance of the government. The committee serves as a moral check on the activities of all departments and ensures that the tax-payer's money is spent efficiently.

Committee on Public Undertaking

Lanka Sundram, an MP suggested the creation of such a committee in 1953. The V.K. Krishna Menon Committee examined the matter in details. Following a series of deliberations, the Lok Sabha adopted a motion to set up a committee on public undertaking (COPU) on May, 1964. The committee has 22 members – 15 drawn from the Lok Sabha and 7 from the Rajya Sabha. As a convention, the committee functions on a non-party basis. The members are elected according to the principle of proportional representation by means of a single transferable vote. The tenure of membership of the committee is 5 years. One-fifth of the members, however, retire by rotation. The functions assigned to the committee are:

(1) To examine the autonomy and efficiency of the public undertakings;
(2) To examine the reports and accounts of public undertakings;
(3) To examine the reports, if any, of the Comptroller and Auditor-General on the public undertakings; and
(4) To consider functions vested in the Public Accounts Committees and the Estimates Committee in relation to the public undertakings.

Initially, the committee had its jurisdiction over a dozen public corporations:

(1) Central Warehousing Corporation
(2) Industrial Finance Corporation
(3) Oil and Natural Gas Corporation
(4) Damodar Valley Corporation
(5) Mazagon Docks, Mumbai
(6) Garden Reach Workshop, Kolkata
(7) Air India International
(8) All government companies
(9) Bharat Electronics
(10) Life Insurance Corporation of India
(11) Indian Airlines Corporation
(12) Hindustan Aircraft Limited

The committee is not expected to discuss matters of government policy as well as matters of day-to-day administration. Also, it has no jurisdiction over those companies in which the government has the largest single share. The committee brought out its first report in April, 1965, and has since been publishing reports along with recommendations. It is a fact-finding committee and its function, essentially, is to help Parliament to have a more effective annual debate on the working of the public undertakings. The committee has submitted scores of report which constitute a rich mine of information to evaluate the working of Public Enterprises in India in the Pre LPG era. These reports can be classified into three categories.

(1) The reports that relate to individual central enterprises.
(2) The horizontal studies.
(3) The 'Action Taken Reports'.

In the first category reports, focusing on individual enterprises, references are made to all significant operational aspects of the undertaking. Numerous shortcomings in the management have been pointed out in relation to problems common to several undertakings. The horizontal reports of COPU have been of this nature. Most of the recommendations of the committee have been accepted by the government. The COPU has also made useful recommendations regarding the personnel departments of public enterprises. Some MPs want that the COPU should have co-equal powers with the Public Accounts Committee and the Estimates. The Administrative Reforms Commission had recommended that "the COPU should take up a group of undertakings falling within one area of enterprise and bring out one consolidated report on that particular public sector industry as a whole". The Parliament should focus its attention on core issues. The COPU should be backward-looking as well as forward-looking. The committee has also promoted a greater understanding between the members of Parliament and the management of undertakings. It has made public accountability of government enterprises effective but the committee has not been able to examine all the undertakings falling in its area of investigation. It could examine only about 50 per cent of appraisal reports on individual undertakings in the past. Moreover several important public undertakings in defence establishments have been kept outside the committee's jurisdiction. The government has failed to accept the COPU's recommendations and even those accepted have not been implemented. The one-year tenure of members of COPU has deprived MPs from developing specialisation in public enterprises. The ministers do not appear before parliamentary committees, and hence the executive accountability to Parliament has remained incomplete. The non-acceptance or non-implementation of COPU's recommendations are not even discussed in the Parliament. The tone and content of the reports of the committee have been unduly harsh. Often these recommendations have lacked consistency and have revealed that these have not always been negative. The policies of liberalisation and disinvestment of public sector enterprises have pushed this committee into oblivion. Yet the core sectors and the Navratana management is duly supervised by the Parliament through this committee.

Standing Committees

The standing committee system in the Indian Parliament got started in 1993. Seventeen standing committees, with 45 members each, 30 drawn from the Lok Sabha and 15 from the Rajya Sabha have been created. Half of the chairpersons of these committees come from opposition parties. The members are drawn from all the political parties in the Parliament and change annually. The committees have extensive powers to summon and grill public servants. These committees make the government departments more accountable. They screen legislation, assess policy statements and verify the claims made by the departments in their annual reports. Combining the British and the American legislative systems, the function of the Indian parliamentary standing committees is to scrutinise the demand for grants made by various ministries. The lack of legislative scrutiny of the executive's spending proposals requires scrutiny before hand. The major functions of these committees are (1) a non-partisan examination of functioning of government (2) monitoring and evaluation of performance (3) examination of supplementary estimates and feedback to Parliament and government on economic proposals. They make close scrutiny of legislative proposals, review of the implementation of laws, develop second line leadership/generate specialisation and expertise among members.

The standing committee system has radically altered the way of parliament's functioning and has strengthened the Parliament vis-à-vis the executive. The ministries and departments have become more careful in framing their demands. Even though, a majority of demands continue to be guillotined, the committees ensure that they are examined at least once. In the working of these standing committees most of the ruling party members have behaved in a non-partisan manner while questioning officials and preparing reports. The committees screen legislation, assess policy statements and verify the claims made by the departments in their annual reports. When the demands have been scrutinised beforehand, Parliament will have to spend less time on discussing the grants for each ministry. The reports of these committees though a "persuasive in value", help the government to take an informed view of subjects. These standing committees should embrace the entire spectrum of administration. They should provide:

(1) monitoring and evaluation of performance and examination of supplementary estimates;
(2) feedback of Parliament and government on economic proposals;

(3) close pre-budget scrutiny of all estimates and expenditure being voted;
(4) non-partisan examination of functioning of government departments;
(5) development of leadership, including its second line, in parliament;
(6) development of specialisation and expertise among members;
(7) review of the implementation of laws passed by parliament; and
(8) close scrutiny of legislative proposals.

The standing committee system is useful in many ways by altering the way of parliament's functioning. The ministries are more careful in framing their demands to avoid being pulled up for excessive wasteful and irrational demands. A majority of demands may continue to be guillotined but the committees ensure that they are examined. Even Atomic energy officials are asked to justify their demands. Most of the ruling party members of these committees behaved in a non-partisan manner. The parliamentary experience and organising ability is regarded as the test for the choice of the chairperson. Attempts are being made to ensure full attendance and the reports are submitted to the Parliament in time.

Thus, the budget in a parliamentary system has its procedures of executive and parliamentary control. The revenues raised and public expenditure incurred has to be accounted for and duly controlled by finance ministry and by Parliament through the instrumentality of the C&AG of India. When both the houses of Parliament finally pass the reports of PAC, the budget of the previous year stands executed and the process continues every year. The finance ministry and the executive departments have to take actions on the recommendations of Parliament committee reports and avoid the lapses in future.

Sunset legislation, ZBB, PB and PPBS are some of the recent techniques suggested as budgetary reforms by Hoover Commission in USA and Peter A. Phyn of a private company. The presidential system, because of separation of power does not have minister/secretary in the House of Congress to monitor the budget of the President. So the budget has to be self-explanatory to muster support of Congressmen and senators on the basis of its performance standards. Similarly, programme planning is needed in the American system where budget encounters ad hocism and deficit budgeting is to be avoided in the era of global spending by the President. In India, all these techniques were easily adopted because of their obvious advantages in a deficit economy and the availability of planned economy.

Sunset Legislation

Eliminating of undesired, outdated, redundant and irrelevant programmes requires a formal process of policy review. "It embodies the concept of self-retiring government programmes by providing for the termination of statutory authorisation of programmes. This is achieved by placing time limits on government programmes in the legislative enactments themselves and providing for their automatic termination on the prescribed dates unless, affirmatively recreated by legislature after conducting a detailed review." The sunset legislation with expiry dates ensures economy in government expenditure and avoids unnecessary expansion of government activities. It makes the financial resources available for new programmes and ensures administrative rationality by facilitating the reallocation of limited funds on a continuous basis. The sunset laws enacted by Parliament helps in overcoming the resistance met within the executive for eliminating an ongoing programme by shifting the major responsibility for its evaluation to the legislature.

Performance Budgeting of Hoover Commission

Earlier called as functional budgeting or activity budgeting the PB originated in USA. The term 'performance budget' was coined by the First Hoover Commission in 1949 which recommended the adoption of performance budgeting to make effective management approach to budget process. President Truman introduced it in the Congress in 1950. The concept of a PB is of recent origin but has become an integral part of the processes of reform in financial administration. This budget is radically different from the traditional budget, called 'line item budget'. It used to be prepared with a focus on the objects of expenditure, such as staff, buildings, equipment, etc. In sharp contrast of classifying the budgetary allocations, a performance budget undertakes allocations of expenditure by reference to particular objectives and functions. The shift in budgeting from itemwise expenditure to functions or activities has a profound significance in modern public administration. The performance budget presents public expenditure in terms of functions, programmes and activities, and stands out from the line item budget which used to emphasises staff, furniture and equipments. The ARC defines a performance budget as a technique for presenting government operations in terms of functions, programmes, activities and projects.

At a broad definitional level, performance budgeting can be most appropriately associated with a budget classification that emphasises the things which government does, rather than the things which government buys. Performance budget shifts the emphasis from the means of accomplishment to the accomplishment itself. A performance budget, starts off by analysing objectives of an organisation and decides under what general headings the expenditure can best be analysed functionally. (1) A *function*, in this context, means a major grouping or division of the total organised effort which is directed towards the accomplishment of organisation's purpose. (2) A *programme* is a segment of a function, whereas, (3) an activity or project is a division of a programme into homogeneous units of work. For instance health is a *function* which can be broken up into *categories* like: (1) Preventive Care and (2) Curative Facilities. These categories can be further split into *units* such as: (1) Outdoor Service (2) Indoor Care and (3) Intensive Care Unit. These unit of *activities* can again be classified into *programmes* or projects like: (1) Mother and Child Care (2) Anti-malaria Campaign, (3) Family Planning Programme and (4) AIDS Eradication Project, etc. The unit cost of each activity, though difficult but can be worked out. This can be multiplied to the patients served and an annual figure may be arrived at for allocation in the budget. Then in place of items like salary, food, medicine and equipment, the performance becomes the basis for budget formulation.

'Functional budgeting', 'activity budgeting', 'performance budgeting' are also called as 'programme budgeting'. To begin with they were synonymous expressions but of late the writers have begun to regard programme budgeting as an improvement on performance budgeting. (1) A performance budget focuses on works and activities of an organisation whereas programme budget or PPBS treats them as 'intermediate aspects' and concentrates on output analysis. (2) A performance budget strives for an improvement of the internal management of an organisation by using techniques like cost accounting, work measurement, and performance standards. As against this, a programme budget is a tool of management devised to measure an organisation's effectiveness. A programme budget, on the other hand, is basically an allocative device. The work done by the two Hoover Commissions in this field is original and is, of pioneering significance. Since 1950, the United States government has adopted the performance budget and several countries of Asia, Africa and Latin America have switched over to this technique of performance budgeting.

In India, the performance budget movement began in the fifties. The Estimates Committee of Second Lok Sabha in its twentieth report, recommended: "Performance-cum-programme system of budgeting would be ideal for a proper appreciation and the scheme of outlays included in the budget especially in the case of large-scale developmental activities." Pressed by the inadequacies of the existing budgetary practices, the Union government adopted the performance budgeting. Later on an American expert, Frank W. Krause, and the ARC Report on Finance, Accounts and Audit (1968) also recommended an early introduction of performance budgeting both at the Centre and in the states. The ARC suggested that the ministry of finance should assume responsibility for introducing the system and also to give lead to the states in the matter. The Central government announced its decision to introduce performance budgeting in four central ministries in 1968. In 1977–78, about 32 developmental departments in the Central government introduced performance budgeting in their selected units.

The concept of performance budgeting had aroused extravagant hopes. Its implementation has been deficient in many ways. The unit cost data have not been worked out properly. Though many projects extend over a period of years, the future years costs have not been shown in the performance budget. There is no correlation between inputs and outputs and setting of targets and measuring of performance is not very scientific in the absence of norms and standards. The technique has not been followed right down to each cost centre.

To make performance budget a useful tool for administrative management and financial control, in the implementation of programmes and evaluating of performance, it is necessary that the Parliament should make the executive accountable to it. The phases of performance budgeting need establishing a functional classification of governmental operations. Cost accounting and financial management should accord with functional classification. Quantitative hours and yardsticks of performance and unit costs provide timely feedback to the programme managers. The process of classification requires a comprehensive list of all the objectives and scope of work of the ministry. The functional classification should indicate the range of work of the ministry and lay down the programmes for allocation of funds on priority basis. The classification should facilitate the compilation of accounts and computation of costs.

If administrated properly the performance budget can show the results of the previous year and their unit costs. It can provide a true picture of spending and revenue alternatives and fix the responsibility very precisely. It shows who was responsible for what. The ARC (1966–70) lists the benefits of performance budgeting as under:

(1) It presents clearly the purposes and objectives for which the funds are sought and the programmes are designed in financial terms.
(2) It helps in better understanding and better review of the budget by the legislators.
(3) It improves the formulation of the budget and facilitates decision-making at all levels of government.
(4) It enhances accountability and provides an additional tool to management in financial operations.
(5) It renders performance audit more effective.

Unlike the line item budgeting, the performance budgeting emphasises on the purpose rather than the expenditure. It presents budget in terms of functions, programmes, activities and projects and establishes a correlation between the physical (performance) and financial aspects of each programme and activity.

The reports of Estimate Committees, Frank W. Krause and ARC point out the utility of performance budgeting, the purposes and objectives, the programmes and accomplishments the improved formulation of budget and the accountability of the management, render performance audit a purposeful and effective tool in modern fiscal administration. It has contributed to legislative literacy, better executive accountability and social audit of budget in a democratic polity.

Programme Budgeting (PPBS)

Performance budgeting or programme budgeting also known as planning-programming-budgeting system (PPBS) owe their origin to Hoover reforms. President of USA, Johnson introduced them but they were later abandoned in 1971. The PPBS was an attempt to integrate budgeting with overall planning for the government as a whole, and to make the planning, execution, and evaluation of government policies as systematic as possible. It has its roots in industry, where it was practised by the American automobile company – General Motors – since 1924. The department of defence adopted it in 1964. President Johnson prescribed PPB system for the entire federal budget in 1965.

The PPB laid adequate weightage on relative merits of alternative goals, programmes and projects and the different ways of carrying them out. It is viewed as an input-output system based on rigorous analysis which seeks to discover the relative advantage of given solutions compared with other alternatives. The centre for PPB is the budget. The methods used are planning and decision-making. The purpose can be called a more viable economy and improved coordination. The four main features of PPBS were identified as:

(1) Goals or the government and its programmes;
(2) the future year implications of the programmes;
(3) the analysis of pertinent costs; and
(4) the analysis of alternative courses of action and anticipated outcomes.

PPB lays down socio-economic objectives at each level and for each project and programme in the light of national objectives. It stresses identification of alternatives with their respective cost-benefit analysis. It requires continuous inter-agency coordination and periodic reviews and evaluations in terms of national goals. The problem that lead to decline of PPBs is its analytical nature which does not appeal to public servants. This system integrates the planning, programming and budgeting functions and incorporates a scheme of planning in the budgeting process. "PPBS emphasises the planning aspect of budgeting for selecting the best out of a number of available programmes and for optimising the choice in economic terms while allocating funds in the budget. It treats budgeting as allocative process among competing claims by using relevant planning techniques."

In India PPBS has been easy to get incorporated in national and state planning. Unlike USA, India has a Standing Planning Commission which undertakes a systematic exercise of planned development through regular Five-Year Plans. Each year the budget estimates are accommodated with plan allocations at each level and the programme planning done by the Planning Commission gets its authorisation by the National Parliament. The Five-Year Plan represents the capital budget and the fiscal arrangement decreed by the Finance Commission every fifth year is systematically annualised with additions, subtractions and alterations in the Budget. This streamlines the budgetary process with programmes and plans which was also the intention of Hoover Commission.

Zero-Based Budgeting (ZBB)

The ZBB also originated in USA and was developed by Peter A. Phyrr, a manager of a private industry in 1989. It was introduced in the US government by President Jimmy Carter in 1978. Like the performance budgeting or PPBS, the ZBB can also be called a rational system of budget making. Under this system, every scheme is reviewed critically and re-justified totally from zero, i.e., the scratch before being included in the budget.

ZBB is an attempt to base budgetary evaluation of all programmes and expenditures in terms of the entire budget request in details. It is different from conventional budgeting because in ZBB an administrator has to justify all the new proposals, and also the ongoing activities and the requirements of funds for them. To quote Peter A. Phyrr, "Zero base budget means the evaluation of all programmes. The evaluation of all alternatives and programme performance may occasionally lead us to completely rethink and redirect a programme in which case we 'throw everything out and start all over again'. However, in majority of cases, programmes may continue, incorporating modifications and improvements. For the majority of programmes, we will concentrate our analysis on evaluating programme efficiency and effectiveness and the evaluation and prioritisation of different levels of effort." ZBB technique involves a critical review of each scheme before a budgetary provision is made for the same. It requires each organisation to evaluate and review all its programmes and activities current or new on the basis of cost as well as performance. A scheme will not be funded merely on the ground that it was in the operation during the previous year and current year. Its utility, justification and performance will have to be established. The main idea behind ZBB is that the agency should justify its entire budget from the ground zero each year.

The peculiar features which make ZBB useful are:

(1) A comprehensive analysis of priorities, goals and objectives which make it realistic;
(2) Scrutiny of all new proposals and the continuing expenditures on existing activities and rejustification for the removal of unnecessary dead heads of expenditure;
(3) Optimum use of limited resources basing the ranking of the completed budget on relative cost benefit analysis;
(4) A pragmatic approach which offers a flexible management tone leading to savings;
(5) Programme effectiveness which make administration more responsible and responsive; and
(6) Better participation of executives in the budgetary process.

Similarly the problem areas of ZBB have been identified as under:

(1) Costly infrastructure and trained personnel;
(2) Ranking of decisions when costs and benefits are not quantifiable;
(3) Handling of large data-making which is a tough task; and
(4) Human bias in the selection of decision packages.

In India, the decision of introducing ZBB was taken by the Finance Minister, V.P. Singh in 1986. ZBB was adopted by major departments at the union level in 1987–88. The huge and unmanageable deficit was not only to be reduced but the detailed budgetary process was put on the wheels. It required (1) Clustering of departments, (2) Pruning of wasteful activities, (3) Closure and transfer of projects, (4) Renewed weightage on ongoing activities, etc. The new budgets started with a zero base and arrears were stretched over a period of time.

Thus, the ZBB involves a total re-examination of all schemes afresh from base zero instead of following the incremental approach to budgeting which beams with the estimation of the current expenditure. "The basic feature of a zero-based budget is that the departments, while preparing their budgets, should not take anything for granted and, therefore, should start on a clean slate. The budget making for the ensuing year should be started from zero instead of treating the current budget as the base or the starting point. The ZBB is an operating, planning and budgeting process which requires each manager to justify his entire budget request in detail from scratch and shifts the burden of proof to each manager, to justify why he should spend any money at all, as well as how the job can be done better." The ZBB technique eliminates or minimises the low priority programmes to improve programme effectiveness. In fact, it makes high impact programmes to obtain more finances by reducing tax increase. It facilitates critical review of schemes in terms of their cost-effectiveness and cost benefits to provide for quick budget adjustments during the year. It allocates the scarce resources rationally and has increased the participation of the line personnel in the preparation of budget.

The ARC Reforms

The department of science and technology was the first to introduce ZBB in India in 1983 and other ministries followed in the year 1986–87 fiscal year. The ARC's team on finance accounting and auditing examined the fiscal administration in depth and identified the ailments that afflict the fiscal system. Over a period of time, these problems have multiplied and cumulated into serious threats which need to be rectified by budgetary reforms. Some of these problems are:

(1) Tax evasion,
(2) Non-realisation of tax arrears,
(3) Black money in the economy,
(4) Corruption in administration, and
(5) Ineffectivity of control measures.

Since 1968, these problems have deepened and the policies of liberalisation and globalisation have added a number of new dimensions to tax policies, loan liabilities and scientific management of public revenues and expenditure. The ARC suggested:

(1) Financial year from November 1 to October 31, to have a better appreciation of fiscal resources.
(2) Performance budgeting to make the executive responsible and legislators better informed.
(3) Separation of audit and accounts which has already been done in 1976 with the appointment of integrated finance advisors to assist the head as chief accounting officer.
(4) Economic classification of central budget so that administrative efforts of the ministries get reflected in the budget. The suggestion has been accepted by the government.
(5) The Public Accounts Committee must undertake a positive exercise to review the implementation work of ministries involved in fiscal administration.
(6) The three audits or propriety audit should have an extended realm bordering on continuous budgetary reforms.

Thus, fiscal administration in India passes through the throes of change. The closed economy has opened itself to globalisation. The budget as a tool of coordination has become more relevant today than budget as a tool of control of the past. The managerial reforms presuppose tax reforms and radical change in budgetary processes of a parliamentary democracy. Development budgets have to be dove tailed with regulatory restraints of a deficit economy. Democratic development is what should be writ large on the budgetary theory of a fast transforming society in India.

13

Administration of Welfare and Development in India

One crucial component of Indian administration after independence is development administration including the administration of welfare of the teeming millions. It has caused a dichotomy of regulatory administration versus development administration which is euphemistically also called as plan and non-plan administrations. During Nehru period, community development was synonymous with planned effort for development and every Five-Year Plan inaugurated a series of welfare programmes or rural developments projects for socio-economic transformations in the countryside. The founding fathers while hammering out the Constitution realised the problems of economic poverty and social backwardness of the country and laid down 'Directive Principles' which had governed the principles of state policy in the operational fields of public policies during last several decades. The economic directives like 'equal pay for equal work', 'equitable distribution of national wealth', improvement in the standards of living and social security urged upon the governments to commit themselves to social change and welfare. Additionally, there are socio-cultural directive which enjoin upon the future rulers of the state to establish an equalitarian and humane society without distinctions and discriminations of caste, colour, sex and creed. The social justice and social welfare have been conceptualised as 'dignity of the individual' with socio-cultural rights consitutionally guaranteed by the right to equality before law and equality of opportunity for all. The weak, the women and the handicapped constitute a large section of Indian society and the republican polity is struggling to ensure justice – social, economic and political. The medieval backwardness, which hangs as a standing shame in the development of scientific temper, needs the eradication of poverty, massive efforts for social awareness and a humanistic revolution against brutalities and parochial behaviours. The Indian state launched this twin campaign of development and welfare right in 1950 and the movements gained momentum with every successive Five-Year Plan. The effective implementation of welfare plan projects required a strong developmental infrastructure to accelerate the pace of change in the countryside. The rural development was conceived as a strategy to enable specific target groups of people, poor, rural, women and backward, to gain for themselves more of what they need and deserve. It involved helping the poorest amongst those who must control more of the benefits of the rural development programmes purposely designed to facilitate a multi-faceted growth. The rural poor were to be provided opportunities for the utilisation of their potential in the process of goal-oriented change. It aimed to reduce pressure on cities to enable the use of resources and to reduce spatial disparities.

The problems like poverty, unemployment and backwardness were to be solved through democratic decentralisation, community development and Panchayati Raj. Initially rural development was somewhat synonymous with agricultural development but gradually it acquired a wider meaning in terms of holistic change, people's involvement and human empowerment for sustainable development.

Development has been defined by experts as a phenomenon of change plus growth. The change has to be socio-cultural while the growth can be measured in terms of per capita income, GDP and GNP. The government can initiate and monitor this change leading to growth or the vice versa. Once the infrastructure becomes conducive to the elimination of poverty and illiteracy, the welfare measures can be launched for the weak and the deprived and also for the welfare of the people in the main stream. The Constitution tries to identify these weaker sections or deprived people as members of Scheduled Castes and Scheduled Tribes. The later developments have added members of the OBC (other backward classes) minority communities and handicapped individuals. According to Kaka Kalelkar Report, women as a class are backward in India and all sorts of welfare programmes for these deprived or underprivileged groups constitute the core of welfare administration. Thus, broadly speaking, development administration and welfare administration are intimately interlinked, but they cannot be called 'synonymous'. The chart below explain the linkage between the two:

Articles 38, 39 and 46 of the Constitution envisage India as a welfare state, committed to the welfare and development of its people in general and of vulnerable sections of society in particular. The welfare programmes in the beginning were directed to provide some curative and rehabilitative services. But later on they got oriented towards empowering the disadvantaged and marginalised sections of Indian society. The ministry of welfare constituted in 1985 was renamed as the ministry of social justice and empowerment in 1998. Animal welfare was given to the ministry as an additional charge but the development of Scheduled Tribes was transferred to the ministry of tribal affairs in 1999. The responsibility for implementation of the schemes is shared between the Central and state governments. The Central government is responsible for formulating the policies and programmes besides coordinating and promoting implementation of allied services by the states.

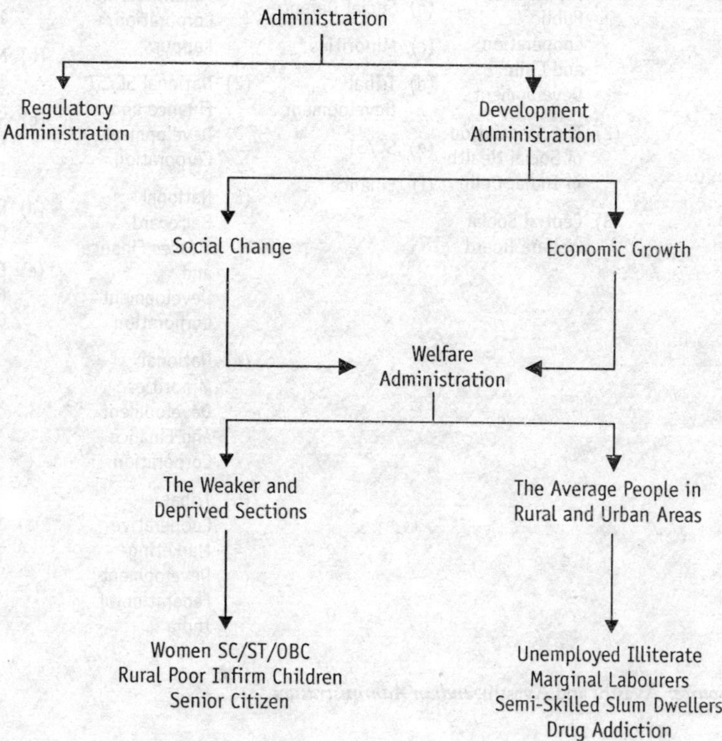

The Ministry of Social Justice and Empowerment

The ministry of welfare was carved out by integrating three specific areas: (1) welfare of SC/ST/OBC, (2) welfare of the disabled, women and handicapped, and (3) administration of *wakf*. After several reorganisations, today it stands as a ministry of welfare with departments of welfare and department of women and child development. The chart below explains the administrative organisation of the ministry:

Ministry of Social Justice and Empowerment: Administrative Organisation

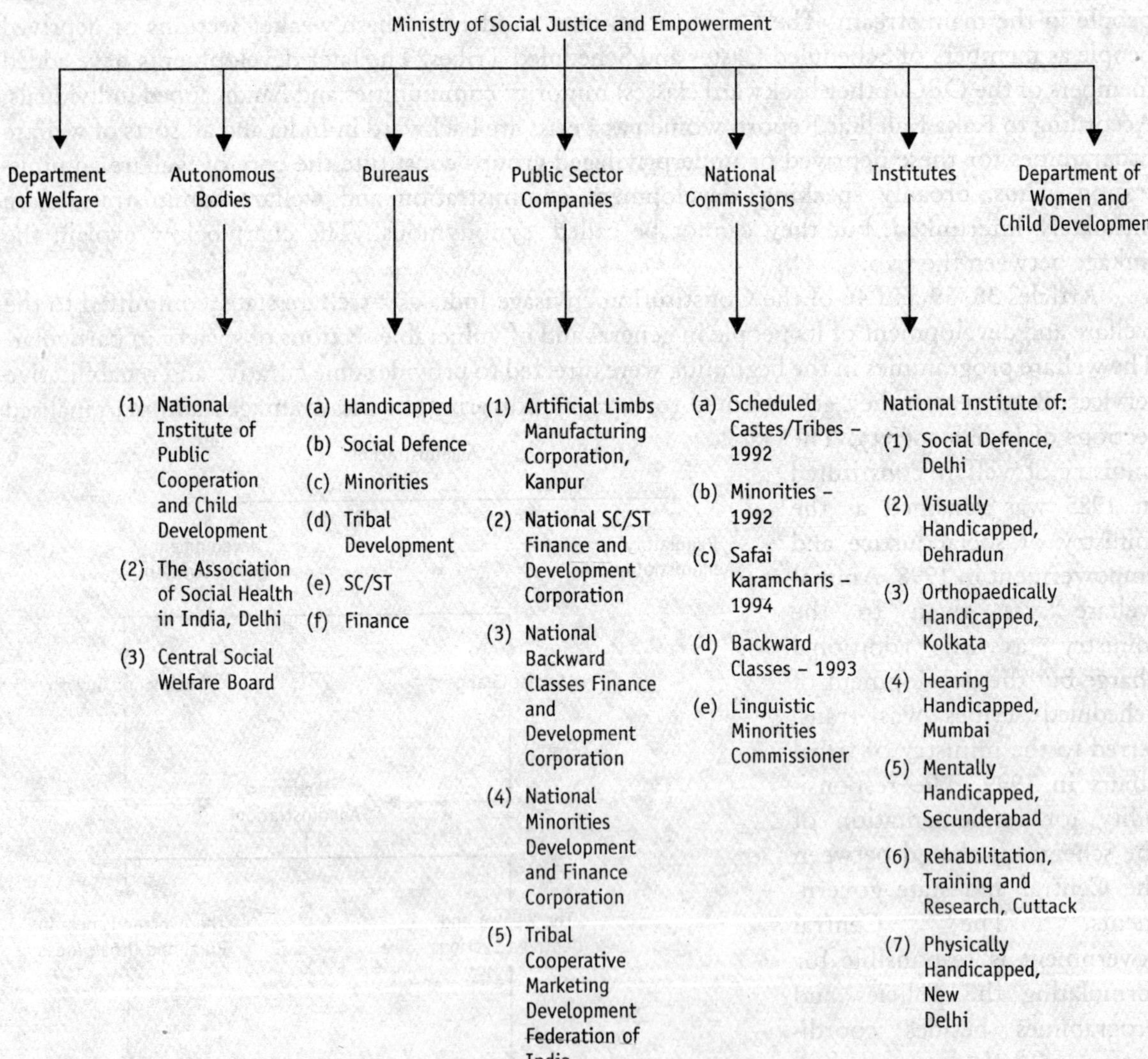

Source: Avasthi and Avasthi, *Indian Administration*.

The ministry is a nodal agency and much of its work is accomplished through field units and national commissions engaged in the tasks of coordination, training and facilitation to the target groups. (1) The two departments explain the focus of the ministry. (2) The seven institutes offer training and provide shelter houses. (3) The six bureaus function as administrative agencies. (4) The five commissions and three autonomous bodies handle policy matters and (5) five public sector undertakings arrange for finances, and facilities for development. As the governments' commitment to public welfare has increased, the ministry has developed a variety of staff and line agencies for policy making and policy monitoring in the field. The states have their respective parallel organisations and notwithstanding the overlap in functions, the social welfare administration of union and state governments have come out with innumerable scheme and projects for the welfare of the weak, the women and the deprived. Most of these commission's bureaus, institutes and corporations work in their respective fields and receive aids, grants and sponsored projects which they manage at their own. The autonomy of the field units is enhanced by the fact that the two departments of the ministry are far away in Delhi or in state capitals. The Central Social Welfare Board and National Commissions are directly concerned with the administrative coordination and supervision of schemes and projects in the field. Even policy formulation exercise is undertaken by the board and commissions. The bureau and institutes primarily take care of implementational aspects of policy in the area of social welfare.

Central Social Welfare Board (CSWB)

The Central Social Welfare Board is the key organisation in the field of social welfare in India. Created in 1953 it comprises of a full-time chairperson and members representing state and union territories. Its general body consists of 51 members headed by the chairperson. She is appointed by the government in consultation with the ministry of social welfare from amongst prominent women social workers. The general body consists of representatives nominated by state governments, social scientists, representatives from the ministries of finance, rural reconstruction, health education and social welfare and one member from Planning Commission. In addition three members of Parliament, social workers, social scientists and social welfare administrators are also included in the general body. The administration of the affairs of the CSWB is vested in an executive committee nominated by the government from amongst the members of the CSWB. The executive committee comprises of 15 members including the executive director.

The Board is administratively organised in a number of divisions and sections. The chairman is aided by a secretary who is of the rank of the deputy secretary or director in the Government of India. The CSWB has three joint directors, one financial advisor-cum-chief accounts officer, chief administrative officer and a public relations officer. The board assists in the improvement and development of social welfare activities. Its statutory functions are:

(1) To survey the need and requirements of social welfare organisations.
(2) To promote the setting up of social welfare institutions in remote areas.
(3) To promote programmes of training and organise pilot projects in social work.
(4) To subsidise hostels for working women and the blind.
(5) To give grants-in-aid to voluntary institutions and NGOs providing welfare service to vulnerable sections of society.
(6) To coordinate assistance extended to welfare agencies by Union and state governments.

The board coordinates between the programmes of the CSWB and other departments and also, between voluntary organisations and the governments. It is funded by the Government of India and the funds for the programmes as well as non-plan expenditure of the board are a part of the budget of the department of social welfare. There has been a significant increase in the total expenditure in the programmes of the board during last few decades. The nine divisions, two sections and one unit which constitute the organisation of the ministry can be presented as under:

Organisation of Central Social Welfare Board

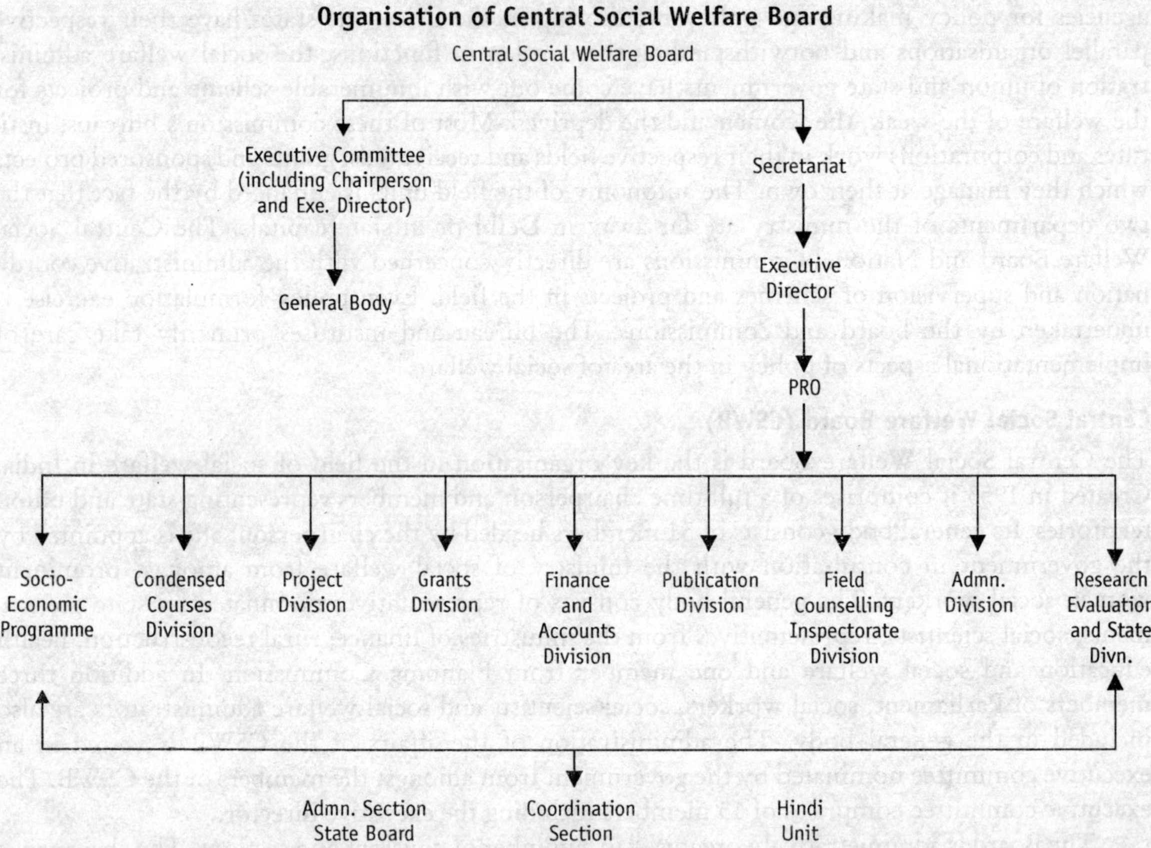

The names of the division are self-explanatory. For instance, project division looks after projects while grants-in-aids division processes and administers the distribution of grants the accounts of which are submitted to the finance and accounts division. Coordination and administration of state boards are handled by sections and Hindi unit is for assistance to all the divisions and their units in the field. The state social welfare boards have a similar and parallel structure but the regional and state variations exist in northern and southern states. The state social welfare boards have been established purely as advisory boards to advise the CSWB on the institutions requiring assistance and their eligibility to get such assistance, while the grants were sanctioned directly to the organisations by the CSWBs. These boards are also responsible to supervise, guide and advise the voluntary organisations in the welfare programmes in their respective areas. The CSWB has a wide network of its activities ranging from anganbaris to family welfare camps. Some of these welfare activities of the target groups are:

(1) Running of rehabilitation centres and cooperative societies for destitute, widows, orphans and deserted women and children.
(2) Educating and training women to acquire vocational skills to become employable.
(3) Organising family welfare camps to promote small family norm through opinion leads.
(4) Providing hostels for working women of low income groups with adequate security.
(5) Operating urban welfare centres in towns for recreational activities and learning programmes for women and children.
(6) Supplying nutritional supplementary diet and tonics to malnourished mothers and children below 5 years through balwadis and day care centres.

The CSWB consolidates the work done by voluntary agencies. It funds specific projects and strengthens welfare services for children, women and handicapped. The victims of drug abuse, infirm and retarded children and vulnerable groups of minorities are offered extra protection by the programmes of the ministry which directly as well as indirectly contribute to empowerment of the deprived.

The National Commission for SCs and STs

According to 2001 census, persons belonging to Scheduled Castes (SCs) constitute 16.48 per cent of population in the country. They fall in the category of weaker and marginalised sections of society. The Constitution of India guarantees equality before law to all. Social equality, right to education and reservation in employment and economic development are ensured by Article 46. Similarly, they have been given the right of political representation in the houses of Parliament, legislative assemblies and Panchayati Raj institutions. The National Commission for SCs and STs has a chairperson, a vice-chairperson and five other members. The responsibilities of the commission as enumerated in the act are:

(1) To investigate and monitor all matters relating to the safeguards provided for the Scheduled Castes and Scheduled Tribes under the Constitution or under any other law;
(2) To present to the President annually, and at such other times as the Commission may deem fit, reports upon working of these safeguards;
(3) To enquire into specific complaints with respect to the deprivation of rights and safeguards of the Scheduled Castes and Scheduled Tribes;
(4) To participate and advise on the planning process of socio-economic development of the Scheduled Castes and Scheduled Tribes; and to evaluate the progress of their development under the union and any state;
(5) To make in such reports/recommendations as to the measures that should be taken by the union or any state for the effective implementation of those safeguards and other measures for the protection, welfare and socio-economic development of the Scheduled Castes and Scheduled Tribes; and
(6) To discharge such other functions in relation to the protection, welfare and development and advancement of the Scheduled Castes and Scheduled Tribes as the President may, by rule, specify.

The commission while investigating and monitoring matters relating to safeguards under law have powers of a civil court trying a suit. The government consults the commission on policy matters affecting Scheduled Castes and Scheduled Tribes.

The National Commission for Safai Karamcharis

The National Commission for Safai Karamcharis was constituted in 1994 under the provisions of the National Commission for Safai Karamcharis Act (1993), to promote and safeguard the interest and rights of safai karamcharis or sweepers. It is empowered to investigate specific grievances and matters relating to implementation of programmes and schemes for welfare of janitors. The Commission is consulted on major policy matters affecting safai karamcharis, who suffer social humiliation and inhuman atrocities. The Untouchability (Offences) Act 1955 of the Parliament was thoroughly amended and renamed as Protection of Civil Rights (PCR) Act since 1976. The Act is administered by the state governments and some of the following measures have been taken by all the states and the union territories in the country:

(1) The Union government provides cent per cent matching grant to state governments against the expenditure incurred in the implementation of PCR Act.
(2) Effective guidelines and instructions are issued by the executive authorities to implement the provisions of PCR Act of the Parliament.
(3) Legal aid is provided to victims of untouchability by the state in specific cases.
(4) Special committees are making periodic reviews of the problems of untouchability and have made suggestions in all states.
(5) Special cells and squads have been established for initiating and supervising prosecution under PCR Act.
(6) Special mobile courts are functioning in untouchability prone areas of backward states.

The Prevention of Atrocities Act (1995)

Another significant landmark in the area came on Mahatma Gandhi's martyr day in 1990 when the Indian Parliament specified the offences in the category of atrocities and provided deterrent punishments for commission of the same. This Act known as POA (Prevention of Atrocities Act) has been in vogue since 1995. The rules, the special courts and the severe punishments under the Act go a long way to check atrocities against members of SCs and STs in different parts of the country. The parliamentary committee has been overseeing these measures and its recommendations are incorporated in the rules and regulations made to implement the constitutional safeguards. On the positive side, the National Commission along with National Scheduled Caste Finance and Development Corporation advances a varieties of grants and assistance funds to pull out the SC and ST people living below the poverty line.

Welfare of Scheduled Tribes

The Union government has a separate ministry for tribal welfare constituted in 1999. The ministry of tribal affairs has branched off from the parent ministry of social justice and empowerment. It is also a nodal agency for overall policy planning and coordination of programmes and projects for the welfare of the members of Scheduled Tribes. The districts where ST population is more than 50 per cent have been identified for modified area development approach. Pockets thickly populated by ST groups have been organised into clusters as special targets. Some of the programmes in the area of tribal welfare administration are:

(1) Schemes for tribal groups
(2) Special cent_al assistance programmes

(3) Grants-in-aid for tribal sub-plans
(4) Forest produce operations
(5) ST hostels and ST ashrams schools in tribal areas
(6) Tribal research institutions

As financial resources have been the usual alibi, the Government of India has come out with the Tribal Cooperative Marketing Development Federation of India with a chain of Gram banks to ensure remunerative prices of produce and financial support to the enterprising tribals. The National Commission and Finance Development Corporation (NSTFDC) is engaged in developing plan projects and monitoring their implementation through special funds and grants in sectors of tribal welfare and tribal development. Notwithstanding the criticisms of poor and dishonest performance, the following measure speak of governments efforts for the welfare of the tribals:

(1) A separate National Commissions for Scheduled Areas and Scheduled Tribes (NCSAST) has notified Scheduled Areas for Jharkhand, Chattisgarh and Madhya Pradesh. Empowerment of ST in 9 major states (AP, Jharkhand, Gujarat, MP, Chattisgarh, Maharashtra, Orissa, Rajasthan and HP) can be measured by allocation of 2,40,400 seats for tribal candidates in Panchayati Raj Institutions. In fact, 2,22,600 tribal leaders are participating in rural governance at the hustings.
(2) NSTFDC, a government undertaking with an authorised share capital of Rs 500 crores extends financial assistance to Scheduled Tribes at concessional rate for income generating schemes costing up to 10 lakh per unit. It provides grants for skill development programme for STs and fill the critical gaps by providing backward and forward linkages for activities undertaken by the target group
(3) A scheme known as Adivasi Mahila Sashaktikaran Yojana assists the Scheduled Tribe women below poverty line for small economic activities to augment their income with a loan of up to Rs 50,000 at an interest rate of four per cent per annum.
(4) Increased allocation of funds, availability of loans, grants for marketing support from NSTFDC have been to the tune of Rs 28 crores in 2002 and 42 crores in 2003.
(5) The SC and ST Order Amendment Act 2002 has modified the list of ST communities into 270 tribes by several inclusions and exclusions on the basis of experience of last several decades.
(6) Feature films like Abu Birsa and hundred documentaries have been produced for TV screening to create awareness about problems of tribal societies.
(7) Adivasi Mahila Sasaktikaran Yojana offers financial assistance up to Rs 50,000 to eligible ST women at a subsidised rate of interest, i.e., 4 per cent.
(8) The NGOs working for tribal development have not only been funded but their leaders have been trained through schemes like exchange of visits by tribals (EVT) and projects for educational modernisation.
(9) Special funds have been made available for quality education through Eklavya Model School, post-high school scholarships, equipped hostels for girls and boys, teachers quarters, and construction of modern educational complexes in tribal areas. Billions of rupees have been spent and thousands of jobs have been created with substantial investment in human resource development.
(10) Special assistance programmes have developed tribal sub-plans and crores of rupees have been invested in infrastructural development of tribal belts.

In the year 2000, the number of projects implemented through NGOs were more than 900. Over 0.25 lakh tribal students availed the benefits of free education from 106 residential school, 56 non-residential school and 95 hostels. Approximately, 1,115 teaching and over 2,000 non-teaching personnel were employed in these schools and hostels through NGO-run projects by the ministry.

Welfare of Other Backward Classes (OBC)

Ever since the Mandal Commission Report highlighted the problems of backward classes a new category called OBC has emerged in welfare administration of the country. The Constitution empowers the state to make provisions for reservation of posts in favour of any backward class or classes of citizens. The government has taken several steps for the socio-economic empowerment of the backward classes through implementation of schemes for educational development and concessional financial assistance for supporting their welfare activities.

The National Commission for Backward Classes Act, 1993 was enacted by Government of India for entertaining, examining and advising the Government of India on requests for inclusion and complaints of over-inclusion and under-inclusion in the lists of OBC of citizens. National Backward Classes Finance and Development Corporation has been established with the objective of providing concessional finance to the members of backward classes living below the poverty line. Some other schemes for educational advancement of the OBC students are:

(1) Pre-Matric Scholarship
(2) Post-Matric Scholarship
(3) Pre-Examination Coaching
(4) Hostels for OBC Boys/Girls
(5) Assistance to Voluntary Organisation for Welfare of OBCs

More recently a revision in the Reservation Policy is being contemplated for OBC candidates in private sector employment and technical education institutes. The government has increased the number of seats and access to higher and technical education is being encouraged to students belonging to the OBC sector.

Welfare of National Minorities

The government has notified and accepted five communities namely, Muslims, Sikhs, Christians, Buddhists and Zoroastrians as accredited minorities at the national level. The Constitution protects the interest of these minorities and recognises their rights to conserve their languages, scripts and culture and establish and administer educational institutions of their choice. Constitutional safeguards have been provided to minorities by setting up a National Commission for Minorities and Commissioner for Linguistic Minorities since 1992. The Commission review the implementation of policies of Union and state governments towards minorities and submits annual reports to the Union government. The Commission has a chairperson, a vice-chairperson and five members nominated from amongst persons of eminence, ability and integrity. The Commission endeavours for the welfare of the minority communities in varied ways. Its 15-point programme aims at:

(1) Promoting communal harmony and goodwill through socio-economic reforms,
(2) Ensuring adequate representation of minority communities in government employment, and
(3) Devising ways to present communal riots.

The Maulana Azad Education Foundation and National Minorities Development Finance Corporation are working in this direction. The ministry of social justice and empowerment has the responsibility of administration of Wakf Act, 1995 which governs the management of holy shrines and movable and immovable properties of Muslims recognised as religious, pious and charitable by Muslim law. The Durgah Khwaja Sahib Act, 1955 governs the administration of Ajmer Shrine. The Act does not apply to wakf properties located in the state of Jammu & Kashmir. The office of commissioner for linguistic minorities was created in 1957 in pursuance of Article 350-B of the Constitution which came into existence as a result of the recommendations of the State Reorganisation Commission. It looks into representations and complaints received from associations and individuals belonging to linguistic minorities. The Commission has its headquarters at Allahabad with regional offices at Kolkata, Belgaun and Chennai.

Welfare Administration for Women and Children

Women and minor children are accepted as a special group of citizens, who need protection and promotion at the hands of the state for the development of their social and moral health in society. The Directive Principles of State Policy of the Constitution talk about it and a special department of women and child development exists as a part of the ministry of human resource and development. The department formulates plans, policies and strategies for this special effort by the government. Legislation is being enacted and administrative coordination of efforts in private and public sectors is attempted to make conditions conducive for the development and welfare of the mother and the child. It is a nodal agency which initiates programmes and pursues follow-up measures. The welfare programmes include:

(1) support services,
(2) training for employment and income generation,
(3) gender sensitisation,
(4) awareness creation,
(5) capacity-building, and
(6) welfare of the target groups in vulnerable age situations.

The department has three autonomous organisations attached to it. They are: (1) National Institute of Public Cooperation and Child Development, (2) Central Social Welfare Board, and (3) Rashtriya Mahila Kosh. All of them work for the stated objectives.

National Children's Board (1974)

The Board is headed by the prime minister as chairman and has the minister of human resource development as vice-chairman. The functions of the Board are:

(1) to plan and review implementation of programmes for welfare and development of children;
(2) to act as high-powered national body to symbolise the commitment of the nation to the welfare and development of children. The Board serves as a national forum for interaction between voluntary agencies and the department.
(3) to coordinate efforts made by different governmental and private agencies in implementing programmes for welfare and development of children;
(4) to locate gaps in the existing services and suggest measures to eliminate such gaps;
(5) to suggest changes needed in priorities accorded to different programmes, and

The Nutrition and Child Development Bureau (NCDB)

The NCDB undertakes integrated child development services. The main programme for children is Integrated Child Development Services (ICDS) programme which is a centrally sponsored scheme. The scheme is the largest child development programme in the world which was launched in 1975. The objectives of ICDS are:

(1) Reducing incidence of mortality, morbidity, malnutrition and school dropouts;
(2) Enhancing capability of mothers to look after normal health and nutritional needs of child through proper health and nutrition education;
(3) Improving nutritional and health status of children in the age group 0–6;
(4) Laying foundation for proper psychological and social development of child; and
(5) Achieving affective coordination of policy and implementation among various departments to promote child development.

The ICDS programme offers a package of delivery of services to pregnant and wet mothers and their children below 6 years of age. The package includes:

(1) Health check-ups,
(2) Immunisation facilities,
(3) Health education to women,
(4) Supplementary nutritious meals, and
(5) Free preschool non-formal education,

The programme which started from tribal areas now covers hundred of villages through ICDS projects. Organisations like WFP (World Food Programme) and CARE (Cooperative for American Relief Everywhere) provide the support structure to this centrally sponsored scheme. The results have been spectacular as is evident in sharp decline in infant mortality rate and birth rate in the ICDS villages.

Day centres and creches for children of poor working or ailing mothers is another venture which the administration operates with the cooperation of voluntary organisations. The grants are provided to central social welfare board which engages NGOs to implement the scheme for children below 5 years of age. The crèches and day care centres provide immunisation and recreation facilities. The children can come and sleep here and got free meals and medical facilitation also. Several national organisations like Bhartiya Adimjat Sevak Sangh and Indian Council for Child Welfare have volunteered to implement the programme, whose services spread to all the states in the country. The programme started with 247 crèches covering 6,175 children in 1975, today has thousands of centres and lakhs of child beneficiaries in every state.

The ECE (Early Childhood Education) is a useful child help programme designed to improve communicative and cognitional skills as a preparation for primary school entry. The NGOs run these schools in rural areas and assistance is offered by the central government. Educationally backward states are preferred and thousands of these ESE centres which were formerly run by the ministry of education are now being managed by department of women and child development under new education policy since 1987–88.

Another programme known as wheat-based supplementary nutrition for preschool children and nursing and expectant mothers make use of surplus wheat stocks to improve nutritional status of children and mothers belonging to the weaker sections. This programme is meant to expand the existing supplementary feeding services by covering additional beneficiaries. Central assistance for the programme comprises supply of free wheat and supportive costs for other ingredients, cooking, transport, etc. The state governments are given wheat at issue price fully paid by them. The programme is completely aligned with ICDS and its nutrition programmes are being implemented since 1970 through five national level voluntary organisations, namely, Central Social Welfare Board, Indian Council for Child Welfare, Harijan Sevak Sangh, Bhartiya Adimjati Sevak Sangh and Kasturba Gandhi National Memorial Trust. Grant-in-aid under this programme is given towards honorarium for balsevikas/helpers and supplementary feeding of children. Children in the age group of 3–5 are covered under this programme. Supplementary nutrition consisting of 300 calories and 10 grams of protein per child per day is given for 270 days a year, besides social and emotional development of children.

Child Labour

The Constitution of India enjoins upon the government that children are protected against exploitation and against moral and material abandonment. Right against exploitation specifically prohibits 'Begar' and right to free compulsory primary education is accepted as a fundamental right. Still millions of children work in factories and are engaged in hazardous employment. Studies and surveys show appalling conditions. A majority of the working children are found in rural areas. In urban areas, they are found in canteens/restaurants or are found engaged in picking rags and hawking goods on footpath. But some children are working in highly hazardous conditions. For example, fireworks and matchbox units in Sivakasi in Ramanathapuram district in Tamil Nadu employ 45,000 children. A large number of children are working in stone polishing units in Jaipur, brassware industry in Moradabad, lock making units in Aligarh, slate industry in Markapur (Andhra Pradesh), Mandsaur (Madhya Pradesh) and the carpet making in Jammu & Kashmir. The government has initiated progressive legislation by asking the Parliament to enact:

(1) Factory Act, 1881 (hours of work)
(2) Child Labour Act, 1933 (prohibition of employment to minors)
(3) Factory Act, 1948 (safeguards to child labour)
(4) Child Labour Act, 1986 (regulation of condition of work)
(5) Juvenile Justice Act, 1987

The old acts have been radically revised. The national policy on child labour assures the elimination of child labour and even Supreme Court of India has severely punished the offending employers. The right to education goes a long way to offer opportunities to a child to develop his or her personality through capacity building which is the basic role of education. The Child Commission of India, on the lines of Women's Commission and Human Rights Commission should protect the interests of children and still more promote conditions conducive for versatile development of all children in varying age groups.

Welfare of Women

Women as a category need special treatment because of gender problems and motherhood liabilities. In India they have been subjected to cultural discrimination and being economically dependent on father, husband and son. Their development as an individual human being is a long journey for which special measures are needed. The Constitution makes a heroic proclamation that gender distinctions stand abolished and equality of sexes is guaranteed by the Constitution. Yet, in social life, evils like child marriage, sati, dowry, immoral traffic, sexual abuse and crimes of rape and violence are on the increase. The Constitution enjoin upon the government to protect the personality of woman, give her special facilities to become a citizen. This notion of welfare has created a special ministry for women and children in the Union government and the social welfare departments in state administration have a variety of laws, projects and scheme to administer in this regard. After 1950, enough has been done to promote female education, but the following measures deserve special mention:

(1) Criminal laws, namely, the Indian Evidence Act, the Indian Penal Code and the Criminal Procedure Code have been amended to make penal provisions against the offence of rape and other crimes against women, more stringent and also to make a new provision in the Indian Penal Code to make cruelty against women by husband and other relations punishable. Consequential amendments arising out of the Dowry Prohibition (Amendment) Act, 1986 have been carried out in the CRPC and the Indian Evidence Act. A new offence 'dowry death' has been included in the Indian Penal Code.

(2) A scheme for assisting the setting up of women's development corporations (WDCs) in all the states has been launched. Identification of women as individuals or in groups, preparation of viable projects, facilitating training, credit and marketing, etc., are some functions to be carried out by the proposed corporation.

(3) To train destitute women in the age group 18–50 in marketable skills, a scheme for setting up rehabilitation centres for women in distress have been started. The training is provided on residential and non-residential basis as per requirement. The scheme envisages training in both traditional and non-traditional trades for a period of not more than one year. It is implemented through voluntary organisations which are given 90 per cent assistance, shared equally by Central and state governments.

(4) To train women belonging to weaker sections and provide them employment on sustained basis, programme of income and employment generation is implemented through public sector undertakings/corporations/autonomous bodies/voluntary organisations. Assistance for the programme comes from Norwegian Agency for International Development (NORAD).

(5) To provide cheap and safe accommodation for working women belonging to low-income group, a scheme of construction/expansion of hostel buildings provides assistance for day-care centre for children attached to working women's hostels. It provides assistance to voluntary organisations to the extent of 50 per cent of the cost of land and 75 per cent of the cost of construction of buildings. A resident can stay in a hostel for a period of three years, extendable up to five years.

(6) The Suppression of Immoral Traffic in Women and Girls Act, 1956 as amended in 1978 and 1986 makes the provisions more effective and stringent and extend the scope of the Act to cover all persons whether male or female who are exploited sexually for commercial purposes. The Act is now called the Immoral Traffic (Prevention) Act, 1956. The Dowry Prohibition Act, 1961 as amended in 1984 and 1986 makes the offence cognisable, and enhances penalty of both fine and imprisonment and widens the scope of the Act to make it more effective. The Indecent Representation of Women (Prohibition) Act, 1986 seeks to prevent indecent display

of women through advertisements, books, posters, etc. The Commission of Sati (Prevention) Act, 1987 was a landmark legislation to prohibit commission of sati. It provides for more effective prevention of the commission of sati and its glorification. Punishment of any act of glorification of sati is imprisonment for a term which shall not be less than one year but which may extend to seven years and with a fine which shall not be less than Rs 5,000 but which may extend to Rs 30,000.

(7) The Family Courts Act was passed in 1984 for setting up of family courts in the country with a view to promoting conciliation in and securing speedy settlement of disputes relating to marriage and family affairs and for matters connected therewith. Department of women and child development has the nodal responsibility of CARE assistance in discrimination on ground of sex against women in employment. To prevent discrimination against women both at the time of recruitment and after, the Parliament has enacted the necessary law in 1987.

Thus, the administration of welfare has its roots in the Constitution. Today, it has developed into a huge countrywide network of organisations offering facilitations, services and infrastructural growth centre for welfare and development. The welfare state in India is a philosophy of the Constitution and the Fundamental Rights and Directive Principles of State Policy along with judicial activism have made it obligatory for the state to work in this direction. The various ministries, commissioners, departments and agencies at Union and state levels are actively engaged in formulating policies, implementing places and scheme and developing strategies to induct and monitor this desirable change so that the weaker sections may join the national mainstream and the average citizens also get empowered to undertake individual and social welfare. The Constitution identified these categories of people as members of SC and ST and over the years the concept of welfare administration has developed a variety of services for the underprivileged. Reservation policy has been the hall mark of social justice and the welfare administration in India remains dedicated to the protection and promotion of special interests of the members of Scheduled Castes, Scheduled Tribes, Other Backward Classes, minority communities, women and children, and infirm and handicapped citizens.

The welfare administrators in various ministries and autonomous organisations are supposed to protect the interests of these groups and their members in distress. Conversely, they should take positive measures to enable them to better their lot and face the social struggle with confidence. The problems being social and cultural, the welfare administration can do pretty little and the bureaucrats in social administration are often condemned for their callousness, apathy and jaundiced attitudes. The critics find social administration too bureaucratic to deliver goods and most of these services have discretionary pockets causing corruption and crime against the victims of social injustice. Yet, the welfare state can handle or size up these problems only through the machinery of the state. Even if the administration is weak, the other organisations like NGOs, political parties and interest groups are weaker. Even, the local bodies or private philanthropic or religious groups are unorganised and whatever grants are doled out by bureaucracy of social administration is not spent in an accountable way. The experience being mixed the social administration is being allowed to proliferate and new categories of target groups are being included. More and more funds are placed at the disposal of civil servants and non-government organisations to undertake this Herculean task with popular participation. In fact, it should become easier, if and when the country develops economically. The projections are that by the year 2020 the people below poverty line will be manageable, female literacy will touch encouraging limits and urbanisation along with technology will make India a developed country at par with the rest of the world. One may call it a dream but economic development is the surest way of social welfare also. Indian administration has been deeply engaged in this development exercise through planning. The transition has been too long but it was somewhat inevitable.

Administration of Development

Development has been viewed as a complex phenomenon of change that needs high investment in social values. As a concept of cherished change for higher values, it is a responsibility of family, school, religion and political system which shape human personality through socialisation. This requires initiation and monitoring which the state has to do in developing countries which are seeped in social stagnation. The students of development administration call it the administration of development which in simpler words means administration of those government sponsored schemes and plan projects which ultimately catalyse change. The administrators in India, who are well trained in the management of *status quo*, dread change and development in their hands has been rather too slow. Riggs call this phenomenon as the lack of administrative development. The civil servants in developing countries like India do not possess the capacity and will to initiate requisite and desired change. The result has been that the administration which does not want change is paradoxically looking after the administration of change or development. The Government of India launched dozens of schemes and projects for rural development which the state and district administrations are implementing haltingly without much administrative development of their public services.

Having failed to induct Planning Commission in the Constitution of India in 1950, Pandit Nehru took to the road of community development under the aegis of bureaucracy. Several programmes of intensive agricultural development, marginal farmers and labourers development and small farmers development were conceived and launched in selected blocks for specific target groups. The advent of the Green Revolution helped in changing the scenario further and as the names suggest the farm and farmer's development was the priority. Intensive Agriculture Area District Programme (IADP), Small Farmer Development Agency (SFDA), Marginal Farmers and Agricultural Labourers Development Agency (MFALDA) identified small areas and stressed upon marginal farmers. As the agricultural revolution advanced in the country, several allied areas got added up to these schemes and new programmes like Command Area Development (CAD), Desert Development Programme (DDP), National Rural Employment Programme (NREP) and Training for Self-Employment (TRSEM), etc., were launched for poverty alleviation.

It is difficult to classify these development programmes of administration into specific categories. Some of them have been production-oriented while others have objectives like equity, infrastructural development and institution building. During Indira Gandhi period, these programmes developed populist overtones and the phase of Janta government added new components through dozens of new projects and schemes for social justice. Rao government had to continue with this policy of rural development and the Integrated Rural Development Programme (IRDP) of 1978–79 which it received as a legacy, gradually got linked up with the constitutionalised version of Panchayati Raj for its district level implementation. The beneficiary group-oriented programmes aimed only at employment generation (NREP, JRY, Food for Work, etc.) or at poverty alleviation (SFDA, MFAI) or at social change (DWACRA). The area development programmes did not neglect the target beneficiary group orientation and programmes like CAD, DPAD, and DDP had facilities as sub-components with water management and infrastructural expansion as their key priorities. A break-up of these programmes from the point of view of development administration in India can be attempted as under:

During Nehru Period (1950–65)

The Congress governments emphasised upon agricultural production and community participation as is evidenced by some of the schemes listed below:

(1) Bhoodan Movement 1951
(2) Gramdan Movement 1952
(3) Community Development Programme (CDP) 1952
(4) National Extension Service (NES) 1953
(5) Applied Nutrition Programme (ANP) 1958
(6) Panchayati Raj (PR) 1959
(7) Intensive Agriculture District Programme (IADP) 1960
(8) Hill Area Development Programme (HADP) 1960
(9) Tribal Area Development Programme (TADP) 1962
(10) Intensive Agricultural Area Programme (IAAP) 1964
(11) High Yielding Variety Programme (HYVP) 1965
(12) Intensive Area Development Scheme (IAD) 1965

During Indira Gandhi Period (1965–1980)

The emphasis shifted to Garibi Hatao and 20-point programme for the benefit of teeming millions. This led to a spate of programme enumerated below:

(1) Small Farmers Development Agency (SFDA) 1969
(2) Agency for the Development of Marginal Farmers and Agricultural Labourers (MFAL) 1969
(3) Drought-Prone Area Programme (DPAP) 1970
(4) Rural Works Programme (RWP) 1971
(5) Crash Scheme for Rural Employment (CSRE) 1971
(6) Pilot Intensive Rural Employment Projects (PIREP) 1972
(7) Employment Guarantee Scheme (EGS) 1972
(8) Command Area Development Programme (CADP) 1973
(9) Minimum Needs Programme (MNP) 1974
(10) Twenty-Point Programme 1975
(11) Habitat Movement 1975
(12) Food for Work Programme(FWP) 1976
(13) Antyodaya 1977
(14) Desert Development Programme 1977
(15) Operation Barga 1977

(16)	Comprehensive Area Development Programme	1978
(17)	District Industries Centre (DIC)	1978
(18)	Integrated Rural Development Programme (IRDP)	1978
(19)	National Rural Employment Programme (NREP)	1980
(20)	Training of Rural Youth for Self-employment (TRYSEM)	1980
(21)	Whole Village Development Programme (WVDP)	1980
(22)	Special Programmes for Women and Children (SPWC)	—
(23)	Programmes for Depressed Areas (PDA)	—
(24)	Tribal Area Development (TAD)	—
(25)	National Seeds Programme (NSP)	—
(26)	Scheme for Development of Women and Children in Rural Areas (DWCRA)	—
(27)	Intensive Pulses Development Programme (IPDP)	—
(28)	Summer Moong Production Programme (SMPP)	—
(29)	Intensive Cotton Development Programme (ICDP)	—
(30)	Village Small Industries (VSI)	—
(31)	Khadi and Village Industries Programmes (KVIP)	—
(32)	Dairy Development Programme	—
(33)	Bio-Gas Programme (BGP)	1981

During Post-Indira Period (1980–2000)

After the lifting of national emergency, the Janta government and (late) P.V. Narsimha Rao government took to the philosophy of social justice and Panchayati Raj and some of the welfare programme bear a testimony to this change:

(1)	Self-Employment to Educated Unemployed Youth Programme (SEEUYP)	1983
(2)	Rural Landless Employment Guarantee Programme (RLEGP)	1983
(3)	Economic Rehabilitation of the Rural Poor (ERRP)	—
(4)	Planning for Development of Villages Programme (PDVP)	—
(5)	Integrated Rural Energy Programme (IREP)	1981
(6)	Western Ghats Development Programme (WGDP)	—
(7)	National Wasteland Development Programme (NWDP)	—
(8)	Special Incentive Programme for the Industrially Backward Areas	—
(9)	Rural Labour Employment Guarantee Programme (RLEGP)	—
(10)	Accelerated Rural Water Supply Programme (ARWSP)	—
(11)	People's Action for Development (India) (PADI)	—
(12)	The Social Forestry Programme (SFP)	—
(13)	A Tree for Every Child Programme	—
(14)	Operation Flood I (OF I)	—
(15)	Operation Flood II (OF II)	—
(16)	Rural Growth Centres (RGC)	—

(17) Renewable sources of Energy in Rural Areas (RSERA) —
(18) Special Inputs in Area Development —
(19) Special Food Grains Production Programme (SFPP) 1986
(20) Special Rice Production Programme (SRPP) 1986
(21) Forest Farming for Rural Poor (FFRR) 1986
(22) Indira Awas Yojana (IAY) 1986

During Bajpai Period and Later (since 1999)

From Narsimha Rao to Bajpai was a big political change but the BJP government and later on the Manmohan Singh government have continued with the erstwhile programmes. The advent of Panchayati Raj has caused a big difference in the political scenario. Naturally, the contents, directions and strategies have changed. Some of these programmes are:

(1) National Oil Seed Development Programme
(2) Massive Programme for Assistance to Small and Marginal Farmers for Agricultural Development
(3) Special Animal Husbandry Programme/Livestock Production Programme
(4) Assistance to Allottees of Ceiling Surplus Lands
(5) Minor Irrigation Subsidies for Solar Pump, Windmill, Drip, Sprinkler, Man and Animal Powered Lifting Devices
(6) Bonded Labour Rehabilitation Scheme (BLRS)
(7) Integrated Child Development Scheme (ICDS)
(8) Adult Education, Functional Literacy, Shikshakarmi Schemes
(9) Women Development Programme (WDP)
(10) Rural Artisans Programme
(11) Krishi Gyan Kendra (KGK) and Krishi Vigyan Kendra (KVK) Scheme
(12) Lab to Land Programme
(13) Jawahar Rozgar Yojana (JRY)
(14) Swach Jaldhara
(15) Swarna Jayanti Gram Yojana
(16) Antyodaya Yojana

Most of these schemes once launched, continued or later got amalgamated in other schemes. They have little to do with political ideology but the successive governments in India changed their strategies or nomenclatures to claim credit for achievements. All these schemes are ministry-based or ministry sponsored for which funds are allocated in the Five-Year Plans. After 1993, the concept of DRDA has redefined some of these schemes and like IRDP, they are being reintegrated with the distinct level plans of development assigned to Panchayati Raj bodies.

The main objective of administration of government sponsored development was to pull out the rural folks from poverty and ignorance which reinforce each other. Most of these schemes were conceived at union level or by the Planning Commission but their implementation had to be done by officials of state or district administrations, along with NGOs and Panchayati Raj bodies. Planning from below was the rhetoric but centralised planning kept on determining priorities and providing funds which civil servants spent for fixed targets in a time bound manner. The implementing machinery, being far away in the field, the review committees or coordinating agencies kept on shifting the approach to rural development with the result that by 1980 the Sixth Five-Year Plan had to come out with integrated rural development plan in place of diffused schemes in the field. The purpose was to make rural development balanced and rounded one and the IRDP was conceived as development of the rural society in all its facets. The IRDP was invented to remind all concerned that the new approach stands for integrated performance, an integral part of totality of national economy. It implied total development of the area and the people through institutional and attitudinal changes in a package of services. For this, the extension methods will include expansion of infrastructure and allied services in areas like health, education, basic civic amenities and family planning. The ultimate objective will be to improve the quality of life in the rural areas.

The Integrated Rural Development Plan

IRDP has been a major programme that provides a key component to development administration. It covered the primary sector like agriculture, irrigation, animal husbandry and minor projects in non-farm sector. In the secondary sector, IRDP concentrated upon village industries, *siri* culture and training for self-employment. The tertiary sector took care of shops and cottage industries at village level. The special beneficiaries under IRDP are the members of SC, ST and women. Special provisions for a specific percentage of the total funds are allocated for these categories. The IRDP has been self-employment-oriented and the development of infrastructure has established linkages through district supply and marketing societies (DSMS) to DRDP beneficiaries. The women have been accorded special treatment under rural development programmes. For instance DWCRA, i.e., development of women and children in rural areas is a part of IRDP. It provides skills, training, employment and credit to women. The Jawahar Rozgar Yojana reserves 30 per cent employment opportunities for women. Under the programme TRYSEM, the minimum coverage has been 40 per cent. The IRDP provides productive assets and inputs to target groups. Financial assistance in the form of subsidies is provided by the government and financial institutions. The subsidies are advanced and their limits vary for small farmers, agricultural labourers and rural artisans and people belonging to the Scheduled Tribes. Minor irrigation projects are free from ceiling limits. Training to the eligible beneficiaries for capacity building and technology has enabled the beneficiaries to take benefits from these schemes. These integrative programme of development, have brought varieties of people to their fold and the BPL beneficiaries have come out in increasing numbers with every Five-Year Plan.

Command Area Development (CAD)

Year of Launch	1973
Objectives	All round development of the command area of the major irrigation projects.
Strategy	One administrative unit based on natural resources of activity and cutting across administrative boundaries.
Activities	Water management, groundwater exploitation, consolidation of field channels, scientific drainage, enforcement of cropping pattern, timely supply of inputs, creation of support services and extension of training.
Functional Components	(1) improvement in irrigation system through development of canals, (2) as construction and maintenance of drains, (3) on-farm development including water development, updating land records and realignment of field boundaries, (4) agricultural extension system, research and agricultural cooperatives, and (5) command area development including processing of industries, forestry, pastures, care of animals and control of diseases.
Weakness	Rich farmers reaped the benefits, weak cooperatives, marketing problems.

Desert Development Programme (DDP)

Year of Launch	1977–78
Scope	Hot and desert districts of Gujarat, Rajasthan and Haryana and cold deserts of Himachal Pradesh and Jammu & Kashmir.
Objective	Controlling the desert, restoring ecological balance, stabilising sand dunes, improving economic conditions.
Activities	Afforestation, groundwater development, water harvesting, rural electrification, development of horticulture, semi-culture.
Functioning Agencies	Union and state governments implementation through DRDA since Seventh Five-Year Plan.

The Drought Prone Area Programme (DPAP)

Year of Launch	As rural works programme in 1970–71 converted into DPAP in 1973.
Objectives	(1) Promoting development works to end drought rather than schemes of employment, generation. (2) Water resources development of the area; (3) Afforestation through farm forestry and pasture development; (4) Productive use of water resources; (5) Soil and moisture conservation including water harvesting; and (6) Encouragement to dairy, forestry and fisheries.
Funding	Shared by Union and state governments.
Activities	Moisture soil and water conservation, checking of soil erosion, preventing floods, recharge of groundwater, and increase areas under irrigation.
Operational weaknesses	Watershed identification caused conflicts, non-availability of bank credits, loan system defects and defaulters untrained staff, unbankable proposals, no timely action for recovery of dues.

Small Farmers Development Agency (SFDA) and Marginal Farmer and Agricultural Labourers Development Agency (MFALDA)

Year of Launch	1969 (small and marginal farmers identified on the basis of land holdings as recommended by National Commission on Agriculture).
Objectives	Agriculture and horticulture development, change in cropping patterns, soil conservation, land shaping, poultry and dairy development – goat and sheep rearing.
Activities	At district level, funded by union government and administered by state agencies.
Weakness	(1) Lack of publicity, (2) Absence of land reforms, (3) Red tape of procedures, and (4) Wrong identification of beneficiaries. (5) Selective coverage of districts by SFDA and MFAL in DPAP districts. The DDAs, SFDAs, MFALs – all became DRDAs when IRD covered the country.

National Rural Employment Programme (NREP)

Year of Launch	1980
Objectives	(1) Strengthening the rural infrastructure, (2) Improvement of the nutritional standards, (3) Creation of durable community assets, and (4) Generation of gainful employment.
Activities	Social forestry, soil and water conservation, minor irrigation works, construction of primary school buildings, rural water supply works, land shaping and water management.
Funding	50:50 sharing basis between central and states through DRDA and Panchayati Raj Institutions.
Weakness	Absence of proper survey, non-need basis of projects – magnitude of rural unemployment, poor assessment by Gram Sabhas.

Rural Landless Employment Guarantee Programme (RLEGP)

Year of Launch	1983
Basic Objectives	Employment opportunities for rural landless, creation of durable assets, strengthening of rural infrastructure.
Funding	Hundred per cent by Central governments partly in cash, partly in kind (food grain).
Activities	Construction and reclamation of watersheds, social forestry, minor irrigation, works employment up to 100 days in a year for one member of the family – wells for SC and ST.
Weakness	Too ambitious – administrative procedures and multiple supervision.

Jawahar Rozgar Yojana (JRY)

Year of Launch	April, 1989
Objectives of the Yojana	Generation of employment to the unemployed and underemployed in rural areas, strengthening of rural infrastructure, assets formation and better quality of life.
Scope	One member per family, below poverty line sector to have employment for 50 to 100 days in a year covering 44 million families in 120 districts.
Activities	Rs 80 to 100 thousand rupees annual aid to every panchayat. Asset building works: (i) having potential of benefits to the poverty group, (ii) those who directly use the assets, (iii) sale of facilities created by the assets to ensure continuing income, and (iv) construction of houses, social forestry, minor irrigation and soil and water preservation works.

Strategy: Special preference has been given to SC/ST and freed bonded labour for employment. Thirty per cent of the jobs are reserved for women in programmes, DRDAs and Panchayati Raj institutions. The Million Wells Scheme (MWS) provides irrigation wells, free of cost to poor and Indira Awas Yojana (IAY) provides construction of dwelling units, free of cost, for the poorest of the poor belonging to SC/ST and freed bonded labourers. The achievements of the JRY have been outstanding in the areas of employment generation and infrastructure building in countryside with its focus on weaker sections.

Training of Rural Youth for Self-Employment (TRYSEM)

As the name shows, the target groups for TRYSEM are rural youth who are employable but lack training to get employed.

Year of Launch	August, 1979
Objectives	Training rural youth in agriculture, business and services in the age group from 18 to 35 years.
Scope	Trainees from amongst small farmers, agricultural labourers, landless rural artisans, women, SC and ST groups.
Training Areas	Handloom printing, weaving, oil extracting, tailoring, poultry through poly techniques and workshops for few days or week with monthly stipend.
Strategies	VLW identifies the potential beneficiary, block selection committee interviews and selects after training, credit support is provided, repayment procedure are liberal. Follow up programmes are organised.
Weakness	(1) Improper selection of trainees (2) Undue concentration on a few vocations (3) Neglect of the aptitude of the trainees, (4) Poor infrastructural support to the trainees, and (5) Lack of follow-up of the trained youth.

As a part of JRY, the TRYSEM programmes have been revised and modified several times with addition allocation and innovative projects. The earmarking of funds under IAY has been increased and the benefits have also been extended to non-SC and ST families. A part of the wages paid to the skilled labourers has been included under the wage component. The expenditure on a house under Indira Awas Yojana has been increased in the plains and in remote hilly areas. The district collector inspects and his senior officers visit the sites and ascertain the execution.

Rural development through rural roads is a part of the minimum needs programme in the state sector. For providing safe drinking water to rural folks, the Union government sponsors Accelerated Rural Water Supply Programme (ARWSP). The national mission on drinking water has been active since 2000. Efforts are made to provide one source of water. It can be one tubewell with handpump for 150 persons. Similarly, programmes of rural electrification have been activated and more than 85 per cent of villages have been covered. Agricultural marketing regulations, information about prices, development of market yards are undertaken by the directorate of agriculture marketing in the states and Krishi Upaj Mandi Samitis. The scheme conducts market research and undertake market planning and design. The land reforms policy stands outlined as under:

(1) Abolition of intermediary tenures like zamindars and jagirdars.
(2) Ceiling on agricultural land holdings and distribution of surplus land.
(3) Tenancy reforms.
(4) Consolidation of land holdings, for rationalisation of agriculture, and
(5) Updating of land records through computerisation.

The ministry of rural development of the Government of India sanctions funds for assistance to allottees of ceiling surplus which is processed through DRDAs. Biogas is being harnessed as an alternative source of energy through decomposition of animal and vegetable wastes. The BDOs motivate the farmers, prepare their loan applications and submit them to the concerned banks for sanction under the aegis of DRDA.

The Pre-Panchayati Raj Era

All these development schemes and the administration of development and social welfare in the pre-Panchayati Raj era has a special significance because it paved the way for neo-development administration under Panchayati Raj. Before the passing of two Amendments 73rd and 74th, the development projects were a near preserve of bureaucracy and the funding came from the Union government and its ministries to initiate rural transformation. The state government as a middle level tier supervised this development exercise through district collector and other functionaries like BDO and VLW at levels below. The machinery for the implementation of the development plan projects did not follow any uniform pattern. The ministries at Central or state levels played the nodal agency and the bureaucracy engaged in operational activities also supplied inputs for new plan formulations which was called planning from below. The inauguration of Panchayati Raj in 1959 and its later setbacks kept the state and district machinery in command and all schemes integrated as IRDP or centrally sponsored schemes made their cumulative contributions for holistic development by mitigating poverty, removing backwardness and generating employment for rural people in general and weaker sections in particular.

Four decades of community development through government monitoring and intervention (1952–1992) has created a healthy and productive unrest in the countryside. Notwithstanding the debate that rural bureaucracy was corrupt, elitist and inefficient the fact remains that the present administration of development and social welfare through Panchayati Raj have been unworkable had the administration of plan projects not preceded it earlier. The ministry of rural reconstruction was set up in 1979 as a department in the central ministry of agriculture and irrigation. In 1982, it was given a nomenclature, i.e., the department of rural development under the ministry of agriculture. The other departments of the ministry were the wasteland development department and the department of rural employment and poverty alleviation. It has the nodal responsibility of planning and monitoring development projects relating to rural development. The central committee for IRDP has nominees of the home ministry and the Planning Commission. In fact, almost all ministries involved in development administration have a direct concern with the formulation and execution of the programmes.

The states have separate departments to deal with the problems of rural development. The rural development departments looked after the programmes of the centre and the matters relating to Panchayati Raj. Some states has development commissioner to co-ordinate the developmental activities. In other states, the chief secretary acted as the development commissioner. The State Level Coordination Committees guided the department of IRD and other special schemes. In each district, IRDP was implemented by the DRDA. The organisation for the implementation of the IRDP was located at the district level. The collector presided over the district 20-Point Programme committee. At the block level, below the BDO, and a variety of technical extension officers, executed developmental programmes in areas like agriculture, cooperatives and industry. The VLW at the cutting edge acted as field agent for implementation of IRDP schemes and the targeted groups. The voluntary agencies of farmers were encouraged to participate. The Reserve Bank of India sponsored National Apex Bank for Agriculture and Rural Development (NABARD), which advanced credit for rural projects and undertook the responsibility of training and research in rural development activities.

The development administration in India has essentially been an integral part of plan administration for which the Planning Commission evolved a very elaborate mechanism at Yojana Bhawan. As the Planning Commission was an extraconstitutional body the central ministries collaborated in the plan process and made funds available but there was no corresponding machinery at the state level to assist and report. Some states constituted state planning boards which worked with development commissioners and development department of states with varying levels of effectivity and success. For instance, Bihar Planning Board set up in 1973 remained dysfunctional all along. The Gujarat Planning Board (1980) worked for five years only. Tamil Nadu had a full time non-official chairman in its Planning Board. Karnataka Planning Board performed advisory functions. The Madhya Pradesh Planning Board was too weak but the Maharashtra state appointed only a sub-committee of a dozen ministers under the chief minister which functioned effectively. The experience of UP, Punjab, Haryana was disappointing. Rajasthan state constituted the Board in 1973 but reorganised the same in 1990 with chief minister as chairman and planning minister as vice-chairman. The other members were chief secretary, development commissioner, finance secretary, secretary (policy planning), secretary (special schemes), organisation, and special secretary (planning). The other members were finance minister of state for planning and 18–20 part-time members out of whom 8–10 would be experts in different subjects/fields and 8–10 people's representatives/distinguished persons/of social service institutions, etc. Most of these Boards in states were entrusted with functions like perspective planning, policy-formulation and determination of sectorwise priorities of state plans. To strengthen the base of plan formulation the board offered guidance to the implementation of plan programmes. They identified the regional imbalances in developmental sectors and suggested measures to mitigate them.

The state planning boards, during the pre-panchayati phase, were a dismal failure. The state chief ministers took little interests and used the boards as agencies to extract funds from Union treasury. Planning at state level was the responsibility of development commissioner and his bureaucracy with the result development became doling out funds and receiving statistical reports of performance from the district authorities and below. Most of the problems of development administration or management of welfare projects emanated from this tier which administered development like a traditional department of revenue or agriculture. The state boards were flooded with non-experts and the efforts concentrated on receiving projects and funds and passing them on to the district administration.

The story at district and block levels is not very different partly because a busy and over-worked collector passed on the responsibility to his administrative junior and the accountability pattern was neither adequate nor rigorous. The block level hierarchy of the BDO concerned itself to the rules and the beneficiary groups were ignored as unwilling partners. Before 1993, the collector, the BDO and the VLW along with a team of extension officers spent crores of rupees under various plan projects. Some of its result are more than visible but obviously much more could have been accomplished if district administration would have responded to the call and intentions of the union government.

Pressured by the reports of review committee, the state governments gradually realised the non-bureaucratic or political awareness aspect of development and a beginning was made by constituting district rural development agency (DRDA) for the implementation of IRDP. Each district was to have its own DRDA registered under the Societies Act (1958). But it functioned like a government department. The collector has been the chairman and his planning team consisted of economists, rural industries officer, district superintending engineer along with members of panchayat samitis. A typical DRDA in most of the states had been constituted as follow:

The District Collector as its chairman. The other members includes MPs and MLAs of the district. Head of the central cooperative bank project director-cum-additional collector (development) are added to provide the beneficiary component. Chairman, regional rural bank and the Zila Pramukh, senior-most officer of the leading bank general manager, District Industries Centre, District Family Welfare Officer, Regional District Officer, Scheduled Caste Finance Corporation, representative, district milk union are also members to make it broad based. Two representatives of the weaker sections, one of whom may be drawn from among the SC/ST beneficiaries of the programmes and one representative of rural women are also added.

As a governing body, the DRDA formulates policies and coordinate district level plans and schemes sponsored by various agencies. Its functions and roles have been varied. Implementation of IRDP being the major responsibility the DRDA normally performs the following functions:

(1) The information feedback to district and block level agencies about requirements of programmes.
(2) Submission of a periodical report of its working to the state government.
(3) Plan and project formulation by obtaining proposals and coordinating them at the state level committee.
(4) Preparation of blockwise development plans in the district.
(5) Institutional credit to beneficiaries for financing plans.
(6) Identification of BPL families.
(7) Securing inter-sectoral and inter-departmental coordination.
(8) Publicity to the achievements made under the programme.
(9) Implementation of area-based, and combined programmes.

The executive committee of every DRDA works through an executive committee which finalises the sectoral annual plans which are later inducted into the Annual Action Plan of the district. The committee finalises the input requirements, training programmes and infrastructural facilities needed. The DRDA works in cooperation with various kinds of rural officials like additional collectors, district planning officers, assistant engineers, and project manager.

The DRDA review the progress of IRDP and takes decisions about sectoral plans and annual action plans. It approves the list of beneficiaries and takes stock of funds and expenditures incurred on projects. The departments concerned with IRDP at the state level can send its representatives to the committee, while the relevant district level officers are included as members of the executive committee. The IRDP programme has a wide spectrum and the DRDA implements the schemes under the umbrella in phases. The identification of genuine beneficiaries or deserving persons and household needs screening through the gram sabhas and panchayats. The final lists are approved by panchayat samitis and state departments of rural development. Credit planning and management for IRDP schemes is done with the collaboration of cooperatives, commercial banks and regional rural banks and NABARD. The subsidy share is passed on to the beneficiary in kind and not in cash. The subsidy is disbursed along with the loan and a purchase committee is constituted for the purchase of assets. The after care and follow-up plans are executed by various kind of official of developmental bureaucracy. As per rules, the progress of beneficiaries is monitored and evaluated in a planned manner. Quarterly and monthly reports on the programmes are sent to the Government of India and the Planning Commission. The progress is also monitored through a computerised rural information system (CRISP) with the National Informatics Centre (NIC). Its findings are that a substantial part of assistance has gone to the weaker sections of Indian society. A Reserve Bank of India study identified some areas of non-achievements of IRDP. They were:

(1) non-homogeneity of the poor
(2) poor resource endowment of weaker sections and
(3) unpreparedness of the poor to deal with their benefactors and with the market.

The study report recommended a tightening of the loan-disbursed process and linking subsidies to performance. Credit mobilisation and per capita investment have been accepted as yardstick for measuring success in IRDP.

The Post-Panchayati Raj Era

The post-panchayati phase of development administration in India commences since the introduction of Amendments 73rd and 74th in the Constitution in 1993. The three-tier constitutionalised federalism being a novel experiment makes it obligatory on the rulers at centre and in states to classify their position and thinking about the third tier. The amendments only out line the structure of district polity but how should it operate and develop relations with other tiers is a matter of constitutional conventions and practices. During last ten years, two elections of Panchayati Raj bodies in all the states have taken place and it has destabilised the system of district administration and state level polity in its political complexion. The political leaders of state and district level bureaucracy see a direct threat to their power and are apathetic, if not hostile to this democratic development. The panchayati change being irreversible is being scandalised by vested interests who find rural India ill-prepared for a democratic transformation in the countryside. On the contrary, the new forces are not satisfied with mere development administration but have started struggling for the end of diarchy. The demand from district administration to district governance is being voiced and development administration is accepted as a training ground for emerging panchayati leadership of rural India. Naturally, the old system of plan projects, grants-in-aid and sponsored schemes has to be reorganised to strengthen Panchayati Raj bodies. The union government has decided to funnel all its resources directly to elected bodies of Panchayati Raj and the collector and the development commissioner as intermediary in the disbursement of funds allotted to MPs and MLAs, etc., will be dispensed with. As and when this change comes the Panchayati Raj bodies should scan the previous experiences of development administration and pin point the specific reforms needed to intensify development and social welfare. Although, no catalogue can be prepared about the inadequacies and ineffectiveness of rural development programmes, but an objective analysis reveals that much more could have been accomplished had there been a political will and an administrative strategy to indent change in the stagnant rural society of India. Some of the following lacunas, if studied with care, can keep panchayati bodies of future to plan a view and to be conscious about:

(1) Rural development in India through its ill-trained, elitist and urban bureaucracy is an anathema and a contradiction of perspectives. Most of the development projects launched and implemented without testing their feasibility have remained on paper and ultimate lost in the corruption of the pipeline.

(2) The rural development plans schemes, projects ill-conceived at Delhi or state capitals could not identify the beneficiary target groups and the benefits went to the affluent and the influential. Wherever it went to the real poor the recovery system of the banks has caused bad debts of public funds.

(3) The poor and shoddy implementation of rural development scheme generated a wave of frustration among villagers because the efforts aroused a mounting tide of expectations without corresponding results.

(4) The most serious weakness of development administration was voiced by Balwant Rai Mehta and Ashok Mehta reports, which documented absolute non-involvement of people with the bureaucratic claptrap of officials. Even, the VLW proved a sort of patwari who rural 'sahabs' than the real poor. The people feel that development is a dole distribution by district officials.

(5) The developmental bureaucracy had an alibi that there were no non-government organisations or voluntary groups at block level. Naturally, popular non-government leadership will take its time. But, the worse is that whatever community participation is available at village level is ill-motivated and corrupt which makes development exercise vulnerable to further exploitation of the weak and the poor.

(6) The administrative cost of rural developmental plans has been prohibitive. The administrative procedures have been alien to the induction of technology. Even the most sophisticated scheme were lost because the infrastructure could not be built in the absence of the basic infrastructure.

Thus, the road to hell was found paved with best institutions. The district officials claim that they worked against extraordinary odds which do not exist today. The people can be excused that they could not perceive the change and did not distinguish between wolves in sheep's clothing. The centre and state governments assert that they pumped colossal amount of money in rural development and had very honest intentions for a genuine transformation. Thus, nobody can be blamed but the fact is that even the most reasonable or even the minimum has not happened with exorbitant costs in sixty years time. This raises basic questions like should rural development be attempted by government through special project agencies or should the extension services be multidisciplinary or single department oriented? What roles the NGOs informal groups, government agencies and Panchayati Raj bodies should play in the process of rural development? The search of, coordination and efficacy in rural change is an endless process of experimentation. It should stop at some point.

With the advent of Panchayati Raj, the administration of economic development and social welfare in India has entered into a new phase democratic change and popular participatory development. In place of administrative coordination, the problems of holistic and sustainable development has to be worked out in terms of policies. The models of decentralised planning in states like Gujarat, Karnataka and West Bengal reflect attempts of diffused programmes and funds at district level. The rationale of district planning has to rest on the involvement and participation of the people of the district. The grass roots planning must generate a psychology of development and a movement for socio economic change through popular participation. Decentralisation through district planning must enable a better perception of the needs of the local areas. Better informed decision-making should lead to achieve better coordination and integration, ensuring effective participation of the people for improved productivity.

A district in India is large enough to serve as a viable planning unit. It has a pattern of administration with internal consistency and administrative relationships. The delimitation of panchayati, parliamentary and legislative constituencies are broadly close to the boundaries of the district. All information about land records, irrigation works, development and social services is organised on a district basis. Naturally, district level planning of development through PRIs will have to the destiny of the present-day dyarchy, which should get dissolved, with development. The states should have regular and standing Planning Commission of experts to tag district plans to the state plans of the planning commissions. An integrated approach to district development should lead to organisational integration and coordinated devolution. The district planning will have to have an extended role in spatial planning with overall responsibilities pertaining to identification of local needs; taking stock of resources of the district and mapping of amenities at every level. Formulation of district plans and policies in their socio-economic, spatial and temporal dimensions; and coordination, monitoring and overseeing of the implementation of the district plan and programmes deserve special emphasis. The people and panchayat leaders should be active participants in this process of planning for district development. The comprehensive planning should earmark the share of every participant and the beneficiary. A single but rigorous methodology will have to be adopted. It should involve: district profiles, objectives, data, strategy and thrust areas, inter-block balance, physical and financial components of the plan with assessment of resources.

Of course, the state government will finally decide about the nature and scope of district level planning. But then, it is certain that as PRIs get their roots in the soil the conditions, situations and role of the union government will be decisive factors in the organisation and process of district level planning for rural development. The role of the collector and technical services with and should undergo a sea change if the panchayati civil services are constituted by the states. The tenure system may continue but a new state development service will be the need for the administration of development at district and below. The operational phases may take a few decades but the initiation limited decentralisation and autonomous development will be an evolutionary process of planned development. The state governments committed to the strengthening of Panchayati Raj must define the scope of district planning and sectoral schemes, disaggregate plan funds and formulate criteria for inter-district allocations. Strengthening plan capability and horizontal monitoring machinery below and linking it with monitoring mechanisms at higher levels by setting up district planning board of popular representatives can result in establishing planning procedures for Five-Year Plans and annual plans of state and Centre.

Gradually, it will lead to sectoral planning within the frame of district planning. It will introduce the concept of free funds and encourage limited localism in district planning. The delegation of extensive powers and streamlined procedures for dovetailing of district plans into state plan will help the annual plan budget of the Five-Year Plan. As the Madhya Pradesh Digvijay Singh Model suggests that the shift from district administration to district government will be a logical culmination of the evolutionary parliamentary process, the district planning system will enlarge localism to cover decision-making in all sectoral activities. It may involve administrative reforms to delegate decision-making powers at the district level. The encouragement and facilitation of a high level of popular participation will develop budgetary practices that would encourage local initiation, regional collaboration and national perspective.

Thus India, in 21st century, will be operating a polity wedded to the ideals of democracy, development and social justice. The welfare state concept which had to be administrative before 1993 will have to be accommodated with panchayati politics at the lustings. This three-tier federation has been ushered into ensure self-government and social welfare through economic development and scientific change in rural patterns of living and working. Once the development thrust gets debureaucratised and local people address themselves to the challenge of local development, the problems of social injustice and cultural stagnation will give way to a modern technological society which the agricultural and caste-driven society of India has never been since the Vedic times. It is the second war of Indian independence of the Indian people against their elitist rulers. The objectives of a Gandhian revolution will remain incomplete unless villagers manage their own affairs through panchayats and have effective participation in their rural governance to develop their potential to the full and eradicate poverty exploitation and discriminations from the rural life of their countrymen. The administration of development and social welfare has played its catalytic role and now it should cooperate, facilitate and enhance this metamorphosis of change and growth.

14

Public Enterprises in Liberal Economy of India

One natural and inevitable consequence of planned development in India has been the phenomenal growth and extension of public undertakings in varied fields of developmental activities. The positive intervention of the welfare state in the economic activities necessitated the strengthening of the core infrastructure to facilitate enhanced production, equitable distribution and improved consumptive patterns for a qualitative life. The successive Five-Year Plans not only raised the funding inputs but radically revised and diversified the production portfolio for local, national and global markets. Varied reasons such as the need of widening the narrow industrial base, mobilisation of public resources, ensurement of social justice and assisting the private sector to augment production prompted the government to enter into business of development. Over the years, public sector enterprises have been created to fill the gaps in the economy. These units have been engaged directly as well as indirectly in advancing loans, regulating trade, organising developmental activities, manufacturing heavy machine tools, instruments, electrical equipment, chemicals, drugs and fertilizers, drilling for oil and refining crude oil, operating air, sea and road transport, mining of mineral ores, smelting steel, production and distribution of milk, trading, markets, hotels and the like. As the Indian economy started marching towards commanding heights, the outlays of successive Five-Year Plans also escalated giving a proud place to the public sector and its undertakings. The adjacent table presents the mounting graph.

Five-Year Plans	*Public Sector Outlay (in crore rupees)*
First	1,960
Second	4,672
Third	8,577
Fourth	15,724
Fifth	18,225
Sixth	84,000
Seventh	7,43,000
Eighth	7,98,000
Ninth	10,00,000

Out of these bulging public sector allocations of the plans, a large share has flowed to the creation and expansion of public enterprises which were owned wholly or partly by the central government or state governments or jointly by central and state governments. Most of them are engaged in the industrial, agricultural, commercial or financial activities having self-management. They constitute a big segment characterised by significant patterns and managerial practices. They cover fields like manufacturing, mining, petroleum, chemicals, and pharmaceuticals, infrastructural, financial and insurance services. Different organisational forms have been evolved to suit individual requirements and needs. Some are purely promotional and others are engaged in production and expected to earn profits. There are thus inherent differences in their scope and nature. The adjacent table shows the growth of public enterprises in the Central government since 1950.

The statistical figures exclude departmentally managed enterprises like railways and ordnance factories. Of the 246 public enterprises in the Central government, the ten top are asset-holding enterprises. They are:

(1) Indian Oil Corporation
(2) Steel Authority of India
(3) Oil and Natural Gas Commission
(4) Coal India
(5) National Thermal Power Commission
(6) Food Corporation of India
(7) National Hydro Electric Corporation
(8) Bharat Heavy Electricals
(9) Neyveli Lignite Corporation
(10) Mahanagar Telephone

Public Enterprises in India

Year	*Number of Public Enterprises*	*Total Investment (in million rupees)*
1951	5	290
1956	21	810
1961	48	9,530
1966	74	24,150
1971	101	35,510
2000	235	23,00,000

It is difficult to group all these 246 units into specific or exclusive categories. Some of these public sector units have been sold under the new dispensation. Several are in the process of construction. The traditional classification of public enterprises engaged in producing or manufacturing goods and rendering services does not neatly apply on the mixed and changing scenario. Yet, their number denotes the kind of priorities the government has shown in developing the public sector as a whole.

In fact, the organisation and management of public enterprise units could not be uniform. Diversity was implicit in the industrial and commercial nature of their management. The effort was to combine efficiency and profitability of the private sector with the public accountability of public administration of government. In practice, four kinds of patterns of management were evolved for different kinds of enterprises, each with significant variations. These patterns were:

(1) Departmental undertakings,
(2) Public corporations,
(3) Government companies, and
(4) Holding companies.

In addition, a number of minor kinds of patterns like control boards, public trusts, commissions, commodity boards and cooperative societies were also established to administer public enterprises of various sorts.

Departmental Undertakings

Government participation in manufacturing and other organised business before was very limited and it was organised as part of government departments. Railways, posts and telegraphs, defence production units, All India Radio, and other industrial units were all departmental units. Only the

	Allied Group	*Total Enterprises*		*Allied Group*	*Total Enterprises*
I.	Enterprises yet to be completed	9	III.	Service Enterprises	
II.	Goods Manufacturing/Producing Enterprises			(1) Contract and Construction Services	8
	(1) Power	4		(2) Tourist Services	8
	(2) Petroleum	14		(3) Telecommunication Services	2
	(3) Transportation Equipment	13		(4) Industrial and Technical Consultancy Services	12
	(4) Textiles	14		(5) Trading and Marketing	19
	(5) Chemicals and Pharmaceuticals	20		(6) Financial Services	7
	(6) Minerals and Metals	13		(7) Transportation Services	12
	(7) Steel	9		(8) Section 25 Companies	2
	(8) Coal and Lignite	8		Total	70
	(9) Fertilizers	8			
	(10) Agro-Based Industries	4			
	(11) Heavy Engineering	16			
	(12) Consumer Goods	19			
	(13) Medium and Light Engineering	23			
	Total	174			

Hindustan Aircraft Limited was organised as a company. It was a private company taken over by the government to meet the exigencies of war. This process has continued even after independence. New projects like the telephone factory and the fertilizer factory were organised as departmental units in their early stage of development and other newly started units like the Chittranjan Locomotive Works, Diesel Locomotive Works and Integral Coach Factory were made a part of the departmentally run railway organisation. This form is still commonly employed when the main purpose of the enterprise is to provide revenue. It is financed by annual appropriations from the budget and its revenues, are paid into the treasury. It is subject to the budget accounting and audit controls, applicable to government activities. Its permanent staff consists of civil servants and their conditions of recruitment and services are somewhat similar to those of other government servants. The enterprise is generally organised as a major subdivision of one of the central departments of government and is subject to the direct control of the head of the department. Legally speaking, the enterprise possesses the sovereign immunity of the state and can be sued only by following the procedure for filing suits against the government. It possesses sovereign immunity of the state and cannot be sued without the consent of the government. It is created by an executive resolution and prior approval of the Parliament is not required to create it.

This pattern of public undertaking provides for a maximum degree of control by a minister who is politically responsible to the Parliament. It facilitates a clear relationship with other parts of the governmental structure and enables the government to have better control over its funds. It prevents the public money from being misappropriated and misused. It is well known form of organisation, having fixed rules and standard patterns and has been found suitable for those enterprises which are set-up for special reasons like defence, strategic importance, national security, economic control, financial control, safeguarding public interest, etc.

The critics of departmental pattern argue that it directly negates the requirements of autonomy due to excessive control and militates against initiative and flexibility of the enterprise. It leads to rigid financial and budgetary control and suffers from rigidity of rules and regulations and bureaucratic red tape leading to delays. Because of centralisation it does not facilitate sufficient delegation of authority and hence not used for economic and financial enterprises in recent times. Its inherent characteristics are rigidity and red tape.

Public Corporation Pattern

A public corporation as a form of public enterprise was developed in the second half of 20th century. W.A. Robson calls it "the most important invention of the 20th century in the sphere of government institutions." Herbert Morrison views it as "a combination of public ownership, public accountability and business management for public ends. In fact, it is clothed with the power of government but possesses the flexibility and initiative of a private enterprise." Some of the important public corporation established by the Union government are:

(1) Reserve Bank of India (1935)
(2) Damodar Valley Corporation (1948)
(3) Industrial Finance Corporation of India (1948)
(4) Indian Airlines Corporation (1953)
(5) Air India International (1953)
(6) State Bank of India (1955)
(7) Life Insurance Corporation of India (1956)
(8) Central Warehousing Corporation (1957)
(9) Oil and Natural Gas Commission (1959)
(10) Food Corporation of India (1964)

Some of the important public corporations established by state governments are:

(1) State Financial Corporations
(2) State Road Transport Corporations
(3) State Land Mortgage Banks
(4) State Electricity Boards

A public corporation is wholly owned by state, that is, its entire capital is provided by the government. It is created by a special law of legislature which may be enacted by Central or state governments. This special statute defines its objectives, powers, duties and privileges and also prescribes the form of management and its relationship to the government departments as a corporate body. It is a separate entity for legal purposes and can sue and be sued, enter into contracts and acquire property in its corporate name. It is usually independently financed except for appropriations to provide capital or to cover losses. It obtains its funds from borrowing which may be from the treasury or from the public and from revenues derived from the sale of its goods and services. It is authorised to use and reuse its revenues. The public corporation are generally exempt from regulatory and prohibitory statutes applicable to the expenditure of public funds and are not subject to budget, accounting and audit procedures which are applicable to non-corporate agencies. The employees of corporate bodies are not civil servants. They are recruited and remunerated under terms and conditions which are determined by the corporation itself. More significantly corporation enjoys functional autonomy and is not subject to direct control of the head of the department in its normal operations. Except for the formal policy directions issued to it by a minister, it is guided by the statute which created it. It is managed by a board of directors appointed by the government. One of the directors is appointed to function as the chairman of the board.

A public corporation form of organisation facilitates autonomy in its day-to-day administration and provides freedom from political influences and partisan considerations. It provides for a healthy mix of commercial efficiency of a private enterprise with public accountability of a government department and provides freedom from unsuitable rules, regulations and controls of the government. The corporation pattern facilitates a high degree of financial flexibility and personal mobility and serves as a valuable instrument for social control of economic life. But the critics maintain that it is inherently rigid and ill-suited to meet the requirements of changing times because the changes in its structure or procedure can be affected only by a statutory amendment. This fact gives rise to the problems of reconciling administrative autonomy with public accountability. Naturally this does not facilitate clear distinction between the "matters of policy" and "matters of day-to-day administration". The corporations place significant political power in the hands of a small unrepresentative and a self-perpetuating group which controls and manages it. In actual practice they do not facilitate flexibility and autonomy in both financial and administrative aspects. The ministries in India look upon the corporation as their wings or branches and issue orders and directions in a similar way. The Estimates Committees (Second Lok Sabha) in its eightieth report observed that no well-defined principles had been followed in determining the form of organisation of public undertakings. The committee suggested that

> wholly owned government undertakings should ordinarily be organised in the form of statutory corporations. The departmental management was found justified for special reasons like defence, strategic or security needs or for purposes of economic control and the company form should have been an exception for organisations of specific nature.

The Krishna Menon Committee Report on State Undertakings in India found the weaker side of corporation form in the departmental methods of purchase of raw materials and sale of products. Their permanent staff has been subject to rules and regulations applicable to civil servants. Putting of cash receipts into government account has resulted in tardy procedures of arranging funds, and sanctions for expenditure. The system of accounting and audit has been cumbersome and dilatory. Still the public corporation as an organisational device for the administration of public undertakings, has won acclaim both in India and abroad. In Britain, most of the nationalised industries like British Broadcasting Corporation, British Overseas Airways Corporation, Overseas Food Corporation, etc., have been organised as public corporations. Countries like France, Canada, Italy, and the United States have also adopted this form of organisation for their public enterprises. Independent India has followed this pattern. The Damodar Valley Corporation, Indian Airlines Corporation, Air India, Life Insurance Corporation, Central Warehousing Corporation, Food Corporation of India, Industrial Finance Corporation, etc., are the well known examples in point. In addition, state governments have set up their own corporations, the most important of which are the electricity board and the state roadways transport corporation. The Public Corporations form is acceptable to all political parties, right as well as left, as appropriate instruments for operating nationally owned undertakings.

The Study Team on Public Sector Undertakings of ARC examined the entire issue in depth and observed: "The departmental form is one that is generally regarded suitable only for undertakings that provide services affecting the totality of the community. The undertakings that require a high degree of freedom, boldness and enterprise in management must be free from the circumspection and cumbersome, time-consuming and vexatious procedures of departmental administration. Both the company form and the Public Corporation form can provide for this flexibility and autonomy. It is not, therefore, possible to prescribe one of these forms as applicable for all types of undertakings and under all circumstances. We therefore, recommend that the government should adopt the form of Public Corporation as the general rule for the industrial and commercial undertakings in the public sector in India." The Administrative Reforms Commission itself in its report of 1968 recommended that:

(1) Undertakings which are predominantly trading concerns or areas of business, may have the company form of organisation.
(2) Development agencies should, be run as statutory corporations or as departmental undertakings.
(3) Statutory corporations should be adopted in the industrial and manufacturing fields.
(4) A government company form of organisation may be adopted for projects to encourage private participation.

The government's decision on these recommendations was: "For certain enterprises providing public utilities which are primarily intended to develop the basic infrastructure facilities, the statutory corporation form of management may be preferable. For other enterprises including those operating in the monopolistic field but where the commercial aspect is predominant, the present form of a company may allow more flexibility. The government, therefore, does not consider that this form of statutory corporation should in general be adopted for public enterprises". The government has thus decided to continue with its earlier policy of supporting the company form of organisation for state undertakings.

The Issue of Internal Autonomy

The autonomy of public corporation raised a great debate about their internal working and external relation with the ministers and the Parliament. The internal autonomy was asserted in:

(1) Policy matters,
(2) Day-to-day routine operations,
(3) Personnel policies and service conditions, and
(4) Commercial audit.

Similarly, ministerial control was resisted and limited powers of the concerned minister were haltingly accepted. The government has the authority to frame rules and regulations to facilitate the working of these enterprises. It can prescribe forms, lay down procedures and even prescribe the activities to be undertaken. The government stands empowered to appoint the chairman and members of the board of management and the managing director. In addition, it retains the power of approval of appointment to posts carrying salaries above a certain limit. The government can institute enquiries into the working of a corporation. The government can remove from office any member of the management board under certain conditions. The government can supercede a board if a particular board of management fails to carry out the purposes for which it was created or if it fails to carry out the directives issued by the government. Similarly the power of issuing directives is the most important power which is exercised by a minister. A sub-clause of the same clause lays down that, if any dispute arises between the Central government and the corporation, the decision of the Central government shall be final and binding.

The financial powers of the minister were narrowed down to advice, sanction and prior approval. Ministers are authorised to appoint a financial adviser on the governing board of a corporation. Such adviser can exercise a sort of veto over affecting expenditure and the financial policy of the government. The sanction of the government is necessary to sanction capital expenditure above a certain amount, and for matters connected with borrowings, investments, securities, distribution of profits, etc. The approval of the government is required about the forms for maintaining the accounts of the enterprise and for their audit. Usually, the audit of accounts is done by the auditors appointed by the government. The government also controls the fixation of prices of goods produced by the enterprises as well as the quantum and rate of payment for services rendered.

The relationship between ministers and public undertakings has not worked smoothly. The ministers usually issue clear directives in writing as they are supposed to do and take responsibility for such directives before the Parliament. They have also chosen to depend upon influence and secure compliance of their wishes through informal means like appointment of officials and non-officials as chairman and members of governing boards; deputising serving government officers to executive posts in public undertakings.

The Parliamentary Control

The parliamentary control over public undertaking has been unsystematic, haphazard and ineffective. It operates through the instrumentalities of:

(a) Question hour
(b) Adjournment motions
(c) Parliamentary debates
(d) Discussions on reports
(e) Parliamentary committees especially the CPU

Committee on Public Undertakings

In addition to Public Accounts and Estimate Committees, a special committee on public undertaking was constituted by the Indian Parliament in May 1964. It consists of not more than fifteen members, ten from the Lok Sabha and five from the Rajya Sabha, elected by the concerned house every year from amongst its members according to the principle of proportional representation by means of the single transferable vote. However, a minister cannot be elected as a member and in case a member of the committee becomes a minister in future he ceases to be a member of the committee with immediate effect. The term of office is one year but there is no bar to re-election of the same members. One of the members is elected as the chairman of the committee. The functions of the committee are:

(1) To examine whether the affairs of public undertakings are being managed in accordance with sound business principles and prudent commercial practices.
(2) To examine the reports and accounts of the public undertakings.
(3) To examine the reports, if any, of the Comptroller and Auditor-General on public undertakings.
(4) To exercise such other functions vested in the committee on public accounts and the committee on estimates in relation to the specified public undertakings as may be allotted to the committee by the speaker from time to time.

The committee decided to select a few undertakings for detailed study each year. It takes up one subject on the working of undertaking for horizontal study, e.g., materials management, each year. The committee may also examine the working of state government owned industries in the public sector on request. The Administrative Reforms Commission felt that "this detailed and continuous scrutiny by Parliament, pushes the minister to keep himself informed on all matters that relate to a public enterprise including matters of day-to-day administration". The scrutiny that Parliament exercises over the working of public enterprises cannot be matters of day-to-day administration. This principle has been incorporated in the rules framed by Parliament on the 'scope of admissibility of questions' and the rules governing the working of the committee on public undertakings. The regulatory and prohibitory statutes do not apply on the expenditure of corporation funds which are not subjected to budgeting and audit procedures applicable to governmental agencies. The budgets of such corporation are not voted by parliament; only the capital investment programmes financed by the government are put to vote. The accountability of autonomous statutory corporations is, assured by their audit by an independent authority and they fall under three categories:

(1) Corporations in respect of which the responsibility of audit has been entrusted entirely to the C&AG, e.g., DVC and JAC.
(2) Corporations whose audit is done by professional auditors, i.e., private firms of chartered accountants. These auditors are appointed by the Central government in consultation with the C&AG, who retains the right to undertake supplementary audit.
(3) Other corporations for which the audit is done exclusively by the private firms of chartered accountants and the C&AG does not come into the picture at all such as the RBI, LIC and FCI submit their annual reports and accounts directly to Parliament.

Government Sponsored Company

The manufacturing concerns in public sector often use the joint stock company form. It is incorporated under the Companies Act, 1956. Section 617 of this Act states that "a government company is that in which not less than 51 per cent of the paid-up share capital is held up by the central government and by any state government or governments or partly by the central government and by one or more state governments". This Act recognises two forms of companies: (1) private limited, and (2) public limited. The private limited company needs minimum two shareholders while a public limited company has to have minimum seven. There is no upper limit about the maximum number in a public limited company, but the private limited companies cannot have more than fifty members. There is restriction on the right of a shareholder to transfer his shares in private company but public limited companies do not have any restriction. The private limited form is also known as mixed ownership company which includes joint enterprises shared between the government and private interests, national or foreign.

The Estimates Committee of Second Lok Sabha (The Eighteen Report) advanced reasons for the adoption of the company form of organisation. The takeover of an enterprise is justified if there is an emergency; It is advisable to launch an enterprise in association with private capital; or to start with a view to eventually transferring it to private hands. Such industrial undertakings whittle away parliamentary control over public money. They have been called a small kingdom, completely assigned to the over lordship of a managing director. It has even been criticised as "a fraud on the Company's Act and the Constitution". Its major weaknesses are that it evades the constitutional responsibilities which a state-controlled enterprise has in a democratic society to the government and Parliament. In practice it becomes a mere fiction because the company law makes financial flexibility and autonomy a myth than a reality. The undefined and unrestricted powers exercised by the government department is responsible for treating them like subordinate offices of the ministry concerned.

In India, this pattern has proved to be the most popular and extensively used form of organisation for management of public enterprises – industrial as well as commercial. In a joint enterprise the capital is shared between the government and the private interests, which can be either national or foreign. By acquiring 51 per cent or above of the share capital, the government becomes the *de facto* controller of the affairs of the mixed ownership company. That is why it is called a government company. While a public limited company requires a minimum of seven shareholders for its formation, the shareholder's right to transfer his shares is not restricted and the maximum number of shareholders can be any. Naturally, a private limited company is more suitable than the public limited company for organising a public enterprise.

Some of these important government companies are:

(1) Hindustan Machine Tools (Private) Limited
(2) Bharat Electronics (Private) Limited
(3) Bharat Heavy Electricals (Private) Limited
(4) Hindustan Cable (Private) Limited
(5) Hindustan Housing Factory (Private) Limited
(6) Rashtriya Fertilizers and Chemicals (Private) Limited
(7) Hindustan Antibiotics Limited
(8) Indian Tourism Development Corporation
(9) Indian Telephone Industries Limited
(10) Indian Oil Corporation
(11) Heavy Engineering Corporation
(12) National Coal Development Corporation
(13) Hindustan Insecticides (Private) Limited
(14) Fertilizer Corporation of India Limited
(15) Hindustan Shipyard Limited
(16) Shipping Corporation of India Limited
(17) Maruti Udyog Limited

Some of the government companies use the term 'corporation', but in actual practice they are organised as government companies. Fertilizer Corporation of India, Indian Oil Corporation can be cited as examples in point. A government company form of organisation possesses most of the features of private limited company. It is either wholly owned by the government or 51 per cent (or above) of the capital stock is owned by the government. In fact it is created by an executive resolution under the Indian Companies Act of 1956. It is a body corporate and has a separate entity for legal purposes and can sue and be sued, enter into contracts and acquire property in its name. Its Articles of Association (which lays down the rules of internal management) are drawn up and revisable by the government. Funds are obtained from the government and, in some cases, from private shareholders. It is ordinarily not subject to budget, accounting and audit and procedures which are applicable to government departments and employees are not civil servants and are recruited and remunerated under terms and conditions which are determined by the company itself. All the directors or a majority of them are appointed by the government depending upon the extent to which private capital is participating in the enterprises. It can be created by an executive decision without parliamentary approval. It provides for sufficient government control and enables association with private enterprise. It facilitates autonomy in day-to-day administration with a high degree of financial flexibility and personnel autonomy for expansion and extension.

The other side of the picture is that it evades constitutional responsibilities which a state-controlled enterprise has to have in a democratic society towards the government and to the Parliament. This is the reason why it was described by Ashok Chanda, as "a fraud on the Company's Act and on the Constitution of India". The use of the company form and of the law regulating commercial companies, usually becomes a mere fiction because all or most of the functions normally vested in the shareholders and in the management are reserved to the government by the statue setting up the company. In practice, it does not facilitate flexibility and autonomy in financial and administrative aspects. The Estimates Committee of Lok Sabha maintained that, "the companies are more or less extensions of departments and are run amuse on the same pattern, with minor changes here and there". Gorwala in his Report on the Efficient Conduct of State Enterprises (1951) considered government company form superior to public corporation form because of its flexibility. The First Five-Year Plan document supported the adoption of government company form. The Administrative Reforms Commission favoured the adoption of public corporation form in general for public enterprises but the company form may also be adopted when an enterprise is small in size or is being established with an element of private participation. It suits to an enterprise if it is predominantly a trading concern. The government did not accept the recommendations of ARC and continued its earlier policy of adopting the company form of organisation for public enterprises.

Holding Companies

A holding company form of organisation involves integration of all the companies which are operating in the same field or which have strong technical and commercial affinities with each other under a common management. Such companies called as subsidiaries are brought under the common management of a holding company. It is one company which has acquired a majority share in the ownership capital and which by virtue of its share ownership is able to control the management of subsidiary companies. Some of the successful examples of holding companies in India are:

(1) Coal Authority of India Limited
(2) Gas Authority of India Limited

(3) State Trading Corporation of India
(4) Steel Authority of India Limited (1973)
(5) General Insurance Corporation of India

A 'sector corporation' form of organisation which was recommended by the Administrative Reforms Commission is analogous to the holding company form of organisations. The Arjun Sengupta Committee (1986) recommended the establishment of holding companies or sector corporation in main areas of economy.

There are other forms of public enterprises. They may be boards, trusts, commissions, cooperative societies, etc. The control boards are established for the management of multipurpose river valley projects. They are created by an executive resolution of the Central or a state government. There are 14 control boards in the country like Nagarjunsagar Control Board, Kosi Control Board, Bhakra-Beas Management Board, etc. The public trust are established to undertake development work in their fields. They are created by special acts of Parliament. The examples of such enterprises are Tariff Commission, Khadi and Village Industries Commission, Forward Markets Commission, etc. Recently, some commodity boards have been established to promote industrial development. They are created by special acts of Parliament. The examples of such enterprises are Small-Scale Industries Board, Coffee Board and Rubber Board. The cooperative societies are established to undertake developmental and promotional activities. They are registered under the Societies Registration Act. The examples of such enterprises are Indian National Research Development Corporation. Trade Fair Authority of India, Indian Dairy Development Corporation and many others.

Department of Public Enterprises

The bureau of public enterprises was established in the ministry of finance in 1965. Twenty year later, the bureau was replaced by a full-fledged department of public enterprises under the ministry of industry. It acts as a data bank and a clearing house of information on common matters. As the secretariat of Public Enterprises Selection Board, it assists the enterprises in making selections. It arranges training programmes and advises the enterprises on management development. Technical and expert assistance is also offered on wage structure, service conditions, policies and allied matters. The department submits periodic reports to the Parliament and government on its working and coordinates work pertaining to its examination by parliamentary committees. It maintains liaison with Department of Administrative Reforms.

The Public Enterprise Selection Board

It is an autonomous decision-making body which works under the administrative control of personnel and training department of the ministry of personnel, public grievances and pensions. The secretarial assistance is provided by the department of public enterprises. Its functions are:

(1) To oversee management development activities of public enterprises.
(2) To advise the government on appropriate organisational structure and categorisation of positions at the top.
(3) To make recommendations to the government for appointment to full-time board level posts of executives, functional/executive directors and part-time directors.

The public enterprise were assigned a pre-eminent role in the economic development of India. The scheme of Industrial Policy Resolution of 1956, talks of 'commanding heights of the economy' through public sector enterprises. The economic development and rate of growth were accelerated and sound economic infrastructure for industrialisation was established. The monopolies and concentration of wealth in the hands of few could not be prevented but self-reliance in strategic fields to reduce dependence on foreign technology was attained. Balanced regional development was achieved and regional disparities were reduced. Employment opportunities in different sectors improved the standard of living of people and reduced the pressure on balance of payment through export promotion and import reduction. The development and expansions of small and ancillary industries took place and surplus resources were generated for reinvestment purposes. Even redistribution of income and wealth got boosted. They have witnessed a phenomenal growth and while there were only 5 central enterprises with an investment of Rs 29 crores in 1954, their number increased to 240 with an investment of Rs 2,30,140 crores in 1999. In terms of share in national production, they contribute the entire output of lignite, copper, petroleum, 80 per cent of zinc, 95 per cent of coal, 50 per cent of steel and aluminium and about one-third of fertilizers.

Their role as 'model employers' have provided various social amenities to their employees like housing, schools, hospitals, recreation centres. In 1999, they had a total of 19 lakh employees. They have effectively promoted redistribution of income and wealth through development of backward regions, provision of public utility services at subsidised prices and have helped the economy in earning substantial amount of foreign exchange through import substitution. They account for about one-fourth to one-fifth of the total export earnings. The contribution of public sector towards the government exchequer through dividends, corporation tax, excise duties and custom duties and others has increased. Their record in supplying goods and services like transport, communication, power, irrigation, drugs, cement, etc., has been commendable. They have also played an important role in collecting savings and mobilisation of resources for public investment to speed up economic growth. The important ones in this regard are IDBI, IFCL, LIC, UTI and SBI.

The Debacle

Notwithstanding these achievements, the public enterprises have met with enormous failures, especially in financial performance and managerial efficiency. Of the total 240 central enterprises, about 140 were making profits and 100 were incurring loses in 1990. There were about 50 sick industrial enterprises which have accumulated whooping losses. Some of the reasons for the limited success of the public enterprises have been identified by several committees as under:

(1) Non-rational price policy.
(2) Overmanning of personnel.
(3) Lower utilisation of capacities.
(4) Technological obsolescence.
(5) Lack of autonomy.
(6) Militant trade unionism.
(7) High overhead cost.
(8) Long-gestation periods.
(9) Higher capital intensities.
(10) Inefficient management.

(11) Evils of competitions.
(12) Inefficient inventory management.
(13) Faulty sites due to political considerations.
(14) Over-capitalisation.
(15) Dclay in completion of constructions.

The Post-1991 Scenario

In July 1991, the government of P.V. Narsimha Rao made a public statement about public sector policy. This policy statement contained several historic decisions. It maintained that the portfolio of public sector investment will be reviewed with a view to focus the public sector on strategic high technology and essential infrastructure. The public enterprises which were chronically and continuously sick will be referred to the Board of Industrial and Financial Reconstruction (BIFR) and a social security mechanism will be created to protect the interests of workers likely to be retrenched. A policy of progressive disinvestment will be followed and shareholding in public sector would be offered to financial institutions and general public. The boards of public sector companies will be made more professional and the performance improvement will receive emphasis through a system of memorandum of understanding (MoU) and management will enjoy greater autonomy and will be held accountable. By 1991, 71 public undertakings signed MoUs and this number of public undertakings signing MoUs has continuously been increasing since then.

This New Industrial Policy of 1991 which was conceived in the post-disintegration era of Soviet Union was supposed to take care of the waves of 'New Rightism', popularly known as liberalisation, globalisation and privatisation. The World Bank monitored this world view of new public administration which had its inevitable repercussions on public sector enterprises in India. The New Economic Policy of P.V. Narsimha Rao in 1991 made a radical departure from the Nehruvian economic philosophy contained in the 1956 policy. In fact, it heralded an era of liberalisation which led to privatisation and globalisation. This LPG means free-market economy which marks a change from a restrictionist regime to a free market. It implied reducing, relaxing and dismantling of government's controls and regulation in economic activities. These measures included delicensing of industries, raising of licensing limits, relaxations under the MRTP Act, broad banding relaxations under the FERA (now FEMA) regulations, legislation of additional capacities, relaxations in export-import policy and so forth. Thus, the private sector has been permitted to function freely in respect of investment, production and products. Privatisation implied denationalisation that is changing the ownership of public enterprises fully or partially to the private parties, deregulation, that is, allowing the entry of private sector into areas hitherto exclusively reserved for the public sector and operating contract, that is, entrusting the management and control of public enterprises to the private parties on agreed remuneration. The contest of globalisation added progressive integration of Indian economy with the world economy. This implies opening up the Indian economy to foreign direct investment. It removes constraints to the entry of multinational companies (MNCs) in India. Thus, the Indian economy has been made a part and parcel of the world economy.

Some of the reasons for this change in the government's policy towards public sector were dismal financial performance of the public sector and poor returns against heavy investments and the government's inability to provide budgetary support to sick enterprises. The need to create competition for public enterprises to earn profits through improved efficiency was urgently felt and the global trend towards liberalisation, privatisation, and globalisation invited the private sector to come forward to invest huge amounts in infrastructure areas. This external factor influenced foreign governments, MNCs, World Bank, IMF and other foreign agencies to discover new market in the closed economy of India.

Under the New Policy in post-1991 phase, the government decided to confine public sector investments to strategic, hi-tech and essential infrastructure areas. Some of the areas reserved for public sector were opened up to the private sector selectively and public sector was allowed to enter in areas not reserved for it. Sick public enterprises were referred to the Board for Industrial and Financial Reconstruction (BIFR) for formulation of revival and rehabilitation schemes and a social security mechanism has been created to protect the interests of workers likely to be affected by such rehabilitation schemes. A part of the government's share-holding in the public sector has been offered to mutual funds, financial institutions, general public and workers and the boards of public sector companies have been made more professional with more powers. Through the MoU system, management has been granted greater autonomy and made accountable for results. This has led to decline in budgetary support to public enterprises.

The Liberal Economy Reforms

As a follow-up of this new policy and a series of macroeconomic policy reforms leading to the liberalisation of the Indian Economy, the government had taken various measures to reform the public enterprises. Some of these reform measures are:

(1) The Policy of Dereservations
(2) Closer or Revival of Sick Units
(3) Golden Handshakes
(4) The Policy of Disinvestment
(5) Choosing and Strengthening the Navratanas
(6) Support to Miniratnas
(7) Signing of MoU

(a) Closer of Sick Units

In 1991, the number of industries reserved for the public sector was reduced from 17 to 8. Two years later, two more items were deleted from the reserved list. Again in 1998, another two items were dereserved. In May 2001, the government opened up one more area to the private sector participation. Thus, by 2004 only 3 areas stood reserved, viz., (i) atomic energy, (ii) minerals specified to the atomic energy (control of production and use) order, 1953, and (iii) rail transport.

(b) Privatisation

Additionally, some of the dereserved areas are opened not only to domestic private enterprises but also to foreign private enterprises. The Sick Industrial Companies Act (SICA, 1985) was amended in 1991 to enable the sick public enterprises to be referred to the Board for Industrial and Financial Reconstruction (BIFR, 1987) for revival or closure. Till the end of 2000, out of 74 sick units, winding up was recommended in 13 cases and 3 units were found earning profits.

(c) The Golden Handshake

In 1992, the government initiated the voluntary retirement scheme (VRS) to help the public sector enterprises to shed manpower. This scheme came to be popularly known as 'Golden Handshake' Policy as the workers get a handsome amount from the enterprises at the time of dissociation. The National Renewal Fund (NRF) was created in 1992 for training and redeployment of retrenched workers, besides providing compensation to the persons seeking voluntary retirement. As a result, the number of employees came down from 22 lakhs in 1991 to 19 lakhs in 1999.

(d) The Disinvestment Programme

The disinvestment programme started in 1991–92 had the objective of raising non-inflationary kind of finance for the government budget. Disinvestment can be seen as a process whereby the government withdraws a portion or the total of its equity in a public enterprise. The Government of India appointed a 'Committee on Disinvestment of Shares in Public Sector Enterprises' (1992) under the chairmanship of C. Ranagarajan to suggest measures with regard to the disinvestment programme. On its recommendation, a 'Commission on Public Sector Disinvestment' was set up under G.V. Ramakrishnan which prepared a long-term plan of disinvestment of public sector enterprises Till 1999, the government raised Rs 18,638 crores from various rounds of disinvestment and reduced its equity in non-strategic public sector enterprises to 26 per cent or less from 2000.

(e) The Navratna Status

Long last, the government has identified nine leading well-performing and high profit-making public sector enterprises as the 'Navaratnas' (nine precious jewels). In 1997, two more have been added to the list. They were granted substantial enhanced autonomy and operational freedom in financial, commercial, managerial and organisational fields to facilitate their becoming global players. Their boards have also been professionalised by induction of non-official part-time professional directors.

There are 11 public sector enterprises which have been included in the category of 'Navaratans'. They are:

(1) Indian Oil Corporation Ltd. (IOC)
(2) Gas Authority of India Ltd. (GAIL)
(3) Steel Authority of India (SAIL)
(4) Videsh Sanchar Nigam Ltd. (VSNL)
(5) Indian Petro-Chemicals Corporation Ltd. (IPCL)
(6) Oil and Natural Gas Commission (ONGC)
(7) Hindustan Petroleum Corporation Ltd. (HPCL)
(8) Mahanagar Telephone Nigam Ltd. (MTNL)
(9) Bharat Petroleum Corporation Ltd. (BPCL)
(10) Bharat Heavy Electricals Ltd. (BHEL)
(11) National Thermal Power Corporation Ltd. (NTPC)

These 'Navaratnas' have been given special freedom to incur capital expenditure without any monetary ceiling. They can enter into technology joint ventures or strategic alliances to obtain technology. To effect organisational restructuring they can establish profit centres in India and abroad. They can also create and wind-up posts below board level and raise capital from the domestic and international markets. Permission has been accorded to them to establish financial joint ventures and wholly owned subsidiaries in India and abroad with equity investment up to Rs 200 crores and deal with manpower management.

(f) The Miniratnas

The 'Navaratnas' account for nearly 80 per cent of the profits of total public sector enterprises and Rs 1,40,000 crores of annual turnover. In 1999, they earned a net profit of Rs 12,073 crores. In the year 1997, the Government of India identified another 97 profit making public sector enterprises as the 'Miniratnas' (small precious jewels) and granted them financial, managerial, and operational autonomy. These enterprises are divided into two sub-categories depending on their recent performance. (1) The first category of Miniratnas are the enterprises which have earned profits continuously for the last three years and have earned a net profit of Rs 30 crores or more in one of the three years. (2) The second category of Miniratnas are the enterprises which have earned profits continuously for the last three years.

In addition to these categories, there are units which have positive network and have not defaulted in repayment of loans/interest to the government and have not sought any budgetary support. Both these categories have freedom to incur capital expenditure without government approval upto Rs 300 crores or upto their net worth and upto Rs 150 crores or upto 50 per cent of their net worth whichever is lower in the two categories respectively. They can also enter into financial joint ventures and establish subsidiary companies and overseas offices. They can sign technology joint ventures, and work out their own personnel policies.

Since 2001, the government has launched a periodic review of the Navratna and Miniratna status of the public enterprises on the basis of their performance of last three years. The system of MoU was introduced in 1987–88 and has grown at a steady rate from 4 MoUs to 108 MoUs. The rating of which was as under:

(1) Excellent – 48
(2) Very good – 28
(3) Good – 9
(4) Fair – 17
(5) Poor – 4

A MoU is an agreement between the ministry and the public enterprise management to grant autonomy to the latter. It defines obligations of both the parties for improving performance of public enterprises and makes public enterprise managements responsible and accountable for results. It is a sort of annual performance contract between the ministry and the enterprise. The Sengupta Committee recommended it in 1985. It has been called the Indian version of the French 'Performance Contract System' and is also comparable with the 'Signalling System' of Korean economy.

Some protagonists of new economic reforms give credit to Prime Minister Rajiv Gandhi who in his first national broadcast to the nation said: "The public sector has entered into too many areas where it should not be. We shall open the economy to the private sector in several areas hitherto restricted to it." Consequently, a number of measures were taken to remove controls, open areas to private sector players. This was the first phase of liberalisation when government decontrolled cement and licences were issued to private sector units to produce cement. The share of free sale sugar was increased to help the sugar industry and the ceiling asset of big business houses was raised from Rs 20 crores to Rs 100 crores. Prime Minister Rao not only furthered the policy but concretised the idea to dismantle the licence permit Raj. The Babu bureaucracy was given a go by and asset limits of MRTP companies was raised to 1,000 crores. It forced the large private corporate bureaucracy and industrial licensing was abolished for all the projects except for 18 industries of core variety.

Globalisation of Indian Markets

Similarly, globalisation was conceived to integrate the Indian economy with the world markets. Its parameters included reduction of trade barriers for a free-flow of goods and services across national frontiers and the creation of conditions conducive. It required free-flow of technology and a free movement of labour in different countries of the world although WTO was opposed to it. The government has attempted to dismantle quantitative restriction on imports and exports to adjust exchange rate to remove over-valuation of currency. Restrictions on 162 items for imports were removed and 69 items were moved from Special Import Licence (SIL) to free imports. The government took measures to encourage foreign investment. For instance, approval was given for direct investment up to 51 per cent foreign equity in high priority industries. To provide access to international markets, majority foreign equity holding up to 51 per cent equity has been allowed for trading companies primarily engaged in export activities.

Automatic permission is given now for foreign technology agreements in high priority industries upto a lump sum payment of Rs 1 crore, 5 per cent royalty for domestic sales and 8 per cent for exports. Other industries have automatic permission if no free foreign exchange is required for payments. No permission is necessary for hiring of foreign technicians and foreign testing of indigenously developed technologies. The degree of privatisation is judged by the extent of ownership transferred from the public enterprises to the private sector. Today hundred per cent transfer of ownership, partial transfer of a public enterprise to the private sector with variants like 25, 51 and 74 per cent transfer to the private sector in joint ventures is permissible. The sale of assets has been allowed to any person who may use them for any purpose. Ownership of enterprises can be transferred to workers who may form cooperatives to run the enterprise. A holding company structure can be designed to permit government to control top level decisions and leaves adequate degree of autonomy for operating companies in their day to day operations. Similarly, in a leasing management the government has agreed to transfer the use of assets of a public sector enterprise to a private bidder for a specific period.

Even financial restructuring has been permitted to write-off accumulated losses and rationalisation of capital composition in respect of debt-equity ratio. If the public enterprise decides to shed some of its activities it can do basic restructuring. The operational measures include: grant of autonomy in decision-making, provision of incentives for workers, freedom to acquire inputs from the markets, development of criteria for investment planning, and permission to raise resources from the capital market. Privatisation in a narrow sense indicates transfer of ownership of a public sector undertaking to private sector. But in another sense, it implies the opening up of the private sector to areas which were hitherto reserved for the public sector. The basic purpose is to limit the areas of the public sector and to extend the areas of private sector operation, including heavy industries and infrastructure.

The New Policy of 1991 aims to achieve certain ends of the society. These ends are achievement of high rate of growth of national and per capita income and full employment to all. It strives to work for self-reliance and reduction of inequality of income and wealth. The number of people living below the poverty line has to come down and a society based on equality without exploitation has to be evolved. The operation of the public sector and the regulatory framework is being tightened to cut down the excessive development of bureaucratic controls and overstaffing in public sector enterprises. The low rate of return in investment in public sector has to be enhanced and poor work ethic in public sector enterprises needs to be changed. It has resulted in the entry of public sector in areas of consumer goods for which it was never meant. High growth rate of over 6 per cent during 1992 to 1997 has been an unprecedented achievement of economic reforms in India. Overstaffing has been reduced in public sector units by voluntary retirement scheme (VRS), and National Renewal Fund (NRF) has been created as a safety net. Cases of sick PSUs were referred to BIFR which recommended revival packages in units considered viable and winding up of unviable units. MoUs were signed with 99 public sector enterprises and more autonomy was granted. Disinvestment of 31 selected PSUs was undertaken, varying from 5 per cent to 20 per cent, and the equity was offered to mutual funds and financial institution. The major flow of the disinvestment programme was that its proceeds were used to finance budget deficits and it is called as 'deficit privatisation'. Out of the total foreign capital inflow, nearly 69 per cent was in the form of portfolio investment and only 31 per cent in the form of foreign direct investment (FDI), adjusting for 10 per cent received from NRIs. The net share of foreigners in FDI has been around 21 per cent. Moreover, 39 per cent of foreign investment is in the non-priority sector. Multinationals are keen to enter these areas which involve short gestation period and high profitability. The reform process has led to higher growth of exports along with much higher growth of imports. Although, the reform process has not succeeded in controlling fiscal deficit but the exchange value of the Rupee vis-à-vis US $ has moved up. In sum, the reform process has led to increase in foreign exchange reserves. Policies of economic reforms have concentrated on short-term objectives of balance of payments, inflation, foreign exchange reserves, and reducing fiscal deficits. However, the long-term goals of reducing poverty, achieving full employment and growth with social justice are yet to be achieved.

Globalisation today represents decolonisation rather than neo-imperialism. Taking advantage of it, India has attained greater and better assimilation of connectivity, commerce, cultures and creativity. Foreign investor's have started coming to the potential Indian market even without making huge profits. The success stories of Indian entrepreneurs bags several awards adding sunrise industries. The IT or BPO hub is a feather in India's cap. Notwithstanding hue and cry against 'outsourcing', the NASSCOM estimate finds over 50 per cent of the Fortune companies taking to outsourcing India as their development base. With an army of 100,000 IT professionals, doctors and scientists, India has almost made a dent in Harvard Business School, NASA, UK hospitals and TNCs. The so-called 'Hindu rate of growth' has touched around 8.1 per cent in 2002–2004. Still the fact remains that the poorest 20 per cent of the world live in India and are content with one per cent of GDP and FDI. The gap between rich and poor has jumped from 11 times to 58 times. Employment opportunities though expanding are not matching. The global village maintains globalisation without a face. Because the phenomenon of Dollarisation keeps 5 per cent of world's affluence population consuming 85 per cent of world resources. This toothless, rootless, jobless and ruthless globalisation brings India face to face with a grim reality. The dark facts speak that:

(1) as many as 26 per cent of population live below poverty line;
(2) despite food surplus not less than 200 million face the rude shock of hunger;
(3) as of now per capita food availability is less than what it was in the 1940s;
(4) illiteracy ratio is as high as 35 per cent;
(5) one-third of MMRs (maternal mortality ratio) of the world is a blot on our public healthcare system;
(6) employment elasticity has fallen from 0.52 in 1983–84 to 0.16 during 1993–2000;
(7) annual growth of employment has decreased from 2.04 per cent during 1983–94 to about one per cent during 1994–2000;
(8) combined fiscal deficit of the centre and states has gone up from 9.3 per cent of GDP in 1990–91 to 10.4 per cent in 2002–03 (some respite in 2003–04);
(9) revenue deficit as a share of fiscal deficits 77 per cent; and
(10) interest payments are close to 50 per cent of centre's total revenue receipts.

Obviously, the answers lie in long and short-term strategies, timely and discernable protection, ongoing, rigorous and vigorous programmes, competitive strength through innovation, strategic alliances and flexible labour laws. India cannot afford to be a peninsula in the vast ocean of global poverty, nor can islands of adherence be tolerated in the sea of mass poverty at national level. Economic reforms with a human face imply an all out-effort in areas like labour, infrastructure, transaction costs power, interest rates and taxation (what FICCI, calls LITPIT reforms). The public sector has a key role to regulate, reform and monitor these welcome changes in the Indian economy. The Manmohan Singh-Chidambaram initiatives have not cut much ice. On the contrary the escalation of oil prices and inflation in the economy demand intervention of the Planning Commission. Although Montek Singh Ahluwalia is more proactive than his predecessor K.C. Pant, yet the position of oil corporations by and large remain unchanged as public sector enterprises. Globalisation has caused uncertainty in the economy and public sector in areas like air transport, communication, insurance, health and education confronts the challenge of competition and reordering of priorities. The regulatory authorities are emerging in these areas and the government policies are ambivalent in restructuring the public sector units due to leftist pressures on the coalition. The Common Minimum Programme experience should evolve a midway for growth of public enterprises with private partnership and adequate regulation through mission oriented 'bureaucracy'.

15

Administrative Reforms and Good Governance in India

The term 'reform' literally means forming again. The form can be a structure or a construct mentally conceived as a picture. This rebuilding or reorganising exercise is called reform because it presents the old form in a new way which may be renovation, readjustment or renewal. The Hindi translation 'Sudhar' stresses upon another aspect of reforming, i.e., bringing the structure to the main stream or the 'Dhara' that goes on. Reforming the obsolescent or outdated practices, working methods, procedures of work or the out work structures in such a way that they become vibrant goal-oriented and effectively functional that is what a reform stands for. Reforms can be political, social, economic and administrative depending upon the contents, contexts and emphasis that the exercise lies upon. To some reforms represent change while other may view them as change within the framework of continuity. Old wine in new bottles or new wine in old bottles or new wine in new bottles may be reform strategies in a system but every reform presupposes a form. These forms keep growing, expanding and decaying. A reform is needed to keep the old form serving the new purpose. Theoretically speaking, a reform can be an innovation or renewal but in each case it requires an artificial inducement for transformation against resistance. In other words, evolution is not reform, but if not attempted the evolution may ultimately lead to it. A reform has to be an artificial human devise to induct change or catalyse the phenomenon in such a way that desired results may follow the speeding of change or manipulation of change or skipping the stages or growth through artificial methods evokes resistance by all those who are accustomed to culturised ways of status quo. Hence, all reforms have to be conceived of as desired changes in desired directions through manipulative means.

Administrative reforms naturally imply a change process in the organisation and working of the bureaucratic machinery and its procedures of work in relation to other organisation of government and the people at large. Like constitutional or political reforms, the administrative reforms need an atonement of the administrative system to the goals of the polity or its constitutional commitments. Even socio-economic reforms like liberalisation or globalisation generate expectations from administration which has to be responsive and goal achieving. As a sub-system of the political system, public administration has to be revamped and updated as a support structure. Viewed in this perspective, an administrative reform is an exercise in:

(a) Restructuring old structure of government by additions, alterations or dismantling of the outdated departments, agencies, bureaus, boards or corporations,

(b) Changing personnel system of recruitment, promotion, training, career planning and evaluation of performance of public servants,
(c) Streaming procedures of work to heighten efficiency, economy and affectivity in the tasks accomplished, and
(d) Redefining relations among various organs, different structures and with the client public to whom the administration seeks to serve and provide facilitations.

The nature of polity decides the nature of administration. The constitutional amendments facilitate political change and this makes it imperative for the administrative system to respond to change and absorb the need as a reform. Such attempts may assume three forms:

(1) The traditional approach has been that one waited for a problem to come up and then placed a competent person to solve it. This approach, has been called the 'management process' where the top executive brings about significant reforms.
(2) It was replaced by the committee process, namely, appointment of ad hoc committees or commissions to investigate problems of administrative reforms and make recommendations. Haldane Committee in UK (1918), the Hoover Commission (1949 and 1955) in USA, the Administrative Reforms Commission (1966) and Veerappa Moily Commission (2006) in India are the examples.
(3) The third approach is the setting up of organisation and methods (O&M) units in administrative agencies or/and the establishment of full-fledged departments of administrative reforms. This is a post-Second World War phenomenon that is found in all countries including UK, USA and India.

India has followed all the three approaches to administrative reforms. The ancient and Mughal periods of Indian history kept the structure growing and adjusting with the needs and demands of the empire. But what can seemingly be called an administrative reform commended as a deliberate rational attempt since the advent of the British in India. As foreign rulers they build the administrative system at the scratch and reviewed it periodically to become more effective for the promotion of their colonial interests. Moreover, they imposed a new administrative structure in an alien land and institutions like secretariat, merit-based civil service, police and criminal justice system, army, education and financial management were ventured as basic reforms which the company administration and later the Crowns government gradually improved through administrative innovations. As the nature and structure of the government changed in the years, 1857, 1909, 1919 and 1935, the administration in India was given an overhand. An evolutionary perspective on secretariat and civil service reforms since 1857 is indicative of British intentions of developing an administrative system in India which should be an amalgam of traditional, colonial and liberal administrations. So they retained the Mughal system in the district but tinkered with it to make it rewarding for the mother country. Macaulay conceived of a variety of civil service reforms, partly because the liberal philosophy of administration was to be inducted but primarily because the colony was to be well-governed and effectively administered by the Britishers in collaboration with the loyalist natives. The collectors, the Governors, the Governor-Generals and the secretaries of State of India were individually and collectively imagined the reform exercise which never lost sight of the basic objective. A host of study groups, committees, commissions and reform groups appointed between 1857 to 1947 chronologically explain the reform efforts made in the Indian administration with varying successes. Some of these reform exercises were:

(1) 1854 Committee on Indian Civil Service
(2) 1860 Committee on Civil Service Salaries
(3) 1876 Committee on Selection and Training of Candidates for ICS
(4) 1887 Study group for Public Service Commissions
(5) 1909 Commission of Decentralisation
(6) 1911 Pike Committee on Work Simplification at District Level
(7) 1915 Lee of Faruham Commission on Public Service in India
(8) 1919 Smith Committee on Secretariat
(9) 1930 Wheeler Committee on Secretariat Reorganisation
(10) 1936 Maxwell Committee on Organisation and Procedures of Government
(11) 1945–46 Tottenham Committee on Reorganisation of Secretariat Department and Working of Tenure System

All these reforms committees and commissions were constituted by the British to concretise the administrative problems about which they had little knowledge but mostly because the reforms needed the approval of the Secretary of State for India who was a responsible minister answerable to the British Parliament. Naturally, the process was slow and every step was taken with this end in view that the long-term implications of reform were thrashed out in advance and its implementability can be tested under Indian conditions. The trends of administrative reforms from 1857 to 1947 indicate that English rulers were interested in:

(a) Developing a merit-based civil service with which they were experimenting in their own country, and
(b) Building efficiency-oriented administrative system for which a network of rational rules and regulations was a prerequisite.

The colonial goals were not compatible with liberalism and welfare of the natives. Moreover, peoples participation in administration was neither possible nor desirable in a colony violently as well as non-violently engaged in throwing away the rulers and their administration. Hence, a piecemeal approach to reforms was adopted and the administrative system was deliberately kept elitist, rule-oriented and awe-inspiring.

The Post-Independence Endeavours

The advent of independence in 1947 shook Indian administration from its moorings. Several events happened and the scenario changed so fast that India almost slipped into post-partition anarchy of communal violence. The Nehru period of 1947 to 1964 was not conducive for any nucleus change in administrative set up of the country. The prime concern was to preserve the nation-state and lay the foundations of a democratic polity which was too alien to seek participation from citizens of free India. Yet, it can be said to the credit of the political rulers of freedom struggle that they did not put administrative reforms on back burner. Rather they conceived of administrative changes in the context of the following circumstances which unfolded in sequence:

(1) Partition of the country and consolidation of administrative system to handle communal violence and refugee rehabilitations on a mass scale.
(2) Departure of senior civil servants to London and Pakistan and fill the wide gap created by their exit.
(3) Integration of princely states and administrative integration of their chaotic cadres into state and all India service.
(4) Framing of the Republican Constitution and adjustment of colonial structures and behaviours with the emergent democratic institutions of the country and aspirations of the people.

This context of political change brought immense pressure on the working of Indian administration at its policy formulation and operational levels. The state administrations also found them out of place to take new measures which were inevitable and hard pressing. Consequently, the elected governments in states started their administrative inquests and the reform committees were constituted to come out with suggestions.

(1) Kerala Administrative Reforms Commission, 1958
(2) Andhra Pradesh Reforms Enquiry Committee, 1960
(3) Rajasthan Administrative Reforms Committee, 1963
(4) Administrative Reforms Committee of West Bengal 1963

These random initiatives taken by political leaders and bureaucrats generated a climate and highlighted the need for change to achieve results. The Government of India, notwithstanding the gigantic challenges of refugee rehabilitation, launched upon its planned developmental journey with the establishment of the Planning Commission in 1950. A whole new area of development administration and administration of social welfare through community development scheme assigned a new and unprecedented responsibility on the shoulders of bureaucracy, which was ill-equipped to undertake the challenge. Naturally, an innovation trained and positive administration was envisaged and demanded which lead to serious and objective inquests in the capability of the system and instant efforts to reinvigorate it. The union ministries, the state coordinators and the district executives were to be streamlined and redefined under the new dispensation of decentralised democracy and planned development. The Nehru era perceived this tension and appointed the following committees and commissions for administrative reforms:

(1) The Secretariat Reorganisation Committee (Girja Shankar Bajpai), 1947.
(2) The Central Pay Commission (Varadachariar), 1946–47.
(3) The Economy Committee (Kasturbhai Lalbhai), 1948.
(4) Advisory Planning Board (K.C. Neogi), 1949.
(5) The Committee on Reorganisation of the Machinery of Government (Gopalaswami Ayyangar), 1949.
(6) Estimates Committee on Reorganisation of the Secretariat and Departments of the Government of India (First Lok Sabha), 1950–51.
(7) Committee on Public Administration (A.D. Gorwala), 1951.
(8) Committee on the Efficient Conduct of State Enterprises (A.D. Gorwala), 1951.
(9) The Machinery of Government: Improvement of Efficiency (R.A. Gopalaswami), 1952.
(10) Committee on Indian and State Administrative Services and Problems of District Administration (V.T. Krishnamachari), 1952.

(11) Public Administration in India – Report of a Survey (Paul H. Appleby), 1953.
(12) Estimates Committee (Ninth Report) and Administrative, Financial and other Reforms (First Lok Sabha), 1953–54.
(13) Re-examination of India's Administrative System with Special Reference to Administration of Governments' Industrial and Commercial Enterprises (Paul H. Appleby), 1956.
(14) The Railway Corruption Enquiry Committee (J.B. Kripalani), 1955.
(15) The Public Service (Qualification for Recruitment) Committee (A. Ramaswami Mudaliar), 1956.
(16) The Commission of Enquiry on Emoluments and Conditions of Service of Central Government Employees (Jagannath Das), 1959.
(17) The Staff Welfare Review Committee (Fateh Singh), 1961.
(18) The Committee on Prevention of Corruption (K. Santhanam), 1964.
(19) The Committee (Ninety-third) on Public Services (Third Lok Sabha), 1964.
(20) The Administrative Reforms Commission, 1966–70.
(21) The Administrative Reform Commission, 2006.

All these reform exercises during Nehru period (1947–64) and later mostly concentrate on the reorganisation of government machinery and personnel system as bequeathed by the British rule. G.S. Bajpai and Gopalaswami Ayyangar streamlined the cabinet and central secretariats. Gorwala and Lalbhai underlined the need of an efficient administrative system in the area of public enterprise and industrial administration. Ashok Chanda and Vardachariar Pay Commissions stressed upon financial reforms and pay package of public servants. The Estimate Committee reports suggested reforms for economy which go a long way to effect efficiency and accountability in the area of public expenditure. It was Dean Paul H. Appleby of Syracuse University who presented his report of a survey and suggested for leading reforms like O&M division in the Union government and establishment of Indian Institute of Public Administration at Delhi for training, research and reforms in administration on a permanent basis. Dean Appleby gave a clean chit to Indian administration but took his cudgels against Comptroller and Auditor-General of India and the Union Public Service Commission for their negativism in administrative control and recruitment policies of civil servants. He calls the Indian administration archaic, feudalistic and unimaginative because of methods of UPSC recruitment through advertisements. He also criticised the tendency of the ministry of finance to centralise powers and not to delegate them to the operational ministries. Besides, he frowned at the working of the office of the C&AG and advocated greater coordination among the ministries. Appleby favoured a system of specifying administrative responsibility for the completion of community development projects. K. Santhanam's report on prevention of corruption is regarded as the most comprehensive survey of an all-pervading phenomenon which has paralysed the public services of India. The Pay Commissions went far enough to suggest Whitely type organisations to redress the grievances of public servants. All these fertilising reforms ploughed the social and created conditions conducive for the major landmark exercise of 1966.

ARC: The Mega Exercise

The major achievement of the Nehru era can be called the establishment of the Department of Administrative Reforms. It offered management advice and facilitated the implementation of reform policies through coordination and liaison work training in administration got a boost and administrative information management could provide a reliable resource for reform. On Nehru's demise in 1964 and a brief stint of Lal Bahadur Shastri as Prime Minister, Morarji Desai was the most senior political leader on whom fell the responsibility of revamping the administrative organisation of India. On 5th January, 1966 the President set up a commission of enquiry which is popularly known as the Administrative Reforms Commission. It consisted of Morarji Desai as chairman and K. Hanumanthaiya, H.C. Mathur, G.S. Pathak and H.V. Kamath as members. All of them were members of Parliament at that time. A senior civilian, V. Shankar, was appointed member-secretary of the commission. Unfortunately, due to various reasons, the membership of the commission suffered frequent causalities needing replacements. The first to leave the commission was G.S. Pathak on his joining the Central cabinet in January. He was replaced by Debabrata Mookerjee. In March 1967, Morarji Desai himself joined the Central cabinet as Deputy Prime Minister and K. Hanumanthaiya succeeded him as chairman. A little later, after the death of H.C. Mathur, T.N. Singh was appointed as member in his place. The ARC as it is popularly known was given a very wide and comprehensive terms of reference. It was specifically asked to examine the public administration of the country and make recommendations for reform and reorganisation where necessary. Sectors of administration mentioned in the terms of reference included:

(1) The machinery of the Government of India and its procedure of work,
(2) The machinery for planning at all levels,
(3) Centre-state relationships,
(4) Financial administration,
(5) Personnel administration,
(6) Economic administration,
(7) Administration at the state level,
(8) District administration,
(9) Agriculture administration, and
(10) Problems of redressal of citizens' grievances.

To facilitate the work of the commission a resolution of the government detailed each of the above ten areas for specific recommendations. Some of the issues to be examined under each head were:

(1) The machinery of the Government of India and its procedures of work:
    (a) The grouping of subjects in department,
    (b) The role of the Cabinet secretariat,
    (c) Problems of inter-ministry coordination,
    (d) Staffing patterns and methods of work within ministries and departments,
    (e) Relationship between ministries and their attached and subordinate offices.
(2) The machinery for planning at all levels:
    (a) Planning organisations and procedures at the Centre and the states, and
    (b) the relationship of the Planning Commission at the centre and planning agencies in the states with other agencies.
(3) Centre-state relationship:
    (a) Centre-state relationship in the realm of planning and development, with particular reference to the growth of central agencies handling subjects in the Concurrent and State Lists,

(b) Centre-state relationship in other spheres, with particular reference to the needs of national integration and of maintaining efficient standards of administration throughout the country.

(4) Financial administration:
   (a) Budgetary reform,
   (b) Reform in the administration of accounts,
   (c) The role of audit,
   (d) The system of expenditure control, including procedures for sanctioning schemes and the problem of financial delegation and decentralisation,
   (e) Procedures governing financial relations between the Centre and the state.

(5) Personnel administration:
   (a) Personnel planning and organisation for it,
   (b) Recruitment policies and procedures, including selected techniques,
   (c) The Union Public Service Commission and the State Public Service Commissions,
   (d) Promotion policies and incentives,
   (e) Policy and rules to ensure efficiency, honesty and maintenance of morale,
   (f) Training,
   (g) Role of the Cabinet Secretary and the ministries of home affairs and finance,
   (h) Personnel management of public sector enterprises.

(6) Economic administration:
   (a) Economic coordination and role of departments of economic affairs and coordination, Planning Commission and the department of industry,
   (b) Administration of foreign exchange,
   (c) Export promotion and role of the concerned departments,
   (d) Review of the mechanism and procedures of economic controls,
   (e) Role of the ministry of industry and supply vis-à-vis other ministries,
   (f) Organisation for promoting industries in the private sector.

(7) Administration at state level:
   (a) Examination of organisation and procedures of state government with special reference to problems of allied nature,
   (b) The need to strengthen administration in the states at all levels.

(8) District administration:
   (a) The role of the collector in respect of general administration and development administration, and as the agent of the state government,
   (b) The role of the collector in the matter of public grievances and complaints,
   (c) The relationship between the collector and Panchayati Raj institutions,
   (d) The relationship between the collector and departmental heads at the district and supra-district levels,
   (e) The size of districts,
   (f) Personnel policies in relation to the post of collector.

(9) Agricultural administration:
   (a) The role of the ministry of food and agriculture and other ministries concerned with agricultural production, and coordination between them,

(b) Inter-relationships between state agriculture departments, community development organisations and other organisations concerned with agricultural production in the states,
(c) Organisation for agricultural administration at the state and district levels,
(d) Coordination between research and extension organisations.

(10) Problems of redressal of citizens' grievances:
(a) The adequacy of the existing arrangements for the redressal of grievances,
(b) Need for introduction of any new machinery of special institution for redress of grievances.

The details helped the Commission to constitute study teams and develop a dialogue with knowledgeable people and an active interface among the members of the Commission. Morarji Desai remained the chairman of the Commission for few months and was later succeeded by K. Hanumanthaiya. The government asked the commission to consider the need for ensuring the highest standards of efficiency and integrity in the public services, and for making public administration a fit instrument for carrying out the social and economic policies of the government. A comprehensive enquiry of this type was to be undertaken in India for the first time. The government left the commission free to "devise its own procedures, and appoint committees and advisers to assist it". The Commission worked from January 1966 to June 1970. It set up 20 study teams, 13 working groups, 4 expert groups and 1 task force to investigate into specified problems and suggest reforms. The association of a large number of knowledgeable persons in public life of the country worked with these teams and groups which made the commission available a variety of insights on different aspects of administrative reforms. The commission submitted 20 reports in all to the Central government which comprised 578 recommendations. The reports of the commission came on the following subjects in the years noted against each:

(1) Problems of Redress of Citizen's Grievances (1966)
(2) Machinery of Planning (Interim) (1967)
(3) Public Undertakings (1967)
(4) Finance, Accounts and Audit (1968)
(5) Economic Administration (1968)
(6) Machinery of Government of India and its Procedures of Work (1968)
(7) Life Insurance Corporation (1968)
(8) Machinery for Planning (1968)
(9) Central Direct Tax Administration (1969)
(10) Administration of Union Territories and NEFA (1969)
(11) Personnel Administration (1969)
(12) Delegation of Financial and Administrative Powers (1969)
(13) Centre-state Relations (1969)
(14) State Administration (1969)
(15) Small Scale Sector (1969)
(16) Railways (1970)
(17) Treasuries (1970)
(18) Reserve Bank of India (1970)
(19) Post and Telegraphs (1970)
(20) Scientific Departments (1970)

Additionally, the ARC produced 33 reports of the study teams and working groups. Out of about 580 recommendations of the ARC, most of them were of a procedural nature or restated the well-known positions of the commission. The commission recommended actions and study team reports have a mine of ideas which go a long way to induct specialisation, professionalisation and de-centralisation in administration. The concern for efficiency, effectivity and economy is writ large on all these recommendations, the commissions has finalised. The earlier reports in varied areas have been re-examined and the conclusions tend to further the reform process initiated by Dean Paul Appleby. The abstract of the major reports of ARC are reproduced here:

(1) The Machinery of Government:
   (i) The size of the council of ministers should be determined by administrative needs, and national combination of subjects into ministerial portfolios be encouraged.
   (ii) The Cabinet Secretary should be a general co-ordinator and principal staff adviser to the prime minister, the cabinet and the cabinet committees.
   (iii) A department of personnel should be set up under the prime minister and its functions should be the formulation of personnel policies and review of their implementation, talent-hunting, development of personnel manpower planning, training and career development.
   (iv) There should be only two levels of consideration below the minister, namely, (i) under secretary/deputy secretary, and (ii) joint secretary/additional secretary/secretary with a 'desk-officer' system.
   (v) Responsibility for overall coordination within a ministry should be assigned to one of the department/secretaries appropriate for this purpose.
   (vi) The department of administrative reforms should be placed under the deputy prime minister.
   (vii) The existing O&M units should be reactivised.
(2) Centre-states Relationships:
   (i) An Inter-state council consisting of the prime minister as chairman, the finance minister, the home minister, the leader of the opposition in the Lok Sabha and five representatives, one each from the five zonal councils should perform functions under Article 263 of the Constitution.
   (ii) The Finance Commission should make recommendations on the principles which should govern the distribution of plan grants to the states.
   (iii) Powers should be delegated to the maximum extent to the states with regard to their work on projects in which the Centre is interested or which are carried out by them.
(3) Personnel Administration:
   (i) There should be a unified grading structure for the entire civil service so as to facilitate the movement of officers from one area to another as per need or competence.
   (ii) Greater opportunities should be provided to government servants of lower ranks to rise rapidly as high as their competence and performance warrant.
   (iii) Wherever the members involved in a particular function are viable, the posts should be grouped into regularly constituted services.

(iv) The present system of confidential reports is replaced by performance reports to get civil servants merit properly assessed (The Manmohan Singh government has accepted it with sweeping modifications).

(v) The public servants should not have a right to strike and their grievance should be settled through a joint consultative machinery and administrative tribunals.

(vi) There should be an improvement of recruitment policies and procedures, pruning of excessive personnel, abolition of unnecessary and ineffective organisations, fixation of work norms, simplification and codification of rules, rationalisation of holidays and strict limitation of overtime work and transfers.

(vii) A functional field must be carved out for the IAS.

(viii) Central training division in the department of personnel be created.

(ix) Both the husband and wife should not be employed under government at the same time.

(x) A civil servant may be allowed to retire voluntarily after he has completed 5 years of service and given proportionate pension and gratuity.

(xi) The quantum of pension admissible may be raised to three sixths of the average emoluments of the last three years as against the existing three-eighths.

(4) Finance, Accounts and Audit:

(i) The November 1 should begin the financial year to facilitate a more realistic assessment of revenue and an even spread of expenditure.

(ii) The departments and organisations should introduce performance budgeting, which would inter-relate financial outlays with physical targets and achievements and present estimates and expenditure on terms of functions, programmes, activities and projects.

(iii) Audit should aim at a positive and constructive approach to see improvements in organisational efficiency and effectiveness of financial rules and procedures.

(iv) The Commission did not consider the question of separation of audit from accounts.

(v) The system of internal financial advice should be strengthened to develop financial competence within each department of ministry.

Economic Administration

(i) Innovative measures for constructive discipline and productive punishment for personnel can mitigate alienation, monotony, stress and frustration among the members of government organisations.

(ii) A culture of initiative and enterprise, particularly among the higher middle and higher levels of bureaucracy needs to be encouraged. The system of consultation, consensus, collaboration and cooperating among personnel in the decisional process should be organisationally.

(iii) Appropriate measures for job enrichment, job rotation, time management and mastering the art of work should percolate to all levels.

(iv) Strong themed efficacious mechanism of conflict resolution at the inter-organisational and intra-organisational levels can evolve an integrated perspective of HRD which would include, and yet transcend, all the salient dimensions of personnel administration, including manpower planning. Job descriptions and specifying roles for greater role-clarity for all-important positions in government organisations can go a long way to facilitate inter-level mobility among personnel and lateral entry into and exit from government organisation.

(v) Improvement in knowledge and skills of (babu) bureaucracy should adopt positive attitudes towards society and work.

(vi) A high-power commission on 'Prices, Cost and Tariff' should be set up to assist the government in evolving rational price policies and in creating a climate of consciousness and also to take over the function of the Tariff Commission.

(vii) In its detailed study reports, the ARC stressed upon developing a positive organisational culture and a motivational climate in government organisations and devising non-monetary rewards and incentives for personnel with a view to recognising good work.

(viii) Rigorous career planning for organisational personnel and establishing a network of action research and training in public systems can impart appropriate pre-entry, induction and in-service training to the personnel belonging to the less privileged sections of Indian society.

(5) Public Sector Undertakings:

(i) Four or five audit boards should be constituted, each for a specific section of public enterprises, for conducting efficiency audit and appraisal of performance.

(ii) The Bureau of Public Enterprises should be reorganised so as to make it a more effective service agency for the ministries and the public undertakings.

(iii) 'Sector Corporations', should be set up with the main function of promotion and development in that area, including the setting up of new projects.

(iv) The practice of deputing government officers for temporary service in public undertakings should cease.

(6) The Planning Commission:

(i) The National Development Council which is at present composed of the prime minister, and of the chief ministers of all the states, should have also the union ministers of ten important departments.

(ii) The Planning Commission should confine itself to formulation of plans and evaluation of plan performance without executive function and authority.

(7) Redress of Citizens' Grievances:

(i) There should be another authority – Lok Ayukta – in each state and at the Centre for dealing with complaints against the administrative acts of other officials.

(ii) Special officers should redress citizens' grievances. There should be one authority – Lokpal – dealing with complaints against the administrative acts for ministers or secretaries to government at the Centre and in the states.

The Commission felt concerned about the effectiveness of the committee system and stored for eliminating unwarranted secrecy to promote openness in government decision-making. It advocated the involvement of consumers/clients/beneficiaries of government systems in the formulation of concerned policies and decisions and their implementation. High standards of performance at the individual and group levels should evaluate leadership and promote effective superior subordinate relations encouraging the formation of groups and quality circles to promote group effectiveness and team building.

(8) State Administration:
   (i) The council of ministers in a state should be compact and homogeneous, its size in big states, may range between 8 and 12.
   (ii) There should also be a policy advisory committee in each department.
   (iii) The standing committees of state legislatures may be set up in selected areas of administrative activity for promoting detailed legislative review.
   (iv) The proliferation of personnel under the state governments must be checked and O&M division must be activised.
   (v) In departments dealing with specific subjects, there should be two staff cells, namely, (i) combined cell on planning and policy, and (ii) a finance cell.
   (vi) Steps should be taken by the Union government and the state governments to reduce expenditure on governors and Raj Bhavans.
   (vii) A convention should be established whereby the public service commissions are consulted by state governments before the latter exempt any case or type of cases from the purview of the state PSC.
   (viii) The existing executive department should be so reorganised and needless multiplicity is removed to avoid diffusion of functions and responsibility.
   (ix) A department of personnel should be set up under the charge of the chief secretary and be placed under the chief minister.
   (x) The full cabinet should meet at least twice a month.
   (xi) Ministers should not intervene in the day-to-day administration except in cases of grave injustice, serious default or maladministration on the part of civil servants.

(9) District Administration:
   (i) The decision-making in district administration should have two centres (a) The tehsil/taluka, and (b) The district headquarter.
   (ii) The diarchy in district administration should clearly demarcate regulatory work for the collector and development functions to Panchayati Raj institutions.
   (iii) The district level development office should be transferred to the zila parishad.
   (iv) The judicial work of the collector should be transferred to the district judge.
   (v) The DCO should be a senior official to work as chief executive of zila parishad.
   (vi) A district tribunal consisting of the collector and a subordinate judge should hold enquiries where removal of elected members of panchayati bodies is involved. In fact, the nascent stage of Panchayati Raj in Indian federal polity requires the linking each organisation's role to the wider objectives of government. A proactive approach and a futuristic orientation among organisations were to be promoted to create an inbuilt mechanism to strengthen this perspective.

Alternative models of organisations with varying sizes, designs, authority network, autonomy patterns, decisional systems, were to be experimented to strengthen the ethical base of government and its institutions and personnel. A sound systems of policy making, based on rationality and assigned appreciation of reality can be possible if more powers and a greater role are assigned to the specialist for professionalism in policy and decisional systems. An effective antenna device can create a sound system of intelligence in administrative organisations.

The Post-ARC Efforts

The ARC completed its labours in 1970. It was the crucial phase of transition when Prime Minister Indira Gandhi was tightening her grip on the government in the midst of fierce opposition and split in the Congress Party. She should hardly peruse and process the reports of the ARC when Pakistan pushed millions of Bangladeshi refugees into Indian border and forced a war which dislocated the stability of economy beyond repair. The country tumbled through the shock when internal turmoil forced Mrs Gandhi to clamp National Emergency on the country in 1975. Later, when emergency was lifted in 1976, Mrs Gandhi was swept away at the lustings and the interregnum was filled by the SVD government of Morarji Desai and Chaudhury Charan Singh. The experiment had its initial pinpricks and when Mrs Gandhi staged a comeback the Blue Star Operation took the tally of her life. All this made the government forget about the Administrative Reform Commission's reports and in the meantime the secretaries in the ministries of the Union government made a systematic bid to pigeon hole all those precious documents which were prepared with hard labour. Mrs Gandhi never had the time or leisure to read these reform reports. Her colleagues in the prime minister's office allowed the reform exercise to lapse. Whatever new efforts Desai and Charan Singh initiated through the constitutions of Ashok Mehta Committee on Panchayati Raj and National Police Commission under Dharmveer could not find favour with post-emergency rule of Mrs Gandhi. Even, Rajeev Gandhi in his brief spell could not touch these reports with a pair of tongs. It was P.V. Narsimha Rao who could usher the country into a era of peace and stability. Economic reforms of liberalisation and globalisation were high on his agenda and Panchayati Raj could get constitutionalised by his heroic efforts. The social justice agenda was too big and the successive government of Bajpai could do nothing but to continue Narsimha Rao reform efforts. The Y.K. Alagh Committee, followed by Hota Committee were constituted to recreate some of the reforms vigorously. The Ramaswami Commission reforms for constitutional change proved abortive and administration was downsized with catch phrases like debureaucratisation, deregulation, disinvestment and corporatisation with open economy of market place. Again the political shift to Congress rule brings the philosophy of reform with a human face. The Planning Commission has been revamped and the economic reforms of liberalisation have been hastened with a more responsible and accountable bureaucracy. Prime Minister Manmohan Singh has already announced a broad based performance appraisal plan for senior civil servants and a new Administrative Reforms Commission in on the anvil to take India to the developed world of 2020.

Although, the record of administrative reforms in India since 1970 is not very encouraging but sporadic and compulsive efforts have been made in response to political changes like national emergency and demands for openness and accountability of administration through public participation. The list below catalogues the committees and commissions constituted since 1970 in the area of administrative reform:

(1) Third Pay Commission (Raghuvir Dayal)
(2) Committee on Efficiency in Administration (Singh and Jha)
(3) Committee on Recruitment Policy and Selection Methods (D.S. Kothari) 1976
(4) National Police Commission (Dharam Veer) 1977–80
(5) Committee on Public Enterprises (Fazal Ali) 1980–82
(6) Commission on Accountability in Public Sector (L.K. Jha) 1981–85
(7) Commission on Centre-state Relations (Justice R.S. Sarkaria) 1984–88

(8) Committee on Recruitment Policy and Selection Methods (Satish Chandra) 1989.
(9) Committee on Panchayati Raj (L.M. Singhi) 1990
(10) Tax Reforms Committee (Dr Raja J. Chelliah) 1992
(11) Pay Commissions (Fourth, Fifth and Sixth) 1986, 1997 and 2006
(12) Committee on Recruitment Policy and Selection Methods (Alagh and Hota) 2000

These reform exercises of the tumultuous era represent a sincere attempt that could make a little dent in the system. The Panchayati Raj reform could take the shape of constitutional amendment. The Kothari and Satish Chandra reports have totally been processed for reforms in all India central services of the country. The L.K. Jha and Challiah reports were serious attempts to reform the economy. The Pay Commissions screened the service conditions and come out with reports which gave fair deal to public servants in the era of liberalised economy. Justice Sarkaria presented his objective point of view about union-state relations, Article 356 and the office of the governor which need clarity in the context of coalitional politics of alliances and hung parliaments with regional political parties. The Dharam Veer reports on Indian police is a milestone, perhaps the only historic effort of 20th century to streamline the most archaic and dilapidated system of Indian police since the days of 1864 and 1902. The reports of the National Police Commission quite boldly breaks the ice and effectively deals with the live problems of police politicisation and politicisation of crime in free India. All these reform reports essentially stress upon:

(a) Democratisation of public administration.
(b) Openness and accountability of public servants at all levels.
(c) Integrity in public services through professionalisation and specialisation, and
(d) Popular participation and decentralisation of administrative structure.

Obviously, this shift from efficiency, effectivity and coordination to accountability, integrity and participation in administrative reform exercise is a qualitative tilt which Gerald Caiden will call an *episodic reform*. The old concept of reform which skirted around design, rationalisation and updating of administrative technology has gone beyond the classical theory of administrative reform. Democratic administration is more than decentralisation and use of cybernetics. It is not mere debureaucratisation or interagency coordination. Like the political system, the administrative system has to be managed for the people and that too with their active participation through MBO. The macro and micro levels of structures have to be responsible, responsive and accountable. The productive organisations and innovative public servants alone can compete for good governance in a liberal policy.

The Bottlenecks

Administrative reforms in free India suffered from a number of handicaps and jaundiced perspectives. Very rarely, they were hazarded with a spirit of adventure. The politicians, the civil servants and even the people took them with a pinch of salt and watched the experiments with a subdued spirit of pessimism and cynicism. Naturally, the desired results could not follow and the reasons can be enumerated as under:

(1) Lack of strong political will.
(2) Vested interests of privileged civil servants.
(3) Popular ignorance, apathy and distrust of people in administration change.
(4) Perceived threats to power positions of rules.

(5) Adhocism as a philosophy of administrative reform.
(6) Short range perspectives without basic nucleus change.
(7) elitist notions of change imposed from above without acceptance from below.
(8) lack of follow-up reforms which renders the initial reform counter productive.
(9) Reforms without institutionalisation process because of which change became abortive and expensive.
(10) Ambiguity and inflexibility of administration reforms which keep them unimplementable and far from being realistic.

The success story of administrative reforms in India is generally lost in the quagmire of history and political milieu of the country. The political masters are blamed for their myopic electoral vision, but the reformers in developing societies reform of the martyrs. The soft pedalling of change renders it to innocuous rhetoric's and worse still the reform become too prohibitive to afford. Evaluations and appraisals of reforms are used as delaying tactics and by the time the new reforms become visible or desirable they are condemned by the initiators of change. The orthodox approach does not break a new ground but only tinkers and modifies the existing structures and processes.

The Indian leadership has adopted a guarded and incremental approach to administrative reforms. The pressures of democracy restrain this process of administrative change. Most of the administrative reforms have been consequential and piecemeal. Institutionalisation of reforms has been obstructed by the impact of personalities. The Indian administrative system lacks the capacity to internalise change and proved more effective than innovation. The administrative reforms come with a lot of fanfare but get diluted and dissipated on the table of Babus.

The episodic reforms according to Caiden require a nurturing climate and a fertile field in which innovative reforms can take roots and draw sustenance. The reform phenomenon being a process requires commitment from future administrators on a continuous basis. Moreover, the inbuilt tendency of resistance based on fear puts the imposed reform in 'jeopardy'. The outside idea howsoever brilliant is shunned and takes time in getting internalised. Hence, comes the need of O&M which has been aptly called administrative reform of administration for the good of administration and by the administrators in their own way. In India, the O&M unit of Administrative Reforms Department is fairly old and its achievements have been evaluated as satisfactory. In fact, the future of committee/commission reforms also depends upon the way the O&M welcomes and handles them in their field operations.

Organisation and Methods

The concept of O&M implies a reorganisation of forms and rediscovery of methods to attain the stated objectives. The structures become obsolete and so becomes the urgency to innovate new methods to supplement or replace the old. The administrators are the best judge of administrative practices and they should constantly be vigilant and productive to identify the facilitators of change. It is not change per se but change in terms of continuity and applicability that O&M units are envisaged to induct new methods to yield better results. The main objective of O&M is to initiate and to sustain a concerted effort to improve administrative efficiency in all branches of government. It calls for continuous attention to the nature and volume of work to be done, the speed and quality of performance, and other factors, The number, quality and mutual relationship of the persons responsible for decision and/or action, flow of work and workload need study. The simplification and ratification of procedures, time and labour saving techniques and alliances are equally important. The main effort in this direction come from within each of its parts. The main task of the O&M division is to supply leadership and drive and by a cooperative effort, to build up a common fund of information, experience and competence in O&M work. The O&M keep close touch with each other and with the director of the O&M division and form a study group and a task force carrying out a series of progressive and planned operations. The O&M officer in each unit selects one section in his own ministry/department and inspects it for assessing defects in speed and quality of performance. The O&M officers suggest ways and means of improving the speed of disposal without any radical change in the existing organisation and procedures. These suggestions are discussed and examined by the group and introduced as pilot projects in the very sections in which the defects were first noticed. O&M officer conducts a census and scrutiny of all the incoming and outgoing inter-departmental references and the extent of the delays through superfluous and unnecessary references are detected. A critical examination of the working of the ministry as a whole may reveal defects in speed and quality of disposal which are due to faults in the organisation and methods, particularly with reference to the handling of correspondence, filing system, movement of papers. The O&M works on the belief that the efforts for administrative efficiency must necessarily come from the administrative unit itself. The O&M division or cell merely supplies leadership and drive by a cooperative effort to build up a common fund of information, experience and competence in O&M work.

In India, the Central government became conscious of this O&M need in the fifties and the O&M division was established in the central government in 1954. Several factors that made it imperative were:

(1) Quantitative expansion of government departments after the Second World War, because of unprecedented increase in the range and volume of governmental activity.
(2) Qualitative deterioration of efficiency in administration after independence because of the exit of European and Muslim officers unblock, causing a vacuum in administrative linearly of the central secretariat.

Obviously, a functional unit was needed to initiate, concentrate and sustain a drive for improvement in efficiency. The Officer Shortage Committee recommended the creation of a directorate DF methods, organisation and training in Central government. In 1948, N. Gopalswami Ayyangar set up an O&M unit in the ministry of transport and later recommended the creation of O&M division as a part of the ministry of home affairs in his report on the reorganisation of the machinery of government in 1949. The A.D. Gorwala (1951) report crystallised the issue and the directorate of training and O&M was to have two branches, one for exclusive O&M work. The report specified details by maintaining that personal approach from an equal level is the essence of work. The directorate would take up each ministry and after a careful study of the method of work, make its own suggestion on the spot. In case of difference of opinion between the director and the ministry, the matter would have to be referred to the cabinet. The directorate would keep a watch to see that they are carried out.

The First Five-Year Plan document (1952) envisaged the need of an effective machinery for plan implementation. The document said that "careful study and review of organisation and methods can lead to greater economy and efficiency. We recommend that the Central government should have an organisation and methods division which would work in close cooperation with the personnel sections in the different ministries". While detailing the specific areas of administrative reforms the plan document continued, "Among the problems which need early attention in the field of methods are the problems of simplifying office procedures, elimination of delays, the system of records maintained in the central ministries, the movement of files, and procedures for efficiency audit in organisations of different kinds." The stress continued and when Dean Paul Appleby presented his survey in his first report in 1953, he pointedly observed:

"... I recommend that the Government of India give consideration to the establishment of a central office charged with responsibility for giving both extensive and intensive leadership in respect to structures, management and procedures. At one level of a highly technical and specific sort, it would give attention to work measurement, work flow, office management, filing systems, space arrangement, and the like; at another level it would be charged with general governmental studies and proposals."

Created in the year 1954, the O&M division was asked to study and deal with problems. Like office procedures and their simplification, techniques for the elimination of delays in like disposals, maintenance of office records and movement of files in the secretariat. But the O&M division in practice chose to keep itself preoccupied with control measures, exercise of general supervisory checks, receipt and compilation of statistical data regarding the volume of disposal of work, and follow-up action on decisions taken at O&M meetings. The organisational studies were missing and the division betrayed a lack of perspective and a holistic approach in planning its own house in order. It could never map out a long-term programme of action, as the top leadership kept on changing with a disturbingly fast frequency. In its total existence of ten years, the O&M division had seven directors, some of them continuing for just six months. Its field of operation was also restrictively drawn, as there were two other organisation in existence engaged in the performance of similar tasks – the special reorganisation unit in the finance ministry, and the committee on Plan Projects in the Planning Commission. Still the efforts to reform the reformers continued and in March 1964, the O&M division got separated from the Cabinet secretariat and merged with the newly created department of administrative reforms as a part of the ministry of personnel, public grievances and pensions. This destroyed the unified O&M set-up because when O&M was given to the new department, special reorganisation unit (SRU) became special inspection unit (SIU) concerned with staff assessment of work measurement. Similarly, the Committee on Plan Projects was separated from the O&M division and the reform perspective changed from routine office jobs to broader administrative reforms. The department of administrative reforms as a part of home ministry gave a higher status and importance to reform work and research work could be taken up in a more systematic manner. The department worked in a dual capacity of a staff agency advising on reforms and as a line agency carrying out studies and seeing to the implementation of their accepted recommendations.

The department of Administrative Reforms functioned under the general guidance of the committee of administration which was set up in August 1961 to integrate the activities of the O&M group. It consisted of the Cabinet Secretary as the chairman, six senior secretaries, and the joint secretary of the department as member secretary. This group of top officials was expected to look continuously into the question of improving administration. It did so by keeping a watch and acting as a clearing house for ad hoc problems that arose. It also submitted reports on specific problems to the cabinet.

The department was entrusted:

(1) To continue the earlier work of the organisation and methods division.
(2) To locate important problems and initiate studies in respect of them.
(3) To examine the organisation and procedures of selected departments with the object of eliminating problems of corruption at different points of the administrative machinery.
(4) To make a rapid scrutiny of past recommendations and conclusions of committees/commissions/individuals with the object of picking up points that could and should be implemented without further enquiry.
(5) To examine the question of setting up of a machinery for the redress of grievances of citizens.
(6) To prepare simultaneously the ground for a comprehensive investigation of the entire administrative system in the country.

In 1973, the terms of reference of the department of Administrative Reforms were revised. Its revised functions were stated as under:

(1) Coordinating the work of processing of the recommendations of the Administrative Reforms Commission.
(2) Promotion and development of O&M and work study and setting up of management service units suited to the special needs of sectoral administration.
(3) Providing management consultancy services to the organisations of the Central government, the state governments, public sector and local bodies.
(4) Advising the Central government on policy matters concerning Administrative Reforms.
(5) Imparting management education and disseminating information on administrative practice and modern management techniques.

The activities and approach of the department are that Administrative Reforms must be preceded by a process of critical and detailed analysis of the entire administrative situation in the field. Thus, the department has evolved four tests in accordance to which recommendations or reforms must be measured. They are:

(1) They should be inherently sound,
(2) They should take into account the jobs practised,
(3) They should be expressed in corporate terms, and
(4) They should be capable to be put into effect.

From 1964 to 1973, the Administrative Reforms Department of the Home Ministry worked under the aegis of a highly empowered committee which consisted of

(1) A Member of Parliament as its chairman.
(2) The head of the organisation to be studied.
(3) A representative of the ministry of finance.
(4) A representative of the Department of Administrative Reforms.

The study teams constituted submitted their reports to the committee and the involvement of the finance ministry and the Parliament made reforms palatable and workable to the government in general and organisation in particular. This reformed procedure of reforms could bring the relevant people together and their interface could generate consensus which alone can be a guarantee for sustainable reform. The finance ministry as a coordinating agency and Parliament as a law making body took interest in reform exercise and the resultant gain was that reports taking one to three years for acceptance and processing could get implemented in few months time.

The Ayyangar Committee transferred the department of A.R. to the Cabinet secretariat (1973) because the report maintained that it was not possible to separate questions relating to organisation of establishment from those relating to organisation of services. So the O&M responsibility was shifted to the home services department of the ministry of home affairs. Four years later (1977), the Janta Party regime retransferred it to department of personnel and administration reform in the ministry of home affairs.

In 1985, the department was elevated to the status of a regular ministry under the Prime Minister. Its new nomenclature was ministry of personnel, public grievances and pensions. The organisational chart of the ministry has a Minister of State at the apex. The Administrative Reforms Department is headed by an additional secretary, who has four management studies divisions under one director for each of there divisions. The O&M division is presided by a deputy director with analysts and investigators. In addition, there is policy advisory committee with an additional director, four directors and one deputy director who assist choosing projects and preparing research designs.

The ministry has a variety of functions and roles. Its Administrative Reforms work consists of (1) research, (2) studies, (3) services, and (4) publications.

The department studies specific problems of administration which are either refereed to it by a government organisation or selected by it on its own. In the selection of these studies, emphasis is given to areas which have a direct bearing on the citizen's satisfaction and require the administration to have greater interaction with members of the public. These studies cover a range of issues relating to the organisational structure and methods as well as procedure prevailing in the ministries and organisations of the government. As a nodal management service agency, the department officers help and advise in respect of management and O&M activities which include modernisation of government offices through the use of modern aids, reduction in paper work, minimisation of the levels of consideration in the disposal of work, fixing of accountability as well as record management. Some of these functions include modernisation of offices which is one of its major objectives. The department provides incentive to various organisations to take up modernisation of their offices to improve administrative efficiency and productivity. It facilitates accessibility for the public to organisations and units of government with which they interact. Accordingly, a plan scheme has been introduced to help the ministries to improve their work environment through adoption of functional layout, creation of open offices for better supervision. Redressal of public grievances is being attempted through better service to people and more efficient management of data through reduction in paper work and use of modern aids and cost and space effective records management. The scheme helps to set-up model unit of a modern office in selected ministries in a time-bound manner. The additional secretary in charge of the department holds periodic meeting with O&M officers of various units to oversee that O&M functions are performed in a planned manner. The Central Secretariat Manual of Office Procedure provides for inspection of sections, review of reports, returns and manuals, consolidation of instructions, etc. These functions constitute an integral part of the control mechanism for ensuring proper and orderly working of offices. The rules, regulations and manuals from ministries are consolidated and orders are issued from time to time. All the ministries are required to carry out inspections of the departmental record rooms annually in consultation with the National Archives of India. The department monitors the compliance of the procedure laid down in the manual regarding recording, review and weeding out of old records.

Staff Inspection Unit (SIU)

As a part of O&M exercise, the SIU was created as early as 1952 with the sole object of reviewing the staff requirements of ministries and to recommend man power to ensure efficiency and economy in the government. The unit follows work study and method study techniques. These techniques include: (1) a study of the organisational network in offices of government, (2) a scientific analysis of their operations, (3) programmes of work simplification and standardisation, and (4) standards of performance to evaluate staff requirements. The SIU has an effective network operating under a director, supervised by a joint secretary. Seventeen study teams work under the director and two deputy secretaries. Each team consists of

(1) A junior analyst,
(2) Two technical assistants, and
(3) One investigator.

An under secretary or a senior analyst heads the team. In all, there are seven under secretaries or senior analysts who are engaged in doing SIU functions. These functions include:

(1) Prescribed standards of performance,
(2) Making arrangement of inspection and ad hoc studies to review the government organisation's staffing, and
(3) Determining and classifying the jobs and grades of required staff.

The SIU is primarily concerned with the measurement of work. This develops workloads to be assessed with its establishment concerning the staff's strength in order to ensure adequacy of workload for each functionary and also to ensure that the workload requires lesser or greater number of staff. The SRU was converted into SIU in 1964 to secure economy in staff consistent with administrative efficiency. The words 'consistent with efficiency' are important – as important as words 'securing economy in staff'. While the two seem to be apparently conflicting, in practice efficiency and economy have to go together.

Staffing Patterns

The O&M man has to be more than an average public servant in his intelligence and imagination to express himself verbally as well as in writing. He should be quite, steady, well balanced, poised and thought provoking in collecting and sorting out his facts. In choosing the alternatives to be recommended, he must be creative and have good judgement. He is expected to be very patient, studious, compromising, resourceful and always desirous of cooperation from all quarters concerned. He should also have the aptitude to direct and coordinate the efforts of O&M task forces, working groups, committees, etc.

Every country recruits its O&M men as per needs of its administrative system. In Great Britain, normally, the staff for a department O&M branch is found by transfer from within ordinary departmental work. The central O&M divisions obtains their staff from other departments. The O&M personnel are drawn from a wider background in Scandinavian countries. These are the men qualified as economists or graduates from technology institutes or civil servants or military officers. In Canada, the recruitment of O&M personnel was done by means of competitive examinations by the organisation and methods service. This experiment failed and Canada has to adopt the US pattern in a revised manner. The central O&M division, in India, stands amalgamated in the ministry of personnel, public grievances and pensions. The special reorganisation unit now is known as staff inspection unit, comprises the staff of the central secretariat services and the SRU personnel mostly from the central field services. O&M cells in ministries, are under the charge of an officer of the rank of deputy secretary designated as O&M officer. This officer looks after the affairs of O&M besides his other responsibilities. Thus, O&M is a sort of part-time job at the levels of the ministries. Its training functions are in decline and various national training institutes have merged to push this O&M role on the margin. Moreover, research in government has a low priority and the section officer variety of officers have downgraded the significance of the enterprise.

O&M Cells

O&M cells are found in the ministries and attached offices. They are headed by an officer-in-charge of the establishment work. The O&M units point out administrative bottlenecks to the ministry concerned and strive to remedy them by suggesting requisite ways and means. The evolution of O&M machinery as a part of administrative reform exercise in India is a sad story of honest intentions. Right from the year 1954, the stalwarts like G. Ayyangar, Dean Paul Appleby, T. Krishanamachari and host of others not only justified the creation of O&M division but suggested detailed concrete plans for reforms. These efforts inspired the well-intentioned administrators who successfully brought the situation to the establishment of the Department of Administrative Reforms in 1964. The functions of the department are:

(1) Making a scrutiny of past recommendations and conclusions of committees/commissions/individuals,
(2) Examining the organisation and procedures of selected departments,
(3) Locating important problems and initiating studies,
(4) Examining the question of setting up of a machinery for the redress of grievances of citizens,
(5) Preparing ground for investigation of the entire administrative system, and
(6) Continuing the earlier work of the organisation and methods division.

The move was inspired by a noble cause of reform but the efforts bogged down against the hard rock of power seeking and procedure conscious bureaucracy. From a division to department, it kept on shuttling from cabinet secretariat to home minister to an independent department, the secretaries repaired it as additional burden but never liked to pass it on to the right kind of reformer because of the potential threat that the reforms could pose to their privileged position. Empowered committee was created but the aphorism of the reform exercise was left to junior functionaries. Naturally, ill-luck dogged the footsteps of the O&M set-up from its very inception and it remained unwept, unkept and unsung almost for a decade from 1954 to 1965.

Because of its shifting locations two O&M division could not develop a niche and the controversy between a headquarter directors of O&M and separate O&M units attached to ministries and department obstinate its effective functioning. Section officers and under secretaries continued with part-time assignments and their suggestions or reports were given their due by their hierarchical seniors. The reform ideas became clerical notes and the part-time directors systematically indulged in infanticide operations of the new ideas. Dean Paul Appleby hoped that "the O&M experiment at national level would have a charter of responsibility for the enhancement of democratic manner and methods within the bureaucracy and between the bureaucracy and the public." As a first step, it was to carry out pilot investigations in suitably selected offices which will provide some experience for O&M work to the group of workers selected for the purpose. Secondly it was to train a group of workers who will form the nucleus of the directorate; to popularise the fundamentals of O&M work among units; and maintain contact with organisation and methods activities in other countries. But the division undertook full-fledged programmes of carrying out investigations of offices on request and of arranging for the training of O&M workers in the central ministries and state governments with the result that it itself became a bureaucratic organisation needing serious reforms.

In the early years, the part-time director was assisted by three deputies, one in charge of the publication of the O&M journal; the second responsible for organising training programmes; and the third concerned with the study of special projects. These officers had a supporting staff of section officers, assistants, clerks, stenographers and messengers. There were no administrative analysts on the staff of the O&M division with scientific training in O&M techniques. The ill-trained babu bureaucracy, flooded with officers on special duty and part-time investigators rendered the O&M division a preserve for surplus staff, scrumbling for allowances and trade unionism.

The O&M division in India in its career of decades never had an elaborate staff of its own. It started with a part-time director who belonged to the Indian Civil Service and had the rank of a joint secretary assisted by an assistant to the director of the rank of an under secretary and supporting clerical staff. Later, a deputy director of the rank of deputy secretary was added with the purpose of carrying out inspections of ministries and departments. Later, one more assistant director of the status of under secretary was appointed and all the three officers belonged to the Central Secretariat Service of the secretariat establishment. However, an officer on special duty was recruited from outside the civil service with a legal background and experience of working in a public enterprise. The juristic approach of junior functionaries did not allow the academic vigour of research to prevail. Consequently, the so-called work and work load increased and there come the bureaucratic suggestion to crate a separate department which could take care of large range of varied activities and handle complex problems.

The Department of Administrative Reforms is a distinct administrative and budgetary entity. Its work has been different from that of the ministry proper and it has developed its own distinctive, organisational pattern. Operationally, the department's work is looked after by a full-time joint secretary who functions under the secretary. Within the department, the staffing pattern is study-oriented and it has a small secretariat staff to attend to its general policy and administrative work. It consists mainly of study teams composed of research staff of various grades which collect and analyse data, uncover issues and prepare documented papers for discussions and decisions.

The Santhanam Committee traced the origins of corruption in administrative delays and harassment and this was used as a plough to expand the activities of the department of administration reforms. Management advice, implementation, liaison and coordination, training, administrative intelligence, assisting Administrative Reforms Commission were identified as core areas for monitoring and innovation. The sick department spread infection and the physician had difficulties in healing his own malaise.

The O&M division had serious dissensions in its ranks about it philosophy, scope and nature of operation. The idea of having a nucleus of persons trained in organisation and methods techniques was abandoned at the very outset on the grounds of non-availability of trained personnel in adequate numbers and the time-consuming nature of the process. The division thus started its work with a three-fold plan of action: to make all concerned conscious of the prevailing inefficiency and of the need and scope for improvement; to find out facts and to see what was actually wrong and to locate the causes adversely affecting: and to devise and apply appropriate remedies. Though the three bodies, namely, the central O&M division, the special reorganisation unit and the committee on Plan Projects were engaged in useful tasks in their respective spheres of work, yet they worked in isolation.

More recently the Manmohan Singh government has felt the need of Administrative Reforms to update the system. Veerappa Moily, a Member of Parliament has been asked to head the administrative commission and another reform panel to go into the implications of revised policy of reservation for the member of OBC in educational institutions. When civil service is going to be subjected to a more rigorous administrative discipline and the nuances of social audit, the Sixth Pay Commission gave some relief along with ancillary reforms or fringe benefits to the public servants. These two commissions come at a time when public administration confronts a challenge of competition downsizing and de-bureaucratisation. The new reforms of the new era must make the administration creative and still more productive.

All reforms whether social, political or administrative need a philosophy to spell out their contents, contexts, speed and price. Viewed from a holistic angle, the Administrative Reforms per se have little segmental meaning. The socio-political changes demand administrative transformations and unless the former are well thought out and visible the latter remain a rhetoric to be paraded by the ruling elites of the system. In UK, USA or France, the administrative change has followed political change and it will be erroneous to expect it the other way round. Fifty years of working of the Republican Constitution has enabled the people of India to have an acquaintance with the democratic philosophy of political governance. This is yet to reach to the elitist administration which has its own alibis to resist democratic reforms. The Weber Taylor perspective of efficiency and economy is repaired as the End of reform exercise in administration. The philosophy of nucleus change is dreaded in the context of political stability and the status quoits philosophy dominates the administration of democratic polity.

Moreover, Administrative Reforms in India is regarded as a preserve of self-reform by the bureaucracy which has its elitist perspective on change. Development and welfare administrations are the example in point where civil service seeks to change the lives of people below poverty line and regards administration as a tool of economic change in society. Little wonder that administrative reform exercise does not extend beyond O&M and there too refuses to penetrate in the thought process of bureaucracy beyond joint secretary's level. The senior civil servants find little wrong with the administration and to them 'grievance redressal' of Administrative Reforms. When pushed further they blame political leaders for the chaos and find people unenthusiastic or unworthy of any worthwhile reforms. This elitist perspective on administrative reform places the entire blame on 'the lack of political will' of the peoples representatives, who to a great extent find themselves instable in facing political change at the hustings. Administration is their saviour and they shun Administrative Reforms on the advise of their secretaries who see threat to their privileged position in reform exercise. The political will is fragile and the administrative reformers.fears are genuine. So, it works out to delay reforms and to accept them only as the last resort. Panchayati Raj experiment and dyarchy in the district is an example that proves that even obvious and inevitable reforms are purposely delayed and sabotaged by appointing committees and pigeon holing their reports. The lack of political will for Administrative Reforms is heightened by the fact that political leaders cannot visualise the distant future and the administration has a strategy to block reforms and delay them so that they become irrelevant. Civil service reforms and reports of committees after committees bear testimony to the fact that Maculay's philosophy and fears are asserted adnautium to redefine merit with reservations so that 'aristocratic vestiges of privileges' may not get dismantled by the onslaught of human rights and dignity of the individual.

Eloquent rhetorics apart, Administrative Reforms in India has been used to justify status quo. The O&M exercise is too elaborate to kill any episodic reform of ARC's dimensions. The reports of National Police Commission were whetted by a number of bureaucratic bodies and the ARC reports were successfully diluted with the passage of time and change in the political complexions of the government. Gradualness of reform is the watch word of administrative change and the history bears a testimony that Gorwala, Appleby and Hanumanthaiya are decorational names. Follow-up reforms are taken up only when it suits to the administration as was the case with Kothari, Satish Chandra and Dharam Veer reforms. The price of reforms which is always worked out by bureaucracy is too heavy to be acceptable in the present. This leads to piecemealing of the reform package and the contradictions cause neutralisation, leaving little impact of the basic idea. The opponents of reforms have used this technique to slow down Administrative Reforms.

The students of Administrative Reforms in India keep writing on the theme of Reforms Revisited and Reforming the Reformers. This literature is indicative of the fact that reform efforts through bureaucracy develop the same drawbacks which they seek to mitigate. The dilemma of Administrative Reforms in India is that, those who can bring reforms do not want them and those who plead for them, can do pretty little except writing a research piece which nobody reads and still less pursues. The plain fact is that administrative reformers do not want to commit suicide. It may look cynical but the net result of all administrative exercise for administrative innovation has led to the expansion of bureaucracy and dysfunctionalism of reform structures. Yet the optimist must continue to hold the fort, believing that something positive emerges even from the misfortunes and honest efforts. The culture of Administrative Reforms takes its own time and the tinkering of the system has forced the reformers to think of lesser evils or alternatives at lesser price. The department of administrative reform and its research projects might have not attained the ideal but their contribution to enhance awareness and make the field fertile for change goes without sayings.

Appendix

Landmarks in Administrative Developments in India

Year	*Events*
321–296 BC	Kautilya's Arthshastra
16th Cent. AD	Machiandri's Prince
1206–1290	The Slave Dynasty
1290–1320	The Khilji Dynasty
1320–1414	The Tughlak Dynasty
1414–1451	The Saiyyad Dynasty
1451–1526	The Lodi Dynasty
1564	Jajia Tax on Hindus was abolished by Akbar
1558–1707	Mansabdari system of military service prevailed in Mughal India
1582	Todarmal's revenue system created in
1858	Last Mughal King Bahadur Shah Jafar was dethroned and exiled
1556–1707	Administrative landmarks of Mughal period can be glanced from *Ain-i-Akbari*, *Tuzuk-i-Jhanagiri*, *Tarikh-i-Shahajahani* and other accounts of foreigners like Bernier, Thomas Roe and Hawkings
1600	East India Company comes to India
1669	East India Company classified positions
1688	Madras Municipal Corporation created
1720	Presidency towns given a court system
1726	Bombay Municipal Corporation established
1753	Department of Audit and Accounts created
1756	Central Secretariat at Fort William gets birth
1771	Merit with seniority accepted
1771	Comptrolling Committee of Revenue constituted

Year	Events
1772	District Collector's post created (abolished in 1773)
1773	The Regulating Act passed
1773	Warren Hastings made the first Governor-General of India
1781	Collector's post revived
1781	Board of Revenue established
1784	Pitt's India Act placed Indian Affairs under Board of Control, representing the British Cabinet
1786	The Board of Revenue established in Bengal
1786	Districts becomes fiscal units
1787	The office of District Collector gets revenue, justice and magistracy
1793	Judicial power of Collectors snatched under Cornwillis code
1800	Fort William College established
1802	Fort William College abolished (but continued as language school till 1854)
1806	East India College established at Hartfold Castle.
1809	East India College transferred to Hailebury
1810	Department of Finance created in the Supreme Government of India
1829	Calcutta Board of Revenue becomes Sadar Board of Revenue
1829	Divisional Commissioners to supervise Collectors and stay responsible to Board of Revenue
1833	Governor General of Bengal took over as Governor of India
1833	Deputy Collectors on non-covenanted posts were appointed
1833	Second Board of Revenue created at Allahabad
1835	A legislative department was created
1843	Secretariats of Indian Government and Bengal Government separated
1843	Four departments created in the Central Secretariat
1844	Deputy Magistrates on non-covenanted posts were appointed
1846	The Secretary Finance Department became ex-officio Accountant General of India
1853	The Charter Act enacted
1853	Patronage system abolished and competitive examination introduced
1854	Macaulay Committee on Recruitment and Indian Civil Service reported
1854	Civil Service Commission established in London
1855	Competitive examination in London held for the first time
1857	The office of Comptroller and Auditor General of India created
1858	Transfer of territory from the Company to the Crown
1858	Hailebury College closed and training transferred to British universities
1860	Indian Penal Code passed
1860	Reports of Special Committee on Civil Services

Year	Events
1860	Annual budget introduced
1860	Central Revenue Department created. Posts of Auditor General and Accountant General got unified
1860	Report of the Special Committee on Civil Service Salaries
1861	The Government of India Act
1861	Indian Police Act: constabulary created; Code of Criminal procedure passed
1861	The Indian Councils Act – Viceroy Canning introduced portfolios system
1864	Local self-government resolution adopted
1870	Devolution of financial powers to panchayats by Viceroy Mayo
1870	Lord Mayo's resolution of municipal institutions
1870	Open competition for normal recruitment
1871	New Municipal Acts (1871–1874) introduced elective principle
1872	Indian Evidence Act
1876	The Committee on the Selection and Training of Candidates for the Indian Civil Service reported
1882	District treasury to be controlled by the Collector
1882	Magna Carta of local government (18th May) came as Ripon resolution
1882	Comptroller General designated as Comptroller and Auditor General
1888	Classification of services into ICS, PCS and SCS by Aitchison Commission of 1886
1892	The Indian Council Act with enlarged functions of Legislative Councils and Right to ask questions
1892	Covenanted Civil Service and Uncovenanted Civil Service given new nomenclatures of Indian Civil Service and Provincial Civil Service
1898	Criminal Procedure Code
1902–3	Police Commission Report
1902	Indian Police Commission reported
1905	The Railway Board for Railway Administration
1905	Deputy Superintendents of Police added
1905	The tenure system was created by Lord Curzon
1909	Morley-Minto Reforms enlarged the streoy of Legislative Councils
1909	Royal Commission upon Decentralisation (1907) reported three-tier system
1911	Pike Committee for district level work simplification
1912	Islington Commission on Training
1914	The Special Police Establishment was born
1915	The Royal Commission on Public Service in India (1912–15) reported
1918	Civil Servants pay for 'superior' and 'inferior' posts classified
1919	Government of India Act
1919	'Dyarchy' introduced

Year	*Events*
1919	Pyramidal organisation for department was recommended by Secretariat Procedures Committee (Lewellyn Smith)
1919	Central Staff Selection Board established for recruitment to Imperial Civil Service.
1919	Laws on village panchayats enacted in all provinces
1919	CAG was made responsible to the Central Legislature
1920	Lewellyn Smith Committee report prescribed a four year tenure for Secretaries and Deputy Secretaries
1921	Railway and General Budget separated
1921	System of independent audit created
1921	Public Accounts Committee and Standing Finance Committee created
1923	Royal Commission on Superior Civil Services under Lee of Feudalism constituted
1924	The Royal Commission on Superior Civil Service argued for the establishment of a Public Service Commission in India
1924	The separation of accounts from audit was recommended by Muddiman Committee
1926	Federal Public Service Commission created
1926	Staff Selection Board abolished and its function transferred to Federal Public Service Commission
1929	The Madras Public Service Commission was born. Regular system started in 1935
1929	Simon Commission recommended separation of accounts from audit
1930	Wheeler Committee on Secretariat organisation was set up (Simon Commission argued in favour of a strong Collector)
1934	Reserve Bank of India created
1935	The Government of India Act
1935	Dyarchy abolished
1935	Union, State and Concurrent Lists drawn
1935	Wheeler Committee recommended double noting
1935	Private Secretary to Governor-General attended cabinet meeting – A beginning of Cabinet Secretariat
1935	A Public Service Commission in each province was created for recruitment work
1936	Wheeler Committee supported the tenure system
1937	The Maxwell Committee on Organisation and Procedure. It suggested that a Secretary be made responsible to the Minister
1937	The division of clerical staff into assistants and clerks was made
1937	Provincial autonomy introduced on 1st April
1938	Formation of the Finance and Commerce Pool of Officers to, and specialise in, matters concerning finance and commerce
1940	Training of Civil Servants in India only
1941	ICS officers training school at Dehradun

Year	Events
1944	Department of Planning created but abolished in 1946
1944	Assheton Committee on training of civil servants reported
1945	Council Secretariat as Coordination Committee of the Council was established
1945	Tottanham Committee on reorganisation of Central Secretariat (First Report 1945, Second Report 1946)
1946	Change in Staffing pattern of the Central Secretariat and duties for offices of different grades
1946	Advisory Planning Board under K.C. Neogi created
1947	The Indian Independence Act passed (18th July)
1947	Cabinet Secretariat was born in August 1947
1947	Prime Minister's Secretariat created on 15th August
1947	Departments in the Government of India designated as Ministries on 29th August
1947	Bajpai Secretariat Reorganisation Committee report
1947	Indian Administrative Service takes over from ICS
1947	First competitive examination for the IAS by UPSC was held in July
1947	Metcalfe House started serving as IAS Training School at Delhi
1947	Prevention of Corruption Act enacted
1947	Report of the First Pay Commission (Chairman: Vardachariar)
1948	Industrial Policy Resolution
1948	Central Secretariat Training School New Delhi established
1948	Damodar Valley Corporation started functioning
1948	Kasturbhai Lalbhai Economy Committee
1949	Gopalaswami Ayyangar Committee on the Reorganisation of the Government of India
1949	Tek Chand Committee on Corruption
1949	Department of External Affairs and Commonwealth Relations was christened as Ministry of External Affairs
1950	The Constitution of India came in operation (26th January)
1950	The Central Secretariat Service was born
1950	Planning Commission inaugurated
1950	First Estimate Committee elected
1950	Contingency Fund created by Contingency Fund Act of India, 1950
1950	N.R. Pillai appointed as first Cabinet Secretary of India
1951	All India Services Act enacted
1951	Local Finance Enquiry Committee reported
1951	Gorwala Report on Public Administration in India and efficient conduct of state enterprises
1951	The First Finance Commission (K.C. Neogi) was set up
1952	National Development Council created

Year	Events
1952	R.A. Gopalaswami Memorandum on efficiency in the secretariat
1952	Presidential and Vice Presidential Election Act
1952	Community Development Programme launched
1953	Scheme of National Extension Service (NES) started
1953	A select committee on Nationalised Industries was suggested by Lanka Sundaram (MP)
1953	Paul Appleby's report on Public Administration in India. First Report
1953	Committee on subordinate legislation created
1953	Committee on Government Assurances started functioning in Parliament
1954	Rajya Sabha members also become members of Public Accounts Committee
1954	Indian Institute of Public Administration was established in New Delhi
1954	Taxation Enquiry Commission
1954	Organisation and Methods Division created
1954	The Central Council of Local Self-government set up
1955	IAS Staff College established at Shimla
1955	Amendment to Prevention of Corruption Act
1955	Kriplani Committee on Railway Corruption
1955	Central Vigilance Division and vigilance units set up
1956	Industrial Policy Resolution of April
1956	Paul Appleby's Second Report on Public Enterprises
1956	Mudaliar Committee Report of the Public Service
1956	Vivian Bose Commission
1957	Balwantrai Mehta Committee (16th January to 24th November) reported to NDC
1957	U.P., Bihar and Rajasthan created civil service training institutes
1957	Administrative Staff College established in Hyderabad
1959	Panchayati Raj first launched at Nagaur, Rajasthan (2nd October); Andhra Pradesh followed
1959	Jagannath Das Second Pay Commission reported
1959	IAS Staff College abolished and IAS Training School, Delhi merged into the National Academy of Administration, Mussoorie
1960	Joint Consultative Machinery set up
1960	Cell (officer-oriented) system started
1960	Intensive Agricultural District Programme (IADP) inaugurated
1961	Allocation of Business Rules adopted
1961	Central Statistical Organisation set up
1961	PM's office given the status of a department of the GoI under the Allocation of Business Rules 1961
1964	Santhanam Committee on the Prevention of Corruption report
1964	Central Vigilance Commission created

Year	*Events*
1964	Vigilance Commissions set up in states on the central model
1964	The Department of Administrative Reforms was born
1964	Sadiq Ali Committee Report on Panchayati Raj
1964	Committee on Public Undertakings of Parliament created
1965	Bureau of Public Enterprises was set up
1966	Indian Forest Service created as the third all-India service
1966	Administrative Reforms Commission (ARC) constituted
1966	Rural Urban Relationship Committee
1966	Kohli Committee on Central Police College
1966	Pillai Committee on Indian Foreign Service
1966	ARC report on Citizens' Grievances
1966	Scheme of Joint Consultative Machinery and Compulsory Arbitration for Central Government Employees launched
1967	ARC Report on Public Undertakings
1968	ARC Report on Machinery for Planning (Interim Report: 1967)
1968	Committee on Service Conditions of Municipal Employees Report (1965)
1968	ARC Report on Machinery of Government and Procedure of Work
1969	'Sandwich Pattern' of training started for the IAS probationers
1969	ARC Report on Personnel Administration
1969	ARC Report on Centre-State relations
1970	ARC disbanded
1970	Department of Personnel created in the Cabinet Secretariat
1971	Secretariat Training School becomes Institute of Secretariat Training and Management
1971	NE Council Act passed
1972	National Academy of Administration at Mussoorie renamed as the Lal Bahadur Shastri National Academy of Administration
1973	Department of Personnel, born in 1970, renamed as Department of Personnel and Administrative Reforms
1973	The Steel Authority of India Ltd. created
1973	Chief Secretary becomes the senior-most civil servant of the state and given the status of a Secretary to the Government of India
1973	Lok Ayukta set up in Rajasthan
1973	R. Dayal – Third Pay Commission
1973	Command Area Development Programme started
1973	Criminal Procedure Code revised
1973	Committee on the Welfare of Scheduled Castes and Scheduled Tribes appointed in the Indian Parliament

Year	*Events*
1974	Gore Committee on Police Training
1974	APPA course at IIPA
1975	The Staff Selection Commission constituted
1975	L.P. Singh and L.K. Jha Reports on Administration Improvement
1976	Precedence to Directive Principles over Fundamental Rights (42nd Amendment) and Fundamental Duties enshrined in the Constitution
1976	Kothari Committee 1974 on Recruitment Policy and Selection Methods reported
1976	Accounts and Audit functions separated and Controller General of Accounts (CGA) created
1977	Asoka Mehta Committee on Panchayati Raj
1977	Prime Minister's Secretariat becomes Prime Minister's Office
1977	National Police Commission (under Dharam Veer) appointed
1978	Constitution (44th Amendment) Act.
1978	Police Commissioner appointed in metropolitan cities
1978	Asoka Mehta Committee report on Panchayati Raj
1979	Revised three tier scheme of examination on the basis of Kothari Committee
1979	Engineers and doctors allowed to compete for all India and Central Services
1980	IRDP started
1980	National Police Commission reported
1981	L.K. Jha Economic Reforms Commission reports
1984	Rao Working Group on District Planning
1985	The Ministry of Personnel, Public Grievances and Pension reorganised
1985	One-week refresher courses and three week training programmes for the IAS
1985	Committee on Administrative Arrangement for Rural Development (CAARD) set up under the Chairmanship of GVK Rao
1985	Radical restructuring of Panchayati Raj in Karnataka
1986	CAPART created
1986	'Sandwich' pattern of training for IPS
1986	Singhal Pay Commission (Fourth)
1986	L.M. Singhvi Committee on Rural Development
1986	Restructured Panchayati Raj in Andhra Pradesh
1988	National Perspective on Women designed
1988	President of India's salary revised
1988	National Commission on Urbanisation Report
1988	Directorate of Public Grievances in the Cabinet Secretariat
1988	Sarkaria Commission (1984–88) on Centre-State Relations
1989	Constitution 64th and 65th Amendment Bills defeated in the Rajya Sabha

Year	Events
1989	Satish Chandra Committee (1988) on Recruitment Procedure for Higher Civil Services
1989	Election Commission become multi-member body
1990	National Integration Council set up
1991	Policy of economic liberalisation
1992	'Indicative Planning' introduced
1992	Constitution 73rd Amendment Act (Rural governance)
1992	Constitution 74th Amendment Act (Urban governance)
1993	Satish Chandra Committee report implemented
1993	Constitution 73rd Amendment Bill and Constitution 74th Amendment Bill (20 April) asserted by President
1993	Seventeen Standing Committees of Parliament started functioning
1993	Human Rights Commission constituted (October)
1993	Liberalisation, Privatisation and Globalisation Policies launched
1994	Department of Jammu & Kashmir Affair created in PMO
1994	Fifth Pay Commission appointed (Chairman Justice Ratnavel Pandian)
1998	2nd Nuclear Explosion at Pokharan by India (11th May)
1998	National Security Council Constituted
2000	Justice Venkatswami Report on the desirability of presidential form of Government in India
2003	Justice Malimath Committee Report on Criminal Justice Administration Reforms
2004	Right to Information Act passed
2006	Veerappa Moily Commission on Administrative Reforms
2006	National Minimum Employment Guarantee Scheme introduced
2006	Old Age Pension Security ensured
2006	Justice B.N. Krishna Seventh Pay Commission appointed
2007	Justice Rajendra Sacehar Report on Minorities
2007	Protection of Women Against Domestic (Marital) Violence Act

Select Bibliography

Agarwal, A.N., *Indian Economy*, New Delhi, Wiley Eastern, 1994.

Ahluwalia, I.J., *New Economic Policies DSE and Privatisation in India*, CPR, New Delhi, 1994.

Alexander, P.C., *The Pen of Democracy*, Bombay, Somayaya, 1995.

Annual Reports of Department of Rural Development, Government of India, New Delhi, 1993-94.

Annual Reports of Ministries of Home, Finance, Defence and External Affairs, Government of India, New Delhi.

Annual Reports of Planning Commission, Government of India, New Delhi.

Annual Reports of Union Public Service Commission.

Appleby, Dean Paul, *Public Administration in India*, Government of India, 1953.

Arora, R.K. and R. Goyal, *Indian Public Administration: Institutions and Issues*, New Age International, New Delhi, 2003.

Arvind, S., *Indian Administration*, Bombay, Himalaya, 1992.

Avasthi, A., *Central Administration*, New Delhi, Tata McGraw Hill, 1980.

Avasthi, A. and A.P. Avasthi, *Indian Administration*, Laxmi Narayan Agarwal, Agra, 1995.

Bailey, D.H., *Police and Political Development in India*, New Jersey, Princeton University, 1968.

Banerjee, A.N., *Public Administration in Ancient India*.

Banerjee, D.N., *Early Administrative System of the East India Company in Bengal*, Longmans, Green and Company, 1943.

Barthwal, P.C., *Public Administration in India*, New Delhi, Ashish, 1993.

Basu, D.D., *Introduction to the Constitution of India*, Nagpur, Wadhawa, 2004.

Bawa, P.S., *Policing People*, New Delhi, Rupa, 1989.

Bhasham, A.L., *Adhbhut Bharat*, Agra, Shivlal Agarwal, 1998.

Bhattacharya and Dutt, *Governing Rural India*, New Delhi, Uppal, 1991.

Blunt, Edward, *The I.C.S.*, London, Faber, 1937.

Chambers, Robert, *Rural Development*, London, Longman, 1983.

Chanda, Ashok, *Indian Administration*, London, Allen and Unwin, 1967.

Chanda, Ashok, *Federalism in India*, London, Allen and Unwin, 1972.

Chandrahas, Singh, *The Civil Service in India: A Historical Study*, New Delhi, Atma Ram, 1989.

Chaturvedi and Jain (eds.), *District Administrative*, IIPA, New Delhi, 1980.

Chaturvedi, S.K., *Rural Policing in India*, New Delhi, B.R. Publishing, 1988.

Desai, Vasant, *Fundamentals of Rural Development*, Bombay, Himalaya, 1991.

Despatches from G.G. to S.S. (Home) Shimla, 1884.

Dhingra, I.C., *The Indian Economy: Reserve Planning, Development and Problems.*
Dodwell, H., *Cambridge History of India*, Vol. V, London, University Press, 1929.
Dubhashi, P.R., *Grammar of Planning*, IIPA , New Delhi, 1983.
Dubleshi, P.R., "Politics and Crime: Beyond Vohra Committee Report", *Statesman*, Kolkata, December, 1995.
Dutt, Abhijit, *Municipal Finances in India*, IIPA , New Delhi, 1984.
Eames and Saran, *District Administration in India*, New Delhi, Vikas, 1989.
42nd and 44th Amendments in Indian Constitution.
Gorwala, A.D., *Report on the Efficient Conduct of State Enterprises*, Government of India, New Delhi, 1951.
Halachami and Bouckairt (eds.), *The Enduring Challenge in Public Management*, IIAS, San Francisco, 1995.
Hanson, A.H., *The Process of Planning*, London, OUP, 1966.
Hasnet, A. Hye, *Integral Approach to Rural Development*, New Delhi, Sterling, 1986.
Jacob, George, *Readings in Panchayati Raj*, NIRO, Hyderabad, 1967.
Jain, H.M., *The Union Executive*, Allahabad, Chaitanya, 1969.
Kangh, R.P. (tr.), *The Kautilaya Arthshastra*, New Delhi, Motilal Banarasi Das, 1972.
Keith, A.B., *A Constitutional History of India*, London, 1936.
Khera, S.S., *Central Executive*, New Delhi.
Khera, S.S., *District Administration in India*, Bombay, Asia, 1964.
Khosla, R.P., *Administrative Structure of Great Mughals*, New Delhi, Kanti Publications, 1991.
Lewis, J.P., *Indian Political Economy: Governance and Reform*, New Delhi, OUP, 1995.
Lewis, N. and Singh, S.S. (eds.), *Ombudsman: India and the World Community*, IIPA, New Delhi, 1995.
Lynton, Rolph P. and Udai Pareek, *Facilitating Development*, New Delhi, Sage, 1992.
Maculay Committee Report, Parliamentary papers, London, 1855.
Madan, J.C., *Indian Police*, New Delhi, Uppal, 1980.
Maheshwari, S.R., *Rural Development in India*, New Delhi, Sage, 1985.
Maheshwari, S.R., *The Administrative Reforms Commission*, Agra, L.N. Agarwal, 1972.
Malhotra, B.B., *In-Service Training of Civil Servants*, IIPA , New Delhi.
Mansukhani, H.L., *Corruption and Public Servants*, New Delhi, Vikas, 1979.
Mathur, K.P., *Administration of Police Training in India*, New Delhi, Gyan, 1987.
Mathur, Y.B., *Rural Development in India*, NIRD, Hyderabad, 1985.
Mehta and Batra, *Administration for Rural Development*, Jaipur, 1984.
Mehta, Usha, *Kautilaya and His Arthshastra*, New Delhi, S. Chand and Co., 1980.
Mishra, B.B., *Bureaucracy in India*, New Delhi, Oxford, 1977.
Mishra, B.B., *The Administrative History of India*, New Delhi, Oxford, 1970.
Mishra, B.B., *The Central Administration of the East India Company*, London, Manchester Press, 1959.
Mishra, C.P., "Process of Planning in India" in K.N. Dubey (ed.), *Planning and Development in India*, New Delhi, Ashish, 1990.
Mishra, N.L., *Responsive Administration*, Jaipur, Amar Jyoti, 1989.
Mishra, Sweta, *Democratic Decentralisation in India*, New Delhi, Mittal Publications, 1994.
N.N. Vohra Committee Report, Government of India, New Delhi.
Nandi, Raj, *Developing Small and Medium Towns*, IIPA , New Delhi, 1985.
Organisation of Government of India, IIPA, New Delhi, 1980.
Organisational Set-up and Functions of Ministries, Government of India, Delhi Institute of Secretarial Training and Management, 1974.
Osbone, David and Gaeller, Ted, *Reinventing Government*, Prentice Hall, New Delhi, 1992. Also see Reddy *Reinventing Government* by P. Druckal Span, December, 1995, pp. 11-15.

Pande, P.N., *Self-Employment Programme in India*, New Delhi, Ashish, 1988.

Paul, Appleby Dean, *A Reorganization of Indian Administrative System*, Government of India, New Delhi, 1954.

Paylee, M.V., *Constitutional Government in India*, Bombay, Asia, 1968.

Pranapjya, H.K., *The Planning Commission*, IIPA, New Delhi, 1987.

Puri, B.N., *History of Indian Administration*, Bombay, Vidya Bhawan, 1968.

Pylce, M.V., *Constitutional Government in India*, Bombay, Asia, 1968.

Rai and Singh, *Current Ideas and Issues in Indian Administration*, New Delhi, Uppal, 1979.

Rai, Hallayya, *Corruption in India,* Madras, E.W. Press, 1985.

Rama Reddy, G., *Patterns of Panchayati Raj in India*, New Delhi, Macmillan, 1977.

Ray, Anirudh, *Some Aspects of Mughal Administration,* New Delhi, Kalayani, 1984.

Reddy, Y. Venugopal, *Multi Planning and India*, New Delhi, Vikas, 1979.

Relevant Reports of ARC, Government of India, New Delhi, 1969.

Relevant Reports of Finance Commissions.

Report of ARC on Personal Administration, Government of India, New Delhi, 1969.

Report of the ARC on Accounting and Audit, Government of India, New Delhi, 1968.

Report on the Government of India and its Procedures of Work, New Delhi, 1969.

Report on the Machinery of the Government of India and its Procedures of Work, ARC, Government of India, New Delhi, 1968.

Report on the Reorganisation of the Machinery of Government of India, New Delhi, 1949 (Gopalaswami Ayyangar Report).

Reports of Central Vigilance Commission.

Reports of Finance Commissions of India

Reports of Maxwell, Ayyangar, Tottenham, Wheeler Committees, Government of India, New Delhi.

Reports of Ministries, Government of India, New Delhi, (Annual Reports).

Reports of National Police Commission, Government of India, New Delhi, 1985.

Reports of the Administrative Reforms Commission, Government of India, New Delhi.

Reports: B.R. Mehta, Ashok Mehta and L.M. Singhvi, Government of India Publications, New Delhi.

Roberts, P.E., *India Under Wellesley,* (tr.) by Uma Rao, Lucknow, Hindi Akademy, 1971.

Roy, N.C., *Civil Service in India*, Calcutta, K. Mukherjee, 1958.

Sachdeva, Pradeep, *Urban Local Government and Administration in India*, Allahabad, Kitab Mahal, 1993.

Santhanam Committee Report, Government of India, New Delhi.

Sarkar, J.N., *Mughal Administration,* Calcutta, M.C. Sarkar, 1935.

Sarkaria Commission Report, New Delhi, 1988.

Sarulia, Shankar, *Grameen Police*, BPRRD, New Delhi, 1989.

Seerrai, H.M., *Constitutional Law of India*, Bombay, Tripathi, 1983.

Sen, Shankar, *Indian Police Today*, New Delhi, Atlantic Publishers, 1997.

Sethi, J.D., "Autonomy of the Planning Commission", *Mainstream*, March 14, 1992; *Planning Machinery in India*, INPA, VII, 1961.

Shakhdhar, M.L., *Budgeting in India*, IIPA, New Delhi, 1960.

Shakhdhar, M.L., *The Organization of the Government of India*, IIPA, New Delhi, 1968.

Shamaleb, A., *Administration of Training in India*, Jaipur, Arihant, 1994.

Sharma, P.D., *Indian Police and Internal Security*, New Delhi, Uppal, 1987.

Sharma, P.D., *Police and Criminal Justice in India*, New Delhi, Uppal, 1983.

Sharma, P.D., *Police, Polity and People in India*, New Delhi, Uppal, 1968.

Sharma, S.K. and Malhotra, S.L., *Integrated Rural Development*, New Delhi, Abhinav, 1977.
Shastri, Nilkant, *History of India*, I, Madras, Vishwanathan, 1950.
Shriramkrishna and Green, *Metropolitan Management*, New York, Oxford, 1986.
Shrivastava, A.L., *Bharat Ka Itihas*, Agra, Shiv Lal Agarwal, 1990.
Shukla, J.D., *State and District Administration in India*, IIPA, New Delhi, 1976.
Singh, Katar, *Rural Development: Principles Policies and Management*, New Delhi, Sage, 1986.
Singh, Manohar, *Rural Development Administration*, New Delhi, Deep and Deep, 1988.
Singh, U.B., *Administrative System in India*, New Delhi, APH Corporation, 1998.
Smith, M.P., *Nationalism and Reforms in India*, New Haven, Yale University Press, 1938.
Thapar, Romila, *Bharat Ka Itihas*, New Delhi, Raj Kamal, 1996.
The East Asian Miracle: A World Bank Policy Report, New York, OUP, 1993, pp. 157-89.
Tottenham, R., Reports on the Reorganisations of Central Government (1945-46), Government of India, New Delhi, 1955.
Tripathi, M., *Kautilaya Ka Arthic Chintan*, Jaipur, Classics, 1994.
Tummala, K.K., *Public Administration in India*, Singapore, Time Academic Press, 1994, pp. 275-80.
Varma, V.P., *Ancient and Mediaeval Political Thought*, Agra, Laxmi Narain Agarwal.
Wade, Robert, *World Development*, 1985.
Woodruff, Philip, *The Men Who Ruled India*, London, Jonathan Cape, 1953.
Wool Cott, J.E., *British Rule in India*, New Delhi, Anmol, 1986.
Yugandhar and Mukerjee, *Decentralised Planning*, New Delhi, Concept, 1991.